Property of
Dept. of Transportation
Environmental Analysis

GRAND OLD
AMERICAN
BOTTLES

First Edition limited to 1000 copies.

Second printing in response to demand.

FROM MAN TO MACHINE

Worker's Crypt—Bottle Blowing of the 18th Century.

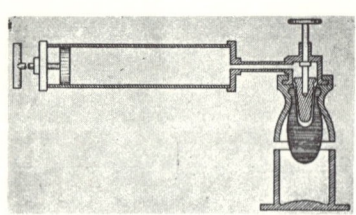

STUDY IN CONTRASTS.

In 1903, the first fully automatic machine for making bottles was invented, and the glass container industry progressed further than it had at any time since the invention of the blow-pipe 2,000 years earlier.

GRAND OLD AMERICAN BOTTLES

Descriptive listings of Glass Bottle Types from Colonial Times to the Present. Lavishly Illustrated, Encyclopedic

By Dr. Larry Freeman

Copyright 1964

No part of this book may be reproduced without permission from the publisher.
Library of Congress Card Number 23066-63.

Century House

Watkins Glen, N. Y.

TABLE OF CONTENTS

INTRODUCTION, why 4 bottle groups 5
A—WHISKEY; B—MEDICINAL; C—HOUSEHOLD; D—FIGURAL
CHAPTER I   DEMIJOHNS & CARBOYS . . 13
CHAPTER II   EARLY SEAL BOTTLES . . . 17
CHAPTER III   WINE DECANTERS 23
CHAPTER IV   EARLY AMERICAN POCKET FLASKS 31
    Chestnut type (Wistarbergs, Stiegels, Pitkins)
CHAPTER V   FULL-BLOWN FLASKS . . . 42
    Masonics, Violins, Scrolls, Sunbursts
CHAPTER VI   HISTORICAL & PICTORIAL FLASKS 55
    Varied Van Rensselaer Historicals: Eagles, Washingtons, Pikes' Peaks, Cornucopias, etc.; Ovoids and Calabashes
CHAPTER VII   19th C. MARKED IN GLASS WHISKEYS 113
CHAPTER VIII   20th CENTURY WHISKEYS . . 151
    Bar Bottles, home and hip flasks, modern gift decanters
CHAPTER IX   BITTERS BOTTLES 177
    Original Thompson check list and 166 new forms
CHAPTER X   OTHER MEDICINALS . . . 250
    Check-list Sarpsaparilla and other tonics not specifically marked Bitters; also proprietary medicine bottles before 1875
CHAPTER XI   INTRODUCING HOUSEH'LD BOTTLES 295
CHAPTER XIa   PERFUMES AND SCENTS . . 300
CHAPTER XII   MINERAL WATER BOTTLES . . 300
    Saratoga and other mineral Spring Bottles, soda pop & vinegar
CHAPTER XIII   FOOD CONTAINERS . . . 345
    Milk, ale, pickle and syrup bottles, fruit jars
CHAPTER XIV   HOUSEHOLD AIDS—NECESSITIES 317
    Ink, hair dye and blacking, target, nursing and testing bottles
CHAPTER XV   DRUG TRADE BOTTLES . . 372
    All types of bottles made for store trade from reproduced catalogs of 1890
CHAPTER XVI   HEALTH-HELP BOTTLES . . 429
    Liniments, ammonia and miscellaneous not previously covered
CHAPTER XVII   FIGURAL BOTTLES 435
    Selected listings of bottles formed in shape of some figure—Group Hu—Human; Ob—Other objects; Group An—Animals
CHAPTER XVIII COLLATERAL MATERIALS . . 475
    Advertising and other pictorials associated with bottle collecting
CHAPTER XIX   BOTTLE MAKING 480
APPENDIX 487
    Note on book's format; chronology of bottle making; check lists
GLOSSARY OF TERMS 488
BIBLIOGRAPHY 494
SUBJECT INDEX 500

INTRODUCTION: WHY FOUR GROUPS

The writer is a long-time collector of Old Bottles, especially those which housed the nostrums and phony cure-alls for "Female Complaints", "Lost Manhood" and "Health Bitters." In an earlier volume, "The Medicine Showman and His Bottles," he told how his father once inherited a company selling these concoctions and listed many marked-in-glass proprietary medicine flasks which are now prime collector items. The present volume goes far deeper into the subject and is more generally inclusive. Years ago he came into personal contact with two great Early American Bottle Collectors (Stephen Van Rensselaer and J. H. Thompson) whose out-of-print books (Early American Bottles and Flasks; Bitters Bottles) brought the first definite order into this field. G. and H. McKearin, H. Revi and other authors have since greatly extended our knowledge of various phases; but because new collectors find much of the old data hard-to-come-by, the present writer has included excerpts from these two pioneer check lists, thereby providing some basic reference material before going on to cover more modern areas, like the medicine, figural, whiskey, and scent bottles which command so much current collector interest. For easy citation and study, the subject is organized under four major groupings.

Group A.—This section covers the containers used primarily to hold strong drink. It begins with a section on carboys, casks and decanters, swings on to Early American-made Chestnuts, through the Historical flasks—the Eagle, Cornucopia and other pictorials of this period, then into the Booz, **Bininger** and other marked whiskey bottles, to end with a section on the late Whiskey Bottles and Gift Decanters now being collected by and from present day imbibers of "Mountain Dew."

Group B.—This covers containers used primarily for Bitters and other aids to health, from the 1800's through the 1890 era of Puritanical Tipplers down to present day consumers of Geratol, Lydia Pinkham and Peruna. It begins with a section on Bitters (Bunkum for Booze), lists many collectable related proprietary medicine bottles, finishes with the vials intended for prescription medicine and various self-help remedies.

Group C.—This is a Miscellany covering all household and personal needs not associated with either strong drink or patent medicine. It begins with a section on milk, oil, pickle, fruit jars, syrups and other staple food containers, then turns to mineral, soda and beverage bottles, including such old standbys as "Pluto Water for the Bowels." A section on perfume, scent and snuff bottles lead to a final roundup for the household heading with descriptions of ink bottles, hair dye, blacking, barber, target, drug store and testing bottles.

Group D.—The last major head has been kept for the object figural bottles and whimseys that are so much in demand by collectors today. Developed for a wide variety of purposes, or even for none other than "just looks," these bottles range all the way from the very early to the very late. Many collectors assign purposes and names to such bottles which may or may not have basis in fact; other collectors reject all hearsay and turn their attention primarily to amassing "association material" —that is, the advertising pamphlets and wall signs that were used to sell the contents of all types of bottles which have been listed in groupings A through D. Because so little has been written on this phase, here is included a large section on bottle advertising and labels; then it goes on to a brief resume of the entire bottle field with some special notes on "how to gauge the age of a bottle," a glossary of bottle-terms and an extensive bibliography.

Early American Bottles carried varied contents other than the corn whiskey and Yankee brewed Jamaica rum. But equally worthy of attention (and often just as old) were the apothecary and bitters bottles that followed this Group A trend; handled glass jugs, many with original labels, grenade fire extinguishers, pickle bottles, some with gothic arches on all four sides, peppersauce bottles, mineral water bottles and hundreds of patent medicines, which in the main originally contained bourbon whiskey with a dash of herbs to cover the law, demijohns in cylindrical, globular and kidney shapes, drug bottles and jars, chestnut bottles, so-called because they resemble a chestnut in form, the New England and Mid Western type of swirled and ribbed Pitkins, inks, scents, many of them in the shape of small figures, Mid Western quilted, ribbed or swirled bottles and flasks and the very early types of black squat bottles, some from Indian graves and others bearing dates seals on their sides from 1716 to 1846, the earliest unmarked speciments dating back to 1660, pottery book bottles, produced in great numbers at Bennington, Vt., and figure or character bottles which are a field in themselves.

Study of the perfume bottles and toilet sets purveyed to our great grandmothers, the small scent and smelling salt bottles for handbags or reticule, pickle and ink bottles, also the snuff and pill bottles, the old heirloom decanters and carafes, the family fruit jars, nursing bottles, and milk jars, the syrup, oil and vinegar bottles of colonial days, the "pop" and soda siphons, the ginger beer and mineral waters that were sold in special containers leads finally to proprietary medicine and the figural bottles which are now in such collector demand. All of these, to say nothing of special character whimseys and fantasies in glass deserve more than a passing mention in this book. Our concentration is on American Glass Bottles, and precludes study of the leather and stone bottles of all types which preceded. We need not go into the early glass bottle blowing of the Egyptians, the Roman Empire types and those of the Venetian and German enameled periods. These are already well covered else-

— GROUP A: LIQUORS

where. We do devote a partial chapter to English bottle making simply because so much of this product found its way into America and is collected today often as American Glass. Thereafter our main interest will be the color, shape and contents of American made bottles during the full stretch of our nationhood from its beginning down to present day, but with first attention upon its whiskey and so-called "medicinal" containers.

Never before has anyone attempted the full story of American Glass bottle making from pioneer day (when every man kept up his spirits by liberal nips from a hand-blown flask) on down to today's home party (its bar or cocktail table overflowing with gift 'decanters' made for various modern distillers). But this book is much more than a tale of why whiskey flasks and now empty proprietary medicine bottles are now collected; it lays bare the sources of a great American industry, aids the identification of different types produced and instead of stopping with the rare and scarcely attainable early varieties, traces developments through the Bitters, Bunkum and Booz Era to the present rage for preserving old Mason fruit jars and recent character bottles. Many of the latter's original contents were, true to form, at least slightly alcoholic.

Readers whose avocation is neither in collecting nor sampling the contents of various bottle-types will find here much exciting Americana Lore. For whereas the mass-promoted taste now veres to the zip-sip tin beer can and the status bid of a scotch highball, the Grand Old 'Corn for the World' bottle will always have its nostalgic following. In the pages which follow, and especially in the captioned bottle-pictures which are so liberally interspersed, students can trace our Nation's History from the Moonshiners Mountain Dew and Yankee Rum down through the patent medicine craze to modern times when even the design of perfume and household food containers has been used to shape both taste and demand.

In conclusion, it should be emphasized that the writer has not been especially interested in the details of proper attribution for different types of bottles, i.e., "who made this and when." Attempts at such definite attribution for special bottle types has already been undertaken by others. Here instead, he invites both the neophyte to bottle collecting and the seasoned expert to see what a wealth of bottle-variety in which an individual can specialize. Verily, this is better than the fine points of stamp collecting. For old bottles lie around everywhere, and even many recent discards will be the rarities of tomorrow. In fact the entire subject is so vast that this limited deluxe edition has had to be arranged as four books in one, with each of its major groupings given its own classification system.

Yorker Yankee Village
Watkins Glen, N. Y.

Larry Freeman

CABINET OF A BOTTLE-COLLECTOR.

— GROUP A: LIQUORS

BOTTLE COLLATERALS

THE PIONEER BOTTLE COLLECTORS

Somewhere the writer should pay tribute to all the pioneer bottle collectors whose interest and preservation tendencies have kept a very ephemeral object from being lost to posterity. Five names come to mind, and all but the last, Charles Gardner, are no longer with us. Stephan Van Rensselaer and James Thompson were well known to the writer, George McKearin and Edwin LeFever almost not at all. We commemorate the classificatory work of Van Rensselaer and Thompson in special sections devoted to their pursuits of Flasks and Bitters Bottles. Edwin LeFevre, who wrote among other things the famous 1929 Saturday Evening Post article, "Why I Collect Empty Bottles," was seen in an Antique shop that year, haggling over prices. George McKearin, who was prevailed upon to open his shop door late one night in 1940, had by that time become the outstanding authority in the field. Having tried out every kind or type of bottle collecting and settled on the Historical Flask as his great specialty, he was not much interested in the writer's drive for 1900 specimens. Speaking of this encounter with the Van Rensselaers, he was told this interesting anecdote: "When George was first getting interested in old glass he brought a blown object into our New York City shop and described it as a drinking vessel; actually it was an early telegraph wire insulator; yet in this way was a connoisseur's knowledge first born." Then there is Mr. Gardner, without whose aid this book could not have been written. Since he is the last one left of the great pioneer bottle collectors, below is an interview conducted recently in his New London, Connecticut home where he holds court for his bottle friends and displays a collection which your writer calls "the greatest."

"In 1929, Mrs. Gardner and I called on friends with a window full of colored bottles which they had accumulated from various sources. Our hostess explained the meaning of a pontil mark which appeared on the bases of these. Then and there I became interested in old bottles and since that time I have been an ardent collector.

"Prior to bottle collecting I had collected guns. One day Stephen Van Rensselaer, who had written a book on the subject of old bottles, came to see my collection. As he dealt in old guns, I parted with a station-wagonload of these in exchange for his bottles. This gave me a very good start. My collection has since grown in size and importance to the point it numbers some four thousand specimens, and requires two floors of an addition I had built for the purpose of properly displaying these treasures.

— MORTGAGING THE FARM

From a lithograph by D. W. Kellogg & Company of Hartford. Quite obviously the title of this print is one of implication mortgaged; but it will be if Hiram stops at the dram shop on his homeward way from the hayfield. The industry of hen her brood is by no means an accidental feature. It is intended to convey a lesson. So, too, is the representation of the watering trough, while their master's nose is pointed toward the aromas wafted from the open bar.

— GROUP A: LIQUORS

"Unlike some hobbies, bottle collecting can be a profitable investment. At the present market my collection would bring around $50,000. Needless to say I did not invest that much. I hope, Dr. Freeman, you will not attempt a price guide in your book, for values are ever changing. As examples of the increase in value over the years I would cite three instances. In 1931 I purchased a flask known as the Jared Spencer and marked Manchester, Conn., from Stephen Van Rensselaer for $75.00. A few years later, a friend collector offered me a $500 G. E. refrigerator for this flask and right away the wife made up my mind to accept. About three years later the same friend obtained a duplicate of the flask and traded it back to me for three flasks that cost me a total of $45.00. In 1956 a duplicate of this flask was sold for $570.00. These four bottles together with a few unimportant inks are the only bottles I have ever parted with from my collection. Another time a picker brought me in a flask tightly clasped in his hand and said he was going to sell it to me sight unseen. Seems he called a local dealer on the phone and was offered $2.50 for a flask with cornucopia on one side and eagle on the other. Since he heard I was a beginner he thought to take advantage of my ignorance for $8.00. I am mighty glad he did; a similar flask sold a year ago for $290.00. I also purchased a Stiegel amethyst Daisy in Square at $250.00 and the latest selling price for a similar bottle was $700.00. To enjoy the fun of collecting and at the same time be aware you are actually making a profitable investment explains one of the important advantages of this hobby. As one old chap said when I asked him how he could bear to part with his collection: "I have had all the pleasure of collecting them and admiring them over the years and now I can have the fun of spending the money I get for them."

"I have had an opportunity to watch glass blowing in several factories and it is a most interesting sight. Knowing how my bottles were actually made lends added charm. I have also visited a number of glass house sites where the former factories stood and have gathered fragments of glass that identified certain bottles in my collection.

"One interesting sidelight on bottle collecting is the number of reproductions on the market. These bottles are produced in part by Clevenger of Clayton, N. J., manufactured with no intent to fool the public but as decorators' material, attractive bright colored bottles in the old designs at a very low price.

"I think a hobby of some kind is an absolute necessity to a person who has passed middle age. I am now over seventy and look forward every day to the prospect of finding something to add to my collection. Every motor trip we take or every visit to another city offers the chance for such a thrill; and when one grows old, thrills are worth seeking. This remark of Homer Keyes, founder of Antiques Magazine, also sticks with me: 'It is a pleasure to meet a collector who appreciates a full bottle as well as an empty one.' "

GRAND OLD AMERICAN BOTTLES

Demijohns

Illustrating the off-hand and mold-blown technique.

The heavy bottle which was probably a failure.

— GROUP A: LIQUORS

CHAPTER 1 DEMIJOHNS & CARBOYS

If anyone sets out to get a sample collection of all types of bottles that have been made or used to hold a certain kind of liquid, he will find a fascinating study ahead: Let us confine ourselves first to the bottles intended for "spirits" (whiskey, wines, gin and hard liquors). The first spirit bottles to be found in America are plain and cut-glass decanters, practically all of English origin. A sample of this type together with the chained wine labels in Sheffield or solid plate belong in any spirit bottle collection. So, too, might be the carboys and wicker covered demijohns that carried hard liquor contents in quantity from across the sea and from which the wine merchant or tavern keeper rebottled. Next would come some of the early free-blown bubble bottles, then the blown-molded ones extending through the various periods from those with and without pontil showing, to the expanded-mold flasks and finally to the products of full blown mold and bottle pressing machines. Here variety ranges from so-called Historical flasks to Booz and Bininger whiskey bottles, the hip flasks of pre and post Volstead Act days even into the collecting of modern "nips," as well as the special character types and Christmas gift decanters put out at the present time.

Into a spirit bottle collection inevitably fall some which may not have been designed for hard liquors but were used first to sell pop, syrups, even ammonia and hair dyes. All of these other bottle types are covered in detail in later sections. Always know, however, which ones are modern reproductions and which old. For instance you can get a modern Aunt Jemima syrup bottle at the super market for fifty-nine cents, or wait and see it offered for $1.50 and up at some so-called antique shop (and really worth it too).

Our first or A Grouping covers only the array of whiskey types. In one hundred or more years of collecting bottles after their contents have gone down the drain, we pause with each spirit bottle type and period to list as many different forms as possible. However, we are not going to try to assign each a maker, place or time, especially since variations of the same type sometimes appears endless. Far better each type be given a representative sampling and have some blank space left where the collector (using our system) can put added notes he unearths for self. While both Egyptians and Romans made glass bottles (usually small) the earliest spirit and wine bottles related to our own Colonial Period came from 15th and 16th Century Europe. England was not far behind the Dutch, northern German enamelers and Venetian glass makers, especially when it came to turning out the crude heavy bubble bottles or demijohns used to carry potable liquors to the American market. In fact, the English tried to keep the Colonies from making any manufactured articles; carboys and wicker-covered glass demijohns were no exception. It is doubtful if many of the larger demijohns (holding several gallons) that one sees in collections and antique shops are even very ancient. Most are 19th Century; but a few of the heavy dark ones might just be 18th Century English. If one wants a truly old bottle of the Colonial period, he searches for a type of smaller container in which the name and vintage date of the original consignor or owner is "sealed" on the glass. In an accompanying page we show samples of these early hand-blown bubble-bottles coming here from England, including the so-called 11th dated 1690 bottle found in 1933." Since that discovery several others have been turned up, at least one in America. We also show the gradual evolution of liquor bottle shapes from the crude blown bubbles of that period to a form almost identical with that of many modern bottles.

Demand for these first heavy black glass "Hogarth's" or crude wine-serving bottles grew so rapidly that by 1695 over 240,000 dozen such products were being made in England each year. In his history of English Glass Making, H. J. Powell reports there were nine such bottle houses in the London district, five each in Bristol, Newcastle and Stourridge, two each in Newnham, Gloucester, Silkstone and Yorkshire. He also reports how they were first made; "from the 13th Century on, bottles were merely a bubble with a neck, the blowing tube used to form a large bladder, then 'thrown' so to stretch the neck before separating it (from the blow pipe with a wet stick) and putting it in the annealing furnace." Of course, even before these crude black glass bottles were invented, wine and spirits were carried by animal bladders and in leather bottles. The 16th Century glass-type improvement seems to have been largely in giving a slight push-up to the bottom of the bottle, which greatly increased its strength in withstanding breakage. One will note that this 'kick-up' is still used today with many wines and liquors. For correct bottle terms consult the glossary.

Of the various early bottle types we have shown, (1) the tall and squat bottles with kick-up bottoms, (2) then the more squatty types with rather long necks (1730) on to (3) those made before the turn of the century with a tapering cylindrical neck and very high kick-up, most of which are presumable English in origin. Those so-called Blob or Dutch bottles (where surface decorations in terms of small blobs of glass were applied on the outside of the bottle), should really be called punts and are best studied as "seals" or "bosses."

On another page we show by way of contrast German Enameled, Spanish, Venetian and other early foreign bottles used for Brandy and Spirits. While not American, many of these gave names to bottle types which later were sometimes made by American glasshouses. Note the

— GROUP A: LIQUORS

Holland Gin Bottles—square faced gins or spirits which belong in every bottle collection. Usually the ones you find are quarts and some are fairly late. These bottles are properly labeled square-faced spirit bottles and besides being imported, they were extensively made in early America. Such bottles were blown in an open—topped mold—the easiest type for a glass blower to handle; the gather was blown in from the top and then easily lifted out at the top because the sides were tapered. These bottles were usually sent empty from the glass house. They were packed a dozen to a wooden case, fully partitioned to prevent breakage. Tavern keepers and grocers bought a quantity and put in whatever contents they wished (usually gin or rum drawn from casks) to sell to the thirsty public.

Perhaps one of the rarest of these intact cased lots was found by Mr. Charles Gardner long ago. It carries 15 oversize gin bottles, their size is 19¾ high by 7¾ inches square—all nicely set in a dovetailed pine chest. Who has or can find another? Anyway, happy hunting!

While the English entered the bottle game fairly late, by early 18th Century the products of Nailsea and Bristol were so well received in Colonial America that most townhouses sported Bristol glass decanters and Nailsea flasks. And while an expert in the decanter field can show you early French-type decanters, the really high-styles were those of cut Waterford, Cork and Irish glass in contrast to the Bristol types (either slightly ovoid or of taper shape). It is thought that the broader and shouldered barrel form (which we usually associate with Irish decanters) came in around 1770, with the applied neck rings or colors being made after 1790. But whether these were prominent before or just after American Independence, we do know that many of each type reached these shores. Rather than bother with specific foreign attributions, it is now time to move into American made products. We find bottles as the principal commercial product of most glasshouses operating here from the late 18th century through the first half of the 19th. Before that time, if any glass was made in America, it was largely for windows with perhaps the remainder of the day's mix given to the glass blower. He could take an offhand blown piece away free and exchange it for "spirits" from the home brewer's still, or to use at the store for a refill.

The history of English bottle making goes back to around 1557; but it was difficult to get the secrets of the glass mix into any other hands. Their first patent for the manufacture of glass was March 26, 1623 and throughout the Colonial period of our history, England would allow neither artisans nor formulas to leave the Mother Country. Instead, English glass plants made many carboys and heavy flasks which they filled with whiskey and sent to America in large quantity. Everything was done to discourage local industry. It was not until after the Revolution that America began to make the bottles which would carry the whiskey, rum and other spirits that the hearty pioneers of the West needed and loved.

EARLY AMERICAN BOTTLES AND FLASKS

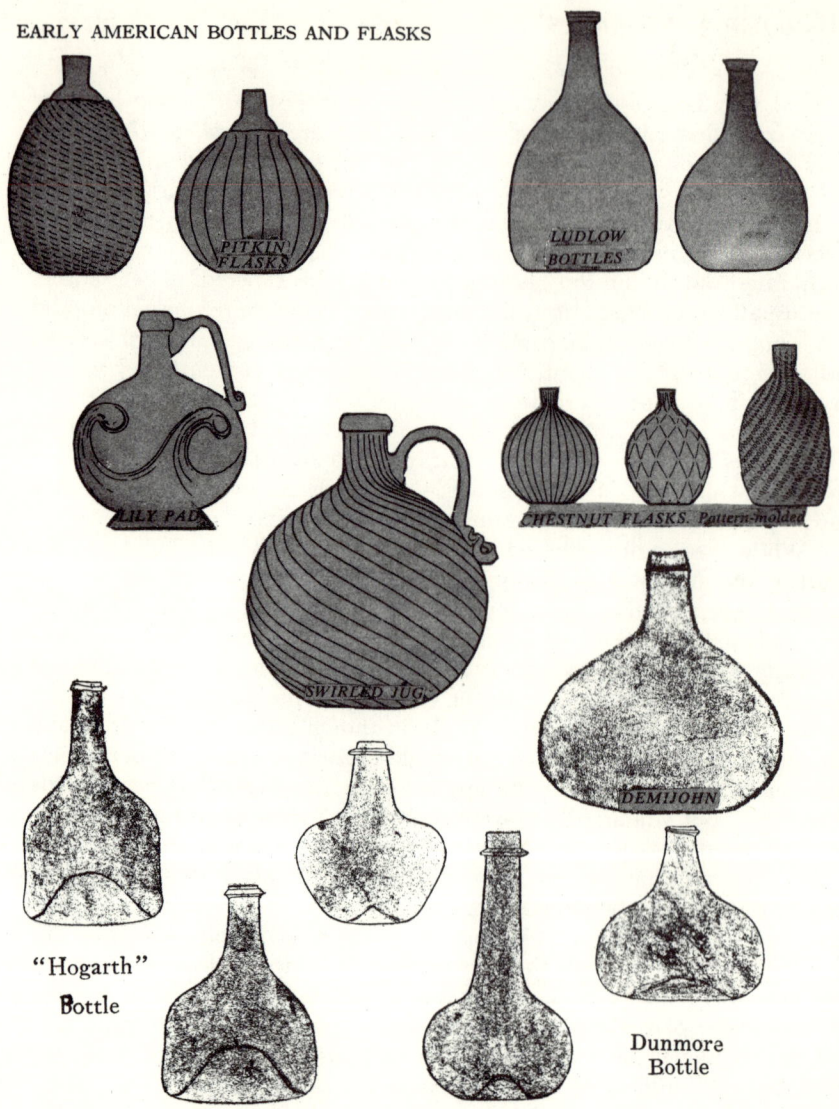

The big demand was for window glass to help light the homes being erected in the wilderness and soon producers of such a commodity were also being asked to blow some pocket flasks needed to hold daily pint of corn whiskey or other heady spirits as required by frontiersmen. Here you have the origin of the Great American Bottle—a "sustainer of life" and an article of commerce still going strong. As much as the contents of such bottled euphoria were loved, so people have always craved to collect these pocket containers as well. This leads us into an account of "seal" bottles and high style home decanters which are the flasks forerunner and counterpart.

— GROUP A: LIQUORS   17

THE EARLY "SEAL" BOTTLES

THE ELEVENTH BOTTLE

I thought it might be of interest to your readers to learn that another of these rare bottles has turned up, and was recently on show at the Wine Trade Exhibition at Vintners' Hall, although it arrived too late to be included in the exhibition catalogue. The ten recorded dated English glass wine bottles of this century are now increased to eleven.

The bottle in question is the property of Mrs. K. S. Cassels of Minehead. It is of the usual dark bottle-green glass, 7ins. high, and of the half dumpy shape typical of its date. The seal or lozenge on the shoulder contains

PENNSYLVANIA AQUAMARINE RIB BOTTLE
Club-shaped, the sides overlaid with ribbed strap medallion containing the initials "R. G." Tapered Possibly the initials indicate Ralph Galagher, for Lorenz & Wightman in the early 19th century. Rare.

Early Seal Bottles from the Gardner Collection: One dated 1716 is the Seal of Jonathan Swift—author of Gulliver's Travels, an English Bottle found in an Early R.L. Indian Grave, also three late Seal Bottles (see text).

— GROUP A: LIQUORS

CHAPTER II EARLY SEAL BOTTLES

THE EARLY "SEAL" BOTTLES

To the collector who hankers to add the earliest known type of bottle to his hoard, the way is very rough. Practically all the earliest of those "bottle blobs" in black (dark green) glass which have an impressed seal showing date of making are in museums. We have already mentioned that these seals, usually circular, were pressed into a hot blob of glass to show either the name of the owner (Lord Hume) whose wine it would hold or the year of vintage it held (Medoc 1779). Such bottles as have been dug up were usually small, holding only a pint of liquor and were stored in the master's cellar. While the writer was a Fellow at Cambridge University recently, he was privileged to see the wine cellar of one of the oldest colleges, and there amid dark and cobwebs was such a dated bottle with its contents still intact. Unfortunately the light in said crypt was so feeble one could not make out the date. We do know, however, that the number of early dated (seal) bottles left in England are so few that every discovery is subject to a special news item. For instance, an accompanying page shows a report (from Connoisseur—July 1933) of the eleventh dated bottle find. The seal or lozenge on the shoulder carries the date 1690.

Anyone interested in this type of early bottle should visit or consult the out-of-print book on this subject reported in the bibliography, "The Wine Trade Exposition" at Vintners Hall in London, holds the key here. We show a page of an early exhibition folio from such a work. It is possible to find some such items made as late as the early 19th century. These and bottles with small blobs of glass applied over the outside surface of a free blown piece would probably be quite early. They are quite different from applied glass decorations in the Venetian manner, the latter (of course) in contrast with the early English decanters mentioned earlier in this chapter.

In conclusion it is presumed that most of the bottles described in our first A Grouping chapter, and made to hold wine or spirits, were free blown or early blown-molded. Casks and carboys in wicker may of course be much later in origin. Glass cutting and wheel engraving was practiced on some early decanter types, even occasionally on blown-pattern molded ones. If the reader is not already familiar with the methods used to produce bottles of these types, he can consult both the introductory pictures and an appendix at the end. Certainly very few of the really old ones described as seal bottles were American made.

–HOW TO JUDGE AGE OF EARLY SPIRITS BOTTLES

A final recapitulation is here given to this chapter's study of carboys, casks, demijohns, decanter and "seal" bottles. In the interests of systematic nomenclature the term "casks" should properly refer only to the oak kegs in which spirits were shipped for later decanting. A carboy is usually thought of as a very large bottle (holding up to or beyond ten gallons), while demijohns hold smaller amounts, usually under four gallons. The latter were shipped into the Colonies (with and without liquid contents), often originally covered with wicker to prevent breakage. All early ones were globular in shape and free blown. The typical English demijohn has very slanting shoulders, the heavy base forming the bottle of the triangle. Less slanting sides form the kidney-shaped demijohn and the smaller 18th century English free blowns are sometimes called egg-shaped. In contrast, Italian demijohns are more pear-shaped and often "pinched in." Free blown or partly molded demijohns are found with a sheered top; early ones have an applied ring and later ones a sloping collared mouth. Of course a large number of these demijohns were actually made in America rather than imported. They were general purpose bottles, as were the carboys, to replace the contents carried in oaken casks or kegs that often leaked. One can be assured that a great deal of *American Corn Whiskey* and *Jamaica Rum* found its way into those demijohns sent to tavern keepers and now displayed as empty bottles. Not so, however, the original contents of the smaller "seal" bottles; these held special wine or brandy spirits described below.

The items which have special significance for a collector of really early bottles, are those small heavy black glass long-necked blob bottles of the 17th and 18th century on the shoulder of which is impressed a seal in the glass which often dates the bottle, its contents or the original owner. Early dated sealed bottles are extremely rare. In fact we have already mentioned how the eleventh one of these rarities (dated 1690) was discovered in England back in 1933. Of this Mr. Charles Gardner of New London, Connecticut recently said, "must be I found the 12th dated seal (1696), about the same time. One dated along with the initial J. S., was later identified by Vintners Hall lists as being the seal of Johnathon Swift, author of Gullivers Travels." Just how Mr. Gardner's bottle arrived in America remains a mystery. Of course it could have been stolen from Swift's private stock; or its contents having been downed and the bottle discarded, it could have been used to ship "firewater" to the Indians. Whatever its history, Mr. Gardner reports he did get one sealed bottle out of an Indian grave in Rhode Island. It's more squatty shape indicates an early 18th century date and the initials TCD tend to indicate a tavern keeper named Drinkwater whose descendants ran a "pub" at Southwalk, England on the Thames entrance to London for many generations. The inscription on this 8-inch bottle is, "The

— GROUP A: LIQUORS

White Bear at Bridge Fort," and this encircles the figure of a bear; research has proved this the sign of the tavern that T. C. Drinkwater ran.

Three later sealed bottles are also in Mr. Gardner's collection. One is a wine bottle dated 1846, another held enough wine for a dual serving —it carries the seal of Lincoln College, England and has no date. Special attention is due his third example which bears the seal of the Lenox family, early New Yorkers, whose books and money started New York Public Library. The original label below the seal reads as follows: "Imported Maderia by the late Robert Lenox, esq., by Ship Grace via India in April 1804, put in demijohn Oct. 1805. Bottled March 1816, Rebottled (and used) June 1888"—surely quite an aged drink and an even better bottle empty! As you can see by the examples shown, seal bottles vary in shape with the age of manufacture. Collectors seeking the early 17th century types may have to settle for small single serving examples such as is shown together with the 6-inch measuring tape. These are old and also expensive even though they carry no seal. The Bibliography at end of book tells where you can find added information on early seal bottles, decanters and demijohns. Collecting in this part of the field is tough.

Perhaps one of the rarest of these intact cased lots was found Mr. Charles Gardner long ago. It carries 15 oversize gin bottles.

Blue Glass Decanters: late eighteenth century

Spanish, Venetian and other early foreign bottles used for Brandy and Spirits. While not American, many of these gave names to bottle types which later were sometimes made by American glasshouses. Note the

— GROUP A: LIQUORS

CHAPTER III WINE DECANTERS

AMERICAN WINE BOTTLES AND DECANTERS

Stiegel and the Philadelphia Glass Works both advertised decanters of many sizes in the 1770's, but not one extant specimen is authoritively attributed. A few may have been free-blown, but the great majority were probably blown-molded in Sandwich, Massachusetts, and Keene, New Hampshire in clear glass in imitation of the Irish cut glass decanters. We do know that bottles for both table and pocket were a principal product of most American Glass Houses from 1750 to 1850. The first free blowns were from a bottle glass (usually dark green). The glass blower turned to clear soda lime and flint glass only to make his decanters. The idea of blowing decanters in a smooth mold probably came along with other early pocket flasks. Next came the blown pattern mold, and this could be further elaborated by redipping in molten glass for further strengthening and also expanding the already molded pattern. The expanded pattern-mold type of blown decanter is a quite offhand piece, while the major American examples found are of the blown full pattern mold types. These were widely made by many glasshouses, along with other spirit containers, including swirled jugs, wine bottles and large demijohns some of which took the place of imported ones to carry liquor in quantity from country inns. Liquor came to bars in barrels and customers either brought or bought a bottle or demijohn to carry off their liquor. Naturally it is difficult in this opening section to keep entirely off the subject of the small individual flasks. We must remember that all types were often made by the same glass house and that fine decanters, even those free blown and with hand-cut engraving may have as its cousin a very prosaic carboy-demijohn or free blown flask. Probably not many bottles (if any), were made in early America with a wine seal attached. "Corn licker" did not require a labeled glass bottle as it does today and the only glass name put on some decanters would be the intaglio pattern word, Gin or Port.

The collector of Early Decanters will have some difficulty in separating the products of English, Irish and other glasshouses from those made in America. According to McKearin, earliest blown products carried similar shapes originally developed in England up to 1780, these included a long slender shouldered body with slender neck and spire or pointed stopper; the plain or wheel engraved, had slender tapering necks with circular or lozenge stopper and plain rather than flanged lip. It is thought these ovoid taper decanters were gradually replaced beginning about 1775 by the broader and shouldered barrel form and that around

Pittsburgh Glass

Dorflinger Glass displayed at the Centennial Exhibition. —Courtesy Philadelphia Museum of Arts

— GROUP A: LIQUORS

1790 a cylindrical decanter was evolved with nearly vertical sides up to a rounded sloping shoulder and with applied neck rings and mushroom or wheel stoppers. All of these engraved or cut decanters involving much hand work (some Irish), a few Stiegel type continued their vogue well into the 19th centry, when American ingenunity developed a decanter which effectively took the place of the expensive and fashionable imported Irish and English blown glass with wheel cut designs. Through the use of the blown three-mold process, we set out to simulate the cut-glass decanter by adapting such patterns through the medium of a full blown three-mold design which used a three-section contact mold to form both shape and pattern. Decanters were among the first commercial productions of this American contribution to glassmaking; some were even labeled and advertised as "American Waterford." Such three-mold full blown decanters made their appearance around 1820 and were a vogue until late in the 1830's, when the pressing machine tended to take over for most tablewares. We show you on accompanying pages not only the earlier blown and hand cut decanters, but also examples of the three types of blown three-mold decanters as first listed by Mr. Van Rensselaer. We shall not go on to the 1850-1900 pressed wares since these are already adequately listed in the Kamm-Wood Encyclopedia of Pattern (Pressed Table) Glass (see Bibliography). For pressed glass gift decanters of the mid 20th century, made for whiskey manufacturers you will find adequate examples in the last section (chapter 8.) of our present Group A or Spirit Bottle Classification.

[105]   [96]   [107]   [97]

105. KEENE BLOWN THREE-MOLD DECANTER
   Of olive-amber glass, blown in the same mold as the preceding decanter.
96. KEENE BLOWN THREE-MOLD DECANTER   *Circa* 1825
   Olive-amber bottle glass, pint size, in a geometric pattern with Keene sunburst Type 1. These bottle-glass decanters never had stoppers.
106. SMALL OLIVE-AMBER GLASS BOWL
   Rare individual piece from the Keene factory of Justus Perry.
97. KEENE PINT DECANTER
   Like the preceding, but in rare olive-green color.
107. EXTREMELY IMPORTANT BLOWN THREE-MOLD BOTTLE
   Of clear olive-green glass. Believed to be a product of Perry's Keene glass factory.

— GROUP A: LIQUORS

We show you on accompanying pages cut decanters, but also examples of the three types of blown three-mold decanters as first listed by Mr. Van Rensselaer.

DECANTERS

THREE-SECTION MOLD BOTTLES

ARCHED

    1. Quart—clear glass. (U).

    2. Quart—clear glass. (U).

    3. Quart—clear glass, most elaborate of the arched pattern, with central horizontal ribbing, with the addition of entwined serpents. (U).

    4. Quart—clear glass, 10½ inches to top of stopper. (U).

    5. Quart—clear glass. (U).

GEOMETRIC

    6. Half pint—clear glass, 2¾ inches to top of stopper. Sunburst in combination with diamond diapering. (U).

    7. About half pint—clear glass, height 4¾ inches, diamond diapering. (U).

    8. About half pint—clear glass, height 6⅜ inches, semi-horizontal ribbing. (U)

    9. About half pint—sapphire blue, height 6¾ inches, vertical ribbing. (U).

    10. Pint—clear glass, 7 inches to top of stopper, broad band of diamond diapering. (U).

    11. Pint—olive green, height 7 inches, sunburst-in-the-square. (Kn).

    12. Pint—golden amber, height about 7 inches. Alternate squares of diamond diapering and sunburst-in-the-square. Also half pint. (Kn).

    13. Pint—clear glass, height 8½ inches to top of stopper. Broad band of diamond diapering. (U).

    14. Quart—olive amber, height about 9½ inches. Alternate squares of diamond diapering and small squares of diamond diapering with sunburst border. (Kn).

    15. Light amethyst, 10 inches to top of stopper. Same design as No. 14. (U).

    16. Quart—clear glass, 10¼ inches to top of stopper. Same as No. 15. (U).

Upper   19   28   4   23
Lower 24   15   17   18   16

 per   9   11   14   12   8
wer 8   13   20   21   22   10   6

— GROUP A: LIQUORS

17. Quart—clear glass, 10½ inches to top of stopper, sunburst-in-the-square. (U).

18. Quart—clear glass, 10½ inches to top of stopper. Same as No. 16. (U).

19. Quart—clear glass, 10½ inches to top of stopper. Broad band of diamond diapering. (U).

20. Quart—clear glass, 11 inches to top of stopper, horizontal fluting. (U).

21. Quart—amethyst (light), 11 inches to top of stopper. Two series of horizontal fluting. (U).

22. Quart—clear glass, 11 inches to top of stopper, vertical fluting. (U).

23. Quart—light amethyst, 11 inches to top of stopper, large sunburst-in-circle. (U)

24. Quart—clear glass, 11¼ inches to top of stopper. Same as No. 18. (U).

25. Quart—clear glass, sunburst-in-square. (U).

26. Quart—clear glass, the sunburst in combination with diamond diapering and lettered "WINE". (U).

27. Quart—clear glass, the sunburst in combination with diamond diapering and lettered "BRANDY". (U)

28. Quart—clear glass. The sunburst in combination with diamond diapering and lettered "RUM". (U).

29. Pair blue, made 1825 (SW)

30. Group rare pieces, all miniature except the cruet bottles. (U)

BAROQUE

31. Quart—clear glass, horn of plenty. (U).

32. Quart—clear glass. (U).

33. Pint—clear glass. (U).

34. Broad vertical ribbing with banding in center of looped designs, about pint—clear glass, height 8½ inches. Attributed to Fredericktown, Maryland.

GRAND OLD AMERICAN BOTTLES

South Jersey-type.

South Jersey-type bottles

CHAPTER IV   E.A. POCKET FLASKS

Bottles were the principal product of most American glass houses from 1750 to 1860 and the great majority of these were intended for "liquid refreshment" or more impolitely "good corn whiskey" (bourbon). This is not the place to develop the origin of this true American product, still being made in the old sour mash manner, bootleggers, moonshiners and Blue Ridge revenuers not withstanding. We are here interested only in the glass bottle or pocket flask, which every mother's son once used to carry for sustaining his work in the fields or took along on his journey through the Wilderness for frequent replenishing at rude trading posts and taverns along the way. These frontiersmen set a pattern of hard drinking, and a prize collection of the blown flasks they left behind is sought by modern Americans, many of whose thirst for such spirited contents has remained unabated down to the present day.

The neophyte collector is often told to start with a *Pitkin* flask. Actually this type was made at many Eastern glasshouses like Keene and Coventry as well as at Manchester, Connecticut. There is even a difference between New England Pitkins (smaller and thinner) and the Mid-West Pitkins (larger and more canteen-shaped). But if interested only in overall type, say all were usually of pint size and with further blowing from a pattern-mold to obtain typical Pitkin patterns of "vertical ribbing with broken swirl."

Probably Westarburg, N. J. (and not Pitkin) made our first real American glass flasks. From about 1739 until its 1780 failure there was mass-produced gallon, half gallon, quart and pint containers. At first typified by the early long-necked free blown bottles in dark glass as described in a previous chapter, at some later date there began to be blown a more varied *chestnut shape* from a mix which if purified would have been clear instead of light green. One worker (Stenger) established his own plant in nearby Glassboro and gave rise to a variety of flask shapes and colors. Now described as "South Jersey Type Bottles," the colors of these flasks ran from light olive to aquamarine and dark green, while shades of amber ran from deep brown to honey color. The workers were designers as well as makers, hence they introduced many individual or swirled or scroggled overlays that are now prime collector items. All these earliest flasks were free-blown and decorated by manipulation. Since the decoration had to be worked while the glass was still in a plastic state, ornamentation was never quite the same for any two flasks. Today, we recognize at least five types of early decorated chestnut flasks:

(1) *Punts*: applied blobs of glass, swirled or redipped and hand molded into motives such as leaves or shields (includes seals).

The neophyte collector is often told to start with a *Pitkin* flask. Actually this type was made at many Eastern glasshouses like Keene and Coventry as well as at Manchester, Connecticut. There is even a difference between New England Pitkins (smaller and thinner) and the Mid-West Pitkins (larger and more Division I—Pitkin Type next shown only)

Pitkin Type, Division I
Plain and with inside Ribbing, Division II
Single and Double Mouthed, Division III
Side Depressions, Division IV

Division I.—Ribbing to right or left, diapering, and diamond pattern.

PLATE 1
1. Green, diaper pattern 5½ inches.
2. Bright green, heavy diamond pattern running to top of neck, 6½ inches.
3. Very light green elongated diamond pattern, 6 inches.
4. Light sea green spiral ribbing running to left and then to right to top of neck, 6¾ inches.
5. Greenish yellow diaper pattern, 6¼ inches.
6. Clear glass, diaper pattern, 4½ inches.
While several of the above may be Stiegel they can not be definitely classed as such.

PLATE 2
1. Olive. Ribbing running to left. Heihgt 5 inches.
2. Light green, vertical ribs and horizontal ribbing running to right. Height 5½ inches.
3. Light green, bulbous shape. Broad ribbings running to right. Height 5 inches.
4. Amber. Ribbing running to left. Height 5 inches.
5. Olive amber, ribbing running to left. Height 4½ inches.
6. Olive brown, vertical ribbing and horizontal ribbing running to left. Height 5 inches.
7. Bottle green, vertical ribbing. Height 5¾ inches.
8. Dark sea green, vertical ribbing and ribbing running to the left. eight 6¾ inches.
9. Greenish amber, vertical ribbing and ribbing running to left. Height 6¼ inches.
10. Bright green, ribbing running to left. Height 5½ inches.
All the above have inserted necks.

PLATE 3
1. Aquamarine, vertical broad ribs and horizontal ribbing running to right. Height 6 inches.
2. Light amber, vertical ribs and horizontal ribbing running to left. Height 6½ inches.
3. Light green, vertical ribs and ribbing running to right. Height 7⅛ inches.
4. Sea green, vertical ribs, and horizontal ribbing running to left. Height 7⅛ inches.

— GROUP A: LIQUORS 33

    5. Bright olive green, vertical ribs and horizontal ribbing running to right. Height 6 inches.
    6. Amber brown, vertical ribs, horizontal ribbing running to right. Height 7½ inches.
    7. Dark green, heavy vertical ribs, horizontal ribbing running to left. Height 5½ inches.
    8. Bottle green, very fine ribbing running to right. Height 6½ inches.
    9. Dark amber, vertical ribs, and horizontal ribbing running to left. Height 6¾ inches.
    10. Light olive green, vertical ribs and ribbing running to right. Height 6½ inches.
All the above have inserted necks.

PLATE 4
    1. Deep amethyst.
    2. Dark amber.
    3. Dark amber.
    4. Amethyst.

    5. Aquamarine.
    6. Green.
    7. Light blue.
    8. Aquamarine.
About pint size, found in Ohio and typical specimens.

PLATE 4
    (Middle) Yellow green found near Middlebury and undoubtedly made at first factory. (Vt.)

    Clear glass, 4½ inches high.

    Horizontal rows of hob nails. Half pint— s b. (U).

    Half pint—very dark greenish-aquamarine. s m s b.

    Covered with ornaments like four-pointed stars. Pint—beautiful clear glass with very faint shading of yellowish green. Very crude flanged mouth. s b. Height 5¼ inches. (U).

    Another covered with small raised ornamentations, similar to dew drops about ⅛ inch in diameter, the edges are corrugated, coming to a point, and are not rounded. Pint—clear glass and bubbly. s m s b. (U).

DIVISION II.—PLAIN AND WITH INSIDE RIBBING.

PLATE 4
    Found near Middlebury and undoubtedly made at first factory. (Vt.) (Right and left.)

PLATE 117

— GROUP A: LIQUORS

PLATE 4
1. Light olive yellow. Height 8¾ inches. (U).
2. Light green. Decoration of vertically expanded ribbing. Height 8 inches (U).
3. Pale yellow green. Height 7½ inches. (U).
4. Clear light green. Height 6½ inches. (U).
5. Clear light green. Height 5 inches. (U).
6. Pint—smoked amber. f m   s b. from Ohio. (U).

DIVISION III.—SINGLE AND DOUBLE MOUTHED WITH AND WITHOUT QUILLING.

1. PEAR SHAPED (E)
Clear glass. Sides edged with quilling. Height 8½ inches, width 4¼ inches. (U).

2. DOUBLE MOUTHED
Clear, light amber. Height 8⅜ inches, width 3⅝ inches. Footed base. (SJ).

3. Pale yellow green. Height 9⅞ inches, width 4½ inches. (U).

4. Clear glass. Height 8½ inches, width 3⅝ inches. (SJ).

5. Light green, opaque white looping. Height 7¼ inches, width 3⅜ inches. (SJ).

DIVISION IV.—SIDE DEPRESSIONS OR FINGERHOLDS.

1. Pint olive amber. s m   s b.
2. Half pint, light green, swirled ribbing to left. sm s b.
3. Pint light green. f m   s b.
4. Pint light green. s m   s b.
5. Half pint blood amber. s m. s b.

Note: These flasks are attributed to foreign origin but I believe many were made in the United States, probably to satisfy the whim of the blower. The one shown on   is known to have been made at Stoddard, N. H. The flasks shown are less crude than the Tyrolean. The latter were pinched when in a plastic state to give a finger hold and the resulting impressions are much less uniform than those on the bottles on this plate. Furthermore, the necks were inserted instead of being blown with the bottle.

6. Half pint, golden amber. s m   s b. Height 6 inches, slightly sunken on each flat side. Also pint. (U).

7. Another, quarter pint, golden amber. s b. Height 5 inches. (St.)

(2) *Quilting* or trailing: applied wavy lines in swirled or crosshatched (diamond quilted) lines.

(3) *Rigaree*: applied ribbons in parallel lines.

(4) *Threading*: rows of superimposed glass on rim or neck.

(5) *Looping*: threads of glass on body of bottle in a different color.

The major difference between the Pitkin type flask and these early South Jersey types seems to be that Pitkin Chestnuts were pattern-molded i.e., the gather was redipped and blown in a two-part mold to make a ribbing then removed for further swirling of the gather as wished to make a broken swirl, but not to have any glass hand applied. Expanded blown molds are thus the presumed forerunners of many full patterned molded flasks which followed.

In moving towards the varieties of full pattern-molded flasks that challenge the collector, we must turn next to the work of Baron Stiegel, our second great name in bottle making. Just as there is a Wistar (South Jersey) type of free-blown flasks so we also recognize a Stiegel type which is largely expanded pattern-molded. Stiegel made bottles at Manheim, Pennsylvania, from 1763 to 1772, half gallons and pints, also the slightly smaller chestnut shapes known as pocket flasks. At first elaborately flower decorated and enameled on clear flint glass, Stiegel also turned to pattern molding of glass in amethyst and other colors.

Pattern molded glass is formed by blowing a blob of pliable hot glass into a mold which has a design cut in its inner surface. While still on the blow pipe, the impressed glass is released by opening the mold and further shaped by the free blown technique. Some variations in swirling and scroggles can be developed from a simple mold pattern (such as ribbing). But the favorite early Stiegel flask is probably one when the incised diamond-quilted pattern is given the expanded-mold treatment, i.e., blown larger so that the bottles come to full size with the quilting effect enlarged but made at the same time softer. Many people refer to all expanded mold diamond-quilted chestnuts or pocket flasks as Stiegel, especially those found in blue and amethyst. It would be more correct to call the Stiegel types, for the majority now extant were probably made in other Western Pennsylvania and Ohio factories, not at Manheim.

Although this section has given primary attention to free blown and pattern mold flasks in the chestnut shapes, we might mention that contemporaneously with these eighteenth century types, we find early gin, rum, and Dunmore squat wine bottles made in other shapes. Samples of such are shown (usually without attribution) in accompanying pictures. We might also mention that Deeming Jarves (our third great glass name) made blown bottles at Sandwich before and after his 1825 development of the pressing machine.

Remember, however, that this chapter has little implication for the historical and other pictorial flasks which flooded the market in the early 19th century. The typical free blown or expanded pattern mold flasks

GROUP A: LIQUORS

37

1 2 3 4

5 6 7 8

G22 D2 D1 G22 D2

Stiegel Bottles and Flasks

Perfume Bottle

1.4 Amethyst, with expanded pattern mold design of large diamond.

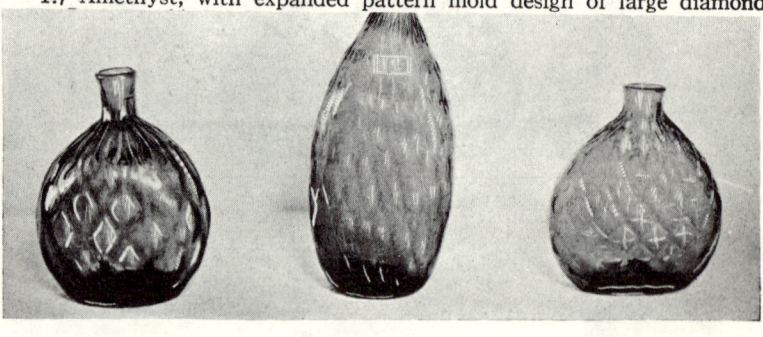

4   10   11

Pocket Flask

5. Amethyst, height 7¼ inches.

6. Clear glass, height 7 inches.

7. Clear glass, height 6½ inches.

8. Light amethyst, fine diamond pattern running (middle). Very rare.

9. Amethyst with pattern mold knobbed design, height 5¼ inches.

10. Green, small diamond type, height 7 inches.

11. Green, small diamond type, height 4½ inches.

The pocket flasks are quite flat. Golden amber is the rarest color. Also found in blue.

12. Clear flint double flask, height 8½ inches.

13. Decorated Stiegel Flask.

— GROUP A: LIQUORS

of the late 18th century carried over (in some places) well into the next century with little more than a conventional ornament suggested by the mold pattern. In fact when trying to date early whiskey flasks one usually passes from the "Stiegel type chestnut" to the first full-pattern-blowns called "sunbursts" and which are only slightly different in shape. It is these "sunbursts" and "Masonic" flasks, including the famed Jared Spencer (impressed name in glass and often wrongly attributed to Pitkin), or the 1810 J.P.F., which probably sparked vogue for later Historicals.

Before entering upon that story, here are some other terms the collector should know when discussing early bottles. (1) A Hogarth bottle is free blown and owes its name to the fact that Hogarth's Rakes Progress prints show a globular bottle with a high neck and crudely collared kick-up. (2) Other early squat bottles are sometimes referred to as Dunmores and those of similar globular shape have been referred to as Ludlow's because for years its was thought they were made about 1815 in a glasshouse at Ludlow, Mass. Actually these seem to have been made for over 100 years in most every glasshouse from Wistar to Stiegel and on well into the 19th century. (3) The thin saddle flask (free blown) is also an early rarity. (4) More examples remain of the chestnut Pitkins than the Stiegel type pocket flask. These are mentioned again to emphasize they were blown pattern molded whereas (5) early sunbursts and Masonics were probably the first flasks blown in a full size mold for decorative purposes.

STYLES AND ERAS IN BOTTLE MAKING

We have already seen something of the age of a bottle in terms of its shape and manner of making. But also one will find that the character of a bottle tends to vary with the style and status symbols set by different eras. In the early 19th century it was the fashion to carry liquid refreshments to the field and other places of business in either a stone handled pottery bottle or, more frequently, a glass flask adorned with some symbol of American independence. Masonic flasks were preferred by townsmen, those of fruit and fowl by the husbandmen. The distillers aided and abetted such a fad, but since their wares could be decantered by any crossroads store from bigger casks, the practice of impressing a company name in the glass did not follow. Instead a few bottle wholesalers selling such wares for packaging whiskey might imprint their own names. In general, however, there are few identifying marks of place of manufacture and so "Stiegel type" or "late Ohio type" make up for better attribution of unmarked early bottles. There is still a great number of these early flasks in private collections, but from such widely dispersed spots one can only conclude that all Western migrating Americans had these Grand Old Bottles and preserved them as a bit of color when new forms took the place of the chestnuts, sunbursts and Masonics described in this chapter. The vogue for Historical flasks held until about the mid 19th century, when emphasis of bitters and medicated liquor drinks took over to be eventually replaced by other types of bottles

Stiegel made bottles at Manheim, to 1772. At first elaborately flower decorated and enameled on clear flint glass, Stiegel also turned to pattern molding of glass in amethyst and other colors.

3

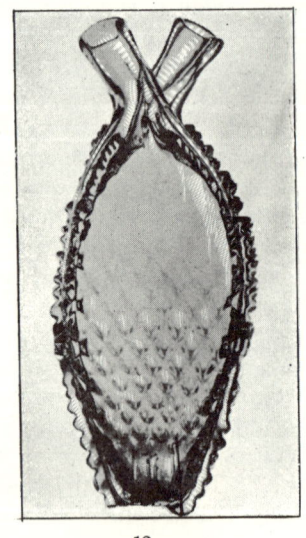

12

14

— GROUP A: LIQUORS

14. Enamelled drug bottle, dark amber, flashed with white, octagonal, height 7⅝ inches.

15. Blue conventionalized floral design, height 6 inches.

16. Clear glass, conventionalized floral design. ("Sebastian Witmer") height 7¼ inches.

17. Cordial bottle, clear glass, dove design, with stopper of clear glass, height 4¾ inches.

The enamelled bottles are found with various decorations, those listed being representative Stiegel examples. Other factories made them also but at this time they can not be designated.

18. Clear glass carafe, height 7¾ inches.

19. Nile green, height 10½ inches, upper left.

20. Dark red amber, height —— inches, upper right.

21. Green, height 11¾ inches, lower left.

22. Olive green, height 14 inches, lower right.

23. Handled Jug. Clear glass, decorated.

24. Another, clear glass, plain with stopper.

25. Cylindrical, narrowing at mouth which is flanged, the base is circular and flat with spread enough to maintain the vial in a vertical position. Clear glass. Height about 10 inches.

The foregoing groups can safely be assigned to Stiegel origin, since nearly all those illustrated are examples shown in "Stiegel Glass" by F. W. Hunter, whose attributions have never been questioned and supplemental research to his very thorough investigation has confirmed his conclusions.

Many of the more ordinary bottles made by Stiegel are so similar to those made elsewhere that a definite and positive statement that a piece was made by him is seldom vouchsafed by anyone who really is an authority or who holds his opinion to be of value. Nevertheless, pieces that have been handed down from generation to generation, that were originally obtained from Stiegel, and those of recognized Stiegel design can also be regarded as of his make.

*Enamelled ware was not made by Stiegel, according to tradition, until 1772. Sebastian Witmer, a crude and rapid worker. The black lines vary greatly in thickness and are quickly and carelessly applied. He executed steeple, floral, fantastic bird, and cow designs. He used the heart and upright branch in his decorations. And he copied European floral designs on the Stiegel drug bottles. (From "Stiegel Glass".)

Rare Early Flasks from Gardner Collection; The Concentric Ring Eagle and the 1810 J.P.F. (Foster was the man who took over the glass works in that year).

— GROUP A: LIQUORS 43

CHAPTER V FULL-BLOWN FLASKS

EARLY TO LATE DECORATIVE FULL-MOLD BLOWN FLASKS

Because most flask collectors have been concerned with pictorial historicals, there is a tendency to neglect a similar but antidating and survival type. Authorities like Van Rensselaer and McKearin have pointed out you can often date flasks by reference to their form. Here is where this takes one.

A.—Because the blown and blown-molded types of flasks could only approximate the same liquid capacity for each piece blown, there was often dispute from buyers of spirits that they were not getting "full measure." This fault of deviation from standard capacity could be corrected if the blower used a full-sized piece mold and did not attempt to alter shape or decoration by taking it out for expansion and pressed on furbelows. When the pieces of a 2-post mold were designed for the size and shape of a full quart container, the glass object formed by blowing the gather against its sides would have the desired uniformity.

B.—Around 1800 there was sufficient interest in such standardization that glasshouses began to think up names or designs which could be pressed into the glass at the same time. Such impersonal and less hand-crafted production began to be practiced extensively in America around 1810 and from then on extensive mechanization of glass bottle making became inevitable. The New Republic had an industrial boom, population expanded westward and the demand for liquor containers was insatiable. At the same time with new glasshouses coming into being over night, old firms had to keep apace with new designs in order to challenge competition with their markets. The result was a rapid proliferation of forms and much design piracy.

C.—It appears that the first of these relief decorations to catch on with the public were the Sunbursts and Masonic Emblems. The date of these forms is usually held around 1815-1825, though of course many were made later, often from the same molds. These decorated flasks from full blown molds were first made in Eastern glasshouses and credit for the prototype is the rare Jared Spencer, though not a Pitkin; see also plate for the J. E. Foster flasks of same period. These and other varieties of same form are shown below including early Lafayette, Liberty Cap, Columbus Eagle and The Eagle Canteen. We give the Van Rensselaer classifications of Sunbursts and Masonics which had their heyday in the second decade of the 19th century. Some of these early form F M B flasks (full mold blown) are extremely rare, but for such valuation you are referred to other authors in the Bibliography.

Van Rensselaer speaks of the earlier bottle as having a sheared mouth and the point where the punty rod was broken off as leaving a jagged scar as a pontil mark, then goes on to say that after 1850 the calabash bottle became the prevailing type for fills and refills rather than the ovoid frame that had held first place. These are our present concern.

.—It appears that the first of these relief decorations to catch on with the public were the Sunbursts and Masonic Emblems. The date of these forms is usually held around 1815-1825, though of course many were made later, often from the same molds.

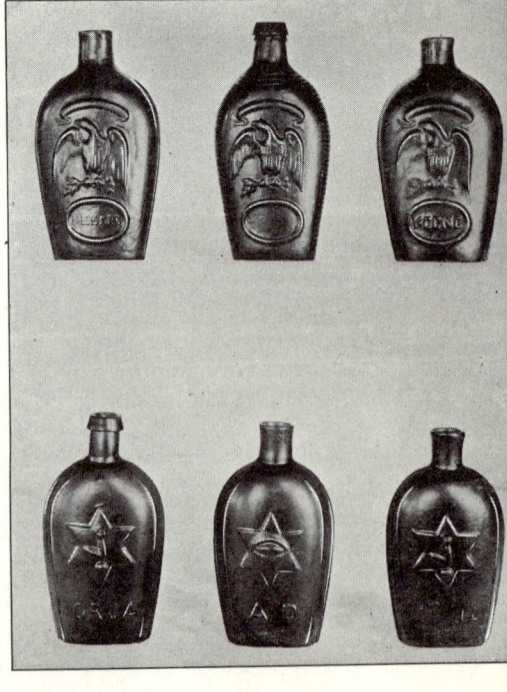

Upper   2   21   1   2   21   1
Lower   1   1

— GROUP A: LIQUORS

Masonic Bottles and Flasks

Division I—Keene

1. Masonic floor of 12 bricks, 6 stars on right outside top of arch and sunburst on left, and below this are crossbones. Reverse: Spread-eagle to left with ribbon, below oval and K C C N C (Keene) large letters. Pint—golden amber. s m s b. (Kn.).

2. 20 bricks, trowel and eye at left of arch between sunburst and crossbones, also bee-hive right lower corner of arch, half moon above the stars at right. Reverse: "Keene" in small letters.

3. Smaller compasses and triangle, outside the arch the bee-hive is smaller and less perfectly modelled, on the left the crossbones are smaller and higher up, the emblems on the right are obscure. Reverse: Oval not lettered. Pint—golden amber. s m s b. (Kn).

4. No trowel to left of Masonic emblems and no bee-hive at base. (Keene on oval).

5. Two dots between crossbones and sun. Reverse: Two dots to right of eagle. Dark amber (Kn).

6. Bee-hive. (Kn).

8. Masonic arch, pavement with 4 rows of bricks; the arch encloses near the top an all-seeing eye, square with compass and sunburst; without the arch are 3 dots and crossbones. Reverse: Spread-eagle to right, ribbon above, large ball feet on eagle, below oval. ½ pint—olive amber. s m s b. (Kn.) Also found with motifs outside omitted.

9. Like 12 but half pint only. Motif below bricks, and to left of bee-hive, looks like dog. Reverse: Elongated horizontal motif in oval. Light green. s m s b. (Kn.).

10. Masonic arch enclosing sunburst with heavy dot in middle, square with compass and triangle. Very large sunburst covering the area between the square and floor and sides of the pillars, with triangle in the centre marked "G". 24 bricks on the floor. On the left side from bottom up is skull and crossbones, trowel and very large sunburst with heavy dot in middle. On the right side from top down sunburst enclosing a half moon, 3 dots and bar paralleling right pillar of the arch. Below the bricks on right is sunburst, to the left Masonic emblems. Reverse: Spread-eagle head to the left, shield on breast, ribbon above, grasping 3 arrows, points of each are very bulbous, and olive branch. Below oval enclosing 8-point floral motif. 5 ribs on sides. Pint—sea green. Very heavy flask with large spreading mouth which is **sheared.** s b. **(Kn).**

3   D2   9   D1   3   D1   8   D2

11. Reverse: Indented ribbon over eagle like bricking. Not so heavy and much smaller mouth   Clear glass   s m   s b.   (U).

12   Reverse: Beaded oval and small motif   Pint—green

13   Shorter neck, heavy lip to mouth   Reverse: Beaded ribbon over eagle.

14. Reverse: Ribbon over eagle's head more of a continuous bar than a ribbon, beading on the oval is heavier and points on floral motif not so long. Pint—sea green.

15. Masonic arch enclosing large sunburst, square with compass and square, very large sunburst with triangle and large "G". 24 bricks in floor. Outside of sunburst on the left side from the bottom up skull and crossbones, trowel, large sunburst. On the right side from the top down 3 stars, large sunburst encircling half moon, 3 stars and bar paralleling side of the arch. Below the bricks on the right is a bee-hive and to the left Masonic emblems. Reverse: Spread-eagle facing to the left with shield on breast, ribbon indented like bricks. Eagle is grasping 3 arrows and an olive branch. Below very large beaded oval, marked "J K B" (perhaps this represents the combined initials of three glass blowers. 5 ribs on sides. Pint—shaded light golden amber. Rolled mouth. s b. A very heavy flask.

16. Smaller lettering in oval on reverse.

17. Much thicker and has clearer designed emblems, ornament in oval like head of key. Pint—amethystine.

18. Masonic arch enclosing large sunburst. compass and square, very large sunburst enclosing triangle with large "G". Below, floor of 20 bricks. On the outside of the arch on the left from the bottom to the top is skull and crossbones, trowel and sunburst. On the right side from top down 4 stars, sunburst, 3 stars and chair. Below the brick floor on the arch is a bee-hive and on the left of the bee-hive Masonic emblem. Reverse: Spread-eagle, shield on breast, to the left, ribbon over head marked "E Pluribus Unum". The eagle is grasping 3 arrows and an olive branch. Below beaded oval enclosing entwined initials "I P" (Justus Perry, the I representing the old time J). 5 heavy ribs on sides. Pint—sea green. s m   s b. A very heavy flask (Kn).

19. Reverse: No beading on oval under eagle also lettered "I P". This flask is of clear glass. (Kn).

20. Beaded oval lettered "H. S." denoting Henry Schoolcraft.

21. Masonic arch enclosing emblems, 20 bricks on floor; no emblems outside the arch except bee-hive on right lower corner. Reverse: Spread-eagle with ribbon to left, perched on arrows and olive branch, oval below. Sides corrugated closely. 3 rings on shoulders being continuation of the corrugation. Pint—very light green, almost clear, green shows on bottom. s m   s b. (Attributed to Kn).

22. Crude bubbly olive green with sloping inserted neck. Thick heavy flask.

— GROUP A: LIQUORS

11, 12, 13, 14, 15, 16, 17 and 22 are usually assigned to Keene origin but possibly several, more particularly the clear glass examples, may have been made by the New England Glass Company or elsewhere. All s m s b.

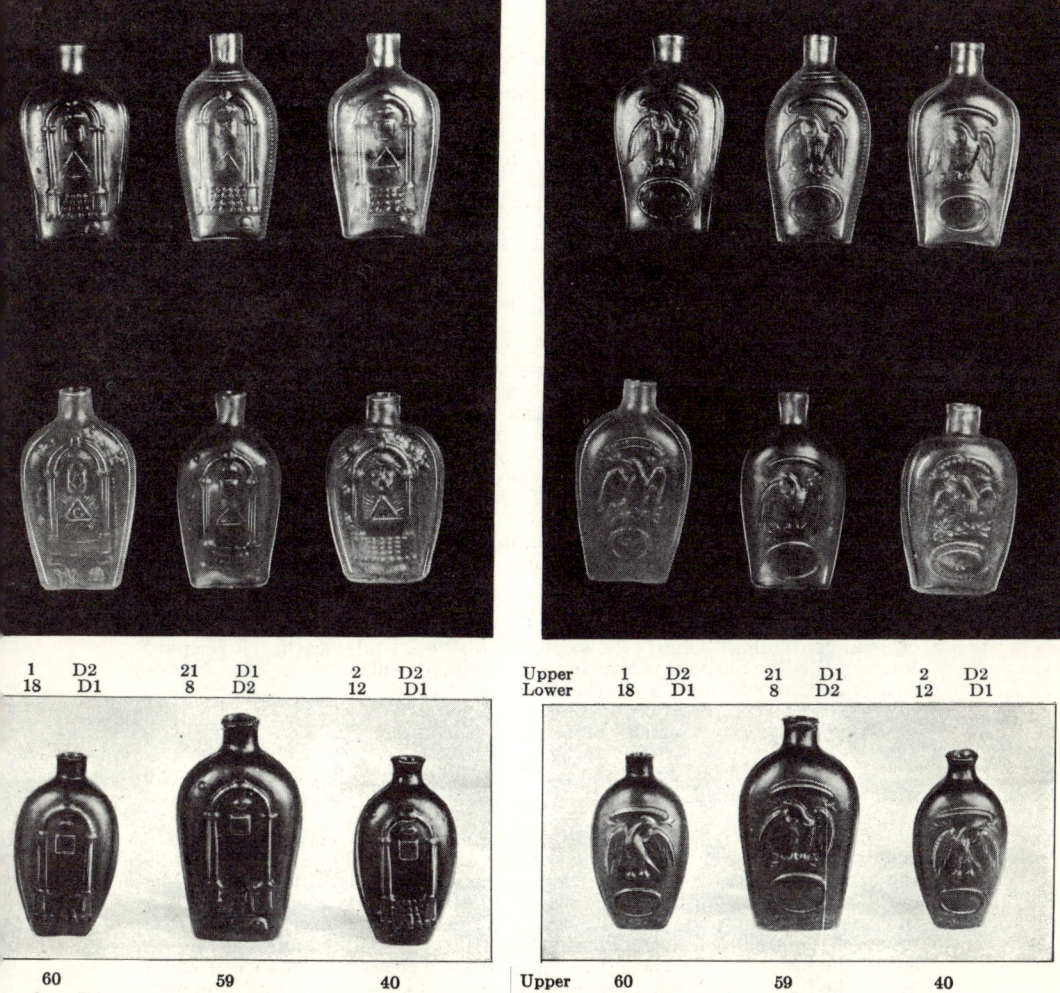

F M B prototype is the rare Jared Spencer, though not a Pitkin; see also plate for the J. E. Foster flasks of same period. These and other varieties of same form are shown below including early Lafayette, Liberty Cap, Columbus Eagle and The Eagle Canteen. We give the Van Rensselaer classifications of Sunbursts and Early Violin Scroll Bottles

---

DIVISION II—MISCELLANEOUS, N. E. G., N. G., ZANESVILLE,

1. Masonic arch, small sunburst, small square with compass and square, triangle with small "G" and small rays around. 20 bricks in pavement. Outside of the arch from bottom up small skull and crossbones, small trowel and small sunburst. On the right side from top down are 8 stars and a half moon. On the lower right hand side of the pavement of bricks is a bee-hive. Reverse: Spread-eagle to the left, shield on breast, ribbon overhead, grasping 3 arrows and an olive branch. Below large beaded oval marked "N. E. G. Co." 6 ribs on the sides. Pint—light green. s m   s b. (N. E. G.)

2. Plain oval with very obscure lettering (perhaps these flasks were blown in an old mold).

3. Masonic arch enclosing a large sunburst enclosing an all-seeing eye, square with compass and square, large sunburst with triangle and very large "G". 30 bricks on pavement. Outside arch bottom up on left side, skull and crossbones, trowel, full moon face surrounded by sunburst. On the right side from the top down 4 stars, smaller sunburst enclosing half moon and 3 stars, bar paralleling right pillar of the arch. Below bricks on the right, bee-hive, on the left Masonic emblems. Reverse: Very slender eagle, facing to the right with head to the left, grasping 3 arrows and olive branch. Large ribbon over the eagle with beading, resembling bricking. Below a large beaded oval marked "N G C". 5 ribs on sides. Pint—light pale green. s m   s b. (U).

4. Masonic arch and pavement. Reverse: Eagle facing to right, perched on oval containing "Ohio"; "Zanesville" above. Underneath, "J. Shepard & Co." ("S" in Shepard is reversed). Prominent central rib on side. Pint—rich golden amber. s m   s b. (Wh).

5. "Murdock & Cassell" replaces "J. Shepard & Co."

6. Masonic arch, containing sunburst, five-pointed ornament, triangle with "G", surrounded. s m   s b.

7. Masonic arch, within on top is a sunburst, below compass on square, below this are rays enclosing large triangle with a very large "G". Outside the arch at base and to the right is a bee-hive and to left of this a log-like motif, and on the right two small obscure motifs, the arch is surmounted by a sunburst on right and left. Reverse: Same except the compass on the square is replaced by a five-pointed motif, also a five-pointed motif at base to left of the bee-hive. To the left of the arch are a trowel, crossed motif and a dot to the right of the arch, dots replace ornaments. ½ pint—bluish aquamarine. s m   s b. (Attributed to Sl).

— GROUP A: LIQUORS

VIOLIN FLASKS

1. VIOLIN
Broad shoulders, large eight-pointed stellar motif, below large dot, then a fleur-de-lis, prominent central rib and small one each side. ½ pint—bluish aquamarine. s m s b. (U).

2. One dot, fleur-de-lis replaces one dot, "B. P. & B." and curled frame to lettering. The initials presumably stand for "Bakewell, Page & Bakewell"

3. Shoulders not so prominent, central side rib broader, particularly near shoulders, round base.

4. Larger stellar motif, slightly narrower shoulders. (No lettering).

5. Small top to fleur-de-lis, small dot.

6. Six pointed stellar motif, no dot.

7. Narrower shoulders, larger motif, also small six-pointed motif top of a heart-shaped panel, having curled ends in the middle, no fleur-de-lis. Quart.

8. Shoulders much thicker through, motif lower down, ends branching from panel frame, heavier and much more curled, one extra rib on sides.

9. Narrow shoulders, eight-pointed motifs.

10. Top motif six-pointed, lower eight-pointed but much heavier.

11. Dots replace the two motifs and there is a crude "C" on obverse. Pint—pale shaded olive green.

12. Broad shoulders, short neck, large anchor, four large dots, these designs within frame with curled ends at base. Reverse: Fleur-de-lis replaces anchor, two dots, same frame, one less rib than preceding on one side.

13. Lettered "Louisville, Ky". Reverse: "Glass Works". On each side the lettering is slightly circular. Half pint and pint.

GRAND OLD AMERICAN BOTTLES

   3   D2   9   D1   3   D1   7   D2

14. Lettering in straight line. Two six-pointed stars. Pint and quart (L).

15. Narrow waisted, urn-shaped frame enclosing "J. R. & Son". Reverse: Fleur-de-lis and curled ornament replaces lettering and urn. Pint—aquamarine. s b. (JR & S).

16. Rounder shoulders. Scroll designs covering flask. Reverse: Same Pint—aquamarine.

17. Different designs. Quart—aquamarine.

18. About like No. 15, lettered "R. Knowles* & Co., Union Factory, Wheeling, S Va." encircling the flask, star above. Reverse: Star and peculiar shaped motif. Pint—light green. s m   s b. (R K).
*"I find Richard Knowles, glass blower in a number of our old directories but no mention anywhere of his operating a factory. An old glass worker, the grandson of S. G. Robinson, the pioneer window glass man, told me that he remembered this Dick Knowles; that he had worked for his grandfather at times. He said sometimes a workman's name was put on a bottle and he thought that might be the solution of that."
(From a letter from Etta M. Roberts, Librarian, Wheeling, W. Va.)

19. Two quart size. Also sapphire blue.

20. In shape of violin. Reverse: Same. Pint—golden amber. c m. (They were sold with bow and neck piece and packed in a special cardboard box.)

21. Another, holds one small drink. Lettered "Pat. apl'd for".

Note: Some of the motifs seem to be four-pointed, but really appear so on account of the sharpness of the design in the mold being worn from usage.
Violin flasks were made at Wheeling, West Virginia; Zanesville, Ohio; Pittsburgh, Pennsylvania and probably at Wellsburg, Steubenville and Martins Ferry, Onio, and some of the smaller factories in Indiana, and of course at Louisville, Kentucky and Lancaster, N. Y.
Many minor and not noteworthy variations occur, denoting a wide range of production.

The variations in the finish of the mouths is very different, sheared, collared and ringed, scarred bases, flat bases, and hollowed bases are noted.

Also found in rose opal, 7 shades of green, violet and purple, and sapphire blue.

| G1 | 55 G1 | 56 G1 | 4 | 75 G1 | 77 G1 | 73 G1 | 76 G1 | 74 G1 |

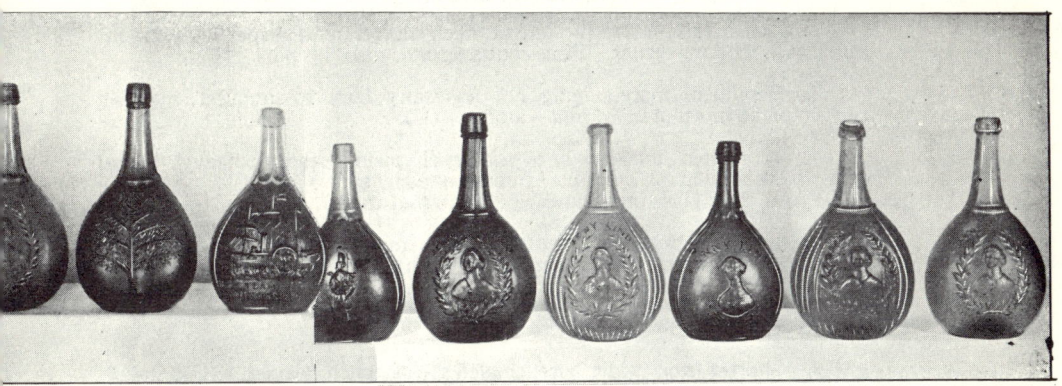

y Violin and Scroll Bottles; also 1850 Calabashes (numbered as G1 Historicals check list).

Sunburst Flasks

1. Sunburst

Large sunburst, on panel, covering side of flask, five pointed motif in center. Reverse: Same. Very prominent central rib and two smaller ones on sides. Pint—claret toned amethyst s m s b. (B).

2. Central rib, not so prominent, neck shorter, oval shaped motif in sunburst with hollow center. Pint—aquamarine, also ½ pint. (U).

3. Shoulders more sloping, not so many bars to sunburst, motif in center spread out more. ½ pint—amber. (U).

4. Elongated sunburst in ovoid panel, inside beading, heavy vertical ribs. Reverse: Same. About ¾ pint—green. s m s b. (U). Also clear glass one known. (Attributed to Vt).

*5. Large sunburst covering flask. Reverse: Same. Corrugated sides, divided by small central rib, long neck (1 inch), narrowing at base. ½ pint—aquamarine. s m s b., also pint.

*6. Same but 3 ribs on sides.

7. Shorter neck, wider base, shaded green, much heavier. (U).

8. Smaller sunburst with raised oval in center, lettered "Keen" (no e). Reverse: Same except oval lettered "P & W". Corrugated edges, two horizontal bars at base each side. Pint—olive green. s m s b. (Kn).

9. Half pint, one bar. (Kn).

10. Broader shoulders and thicker mouth more spreading.

11. Rounder shoulders, corrugation extends up on neck forming two bars, no ovals in center of sunburst, two bars at base. ½ pint—golden amber. (Kn).

12. Smaller, shoulders do not slope as much. Sunburst much heavier no bars at neck. (Kn).

13. Like 10 but squarer. (Kn).

14. Shoulders and corrugations form step-like base to neck. Pint—golden amber. (Kn).

15. Same but square shoulders, 4⅝ inches wide. Very heavy and thick. (Kn).

16. Same but has centre like 13. Smaller sunburst, rounder shoulders, different mouth. Aquamarine. (Kn).

17. Same but no motif in center of sunburst, shorter base to neck. Clear glass, sea green, olive green, golden amber, etc. Very heavy and thick. Shoulders 4⅝ inches wide. (Kn).

18. Large oval panel in center of sunburst, on corrugations on neck. Aquamarine. s d c m. (Kn). Also olive green.

19. Like 17 but smaller and of lighter glass, narrower shoulders. Pint—clear light amber and olive green. (Kn).

(*Attributed to Vt. perhaps made by N. E. G.)

— GROUP A: LIQUORS 53

D.—Leaving the Historicals for the next chapter, we conclude here with some late 1850 calabash types and the earlier Violin Scroll Bottles. Based on the Van Rensselaer classification and pictures one can realize that the early scrolls were not really violin-shaped at all, also that calabashes are a throw-back to the early long neck Hogarth's of an earlier period. Typical check lists of all these early flasks (including Stiegels)

appear in this chapter to make the collector immediately aware of what he is seeking. One must be cautioned however that there have been many reproductions of Stiegel and Pitkin type flasks as well as the full mold-blown "sunbursts" and later "historicals." Recently the writer attended the Pennypacker sale of fakes which top authority G. S. McKearin had assembled in his own lifetime. The verisimilitude of some was unbelievable. One can almost predict they will all be on the market in about 20 years, this time as originals.

Well, how does one distinguish the real thing, someone asks? The answer there is probably another book and a lifetime of examining glass. Best approach might be a visit to Corning Glass Museum to a real look at what early blown glass looks like. Later glass mixes are far less impure. Full blown and pattern molded appear from time to time as modern gift shop flasks and should be quickly spotted.

Van Rensselaer speaks of the earlier bottle as having a sheared mouth and the point where the punty rod was broken off as leaving a jagged scar as a pontil mark, then goes on to say that after 1850 the calabash bottle became the prevailing type for fills and refills rather than the ovoid frame that had held first place. These Historical flasks of the 1825-1850 period are our present concern.

Sheared-lip Keene's from author's collection.

HISTORIC EARLY AMERICAN FLASKS

Authentic reproductions of antique historical portrait flasks that were the rage of the 19th century. Handmade in glass, these beautiful 1½ pint flasks stand 8" high, come in Amber, Amethyst, Peacock Blue or Milk Glass.

REVOLUTIONARY
George Washington on one side, General Taylor on other.

AMERICANA
Eagle and Shield on one side, Cluster of Grapes on other.

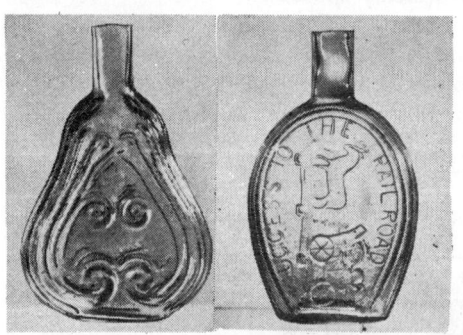

HEART   **RAILROADER**

COLONIAL

FEDERAL

Log Cabin on one side, Lincoln on other.

— GROUP A: LIQUORS

CHAPTER VI   HISTORICAL FLASKS

HISTORICAL AND OTHER PICTORIAL FLASKS

The previous section covered early examples of the relief-decorated flasks which are the prototypes of those collections now designated as "Historicals." All were made by blowing the glass in a full-pattern-mold to assure repetitive size and uniformity. But pints, half-pints and full quarts were blown in such a variety of different patterns and shapes by competing glasshouses that the remaining examples cover several hundred varieties. No one, unless that last of the pioneer bottle collectors (Mr. C. D. Gardner) is out to assemble a complete catalog; his forerunners (Van Rensselaer and G. McKearin) had their own hordes dispersed to museums long ago, and in some cases only 2 or 3 specimens are known to exist. Today's flask collector is usually content with some of the more common varieties, for even these bring high prices.

This chapter does not tell neophytes much about relative rariety. The reason should be obvious, (1) there are no Historical flasks lying around in cellars and attics to be found for a proverbial song; (2) This is a field for experts, where books by McKearin and some others will take a very long time to master all the intricacies; (3) The collector or dealer who wants only the "Really rare" must recognize that styles in bottle collecting change and that today's status symbol for a "rare flask" is finding one that is some slight variant on a long-known example and hence is considered unique. The reader will find very little of such lore in this section. Instead the aim has been to sample rather thoroughly the major types of pictorial flasks which catered to the hard liquor demands of this country from 1825 to the 1860's when the vogue for historicals lost its popularity and was replaced by other types of whiskey containers. If any collector has the notion that an historical flask is one having a Presidential face impressed in the glass, he is in for something of a shock. For some of the earliest flasks shown in the last chapter have faces of G. Washington, A. Jackson and LaFayette but are often regarded as Masonics and not true historicals. The reasons are these: (1) From 1810 to 1825 Masonry was socially important in the East. Washington and Jackson were Masons and these particular flasks are Masonic emblem flasks in which the face shown is quite incidental. (2) Furthermore they were not issued to commemorate an episode or event as were so many later pictorials. (3) Finally, the real craze for the 1825-1860 historical flasks is thought to have been started by an enterprising immigrant, Thomas W. Dyott (M.D.?), who arrived from England about 1806 and by 1825 was using all the newspapers in the land

To Druggists, Booksellers, Country Merchants, Artists, &c.

T. W. DYOTT & Co.
APPOINTED AGENTS
For the European and American Manufactories,
OFFER FOR SALE,
AT THE N. E. CORNER OF SECOND AND RACE-STREETS.
AND NO 341, HIGH-STREET, PHILADELPHIA:

500 dozen Robertson's Elixir of Health	100 groce Laudanum, in vials
500 do do Vegetable Nervous Cordial	100 Antimonial Wine, in vials
500 do do Patent Stomachic Bitters	100 Seneca Oil do
500 do do Rhumatic Drops	100 Oil of Spike do
100 do Tissot's do do	100 Sweet Oil do
500 groce Robert's Worm Lozenges	100 Powdered Jalap do
500 Dyott's Anti-Bilious Pills	100 Calomel Ppt. do
large boxes	100 Red Precipitate do
1000 do do do small do	100 Tartar Emetick do
500 do Patent Itch Ointment	100 Fine Powdered Bark do
500 Mahy's Approved Plaister Cloth	100 Powdered Rhubarb do
300 Circassian Eye Water	300 Tartar Emetick Vomits
300 Dyott's Infallible Tooth Ache	100 Mercurial Ointment in small boxes
Drops	100 Red Precipitate in do
200 Van Butchel's Corn Plaster	200 Ess. Lemon in Vials
100 Paul's Patent Columbian Oil	200 Do Bergamot do
100 Godbold's Vegetable Balm of Life	200 Do Lavender do
400 Bateman's Drops	300 Well's Refined Liquorice in large
50 Essence of Peppermint	boxes
400 British Oil	500 Do do do small do
500 Stoughton's Bitters	500 Pure Lemon Acid
500 Godfey's Cordial	1000 Balsamic Court Plaster
400 Turlington's Balsam of Life	500 Wash Balls, scented
300 Steers Opodeldock	500 Pomatum
1000 Harlem Oil	500 Clout's Durable Ink
300 Balsam de Maltha	1000 Walkden's Ink Powder
300 Golden Tincture	500 Restorative Tooth Powder
300 Dalby's Carminative	500 Levigated Charcoal Dentrifice
700 Worm Tea	200 Tooth Brushes, assorted
200 Oil of Worm Seed	100 Smelling Bottles do
700 Anderson's Pills	1000 Bayley's Patent Blacking Cakes
500 Hooper's do	1000 Do do do Balls
100 Lee's New London do	1000 Camel Hair Pencils
100 Thompson's Eye Water	500 Do do Marking Brushes
50 Do. Aromatic Tooth Paste	1000 doz. Imported Water Colours, consist-
100 Balm of Iberia	ing of 1, 2, 3, and 4 row boxes,
50 Hamilton's Elixir	from the Manufactories of Reeves,
200 Imperial Lip Salve	Ackerman, and Newman
300 Fresh Castor Oil, in vials	2000 groce assorted Toy Paints, for the use of
300 Wine Bitters do	children, &c. &c.
100 Elixir Paregorick do	

Together with an extensive and general assortment of fresh Drugs and approved Chemicals, Glass Furniture, Vials, Paints, Windsor Glass, Dye Stuffs, and Professional Articles of every description, suitable for town and country Merchants, Practitioners, &c. on liberal terms, for cash or at the usual credit.

June 21---dtf

The Democratic Press - Philadelphia   November 20, 1816

— GROUP A: LIQUORS

to promote his nostrums and specially designed historical flasks. We know that by 1812 he had a large drug store and liquor warehouse in Philadelphia. Needing much glassware for his business and unable to get imported supplies due to the War, he bought into a factory (Olive) at Glassboro, N. J. and shortly thereafter became sole agent with a controlling interest in both Gloucester and Kensington factories. This was the period (March 1822) when students find the first advertisement by which historical flasks can be identified. Thinking to sell his glasswares widely (empty as much as filled) Dyott had apparently created a special mold to commemorate the U. S. Frigate FRANKLIN, launched at Philadelphia in 1815. Thus his advertisement identifies an "American Eagle Flask, Ship Franklin; Agricultural and Masonic Pocket Bottles." Strung at the bottom of Dyott appeals to buy his medicines, this ad is the earliest probable date for historical flasks. But with this small fanfare as a start, we find the craze for historicals built almost overnight so that by 1824, Dyott was advertising many added patterns—with the rest of the glasshouse fraternity not far behind.

Using the newspaper medium lavishly and on a country-wide scale Dyott (with his T. W. D. impressed in the glass) also advertised a flask enclosing the Farmers Arms in an agricultural flask, an American eagle in a Mason flask, and memorialized General Lafayette's visit (1824-25) by creating an eagle flask with General Lafayette T. W. D. impressed. Other Dyott historicals of this period which were widely sold to tavern keepers for bottling from demijohn brews include "General Lafayette, Republican Gratitude," and "General Washington, E. Pluribus Unum." Others of this same 1825 period are the Eagle-Cornucopia "T.W.D.", "E. Pluribus Unum: one of many," the Benjamin Franklin, "Where Liberty Dwells There is My Country—T. W. Dyott," and ship "Franklin," "Free Trade and Sailors' Rights."

At the 50th anniversary of our Declaration of Independence, Thomas Jefferson and John Adams died within a few hours of each other and Dyott signalized this event by taking the mold for his Washington flask and having cut above the eagle "E Pluribus Unum" and on the figure side the inscription "Adams and Jefferson, July 4, 1776." This commemorative flask was so popular that even today extant specimens are fairly common. Dyott probably used a Philadelphia moldmaker, and since the molds were wooden, added items could be inscribed in old forms and often were. In fact, so profitable had Dyott made historical flask sales that by 1832 he had erected his own town (Dyottville) with five glass facorties as its core. Forced into bankruptcy in 1837, the fires of the Dyottville furnaces were drawn and Dyott himself never returned to rekindle them. Eventually the factories were opened by other hands and in the 1840's period new commemoratives and historicals (such as Taylor) appeared and are identified with Dyottville. But by now the great promoter was gone and other glassmen took over the field of which many believe he was the first creator.

Rare Historicals from Gardner Collection, "Crossed Keys" and Reverse; "Hard Cider" and Reverse.

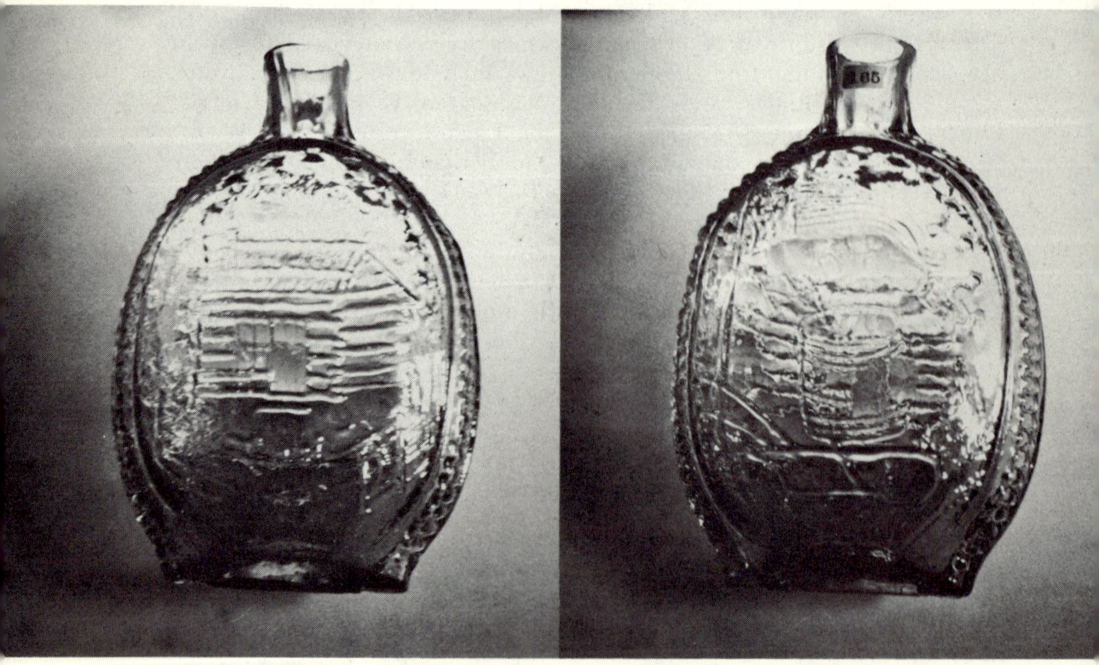

— GROUP A: LIQUORS

HISTORICAL FLASK CLASSIFICATIONS

In the hey-day of pictorial flasks almost any event or idea would give rise to a new mold pattern. Baltimore Glass Works' "Corn For the World," formed a most appropriate wording for Bourbon whiskey containers and any exciting internal improvement such as a railroad, the Bunker Hill Monument or a Free Trade slogan would bring out a new flask for holding hard liquor. Henry Clay's support of high tariff inspired "The American System"— steamship and sheaf of rye with the added words, "Use me but do not abuse me."

Van Rensselaer and other authorities placed the first bottle flasks after the Stiegel and Pitkin chestnuts as being of the sunburst type and probably made at Keene, N. H., on or before 1810. He placed the period from 1808 to 1860 as the hey-day of the fancy pocket flask and gave the first listing of the U. S. glasshouses responsible for these forms including both historicals and other pictorials. Some speak of them as being blown in engraved metal molds, or blown in soap-stone molds, though some may have been made of wood. The attractive designs were used to stimulate mainly liquor sales (still largely untaxed) and by the 1840's the country really went bottle mad, with so many varieties and pirated mold patterns of rival glasshouses that experts are still finding new varieties.

We take it that every bottle collector knows the first true American drink was the rum which the Puritans brewed from West India molasses. But Western expansion after the Revolution brought forth homeplanted grains which soon exceeded the rum trade in potable liquors. The impregnable social position of Mid-Western Rye and Southern Corn Liquor became the 19th Century's counterpoise for the Rum Drinks of Easterners. Frontier people West of the Alleganies were reared from childhood on the family jug. Everyone has heard of "The Little Brown Jug" (at first of local pottery and not until midcentury reproduced in brown glass); but the lure of the Great American Bottle was first not in its shape but its contents. Its pleasant taste and agreeable effects kept people cool in summer and warm in winter when lacking today's central heating. Traditionally involved in both love and fighting, it was almost the backwoods only diversion and enjoyed a high reputation as the Nation's Greatest Therapeutic Agent—effective against fevers, snake bite and general debility. With grain the greatest commodity the New Republic had to offer, its easy economic transfer as whiskey made the bottled product available everywhere. It was dispensed freely during political campaigns, used to seal business and family deals, issued in daily rations to the Army. Even Ministers of the Gospel were sometimes paid in whiskey; for as guardians of a devoted flock, many took their BIBLE straight—especially its admonition to "give strong drink unto him that is ready to perish and wine to him that be of heavy heart." With this motto as guide, small wonder the empties were often also kept and cherished.

GRAND OLD AMERICAN BOTTLES

Every collector, more especially those who have large collections, is particularly interested in bottles in shades of blue, green amethyst and amber. Not so much in the latter unless the shading runs to vaseline color or a very rich golden amber. The two colors sought by all are jade green and opaque blue, possibly a specimen of either color will turn up with a pictorial design. Plain bottles of these and allied colors were made at Sandwich, Mass.

IN MEMORIAM

The Wines they drank from you, old flask,
   Before the revolution
Would fill full many a keg and cask
   With vigorous solution;
But now you're empty and alone,
   Exiled from liquidation,
And not a drop to call your own,
   That's dreamed of fermentation;
The household flagon used to be
   The cheer of every minute,
But now it's part of history
   That there is nothing in it.

Stephen Van Rensselaer

THE LEATHER BOTTEL, ANNE HATHAWAY'S COTTAGE STRATFORD-ON-AVON.

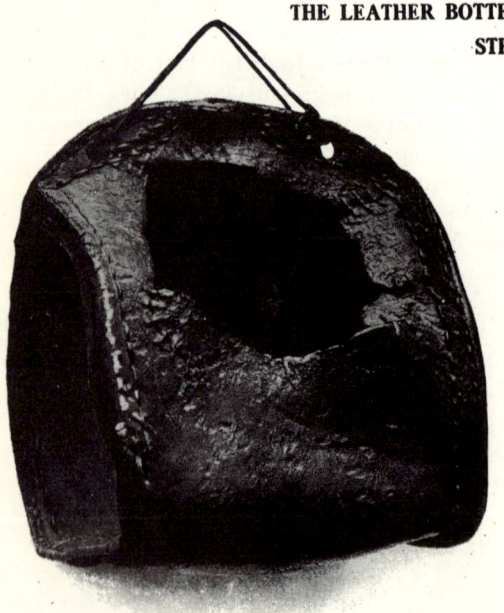

And when at length
    the bottel grows old
And will no longer
    good liquor hold,
Out of the side
    you may make a clout
'To mend your shoes
    when they're worn out:
Then take and hang it
    up on a pin
Twill do to put hinges
    and odd things in:
So we hope his soul
    in Heaven may dwell
Who first found out
    the leather Bottel.

— GROUP A: LIQUORS

THE VAN RENSSELAER DESCRIPTIONS

In 1920, Mr. Stephen Van Rensselaer published in very limited edition, a number of plates picturing both sides of a given flask, together with a brief description of its marking and (when possible) attribution to place of manufacture. It was this now fantastically rare book that first sent collectors in the 1920's in search of historicals. Antiquers in the big eastern centers started bottle hunts that would rival any of the 1960 old bottle diggings that now have California hobbyists enthralled. In Philadelphia, George Horace Lorimer, editor of the then-lush Curtis Publications, and his authors gave untold time, money and space to telling about their finds. The bibliography covering bottle reports by Edwin La Fevre, Kenneth Roberts and others will indicate that flasks like those first described in Van Rensselaer's first book were considered prime copy for Saturday Evening Post articles. We start with a sampling of ten plates from that first book to show how various types of pictorial subjects were first mixed in a grand melee.

Following this first attempt to bring order into a chaotic field, these early listings were superseded in 1926 by a revised edition, bringing out new facts, new bottles and a new numbering system. It is this revised Van Rensselaer method of grouping that is used herein to complete our study of 1825-1865 Pictorial flasks. It begins with a symbol system for identifying the make and lip types of early and late flasks, and carries five subject groupings.

Note that the first grouping I is what was called the true historicals, the next two groupings (II and III) deal with Eagles and Washingtons, while the others (IV and V) cover the Pike's Peak flasks (Jenny Lind calabashes which came near the same time appear in earlier groupings) followed by a listing of so-called non-history pictorials. It might be asked why the writer uses this system when the later one of McKearin is perhaps more complete. His answer is that this is a memorial promised Mrs. Van Rensselaer before her passing. Also, a complete listing of all varieties of the same type is out of place in a general reference book. In fact, the Van Rensselaer classification has itself been somewhat condensed in an effort not to become discursive. The specialist interested only in historicals can make further studies viva the bibliographic references. Here now are the leading examples in this fascinating field, all valuable, some running into many hundreds of dollars and very rare. Photographs from the Van Rensselaer and Gardner collections will serve as aid to the written descriptions. We are also deeply indebted to Corning Glass Museum for copies of line drawings used in their booklet on Historical Flasks which marked the exhibition and acquisition of the famed McKearin bottle collection by that institution. In the sections which follow one will find a total of over 400 individual listings, groupings and sub-groups. Those wishing to use this system in bottle correspondence should mention both number and grouping, i.e., a particular Eagle flask should be referred to as Group II, No. 11.

Mr. Stephen Van Rensselaer published 1920, We start with a sampling of ten plates from that first book to show how various types of pictorial subjects were first mixed in a grand melee.

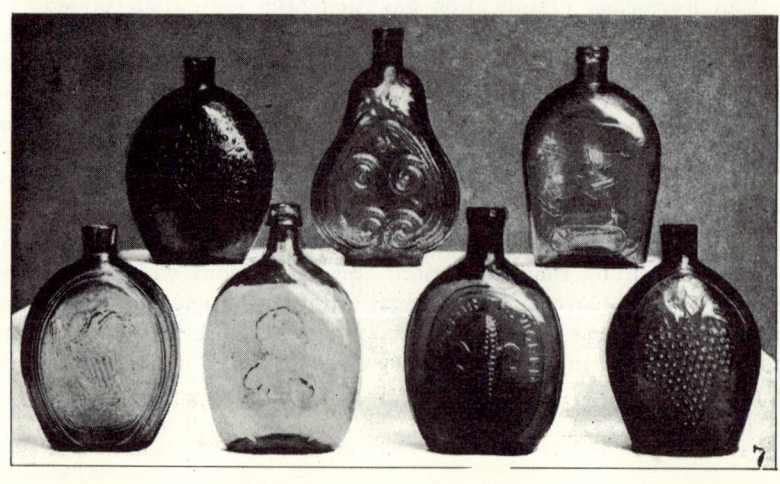

PLATE VII

1. Isabella Flask (I)
   "Isabella" on ribbon; in center, anchor with rope, and below, "Glass Works" on ribbon. Reverse: Picture of glass works. Half pint — light

7. American Eagle Flask (P)
   Spread-eagle with ribbon on arrows and olive branch. Panel below. Reverse: Clasped hands in shield, nine verticle bars above plain oval,

PLATE VIII

1. Columbian Flask (U)
   "Columbian Exposition". Below, bust of Columbus facing to the front. Numerals 1893 below, and below this, "A. E. M. Bros. & Co." Reverse: "Pennsylvania Pure Rye Baker Whiskey." Pint — amber. Collared mouth. Flat shape with high shoulders, oval sides.

2. Pitkin Flask (Pt)
   Corncob pattern, twist to the right, sloping shoulders, rounded body. Pint — sea green. Sheared mouth.

3. Pitkin Flask (Pt)
   Very narrow shoulders. Fluted longitudinally. Pint — very pale greenish aquarmarine.

4. Baltimore Flask (B)
   Baltimore Monument and inscription above, "Baltimore". Reverse: Bust of Taylor and "Fells Point". Pint—aquamarine. Collared mouth.

5. Sunburst Flask (C)
   Large sunburst, oval-shaped, with very prominent bars. High, sharp shoulders. Corrugated sides Much finer quality glass and lighter in weight than the usual run. Pint — olive amber. Sheared mouth. Scarred base.

6. American Eagle Flask (L)
   Eagle perched on arrows, in oval, 2½ X 2 inches. Reverse: Same. The flask is ribbed all over. Pint—aquamarine. Double collared mouth. Scarred base.

7. Columbia Flask (U)
   Bust of Columbia with cap, facing to the left, on panel. Above, 13 stars. Reverse: Large eagle with head to the right, perched on arrows and olive branch. Underneath, "B & W" (script). Central rib on each side. Pint—light olive green. Sheared mouth. Scarred base.

PLATE IX

1. **Baltimore Handled Jug (U)**
Marked "Griffith, Hyatt & Co., Baltimore", with indented panel. Reverse: Flat. Amber. Collared mouth. Scarred base.

2. **Bear Bottle (U)**
In form of a sitting bear, with hands across stomach. Pint—olive amber. Collared mouth.

3. **Flora Temple Flask (U)**
Flora Temple facing to the left. Above, "Flora Temple". Below, "Harness Trot 219½". The picture of the horse and the words "Flora Temple" are contained in a square panel projecting at the top. Reverse: Plain. Pint—dense amber. Collared mouth.

4. **Violin Flask (U)**
In shape of a violin. Pint—clear light amber. Collared mouth.

5. **Stoddard Three-Mould Flask (G)**
Long neck, quilted pattern: Pint—olive amber. Sheared mouth. Scarred base.

6. **Pitkin Flask (Pt)**
Height, 5¾ inches. Pint—clear amber. Sheared mouth. Scarred base.

7. **Crystal Palace Bottle (Un)**
Marked "Crystal Palace Premium Soda Water. W. Eagle, New York". Reverse: Picture of Crystal Palace and inscription "Union Glass Works Phila." About ¾ pint—sea green. Heavy collared mouth.

PLATE X

1. **Masonic Flask (G)**
Masonic Arch, containing sunburst, square, with crossed compasses, and underneath, a diamond, containing letter "G", surrounded by sunburst. Underneath, brick floor of 16 bricks. Outside the Masonic Arch there are numerous Masonic emblems. Reverse: Spread-eagle with head to the left.

2. **Masonic Flask (G)**
Masonic Arch, containing sunburst, five-pointed ornament, triangle with "G", surrounded by sunburst. The arch rests on a closely tessellated pavement. On the outside of the arch on the top is a sunburst each side, and on the bottom a bee-hive with five-pointed ornament. On the left side are two Masonic emblems. Reverse: Same. The sides are beaded with central rib. Half pint—shaded light green. Sheared mouth. Scarred base.

3. **Masonic Flask (G)**
Masonic emblems with five-pointed ornament and bee-hive underneath. Reverse: Spread-eagle with ribbon, and panel enclosing entwined initials "H P". Pint—green. Sheared mouth. Scarred base.

4. **Masonic Flask (K)**
Masonic Arch enclosing sheaf of wheat, shovel, pitch fork and rake. Below, fleur de lis. Reverse: Spread-eagle, with rays, facing to the right, perched on beaded oval, arrows, and olive branch, and initials "T W D" in oval. Ribbed sides. Pint — aquamarine. Sheared mouth. Scarred base.

5. **Masonic Flask (G)**
Masonic Arch, containing sunburst, enclosing triangle with "G", square, with crossed compasses, and underneath, brick floor of 16 bricks. Outside the Masonic Arch there are numerous Masonic emblems. Reverse: Spread-eagle, with head to the left, perched on arrows and olive branch, ribbon above. Oval panel underneath is plain, and contains an eight-pointed ornament. Very heavy flask. Pint—sea green, with large flanged mouth. Scarred base.

6. **Masonic Flask (G)**
Masonic Arch containing sunburst, square, with crossed compasses, and underneath, a diamond, surrounded by sunburst. Underneath, brick floor. The arch is surrounded by various Masonic emblems, skull and cross-bones, sunburst, and bee-hive. Reverse: Spread-eagle perched on arrows and olive branch. Above the eagle is a ribbon marked "E Pluribus Unum". Underneath the eagle is an oval containing entwined "H P". Ribbed sides. Pint — milky white. Sheared mouth. Scarred base.

7. **Masonic Flask (K)**
Masonic Arch enclosing sheaf of wheat, shovel, pitch fork and rake. Below, fleur de lis. Reverse: Full rigged ship and "Franklin". On the sides: "Free Trade and Sailors' Rights. Kensington Glass Works Philadelphia". Three ribs on sides, the inscription being between. Pint — amber. Sheared mouth. Scarred base.

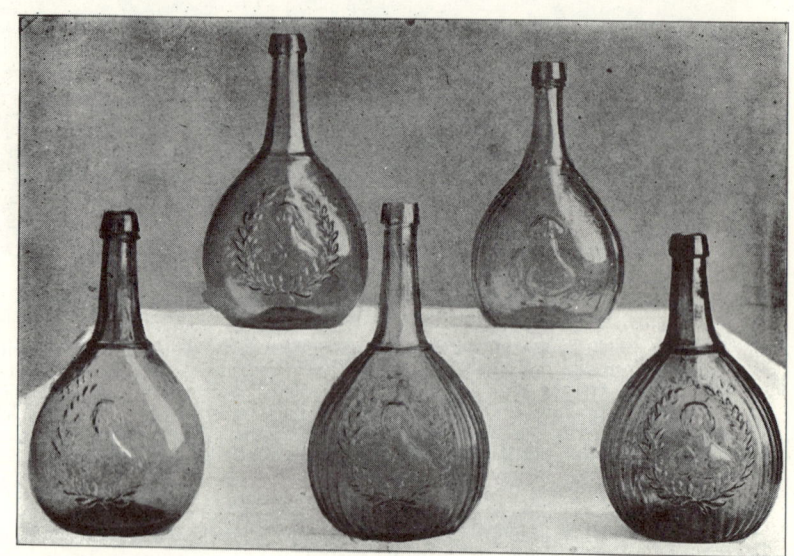

PLATE XI

1. **Jenny Lind Bottle (M)**
"Jenny Lind" above. Bust of Jenny Lind, surrounded by wreath. Reverse: "Milfora G. Works" and picture of glass works. Quart — long neck. Collared mouth. Aquamarine. Scarred base.

2. **Jenny Lind Bottle (F)**
"Jenny Lind" above. Bust of Jenny Lind, with wreath underneath. Reverse: "Fislerville Glass Works". Below, picture of works. Ribbed sides. Quart—long neck. Clear, very light bluish aquamarine. Collared mouth. Scarred base.

3. **Jenny Lind Bottle (H)**
"Jenny Lind" above. Bust of Jenny Lind surrounded by wreath. Reverse: "Kossuth". Underneath, bust of Kossuth facing to the right. Quart—long neck—bluish aquamarine. Collared mouth.

4. **Jenny Lind Bottle (Wn)**
Bust of Jenny Lind, surrounded by wreath. "Jeny Lind" above. Reverse: Picture of glass works; no inscription. Ribbed sides. Quart—long neck—bluish green. Collared mouth. Scarred base.

5. **Jenny Lind Bottle (H)**
Bust of Jenny Lind surrounded by wreath; "Jenny Lind" above. Reverse: Picture of glass factory. Above, "Glass Factory". Six-pointed star between "Glass" and "Factory". Ribbed sides. Quart—long neck - bluish aquamarine. Collared mouth. Scarred base.

— GROUP A: LIQUORS 67

PLATE XII

1. Holtzerman's Bitters Bottle (U)
   In the form of a log cabin with pointed roof, and marked as above. Three sides made to represent a house with shingled roof. The other side plain about ¾ quart—clear amber. Collared mouth.

2. Plantation Bitters Bottle (U)
   In form of a log cabin, marked "Plantation Bitters 1860. Patented 1862". About ¾ quart—dense amber. Collared mouth.

3. Wild Cherry Bitters Bottle (U)
   In form of a log cabin, marked "Wild Cherry" and tree. Reverse: "H. P. Herb Wild Cherry Bitters". Sides plain. On each side of the roof is the word "Bitters". ¾ pint—pea green. Collared mouth.

4. Indian Queen Bottle (U)
   Marked "Brown's Celebrated Indian Herb Bitters Patented 1867". In form of an Indian queen. ¾ quart. Amber. Sheared mouth.

5. Fish Bottle (U)
   Marked "Dr. Fisch's Bitters". Reverse: "W. H. Ware Patented 1866". In shape of a fish. ¾ quart—clear amber. Collared mouth.

6. Dutchman Bottle (U)
   In form of sitting Dutchman. Marked "Van Dunck's Genever Trade Mark Ware & Schmitz". Pint—dense amber. Collared mouth.

7. Corn Cob Bottle (U)
   Tall bottle, in shape of a corn cob. Marked "National Bitters Patented 1867". ¾ quart—clear light amber. Collared mouth. Height, 12½ inches.

PLATE XIII

1. **Pike's Peak Flask (P)**
   "For Pike's Peak" above; below, prospector with overcoat, flat topped hat, pack over right shoulder, cane in left hand, walking to right. Reverse: Same figure, also running deer. Pint—amber. Ringed mouth. (Same as No. 8 on Plate XX.)

2. **Baltimore Flask (B)**
   "Baltimore" on ribbon. Anchor with rope. Underneath, on ribbon, "Glass Works". Reverse: Winged dragon's head and "Resurgam". Pint—amber. Double collared mouth.

3. **Westford Flask (Wf)**
   "Westford Glass Co., Westford, Conn." Reverse: Sheaf of wheat, crossed pitch fork and rake, and five-pointed star. Pint—amber. Double collared mouth. Full of bubbles.

4. **American Eagle Flask (P)**
   Eagle with ribbon and oval underneath. Reverse: Clasped hands and panel in shield. Above, thirteen stars. Branch on each side of shield. Pint—amber. Ringed mouth.

5. **Columbian Jubilee Flask (U)**
   Ship, below figures 1492-1892. Reverse: "Columbian Jubilee" (in script). Pint—amber. Double collared mouth.

6. **All-Seeing-Eye Flask (G)**
   Six-pointed star, eye in the middle. Underneath, "A D". Reverse: Six-pointed star, Masonic arm and emblem, and "G R J A" underneath Three ribs on each side. Pint—light clear amber. Sheared mouth. Scarred base.

7. **American Eagle Flask (P)**

— GROUP A: LIQUORS 69

PLATE XIV

1. **American Eagle Flask (P)**
   Eagle with ribbon, head to left, shield on breast, perched on oval and arrows. Reverse: Same. Pint—very light green. Ringed mouth. Scarred base.

2. **Spring Garden Flask (SG)**
   "Spring Garden" on ribbon. In center, anchor with rope; below, "Glass Works" on ribbon. Heavy raised bar below. Reverse: Log cabin with tree at the right, without leaves. Heavy bar below. Half pint — aquamarine. Collared mouth.

3. **American Eagle Flask (D)**
   Eagle, with ribbon, facing to right, perched on shield, which in turn is resting on rocks. Reverse: "Dyottville Glass Works Philada", (in semi-circle). Pint—bluish aquamarine. Sheared mouth.

4. **Soldier Flask (B)**
   Picture of soldier with musket, bayonet and spiked helmet. Underneath, on raised flat rib, the words "Baltimore, Md." Reverse: Ballet dancer. Underneath, raised flat rib. Pint—aquamarine. Sheared mouth. Scarred base.

5. **Cannon Flask (P)**
   Cannon on two-wheeled carriage; unfurled flag on pole above, and six cannon balls. Reverse: Clasped hands in heart-shaped shield, underneath which is oval-shaped panel with "F. A. & Co." There is a branch on each side of the shield, and above, "Union" and 13 stars. Pint—aquamarine. Ringed mouth.

6. **Bicycle Flask (U)**
   Picture of a woman riding a bicycle, facing to left. Reverse: Eagle with ribbon, perched on arrows, head to right. Below, oval containing "A & D. H. C." Pint—bluish aquamarine. Ringed mouth.

7. **American Eagle Flask (P)**
   Eagle with ribbon, head to left. "Pittsburg, Pa." in oval underneath.

PLATE XV

1. **Washington Flask (K)**
   Washington in uniform, full face to the front, and "General Washington" in semi-circle above. Reverse: Spread-eagle, facing to the right, with rays above, perched on arrows and olive branch on top of beaded oval, enclosing letters "T W D". Pint — bluish aquamarine. Sheared mouth. Scarred base. Ribbed sides.

2. **American Eagle Flask (G)**
   Eagle, with ribbon, perched on log, with arrows. Underneath, oval-shaped panel containing eight-pointed ornament. Above eagle are 14 stars. Reverse: Same. The sides are corrugated, with central rib. Pint — blue. Sheared mouth. Scarred base.

3. **Flag Flask (C & H)**
   Eagle with large shield on breast, facing to the left. Branches underneath: 13 stars above. Reverse: Flag, on which are 13 stars, and underneath, "For Our Country". Ribbed sides. Pint—aquamarine. Sheared mouth. Scarred base.

   Note: There are three different varieties of flags and eagles in this flask.

4. **Wheat, Price & Co. Flask (WP)**
   Bust, facing to right, and in semi-circle around, "Wheat, Price & Co., Wheeling, Va." Reverse: Picture of glass works and "Fair View Works". Corrugated sides with central rib. Pint — green. Sheared mouth. Scarred base.

5. **Ship Flask (K)**
   Full rigged ship. "Franklin" underneath. Reverse: Spread-eagle, rays above, perched on panel with initials "T W D". Ribbed sides. Pint—aquamarine. Sheared mouth. Scarred base.

6. **Ringgold Flask (B)**
   Bust of Major Ringgold in uniform, facing to the left on panel, "Major" above; "Ringgold" below. Reverse: Bust of Taylor, underneath, "Rough and Ready". Pint — puce. Sheared mouth. Scarred base.

7. **Cannon Flask (Br)**
   Cannon on two-wheeled carriage, and cannon balls, on panel with following inscription running around: "Gen'l Taylor Never Surrenders".

— GROUP A: LIQUORS   71-

PLATE XVI

1. **Grape Flask (C & H)**
   Large bunch of grapes. Reverse: Large sheaf of wheat. Ribbed sides, with very prominent central rib. Half pint — clear bluish aquamarine. Sheared mouth. Scarred base.

2. **American Eagle Flask (K)**
   Eagle, head to right, with rays, perched on beaded oval with olive branch and arrows, and "T W D" in oval. Reverse: Cornucopia on panel, and the following on panel on the sides: "E Pluribus Unum"; "One of Many"; "Kensington Glass Works, Philadelphia". Heavy central rib on sides. Half pint—light blue. Sheared mouth. Scarred base.

3. **Sailboat Flask (Br)**
   Picture of sloop rigged sailboat in panel, sailing to the left. Reverse: Eight-pointed star. Ribbed sides. Half pint — aquamarine. Sheared mouth. Scarred base.

4. **Sailboat Flask (B)**
   Picture of sloop rigged sailboat on panel, sailing to the right, and "Fells Point". Reverse: Monument and "Baltimore". Half pint — purple. Sheared mouth. Scarred base.

5. **American Eagle Flask (D)**
   Eagle, with head to left, shield on breast, perched on arrows and olive branch, on panel, surrounded by beading. Reverse: Pine tree surrounded by beading, with "Liberty" above on panel. Central rib. Half pint— shaded light green. Sheared mouth. Scarred base.

6. **Jester Flask (U)**
   Picture of stout man with cane behind his back and high hat, jesting with another man with long-tailed coat and umbrella. Reverse: Full face Dutchman with arm underneath the chin. Half pint—shaded corn flower blue. Sheared mouth. Scarred base

7. **Byron Flask (K) (C)**
   Draped bust of Lord Byron. Reverse: Draped bust of Walter Scott. Half pint—amber. Sheared mouth. Scarred base.

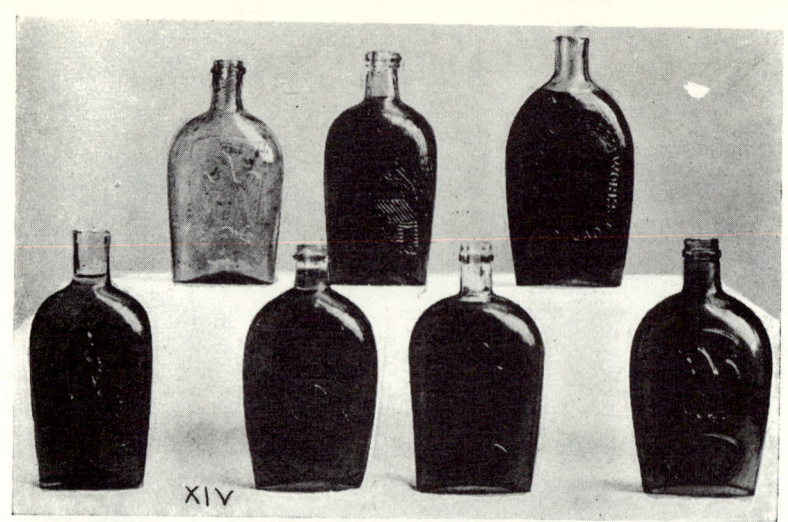

XIV

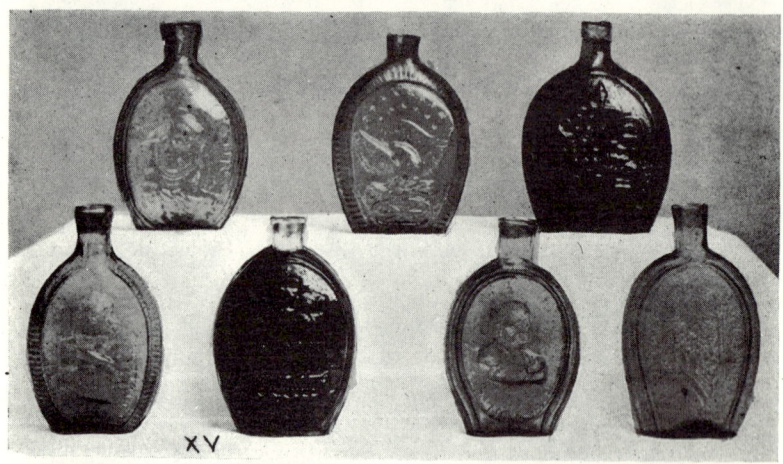

XV

XVI

— GROUP A: LIQUORS

Van Rensselaer method of grouping begins with a symbol system for identifying the make and lip types of early and late flasks, and carries five subject groupings.

Used to denote names of Glass Works and Glass Manufacturers.

A	Albany Glass Works	LZ	Frederick Lorenz
A & Co	Adams & Co.	M	Millford Glass Works
Ag	Arsenal Glass Works	MC & Co.	McCully & Co.
B	Baltimore Glass Works	Md	Medford Glass Works
B. P. & B.	Bakewell, Page & Bakewell	Mn	Mechanic Glass Works
Br	Bridgeton, N. J.	McT	McCarthy & Torreyson
Bs	Bristol Glass Works	M & C	Murdock & Cassel
By	George A. Berry & Co.	N. E. G.	New England Glass Co.
C	A. & D. H. Chambers	N G	New Granite Glass Co.
Ch	J. L. Chapman	N. L.	New London Glass Works
Cl	Clyde Glass Works	P	Pitkin Glass Works
Ct.	Coventry, Conn.	P P	Probably Pittsburgh, Pa.
C & Co	Cunninghams & Co.	R	Ravenna Glass Co.
C & H	Coffin & Hay	Rd	Richmond Glass Works
C & I	Cunninghams & Ihmsen	RK	R. Knowles
D	Dyottville Glass Works	S	Stiegel
E	English	Sa	Saratoga, N. Y.
E W & Co.	E. Wormser & Co.	S G	Spring Garden Glass Works
F	W. Frank & Sons	SJ	Southern New Jersey
F. A. & Co.	Fahnestock, Albree & Co.	Sl	Salisbury Glass Co.
Fr	Foreign	Sm	A. R. Samuels
Fs	Fislerville Glass Works	St.	Stoddard, N. H.
Fw	Freewill Glass Works	Sw	Sandwich
G	Granite Glass Co.	S & C	Stebbins and Chamberlin
G. & H.	Gray and Hemingray	S & D	Sheets & Duffy
H	S. Huffsey	S & S	Stebbins & Stebbins
H S	Henry Schoolcraft	T	Tibby Bros.
Hw	Hawley Glass Works	T S	Thomas Stebbins
H & S	Hancock & Sons	U	Unknown
I	Isabella Glass Works	Uf	Union Factory, Va.
I C	C. Ihmsen	Un	Union Glass Works, Philadelphia
IW	William Ihmsen	Unl.	Union Glass Works, New London
J P	Justus Perry	U n s	Union Glass Works, Somerville
J. P. F.	J. P. Foster	Vt.	Vermont Glass Co.
J. R. & S.	James Rowland & Son	W	Willington Glass Works
J T	James Taylor & Co.	Wb	Wistarberg
K	Kensington Glass Works	Wc	Unknown
Kn	Keene, N. H.	Wd	Waterford Glass Works
K & M	Knox & McKee	Wh	White Glass Works
L	Louisville Glass Works	Wl	Wheeling Glass Works (Union Glass
L. F. & Co.	Unknown	Wn	Whitney Glass Works
Ld	Laird & Co.	WP	Wheat Price & Co.
Lg	Lyndeboro Glass Co.	Wt	Westford Glass Co.
Lk	Lockport Glass Works	Z	Zanesville, O.
Ln	**Lancaster Glass Works**	Zc	Zanesville City Glass Works

Sheared	Mouth	Flattened	Mouth
Collared	"	Ringed	"
Double Collared	"	Flanged	"
Sloping	" "	Spout	"
Long Sloping Collared	"	Banded	"
Rolled	"	Heavy Collared	"
Screw or Thread Mouth		Folded Lip	

s m s b=sheared mouth scarred base, otherwise flat or hollow base

GRAND OLD AMERICAN BOTTLES — 74

Rare Historicals from Gardner Collection; Andrew Jackson ½ Pt., Aqua; American System, Pt. Aqua.

GROUP A: LIQUORS

Rare Historicals from Gardner Collection: John Q. Adams, Pt. Aqua; Hour Glass ½ Pt., Olive Green.

GRAND OLD AMERICAN BOTTLES

GROUP I

Historical Bottles and Flasks

(A few variants completing series not historical included under this head)

Colors and sizes refer to bottles illustrated or described—any attempt to give range of colors in each group is manifestly impossible.

1. ADAMS
Bust of Adams, facing slightly to left. Above "John Q. Adams", in semi-circle. Reverse: Spread eagle, head to right, 13 stars above, perched on arrows and olive branch and beaded oval, underneath oval "J. T. & Co". Beaded sides divided by central rib. The designs on panels. Pint—aquamarine. s m s b. (Sixth President 1825-1829) (J. T.).

2. AGRICULTURE
"Agriculture" in semi-circle. Underneath, sheaf of rye and below this sickle, pitch-fork, rake, scythe and plow. Reverse: "W. Ihmsen's" and below the eagle, which is perched on olive branch, oval marked "Glass". Pint—greenish aquamarine. s m s b (Ih).

3. BALTIMORE
"Baltimore" in semi-circle. Below, Baltimore Monument. Reverse: "Liberty & Union". Designs on panels. Pint. Aquamarine s m s b. (U). P. 1.

4. Baltimore Monument and "Baltimore" on panel. Reverse: "Corn For The World"; underneath stalk of corn in ear, also on panel. Quart—light olive amber. D c m. (B).

5. Baltimore Monument. Reverse: Border of grape vine with fruit surrounding "A little more grape Capt. Bragg". Half pint—aquamarine. s m s b. (B).

6. BRYAN
Bust of Bryan facing to the left. "In Silver We Trust" above. Below, "Bryan Sewall 1896" and 10 stars. Reverse: Spread eagle with wreath. Above eagle "We Shall Vote". Below eagle "16 to 1", and above "United Democratic Ticket". Circular, representing dollar, with milled edge, and oval-shaped base. Half pint—clear glass. d c m (U).

7. CANNON
"Gen. Taylor never surrenders" (three quarters circle) between cannon on wheels facing to the right. 15 cannon balls underneath the cannon, rammer and swab on right side of the wheel, rammer leaning on cannon in front of wheel, small kennel-like building below muzzle of cannon. Reverse: "A little more Grape Capt. Bragg" (last two words in semi-circle), grapes on vines surrounding the lettering—design on panels. Pint—aquamarine. s m s b. (B).

8. Cannon of same design and cannon balls (number obscure but evidently about 15), no accessories or building. Reverse: Fewer bunches of grapes. ½ pint—golden amber, heavy central rib on sides. (B). Also clear glass.

9. Reverse: Monument. Green. (B).

—GROUP A: LIQUORS

10. Cannon mounted on two wheeled carriage to right, rammer leaning on left side, unfurled flag to left over muzzle of cannon, cannon balls (3 rows) forming pedestal, can to right of the pile of cannon balls, (looks more like a floral motif). Reverse: 13 stars, "Union", small letters, shield with clasped hands, bars and oval initialed "F. A. & Co.", olive branch each side of shield. Half pint—aquamarine. r m. Also pint.

11. Half pint has lettering on upper part of oval in quarter circle. Reverse: The powder can is correctly designed. (Fa)

12. Larger cannon, smaller wheels, no can, no rammer. Reverse: Different shield "F. A. & Co" omitted. (Probably F A & Co.).

13. Heavier cannon and carriage to left, flag to right over muzzle. Reverse: Large clasped hands, shorter bars, larger oval, lettering "W. Frank & Sons Pitt". (F).

14. Smaller cannon and carriage, larger flag. Reverse: "Union" larger, clasped hands smaller, fewer bars, smaller oval, lettered "W. Frank & Sons Pitts". Deep claret color (F).

15. CLEVELAND
Bust of Grover Cleveland, in impressed circle, facing to the left. Reverse: Plain. Flat raised rib on sides. Pint—iridescent aquamarine. d c m "A. C. Co." on bottom. (U).

16. Bust on circular panel, "Cleveland" to the left of bust in semi-circle. Reverse: Bust of Hendricks on similar panel, "Hendricks" to right of bust. Pint—clear glass, flanged d c m. On oval (1 inch x 1½ inch) bottom, "J. R. Hartigan's Patent—Pitts." (U)

17. Busts of Cleveland and Stevenson. In panel "Our Choice". Below "Cleve & Steve", Nov. 8, 1892. March 4, 1893. Reverse: Barrel Staves and Rooster. Semi-circular barrel shape. Pint—clear glass. d c m. (U).

18. In form of Bust of Cleveland. Round base marked "Cleveland" About ¾ quart—frosted clear glass. c m (U)

19. COLUMBIA
Bust of Columbia with cap, facing to the left, on panel. Above, 13 stars. Reverse: Large eagle with head to the right, perched on arrows and olive branch. Underneath, "B & W" (script). Central rib on each side. Pint— —light olive green. s m s b. (U).

20. No stars. Reverse: "B & W" omitted. Clear glass. (U).

21. Bust of Columbia with cap, on panel; 13 stars above in semi-circle; "Kensington" underneath. Reverse: Eagle, head to right on panel. Underneath "Union Co", vertical ribbing on base. Broad central rib on sides. Pint —aquamarine. s m s b (Un).

22. "Ashton" instead of "Kensington", reverse "Hough" instead of "Union Co." (U).

23. No lettering—blue (U).

GRAND OLD AMERICAN BOTTLES

EARLY AMERICAN BOTTLES AND FLASKS

24. Columbia differs slightly, reverse eagle is shorter and faces to left, rib on sides not so prominent. Half pint—pale green, almost clear (Un).

25. COFFIN & HAY
"Coffin & Hay" (semi-circle) below "Hammonton, N. J." (semi-circle) plain space between lettering. Reverse: Spread-eagle to right, rays over head, grasping arrows and olive branch, plain oval below. Pint—aquamarine s m s b.

26. COLUMBIAN
"Columbian Exposition". Below, bust of Columbus facing to the front, 1893 below, and below this "A. E. M. Bros. & Co." Reverse: "Pennsylvania Pure Rye Baker Whiskey". Flat shape with high shoulders. Pint —amber. Collared mouth (U).

27. Ship, below 1492-1892. Reverse: "Columbian Jubilee" (in script). Pint—amber. d c m. (U).

28. FLAG
"Coffin & Hay" (semi-circle) large flag on pole, below "Hammonton, N. J." (semi-circle). Reverse: Large spread eagle, head to right, rays above, perched on double framed oval and arrows and olive branch extend to left and right respectively from the claws. Designs on panels. Heavy central rib on sides. Quart—light green. s m s b.

29. Eagle, raised wings in bold relief perched on partly furled flag. Reverse: Branch with flower and leaves, very prominent rib on sides. Pint— light green. d c m. s b. (U).

30. 10 stars in semi-circle and flag. Below the flag is "Hard Cider" in semi-circle, below this is a barrel, and below the barrel is a plow with branch each side. Reverse: Log Cabin with 9 stars above, in semi-circle. Below, fence. Corrugated sides, with heavy central rib. Pint—beautiful clear blue. s m s b. (Ln)

31. Flag on pole to right, 13 stars and 9 bars. Reverse: "New Granite Glass Works" (¾ circle) "Stoddard" (¼ circle), below "N. H." Prominent rib on sides. Pint—golden amber. s m s b. (N. G.) Also half-pint.

32. Smaller flag on pole to left, 16 stars, 13 bars. Reverse: Same as 31, golden amber. Small rib on sides. The flask is flatter and somewhat narrower but the same height (N. G)

33. *Flag with 20 stars. Underneath "For Our Country". Reverse: Spread eagle, head to right, rays above, perched on shield, branches below. Ribbed sides. Pint—aquamarine. s m s b. (C & H).

34. *Flag with 18 stars. Underneath "For Our Country". Reverse: Eagle facing to the left, rays above, perched on large shield, branches below, ribbed sides. Pint—clear aquamarine. s m s b. (C & H).

35. *Flag with 13 stars. Underneath "For Our Country". Reverse: Eagle with large shield on breast facing to the left, ribbed sides. Pint— aquamarine. s m s b. (C & H).

There are so many bottles that might be included in this category that only thees are listed.

CORNUCOPIA FLASKS

1. Cornucopia on panel, to the left. Reverse: Basket of flowers with five bars to the basket. Heavy central rib on sides. ½ pint—olive green. s m s b. Also pint.

—GROUP A: LIQUORS

2. Different design cornucopia, different arrangement of fruit. Reverse: Different design basket having six bars, also different arrangement of fruit.

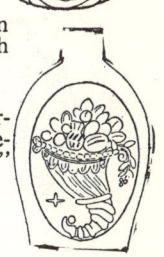

3. Large dot to left of cornucopia. ½ pint.

4. Pointed motif instead of dot. ½ pint.

5. Different design cornucopia to right. Reverse: Different design basket and different arrangement of fruit, also seven bars to basket, which are continuous extending to base. ½ pint—golden amber. s m s b.

6. Different cornucopia to right, from any of the preceding, also different arrangement of fruit. Reverse: Different basket from any of the preceding, also different arrangement of fruit. "Lancaster Glass Works, N. Y." above in semi-circle. Pint—bluish aquamarine. s m s b.

7. Reverse: Lettering omitted. (Ln).

8. Very crude cornucopia, relatively fewer pieces of fruit. Reverse: 7 bars to basket also holding relatively fewer pieces of fruit. ½ pint. (Ln).

9. Large cornucopia to left on panel. Reverse: Large spread-eagle to right, shield on breast with four large bars, perched on rocks, 3 arrows showing at left of rocks and olive branch at right of rocks. Heavy central rib on sides. Pint—olive green. s m s b. (Kn).

10. 2½ inch mouth, body is nearly round and is 3⅝ inches in diameter. Has undoubtedly been reshaped while plastic. Rich golden amber. s m s b. (Kn).

11. Another—panel much less prominent, no frame to panel, very low central rib and four-pointed ornament on left side of cornucopia (usual mouth and shape.) s m s b. (Kn). An opaque one is known.

12. Slender cornucopia with fruit, curled over base, or tail. Reverse: Spread-eagle with shield on breast, facing to the right, right wing foreshortened. Three arrows in claws. Perched on oval with narrow beading which rests on six rays or grass blades. Nine stars above eagle. Corrugated sides with central rib. Pint—green. s m s b. Eagle very similar to No. 4, Group I1, Division II but there is no olive branch in eagle's claws.

13. Large cornucopia. Reverse: Very early type spread-eagle to right, shield on breast, 13 stars above. ½ pint—olive green—corrugated sides. s m s b. (U.

14. Cornucopia on panel, and the following on the sides: "E Pluribus Unum"; "One of Many"; "Kensington Glass Works, Philadelphia". Reverse: Eagle on panel, head to right with rays, perched on beaded oval with olive branch and arrows, and "T W D" in oval. Heavy central rib on sides. Half pint—light blue. s m s b.

15. No rays, plain oval, no lettering, no lettering on sides. s m s b. ½ pint. Aquamarine. (K).

16. "T W D" omitted, ribs inclining slightly to right and left below oval. Reverse: Different cornucopia; end more curled, sharper rib on sides. ½ pint bluish aquamarine. s m s b. (U).

36. FRANKLIN
Large bust of Benj. Franklin, facing to the front, on oval panel. Above "Benjamin Franklin". Reverse: Bust of Dr. Dyott facing to the front, and above "T. W. Dyott, M. D." Central rib on sides between which is "Kensington Glass Works, Philadelphia", and "Eripuit Coelo Fulmen Sceptrumque Tyrannis" (He snatches from the sky the thunderbolt, and the sceptre from tyrants.) Quart—aquamarine. sm s b. (K).

37. No Lettering. (K)

38. "Benjamin Franklin" (semi-circle) below bust of Franklin. Reverse: "T. W. Dyott, M. D." (semi-circle), below bust of Dyott. Central rib on sides between which is "Where Liberty dwells there is my country", "Kensington Glass Works, Philadelphia". Pint—aquamarine. s m   s b. (K).

39. No lettering on sides. (K).

40. Large bust of Franklin facing to the front above "Benjamin Franklin" (semi-circle). Reverse: Unidentified bust facing to the front above "Wheeling Glass Works" (semi-circle). Pint—aquamarine. s m s b. (WL.) N. B. The bust appears to be that of Dr. Dyott.

41. GRAPE
Large bunch of grapes. Reverse: Large sheaf of rye. Ribbed sides, with very prominent central rib. Half pint—clear bluish aquamarine. s m   s b. (C & H).

42. Smaller bunch of grapes. Ribbed sides, c m (U).

43. Narrower bunch of grapes. Reverse: Spread eagle to left, large shield covering lower part of body, 13 stars above, olive branch each lower side of shield. Heavy central rib on sides with 3 small ones either side. Designs on panels (C & H).

44. Large bunch of grapes. Reverse: Large spread eagle, head to left, shield on breast, grasping arrows and olive branch, 13 stars above. Quart—aquamarine. (C & H).

45. Bunch of grapes in depressed 3 inch panel. Reverse: Plain, ½ inch raised rib on sides. Thread mouth. Pint—yellowish amber. (U).

46. GRANT
Crude head of General Grant facing to left, enclosed in double oval frame, outside of which are laurel leaves and bowknot of ribbon below. Reverse: Eagle with outstretched wings facing to left, ribbon above, perched on shield through which a ribbon runs, olive branch extending from each side of shield, below "Union". Pint—aquamarine. r m. (U).

47. HARRISON
Full bust of Harrison in uniform. Above "Wm. H. Harrison" Reverse: Log cabin with cider barrel and plow. Cabin door has latch string out; chimney is capped, and opposite end of cabin from chimney is surmounted by a staff and flag with eight stars. Corrugated sides divided by central rib. Pint—greenish aquamarine. s m   s b. (U).

— GROUP A: LIQUORS

48. INDIAN
Indian with bow and arrow shooting bird perched on tree. Tree without leaves on the left, between the Indian and this tree is a dog. Underneath is the inscription "Cunninghams & Co., Pittsburgh, Pa." Reverse: Spread-eagle perched on top of monument, with ribbon. Eagle is facing to the right. On each side of the monument is a tree with bird perched on it. Underneath the monument is "Continential".—Quart—iridescent aquamarine r m (CN).

49. INDIAN with crown, shooting bird on tree, with bow and arrow. Dog behind. Reverse: Eagle with ribbon on pedestal and serrated flag. Bird on each side. Pint—aquamarine. c m (U).

50. JACKSON
Full bust of Jackson in uniform, facing slightly to the left. Above "General Jackson", in semi-circle. Reverse: Spread-eagle, 13 stars above, head to the right, perched on arrows and olive branch and beaded oval. Underneath oval, "J T & Co." Beaded sides divided by central rib. The designs on panels. Pint—light green. sm s b. (JT).

51. Reverse: "J T & Co" omitted and only 9 stars. (JT).

52. Reverse: Large floral motif showing acorns. (U).

54. Bust of Jackson facing to the right on oval surrounded by Masonic Arch. Below, fleur-de-lis, below outside the oval "Andrew Jackson" in large letters. Reverse: American eagle in oval facing to the left. Perched on arrows and olive branch. Seven stars above eagle, and outside the ova "Wheeling" Knox & McKee". Heavy central rib on sides. Pint—light bluish green. s m s b.

55. KOSSUTH
"Kossuth" above. Below bust of Kossuth facing to the right. Reverse: Tree. Quart—long neck—yellowish amber. Collared mouth. (H).

56. "Louis Kossuth" above. Below, bust of Kossuth with high hat and plume, flag each side. Reverse: Ship. Underneath, "U. S. Steam Frigate Mississippi". Ribbed sides. Quart—long neck—greenish aquamarine. c m. s b, marked "Ph. Doplein Mould Maker 84 Nth 5th St." (H).   (Kossuth the Hungarian Patriot).

57. LA FAYETTE
"La Fayette" (semi-circle) below bust of La Fayette to right, horizontal bar below "T. S." (Thomas Stebbins) two horizontal bars extending across flask. Reverse: "De Witt Clinton" (D reversed) in semi-circle below bust of Clinton to right, "Coventry" (semi-circle) "C-T" between two horizontal bars extending across flask, three horizontal bars extend around shoulders. Corrugated sides. Pint—olive amber s m   s b.

58. No bar below bust "S & C" (Stebbins & Chamberlin) and three bars below. Reverse: D not reversed, "C-T" below bust and 3 bars. ½ pint.

59. Below bust horizontal bar with short vertical ends "T-S" and one bar below. Reverse: Masonic Arch, 12 pointed stellar motif below, two 6 pointed above. ½ pint.

60. Bar and "T. S" omitted. **Reverse:** Arch but no motifs, one central rib on sides instead of corrugation. ½ pint—olive green. (T S)

61. **Reverse:** Different bricking to Masonic pavement (4 rows No. 60 has 3) no bars. Pint—olive amber. (T S)

62. "Covetry" (not Coventry) semi-circle and "C–T" between. **Reverse:** 11 stars (semi-circle) surrounding liberty cap on pole. On the pint are two bars at base. Reverse: Star to left and half moon to right above arch, no motif below. In oval below "S & S" (Stebbins & Stebbins). Two bars extend around, below "C–T". 5 ribs on sides. Pint—golden amber s m s b.

63. Same but "Coventry".

64. Same except "Coventry" instead of "Covetry". Reverse: 9 stars, 3 ribs on sides. ½ pint.

65. Reverse: Stars omitted.

66. Bust of LaFayette facing to the right on oval panel surrounded by Masonic arch. Below, fleur-de-lis, below outside the oval "Gen'l LaFayette" in large letters. Reverse: American eagle in oval facing to the left, perched on arrows and olive branch. Seven stars above eagle, and outside the oval "Wheeling" "Knox & McKee". There are 6 cannon balls below eagle. Heavy central rib on sides. Pint—light bluish green. s m s b. P. 3 and 18.

67. Reverse: "Wheeling" and "Knox and McKee" omitted, also cannon balls. (K & M).

68. Full bust of LaFayette in uniform, facing to the front. "General LaFayette" above (semi-circle). Reverse: Spread-eagle rays above, perched on beaded oval initialed "T W D", grasping arrows and olive branch. Above the rays is "E Pluribus Unum". On the sides divided by central rib "Republican Gratitude"; "Kensington Glass Works, Philadelphia". Pint—aquamarine. s m   s b.

69. Reverse: "E Pluribus Unum" omitted, fewer rays, no lettering on sides. (K).

70. LIBERTY
Figure of Liberty standing, with pole and liberty cap in left hand, and shield in right. Above, "Liberty" in a scroll. At the sides are the letters "U. S." Reverse: Log Cabin, pump, tree and gate. At the base "Liberty" Pint—pale blue. d c m. (U).

71. LINCOLN
"Abraham Lincoln" in semi-circle; below bust. Reverse: bunch of grapes. Quart—amber. c m. (U).

72. JENNY LIND
"Jenny Lind." Below bust surrounded by wreath. Reverse: "Kossuth." Below bust facing to the right. Quart—long neck bluish aquamarine. c m. (H).

— GROUP A: LIQUORS 83

73. "Jenny Lind." Below bust with wreath underneath. Reverse: "Fislerville Glass Works". Below, picture of works. Ribbed sides. Quart—long neck. Clear, very light bluish aquamarine. c m s b. (Fs).

74. "Jenny Lind". Below bust surrounded by wreath. Reverse: "Millfora G. Works" and picture of glass works. Quart—long neck. c m s b. (M).

75. "Jenny Lind". Below bust surrounded by wreath. Reverse: "Glass Works". Below picture of glass works. Below "S. Huffsey" quart —long neck—aquamarine. c m (H).

76. "Jenny Lind". Below bust surrounded by wreath. Reverse: "Glass Factory". Picture of factory below. Six-pointed star between "Glass" and "Factory". Ribbed sides. Quart—long neck—bluish aquamarine. c m s b. (Wn).

77. "Jeny Lind". (One n) Below bust surrounded by wreath. Reverse: (One n) Picture of glass works, no inscription. Ribbed sides. Quart—long neck —bluish green. c m s b. Height 10½ inches. (R).

78. Head and bust narrower and not so well executed, smoky blue, round, rolled collar, hollowed base. Height 9½ inches. (Probably Un. as they show all the characteristics.)

79. Small bust of Jenny Lind below large lyre. Reverse: Same. Shaped something like violin. Pint—sea green. s m s b (Probably M T C).

80. Same except quart and on one side is a wreath-like border. (Probably M T C)

81. LOG CABIN
In form of log cabin, "Tippecanoe" across one side, below door in centre, window on each side, cider barrel under one window. Reverse: "North Bend" across, below same as obverse. Pint—olive amber. c. m. s. b. Height 5½ inches. (U).

82. LOCOMOTIVE*
Early locomotive to left in very bold relief, man between tender or car which appears to have wood in front and 3 mounds on back end. Reverse: Female figure balancing on toes to left emptying cornucopia, wing-like appendages on back and one in front between right raised arm and headdress in form of plumed hat, on the somewhat flattened sides "Success to the railroads". Pint—clear glass. s m s b. Base is 1½ x ¾ inches. (Attributed to B).

83. Crude locomotive to left on rails "Success to the Rail Road" (running from left lower part of the flask over the engine). Reverse: Same Pint—sea green. s m s b. Heavy central rib on sides. (Ln).

84. Not as flat, lettering on bottom XX also CC. Olive green, thin glass. (U). N. B.

*The Camden & Amboy Railroad, chartered by the State of New Jersey Feb. 4, 1830. Its President was Robert L. Stevens, son of the steam-boat and railroad builder, John Stevens. The former was sent to England

soon after the company was organized and ordered a locomotive for the road. This was the "John Bull" put in service Nov. 12, 1831 at Bordentown, New Jersey. It arrived "Knocked down" and a young American mechanic Isaac Dripps, assembled and ran it. It is held that this was the first steam locomotive operated on a railroad in this country. It is apparent how rare and how historically important is this flask, and no wonder profound interest attaches to such a wondrous piece of glass.

85. MCKINLEY
Bust of McKinley, facing to the left. Above, "Sound Money and Protection", below "McKinley & Hobart". Reverse: Bee with numerals 1896 below. Above "In Gold we Trust" in form of a silver dollar. Milled edge and rectangular base. Half pint—shaded amber. d c m. (U).

86. Bust of McKinley facing to the right, surrounded by stars and above: "Gold Standard No Split Dollars". Underneath, "McKinley". Reverse: Bust of Hobart facing to the front, surrounded by stars. Above, "Prosperity Protection"; underneath, "Hobart". Circular (3½ inches), with oblong base. About ¼ pint—clear glass. Threaded mouth. (U).

87. "Genuine Distilled Protection". Bust of McKinley facing to the front, below "McKinley" "For Sound Money Only". Reverse: Bust of Hobart in oval, below "Hobart". Pint—clear glass. f m. Base lettered "Trade Mark Regd. Pat. Ap. For." (U).

88. MONUMENTAL CITY
Marked "The Monumental City 1880 Sesquicentennial". On base "Baltimore Glass Works Est'd 1780. Baker Bros. & Co." Circular. Quart —clear glass. cm s b (B).

89. OLD CONTINENTAL
Continental Soldier, below "1776". Reverse: "Old Continental Whiskey" (Lengthwise) other panels are plain. Square bottle with columns on corners. About ¾ quart. Light clear amber. c m (U).

90. RAIL ROAD FLASK
"Success to the Railroad" (three quarter circle) horse pulling cart on rails to left, the vehicle is loaded with boxes and barrels. Reverse: Large spreadeagle, head to left, covering entire side lengthwise, 17 stars around the eagle. Designs on panel. Pint—golden amber s m   s b.

91. No lettering. Reverse: No Stars.

92. Larger lettering and sunburst in panels on cart. Reverse: Same.

93. Thinner lettering, sunbursts not so plain.

94. Small lettering.

95. "Success" above cart, "To the railroad" below cart.

96. No lettering. Reverse: Same. Clear glass.

97. Cart and horse to the right "Railroad" above "Lowell" below. Reverse: Same as No. 90 except there are but 13 stars. Half pint—golden amber.

All have heavy central rib on sides.

GROUP A: LIQUORS

98. RAMSAY
"Robt Ramsay Wine & Liquor Merchant 281 8th Ave., New York"
Reverse: Bust of Taylor. Pint—aquamarine. s m s b (U).

99. RINGGOLD
On panel bust of Major Ringgold in uniform, facing to the left. "Major" above, "Ringgold" below. Reverse: On panel bust of Taylor, underneath "Rough and Ready". Pint—puce. s m s b. Ribbed sides (B).

100. No side ribs. (B).

101. SAILBOAT
Sloop rigged sailboat sailing to the left, on panel. Reverse: 8-pointed motif. Ribbed sides. Half Pint—aquamarine s m s b. (Br).

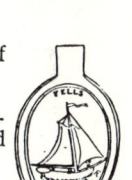

102. No waves under boat. Reverse: Smaller star. Pint—green. (Br).

103. Reverse: "Bridgetown, New Jersey". Motif omitted.

104. Reverse: Bridgeton, New Jersey" (semi-circle), below bust of Kossuth facing to the right. Pint—aquamarine.

105. Boat sailing to the right "Fells" above "Point" below boat. Reverse: Baltimore Monument, below "Balto" ½ pint—aquamarine and amethyst.

106. SHIP
Full rigged ship sailing to right "Franklin" underneath. Reverse: Masonic arch, sheaf of rye, pitch-fork, rake and scythe, below fleur-de-lis type motif. On the sides central rib each side of which is "Free Trade and Sailor's Rights, "Kensington Glass Works, Philadelphia". Pint—aquamarine. s m s b.

107. Beading on sides replaces lettering. (Probably JT).

108. Full rigged ship. "Franklin" underneath. Reverse: Spread-eagle, head to the left, rays above, perched on arrows and olive branch on oval initialed "T W D". Ribbed sides. (3 ribs). Pint—aquamarine. s m s b. (K).

109. STAG
Stag, facing to the left" and Coffin & Hay" above; "Hammonton" below. Reverse: Spread-eagle, with head to right, with olive branch and arrows. Half pint—very pale aquamarine s m s b. Also pint.

110. Stag with large antlers, facing to the right. Underneath, "Good Game". Reverse: Large weeping-willow tree. Ribbed sides. Pint—clear bluish aquamarine. s m s b. (C & H).

111. Stag, dog and hunter, surrounded by foliage. Reverse: Boar's head in circle, surrounded by oak branch and acorns. Flat, circular flask, with beaded sides and small rectangular base. Pint—sapphire blue. Long neck. s m s b. (U).

86   GRAND OLD AMERICAN BOTTLES

112. Stag with big antlers, tree to left "R" at right, no man or dog. Reverse: Boar's head to left in two-thirds circle, gun and horn. Deep sapphire blue. s m sb. (U)

113. Reclining stag to left; branch above. Reverse: Antlers, hunting horn and gun. Deep sapphire blue. s m s b. (U).

114. STEAMBOAT
"The American" below picture of early steamboat with paddle wheels (probably Clermont) steaming to right, flag, probably intended for American, showing, below "System" Reverse: Large open sheaf of rye and around it "Use me but do not abuse me" below narrow rectangular panel with curved ends. Herring-bone sides. Pint—very light, clear shaded olive yellow. s m s b. (U).

115. TAYLOR
"Genl Taylor" (semi-circle) below bust of General Taylor in uniform, facing to left. Reverse: "Fells Point" (semi-circle) at base "Balto", Baltimore Monument between lettering. Pint—aquamarine. s m s b. (B).

116. "Fells" (quarter circle) at base "Point" (large letters slightly curved). Bust of General Taylor with queue, in uniform, facing to left. Reverse: Baltimore Monument, below "Balto". s m s b. (B).

117. "Rough and Ready", below bust (Taylor) in uniform. Reverse: Eagle to right, 10 stars above, perched on three arrows to the left, on beaded oval. Corrugated sides with central rib. Pint—aquamarine. s m s b. (B).

118. No lettering, different bust. Reverse: No stars, eagle lower down on flask, longer neck, narrow base. Pint aquamatine. s m s b. (U).

119. "Rough and Ready" (semi-circle) bust of Taylor (presumably intended for him) below stellar motif. Reverse: "Masterson" (semi-circle), 13 stars, below spread-eagle, head to left grasping 3 arrows and olive branch or other object apparently tied with cord as the loops show. Designs on panels, corrugated sides divided by central rib. Quart—aquamarine. s m s b. (U).

120. "Zachary Taylor". Below, large bust of Zachary Taylor, facing to right. Underneath, "Rough and Ready". Reverse: "Corn for the World" in a semi-circle. Underneath, corn stalk. Pint—aquamarine. s m s b. (B).

121. Bust of Taylor, facing to left, clothing comparatively well up on neck. Reverse: Sheaf of rye, pitch fork and rake. Quart—aquamarine. c m with base ring. (Attributed to Mn).

122. Differing head, clothing less in evidence. Reverse: Narrow top to sheaf. Pint—aquamarine. c m with base ring. (Attributed to Mn).

123. Head slightly elevated. No clothing showing. Reverse: Double headed sheaf, pitch fork and rake omitted. Half pint—aquamarine. c m with base ring (Attributed to Mn).
(The above three flasks have designs on panels).
Note: These three flasks have always been called "Taylor & Sheaf" flasks so I put them under this classification, although there is some question as to the identity of the gentleman shown.

— GROUP A: LIQUORS

GROUP II

DIVISION I—CORRUGATED SIDES.   AMERICAN EAGLE BOTTLES AND FLASKS

Spread eagle head to left, ribbon from beak over head **with five** stars shield with five bars on breast, olive branch in left claw, two arrows in right, crude stellar motif below. Reverse: Same. Corrugated sides divided by central rib. Quart—aquamarine s m s b. (L).

2. Eagle of broader proportions, different motif. Reverse: plain About two and a half quarts—aquamarine. (U).

3. Very similar to (No. 1) but the eagle is more compact, the ribbon from beak does not have stars, two rows of stars (14 in all) are above the ribbon, bars on breast rather obscure, olive branch grasped by right claw and arrows in left (crudely fashioned) eight pointed stellar motif enclosed in rectangle below. Reverse: Same. Pint—aquamarine. (L).

4. Reverse: Stars omitted. Large 12 branched floral motif instead of the eagle. (U).

5. Smaller ribbon marked "Union", eagle has longer neck. Reverse: 14 stars and below a large harp. (U).

6. Very early spread eagle, head to left, ribbon below. The eagle is grasping three arrows in the right claw and an olive branch in the left. Below is an elongated horizontal sunburst. Reverse: "Farley & Taylor, Richmond, Ky." Corrugated sides. Flask holds two quarts, one pint. Aquamarine, s m s b. (L).

7. Eagle, head to right, on panel, perched on oval with arrows. Above eagle are ten stars. Reverse: Same. Corrugated sides with one central rib. Pint—light greenish blue. s m s b. (L).

8. Nine stars, beaded oval. Reverse: Same. (L).

9. Ten stars in semi-circle below spread eagle facing to the right. Three arrows held in right claw, perched on an irregular shaped oval with inside beading. Very large shield which has six bars covers entire breast of the eagle. Below the oval are three bars inclining to the left. Reverse: Same. Corru-

DIVISION II—EAGLE EACH SIDE   10. Same except one side has 9 stars.

1. Eagle with shield and ribbon, oval lettered "Granite Glass Co." Reverse: Eagle with ribbon. In oval "Stoddard, N. H." Pint—deep amber. s m s b.

2. Quart—rich amber, full of bubbles, same as No. 1 except one "d" in Stoddard omitted.

3. Eagle, shield on breast, perched on arrows and olive branch, with ribbon, head to the left. "Stoddard, N. H." in oval. Reverse: Similar, but no inscription. Pint—amber. s m s b.

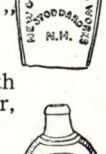

4. No lettering either side. Half pint, pint and quart. One found with 1⅜ inch mouth. (G).

5. Same as No. 4 but has four pointed star on oval. ½ pint. (G).

6. Eagle, head to right, olive branch from beak, extending overhead, small shield on breast, grasping three arrows, underneath "Zanesville"

7. Eagle, head to left, on panel, rays above, perched on beaded oval, with olive branch and arrows. Reverse: Same. Rib on sides. Pint—light green. s m   s b. (K).

8. Spread-eagle, facing to right, ribbon above head, and to left, in beak. Shield on breast, perched on arrows and olive branch. The tips of wings extend below these. Oval below. Reverse: Same. Pint—bluish aquamarine. r m. (U)

9. Eagle with ribbon, head to left, shield on breast, perched on oval and arrows. Reverse: Same. Pint—very light green. r m   s b. (PP)

10. Spread-eagle, head to the left, no feathers showing on wings, bars on breast obscure. The olive branches on which the eagle is perched run together. There is a large oval underneath the eagle. Reverse: Same. Pint rich golden amber. r c m. (U).

11. Eagle to right, small ribbon over head, shield on breast with 7 bars, perched on arrows and olive branch, which extend beyond the wings on right and left. Oval underneath. Reverse: Same. Pint—bluish aquamarine. r m   (U).

12. Spread-eagle, with ribbon to right perched on arrows. Large oval underneath. Short neck 1 1–16 inch, 3 inches at shoulder. Reverse: Same: 2⅛ inch base. ½ pint—light green. c m. (U).

13. Small spread-eagle, head to right, ribbon above from beak, shield on breast, grasping arrows and olive branch, oval below. Reverse: Same. ½ pint—aquamarine. d c m. (U). Also s m.

14. Eagle to left, six small dots over eagle, probably intended for stars, shield on breast, perched on olive branch, small oval below. Reverse: Small eagle in flight head down with snake in beak curling over back and through left wing, designs on panels, heavy central rib, dividing double rows of bull's eyes on sides. Pint— very light aquamarine, almost clear white. s m   s b. Flask narrows at base to 2 x 1⅛ inches. (U).

A peculiar interest attaches to this flask, since the inclusion of the serpent in the design makes it unique. A cut in Gregory and Ginteau's "History and Geography of Ohio" shows an eagle, wings partly raised, with serpent curling over head, held by the eagle's beak and one talon.

"Eagle of Liberty Strangling
the Serpent of CORRUPTION."
This slogan is above and below
"True American Ticket
For President
Wm. Henry Harrison."

The flask, therefore, was undoubtedly produced in 1840 and recalls the spirited campaign of that year.

15. Small eagle, head to right with outstretched wings. Reverse: Same. Designs on panels. Pint—aquamarine. h c m. s b. (U).

16. Rather larger eagle head to right, ribbon from beak over head to left, grasping arrows and olive branch, rectangular oval below. Reverse: Same. ½ pint—aquamarine. r m. (U).

— GROUP A: LIQUORS   89

DIVISION III—LOUISVILLE, KY., VERTICAL, ALSO PITTSBURG CIRCULAR RIBBING

1. AMERICAN EAGLE FLASK
Vertically ribbed, oval panel with large spread-eagle in flight to right, ribbon through beak over head, also extending through shield below on which eagle is perched. Below six-pointed panel lettered "Louisville, Ky. Glass Works" (2 lines). Reverse: Plain. Quart—aquamarine. r m. (L).

2. Vertically ribbed, small spread-eagle grasping arrows and olive branches, raised wings, in oval panel. Reverse: Same. Pint—light aquamarine. s m s b. (L)

3. Vertically ribbed, very small spread-eagle with out-stretched wings, head to right, five stars above, grasping olive branches in right claw and arrows in left. Reverse: Panel lettered "Louisville, Ky. Glass Works" (3 lines) ½ pint—aquamarine. d c m.

4. Spread-eagle, very large wings, head to right, ribbon over head from beak, large shield covering breast, eagle grasping 3 arrows and olive branches. Below: Large oval panel lettered "Louisville, Ky" (2 lines, Louisville in semicircle). Reverse: "Glass Works." Quart—aquamarine. r c m. Also pint.

5. Very early and crude spread-eagle, head turned to right, surrounded by heavy circular ribbing covering entire flask. Reverse: Same. About ¾ quart—pale yellow green. s m s b. (Probably B P & P).
Note: An advertisement of Bakewell's apparently alludes to this flask, which they called the eagle canteen flask, as one of their specialties.

DIVISION IV—REVERSE: CLASPED HANDS OR NAMES OR INITIALS IN PANELS. (FEW OTHERS TO COMPLETE SETS)

1. Spread-eagle with ribbon perched on arrows and olive branch. "A. & Co." on ribbon. Reverse: Large shield, clasped hands, seven flat bars, plain oval, thirteen stars, "Union", large branch each side. Pint—deep amber. d c m. Quart shown.

2. Large eagle facing to right, ribbon above and below through beak, perched on shield directly below through which runs ribbon, arrows and olive branch below. Lettered "Pittsburg, Pa." Reverse: 13 stars, "Union" shield (small letters) clasped hands and oval lettered "A. & D. H. C." branch each side. Pint—aquamarine. r m.

3. Spread-eagle, head to left, ribbon in beak extending over head, perched on arrows. Oval underneath lettered "Geo. A. Berry & Co." Reverse: Same, except oval plain. Pint—light green. r m.

4. Head to right, "G. A. Berry & Co." in oval. ½ pint.

5. Eagle flying to right, long ribbon over head from beak, also double row of elongated dots, eagle is perched on shield (feet do not show), long ribbon goes through shield on a panel. Below is
                C I & Sons
Reverse: Clasped hands, shield 14 bars, long panel rounded ends "Union", above 13 stars. Pint—yellow green. r m.

GRAND OLD AMERICAN BOTTLES

Division V—Reverse Clasped Hands, no Names or Initials

1. Eagle with ribbon, facing to right. Below, panel. Reverse: Clasped hands in shield with branch each side. "Union" in small letters and panel underneath, with clasped hands and "No. 2". Quart—aquamarine. r m. (PP).

2. Spread-eagle with ribbon, on arrows and olive branch. Panel below. Reverse: Clasped hands in shield, nine vertical bars above plain oval, with branch each side. Above fifteen stars. ½ pint—dark amber. r m. (PP).

3. Eagle with ribbon and oval underneath. Reverse: Clasped hands and panel in shield. Above 13 stars. Branch on each side of shield. Pint—amber. r m. (PP).

4. Eagle with ribbon and oval. Reverse: Shield enclosing clasped hands. Oval below, 13 stars above. Branches each side. Pint—amber. c m. (PP).

5. Eagle with ribbon, on arrows and olive branch. Plain oval underneath. Reverse: Shield, clasped hands, fifteen bars on panel, "No. 2", and branch each side. "Union" above; 13 stars. Pint—deep amber. r m. (PP).

6. Eagle in flight, to right. Body in bold relief, ribbon over head, through beak and through shield. Underneath, projecting from shield, are three arrows on right and left olive branch. Reverse: 11 stars "Union", clasped hands within shield, also oval, branch each side. ½ pint—deep amber. r m. (U).

7. Eagle with ribbon above and below head through beak, facing to right, perched on shield through which runs a ribbon slightly to right, olive branch, below panel. Reverse: 13 stars, small "Union" clasped hands on shield 9 bars, oval on shield, branch each side of shield. ½ pint—aquamarine. r m. (PP).

8. Small eagle to right, ribbon through beak above and below, perched on shield through which is ribbon, arrows and olive branch, below plain oval. Reverse: 13 small stars, small "Union", clasped hands, shield, no bars, branch each side. Pint—aquamarine. c m. (PP).

9. Spread-eagle, with ribbon to right, also ribbon below, which goes through shield. Reverse: 11 stars, "Union", clasped hands, small oval, shield which goes to bottom of the flask, branch each side. ½ pint—aquamarine. r m. Eagle near top of flask. (U).

10. No lettering, branch each side of head. Reverse: Spread-eagle, rays and 13 stars above head, no shield on breast, arrows are large and point down, left foot not showing. Crude olive branch extends out under wing, no oval. Green. c m. (U).

Division VI—Reverse Having Motif

1. Eagle to left, 14 stars above, small oval below. Reverse: Tall stem with ten leaves, there is in centre of vertical scroll forming a medallion motif, large bull's eyes on sides. Pint—light green. s m s b. (U).

— GROUP A: LIQUORS

2. Eagle to left, six stars above. Reverse: Circular sunburst, below a small beaded oval, large bull's eyes on sides. (U).

3. Pint—pale yellowish green. s m s b. Very similar to above. (U).

4. Large eagle facing to left. Six stars above, below arrows and olive branch, very small beaded oval. Reverse: Large round sunburst, bull's eyes on edges, divided by central rib. Pint—clear glass. s m s b. (U).

5. Eagle. Reverse: Double circle enclosing 8-pointed stellar motif above scroll, beaded edge divided by central rib. ½ pint aquamarine. s m s b. (U).

6. Eagle on left, raised wings, perched on two partly furled flags. Reverse: Large floral design resembling morning-glory, designs on panels, very prominent rib on sides. Pint—aquamarine. d c m s b. (U).

Note: The flask shown on Plate   is of yellowish-brown pottery, similar to Bennington but it is the same as the glass one described above.

DIVISION VII—MISCELLANEOUS.

1. Small eagle with shield on breast, head to left, perched on arrows Reverse: Plain. ½ pint—amber. Very short neck, with heavy d c m. (U)

2. Spread-eagle head to right, ribbon over head to left, shield on breast with 5 bars, perched on arrows, oval beneath. Reverse: Plain. Quart—olive yellow. r m. (U).

3. Eagle to left. Very long ribbon over head. Eagle has long neck, shield on breast, with four panels, perched on arrows. Reverse: Same. Pint—aquamarine. (U).

4. Small spread-eagle, head to the left, ribbon above, perched on oval composed of branches. Reverse: Same. ½ pint—rich golden amber. r m. (U).

5. Eagle, with ribbon, facing to right, perched on shield, which in turn is resting on rocks. Reverse: "Dyottville Glass Works, Philada" (in semi-circle). Pint—bluish aquamarine. s m.

6. Large eagle perched on arrows and olive branch, lengthwise. Reverse: Same. Central rib on each side. Pint—olive amber. s m s b. (Kn).

7. Wings more upright. ½ pint. (Kn).

I—Washington, Early Specimens, Kensington and Mid-Western

GROUP III

1. WASHINGTON
Washington in uniform, full face. "General Washington" above in semi-circle. Reverse: Spread-eagle, head to the right, rays above, perched on beaded oval initialed "T. W. D." with 5 arrows and very large olive branch. Above, "E. Pluribus Unum" and on the sides ""Adams and Jefferson", July 4, A. D. 1776", also "Kensington Glass Works, Philadelphia".—dark amber.

2. Lettering on sides omitted. Aquamarine (K).

3. Reverse: "E Pluribus Unum" omitted. Aquamarine (K)

4. Larger lettering (those in general being quite crude), larger head. Reverse: No rays, no lettering, corrugated sides, divided by central rib. (U)

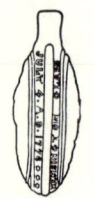

5. Head smaller. Reverse: 9 large stars above, 3 arrows and olive branch very small resembling two dots on stems, no lettering. Corrugated sides divided by central rib. This flask is quite flat. (Stars do not show on P.) (U).

6. "G. Washington". Reverse: 11 stars (smaller), taller eagle, no shield on breast, perched on smaller beaded oval and grasping in right claw 3 small arrows, in left claw small olive branch. Thicker flask than the preceding. (Probably FL).

7. "G. G. Washington" (much spread out). Reverse: 9 stars, 3 arrows. (Probably FL).

8. "G. Geo. Washington". Reverse: 12 stars, larger arrows, very large olive branch, "F. L." in oval, branch underneath extending to each side of oval. Light green. (Looks like "EL" on Plate). (The 2 preceding are so similar it is reasonable to assume they were made by FL).

9. Very unusual bust of Washington, full face to the front, and "G. G. Washington" apparently wearing a wig. The right cheek is very prominent. Reverse: Eagle facing to the left with shield on breast, perched on oval containing "F. L." Above the eagle is "Pittsburgh" (FL).

10. Bust of Washington. Reverse: 10 stars above, eagle to right, below olive branch in eagle's beak, arrows and olive branch in claws, perched on beaded oval marked "JR", below the oval is "Laird & Co. Pitt". (Looks like "LR" on plate). (Ld)

11. Bust with branch each side. No lettering. Reverse: Very early type spread-eagle, head to right, rays and stars above, no oval. Ribbed sides. Pint—aquamarine. (U).

12. Bust of Washington in uniform facing to the front. Reverse: Rather crude eagle, head to the right, large shield with 8 vertical bars on breast, arrows in claws. Corrugated sides divided by central rib. Clear light green. s m a b. (U).

1-12, Pint; aquamarine unless otherwise noted, s m s b.

— GROUP A: LIQUORS

II—Dyottville and Lockport

1. WASHINGTON
Bust of Washington, with queue, facing to the left. "The Father of His Country" above in semi-circle. Reverse: Bust of Taylor, in uniform, facing to left, "General Taylor Never Surrenders" above in semi-circle.

2. On the pints the queue is tied with three ribbons the ends showing.

3. "Dyottville Glass Works, Philada" on reverse omitted. Quart. (D).

4. "Dyottville Glass Works, Philada" on reverse omitted. Queue same as No. 2. Pint, also half pint. On the half pint the neck is longer and face is slightly elevated. (D).

5. Same but all lettering on each side omitted. Pint and half pint.

7. Same but larger bust and quart. 8. Same but longer queue. Quart.

6. Same but queue shorter and without ribbons. Pint and quart.

9. Bust of Washington, with queue, facing to the left. "The Father of His Country" above in semi-circle. Reverse: Bust of General Taylor, in uniform, facing to left. and above "Gen. Z. Taylor". Quart—light sea green. s m   s b. (D).

10. Bust of Washington like No. 2. "Washington" above in semi-circle. Reverse: Bust of Taylor in uniform facing to left. "Gen. Z. Taylor" above in semi-circle. Pint—aquamarine. s m   s b. (D).

11. Same but "Washington" below bust. Reverse: "G. Z. Taylor" below bust. Pint—aquamarine. s m   s b. (D).

12. Bust of Washington with queue, facing to the left. "The Father of His Country" above in semi-circle. Reverse: Bust of Taylor in uniform. "I have endeavored to do my duty" above in semi-circle. Designs on panels. Quart—light olive amber. s m   s b. (D).

13. Different from the usual busts, and on a large circular panel. Quart —aquamarine. s m   s b. (D).

14. Shorter bust, queue is tied with three ribbons, the ends of which show. (D).

15. Bust of Washington, with queue, facing to the left, "The Father of His Country" in semi-circle. Reverse: Bust of Taylor in uniform, facing to the left. "A little more grape Captain Bragg" in semi-circle. Quart— marine blue. s m   s b. Also d c m and s c m with flange at base. (D).

16. Reverse: Bust of Taylor in uniform, no lettering. Pint—aquamarine. d c m. (D).

17. Bust of Washington, with queue, facing to the left on panel. "The Father of His Country" above in semi-circle. Reverse: Plain. Pint—sea green. s m   s b. Also r c m and f c m. (Lk).

18. In the quart the clothing on the bust is different. Reverse: Plain. Panel extends lower on the base. Green—rolled c m. (Lk).

19. Bust of Washington each side, also on one side "Lockport Glass Works". Quart—aquamarine. s m s b.

20. Lettering omitted. (Lk).

Note: While these flasks (1 to 15) in every way similar to those bearing "Dyottville Glass Works" have always been attributed to that factory, yet it is not likely all were made there. It is established that Washington and Taylor flasks were made at Lockport, New York, and Ravenna, Ohio, but in the absence of distinguishing marks it is not safe to say at which place they were produced. The popularity of such flasks must have encouraged the manufacture of them by numerous glass houses.

Division III

Baltimore and Bridgeton

1. Bust of Washington with queue, facing to the left. Reverse: Spread-eagle perched on arrows and large olive branch, with head to the right. 7 stars above, 5 stars below. Heavy central rib on sides. Designs on panels. Quart—bluish aquamarine. s m s b. (Br.).

2. No ribs on sides. (Br.)

3. Large bust of Washington with queue, facing to the right. Above "Fells", below "Point". Reverse: Baltimore Monument, "Balto" below. Designs on panels. Heavy central rib on sides. Quart—aquamarine. s m s b. (Br).

4. Another, same, no lettering. (Br).

5. Bust of Washington, with queue, facing to the right. Above "Bridgetown, New Jersey" in semi-circle. Reverse: Bust of Taylor facing to the right, above "Bridgetown, New Jersey" in semi-circle. Designs on panels. Heavy central rib on sides. Quart—clear aquamarine. s m s b. (Br).

6. Washington, with queue, in uniform, facing to the left. Above, "Washington" in semi-circle. Reverse: Taylor in uniform facing to the left, above "Bridgeton, New Jersey" in semi-circle. Five pointed star between lettering. Ribbed sides. Pint—sea green. s m s b. (Br).

7. Bust of Washington, facing to the left with queue, in uniform (Roman nose). Above in semi-circle "Washington". Reverse: Very tall monument and in semi-circle above "Baltimore Glass Works". Designs on panels. Pint—sea green. s m s b. (B).

— GROUP A: LIQUORS 95

8. Washington, with queue, in uniform, facing to the left. **Above,** "Washington" in semi-circle. Reverse: Taylor in uniform, facing to the left, above "Baltimore Glass Works", large letters. Heavy central rib on sides. Pint—clear amber. s m s b. (B).

9. Bust of Washington in uniform, with queue, facing to the left. "Fells' above, "Point" below. Reverse: Monument, and underneath "Balto". Heavy central rib on sides. Pint—aquamarine. s m s b. (B).

10. Bust of Washington, with queue, facing to right, no lettering. Reverse: Bust of Taylor facing to right, above in semi-circle, large letters "Baltimore Glass Works" (the three "S's" are reversed). Designs on panels, heavy central rib on sides. Quart—aquamarine. s m s b. (B).

11. Same except lettering on obverse.

Division IV

Albany, Stoddard, Calabash, Simons

1. Bust of Washington with high collar, facing to the front, above "Albany Glass Works" in semi-circle, below "Albany, N. Y." Reverse: Full rigged ship sailing to right. Designs on panels. Heavy central rib. Pint—aquamarine. s m s b. also d c m and s c m. (A).

2. Bust of Washington. Reverse: "Albany Glass Works" in semi-circle. Half pint— aquamarine. s m s b. (A).

3. Bust of Washington, in uniform, with long queue, facing to left, "Washington" in semi-circle above, bars on lapel of coat. Reverse: Bust of Jackson in uniform, facing to left "Jackson" in semi-circle above, bars on lapel of coat. Pint—golden amber. s m s b.

4. Bars on lapel of coat omitted each side.

5. Mouth is spread out to 2¼ inches.

6. Smaller lettering and lapel bars omitted each side, otherwise same as 4.

7. Washington facing to right. Reverse: Jackson facing to left. Half pint.

3, 4, 5, 6 and 7 have always been attributed to Stoddard but I believe they were made at Keene. All sm s b.

8. Bust of Washington, full face to the front. Reverse: Tree in leaf. Ribbed sides. Long neck. Quart—aquamarine, 1 c m s b (U).

Pikes Peak Flasks from **Gardner** Collection: W. McC & Co. (Pittsburgh) with reverse; also "**For Pikes Peak**," and "**Pikes Old Rye**."

— GROUP A: LIQUORS

GROUP IV

PIKE'S PEAK FLASKS

1. "For Pike's Peak"; below prospector wearing cap with pack over left shoulder and cane in right hand, walking to left, on oval. Reverse: Spread-eagle with ribbon, head to the left, perched on arrows. Below, oval. Quart—aquamarine. r m. (U).

2. Large lettering slightly different figure. Reverse: Slightly different eagle on longer arrows. Pint—aquamarine. r m. (U).

3. No cane. Reverse: Same as 2. (U).

4. Prospector with pack on left shoulder, and cane in right hand walking to the left, on rectangle lettered "Old Rye". "For Pike's Peak" above. Reverse: Spread-eagle with ribbon, head to the left. Below, oval lettered "Pittsburg, Pa." Half pint—aquamarine. c m. (U). P. 59.

5. No lettering. Reverse: No lettering (U).

6. Slightly different figure. Reverse: Eagle facing to left. Pint—greenish aquamarine. c m. (U).

7. "For Pike's Peak" in semi-circle. Prospector walking to left on rectangle, wearing cap, very small head. Pack on left shoulder, cane in right hand. Reverse: Eagle, short neck, with ribbon to left, perched on arrows, rectangle underneath. Quart—aquamarine. r m. (U).

8. "For Pike's Peak" in semi-circle. Prospector wearing derby and goatee, walking to left, pack over left shoulder, long-tailed coat, right arm does not show. Walking on rectangle. Reverse: Small spread-eagle to left with ribbon, perched on arrows; rectangle below. Pint—bluish aquamarine. r m. (U).

9. "For Pike's Peak" in semi-circle, large letters; below prospector, wearing derby and overcoat, pack over right shoulder, cane in left hand, walking to right. Reverse: Hunter shooting running deer, both to right. No ovals. Pint—bluish aquamarine. r m. (U).

10. Slightly different figure. Reverse: Slightly different figure and deer. Half pint—aquamarine. c m. (U).

11. "For Pike's Peak" in semi-circle; below prospector with pack on his left shoulder, walking on oval to left. Short-tailed coat. Reverse: Plain. Pint—light blue. r m. (U).

12. "For Pike's Peak" in small letters (1-3 circle), prospector high crowned derby walking to left on rectangle, pack over left shoulder, straight cane in right hand, swallow-tailed coat. Reverse: Plain. Half pint—aquamarine. r m. (U).

GRAND OLD AMERICAN BOTTLES

18 24 25 8 6

— GROUP A: LIQUORS 99

20   4   9   1   10

13. "For Pike's Peak" in semi-circle. Prospector walking to left on small rectangle, lower crowned hat, larger man, pack over left shoulder, serpentine cane in right hand, square-tailed coat. Lettering much larger. Reverse: Plain. Pint—aquamarine. r m. (U).

14. "For Pike's Peak" in semi-circle. Prospector walking to left on rectangle, wearing derby. Pack on left shoulder, right arm not showing. Reverse: Plain. Pint—aquamarine. r m. (U).

15. "For Pike's Peak" in semi-circle. Below, prospector, walking to the right, on rectangle. Cane in left hand. Pack over right shoulder and pack on head. Reverse: Eagle with ribbon, perched on arrows facing to the left. Large oval underneath. Pint—aquamarine. r m. (U).

16. Prospector with pack. Shows only arm with pack, no right arm, and no cane. Reverse: Eagle facing to the right. Pint—aquamarine. r m. (U).

17. "Pike's Peak" in slightly curved line, prospector, large head, wearing cap, pack over left shoulder, cane in right hand, long-tailed coat, walking to left on rectangle. Reverse: Spread-eagle to right, ribbon over head from beak, breast covered by 6 bar shield, long wings, eagle perched on arrows, large oval below. Quart—light green. r m. (U).

18. "For Pike's Peak" very large letters in semi-circle, prospector walking on rectangle to left, low crowned cap, small head, pack over left shoulder, cane in right hand, longer-tailed coat, legs bent, cane nearer body. Reverse: Spread-eagle to left with ribbon. Short neck. Wings nearer body. Perched on arrows. Rectangle underneath. Pint—bluish aquamarine. r m. (U).

19. "Pike's Peak" above. Prospector with cap, walking on rectangle to left, pack over left shoulder, cane in right hand. Reverse: Eagle to right, ribbon over head, perched on arrows. Below, oval. Half pint—aquamarine. F m. Short neck. Also r m.

20. "For Pike's Peak" in semi-circle. Prospector, wearing derby, walking to left, on rectangle lettered "Old Rye", cane in right hand. Pack over left shoulder. Reverse: Eagle with ribbon, to right, perched on arrows, oval underneath lettered "Pittsburgh". Half pint—aquamarine. r m. (U).

21. Prospector, low crowned hat, walking to left on rectangle, pack over right shoulder, cane in left hand. No lettering. Reverse: Eagle to left, with ribbon, perched on arrows. Large oval underneath. Pint—light bluish green. r m.

22. "For Pike's Peak". Reverse: Plain, Pint—light green. r m. (U).

23. Prospector wearing derby hat, no lettering, large head, walking to left on rectangle, cane in right hand, pack on left shoulder. Reverse: Eagle to left; below oval lettered "Arsenal Glass Works, Pitts. Pa." Pint—yellowish green. r m.

— GROUP A: LIQUORS

24. Tall prospector, walking to right, wearing pointed derby, pack over right shoulder, cane in left hand. Above, "For Pike's Peak", small letters in semi-circle. Reverse: Large spread eagle, facing to right, shield on breast, arrows and olive branches in claws. 13 stars above. Underneath: "My Country". Pint—bluish aquamarine. r m. (U).

25. "For Pike's Peak" in semi-circle; below prospector, with cap, walking to left, pack over left shoulder, cane in right hand, walking on crude oval, running to bottom edge of flask. Reverse: Spread-eagle, facing to left, with ribbon extending from beak over head, perched on 3 double pointed arrows; below crude oval containing "Ceredo". The eagle is not in centre, but to left of flask. Quart—light green. d c m. Also pint and half-pint, also r m. (U).

26. In the half-pint the lower frame of the panel does not go within a half inch of the bottom of the flask, is more of a rectangle. Reverse: Eagle is nearer to the middle of the flask. (U).

27. Prospector with very large head standing to right, one foot advanced, wearing derby hat, holding bottle opposite lips in right hand, cane in left hand. Reverse: Unusual spread-eagle (lop-sided), has large wings, perched on three arrows. Small shield on breast, branch over head extending from beak with six leaves. Below eagle is a panel. Pint—bluish aquamarine. Rolled c m. (U).

28. Figure similar to the Pike's Peak character, stands on a flat panel with cane, stick over shoulder and elaborately modeled bundle on stick, prominent coat tails, derby hat behind, not on head. Reverse: Eagle, ribbon and arrows above. Crudely rounded panel. No lettering on either side. Pint—aquamarine. r m. (U).

29. "For Pike's Peak" semi-circle, below prospector walking to left on oval (not uniform), wearing cap, cane in right hand, pack over left shoulder. Reverse: Eagle in flight to right, large ribbon over head, very prominent shield on breast, rectangular panel, pointed top and bottom at centre of frame, also projecting corners, lettered "& Co." (name or letter omitted). Pint—aquamarine. d c m. (U).

Note: This group is not entirely complete as in many cases there is a difference in the details of the designs on the three sizes, slight variations that might be due to the mold maker. Not all the Pike's Peak flasks occur in half pint, pint and quart size, but there are so many varieties in which they do occur that a catalogue pointing out these very inconsequential differences would be most confusing. Since there are so many variations it affords the collector much enjoyment to specialize in collecting them.

Zebulon M. Pike, the discoverer of Pike's Peak, in Colorado, then a Lieutenant in the United States Army, commanded twenty-three men who left St. Louis in January, 1806, to explore the territory along the Arkansas and Red rivers, part of the newly acquired Louisiana Purchase. In November of that year Pike, with three of his party climbed to the summit of Cheyenne Mountain, south of what he called "Grand" Peak, which Pike declared "Never would be scaled by man."

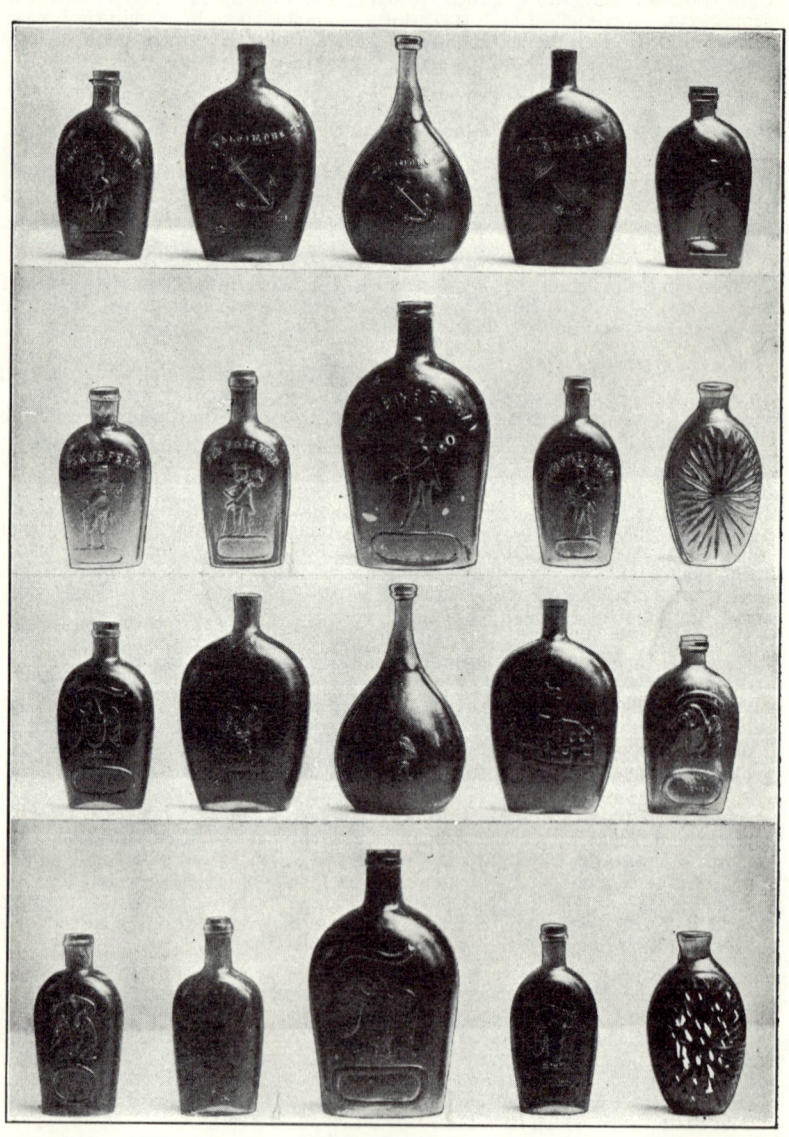

Top Row   2   8   10   48   23
Second Row   17   11   1   7   7
Third and Bottom Row Reverse of above

— GROUP A: LIQUORS 103

CHAPTER VI OTHER PICTORIALS

GROUP V Non-Historical Bottles and Flasks
107   71   70   73   17

1. ALL-SEEING EYE
Six-pointed star, eye in the middle. Underneath, "A. D". Reverse: six-pointed star, Masonic arm and emblem, and "G R J A" underneath. Three ribs on sides. Pint—clear amber. s m s b. (St.)

2. ANCHOR
"New London" on ribbon. In center, anchor and rope, below "Glass Works" on ribbon. Reverse: Bird in flight surrounded by seven stars. Pint—clear olive amber. d c m. (N L).

3. "New London" on ribbon. In center anchor and rope, below "Glass Works" on ribbon. Reverse: Eagle perched on wreath, head to left. Nine stars above. ½ pint—amber, s m s b., also d c m. (N L).

4. "Richmond" on ribbon. Underneath, anchor. Below "Glass Works" on ribbon. Reverse: Picture of glass works. Pint—light green. s m s b. (Rd)

5. Anchor with rope. Reverse: Plain. Raised flat rib on sides. Pint—aquamarine, d c m. (U).

6. Anchor in depressed circular panel, flukes to left "A G Co." on bottom. ½ pint—amber. c m. (U).

7. APOSTLE
The decoration shows the figures of six monks represented standing in Gothic arch-ways, engaged in various devotional exercises. The decoration extends from the base of the bottle half way up. Quart—golden amber, long neck with very small ring, about ¼ inches from the mouth. There is also one with one inch shorter neck, heavier mouth and heavier ring. Color of some of these bottles is a beautiful light golden amber. There is a 1½ inch circular panel for label above the arches. (U).

(The Apostle, or Monk, bottle is an out-standing mistake in modern bottle history, as this bottle was apparently designed to please the Catholic clergy, but it signally fell short of its purpose.)

8. BALTIMORE
"Baltimore" on ribbon; anchor with rope. Underneath, on ribbon, "Glass Works". Reverse: Sheaf of rye with crossed pitch fork and rake. ½ pint—light clear olive amber. s m   s b. Also—aquamarine. r m. (B)

9. Smaller design and nearer to bottom of flask. Pint. (B).

10. Pitchfork and rake omitted. Quart—slender, long neck, ribbed sides. d c m.   s b. (B).

11. Reverse: "Phoenix" and " Resurgam". Pint—amber. d c m. (Ch)

12. Horizontal Barrel surrounded by wreath. Reverse: Plain. Pint —yellow green. d c m. (Probably Ch) Footed base.

13. BICYCLE
Woman riding bicycle, to left. Reverse: Eagle with ribbon, perched on arrows, head to right. Below, oval containing "A & D H C". Pint—bluish aquamarine. r m.

14. BOOZ
On roof "E. G. Booz's Old Cabin Whiskey" (3 lines). Reverse: "1840" (on roof) on side "E. G. Booz's Old Cabin Whiskey" (3 lines). Reverse side "120 Walnut St., Philadelphia" (2 lines). Obverse: door and 3 windows. Reverse 2 plain. About quart—light amber. l c m. (Wn).

15. Gable ends of roof bevelled (Wn).

16. Short neck, found only in aquamarine and yellow green. (U).

Those with the gable ends bevelled are later. Doubtless the first ones with sharp gable ends were hard to remove from the mold, or perhaps these ends were liable to breakage.

17. BYRON
Draped bust of Byron facing to left. Reverse: Draped bust of Walter Scott facing to the right. Designs on panels—prominent central rib on sides. ½ pint—golden amber. s m   s b. (Attributed to Kn).

18. COBWEB
Cobweb interspersed with wheat heads, spider showing near center, covers face of the flask. Reverse: Same. Flat ribs on sides. Pint—amber. c m. (U).

19. COLUMBUS
Bust of Columbus holding globe, facing slightly to left "Columbus" below, on upright oval panel, latticed with beaded edges. Reverse: Same but bust faces slightly to right. Name omitted. ½ pint—clear glass. Threaded mouth, oval footed base. (U).

20. COAT OF ARMS
English coat of arms. Reverse: Branch of tree with acorns. Small vari-shaped lines cover the surface of the flask. The body is more or less rounded, with narrowing base. Pint—clear glass. s m   s b. (U).

— GROUP A: LIQUORS

21. COTTAGE BRAND
Short, square bottle, square base to neck and round above, shingled roof lettered "Cottage Brand" each side. Quart—aquamarine. f m. (like the short necked Booz bottle). (U).

22. COW
Cow facing to the left. Reverse: Large sheaf of rye and pitch-fork and rake. The background of flask each side is latticed. Half pint—very light yellow-greenish tinge. s m s b. (U).

23. CROSSED KEYS
Large five-pointed star and below crossed keys. Reverse: "G" within Masonic square and compass. Corrugated sides. ½ pint—amber. s m s b. (Attributed to J. P. F.)

24. CURRIER
Lion on shield, above 3 birds, ribbon below. Reverse: Original label "Bourbon Whiskey, Edward H. Currier, M. D., Pharmacist, 780, 782 Elm St., Manchester, N. H." Pint—greenish-yellow c m. (3 on bottom). (U).

25. DRAFTED
Prospector walking to left, on semi-circular panel, pointed at ends and centre, hat blown off showing opposite his back, ribbon over head, lettered "Drafted", pack over right shoulder, bag in left hand. Reverse: Eagle with raised wings facing to the right, ribbon over head, perched on shield, arrows and olive branch projecting right and left respectively, also ribbon from bar through shield, oval below pointed top and bottom and at centre. Pint—aquamarine. d c m. (Z).

26. DUTCHMAN
Dutchman with high hat on the back of his head and stick under his arm. Prominent stomach. Reverse: "Ick hab's aber immer gesagt: es muss fort gesoffen werden."
(Translation: "But I've always said so: it must all be drunk up".) Pint—aquamarine. Sloping shoulders. Long neck. s m (U).

28. GENTRY SLOTE
"Gentry Slote & Co." in semi-circle below "New York." Reverse: Horse. Quart—bulbous—olive amber. d c m. (U).

29. GRAPE
Upright bunch of grapes in depressed oval panel. Reverse: Plain. Pint—deep amber. Screw mouth. (U).

30. GREAT WESTERN
Full faced figure of pioneer or trapper in buckskin suit and broad brimmed hat, belt with knife at waist, rifle with butt on ground held in left hand, above "The Great Western". Reverse: Buck with large antlers. facing to the left. Broad, flat rib on sides. Pint—aquamarine. r m. (U).

31. HERZBERG
Tom cat and "Herzberg's Old Tom Gin". Reverse: Plain. Quart—light green. c n s b. (U).

32. HILL
"W. J. Hill—Liquors, Parkersburg, W. Va." in centre, latticed around. Reverse: Latticed. Pint—clear glass—circular, long neck. d c m rectangular base. (U).

33. HORSEMAN
Rider on galloping horse to right, hat flying off. Reverse: Running dog. ½ pint—aquamarine. d c m. Also s m s b. and pint—c m. (U).

34. Rider wearing derby hat. Reverse: Hound walking to right. Pint —light yellowish olive. r m. (U).

35. Horseman riding to right, in soldier's uniform. Reverse: Hound. Quart—bluish aquamarine. c m s b. (U).

36. Has small loop handle. Pint. (U).

37. Horseman riding to right. Reverse: Same. Pint—light greenish. c m. (U).

38. HOUND
A large tree extends up and down the flask with ribbing on the shoulders, and there are two hounds chasing a deer, and the deer is on the reverse side. Near the bottom of the flask on each side are 5 bulls eyes and rays or lines running from these to the bottom of the flask. Pint—clear glass. s m s b. (U).

39. Hound sitting with head raised. Reverse: Buck head surmounted on left by hunting horn; on right by gun, sprays around; beaded sides, divided by rib. Designs on panels. Quart—clear glass. f m. (U).

40. HOUR GLASS
Masonic pillars with 5-pointed ornament between. Hour glass and half moon beneath. Reverse: Same. Corrugated sides. ½ pint—olive amber. s m s b. (Probably C t).

41. HUNTER
Hunter, feather in cap, wearing knicker-bockers, walking to left, gun in right hand, back outward. Reverse: Vine in leaf with fruit resembling blackberries. Sides have four heavy ribs. Pint—deep blue. Sheared, spreading mouth 1½ inches long, the flask tapers to 2¼ inches at base, which is scarred. This one has a hole through rib on each side so the flask could be used as a canteen. Same shape as the Baltimore historical flask. (U).

42. Hunter shooting rabbit, running dog at feet. Reverse: Dog with front paws on tree. Bird in flight above. Pint—cloudy white, narrowing at base. s m s b. (U).

43. Full length figure of hunter, crude skiff at right. Reverse: Two hounds running to left, one ahead of the other. Pint—green. s m s b. (NL).

44. Full figure of hunter covering the entire flask, facing to the left, holding rabbit. Reverse: Laurel wreath and 3 illegible designs. Pint— aquamarine. Heavy ribs on sides. The flask narrows at the base to two inches. c m. (U).

— GROUP A: LIQUORS

45. HUNTER AND FISHERMAN
Hunter, facing to the left, shooting at two birds in flight, two running dogs at feet. Reverse: Fisherman holding fish. Mill to left. Ribbed sides. Quart —long neck—green. Long sloping c m. s m. (Wn).

46. Hunter facing to right, shooting at two birds in flight, one dog. Reverse: Fisherman facing to right, mill and very large tree. l c m. (U).

47. Hunter shooting at a lower angle. Reverse: Fisherman facing to left drawing in hooked fish. No tree or mill. d c m. Also heavy flanged mouth. This one is olive green. (U).

48. ISABELLA
"Isabella" on ribbon; in centre anchor with heavy single fluke with rope and below "Glass Works" on ribbon. Reverse: Picture of glass works. ½ pint—light greenish aquamarine. s m s b. (I).

49. Double fluked anchor "Glass Works" more curved. Reverse: Different glass works, also tree on left and no tower on each end of roof. (I).

50. "Isabella" on ribbon; in center, anchor with rope; and below "Glass Works" on ribbon. Reverse: Sheaf of rye with crossed pitch fork and rake. Pint—green. d c m. (I).

51. JESTER
Picture of stout man wearing high hat with cane behind his back, jesting with another man with long-tailed coat and umbrella. Reverse: Full faced Dutchman with arm underneath the chin. ½ pint—shaded corn flower blue. s m s b. Also clear glass. (U).

51a. Jester below "Manana". Reverse: Figure of a Liar, below double cross. (U).

52. Sides vertically fluted. s m s b. (U). (Like 51).

53. KEY
Key. Reverse: Plain. Flat rib on side. Pint—green. d c m with ring. (U).

54. KEYSTONE
Wreath enclosing keystone. Reverse: Plain. Flat. Rounded shoulders, narrowing slightly at bottom. Convex sides with very narrow rib. Threaded mouth. Pint—dense amber. (U).

55. LATTICED
One side latticed and depressed panel. This side has 17 beads on each edge outside the panel. Reverse: 13 stars, and on the edges outside the panel is a grape-vine with grapes each side. Oval shaped, narrowing to about two inches at the bottom. ½ pint—light puce. s m. (U).

56. LION
Large crown showing lion poised on hind feet with front paws extended and tail elevated. Reverse: Large bunch of grapes. Pint—flattened pear-shape, very light aquamarine, almost white. Narrowing scarred base 2 1-16 inches x 1 5-16 inches. (U).

57. MECHANIC GLASS WORKS
"Mechanic Glass Works Philada". Reverse: Sheaf of rye, crossed rake and pitch fork. Quart—light blue. s m. s b. (Mn).

58. McCARTHY & TORREYSON
"McCarthy & Torreyson", 5-pointed star. "Manufacturers Wellsburg, Va." (first and last lines in semi-circle). Reverse: Large sunflower or sunburst. Pint—dark olive green. s m s b. Also quart. (McC & T).

59. Quart—Reverse plain. (McC & T).

60. MORNING-GLORY
Morning glory, below scrolls. Reverse: Same—quart. s m s b. (U).

61. MOTHER'S PET NURSING
Woman with child in lap. "Mother's" above; "Pet" below. About ½ pint—aquamarine. Sloping shoulders. (U).

62.* MURDOCK & CASSELL
"Murdock" in capital letters in curved line, "Cassel" in capital letters in straight line, "&" between the two names, below a band of short, heavy diagonal ribbing and below this heavy vertical ribbing extending to bottom of flask. Reverse: "Zanesville" in large capital letters in semi-oval formation. "OHIO" below in capital letters in straight line. Same ribbing as obverse. Pint—light green. s m s. b. (M & C).
(The Murdock & Cassel ffask produced at the new glass house was made after 1823).

63. NOT FOR JOE
Woman on old-fashioned high bicycle. In a wreath, seemingly to come from her mouth, "Not For Joe". Reverse: Plain. Pint—amber. c m. (U).

64. OAK
2¼ inch circle enclosing oak tree in leaf. Underneath the tree, within the circle, is "The Oak". Pint—amber. d c m. (U).

65. PINE APPLE
Pine apple design with space for label. Quart—round—deep blood amber. f m s b. (U).

66. Shorter, thicker. Label lettered "W. & Co. N. Y." (2 lines). Clear light amber. d c m s b. (U).

67. No lettering. Amber. s b. (U).

68. Shorter, cupped spout mouth with loop handle. Clear light amber. s b. (U).

69. RAVENNA
"Ravenna Glass Works", 3 lines. Reverse: 5-pointed star. Pint—light green. r m. (R).

70. Reverse: Plain. Olive green. r m. (R).

— GROUP A: LIQUORS 109

71. "Ravenna Glass Co." (¾ circle) 8-pointed star. Reverse: "Traveler's Companion" and 8-pointed star. Pint—amber. Flanged mouth. High shoulders. ½ pint and quart. (R).

72. Rounded shoulders. Quart—aquamarine. r m. (R).

73. "Ravenna" on ribbon. Below anchor and rope. "Glass Company" below—"Company" being on ribbon. Reverse: American eagle with head facing to the left, surrounded by 13 stars. Pint—dense amber. r m s b. Also quart. Pint—blue. (R).

74. SAFE
Safe in circular depressed panel. Reverse: Plain. Flat ribs on sides. Pint—light greenish aquamarine. d c m. (U).

75. SAILOR
Dancing sailor. Below, heavy bar. Reverse: Musician sitting on bench; heavy bar below. ½ pint—amber. Long neck with d c m. (Ch).

76. SHEAF OF RYE
Sheaf of rye, crossed rake and pitch fork. Reverse: 5-pointed star, high up on the flask. Quart—green. d c m. Also pint and ½ pint. s m s b. (Mn).

77. Plain, bottom lettered "Tibby Bros., Pitts. Pa." Pint—clear glass. c m.

78. Large sheaf of rye showing 12 stalks protruding above sheaf. Reverse: Same but only 10 stalks. Pint—aquamarine. r m. (U).

79. "Bart Shea" (semi-circle). Sheaf of rye, below "Philadelphia" (semi-circle). Reverse: Plain. Quart—amber. r m. (U).

80. Latticed, panel in middle containing sheaf. Reverse: Latticed, V-shaped sides. Quart—light bluish aquamarine. d c m. "D S G Co." on bottom. (U).

81. Sheaf of rye, having a flattened sheaf of different design from the others. Oval shaped panel underneath. Reverse: Plain. Pint—aquamarine. c m. (U).

82. Large panel enclosing sheaf of rye with "Liberty" above. Reverse: Large panel enclosing five-pointed star. ½ pint—aquamarine. s m s b. Attributed to (D).

83. Sheaf of rye with clasped hands and panel and "Union". Branch each side. Thirteen stars above. Reverse: Eagle with ribbon facing to right. Ribbed sides. Quart—long neck—bluish aquamarine. (R).

84. Sheaf of rye with crossed pitch fork and rake underneath. Above, spray of rye each side. Reverse: 8-pointed star. Above spray "Sheets & Duffy". Ribbed sides. Quart—aquamarine—long neck. c m s b.

85. Reverse: "Sheets & Duffy" omitted (S & D).

86. Has loop handle—amber. (S & D). P

87. SOLDIER
Soldier with musket, bayonet and wearing spiked helmet. Underneath, on raised flat bar "Baltimore, Md." Reverse: Ballet dancer. Underneath, raised flat horizontal bar. Pint—aquamarine. s m s b. (Ch)

88. Bar under dancer marked "Chapman".

89. Full figure of soldier (or minute man) in uniform, with musket. Reverse: Large 11-pointed star. Ribbed sides. Quart—long neck—bluish green. s c m. s b. (U).

90. Full length figure of soldier with spiked helmet and musket facing to the front. Reverse: Laurel wreath enclosing "So lang dem soldaten dieflasche winkt ihm trotz Hitz oder Kalte der Muth nicht sinkt". ½ pint—aquamarine. s m s b. Very heavy central rib on sides. Base narrows to two inches. (U).

91. SOUTH CAROLINA DISPENSARY
Palmetto tree in the center with seven branches, on the left of the tree "South" on the right "Carolina", below "Dispensary". Reverse: Plain. Raised, flat rib on sides. ½ pint—green. d c m. (U).

92. Circular. Quart—very light green. d c m. (U).

93. Very similar to the first but the branches are much heavier and "S. C." appears instead of "South Carolina". ½ Pint. Amber. d c m. (U).

94. Tree has eight branches, not so heavy as on No. 93. Shoulders and base rounded, oval footed base, marked "C G Co." Pint—clear glass. d c m. (U).

95. Much heavier tree, not quite so prominent a footed base, marked "E. P. Jr. & Co." Pint, clear glass. (U).

96. JARED SPENCER
"Jared Spencer" on round medallion with concave bull's eye in centre. Reverse: Same but lettered "Manchester, Con." (one n). Below the medallion on each side is a motif resembling a round sunburst with geometric design underneath, corrugated sides. Pint—golden amber, s m s b. (P).

97. No lettering, bull's eye with four open spaces, dot instead of sunburst and bulbous base to neck, rounder. Reverse: Same. Pint—golden amber. (P).

98. Large sunburst on medallion. Reverse: Same. Pint—golden amber. (P).

99. SPRING GARDEN
"Spring Garden" on ribbon. In center, anchor with rope; below, "Glass Works" on ribbon. Heavy raised bar below. Reverse: Log cabin with tree at the right, without leaves. Heavy bar below. ½ pint—aquamarine. c m.

— GROUP A: LIQUORS

100. No bars either side. (S G).

101. Ribbons more curved. Reverse: More branches on tree. **Pint**. (S G).

102. STAR
Five-pointed skeleton star. Reverse: Plain. Circular, flat, holds **one** drink, clear glass. c m. Oval base, rib on sides. Height 3½ inches. (U).

103. Star. Reverse: Plain. ½ pint and pint—golden amber. c m. (St).

104. 5-pointed skeleton star. Reverse: Plain. Pint—amber. r m. (U).

105. SWIM
"Will you have a drink, will a"; then a duck; "Swim". Reverse: **Plain**. Flat ribs on sides. Pint—light green. r m. (U).

106. TRAVELER'S COMPANION
"Traveler's Companion". Reverse: "Rail Road Guide". ½ pint—clear glass. c m. (U).

107. "Traveler's (¼ circle) 8-pointed skeleton star below, "Companion" (¼ circle) upcurved. Reverse: Sheaf of rye, crossed pitch fork and rake. Quart—olive amber. c m. (Wd).

108. No star. Reverse: 8-pointed skeleton star. ½ pint—aquamarine. r m. (R).

109. "Traveler's Companion" with 8-pointed star. Reverse: "Lancaster, Erie Co., N. Y." and 8-pointed star. Pint—amber. d c m. (Ln).

110. "Traveler's Companion" between the lettering is a very crude duck. Reverse: "Lockport Glass Works" (3 lines), below the first word is an 8-pointed stellar motif. Pint—rich blue-green. Rolled c m.

111. TREE
Tree in leaf with 14 buds. Reverse: No buds, leaves not the same as to number or position. Quart—light green. s m s b. (D).

112. Bird perched in tree, on right side, "Summer" above tree. Reverse: Tree without leaves, bird on left side of tree, "Winter" above. Designs on oval panel. Pint—aquamarine. l c m. Also r c m s b. (D).

113. Bird and "Summer" omitted. Reverse: "Winter" omitted. ½ pint—aquamarine. c m. Also pint. Also d c m (D).

114. Tree in leaf. Reverse: Same. No bird either side. Pint—aquamarine. s m s b. (D).

115. Same as No. 112 but designs not on panels. d c m. (U).

116. Large tree in leaf. Reverse: Sheaf of rye with crossed rake and pitch fork. Ribbed sides. Quart—long neck—deep claret d c m s b. (S & D).

GRAND OLD AMERICAN BOTTLES

117. Small tree in leaf, bird to right near top. Reverse: Long slender sheaf of rye, with double head, rake and pitch fork. Dark green. (U).

118. Large tree in leaf covering the entire panel. Reverse: Large spread-eagle, head to right perched on arrows and olive branch. Tail of five feathers projects below. Above the eagle are three 4-pointed stars. Very heavy central rib on sides with two smaller ones. Quart—aquamarine. s m s b. (U).

119. Tree in leaf. Reverse: Eagle head to left, rays above, perched on olive branch and arrows, beaded oval. Rib on sides. Pint—aquamarine. s m s b. (K).

120. UNICORN
A square panel surmounted by crown showing a Unicorn with 3 plain spaces across the panel which is ribbed between. Reverse: Bunch of grapes. The flask is covered with very fine ribbing running semi vertically. Pint—blue. s m s b. (U).

121. UNION
13 stars, below "Union", then clasped hands and shield with branch each side, oval below. Reverse: Vertical oval with branch-like frame, laurel branch each side, ribbons below. ½ pint—aquamarine. r m. (U).

122. Reverse: Plain. Quart—light green. c m. (U).

123. Clasped hands in panel, with branch each side. Above "Union" and 13 stars. Reverse: Same. Quart—aquamarine. c m. (U).

124. WHEAT, PRICE & CO.
Bust, facing to right and in semi-circle "Wheat, Price & Co., Wheeling, Va." Reverse: Picture of glass works and "Fair View Works". Corrugated sides with central rib. Pint—green. s m s b.

125. WOLF & SONS
Circular, lettered "S. Wolf & Sons Fine Whiskies". Reverse: Wolf's head base with hole for spigot. 2 quarts—clear glass

12   74   104   29

— GROUP A: LIQUORS

CHAPTER VII MARKED WHISKEYS

Naturally, most flasks described in the two previous chapters carried liquor along with the so-called 'Booz Bottle' (of which more later); but today more people are inclined to credit Bininger with early marking of spirits bottles. His company sold spirits and designed the bottles to hold these for sale. Many early bottle makers carried the name of their glass company or the supplier only. Most early whiskey distillers sold "in the cask" and the tavern keeper could decant into a demijohn or any empty bottle or flask that was handy when a customer came in to carry away his 'basic' refreshment! Sometime before mid-19th century, however, distillers began to take an interest in having a specially designed bottle that would trademark their brand. Unfortunately for the collector of empty bottles, there was immediately rank piracy of similar shapes by competing brands, hence the only way of being assured of the exact original contents is often only by an intact paste-on label.

The fact that an 1850 bottle (a typical date) has marked in glass the name "Old Colony Rye" or only "Pure Corn" does not, of course, dim its charm for the old bottle collector; in fact, as you will see by pages which follow, there is a goodly assortment of marked whiskey sizes and shapes which will make a splendid collection. As for what distillers were used to fill a given type of bottle, one can well imagine that the same brew often appeared in different containers and vice versa; after all, it was not until liquor's return after prohibition that the government cracked down hard on the reuse of whiskey bottles for rebottling. Note that all of today's whiskey bottles carry the words marked in glass "Federal law forbids sale or reuse of this bottle." Also look on underside of same bottle and you usually will have no trouble in finding the original contents marked as "White Horse Scotch," "Hiram Walker's Gin," etc.

If one is going to collect 19th century marked whiskey bottles, he will first need a few pointers on how to estimate age. The most desirable bottles one is after were made after 1850 and are now over a hundred years old. The wide sloping collared mouth was a characteristic and the kick-up bottom of earlier spirit containers had practically disappeared. Bottles of this type were quickly blown in a two part mold and if any figure or printing was to appear in the glass it was done as the glass blob is blown against the pattern side of the mold. Special features such as a handle to form a cruet or jug could be applied to the bottle before it had been annealed and cooled.

Duffy's Pure Malt Whiskey.

1860
★★★

1900
★★★

The One Great Medicinal Whiskey. The only one taxed by the Government as a Medicine.

THE OLDEST MEN IN WORLD KEPT WELL BY DUFFY'S Pure Malt Whiskey

Waco, Texas, Feb. 1, 190

Stephen Joice, who appeared personally before W. L. Tucker, T Collector of McLennan County, aft being duly sworn, said he was 1 years of age. He is a well-know citizen, residing at 623 Main Stree East Waco.

The representative of the "News drove to "Uncle Steve's" residenc where for forty years he has been law giver and a prophet to his peopl

"I was born, on the eastern sho of the Chesapeake, near the Marylar line. While I have always been temperance man, nevertheless, I fir with advancing years a stimulant be good for my stomach and to pr

The above was for 'Medicine.' But an accompanying folder gave these early receipts for an 'Old Time Collation.' Northern taste included Chatham Military Punch, and Manhattans. For the Punch: 1½ Gallons Catawba, ½G. St. Croix, 1 qt. Gordon Gin, 1 qt. Brandy, 1½ qts. Rye Whiskey, ½ pts. Benedictine and 1½ qts. Strong Tea; Mix juice of two dozen lemons and oranges with 2½ pounds of brown sugar, allow to stand 48 hours and then add "a case of champagne." The Confederate Punch used 4 bottles of claret, Brandy and the same lemons and oranges plus 2 pints of Sherry and Rum and three bottles of 'sparkling water.' Rebel Syllabub use a quart of cream and sweet wine, with spice and sugar to taste. Planters Punch mixed 'Southern Comfort' with lemons and 'charged waters.'

Three Variations in the Booz Bottle; Red Amber, Light Aqua, Dark Aqua.

— GROUP A: LIQUORS

One cannot, of course, give a complete catalog of all marked shapes and sizes that are collectable, for new ones turn up all the time. It is best to begin with the list of Biningers and related types originally assembled by Mr. Van Rensselaer, proceed to a photographic sampling of such marked examples in the collection of Mr. Gardner and the writer, then add a few rough line-drawings of still others seen by the writer in his extensive bottle travels. In between we will find time to examine the real story of the famed and dubious 1840 "Booz" bottle including its modern reproductions, to follow the trail of Bininger's whiskey bottlers (who began business in the early 1800's and continued till 1865), to study some famous whiskey bottle types like the shoe-fly, saddle and picnic flasks—even to cover the famous "Pig and Whistle Bottle Hoax" that made such fun for collectors in the early 1930's. All this will give the neophyte as well as advanced collector a lot of 19th century bottle-lore. And what if no such examples appear in shops and cellar hordes? Well, surely all will be able to find early 1860 type whiskey bottles in brown and aqua, even if they bear only the words "full quart" or "full pint." Or turn to even later types in the 20th century in the next chapter with which note our A grouping ends.

One can easily dispose of the Bininger bottles by saying, (A) we are not sure where they were made (note: the letter U in Van Rensselaer descriptions always stands for Unknown), (B) they present the most varied shapes of any spirits bottles extant, (C) they carried cordials and other spirited contents besides whiskey and (D) all brands must have sold in great quantities judged from the number of samples still extant.

As for the 1840 Booz Bottle it never was made in 1840 and it could not have figured in 1840 Harrison Presidential Hard Cider Campaign. Several books have been published stating that this familiar log cabin shape "was developed for a tavern keeper, E. G. Booz, by the Whitney Glass Works to aid the 1840 presidential campaign as this was its symbol where no doubt Booz did a good job selling them filled."

The date, 1840, molded on the bottle, is doubtless responsible for the misconception as to the age of the latter. There is nothing else in the appearance of this container which justifies the inference that it was made as early as 1840. In neither shape nor style does it simulate the log cabin of the Harrison Campaign as it appears upon the log cabin cup plates of that period. The Booz bottle has a smooth base and collar, and exemplifies a rather modern, small, two-story house with shingle roof and plain (not log) walls. The doorway is arched, with double doors, and a modern latch or fastener is indicated. The inscription upon the roof and one of the ends is "Old Cabin Whiskey," not "Log Cabin."

Various other square bottles appeared about 1860. The L. Q. C. Wishart Pine Tree Tar Cordial bottle and the Drake Plantation Bitters bottle are examples. The former bears the date 1859, and the latter

PHILADELPHIA, PA.—THE CENTENNIAL EXPOSITION—EXHIBIT BY THE CORK DISTILLERIES COMPANY OF OLD IRISH WHISKY, IN AGRICULTURAL HALL.—FROM SKETCHES BY OUR SPECIAL ARTISTS.

STYLES AND ERAS IN BOTTLE MAKING

— GROUP A: LIQUORS 117

records a patent in 1862. These bottles, of about the same age as the Booz bottle, resemble the latter in several particulars: none has a pontil mark; the base of each is flat; with a round depression in the center; the collar is tapering and straight, and was joined to the neck after the bottle had been molded, this joint being apparent to the touch; the mold opened diagonally at the base and left a slight ridge or line across the bottom of the bottle from corner to corner, marking the opening of the mold. All these characteristics are likewise apparent in the Booz bottle.

But, if anything further is necessary to prove that this bottle was not made prior to 1860, it will be found in the history of 120 Walnut Street, Philadelphia, which number is inscribed upon the bottle, and in the record of the occupancy of the place by Edmund G. Booz, which was only between 1860 and 1870.

The records of the Register of Wills of Philadelphia show that Edmund G. Booz died in 1870. The files of the Bureau of Vital Statistics of the same city give his age at death at forty-six years. Booz was, therefore, about sixteen years old at the time of the William Henry Harrison presidential campaign in 1840.

An inventory of his estate, filed by his administrators, shows that at the time of his death he had on hand, among other stock in trade, "twenty-five cases of Cabin Whiskey," which were valued at six dollars a case, or at the rate of fifty cents per bottle and contents. The appraisers who fixed this valuation might well be astonished if they knew the prices the empty bottles bring today. Their scarcity is mainly responsible for this. The business of Booz was not large, and his sales, no doubt, were mainly in Philadelphia and its vicinity, so that it is unlikely that any considerable number of these bottles were circulated. In the natural course of events many were broken and destroyed, hence, the survivors at the present time are comparatively few in number.

It is, therefore, clear that the Booz bottle, stamped with the location of his place of business, was made and its contents marketed between 1860 and 1870; and that the date 1840 on the bottle has no application to its age or period.

Notwithstanding impressions to the contrary, the word "booze" did not originate with or descend from the Booz bottle, to which, in fact, it is quite unrelated. It comes instead from Peddlars French "to bowse" or drink. The bottle, however, may have revived or popularized a word which was used in its present sense long before E. G. Booz dispensed his wares. In any event, every collector wants a Booz bottle or reproduction. It was merely a coincidence that Booz chanced to have such an appropriate name, though he was probably not unmindful of the value of the circumstance. Consider the many reproductions of his bottle since its origin. How do you determine the old ones? Well, the three varieties shown in our picture are reputed to be original. Note the chamferred

GRAND OLD AMERICAN BOTTLES

Bininger bottles
collection of Mr. Gardner

— GROUP A: LIQUORS 119

Bininger bottles
collection of Mr. Gardner

120　　　　　　　　　　　　　　GRAND OLD AMERICAN BOTTLES

Note: The A. M. Bininger Co. was established in 1778. The A. Bininger & Co. was established in 1776, according to advertisements.

Bininger Bottles from Gardner Collection.

— GROUP A: LIQUORS

1. BININGER BOTTLE
In center, circular formation "Old Kentucky Bourbon—1849 Reserve". Above "Distilled in 1848" below "A. M. Bininger & Co., 19 Broad St., N. Y." ¾ Quart—dark amber, barrel-shaped d c m. Height 8 inches, base 2⅜ inches, diameter 3⅜ inches.

2. 338 Broadway, N. Y. (U).

3. The series of rings consists of four raised hoops through out instead of four at top and bottom and three in the two middle series as in the smaller ones. Quart. Height 9¼ inches, 3⅜ inches in diameter. c m s b.

4. 19 Broad Street, N. Y. (Small size). (U).

5. "A. M. Bininger & Co. (semi-circle) No. 19 Broad St., New York" (semi-circle) Circular loop handle. About pint—golden amber. d c m. (U).

6. "Bininger's Day Dream, A. M. Bininger & Co. No. 19 Broad N. Y." Quart—loop handle, globular amber, full of bubbles, sloping c m s b. (U).

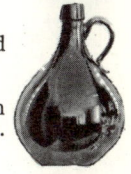

7. "Bininger's Knickerbocker, A. M. Bininger & Co., No. 19 Broad St., N. Y." Pint—dark golden amber. l s c m s b. (U).

8. "A. M. Bininger & Co., No. 19 Broad St., New York". "This in semi-circle) ¾ quart—golden amber. Height 9 inches in shape of vase. (U).

9. BININGER'S HANDLED JUG
With original label marked "Bininger's Pioneer Bourbon" in the middle colored picture of sitting Indian dressed in buckskin with gun, in front of camp fire. "A. M. Bininger & Co., Established 1778, 338 Broadway, New York". ¾ quart—dense amber. r m s b. (U). P.

10. With original label marked "Old Kentucky Bourbon" in the middle colored picture of coat of arms showing children with scythe, top design showing rye. "1849 Reserve A. M. Bininger & Co. 338 Broadway New York" ¾ quart—rich golden amber r m s b. (U).

11. Spout mouth. Note: These jugs had no lettering blown in the glass. (U).

12. Circular, loop handle from neck to slope on shoulder. Lettering below handle. (U).

13. BININGER PEEP O' DAY
"Bininger's Peep O'Day No. 19 Broad St., N. Y. (Semi-circle). Pint dark golden amber, half round, flattened shoulder and base, short neck d c m. (U).

14. BININGER TONIC (U).
"A. M. Bininger & Co. No. 338 Broadway, N. Y." "Bininger's Old Dominion" "Wheat Tonic" (lettering lengthwise on three sides). About ¾ quart—square. bevelled corners—olive green, full of bubbles, l s c m. Height 9½ inches. (U).

15. "A. M. Bininger & Co., No. 375 Broadway, N. Y." Puce (U).

16.* On three sides "Bininger's Old Kentucky Bourbon—1849. Reserve Distilled in 1848. A. M. Bininger & Co., No. 19 Broad St., N. Y." Rectangular, bevelled corners, short neck, ¾ quart, olive green. c m. (U).
  *Another. 338 Broadway.

17. BININGER NIGHT CAP
"Bininger's Night Cap, No. 19 Broad St., New York". Pint, amber. Patent screw top. (U).

GRAND OLD AMERICAN BOTTLES

Bininger Bottles from Gardner Collection.

GROUP A: LIQUORS

18. BININGER
"Bininger, New York" on raised seal, also a cluster of grapes. About quart—circular, dark olive green. c m s b. Height 10½ inches, on edges of base "Bristol Holiketts Glass Works".

19. BININGER CANNON
"In shape of cannon. "A. M. Bininger & Co., 19 Broad St., N. Y." Reverse: Ribbon and underneath a six-pointed star. Quart—amber. s m. Height 12 inches. (U).

20. Lettering omitted. Reverse: different ribbon "N. Y." in place of the star. (U).

21. BININGER'S TRAVELER'S GUIDE
"Bininger's Traveler's Guide, A. M. Bininger & Co., No. 19 Broad St., N. Y." lettering in five lines across. Reverse: Plain. Flat pear-shaped. about half-pint—amber d c m. (U).

22. BININGER CLOCK
"Face of a clock with hands set at eleven. Above "Bininger's" below "Regulator". Reverse: Plain. On sides 19 Broad St., New York". Pint —golden amber. d c m   s b. (U).

NOTE: The original label is lettered BININGER'S REGULATOR BOURBON, A. M. Bininger & Co. Established 1778 (on left of label) (on the right of the label) 19 Broad St., New York. Roman numerals are in gilt, so are BININGERS and BOURBON. Regulator is in black and the lateral lettering also black. The hands and arabesques which decorate the face are gilt. The label was gummed on reverse side.

Abraham Bininger, Grocer, Oswego—market	1801–1803
Abraham Bininger, Grocer, 20 Maiden lane	1803–1809
Abraham Bininger, Grocer, 157 Water St.	1809–
Abraham Bininger, Grocer, 141 Broadway	1846–1847
Abraham Bininger, Grocer, 100 barclay	1846–1847
Abraham Bininger, Grocer, 141 Broadway	1850–1851
Abraham Bininger & Son, Grocers, 14 Maiden Lane	1813–1814
A. Bininger & Son, Tea and Wine Dealer, 12 Maiden Lane	1820–1821
A. Bininger & Son, Wine Merchants, 141 Broadway	1830–1835
A. Bininger & Co. Wines and Grocers, 141 Broadway	1837–1846
A. Bininger & Co. Wines and Grocers, 141 Broadway	1845–1853
A. Bininger & Co. Wine Merchants, 92 Liberty St.	1853–1854
A. Bininger & Co. Wine Merchants and Importers, 92–94 Liberty	1854–1870
A. Bininger & Co. Liquor Importers, 39 Broad St.	1872–1873
A. Bininger & Co. Liquor Importers, 18 Broad St.	1875–
A. G. Bininger, 56 Vesey St.	1846–1847
Abraham M. Bininger & Co., Grocers, 323 Greenwich St.	1850–1851
Andrew G. Bininger, Wine, 12 Vesey St.	1850–1851
Liquors, 2 Warren St.	1856–1857
A. M. Bininger & Co. Importers, 47 Front St.	1878–1882
A. M. Bininger & Co. Grocers, 329 Greenwich St.	1852–1857
A. M. Bininger & Co. Importers of Wines, etc., 17 Broad	1858–1859
A. M. Bininger & Co. Importers, 375 Broadway	1863–1864
A. M. Bininger & Co. Importers of Wines, 15 Beaver	1864–1869
A. M. Bininger & Co. Importers, 39 and 82 Walker	1865–1866
Abraham M. Bininger & Co., Wines, 375 Broadway	1863–1864
Abraham M. Bininger & Co., Wines, 375 Broadway	1864–1865
Frank Bininger & Co., Importers of Wines, 15 Beaver St.,	1863–1864

GRAND OLD AMERICAN BOTTLES

A. M. Bininger & Co., wine and liquor, importers, 19 Broad   1861–63
A. M. Bininger & Co., Liquor dealers, 338 Broadway   1859–60

Bininger Bottles from Gardner Collection.

— GROUP A: LIQUORS

ends of the first two, probably due to the fact that the early glass maker would have had trouble getting a straight roof out of the mold. Next consult pictures of some of the other old Cabin bottles made by other dispensers of whiskey, and finally see if you can buy a Mr. Boston (1950 reproduction) which is sold with liquid contents. Personally, your author would buy no Booz bottle that was offered to him as original!

Other Cabin bottles include one that says Cottage Brand Rye (this is also a Cabin bottle). Another found in both brown and green says *Smokine* on the roof, and lists the importers of this strong drink as "Andressen and Co. of Minneapolis and Winnipeg" (good boundary country for hearty drinkers).

Having disposed of Booz and Binninger we now turn to the eye-catching array of other whiskey and spirit purveyors who marked their brands. Mr. Van Rensselaer gives a list of fifty others to hunt for. Mr. Gardner gives twenty sample photographs which indicate the scope of his personal collection: these types vary all the way from a rare blown saddle flask (sometimes seen with an applied handle) down through the two Indian Queens, one a rare Bitters, the other that even greater rarity, wherein the shoulder shield carries the words *Mohawk Brand Pure Rye*. The two Russian Bears or KIMMELS originally carried a cordial, dated 1875. One of these has an applied face. The Flora Temple whiskey jug is one of the several varieties that have not been reproduced, while the youngish Casper whiskey bottle proclaims in the glass that it is "Made by honest North Carolina people." One wonders, of course, how much of this sort of stuff ever went through the revenue agents. Like the pineapple bottles marked (H. C. & Co., and smelling as definitely of whiskey as of being alleged Bitters) any guess is a good story. Also much sought after is the half-pint and three-fourth quart U. S. Mailbox bottle put out by Rheinstone Brothers in 1875 and labelled Old Rye Whiskey. Don't forget, of course, the Shoe Fly bottle, only a few of which are marked in glass. The distinctive feature of the shoo-fly bottle is its elongated hexagonal base; presumably these could be packed together like close fitting tile and so guard against breakage. Why this bottle (see picture) was ever called shoo-fly is much debated among bottle collectors. But if anyone ever questions the name, there is ample evidence of both letterheads, advertising and story lore that this is the correct label for such a bottle. The writer has spent considerable time in running the term shoo-fly down to sources. Best information to date is about the shoo-fly pie of the Pennsylvania Dutch. This gooey, molasses-like concoction said one Amish friend, always attracted the flies both before and after baking so they got to calling it "shoo-fly." Now this connection to bottles may be very remote, but until shown otherwise, this writer submits that the hexagonal base of the bottle also somewhat resembles a facet of a fly's honeycomb eye—so why not shoo-fly pie and shoo-fly bottles.

126   GRAND OLD AMERICAN BOTTLES

Flora Temple Jug.

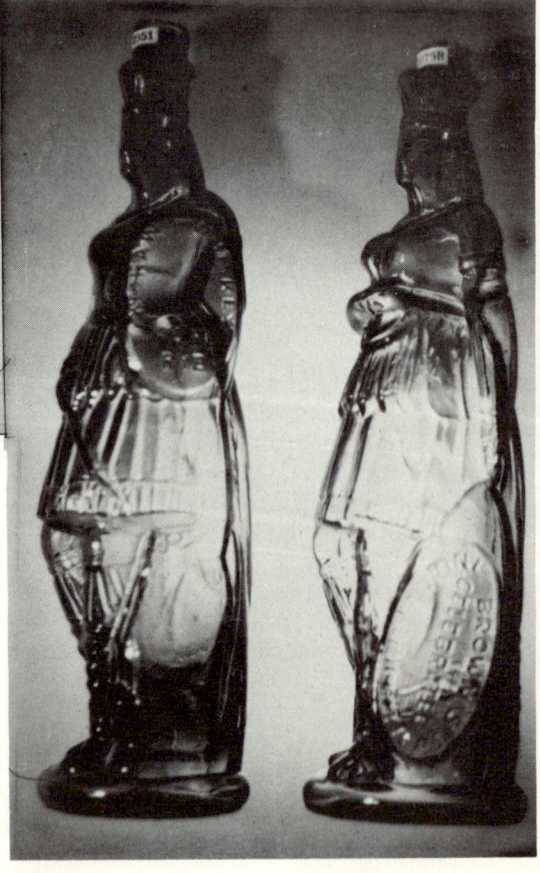

Marked Whiskeys from Gardner Collection: Indian Queen (Mohawk Whiskey on Shoulder Shield; Brown Bitters a competing Mold)

— GROUP A: LIQUORS 127

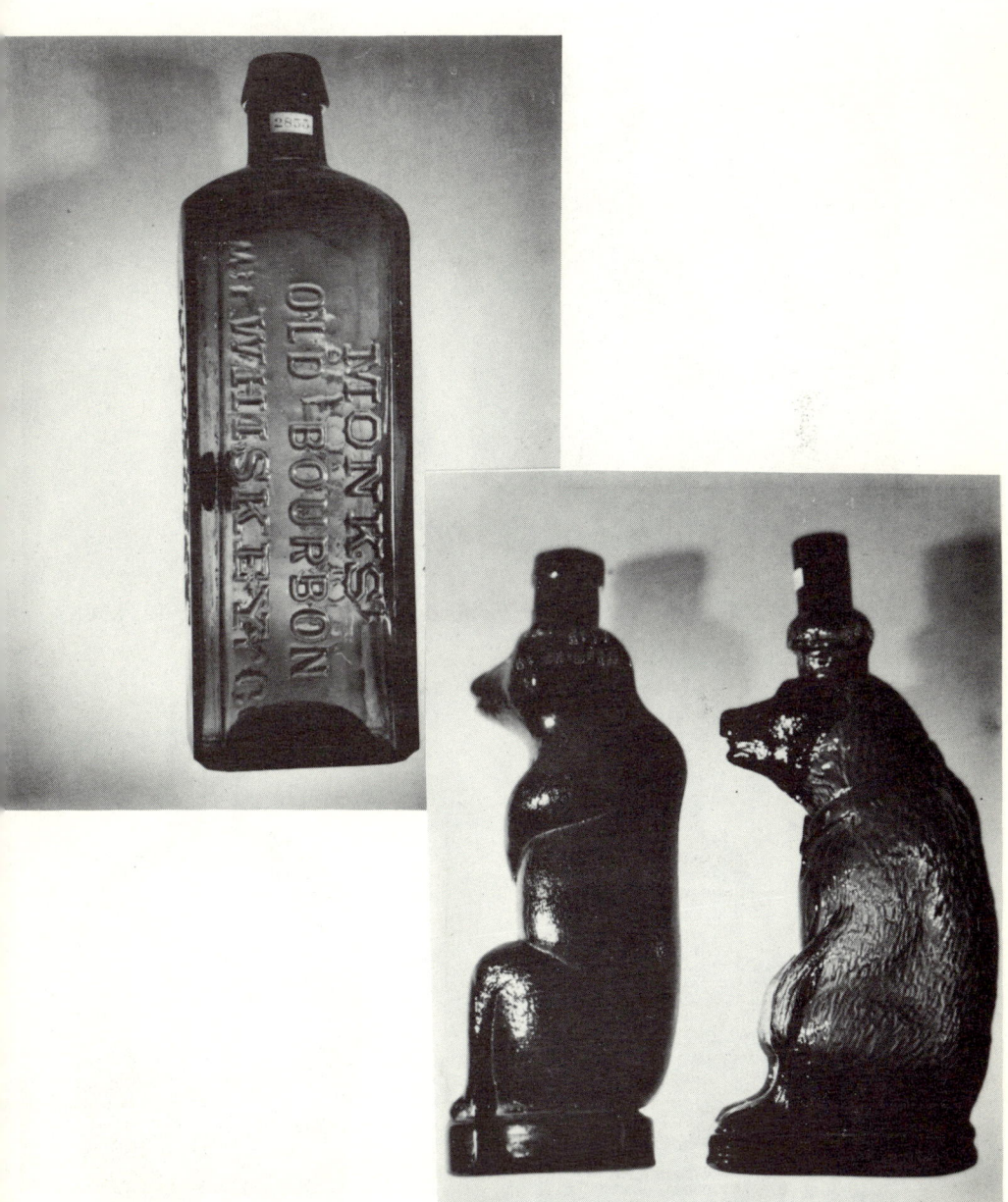

These Russian Kimmel Bottles once held a Cordial—one Russian Bear has an Applied Face; Cf Also Monks Old Bourbon Whiskey.

Marked Whiskeys from Gardner Collection: Sour Mash 1867; W. & C. N. Y.; Shoo-Fly Bottle with Wheat.

— GROUP A: LIQUORS

Branding for some very coarse concoction; a good thing today's collector is more interested in the empty bottle than in its one-time contents.

Illustrations from the collection of David A. Cohen of Darlington, S. C.
This miscellaneous group of South Carolina dispensary bottles shows typical shapes and markings. From left to right is an aquamarine pint, a clear round quart embossed with a monogram, a brown half-pint flask, a one gallon crockery jug, a clear pint flask with label, a clear round quart with a palmetto tree design, and an aquamarine round pint.

SOUTH CAROLINA DISPENSARY BOTTLES

Gov. Tillman, or Pitchfork Ben as he became known in his senatorial days after he verbally threatened President Cleveland with a trident, was forced into seeking a solution for the ever-bothersome liquor question in his state.

Looking around for some sort of compromise between open saloons and prohibition, he learned of a system which originated in Sweden whereby the state bought, bottled, and sold all intoxicants. To him it appeared an ideal arrangement, because it offered both the possibilities of increased revenue and temperance. So through a combination of promises, threats, and skillful political maneuvers, Pitchfork Ben had a dispensary law forced through the state legislature, tested, and declared legal by the courts.

Only two things of the dispensary system remain today, the unusual types of containers used by the state to bottle dispensary whiskey, and a memory to shoot any members of the governor's constabulary who interfered with local grog shops or searched homes for illicit liquors.

— GROUP A: LIQUORS — 131

Bottles Marked Whiskey, early and late.

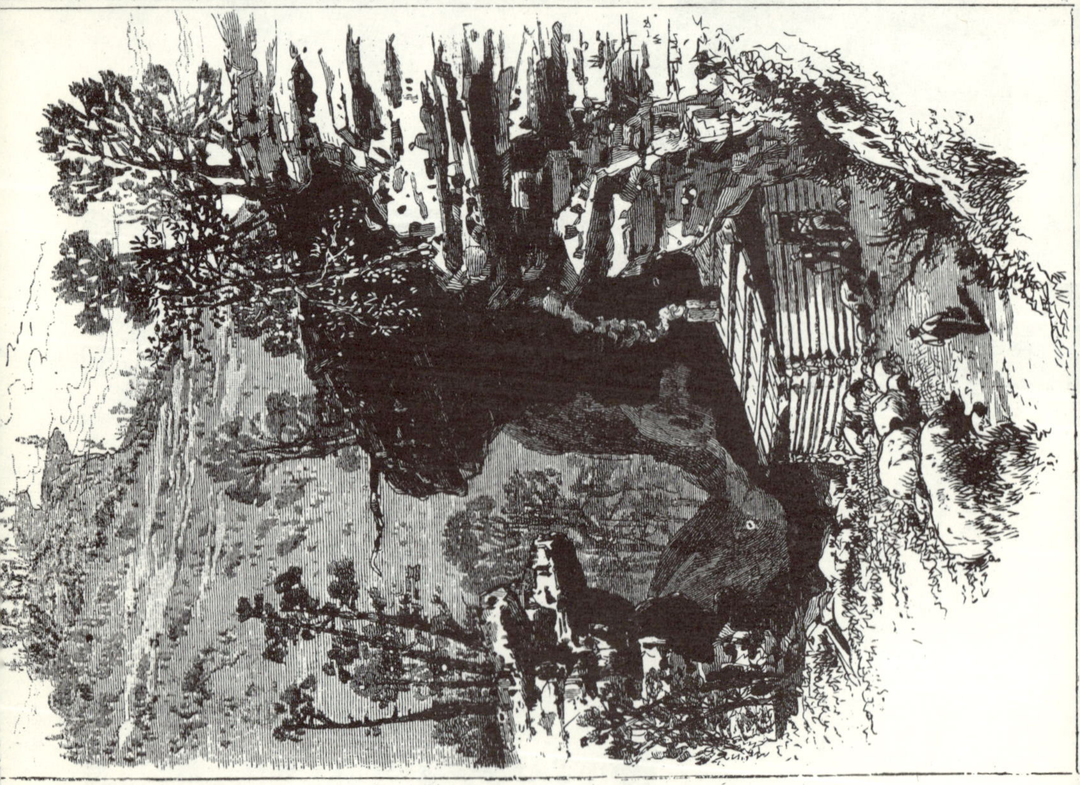

— GROUP A: LIQUORS

When the collector has digested all the luscious bottle-lore carried by foregoing photographs, the 1890 story of South Carolina's Dispensary System and the pictured Revenuer's search for illicit 'mountain dew,' he should give attention to other whiskey commemoratives which deserve at least a casual mention. Some people collect the small "Whiskey Nips." Once given away as salesmen's samples their modern counterparts are now sold as one-shot souvenirs. Space does not permit description of the variety of shapes available; however, the following page does show some of the hard-to-find "Picnics" and "Travelers Companions," along with a very early small saddle flask . . . Also on pages which follow are the descriptive listings of 58 Dated and Lettered Bottles and Flasks of the 19th Century and 53 Labeled Jugs and Cruets that originally carried whiskey.

Finally we call attention in passing to such mid-century bottle rarities like Binninger's Great Gun, Bucannon's Rye and Gayen's Altoona brand of potables: (Photos courtesy the Gardner Collection). These very coarse concoctions make it a good thing today's collector is more interested in such empty bottles than in their one-time contents.

Marked Whiskeys from the Gardner Collection: Picnic Nips, Pocket Jug. an Early Saddle Flask.

GROUP A: LIQUORS

DATED AND LETTERED BOTTLES AND FLASKS

1. "John Bartlett 1756" in circular medallion. ½ gallon, clear green.

2. "David Eustis 1728", circular medallion. About quart—dark olive green, squat shape.

3. FANUEL (U)
Circular medallion lettered:
"B. Fanev   The last one or two letters were omitted due to a mis-
EsqR   judgment of the space available but "il" is probably
1744"   missing since "Faneuil" is an old Boston name—the v
being the old letter for u. The seal is 1½ inches in diameter. About ¾ quart—dark olive green ("black glass") folded lip, deep cavity on the bottom. Height 7½ inches, neck 3½ inches.
    (Dredged up off Long Wharf, Boston, somewhat iridescent from a long immersion in the salt water.

4. "R. S. 1730." About quart—dark green.

5. "John Smith 1750" contained in circular medallion about quart. —olive green. Wb.

6. BRISTOL
Circular, long neck. Quart—olive amber. "Bristol Glass Works" on bottom. s m s b.

7. CASPER'S
Round impressed seal on shoulder lettered "Made by Honest North Carolina People, Casper's Whiskey". Quart—blue. Circular, like modern bottle, but longer neck. 1 c m. .(U).

8. CHAPIN & GORE
Barrel shaped "Chapin & Gore" on the shoulder and on the reverse side of the shoulder "Chicago". In the middle of the bottle is a six-pointed label marked "Sour Mash 1867" and underneath "The Hawley Glass Works, Hawley, Pa." on the bottom "H. Frank's Pat's Aug. 1872". About ¾ quart —light amber. (Hw). f m. (H. Frank, a wine dealer in New York City).

9. "Chicago" omitted and "Hawley Glass Works" omitted.

10. "Hawley Glass Works" omitted.

11. CLYDE
"Clyde Glass Works" in semi-circle and underneath "N. Y." Reverse: Plain. Pint—amber. d c m. Also quart—green.

12. CONTINENTAL
"Continental" (¼ circle) below "1776–1876", lettering is on arched panel. Reverse: Plain. The sides of the bottle are unusual in that they are ovoid. Pint—aquamarine, r m. Five pointed star on bottom. (U).

13. CUNNINGHAMS & IHMSEN
"Cunninghams & Ihmsen (semi-circle) Glassmakers, Pittsburgh Pa." (two horizontal lines). Reverse: Plain. Pint—aquamarine, broad flat rib on sides. r m.

14. DUFFY
Lettered "The Duffy Malt Whiskey Company" (semi-circle) below "Rochester, N. Y." (semi-circle). Large monogram between lettering. Quart—circular—golden amber, short neck, s c m. On bottom "Patd Aug. 24, 1886". (Ln).

15. DYOTTVILLE
Round. On shoulder "Patent" on the base "Dyottville Glass Works Phila". About quart—olive amber. Long s d c m.

16. "Patent" omitted. Olive green—full of bubbles. 1 d c m. Height 11 inches. Usually interesting as it is the last type of Dyottville bottle.

16a. EVANS
"Evans Ale, Hudson, N. Y." Pint—dense amber, spout mouth. (U).

17. FRANK
Lettered "H. Frank, Pat'd Aug. 6th, 1872". ½ pint—amber. Threaded mouth. (U).

18. GRANITE
"Granite Glass Co." Reverse: "Stoddard, N. H." Pint—clear olive amber, full of bubbles. s m   s b. Also quart—1 c m.

— GROUP A: LIQUORS

19. H. F. & B.
Fluted pattern, mellon shape with shield lettered "H. F. & B., N. Y."
About ¾ quart—dense blood red amber. c m with heavy hand around neck.
(U).

20. Haddock
"Haddock & Sons" (2 lines lengthwise). Reverse: Plain. ½ pint—
olive amber. s m   s b. Round with ovoid base. (U).

21. Hart
"Saml Hart & Co., Philadelphia and New York" (4 vertical lines). Pint
—clear glass, fitted with pewter cap on the shoulders for use as a cup. Heart-
shaped impressed mark "S H & Co."   (U).

22. "J. Hauel Philada", on rim. Aquamarine. Height 3½ inches,
1¾ inch base, 1¼ inch mouth. (U).

23. Hawley
Barrel shaped "Hawley Glass Co. 1867" in panel. About ¾ quart—amber.
s c m.

24. Horton
"E. Horton, Avon Spring". Reverse: Plain. Rectangular, bevelled
edges. ½ pint—olive amber. c m   s b. (U).

25. Hospital
"Circular, long neck, lettered on side "U. S. A. Hosp. Dept." Quart—
light amber—c m. Height 9 inches. "S. D. S." on bottom. (U).

26. Hotchkiss
Lettered on the bottom "H. G. Hotchkiss, Lyons, N. Y." Circular,—
deep blue. Height 8¼ inches. c m   s b. (U).

27. Jones and Banks
Square with 3⅜ inches bevelled edges, one side plain, other sides marked
"Jones and Banks, 58 Broad Street, N. Y., Importers". About quart—amber.
Glass screw stopper marked "Pat. Jan. 1861". Height 10¼ inches. (U).
 (1862-3 at 58 Broad St., 1863-4 at 37 Beaver St., New York City.)

28. Kentucky
Pint—aquamarine. r m. "Ky. G. W. Co." on bottom. (L).

29. Lady Hill
"The Hon Lady Hill". Maderia Bottle. Like 3, lower right, P. 105. (U).

30. L. A. M.
Barrel Shaped. "L A M   A & F". Emerald green, r m. (U).

31. Lancaster
Barrel shaped, base lettered "Lancaster Glass Works, Lancaster, N. Y."
About ¾ quart—c n.

32. Louisville
"Louisville, Ky" (semi-circle). Below "Glass Works" (straight line).
Reverse: Plain. Flat rib on sides. Quart—aquamarine. r m.

33. "Louisville, Ky. Glass Works", lettering forms circle running almost to base. Reverse: Plain. Pint—aquamarine. r m.

34. LYNDEBORO
Pint—aquamarine. d c m on base. "L. G. Co."

35. MCCOLLICK
"J. S. McCollick & Co., New York." Barrel shaped. About pint—green. s b. (U).

36. MIST OF THE MORNING
"Mist of the morning, Sole Agents, Barret and Lumley". Barrel shaped. ¾ quart—dark olive brown. 1 c m. (U).

37. "New Life," holds one drink. Amber. d c m. Height 4¼ inches. (U).

38. PATENT
"Patent on side well up on flask. Reverse: Plain. Flat on sides. Pint —olive green. d c m. (St).

39. PERKINS NURSING
"Perkins Patent Vented Nursing Bottle" (semi-circle) below Cow. Reverse: Plain. ½ pint—aquamarine, c m, ring on neck just above shoulder. The neck is slightly out curved from obverse. (U).

40. PICNIC
"Picnic." Reverse: Plain. Flat-shaped flask with high shoulders, rectangular base. ½ pint—aquamarine. d c m. (U).

41. ROBINSON'S
"Geo. W. Robinson, No. 75 Main St., W. Va." in 3 lines, first and last in semi-circle. Reverse: Plain. Heavy flat rib on sides. ½ pint—aquamarine. r m. (U).

42. ROEHLING & SCHULTZ
"Roehling & Schultz Inc." "RE", log cabin shape, one window. About ¾ quart—amber. r m. (U).

43. S. M. & Co.
"S. M. & Co., New York" (2 lines script) on irregular oval medallion held by loop around neck. Bell-shaped, one gallon—golden amber. d c m   s b. Height 15¼ inches, base 6¼ inches. (U).

44. SPIERS & POND
"Spiers & Pond" "Railway" "Purveyors" (3 vertical lines). Reverse: Plain. About ½ pint—clear glass c m. (U).

45. "THAT'S THE STUFF"
Barrel-shape. Space about 3 inches wide in middle, lettered as above. Amber c m s b. (U).

46. THOMPSON
"A. N. Thompson (semi-circle) & Co." below "New York." Quart— long neck. d c m. (U).

— GROUP A: LIQUORS

47. UNION GLASS WORKS
One and a half inches from the bottom on the side is "Union Glass Works."
Quart—long neck—blue, full of bubbles. d c m. (U).

48. "Union Glass Works, New London, Ct." Reverse: Plain. Pint—
d c m. P. 4.

49. WALTON
"W. N. Walton, Pat'd, Sept. 23, 1862." Round foliated design, separated by vertical ribs, octagonal sunken panel for label, floral design stopper. Clear glass. f m. (U).

50. WATERMAN
"Jos. Waterman, No. 1717 Market St. Philada" (3 lines, lower curved). Quart—flattened pear-shape—dense amber. r m s b. (U).

51. WEEKS & GILSON
"Weeks and Gilson, So. Stoddard, N. H." on base. Quart—beautiful rich golden amber, full of small bubbles. c m.

52. WHARTON
"Wharton's Whiskey 1850 Chestnut Grove" (on round panel.) Reverse: Plain. ¼ pint—flat pear shaped, round bottom—blue. d c m. Length 5¾ inches. (Wn).

53. WHEELING
"Wheeling" (semi-circle) "Va". Reverse: "Old Rye" (semi-circle). Pint—olive green. Has rings around neck about a half inch from the mouth, with rather high central rib on sides. (Same type as Keene pint Masonic flask). (Wl).

54. WHITNEY
About quart—olive amber. Long s c m. On the base "Whitney Glass Works".

55. Pint—golden amber. d c m.

56. "Wright" on the neck. Square, two round, sunken panels each side, four indentations on each edge. Height 3¼ inches, 1¼ inches square—aquamarine. (U).

57. WYN
"Constantin Wyn" in raised circular medallion. Reverse: Plain. ½ pint—deep olive amber. s m. (U).

58. ZANESVILLE CITY
Elongated oval with inner and outer border enclosing "Zanesville" above, "Glass Works" below, and "City" in centre. Pint—very pale green—ringed mouth, flat rib on sides. (Zc).

```
   4        1       7       10      19       6      14
         JUGS, CRUETS AND DECANTERS
```

1. Raised circular medallion on left side lettered "Chestnut Grove Whiskey, C. W." (Charles Wharton). Between lettering is a crown-like motif. Reverse: Sunken circular label panel. About ¾ quart—amber. r m s b. (Wn.)

2. Panel on right side omitted, obverse crown-like motif, "Whiskey, C. W." (Wn).

3. "Wharton's Whiskey, 1850, Chestnut Grove". Spout mouth, on bottom "Whitney Glass Works, Glassboro, N. J." Quart—amber. (Wn).

4. No lettering except on bottom. (Wn).

5. Pint, golden amber. r m s b. (U). Original label reads "Bininger's Pioneer Bourbon". Picture of Indian by camp fire, below "A. M. Bininger & Co., Established 1778, 338 Broadway, N. Y."

6. ¾ quart, amber, r m s b. Note: This is a common type and there are many variations such as shape of handle, collars, contour and capacity.

7. On right side ovoid label lettered "Star Whiskey, New York, W. B. Crowell, Jr." (3 lines, first and last semi circles). Quart—golden amber, vertical ribbing. r spout mouth. s b. (U).

8. Inverted bell shape, prominent raised ovoid label marked "S. M. & Co. N. Y." (two lines). About quart and pint—smoked amber. r m s b. Height 9 inches, base 5 inches. (U).

9. "The Old Mill Whitlock & Co." in semi-circle. Inverted bell shape with loop handle, around the neck is a glass cord applied to the bottle and attached to medallion. Quart—dense amber. d c m. s b. (Fr).

10. "Griffith Hyatt & Co." (surrounding on 3 sides semi-circular window with shelf) below (in straight line— "Baltimore". Reverse: Round flattened label. ¾ quart—golden amber, flattened. c m s b. (B).
(Hyatt, Edward & Co., liquor dealers, 376 W. Baltimore St. (From Directories 1856-7; 1858-9, not in 1864).
(Hyatt, Edward &·Co., liquor dealers, 39 S. Frederick St. (From Directory 1855-6.)
(Griffith) (Nicholas R.), Hyatt, (Edward) & Co. importers of liquors, etc. 6 water St. (From Directory 1860 not in next directory 1864.)

11. Calabash shape, round panel, marked "J. F. T. Co., Philad". Vertical ribbing. Quart—light golden amber. c m s b. (U).

12. Golden amber, about ¾ quart. s c m s b. (St.)

13. Golden amber, 1 s c m. s b. (St.)

235

— GROUP A: LIQUORS 141

14. FLORA TEMPLE (See note)
Flora Temple facing to the left. Above "Flora Temple", below "Harness Trot 219¾ inches. The picture of the horse and "Flora Temple" are contained in a square panel projecting at the top. Reverse: Plain. Handle on shoulder. Pint—dense amber. c m.
(Note: Was produced at Lancaster, according to information given by a glass blower who worked there. (See Chapter V), also at Whitney Glass Works. The green ones were only made at the former place.)

15. No handle, pint—green. Also occurs with two raised dots where handle would begin.

16. Dated Oct. 15, 1859, no handle, small dot on right shoulder. Quart and pint. Also occurs with handle.

17. "Pure Malt Whiskey Bourbon Co., Kentucky" (3 lines) top and bottom semi-circular, ¾ quart—smoked amber. r m s b. (U).

18. "R. B. Cutter, Louisville, Ky." (two lines) ¾ quart—olive amber c m. Height 9 inches (U).

19. No spout. c m. No lettering on jug but round label with gilt lettering on blue paper reads "Old Club House 1860 Whiskey, Warranted pure and softened by age only". "Macy & Jenkins, Liberty St. New York, Established 1844". Picture below, (Shown without label).

20. "Ambrosial B. M. & E. A. W. & Co." (on round raised seal). (U).

21. "Original label lettered "The Pride of Kentucky, Fine Old Valambrosial Whiskey, The Travelers Solace from Bourbon County, Manufactured expressly for Woodgate & Co., 93 Water St., N. Y." Quart—light clear amber. r m s b. (U) (1857–1858.)

22. "Ambrosia, E. & W. Co." (two lines on round panel). Reverse: Plain. ¾ quart—smoked amber. c m s b. (U).

23. "Sacket Belcher & Co., 26 Pearl St., N. Y." (2 lines) on raised label. ¾ quart—amber. s m. (U). (Grocers 1851-1852).

24. Wicker design with square space for label, the loop handle is not attached to the neck. Pint—light green. c m. (type 9) (U).

25. Full length figure of priest or king in robes. Underneath the following inscription: "MATKA BOZA KODENSKA". Reverse: Oval containing bust of man with robes and underneath same is the following inscription: "P O D TWOIA OSRONA". Underneath this, picture of a castle and below the following inscription: "SWAITYNIA JASNEJ GORY". About ¾ pint, handle running from the mouth to the shoulder. s m s b. Beautiful brilliant blue. (Fr.).

26. Handled jug, base lettered "F. P. Adams & Co., Boston, Mass., U. S. A." About pint—clear glass, two section mold. Height 9⅜ inches. (SW). P. 51. (The firm name of Francis P. Adams & Co., first appeared in the Boston Directory of 1883 with a place of business at 280 Dover Street. In 1917 the name disappeared from the directory. The concern was engaged in the business of selling flavoring extracts and grocers' sundries.)

27. SARATOGA HANDLED JUG.
Clear, deep green. flecked with opaque and bluish white and pale amber. Pint. s m s b. (Congressville).

28. Lily pad jug, about ¾ quart—sea green, bubbly. r c s s b. **Height 7 inches.** (U)

29. Cruet with stopper, clear glass. (U) Height 8½ inches.

30. Cruet with stopper, wide ribbing slightly twirled to the left on neck. Clear glass. s b. (U) Height 8½ inches.

31. Cruet with stopper, wide ribbing with swirling to the left on neck. Sapphire blue. s b. Height 8½ inches.

32. Sloping sides, enriched with sunk round medallions above broad, short flutings; shoulder serpentining into neck terminating in collar. Ball stopper—clear glass. Height 12 inches. (U).

33. Pair deeply fluted bell-shaped bodies, with collared, incurved necks having flanged lips. Unusual fluted urn-shaped stoppers of clear glass. **Height 13¼ inches.** (U).

Numbers 29, 30 and 31 found in Ohio and undoubtedly made there.

Note: Plain clear glass decanters have not been collected to any extent so I deemed it inadvisable to devote space to them.

11   5   43   54

— **GROUP A: LIQUORS**

Look now for some of the really great additional names one can find marked in glass to commemorate a bygone distiller and which will add lustre to any bottle collection. Shapes are only roughly indicated and we do not pause to tell which will match the identical eagle or other object flasks already shown in earlier chapters; after all, the distinctive feature over any of those is that here we have the name of the whiskey or its maker molded in glass. Most examples pictured are 19th century and antedate the mechanical bottle making machine of 1900.

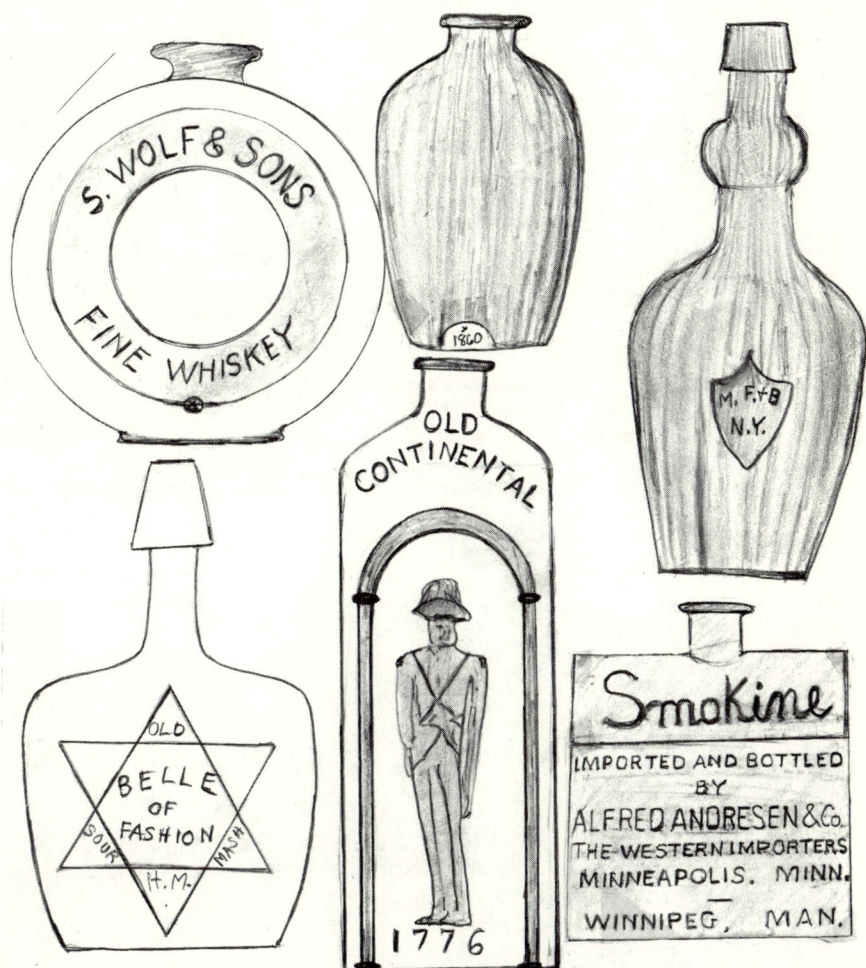

Bottles and association collaterals at writer's Yorker Yankee Village, Watkins Glen, N. Y.

— GROUP A: LIQUORS

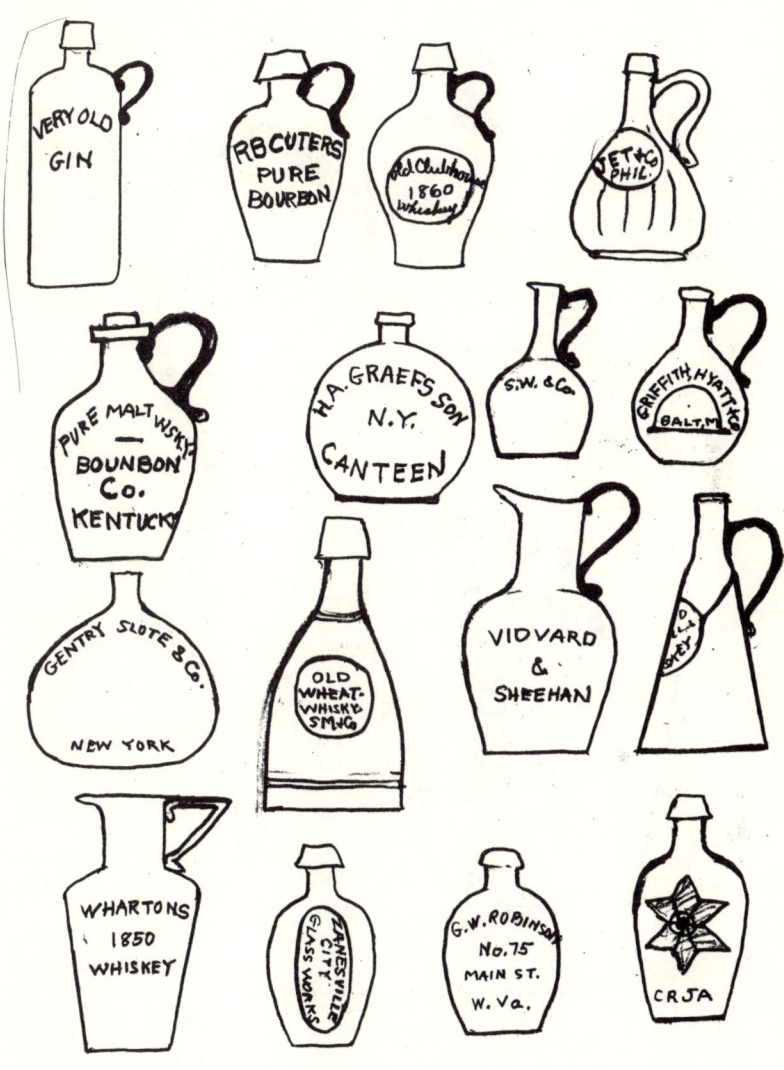

Marked 19th Century Empties uncovered by the writer (besides those traced above) include Ambrosial Whiskey—EAW & Co., Plantation Bourbon—Richards & Co., 99 Washington, Boston. E. & B. Valley Whiskey—Pittston, Pa., Forest Lawn Whiskey (J.H.V.), M.G. Full Quarter—Granite Glass Works, Lancaster Glassworks, Full Quart—Cunningham & Ihmsen, Full Pint—Pittsburgh, Pa.

Marked 19th Century Empties uncovered by the writer (besides those traced above) include The Old Mill Whiskey—Whitlock and Co., Dr. C. V. Cirard's Ginger Brandy, State Whiskey—W. B. Crowell, Jr., New York, Pure Cognac S.W., Gin Cocktail—SM & Co., N. Y., C. & G. Sour Mash Whiskey, Charter Oak Whiskey, J. T. Bickford & Bartlet, Boston, Jones and Banks, 58 Broad St., N. Y., 1861, Superior Bourbon Whiskey, Oct. 15, 1859, also a shoofly type bottle for Old Continental (1776-1876).

— GROUP A: LIQUORS

THE MINER'S FRIEND AND THE PIG BOTTLES

We pause now to consider two of the most interesting types of whiskey bottles that should be in every collection, if one can only find them. The first is the highly sought after *Miner's Friend,* which legend says traveled with the 49'ers in the gold rush to California. The writer has been offered several dark glass jugs with only this inscription, but has found them all alike and quite patent fakes. He suspects that if any such originals exist, they would more likely be dug up in broken pieces around the old California mining camps. As it is now a popular hobby to go bottle digging in these placer mining sites, perhaps something unique will be turned up. Meanwhile, we draw your attention to the only authentic "Miner's Friend" bottle that the author has seen intact. This quart bottle in very heavy "black glass" is of the 1840-50 period and shows two men, one with pick, the other with shovel; around the raised medallion is this legend "'Oldner's Superior Old Rye is the Miner's Protector." Who knows of other Miner's Friend bottles, so marked in the glass?

As for the *Pig Bottles,* it is legend that these little half-pints shaped like a pig could not even be made to stand erect, but were sold in large quantities in the 1870's to the Irish and other burly types who built our Western railroads. Certainly these bottles are to be found mostly in the West and the legends impressed in the glass leave no doubt of their use as a rationed "nip" or of the low humor they expressed. One which memorializes John Gourbaty, a tavern keeper at 115 Christy Ave., St. Louis, actually shows a map with a railroad. Another pig bottle in clear glass shows a crescent on the pig's belly along with the words Jefferson Street Saloon, Louisville, Ky. Since these bottles were blown with the head first, the neck or top opening from which one drank came out the pig's rear. This fact gave rise to the custom of making a little joke of the matter, inscribed in the glass. On one of these small clear pig bottles you find "Compliments of Thomas Netter Distilling Company, Philadelphia . . . Drink while it lasts from the hog's hole." Another in amber says, "Good Old Bourbon from a Hog's A. H." Still another says, "Something good in a hog's hole . . . he won't squeal." In some of these little bottles the pig's eyes are shut and in one version he is actually called "My blind pig."

BLIND PIG TO PINK ELEPHANT

All of which brings us around to a true story of high hoaxing once perpetrated for fun by Homer Keyes (founder of Antiques Magazine) and C. D. Gardner. At an early meeting of the Early American Glass Club in Boston, in jest Mr. Keyes spoke of an alleged *Pig and Whistle glass pattern* that would probably show a blind pig stalking about and tooting a whistle. Participants argued for a pig pattern, (i.e., pig in corn) but questioned the whistle. This was too much for fun-loving G. D. Gardner who actually created such a bottle and sent a photograph which the Boston Transcript printed in 1933. It took quite a time to convince some bottle collectors they were never going to find this flask unless, like the hoax perfectors, they made one themselves . . . in fact one also put a bright pink elephant upon a bottle as a warning to collectors to study their bottles empty or leave the contents of full ones alone.

Branding for some very coarse concoction; a good thing today's collector is more interested in the empty bottle than in its one-time contents.

— GROUP A: LIQUORS

A whole final section of this grouping should well be given over to mid 20th century marked in glass whiskey and related spirit bottles which some neophyte collectors are trying to collect. Most of these are found in such quantity it is doubtful if they will ever have anything more than curiousity value. In the writer's opinion it is far better to concentrate on the more limited issues of modern gift decanters and fin de ciecle whiskies as emphasized in the next chapter. In anticipation there, one might mention such uniques and oddities as the *Hunter* hip flask of the gay 1920's and the replica of the *Poland Water* (Moses) bottle that was used by H. Ricker to convey the first legal gin to thirsty American throats after the long dry spell of the Prohibition era.

Rare and Common Pike's Peak Bottles (Gardner Collection).

Hotel Liquor Cabinet, Virginia City, Nevada, 1898.

— GROUP A: LIQUORS 151

CHAPTER VIII   20TH C. WHISKEYS

INTRODUCTION

With examples of early flasks and mid 19th century marked whiskeys pretty much under wraps, this final chapter of our A Grouping will concentrate on those types which were fashionable from the 1900's and down to the present day. The Whiskey Museum at Bardstown, Kentucky, can show one many collectables of this era; but your writer prefers instead a more intriguing private collection. Through the courtesy of Mr. H. J. Bezette, a lawyer of Louisville, Kentucky, his photographs give one a sweep of personal liquor and bar bottle collecting for the last fifty years. Beginning with handled jugs from the late 19th century (and specialties) we pass rapidly through "fin de ciecle" specialties like wicker handled jugs and pocket flasks—odd shapes identified by label only, down to 1900 with its marked hotel and home bar bottles, the 1920 flasks of the prohibition era and the Hayner lock top bottle that kept ones friends and servants from taking uninvited liberties with its contents.

The bottles shown from the Bezette collection are the ones that every neophyte collector might well start to acquire. They are not easy to assemble, and the ones shown are only a representative sample. Some indeed are quite rare: take for example, the mail box bottles. Even Mr. Charles Gardner's great and very early collection does not have one—yet! Easiest empties of all to collect are the gift decanters of the last few years. Many of these are replicas of early bottles used by the same distiller, others were designed at great price and are truly works of art! Finally, there is the Association Material, liquor signs taken from pre-prohibition barrooms and now often costing much more than the bottled goods they advertise. This chapter then, takes one through all three phases of late whiskey bottle collecting, fin de ciecle plus, late gift decanters and old whiskey signs. Good luck to the new collector of any part of these.

BAR BOTTLES AND OTHER LATE STYLE WHISKEYS

The great variety of colors and shapes of the 20th century whiskey bottles makes a definite listing at this time inadvisable. For one thing, only a few of the thousands of bottles now discarded as soon as their contents are drained are destined to be collector items. For another thing there is often no identification as to maker or distiller marked in the glass, so the same modern form fills the products of various distillers. But if one begins with unique present day selections and works backwards he will eventually have (all) examples which exemplify changes in form from the dawn of the century.

KNOW YOUR LIQUORS

The science of distilling spirits dates back to unrecorded time. It was known to the ancient Egyptians. Long before the Christian era, the Chinese obtained a spirit from rice. The Irish and Scots produced a potable spirit in the British Isles as early as the 6th Century. The word, "Whiskey" is derived from the Irish "uisgebeatha" and the Scottish "uisgebaugh." Both mean the same: "Water of Life." The distillation process was brought to the American Colonies by the early settlers, who first created Straight Rye Whiskey and later, from the distillation of corn and rye grains in early Kentucky, America's Straight Bourbon.

BLENDED WHISKEY One of America's two great Whiskey types — the Whiskey you call "Rye." The Blend is light-bodied, soft, mild in flavor and aroma. It is made by mixing several Whiskies — sometimes many — with Neutral Spirits. By law, the Blend contains a minimum of 20% Straight Whiskey by volume at 100° Proof. Frequently, different types of Whiskies are used. Each is

IRISH WHISKEY Distinctive Whiskey of Ireland, produced in two types: **The traditional,** a blend of straight pot still Whiskies, hearty and full-bodied. **New style,** light, soft and mellow,

RUM America's original liquor, distilled from the fermented juice of sugar cane or molasses. Rum is produced in virtually all of the sugar countries, and in New England (from West Indies molasses). Rums vary in type, from light to heavy. The light Rums are dry, soft, velvety. The heavy Rums are dark, with full rum flavor and bouquet. Rum is enjoyable straight and in highballs. It blends perfectly with fruits and other liquors — makes an ideal base for many cocktails.

GRAND OLD AMERICAN BOTTLES

BOURBON WHISKEY Mellow, flavorful, distinctive American Whiskey, with appreciable body and well defined aroma and bouquet. Bourbon stands with the Blend as one of the country's two great Whiskies. It is distilled from a fermented mash of grain consisting of corn, rye and barley malt. Not less of the mash must be corn. **Straight B** on aged in new charred oak barre mum of 2 years (most are aged 4), and bottled at any legal proof. **Bourbon:** Aristocrat of the Bou 100° Proof, always aged a m

RYE WHISKEY Ble d Whiskey; also a l Wh y type. Straight Ry h died t Bourbon. It is til ented ash of grain cons g barle alt. At least 51% o gra

SCOTCH D Sc nd, renowned as a t Whiskies produ nd light grain W otch is soft, l h the su

154   GRAND OLD AMERICAN BOTTLES

Marked-in-Glass Listings. Late Whiskeys from the Bezette Collection.

— GROUP A: LIQUORS

So we do not exceed space allotted to all whiskies of our A Grouping, (Chapters 1-8, we attempt no definite listing of late bottles, but consider instead some examples of old hotel stuff photographed by Mr. Bezette.

Look first at the typical Bar Bottles of a bygone saloon-keeper. Many have a gold leaf name, and all are now rather difficult to come by. Then see the 2-handled jugs carried home in the 1890's. One in dark green says "very old gin," others in amber are marked in glass as follows: "R. B. Cutters Pure Bourbon," "Old Club House—Whiskey" (Jet and Co. Philadelphia), "H. A. Graef's Son (Canteen), N. Y.", "F. S. W. and Co.," "W. & Co. Cognac," "Cunningham and Inmsen, Pittsburg, Pa.", "Chestnut Grove Whiskey, C. W.", "Old Robison's Rye Whiskey," and so ad infinitum till all look alike. Greater interest and more varied shapes attend those late 19th and early 20th pocket whiskeys which are shown next in this series. "Pure Old Perfection" and "I. W. Harper's Compliments" are followed by the rare half-pint U. S. Mailbox Rye (Rhemstone Brothers of Cincinnati), "Old Shoe Whiskey," "Rare Old Brew, Brookfield Rye," "CH. The Perfect Drink," a McKinley and a Merry Christmas Canteen, both with the turn-of-century screw tops. Below these (reading left to right) is a flask with a painted schoolhouse scene in which a gay drink-time is taking place; the wreaths in the next late flask enclose a barrel; the middle bottle is engraved and from a "Captain Thom, Morrison" with the reverse saying "Old Bourbon"; the tall flask has an oval seal saying, "Here's to you—long life and prosperity"; and the final one is the clock bottle already mentioned in the last chapter. The Wicker covered bottles of the next photo display date from 1880 through 1900; three have handles, the small ones in the middle are wicker covered pocket flasks of 1900. Also of the early 1900 period is "Sam Leger's (wicker covered) Old Bourbon" and his "Old Sour Mash" Edgewater Memorial Bottle. Along with Hyner's and Kellerstraus' lock top bottles (locks not shown) of the 1910-1920 period should go a bottle which attempts to ape the base of the Statue of Liberty in milk glass, probably 1900, but some say it is earlier. Then there is the 1905 amber hip flask commemorating the return of John Paul Jones' body to this country and with a hard rubber cap.

Finally 20th century Bezette bottle photos include those from the prohibition period and 5 "golds" that came before legal whiskey's return. The middle (Thompson) flask is leather covered and the screw top cover marks the usual sign of a hip flask. All other shapes in this final photo roundup typify what we have emphasized before, namely that unless you want to use very modern bottles just for color, or want to show how shape indicates former contents (i.e., the brandies, gin and creme de menthe shapes often differ from scotch and bourbon bottles) there is little point to preserving them.

Having already exceeded our space allotment, later collectors are left to unearth which of today's common bottles will be tomorrow's rareities, here turn next to the more expensive gift decanters.

Late Whiskeys from the Bezette Collection.

Late Whiskeys from the Bezette Collection.

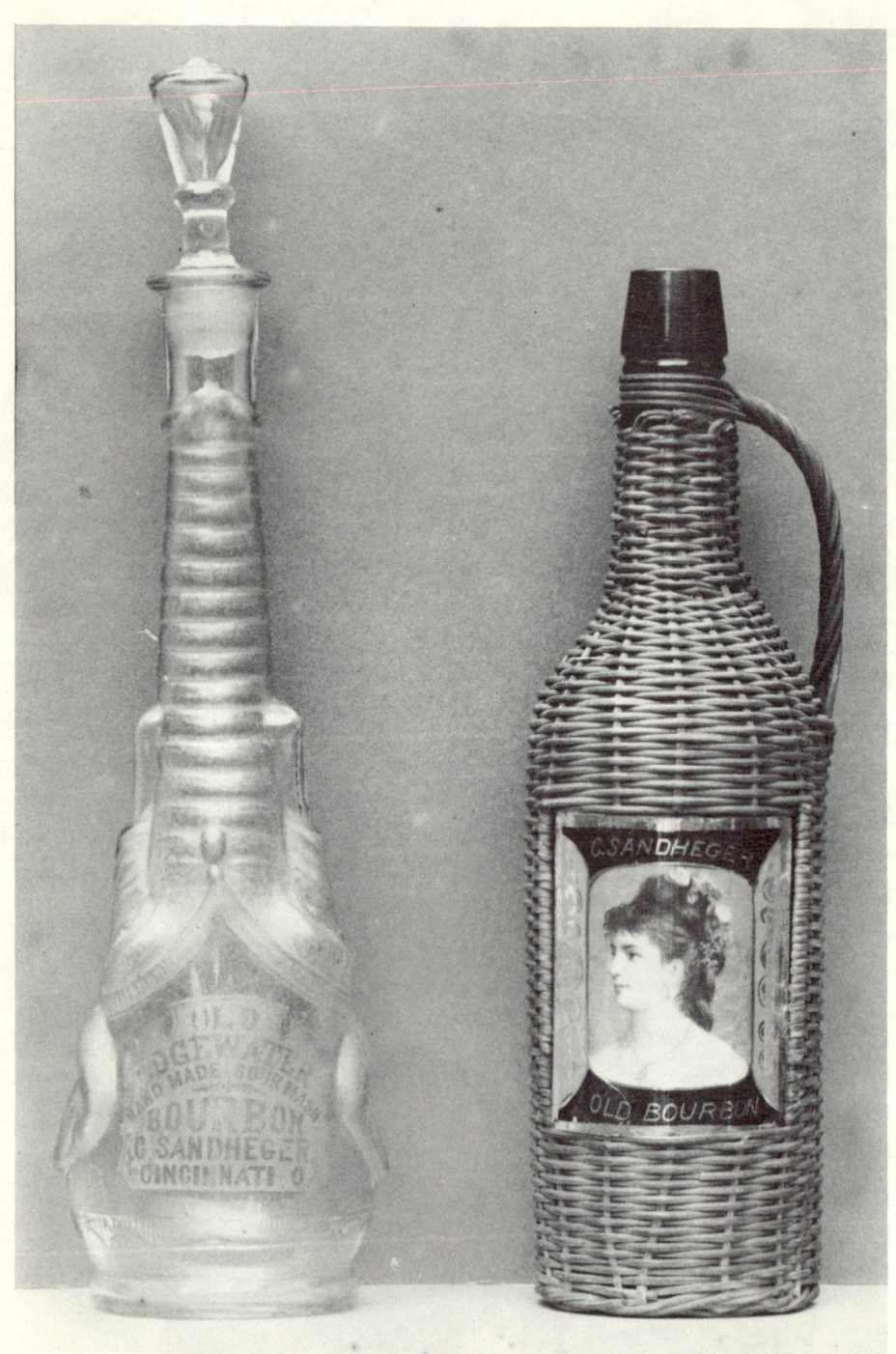

Miniature Liquors
Collect miniature liquor bottles.

Bottles from writers YVY Museum at Watkins Glen, N. Y.

Left : German Rhine-Wine bottles. On the left is a brown HOCK bottle and on MOSELL bottle. *Right :* Typical Stein Wein *Bocksbeutel*. That on the left is blown and is moulded

It should be noted that the 1900 era brought perfection of the mechanical bottle making machine, and at the same time brought in stiffer advertising promotion by rival brands and distillers. As a result one finds a great proliferation of bottles. The government said these could not be refilled or used for resale, but a few may give color in the window.

— GROUP A: LIQUORS

Some of the recent bottles made by Whitall Tatum Company.

GRAND OLD AMERICAN BOTTLES

AMERICA'S MOST WELCOME GIFTS

GIFT CHECK LIST

Give liquors and wines for the truly welcome gift this Holiday. They are always appropriate ... always the distinctive gift ... for almost everyone on everyone's gift list. Easy to buy — no worry about color, size, style or duplication. And always most appreciated! Fine liquors and wines make the ideal gift for Christmas, Birthdays, Anniversaries, Engagements, House Warmings, Bon Voyage and Welcome Home parties, gifts for the Host and Hostess — for every occasion the year around! Use this convenient Check List to plan your gift-giving this Holiday Season.

FAMILY
Father ....
Mother ....
Sisters ....
Brothers ....
Grandparents ....

RELATIVES
Uncles....................
Aunts.....................
Nieces....................
Nephews ....
Cousins ....

BUSINESS ASSOCIATES
Customers ....
Prospects ....
Employer ....
Supervisor ....
Co-Workers ....

FRIENDS
Personal Friends ....

Neighbors ....
Club Members ....
Car Pool Members ....

SERVICE PERSONNEL
Superintendent ....
Porters ....
Elevator Operators ....
Mailman..................
Handyman ....
Sanitation Collectors.......
Gardener ....
Club Attendants...........
Domestic Help............
Telephone Operators.......

TRADES PEOPLE
Milkman..................
Beautician ....
Laundryman ....
Garage Attendants.........
Delivery Men..............

— GROUP A: LIQUORS

THE MODERN GIFT DECANTER

It should be noted that the 1900 era brought perfection of the mechanical bottle making machine, and at the same time brought in stiffer advertising promotion by rival brands and distillers. As a result one finds a great proliferation of bottles. The government said these could not be refilled or used for resale, but a few may give color in the window.

A fast growing and most intriguing aspect of bottle collecting has begun to center around the modern gift decanter. With the custom of exchanging remembrances with dear friends and giving status to valued customers, both individuals and business houses have turned to Holiday Time as a most appropriate occasion. One of the most appreciated tokens has become a Christmas-wrapped gift of bottled spirits. In fact so popular has this type of year-end exchange become that all the leading distillers are putting out their own especially designed whiskey decanters. The fact that these are made in rather limited quantities, and usually changed in shape every year, has made some of these forms already a relative rarity. And even if one were not a bottle collector, some shapes are such quality products that they would be kept in the china closet and used as high style wine or water carafe decanters. One distiller (The House of Calvert) has for the last several years reproduced different early American flask patterns as decanters, with a special blown stopper as a sort of trade mark. As seen by pictures which follow, other distillers use only their regular bottle but dress it up with special boxed Christmas packaging. These naturally will not be the collectors items which specially designed gift decanters will become. Of course we have here given only a representative sample of each type, leaving it for later enthusiasts to make a definite check list. Make no mistake, however, the whiskey bottle collector (whether after rare historical flasks, Waterford Cut glass or Biningers, will not neglect this new field, potentially a "gold mine."

GRAND OLD AMERICAN BOTTLES

— GROUP A: LIQUORS

20th Century Decanters from Writer's Collection.

Hip Flasks—1900 (Paul Jones), 1920 (Silver Mounted) and 1950 (Wickered).

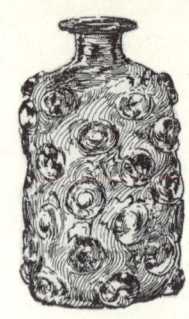

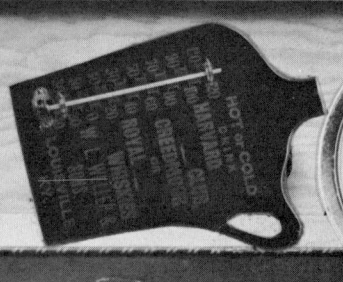

— GROUP A: LIQUORS

PICTORIAL ASSOCIATION MATERIAL

If one is a collector of bottles, especially those whose original contents was whiskey, he can hardly escape the urge to collect pictorial association material. By this we mean those pamphlets, signs, servers and advertising folios which extol the particular virtues of some special brand or type of bygone liquid refreshment. And for anyone with a home bar or fun room, such pictorial embellishments for the walls are rapidly becoming a status "must." The trend is indicated by the ever rising prices which such association material commands when offered at auction. Recently this writer had occasion to attend a Philadelphia sale which dispersed a collection owned by old time movie cowboy Hoot Gibson. Among the effects were numerous whiskey signs once hung in pre-prohibition saloons. Many had only the straight company slogan or identifying trademark; but the pieces most in demand were chromolithos, paintings on tin and simulated oil paintings (paper chromes on canvas backs) that showed a lively home scene. Samples of this type of barroom pictures are shown on other pages with special attention called to one showing a young damsel hiding her face and captioned, "The Morning After" (in the anchor is "D. D. New Hope—Sour Mash—Nelson County, Kentucky). Pictures with this off-beat appeal are in great demand. In fact, at the Hoot Gibson sale, two men got to bidding on a buxom nude chromo-litho and ran the price up to $150 before one quit. Those with an even broader humor may sometime be found. Mr. Gardner reports one owned by some bottle visitor which showed a seated "Mr. Tornbritches" lapping up his favorite brew, while standing up between his spread legs two cats were busy licking him too . . . One of the finest of barroom whiskey signs is found in the Old White Pump Tavern of the Century House old village restoration near Watkins Glen, New York. A reverse painting on glass, it shows the original Pepper distillery in shell work and is valued at over $500.

This same old tavern has a good deal of other association material including a large terra cotta dwarf who holds a local Taylor wine bottle, a "Friar Tuck" cut out that extolls gin, photos of old distilling workers and paintings of The Old Philosopher who is brewing Duffy Pure Malt Whiskey. The latter company sold, primarily through druggists, where it was prescribed a medicine. Sample pages from their "monthly" are shown just to indicate what fascinating byways the pursuit of old empty bottles can lead one into. A further report of advertising ephemera of this type, has of course little place in a reference book on bottles. Let the collector (seasoned or neophyte) check back over the many varieties we have already surveyed in this, our first or A grouping; then if the lure for some of these types is too exacting or costly, let him turn to our next or B grouping. There the late 19th century Bitters and other proprietary medicines (all with strong alcoholic contents) left behind a hoard of empty bottles, only a few of which are already bringing the prices of the earlier historical flasks.

Association Material from writers YVY Museum at Watkins Glen, N. Y.

JAS. E. PEPPER & CO.
PEPPER DISTILLERY
LEXINGTON, KY.

"PEPPER" DISTILLERY HAND MADE SOUR MASH JAS. E. PEPPER & CO. DISTILLERS LEXINGTON KY.

"PEPPER" DISTILLERY HAND MADE SOUR MASH PURE RYE JAS. E. PEPPER & CO. DISTILLERS LEXINGTON KY.

THE OLDEST AND BEST BRAND OF WHISKEY
MADE IN KENTUCKY.

AFTER ONCE USING OUR "TIPPECANOE," PREPARATIONS CALLED "BITTERS," YOU WILL USE NO NESTRUMS NOR TRY "TIPPECANOE."

COPYRIGHT 1883.

DOSE:—One teaspoonful four times a day.

SANMETTO.

THIS remedy is a genito-urinary and nutrient tonic. It ha[s] a special action upon the glands of the reproductive o[r]gans, as the mammæ, ovaries, prostate, testes, etc. Its action [is] that of a great vitalizer, tending to increase their activity, an[d] to promote their secreting faculty. It is specially indicated [in] all cases of wasting of the testes, such as follows varicocele or [is] induced by masturbation, or which is often present in sexu[al] impotency. In gynecological practice it is much used to pr[o]mote the growth of the mammæ; also in uterine atrophy d[e]pendent upon ovarian blight, and in urethritis and gleet, its a[c]tion is unexcelled. But it is upon the prostate gland that th[e] remedy exercises its best effects. Out of every ten men, nin[e] have enlarged prostate, and one has atrophy of the same. Cas[e] after case of both morbid conditions could be recited in whic[h] by the use of **SANMETTO**, the size of the prostate wa[s] equalized, the difficulty of micturition removed, and the sexua[l] power improved. A perfect rejuvenation follows the use of th[e] **SANMETTO**, the general nervous system becomes balanced an[d] reinvigorated. MANUFACTURED BY **OD CHEM. CO.**, 15 Cedar Street, **New York.**

THE GREAT BUILDER
Of Strength and Tissue.

THE STRONGEST AND BEST ON THE MARKET AS PROVEN BY EVERY TEST.

[P]UREMALT stands the test of analysis, the test of climate, the test of market and the

"Drink Only the Purest."

FINE OLD KY. TAYLOR" and "OLD CHARTER"

[o]wn distillation and purity guaranteed by U. S. Government, and [ ] to retail trade. Send for price list and samples.

[TAY]LOR, Sole Owners, Old Charter Distillery,
NELSON CO., KENTUCKY.

R'S LOG CABIN SARSAPARILLA.
R'S LOG CABIN HOPS & BUCHU REMEDY.
R'S LOG CABIN COUGH & CONSUMPTION REMEDY.
(SMALL & LARGE SIZES)
R'S LOG CABIN HAIR TONIC.
R'S LOG CABIN EXTRACT SMALL & LARGE SIZES.
R'S LOG CABIN PLASTERS.
R'S LOG CABIN ROSE CREAM FOR CATARRH.
R'S LOG CABIN LIVER PILLS.

WARNER'S SAFE REMEDIES.

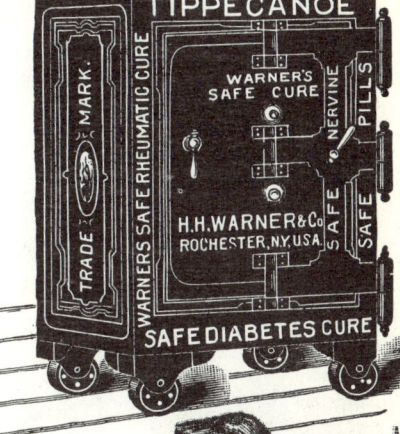

...REMEDY HAS BEEN THE MAINSTAY OF THOUSANDS NOW ADVANCED IN LIFE AND ...ADVANCED AGE WHO OWE THEIR ROBUST HEALTH TO THIS GREAT MEDICINE.

Introducing Group B-Medicinals. All Photos from Gardner Collection. Above Warner's Tippecanoe (#406) & Warners's Safe Bitters (#436).

— GROUP B: MEDICINALS

CHAPTER IX BITTERS BOTTLES

As credit for the first full checklists of Early American Flasks and Whiskey Bottles goes to Mr. Van Rensselaer, so with Bitters Bottles we honor another early pioneer lister,—James H. Thompson. His 1947 out-of-print book on this subject was the first to list and describe 456 marked-in-glass bitters along with classifications as to form and relative rarity. We can do no better than to begin this section with the Thompson classification, appending relevant facts which have come to light since that time, including over 100 additional new forms.

Mr. Thompson drew a sharp line between marked Bitters Bottles and those related 19th century patent medicine panaceas (such as sarsaparilla and Lydia Pinkham) which often had as strong an alcoholic content but were not labeled Bitters marked-in-glass. Since many of the latter are just as old and rare as the 'Bitters' we will give these a descriptive secondary classification; also less well known proprietary medicine bottles made before 1875 and presumably related to Bitters-taking make up a third listing then end this section by a quick look at collateral association material — the almanac advertising signs, and pamphlets which provide such a wealth of information and entertainment for collectors of bottle residua from this era of Medical Quackery and Puritanical tippling.

ORIGIN OF BITTERS AND MEDICINES

Under the Hanoverian King George II, the English government tried to quell the widespread gin drinking on London streets. Previously it was sold for a song, tax free, as a way of keeping the lower classes happy and not interfering with the pursuits and wasted spending of the elite. Now a drastic tax was set up to drive gin out of business and the number of pubs to a mile was drastically restricted. So the gin peddlers could still stay in business, they opened a chain of apothecary shops (many right around St. Paul's Cathedral), put a little herbal bitters in a bottle and sold it very cheap under head of medicinal liquor. The new product was called "Coltick Water," "Gripe Water" or "Bitters." The labels stated, "Easy to take" . . . 2 or 3 spoonfuls each day, or as the fit takes you." And the fits were frequent. When one vendor was called into court and questioned "on the surprising number of people coming to you for medicine," he answered, "Sar, the late tax has given many people the cholick, and that's the reason I now have so many patients."

In Colonial America, the gin, or more usually West Indian rum, was taxed very little. And so, because everyone from Clergyman to Town

Mr. Gardner regards this as his Number One Bitters; the writer finds reading the surrounding ads as more fun than its contents.

— GROUP B: MEDICINALS

Squire and Frontiersman imbibed strong spirits, there was little occasion to dilute the product with medicinal herbals under the guise of aiding health. As has been shown in the A grouping, whiskey (either the 'mountain dew" of moonshiners or other spirits legally licensed by the New Republic) was freely used with no thought of wrong doing or question provided a man "could hold his liquor." But as the country grew more civilized and many workmen were found to squander family funds on strong drink, by the mid 19th century their wives turned towards the W.C.T.U. movement and many took the pledge. This, of course, did not work out for those heavily committed to liquid euphoria and so the patent medicine men (many coming over from Victorian England) put in some herbals and America itself was off on a *Bitter Binge*. As shown in subsequent sections, The Great American Bottle received a new 19th century lift as these highly collectable containers of proprietary medicine (practically all of original alcoholic content) hit the stands.

There is so much to this field of Bitters and other related proprietary medicine bottles that any published descriptive check list is likely to show many variations or unlisted items sent back by reader-collectors in the next mail. Mr. Thompson's pioneer listing of 456 marked-in-glass American Bitters Bottles is still retained as the basic check list. Some of these carrying the notation "no description available" (and which are now identified) have the added information on pages following the primary check list, together with an added check list of 173 previously unlisted Bitters. Descriptions on some of these are also "not available." But so far as possible, here as well as with the original check list, an indication of relative rarity and value is given in terms of number of asterisks used. Thus a common bitters bottle has one star, better ones three. 2. The extreme rarities such as Traveller's, Gen. Scott Cannon, etc., should all have a six star mark and the price is whatever the market will bear. There is simply no point of reprinting the Thompson 1947 prices as all of these are exceeded today. In fact, many now bring the same prices as the rare historical flasks. Line drawings are used where possible beside the bottle description. Also we have given much space to actual photographs from Mr. Gardner's collection. Finally, concluding this chapter on Bitters Bottles we give you a classification of forms, a word on shapes, designs and color, also a general analysis of the rarity problem together with a list of the twelve most desirable Bitters bottles in order of their importance . . . happy hunting.

LISTING RARE BITTERS IN ORDER OF IMPORTANCE
1. Gen. Scott's Artillery Bitters
2. Wilson's Berlin Bitters
3. Carey's Grecian Bend Bitters
4 Traveler's Bitters
5. McKeever's Army Bitters
6. Jacob's Cabin Bitters
7. Jackson Stonewall Bitters
8. Seaworth Bitters
9 Whitwell's Temperance Bitters
10. Dingen's Napoleon Bitters
11. Cannon Bitters
12. Moulton's Oloroso Bitters

Reputedly the rarest of all Bitters bottles is that for Traveler Bitters, of which but three specimens are known to exist can hope that with publication of this list collectors will continue to report information as it comes to them.
—James H. Thompson

GROUP B: MEDICINALS

The primary purpose of this check list is that it may be a guide to the collector of bitters bottles; a secondary purpose is to supply a sources from which may spring a more conclusive report of the many phases of the so-called "patent medicine mania" in America. Because of these two purposes, sometimes at conflict, those interested in bottles alone and their collection should not complain because there has been added to the data they deem necessary to their purposes other and unrelated information. The list, it is hoped, will prove itself useful to both acquisitive and inquisitive collectors.

* Listings in the following are marked to indicate estimations of rarity of Bitters bottles by use of asterisks as follows: Common*, Comparatively Scarce**, Scarce***, Rare*****. Divisions of line of title lettering are indicated by use of a diagonal mark (/).

1—**Abbott's Bitters*****
Round amber. Marked: "C. W. Abbott / Baltimore" in two lines around shoulder. In base: "C. W. Abbott & Co., Baltimore, Md" in circle.

2—**Alps Bitters**
No description available.

3—**American Life Bitters******
Amber log cabin shape. Marked: "American Life Bitters / Eiler / Manufacturer / Tiffin, Ohio," in four lines.

4—**American Stomach Bitters**
No description available.

5—**David Andrew's Vegetable Jaundice Bitters****
Clear rectangular flat. Pint. Sheared mouth. Scarred base. Marked: "Andrew's Jaundice Bitters / Providence, R. I." in two vertical lines.

5-a—Variation: Collared mouth. 8¼ x 4½. Marked: "David Andrews' Vegetable Jaundice Bitters / Providence, R. I." in two vertical lines.
5-b—Variation: In bluish-aqua with tapered flanged mouth. Marked as others.

6—**Angostura Bitters**
Bitters of this title were for flavoring as distinguished from medicinal bitters. Originals were for Dr. J. G. B. Siebert & Sons, CIRCA 1830 and later. Many imitations under the same name have appeared, and various firm names have been affixed. Many variants of bottles.

7—**Angostura Aromatic Tincture Bitters**
No description available.

GRAND OLD AMERICAN BOTTLES

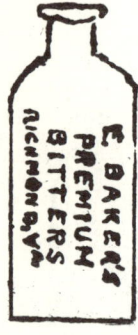

8—**Pure Apple Brandy Bitters***
Barrel shape clear. Flat base with 1½ inch circular depression. Obverse flat. On rounded side single hoops near base and shoulder. Three concentric hoops in two sets at middle of body. Ringed neck. Straight mouth. Bottle identified by label on flat face. Two variations of labels, one lithographed with bright red apple and green leaves. Marked: "Pure Apple Brandy Bitters / Prepared only by Sanford, Chamberlain & Albers / Knoxville, Tenn." 7½ x 3½.

9—**Arbaugh's Newport Bitters****
No description available.

10—**Aromatic Bitters****
Round amber. Long neck bulged. Heavy flanged mouth. About quart. Identified by label alone. Label in blue and gold. Over large "B" is "Aromatic Stomach Bitters."

AROMATIC BITTERS—See Angostura, Aromatic, Blake, Brown, Deutscher, Folger, Price, Sazar, Sazerac, Simon.

11—**Aroma Stomach Bitters**
No description available.

ARMY BITTERS—See McKeever.

12—**Atwood's Jaundice Bitters***
Twelve-sided aqua. Marked: "Atwood's Jaundice Bitters / Moses Atwood / Georgetown, Mass." in five vertical lines and in five panels. Scarred base. Collared mouth. 6½ x 2¼.
12-a—Variation: Twelve-sided aqua. Flanged and ringed mouth. Domed base. Marked: "Atwood's Jaundice Bitters / Formerly made by / Moses Atwood / Georgetown, Mass" in five vertical lines on five panels. 6 x 2¼.

12-b—Variation: Flat rectangular aqua. Beveled corners. Rounded shoulder. Straight neck. Applied tapered flanged mouth. Three sides with arched panels. Other side plain. Marked: "Vegetable / Jaundice Bitters'" in two vertical lines in face panel; reverse plain; in two side panels, "Atwood's" and Georgetown, Ms." Pontil scar in base.

12-c—Variation. Twelve-sided aqua. Marked: "Atwood's Physical Jaundice Bitters.' This title appears on label and broadside wrapper of bottle same as 12-a.
12-d—Variation: Twelve-sided aqua. Panels arched at shoulder. Domed shoulder. Flat base. Screw top. Marked: "Atwood's / Jannaice Bitters / Formerly made by Moses Atwood / Georgetown, Mass." in five vertical lines on five panels. Metal screw cap with portrait of John E. Henry, New York. Pirated brand. Note: Many other variations with slight differences in dimensions due to continual production over long period of years. Also miniature sample bottles.

13—**Atwood's Quinine Tonic Bitters****
Circa 1870. No description available.

← GROUP B: MEDICINALS 185

14—Augauer Bitters***
Rectangular apple green. Marked: "Augauer Bitters" in one vertical line in side panel. Reverse: "Augauer Bitters Co. / Chicago" in two vertical lines. Arch-top panels on two faces. Heavily beveled corners with vertical ribbings. Diogonal mould. Paneled base with "E". Tapered neck. Flanged mouth. 7⅞ x ⅜4 x 2½.
Note: Identical save for marking with bottle for Pepsin Calisaya Bitters, which was original title for these bitters.

15—Augustiner Health and Stomach Bitters**
No description available.

16—Austen's Oswego Bitters***
No description available. Circa 1865.

17—Dr. M. C. Ayer's Restorative Bitters***
Rectangular aqua. Marked: "Dr. M. C. Ayer's / Restorative Bitters / Boston, Mass." 9 x 5 x 2.

18—Dr. Babcock's Liver Bitters**
No description available. Circa 1875.

19—Baker's Orange Grove Bitters***
Deep amber square. Roped corners. Collared mouth. Marked: "Baker's Orange Grove" in one vertical line. Reverse: "Bitters" in one vertical line. 9½ x 3.

20—E. Baker's Premium Bitters***
Round aqua. Marked: "E. Baker's Premium / Bitters / Richmond, Va." in four vertical lines. 6½ x 3.

21—Dr. Ball's Stomachic Bitters***
Rectangular aqua. Panelled on three sides. Folded mouth. Scarred base. Marked: "Dr. Ball's Stomachic Bitters / Northboro, Mass." in two panels. 7 x 2½. Circa 1820.

22—Dr. Baxter's Mandrake Bitters**
Twelve-sided aqua. Flat scarred base. Domed shoulder. Straight neck. Double collared mouth. Marked: "Dr. Baxter's / Mandrake Bitters / Lord Bros. / Proprietors / Burlington, Vt." in five vertical lines in five panels. Circa 1865. 6½ x 2⅛.
22-a—Variation: Same in amber.

23—Dr. Bell's Blood Purifying Bitters**
Rectangular amber. Sunken panels. Flanged mouth. About ¾ quart. Marked: "Dr. Bell's / Blood Purifying Bitters / The Great English Remedy" on four sides.

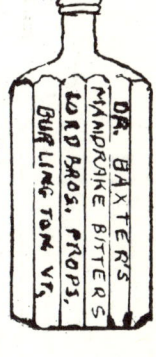

24—Belt's Bitters***
Marked: "Belt's Bitters / The Great Anodyne and Nervine / Trueman Belt & Sons / 13 Camden St., Baltimore, Md." 1870.

25—Belverdee Stomach Bitters
No description available.

26—Bender's Bitters**
Flat rectangular aqua with peaked roof. Marked: "Bender's Bitters / Cincinnati, O." 10½ x 3½ x 2.
Ben Franklin Bitters—See Franklin.

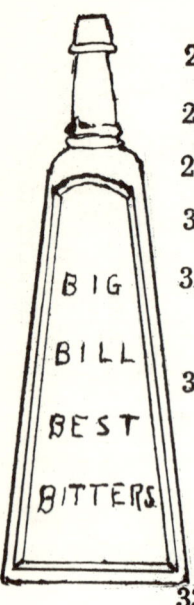

27—Ben Hur Kidney and Liver Bitters
No description available.

28—Berg's Hawkeye Bitters
No description available.

29—Dr. Bergelt's Magen Bitters
No description available.

30—Bertram's Long Life Bitters***
No description available. Circa. 1870.

31—Berkshire Bitters****
Amber. In shape of pig. About pint. Marked: "BERKSHIRE Bitters / A. Mann & Co, / Cincinnati, Ohio." Circa. 1853.
31-a—Variation: In golden amber.

32—Big Bill Best Bitters***
Square golden amber. Tapered from base to shoulder. Rounded corners. Slightly domed base. Two rings at base of neck. Flanged and ringed mouth. Two sides plain; two with arch-top panels. Marked: "Big / Bill / Best / Bitters" in four horizontal lines in two panels. 12 x 3.
32-a—Variations: In various shades of amber.
Note: Label with large picture of man with protuberant stomach.

33—Dr. Birmingham's Anti-Bilious Blood Purifying Bitters****
Round green. Twelve sunken panels. About ¾ quart. **Folded mouth.** Scarred base. Marked: "Dr. Birmingham's / Anti-bilious Blood Purifying / Bitters / This Bottle Not To Be Sold." 8¾ x 3¾.

34—Dr. Bishop's Wahoo Bitters***
Rectangular amber. Steeply roofed shoulder. Beveled corners. Indented panel on face with pointed top. In shoulder on face: "Dr. Bishop's (curved) Wahoo Bitters." In side panels: "Wa-Hoo Bitters Co." and "New Haven, Conn." Square flanged mouth. 10 x 3¾ x 3¾ x 2½.

35—Bismarck Laxative Bitters
No description available.

36—Dr. Blake's Aromatic Bitters**
Rectangular aqua. Heavily champfered corners. Flat base. Arch-top panels. Straight neck. Flanged mouth. Marked: "Dr. Blake's" (in side panel) "Aromatic / Bitters" (two vertical lines in face panel), "New York" (in side panel). 7¼ x 3.

37—G. C. Blake's Anti-Dyspeptic Bitters***
Flask shape aqua. About half pint. Collared neck. Ground pontil scar in base. Marked: "G. C. Blake's / Anti-Dyspeptic Bitters."

38—Blake's Tonic and Diuretic Bitter***
Oval aqua. About quart. Marked: "Blake's Tonic and Diuretic Bitter." Note omission of "s." About 10 in. high. Bottle attributed to Stanger, Glassboro, N. J.

— GROUP B: MEDICINALS

39—Boerhave's Holland Bitters***
Rectangular blue-aqua. Flat base. Beveled corners. Indented panels on three sides. Sloped shoulder. Thin 2½ in. neck. Double collared mouth. Marked: "Boerhave's / Holland Bitters" in two vertical lines in face panel. Reverse plain. In two side panels: "B. Page Jr. & Co." and "Pittsburgh, Pa." Diagonal mould. 7¾ x 2¾ x 1¾.

40—Boker's Stomach Bitters**
Round amber. Long (7½ in.) bulged neck. Domed shoulder. Tapered body. Domed base. Square flanged and ringed mouth. Indentified by labels. Circa. 1870.
40-a—Variation: Earlier bottles bore name of John G. and E. Boker.

41—Bonekamp Stomach Bitters
No description available.

42—Bonekamp Bitters
No description available.

43—Bocnekamp Bitters*
Round amber. Almost flat shoulder. Long straight neck. Square flanged mouth. About ¾ quart. Identified by label which reads: "Boonekamp or Maag-Bitters" and at each side monogram "C.M.F"

44—Botanic Bitters
No description available.

45—Bouvier Buchu Bitters***
Elliptical amber. Ring at base of neck. Collared mouth. About ¾ quart. Marked: "Bouvier (semi-circle) / Bucha Bitters" in sunken panel. "Bouvier Specialty Co. / Louisville, Ky." in three vertical lines. 10½ high.

46—Bourbon Whiskey Bitters***
Deep amber barrel shape. Marked: "Bourbon Whiskey Bitters" in two lines on face. About ¾ quart. Folded mouth. Domed base. With simulated sets of hops at top and bottom of body.
Note: This bottle was probably for either the Greeley or Pollard-Bourbon Whiskey Bitters, but lacks indentfying name of either maker.

47—Dr. Boyce's Tonic Bitters***
Round aqua. Ringed mouth. About pint. Marked: "Dr. Boyce's / Tonic Bitters / Henry, Johnson & Lord / Burlington, Vt."

48—Brazilian Bitters
No description available. McClelland & Cassin, Selma, Ala.

49—Brod's Celery Pepsin Bitters
No description available.

50—Brown's Aromatic Cordial Bitters
No description available.
Brown's Celebrated Indian Herb Bitters—see Indian

51—Brown's Iron Bitters**
Square dark amber. Three sides with deep arch-top panels. Domed base. Domed shoulder. Straight neck. Tapered flanged mouth. Face panel plain for label. Marked: "Iron Bitters" in one vertical line in panel; "Brown Chemical Co.." one line vertical in panel. Baltimore, Md. 8½ x 2¼.
51-a—Variations: in various shades of amber.

52—Dr. Brown's Tonic Bitters
No description available. Circa. 1875.

53—E. Brown Sarsaparilla and Tomato Bitters***
Elliptical aqua. About pint. Scarred base. Sheared mouth. in face panel. Reverse plain.

54—The Bull Wild Cherry Bitters*
Rectangular clear. Indented panels. Beveled corners. Wide 1 in. flanged mouth. Identified by label alone. Circa. 1890.

55—Buckner's Bitters
No description available.

56—Prof. Geo. J. Bryne's Great Universal Compound Stomach Bitters****
Square golden amber. Roped corners. Latticed top to panels. Latticed base. About quart. Marked: "Prof. Geo. J. Byrne's / Great Universal Compound / Stomach Bitters / Patented 1870 / DC / LX / XM"
56-a—Variations: Various shades of amber.
BRYNE'S GLOBE BITTERS—See Globe.

57—Buckeye Bitters
No description available.
BUCKLEN'S BITTERS—See Electric.

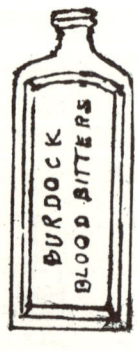

58—Burdock Blood Bitters**
Square aqua. About pint. Double collared mouth. Three sunken panels. Other side plain for label. Marked: "Burdock Blood Bitters / Foster, Milburn & Co. / Buffalo, N.Y." 9¼ tall. Bottle attributed to Lancaster.
58-a—Variation: Rectangular aqua. Beveled corners. Long straight neck. Double ringed applied mouth. Flat base with circle. Marked same as above. 8½ x 2⅝ x 1⅝.
58-b—Variations: Also in shades of amber.
Note: These bottle were produced in great numbers and in many variations in size of letterings and other details. Later issues appeared with screw caps.

59—Burnet's Orange Bitters*
Round clear. Bulged neck. Tapered from domed shoulder to base. Double ringed mouth. Glass topper. Quart. Identified by label which reads: "Burnet's Pure Orange (picture of bulldog) Bitters. James Burnet & Co., London.
BUCHU BITTERS—See Bouvier

60—Dr. Butler's Asparagus Bitters*
Round clear. Tapered neck. Flanged mouth with ring. Quart. Identified by label which reads: "Dr. Butler's Asparagus Bitters, etc." Circa. 1890.

— **GROUP B: MEDICINALS**

Bottles number 56 (Prof. B. Stomach Bitters) and number 69 (Grecian Bend Bitters).

61—Calabash Bitters****
Rectangular aqua. Domed shoulder. Heavy square flanged mouth. Marked: "$ 4 Ounces of / Calabash / (figure of tree) Bitters / The Calabash Bitters Co. / Ogdensburg, N. Y. / Sole Proprietors." In base: "W.T. & Co." (mark of Whitall, Tatum & Company.)

62—Caldwell Great Tonic Herb Bitters***
Triangular dark amber. Three Gothic panels, one latticed others plain. About ¾ quart. Marked: "Caldwell Great Tonic Herb Bitters" in one idented panel. 12½ tall.
62-a—Variations: In various shades of amber.

63—California Grape Bitters**
Rectangular heavy red amber Rounded at sides. Deep indented panels on four sides. Tapered body from base to shoulder. Flat base with 1½ in. depression. Collared neck. Marked: "L. & A. Scharff" in side panel; in reverse side panel "St. Louis, Mo." Large bold letters in vertical lines. On Label: "California Grape Bitters" with bunch of grapes. 9% No description available.

64—California Fig Bitters.
No description available.

65—California Root Bitters
No description available. Circa. 1880.
CALISAYA BITTERS—See Johnson, Henblein, Pepsin, Wahoo.

66—Cannon Bitters****
Dark amber log cabin shape. On three sides six cannons; on another side tent with flag; on roof and four sides two crossed spears and cannon on each corner.

67—Capadura Bitters
Round amber. About half pint. Flanged mouth with ring. Marked: "M. F. & Co." in vertical line on neck. Otherwise identified by label.

68—Capitol Bitters—See Fenner
No description available of brand of this title issued by R. Sternsdorff, Buffalo, N. Y.

69—Carey's Grecian Bend Bitters*****
Rectangular puce. Tapered from base to neck. Roped corners. Raised oval decoration on two sides of shoulder. Arched windows on other sides of shoulder. About ¾ quart. Collared mouth. Marked: "Carey's Grecian Bend Bitters" on one face.
69-a—Variations: In shades of amber.

70—Carpathian Bitters
No description available.

71—Carter's Bitters
No description available. Circa. 1875.

72—Castilian Bitters
Round amber. Tapered body. Slightly hollowed below shoulder. Ring on neck. About ¾ quart. Flanged mouth. Marked: Castilian Bitters" in vertical line. 10 in. tall.
CATAWBA BRANDY STOMACH BITTERS—See Roback.

GROUP B: MEDICINALS

73—Cedron Bitters
No description available. Circa. 1865. Louisville, Ky.

74—Century Bitters**
Square golden amber. Rope-like diamond design on corners. Small horizontal lines at base. On corners above arches bunch of grapes, scissors, battle axe, shield. Slats above. Collared mouth. Marked: "Landenburg's / Century Bitters." Reverse: "A Heller & Bro. / New York," above shield. Spread eagle in arch. Two sides plain. One side with sunburst and "1776"; one side with "1876" in large numerals.
74-a—Variations: In several shades of amber and other colors.

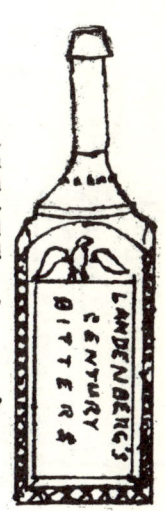

75—Celery Bitters and Angostura
No description available.

76—Celery Bitters
No description available. Steuben County Wine Co.—Celery Bitters—Chicago, Ill.

77—Celery Compound Bitters
No description available.

78—Celery Tonic Bitters
No description available.

79—Dr. Chasteney's Stomach Bitters
No description available.

80—Dr. Chandler's Jamaica Ginger Root Bitters**
Flattened barrel shape amber. About ¾ quart. Double collared mouth. Marked: "Dr. Chandler's Jamaica Ginger Root Bitters / Chas. Nichols, Jr. and Co., Props. / Lowell, Mass."

81—Chapman's Taraxicum Tonic Wine Bitters**
No description available.

82—Chapman's Genuine Bitters**
Rectangular olive amber. Beveled edges Short neck. Folded mouth. About ¾ quart. Marked: "Chapman's Genuine Bitters / No. 4 Salem Street / Boston."
82-a—Variation: With top line: "Only 70 Cents."

83—Genl. Frank Cheatam's Bitters**
Square brown amber. Roofed shoulder with triangular panels. Tapered flanged mouth with ring at base of straight neck. Marked: "Genl. / Frank Cheatam's / Bitters" in three vertical line in face panel. In reverse panel, "Nashville, Tenn." in one vertical line. In depressed circle in base "W. McC. & Co." (Mark of McCulley, Pittsburgh.) 10 x 2¾.

84—Cinchona Bitters
No description available.

85—Clarke's Vegetable Sherry Wine Tonic Bitters**
Rectangular aqua. Collared mouth. Half gallon. From wooden mould. Marked: "Clarke's / Vegetable Sherry Wine / Tonic Bitters / Sharon, Mass."
85-a—Variation: With additional top line: "Only 70 Cents."
85-b—Variation: Full gallon. Aqua. 14 in. tall.
85-c—Other variations in pints, quarts, two quarts of "Mammoth Size" and four quarts of "World's Size." E. R. Clarke, Sharon, Mass. Circa. 1855.

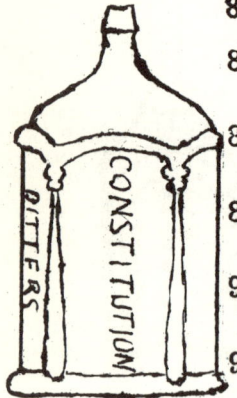

86—Cocoa Bitters
No description available.

87—Cocoainized Pepsin Chinchona Bitters
No description available.
COCKTAIL BITTERS—See Dinger, Napoleon, Fletcher, **Rivaud.**

88—Cocmoke Bitters
No description available.
CENTENNIAL BITTERS—See Simon.

89—Colton's Nervine Strengthening Bitters***
No description available. J. W. Colton, 53 Vesey Street, **New** York. Circa. 1875.

90—Columbo Peptic Bitters
No description available.
CORDIAL BITTERS—See Brown Curtis.

91—Columbo Tonic Bitters
No description available.

92—Clayton & Russell's Stomach Bitters
No description available.
CLOVER BITTERS—See Ryder.

93—Congress Bitters***
Square emerald green. Tapered shoulder. Sunken panels **on** four sides. Marked: "Congress Bitters." Reverse: "William Allen / Fort Edward, N. Y." 10½ x 3½ x 2. Circa. 1865.
93-a—Varation: In bluish aqua.
94-b—Variation: Rectangular green. Three depressed panels. One side plain. Beveled corners. Double collared mouth. 10 in. tall. Marked as above.
94-c—Variation: In pint size.
Note: Paper label on Congress Bitters bottle reads: "1865—Congress Bitters. A Superior tonic, William Allen, manufacturer and proprietor. Wells, Richardson & Co., Wholesale agents, Burlington, Vt."

94—Constitution Bitters****
Round aqua. With decorative scalloped raised ornamentation around shoulders and with four pendants reached to and over base, dividing body into four panels. Marked: "Constitution (one vertical line) / "Bitters" (one vertical line) and "Put up by / B. M. & EAW & CO. / New York" in three vertical lines in panel. Domed shoulder. Tapered flanged mouth. Shallow dome in base. Extended base. 8½ x 4.

95—Constitution Bitters***
Rectangular green. Marked: "Constitution Bitters / Seward & Bentley / Buffalo, N. Y." 9½ x 3½ x 2½.

96—Constitutional Bitters***
Rectangular amber. About ¾ quart. Sloped shoulders. Ring at base of convex neck. Marked: "Constitutional" (semi circle) / "Beverage" on shoulder. Below sunken panel with rolled ribbon at top and bottom. Reverse plain. On sides: "W. Olmstead & Co." and "New York." 10 x 3¾ x 2¼.
Note: While this bottle is not specifically marked as "Bitters," advertising matter referred to the contents as "Constitutional Bitters."

— **GROUP B: MEDICINALS**

Bottles number 100 (Crimean Bitters) and number 105 (Dandelion Bitters).

97—Cooley's Anti Dyspeptic or Jaundice Bitters****
Round aqua. Flask shape. Panelled shoulder. Straight neck. Tapered flanged applied mouth. Marked: "Cooley's / Anti-Dyspeptic / or / Jaundice / Bitters," six lines in ornamental face panel. 6¼ x 2¾.

98—Dr. Copp's White Mountain Bitters***
No description available. Made by Ring's Ambrosia Co., Wilton, N. H.

99—Crescent Tonic Bitters
No description available.

100—Crimean Bitters****
Square golden amber. Columned edges. Square sloped roof with diamond motif in each panel. Square sunken face panels. About ¾ quart. Collared mouth. Marked: "Romaine's Crimean Bitters / Patent 1863" near base, and in vertical line on one face "Crimean Bitters."
100-a—Variation: Square dark amber. Lettering at bottom of each panel: "W. C. Hilton & Co. / Romaine's Crimean Bitters / Patd. 1863." Arrow or spear motif in panels above shoulders. Corners with columns in panels.
100-b—Variations in shades of amber.

101—Curacoa Bitters
No description available. See also Von Hopf.

102—Curtis Cordial Calisaya—Great Stomach Bitters***
Round amber. Marked: "Curtis Cordial Calisaya / The Great Stomach Bitters / 1866." 11¾ x 2¾.

103—Curtis & Perkins Wild Cherry Bitters***
Round aqua. About pint. Collared mouth. Scarred base. Marked: "Curtis & Perkins / Wild Cherry / Bitters" in three vertical lines.
103-a—Variation: In larger size, about ¾ quart.

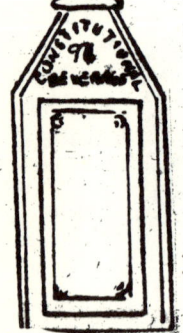

104—Dam (I) Ana Gentian Bitters
No description available.

105—Dandelion Blood Bitters
No description available.
DANDELION BITTERS—See Hamilton, Jerome, Parmalee, Sulphur, Tilton.

106—Deutscher Aromatique Bitters*
Rectangular clear. Straight neck. Ringed mouth. About ¾ quart. Identified by label which reads: "Deutscher Aromatique Feinster Magenbitter / Paris, London, New York / Dr. Bergman."

107—Dewey's Manila Bitters*
Rectangular clear. Straight neck. Ringed mouth. About ¾ quart. Identified by label which reads: "Dewey's Manila (portrait of Admiral Dewey) Bitters" over picture of battleship.

108—De Witt's Stomach Bitters*
Square amber. Rounded corners. Domed shoulder. Tapered neck. Flanged mouth. Domed base. Identified by label. 9 x 2¾.

— GROUP B: MEDICINALS

109—Diamond's Improved Swedish Blood Bitters***
Square amber. Panelled body. Detailed description not available. Origin: Buffalo, N. Y.

110—Didier's Stomach Bitters
No description available.

111—Dingen's Napoleon Cocktail Bitters*****
Greenish aqua. Heavy glass Shape of drum. 4¾ in. neck. Long collared mouth. Bulged neck. Drum 5¾ in. in diameter and 2¾ in. thick. Base extended 3¾ x 2¼ with rounded ends. Marked: "Dingen's Napoleon Cocktail Bitters," on rim of drum. Reverse: "Dingen Brothers, Buffalo, N. Y." Heighth, 10 in. Circa. 1835.
111-a—Variation: In brilliant olive green. With many bubbles in glass.
111-b—Variation: In clear glass.

112—Doty's Mandrake Bitters**
Amber. About ¾ quart. Collared mouth. Marked: "Doty's Mandrake Bitters / C. Doty & Co. / Bradford.
112-a—Variation: Marked: "C. C. Doty & Co., Bradford, Vt." Circa. 1865. Bottle attributed to Stoddard.

113—Dozier's Apple Bitters
No description available.

114—Doyle's Hop Bitters**
Square amber. With roofed shoulders About ¾ quart. Rounded corners. Arch-top panels on each side. Four triangular roof panels. Straight neck. Tapered flanged and ringed mouth. Flat base with dome. Marked in four roof panels: "Doyle's / Hop / Bitters / 1 72." In one face panel hop branch with one large leaf with five points and below two hop flowers, one larger than the other. 9½ x 2½.
114-a—Variation: Hop flowers of about the same size. 2⅝ in. square. In base a ring with "C & Co." (Mark of Cunninghams, Pittsburgh.)
114-b—Variation: Flat base with dome and large four-pointed star. Hop blossoms of nearly same size with one leaf.
114-c—Variation: Four leaves with smaller blossoms. Domed base with "L." Lancaster)
114-d—Variation: Four leaves on one branch and two flowers one much larger than other. Domed base with two parallel pointed lines.
114-e—Variation: One leaf with two connected flowers. Domed base with "E".
114-f—Variation: Four leaves with two connected flowers.
Note: Other variations in arrangement of hop design, in size of letters and in a great variety of base marks. A total of fourteen variants of this bottle have been identified. Made in many factories. Also variations in color. A label from an early bottle reads: "Hop Bitters Manufacturing Co., Rochester, N. Y., Toronto, Ont., London, England."

115—Drake's Bitters
A non-proprietary title used by many independent makers after a formula commonly found in druggists' recipe books. Bottles in imitation of Drake's Plantation Bitters were supplied by druggists' supply houses, but without markings in glass.

Bottles number 85 (Clark's Sherry Wine Bitters) and number 111 (Dinger's Cocktail Bitters).

— GROUP B: MEDICINALS 197

Eight variations in the decorative design on the bottles for Doyle's Hop Bitters (114) in actual size. Fourteen variants of this design have been identified. These nuemerous moulds indicate graphically the number of glass factories required to supply the demand for mass production of bitters.

GRAND OLD AMERICAN BOTTLES

116—Drake's Plantation Bitters**
Square brown-amber. Log Cabin shape. Sloping roof with shingles. Rounded corners. Straight neck. Tapered flanged mouth. Domed base. About quart. Two sides with panels with four horizontal logs above. Marked in roof panel: "S. T. Drake / 1860 / Plantation / X / Bitters." Reverse: "Patented 1862." 10 x 2¾.
116-a—Variation: Golden amber. Vertical shingle lines. Round corners. Faint lettering without the "X". Six logs above face panels.
116-b—Variation: In olive amber.
116-c—Variation: Dark amber with "Drake's" in curved line.
117-d—Variation: Dark amber. Six logs over panels. Scroll decorations at either side of "Drake's".
116-e—Variation: Logs squared at corners instead of rounded. Many other variations in color, size of lettering and base marks. Produced in many factories, including Whitney.

117—Drake's Sazerac Bitters***
No description available. Circa. 1870.
DR. J. BOVEE DOD'S IMPERIAL WINE BITTERS—See Imperial.

118—Druid Bitters****
Rectangular dark amber. About ¾ quart. Collared mouth. Marked: "B. T. / 1866 / Smith's Druid Bitters" in three lines. 9½ in. high.
118-a—Variation: Marked: "B. T. / 1865 / Smith's Druid Bitters."
Other variations in color.

119—Eagle Angostura Bark Bitters*
Globe shape dark amber. One-inch panel at greatest circumference of globe. On neck each of two main panels has four arched sub-panels. Near base sunken circle. Marked: "Patented Feb. 4th, 1902 / Eagle Angostura Bark Bitters Eagle Liquor Distillers." 7 x 11 with 3½ in. neck.
EAST INDIA BITTERS—See Kennedy.
ECLIPSE BITTERS—See Greer.

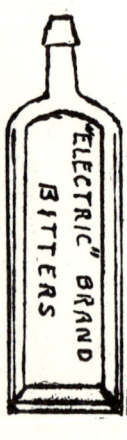

120—E. Z. Laxative Bitters
No description available.
EILER'S BITTERS—See American Life.

121—Electric Brand Bitters**
Square amber. Two sunken panels on faces. Two sides plain. About pint. Domed shoulder. Collared mouth. Marked: "Electric Bitters" in one vertical line. Reverse: "H. E. Bucklen & Co., Chicago."
121-a—Variation: Square golden amber. Rounded shoulders. Tapered flanged mouth. Tapered neck. Beveled edges. Marked: "Electric Brand / Bitters" in two vertical lines in face panel. Reverse: "H. E. Bucklen & Co. / Chicago, Ill." 8½ x 2¼.
121-b—Variation: Square amber. Domed shoulder. Tapered neck. Tapered fllanged mouth. Round corners. Diagonal mould. Four arch-top panels. Marked: "Electric Brand / Bitters" in two vertical lines. Reverse: Same. 8½ x 2⅜.

GROUP B: MEDICINALS

22—English Female Bitters
No description available. Circa. 1870.

23—Eureka Stomach Bitters
No description available.

24—Evans' Quinine Bitters
No description available.

25—Excelsior Herb Bitters***
Rectangular amber. Beveled corners. About ¾ quart. Flanged mouth. Tapered or roofed shoulders. Heavy ring at base of neck. Indented panels. Marked: "Excelsior / Herb Bitters" in two curved lines on shoulder. In two side panels: "J. V. Mattison" and "Washington, N. J." 10 x 3 x 2.

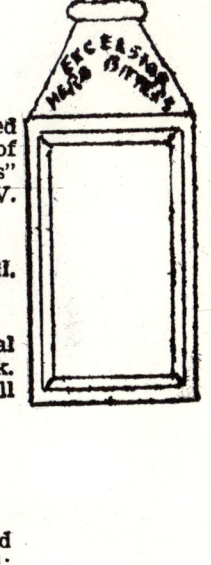

26—Fairbanks Kidney and Liver Bitters*
No description available. T. Fairbanks & Co., Chicago, Ill. After 1906.

27—Favorite Bitters***
Dark amber barrel shape. Pint. Collared mouth. Spiral ribbing. Marked: "Pat. Applied For" in one line on neck. Identified by label which reads: "Favorite Bitters / Powell & Stuthenroth."

FAMOUS WEINER BITTERS—See Weiner.

28—Felsina Bitters
No description available. The Nectar Co.

29—Fenner's Capitol Bitters**
Rectangular aqua. Beveled corners. Domed shoulder. Tapered neck. Flanged mouth. Heavy flat scarred base. Marked: Capitol Bitters" in two vertical lines in beveled arch-top panel in half-inch letters. Reverse plain. In two side panels: "Dr. M. M. Fenner's" and "Fredonia, N. Y." 10⅜ x 3⅜ x 2.

30—Fernet-Bascal Bitters
No description available. Basilea-Calendra Co.

31—Fernet-Branca Bitters
No description available. Maicaltesi, D. & Co.

32—Fernet Extra Bitters
No description available. Bertin & Lepori.

33—Fernet—1—Extra Bitters
No description available. Cordial Panna Co.

34—Fernet-Lenora Bitters
No description available. Liebenthal Bros. & Co.

35—Fernet-Milano Bitters
No description available. Four different makers.

36—Fernet-Universal Bitters
No description available. Venetian Distilling Co.

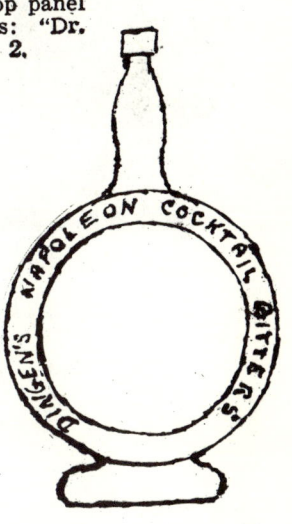

37—Fernet-Carlisi-Fernet Bitters
No description available.

38—Fernet-Chica-Citro Bitters
No description available.

39—Fernet-China-Citro Bitters
No description available.

Bottles number 127 (Favorite Bitters) and number 151 (Ben Franklin Bitters).

— GROUP B: MEDICINALS

140—Fernet-Chica-Carlisi Tonic Bitters
No description available.
141—Ferro-China Bitters
No description available. Six different makers.
142—Ferro-Quina Bitters
No description available.
Note: Numbers 130 to 142 inclusive are identified by markings in the glass and by labels, but the bottles have little collector interest.
143—Dr. Fisch's Bitters
Clear golden amber. Shape of fish. About ¾ quart. Imbricated scales and neck protruded from mouth of fish. Collared mouth. Marked: "Dr. Fish's Bitters" in quarter circle upcurved around eye. Reverse: "H. Ware—Patented 1866." Attributed to Lancaster.
143-a—Variations: In shades of amber.
144—The Fish Bitters****
Dr. amber. Shape of fish. Marked: "The Fish Bitters" in quarter circle around eye. Reverse: "W. H. Ware / Patented 1866." Lettering smaller than 143 and reverse wording repeated in base. Scales rounded and in bolder relief than 143. Fins also different. Heighth 11½ in.
144-a—Variation: In clear glass.
144-b—Variation: In dark green glass.
144-c—Variation: With larger letters.
144-d—Variation: In golden amber
145—Fletcher's Cocktail Bitters*
Round amber Long bulged neck. Flanged mouth with ring. Identified by label which reads: "Fletcher's Cocktail Bitters" with picture of rooster.
146—Fletcher's Celebrated Stomach Bitters*
Square amber. Tapered neck. Flanged mouth. Pint. Identified by label which reads: "Fletcher's Celebrated Stomach Bitters" and has picture of St. George and Dragon.
146-a—Variation: Same in quart size.
147—Foerster's Teutonic Bitters****
Rare amber handled jug. Push-up base. Ring neck. Applied and folded handle. Marked: "Fletcher's" in semi-circle over "Bitters" and "Chicago." 7 x 5 x 3½.
148—Folger's Aromatic Bitters
No description available.
149—Forestine Blood Bitters***
No description available. A. Bloomingdale, Gloversville, N. Y. Circa. 1890.
150—Ben Franklin Temperance Bitters****
No description available.
151—Ben Franklin Bitters****
Barrel shape dark amber. About ¾ quart. Marked: "Ben Franklin Bitters" below bust of Franklin. Reverse: "Poor Richard's Tonic" in rectangle. Pinched label runing at up-angle with "Prove all things." Body tapered from base to domed shoulder. Five hoops below plain belt and seven hoops

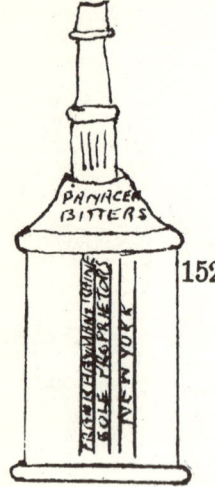

above. Large ring at base of neck. Applied ringed and flanged mouth.
151-a—Variation: In light green glass. Marked: Bust of Franklin and "Ben Franklin Bitters." Reverse: "Poor Richard's Tonic" in depressed panel. On label "Prove all Things." E. Mansfield Rowland, Props. / New Haven, Conn."
151-b—Variation: Marked: G. M. Rowland, New Haven, Conn., Distributors.
151-c—Variations: In shades of amber.

152—Sol Franck's Panacea Bitters**
Round amber. Convex shoulder. Neck panelled to ring then flared to straight mouth. Extended base. Marked: "Sol Franck's / Panacea Bitters" in horizontal line at base of neck. "Frank Hayman & Rhine, Sole Proprietors, New York" vertically on flat ribs or panels of bodys. 10 x 3¼.
152-a—Variation: With marking on convex shoulder: "Sol / Franck's" in two lines; Reverse: "Panacea / Bitters."
152-b—Variations: In shades of amber.
Note: This bottle often referred to as "The Lighthouse Bitters" bottle.

153—Fox & Co. Hygeia Bitters**
Square amber. Heavy collared mouth. Marked: "Fox & Co.'" in vertical line in panel. Reverse: "Hygeia Bitters," in vertical line in panel. Other sides plain. In base "L. & W." Height 9¼ in.

154—Frazier's Root Bitters
No description available.

155—Garry Owen Strengthening Bitters**
No description available. New Orleans, La. Circa. 1869.

156—Gentian Bitters
No description available. See also Damiana.

157—German Hop Bitters
No description available.

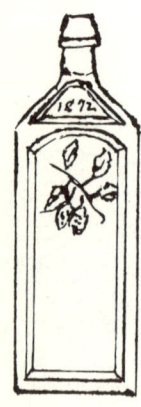

158—German Stomach Bitters
No description available.
German Bitters—See Damiana, Hop, Stomach, Hamilton, Hoofland, Karle, Petzold, Schroeder, VonHumboldt.

159—Germania Bitters**
Rectangular amber. Marked: Wm. C. Oestling / Germania Bitters." 9 x 2¾ x 3¼.

160—Germania Herb, Root and Fruit Tonic Bitters
No description available.

161—Dr. Gerrish's Standard Bitters**
No description available.

162—Ginseng Bitters
No description available. McDowell's Ginseng Bitters, McDowell Ginseng Gardens.

163—The Globe Tonic Bitters**
Square light amber. Four arched panels each of which is plain at base. Rounded corners (pillared). Domed shoulder. Tapered neck. Tapered flanged mouth. Domed base. Marked: "The Globe / Tonic" in two vertical lines of ½ in. letters in

— GROUP B: MEDICINALS

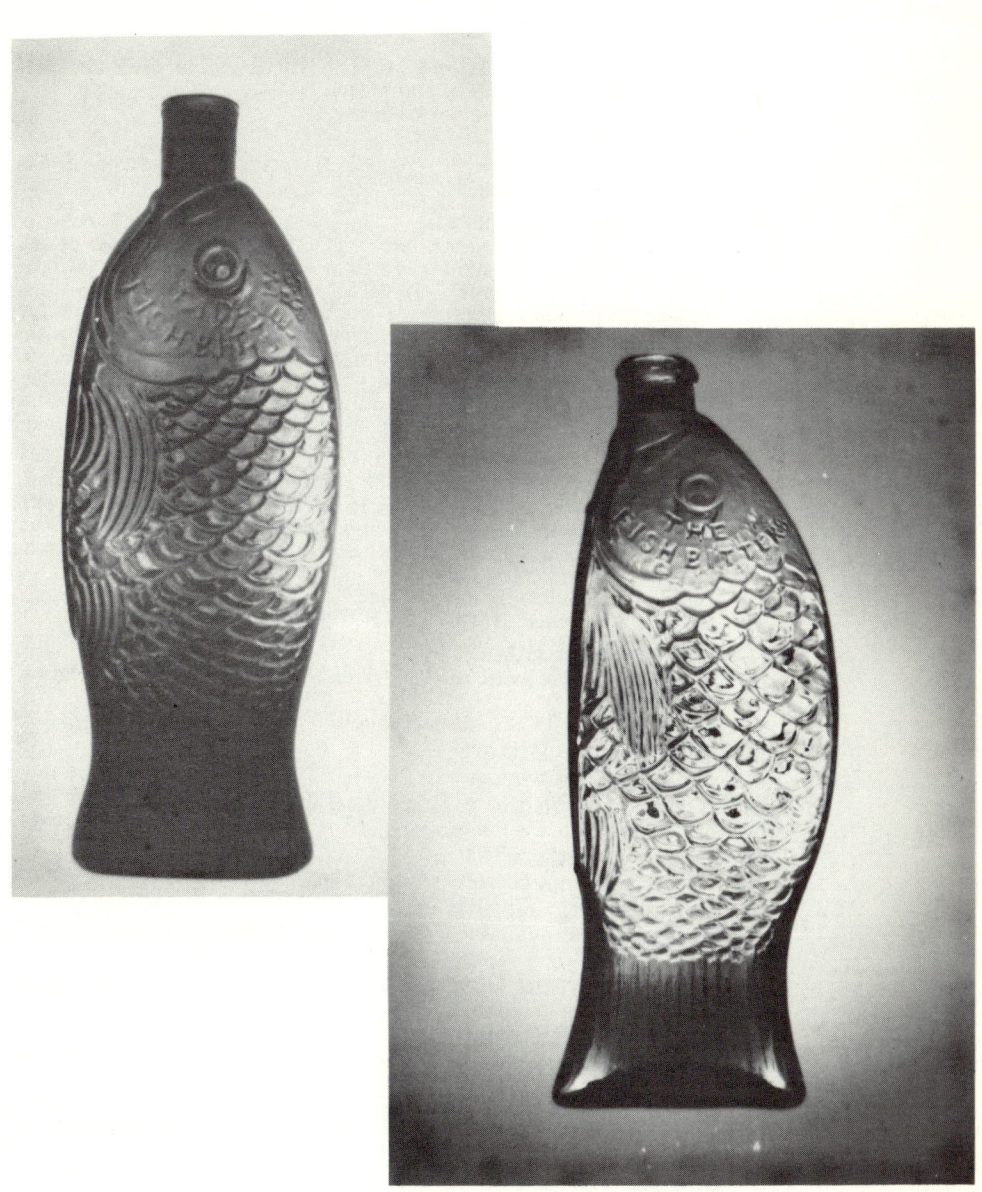

Bottles number 143 (Dr. Fish Bitters) and number 144 (The Fish Bitters).

GRAND OLD AMERICAN BOTTLES

panel. Reverse: "Bitters" in one vertical line of ⅝ in letters. Other two panels plain. 9¾ x 2¾.
163-a—Variation: In dark amber.

164—Globe Bitters
Round amber. Marked: "Globe Bitters / Byrne Bros. & Co. / New York." 10¼ x 3½.

165—Goff's Herb Bitters**
Rectangular aqua. Marked: "S. B. Goff's" in side panel, and "Herb Bitters" in one vertical line in face panel. "Camden, N. J." in side panel. Reverse plain.
165-a—Variation: Miniature or sample bottle. Rectangular aqua. Scarred base. Straight neck. Square flanged mouth. Three sides with panels; other side plain. Marked: "S. B. Goff's one vertical line in side panel; "Herb Bitters," one vertical line in face panel; "Camden, N. J.", one vertical line in side panel. 4 x 1¼ x ⅝.

166—Goff's Bitters
Clear rectangular with one side curved. Two corners beveled. Scarred base with "L." Straight neck. Double collared mouth. Marked: "Goff's Bitters" in over vertical line in fancy italic letters. 5¼ x 2 x 1. S. B. Goff Sons Co., Camden, N. J. Circa. 1872 and later.
166-a—Variation: In larger size.
GOLDEN EAGLE BITTERS—See Tutt.

167—Golden Seal Bitters***
No description available. Golden Seal Bitters Co., Holland, Mich.
GOLDEN BITTERS—See Hubbell

168—Good Hope Bitters
No description available.

169—Old Dr. Goodhue's Root and Herb Bitters***
No description available.

170—Gould's Bitters***
No description available. Circa. 1861.

171—Graefenberg Health Bitters***
No description available. Graefenberg & Co., New York. Circa. 1849.

172—Graham Brand Orange Bitters
No description available.

172 (2) Granger Bitters***
Half pint amber flask. Horizontal anchor on face. Scarred base. Ribboned sides. Double collared neck. Identified by label which reads: "Celebrated Granger Bitters, etc. Boykin, Carmer & Co., Proprietors, 11 and 13 Liberty St., Baltimore, M. D.

173—Graves' Bitters
No description available.

174—Gray Jacket Bitters****
No description available. Circa. 1861.
Note: A brand of bitters issued to appeal to sales in the Confederate States of America.

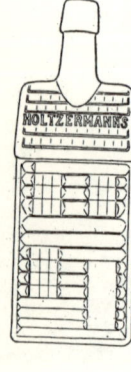

—.GROUP B: MEDICINALS
205

175—Dr. Gray's Tonic Bitters
No description available.
Grecian Bend Bitters—See Carey.

176—Greeley's Bourbon Whiskey Bitters***
Dark amber barrel shape. About ¾ quart. Ten graduated rings (hoops) at top and bottom of plain band at middle of body. Flat base. Short straight neck. Square flanged mouth. Marked: "Greeley's," repeated in two vertical lines on either side of "Bourbon Whiskey" (curved) / Bitters." 9⅛ x 3¼. Circa. 1869.
176-a—Variation: Same bottle in dense amethyst, reddish amethyst, green, amber, puce, light puce and golden amber.

177—Greeley's Bitters***
Golden amber barrel shape. About ¾ quart. Square flanged mouth. Plain band around middle of body; hoops above and below. Marked: "Greeley's / Bitters" in large letters in semicircle on plain band. Barrel of same description as No. 176.
177-a—Variations: In many shades of amber and other colors. Note: Probably a variation of the Greeley's Bourbon Whiskey bottles, issued after public had refused to accept a brand openly labeled as "whiskey."

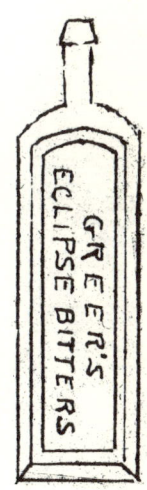

178—Green's Oxygenated Bitters***
Description not available. Circa. 1868.

179—Greer's Eclipse Bitters***
Square amber. One arch-top beveled panel. Other sides plain. Domed shoulder. Straight neck. Tapered flanged mouth. Marked: "Greer's / Eclipse Bitters" in two vertical lines in panel. 8½ x 2¼.

180—Griffith's Opera Bitters****
No description available. Circa. 1870.

181—Dr. Greussie-Altherr's Krauter Bitters*
Round amber. Long bulged neck. Square ringed mouth. About quart. Identified by label which reads: "Dr. Greussie-Altherr's Krauter Bitter" over white cross in shield.
181-a—Variation: In clear glass.

182—Guarana Bitters
Description not available. Circa. 1870.

183—Hagen's Bitters***
Triangular amber. Marked: "Hagen's / Bitters" in two lines. Circa. 1868. Peter Hagen's Liquors, 134 W. 19th St., New York City.

184—Hale's Bitters***
Smoked amber barrel shape. About pint. Marked: "Hale's Bitters."

185—Hall's Bitters***
Amber barrel shape. About ¾ quart. Sets of four hoops at shoulder and base, and two sets of three hoops around body. Square flanged mouth. Short straight neck. Marked: "Hall's Bitters" in circle on face of body; "E. E. Hall, New Haven" near shoulder; "Established 1842" near base. 9 x 3.
185-a—Variation: In golden amber, dark amber, puce and other colors. Some variations in base form in earlier bottles.

186—Hamburg Stomach Bitters
No description available. Weidman Co., Cleveland, Ohio. Circa. 1910.

187—Dr. Hardy's Bottle Bitters
No description available. Cornish Flat, N. H. Circa. 1855.

187 (2)—Dr. Hardy's Cathartic Elect'y or Tonic Bitters
No description available. J. Bush & Co., Cornish Flat, N. H. Circa 1870.

188—Dr. Manly Hardy's Genuine Jaundice Bitters***
Clear rectangular. One-inch champfered corners. Flat base heavily pontil scarred. Domed shoulder. Short straight neck. Tapered flanged mouth applied. Diagonal mould. Rough, bubbly and uneven glass from wooden mould. Marked: "Dr. / Manly Hardy's" in two vertical lines on face. Reverse: "Jaundice / Bitters" in two vertical lines. On two sides: "Genuine" and "Bangor, Me." 6⅞ x 2¼.

189—Hart's Stomach Bitters
No description available. Circa. 1870.

190—Hartshorn's Bitters
No description available. Boston. Circa. 1868.

191—Hart Wild Cherry Bitters
No description available.

192—Hamilton German Bitters*
Square light blue. Beveled corners. Straight neck. Square flanged mouth. Pint. Scarred base. Identified by label. Bottle from Roulette, Pa., factory.

193—Dr. Harter's Wild Cherry Bitters***
Rectangular amber. Indented base with "Design Patented." Sides concaved. Tapered flanged mouth. Marked: "Dr. Harter's / Wild Cherry / Bitters / St. Louis" in four lines in lower half of arch-top face panel. 7⅝ x 4¼ x 2⅜.
193-a—Variations: Pint and half-pint sizes.
193b—Variation: Bottle with "Dayton, Ohio" instead of "St. Louis."

194—Dr. Harter's Cherry Bitters***
Flask shape aqua. Marke "Dr. Harter's Cherry Bitters, St. Louis, Mo."
HAWKEYE BITTERS—See Berg.

195—Harvey's Prairie Bitters****
Square amber. Balustraded corners. Domed shoulder with lattice. Scarred base. Irregular and crooked. Marked: "Harvey's / Prairie / Bitters" in three vertical lines on three sides.
HEALTH BITTERS—See Graefenberg.

196—H. P. Herb Wild Cherry Bitters***
Amber cabin chape. About quart. Marked: "H. P. Herb Wild Cherry Bitters" / "Reading, Pa." in one panel with picture of tree. 8½ x 3.
196-a—Variation: In green glass.
196-b—Variations: In golden amber and other shades.
HERB BITTERS—See Caldwell, Excelsior, Germania, Goff, Goodhue, Stomach, Langley, Mishler, Moore, Mountain.

GROUP B: MEDICINALS

197—Herb Stomach Bitters
No description available.

198—Heublein's Calisaya Bitters
No description available.

199—W. C. Hibbard's Bitters
No description available. Circa. 1870.

200—Highland Bitters and Scot Tonic***
Olive green barrel shape. About ¾ quart. Flanged mouth. Marked: "Highland Bitters / and / Scot Tonic."
200-a—Variation: In amber.

201—Dr. Hoffmann's Golden Bitters
No description available.

202—Dr. Hoffmann's Stomach Bitters
Square amber. Tapered flanged mouth. Beveled corners. About quart. Identified by label which reads: "Dr. Hoffman's Celebrated Stomach Bitters" with picture of female driving chariot.

203—Hollier's Bitters***
Description not available. Auburn, N. Y. Bottle attributed to Clyde.

204—Holtzermann's Patent Stomach Bitters***
Smoked amber cabin shape. Four-sided roof. Bark on logs of cabin. Collared mouth. About ¾ quart. On one face three windows and a door; on two sides one window each; other side plain. Marked: "Holtzermann's" (semi-circle) Reverse: "Patent Stomach Bitters."
204-a—Variation: Golden amber. Two sides to roof. Logs without bark. Flanged mouth. Straight neck. Marked: "Holtzermann's" in horizontal line on roof, and below three bland windows and door. Reverse: "Patent Stomach Bitters" in three lines and below three paned windows and door. J. D. Holtzermann & Son, Piqua, Ohio. 9½ x 3¼ x 2¼.
204-b—Variations: In red amber and other shades.

205—Home Bitters****
Square bronze amber. Flat base with domed circle and four-pointed star. Beveled corners. Arch-top panels. Arched shoulder. Tapered flanged mouth. Mark: "Home Bitters" in vertical line in face panel. Reverse plain. In two side panels: "Jackson, Pfouts and Douglas / Proprietors" and "St. Louis, Mo." 8¾ x 2¾.

206—Home Stomach Bitters
No description available. "The Celebrated Home Stomach Bitters" by same makers as "Home Bitters."
HOP BITTERS—See German, Hops and Malt, Doyle, Iron, Malt and Parmelee.

207—Dr. Hopkins' Union Stomach Bitters***
Square greenish yellow. Marked: "Dr. A. S. Hopkins' Union Stomach Bitters / Hartford, Conn." 10 x 2¾.
207-a—Variation: Square yellow amber. Beveled corners. Straight neck. Tapered flanged mouth. Scarred base. Marked: "Dr. A. S. Hopkins / Union Stomach / Bitters" in three vertical lines in arch-top face panel. Other sides plain. 9½ x 2¾.
207-b—Variations: In shades of amber.

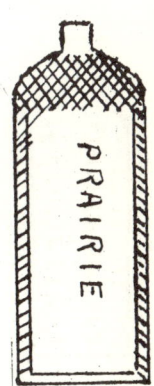

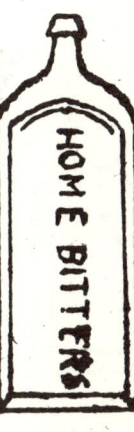

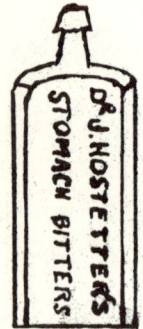

208—Hops and Malt Bitters***
Square amber. About ¾ quart. Four sunken panels on sides. Collared mouth. Marked: "Hops & Malt" above "Trade (sheaf of grain) Mark" / above "Bitters." Three panels without markings. On four shoulder panels "Hops and Malt" over Bitters."

209—Dr. Hortenback Stomach Bitters
No description available.

210—Hostetter's Bitters**
Square dark amber. Collared mouth. Straight neck. Slightly domed shoulder. Rounded corners. Dome in base. Marked: "Dr. J. Hostetter's / Stomach Bitters" in two vertical lines on one face. Marked in base "L. & W." 9 x 2¾.
210-a—Variation: Golden amber with ⅜ in. letters.
210-b—Variation: Smoky amber with ½ in. letters.
211-c—Variation: Dark amber with ½ in. letters and "S. McKee & Co." in base.
210-d—Variation: Golden amber with ¾ in. letters of different design. 8¾ x 2⅝.
210-e—Variation: Olive green. Flat scarred base. ⅜ in. letters. Tapered short neck. Flanged mouth. Crude and wavy glass from wooden mould. 8¾ x 2¾. Probably one of the earliest of Hostetter bottles.
210-f—Variation: With "Contents 14 oz." on one shoulder.
Note: Hostetter's was one of the most widely distributed brands of bitters, and from 1860 to the present has been widely circulated. Bottles were made in many factories, including Pittsburgh, Lancaster and Whitney. A complete list of variants would be too long to undertake here. Made by Hostetter & Smith, 36 Dey St., New York.

211—Hoofland's German Bitters
No description available.

212—Howe's Ague Cure and Tonic Bitters
No description available.

213—Hubbell's Golden Bitters***
Rectangular aqua. Roof shape shoulders. Inset straight neck. Flanged mouth with ring. Flat base with indented oval. Marked: "Golden / Bitters" in two horizontal lines in triangular roof panel. Reverse plain. In two side panels: "George C. Hubbell & Co." in vertical lines. 10 x 3¾ x 2¼.

214—Humulus Bitters***
Square amber. Campfered ⅜ in corners. Collared mouth. Three sides with long sunken panels. Other side plain for label. Marked: "Humulus / Bitters." 9¼ x 2⅝. Stewart D. Howe, Patent Medicines, 171 Canal Street, New York. Circa. 1873-1880.
HYGEIA BITTERS—See Fox.
HYLTON'S WILD CHERRY TONIC BITTERS—See Wild Cherry.
INDIAN BITTERS—See Brown, Stomach, Vegetable, Restorative, Pocanhontas, Pharazyn, Rivenburg, Solomon.

— GROUP B: MEDICINALS

215—Celebrated Indian Herb Bitters**** *
Amber in shape of standing Indian queen. About ¾ quart. Short plain neck protrudes from body dress. One arm across stomach; other arm extended downward to oval shield on which is marked: "Brown's / Celebrated / Indian Herb / Bitters" in three lines. Under flowing dress at rear of figure in three diagonally sloping lines: "Patented / Feb. 11 / 1868". Extended base. Flat scarred bottom. 12 x 3¼.
215-a—Variation: Amber. Marked: "Patented / February 11 / 1867."
215-b—Variation: In green, clear, very dark amber, yellow amber, puce-amber and aqua.
215-c—Variation: Clear, 10¼ in. high. With hair down back and large shield resting on ground at left; left hand on top of shield; right hand across breast holding sword perpendicular.
215-d—Variation: Golden amber. Shield on left side with marking "Mohawk Whiskey / Pure Rye." From same mould as bitters bottles.
215-e—Variation: Shield at figure's left shoulder. Right hand extended downward and holds a rod or arrow. Marked "H. Pharazyn." Also amber and color variations.
Note: Bottles attributed to Whitney, Glassboro. When in golden amber attributed to Agnew & Co., Pittsburgh.

216—Iron and Hop Bitters
No description available.

217—I. X. L. Bitters
No description available.

218—Imperial Wine Bitters***
Complete description lacking. Marked: "Dr. J. Bovee Dod's / Imperial Wine / Bitters" / Charles Widdifield & Co., 78 William Street, New York. Circa. 1861.

219—Indian Stomach Bitters
No description available.

220—Indian Vegetable Sarsaparilla Bitters***
Rectangular aqua. Collared neck. Scarred base. Marked: "George C. Goodwin" in one line on side; reverse side, "Boston." In two lines on face "Indian Vegetable / Sarsaparilla." On reverse face, "Bitters." 8¼ x 2¾ x 1⅞. Circa. 1845.

221—Indian Restorative Bitters***
Rectangular aqua. Beveled corners. About ¾ quart. Marked: "Dr. George Pierce's / Indian Restorative Bitters / Lowell / Mass." in vertical lines.

222—Isaacson, Seixas & Co. Bitters****
Rectangular amber. About ¾ quart. Collared mouth. Marked: Large "C" and "O" intertwined over eye, over "Bitters" and "Isaacson, Seixas & Co. / 66 and 68 Common Street."
IRON BITTERS—See Brown, Pabke, Parmelee.

223—Dr. Jacobs' Bitters***
Rectangular aqua. Scarred base. Marked: "Dr. Jacobs' Bitters / S. A. Spencer / New Haven, Ct." 8¼ x 3 x 1¾.

224—Jacob's Cabin Tonic Bitters***
Clear, shape of log cabin. About ¾ quart. Roof with square shingles. Beveled ends. In face of cabin three four-paned windows and arch-top door. Tooled mouth. Marked: "Jacob's Cabin Tonic Bitters" on shingled roof. Reverse of roof plain. On two sides: "Jacob's Cabin Bitters" and "Laboratory, Philadelphia. Heighth 7½ in.
224-a—Variation: In amethystine glass.
224-b—Variation: With slightly longer neck. Attributed to Whitney, Glassboro.

225—Dr. James Stomach Bitters
No description available.

226—Jenkins' Stomach Bitters
No description available.
JAUNDICE BITTERS—See Andrews, Atwood, Cooley, Kimball, Newton, Richardson.

227—Jerome's Dandelion Stomach Bitters
No description available.

228—Dr. Stephen Jewett's Celebrated Health Restoring Bitters**
Rectangular golden amber. Beveled corners. Pint. Folded mouth. Scarred base. Marked: "Dr. Stephen Jewett's / Celebrated / Health Restoring Bitters / Rindge, N. H." in four lines. Circa. 1830.
228-a—Variation: Rectangular aqua. Letters in three lines. Flanged mouth. Scarred base. Deeply beveled corners. 7½ x 3⅛ x 2⅛.
Attributed to Stoddard.

229—Johnson Calisaya Bitters**
Square claret color. About quart. Collared mouth. Marked: "Johnson Calisaya Bitters." Reverse: "Burlington, Vt." Lettering in two sides. Other sides plain.

230—Jones Stomach Bitters
No description available.

231—Kaiser Wilhelm Bitters**
Round amber. Domed shoulder. Bulged neck. Flanged and ringed mouth. Marked: "Kaiser Wilhelm (semi-circle) / Bitters Co. / Sandusky, O." On reverse on shoulder a raised horseshoe design with opening at top. 10 x 4.

232—Karle's German Stomach Bitters
No description available.

233—Karlsbader Stomach Bitters
No description available.

234—Dr. Kaufmann's Bitters
No description available.

235—S. Kaufmann's Celebrated Anti-Cholera Bitters***
Square puce. Marked: "S. Kaufmann's Celebrated Anti-Cholera Bitters / Patd. 1865." 10 x 2¾.

236—Kaufman' Sulphur Bitters**
No description available. A. P. Ordway & Co., New York.

— GROUP B: MEDICINALS

237—Kelly's Old Cabin Bitters**
Dense amber square cabin shape. About ¾ quart. Collared mouth. Marked: "Kelly's Old Cabin Bitters / Patented 1863."
237-a—Variations: In green and shades of amber.

238—Kelp's Bitters
No description available. Circa. 1861.

239—Kennedy's East India Bitters**
No description available.

240—Keystone Bitters**
Light clear amber, barrel shape. Long neck. Collared mouth. About ¾ quart. Marked: "Keystone / Bitters."

241—Kidder's Bitters**
Oval aqua. Square flanged mouth. Marked: "Kidder's Bitter's / Bailey & Co. / Lowell, Mass."

242—Kimball's Jaundice Bitters**
Olive amber. Marked: "Kimball's Jaundice Bitters / Troy, N. H."
242-a—Variation: Golden amber. Flattened corners. Sheared mouth.
Attributed to Stoddard.
KIDNEY AND LIVER BITTERS—See Babcock, Ben Hur, Fairbanks, Rex.

243—King's 25-Cent Bitters**
Rectangular light green. Beveled corners. Marked: "King's 25-Cent Bitters" in three lines. Reverse plain. King & Co., Rochester, N. Y. 6½ x 2¾.

244—Kingsley's Vegetable Bitters
No description available. Circa. 1868.

245—Koehler's Stomach Bitters
No description available.

246—Kola and Celery Bitters
No description available. Louisville, Ky.

247—Kossuth Bitters
No description available. E. & B. Jacobs, Shreveport, La. Circa. 1870.

248—Kreutzberger's Stomach Bitters
No description available.
KRAUTER BITTERS—See Greussie.

249—Krummel's Boonekamp Maag Bitters
No description available.

250—Kookman's Bitters**
No description available. Louisville, Ky.

251—Landsberg's Bitters**
Square golden amber. Long tapered neck. Two panels, other sides plain. Marked: "M. G. Landsberg's" in one line. Reverse: "Chicago" in one line. Blurred writing. Motifs above three panels like "V.R." Corners at top have cannon balls, crossed swords, battle axe and cannon. Thirteen stars around neck. Sides like "V.R." Base with hexagonal motif. 11 x 2¾.
251-a—Variations: In shades of amber.

212   GRAND OLD AMERICAN BOTTLES

Bottles number 74 (Andsberg's Century Bitters) and number 261 (Litthauer's Stomach Bitters).

— GROUP B: MEDICINALS 213

252—Lacour's Bitters—Sarsapariphere***
Cylindrical dark amber. Column or pillar shape. Hollow base. Three rings at base and one ring at shoulder. Arched panel on either side with two oblong panels between, one marked "Locour's Bitters" and the other "Sarsapariphere." About ¾ quart. Flanged mouth.

253—Dr. Lamb's Celery and Pepsin Tonic Bitters
No description available.
LANDENBERG'S BITTERS——See Century.

254—Dr. Langley's Root and Herb Bitters***
Round aqua. Scarred base. Folded mouth. Pint. Marked: "Dr. Langley's / Root and Herb / Bitters / 76 Union Street / Boston" in five horizontal lines.
254-a—Variation: With "99 Union Street" and numerals reversed.
254-b—Variation: Round amber. With "99 Union Street." 7 x 2¾.
254-c—Variation: In quart size.
J. C. Langley, Boston. Circa. 1850.

255—Lash's Bitters**
Square light yellow amber. Base depressed with diamond and "T." Crude ragged circle in base. Flanged mouth with ring. Marked: "Lash's Bitters" in large graduated letters on face. Reverse: "Natural Tonic Laxative." 9½ x 2¾.
255-a—Variation: Round clear. Flat scarred base with ring. Tapered flanged mouth. Marked: "Lash's / Bitters Co. / New York, Chicago, San Francisco." in four horizontal lines. 11 x 3.
255-a—Variation: In very dark amber square.

256—Lash's Kidney and Liver Bitters**
Square golden amber. Ring in base. Flanged mouth. Domed shoulders. Marked: "Lash's Kidney and Liver Bitters" in graduated letters on face. Reverse: "The Best Cathartic and Blood Purifier." 9 x 2⅜.

257—Lee's Celebrated Stomach Bitters
No description available.

258—Leipziger Magen Bitters***
Square white milk (opalescent) glass. Tapered from domed shoulder to base. Shape of square-face gin bottle. About ¾ quart. Identified by label which reads: "Leipziger Stomach Bitters / Magen Bitters / Wilhelm Hoffman / London, Paris, Berlin."

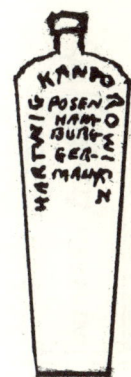

259—Lekko Stomach Bitters
No description available.

260—Liebieg Iron Bitters
No description available.

261—Litthauer Stomach Bitters***
Square milk glass. Tapered from domed shoulder to base. Shape of square-face gin bottle. Domed base. Straight neck. Flanged mouth. Marked: "Hartwig Kantorowicz" in horseshoe-shape; "Posen, Hamburg / Germany" in fi horizontal lines within horseshoe. Other sides plain. 9 x 2¾.

261-a—Variation: Miniature bottle in replica of above. 3¾x1¼.
LIVER BITTERS—See Babcock.
LONG LIFE BITTERS—See Bertram.

262—**Dr. Lovegood's Family Bitters*****
Square amber. Quart. Beveled corners. Collared mouth. Marked: "XX Lovegood's Family Bitters—Dr."

263—**Dr. Loveridge's Wahoo Bitters******
Square dense amber. About ¾ quart. Collared mouth. Marked: "L. Dexter Loveridge Wahoo Bitters." Reverse: same. One side blank. Another side has eagle in flight with arrow. On roof: "XXX Paid. D.W.D. 1863." Heighth, 9¾.

264—**Lutz Stomach Bitters**
No description available.

265—**Lyon Stomach Bitters**
No description available.

266—**Mackenzie Wild Cherry Bitters**
No description available. Dr. Mackenzie Medicine Co., Chicago.

267—**Magador Bitters**
No description available.

268—**Malakoff Bitters*****
No description available. A. Walz, New Orleans, La. Circa. 1875.
MAGEN BITTERS—See Boonekamp, Bergelt.

269—**Malt Bitters****
Round green. About ¾ quart. 8¼ high. Marked: in base "Malt Bitters Co., Boston, U. S. A."

270—**Malt and Hop Bitters**
No description available.

271—**Marks' Famous Stomach Bitters**
No description available.
MANDRAKE BITTERS—See Baxter, Doty, Parmelee.
MANILA BITTERS—See Dewey.

272—**Masten's Wine Bitters**
No description available. Charles J. Masten, Kingston, N. Y. Circa. 1865.

273—**Mishler's Herb Bitters*****
Rectangular aqua. Rounded shoulder. About half quart. Marked: "Mishler's Herb Bitters" vertically on two sides. Third side with series of small lines marked "Tables of Graduation," above "Dose," and below "Stoeckel's Grad. Pat. Feb. 11, '66." Fourth side plain. Three sides with sunken panels.
273-a—Variation: Square golden amber. Beveled corners. Rounded shoulder. Tapered flanged mouth with ring. Marked: "Mishler's Herb Bitters" in one vertical line in arch-top panel. Reverse: "Mishler Herb Bitters Co." in two vertical lines in panel. In another panel rule-like series of small lines extended over arch to shoulder and marked "Table Spoon Graduation" in vertical line. In base in circle: "Stoeckel's Grad. Pat. Feb. 6, '66." 9 x 2⅝.
273-b—Variations: In shades of amber.

— GROUP B: MEDICINALS

Bottles number 69 (Grecian Bend Bitters) and number 281 (Morning Star Bitters).

274—Melvin's Bitters***
No description available. Noah D. Melvin, West Plymouth, N. H. Circa. 1866.

275—Mexican Stomach Bitters
No description available.

276—Milburn's Kola and Celery Bitters
No description available.

277—Mitchell's Bitters
No description available. Invoices indicate that this brand was also sold in powder or dry form with directions to dissolve in whiskey or wine.

278—Miller Brand Bitters
No description available.

279—Moore's Herb Bitters
No description available. Moore Drug Co.

280—Mountain Herb and Root Bitters***
Square amber. Flat scarred base with indent. Beveled corners and base. Round shoulder. Flanged applied mouth. Marked: "Mountain / Herb and Root Bitters" in two vertical lines in arch-top panel. Reverse: "Dr. J. Henry Salisbury / Hinsdale, N. Y." in two vertical lines in panel. Third side panelled; one side plain. On three sides near base "I.S.P. / I.N. / 1869." 9¼ x 2⅜.

281—Morning Bitters****
Triangular smoky amber. One side ribbed on slant. Another side with lettering and ribbing at top. Third side with sunken panels. Long neck. About ¾ quart. Heighth 12¾ in. Marked: "Morning Bitters / Inceptum 1869," and "Patented 1869."

282—McKeever's Army Bitters****
Dense amber. Lower half round to represent drum, showing strings. Upper half with cannon balls. About ¾ quart. Collared mouth. Marked: "McKeever's Army Bitters" on broad band. Heighth 10½ in. Anna McKeever, Liquors, 296 W. 17th St., New York. Circa. 1860-1880.

McDOWELL'S GINSENG BITTERS—See Ginseng.

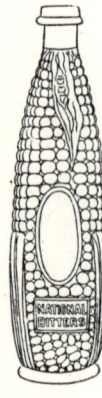

283—National Bitters***
Light clear amber in shape of ear of corn. About ¾ quart. Long leaf extended from base to neck. Two folded leaves half way up sides. Base extended in ring. On face oval blank panel below rectangular panel in which is marked "National / Bitters." In base "Patent 1867." Ring at base of neck. Flanged and ringed mouth. All-over kernels of corn. 12½ x 2¾. Walton & Co., Proprietors, 9 North 7th St., Philadelphia.

283-a—Variations: In clear, aqua, olive amber, red amber, dark amber and blue-aqua.

283-b—Variation: One without lettering, Heighth 10 in.

283-c—Variation: With large square label panel. Clear. 3¼ in. base.

283-d—Variation: Rectangular label panel. Small loop handle. Slightly ribbed from shoulder to neck. Heighth 8½ in. Dark green and clear.

— GROUP B: MEDICINALS

283-e—Variation: Plain section shorter and thicker.
Attributed to Whitney, Glassboro, and other factories.
NAPOLEON COCKTAIL BITTERS—See Dinger.
NATIONAL BITTERS—See Stoughton.

284—**National Tonic Bitters****
Golden amber square. Roped edges About ¾ quart. Collared mouth. Marked: "National / Tonic Bitters" in two vertical lines on two sides.
NEWPORT BITTERS—See Arbaugh.

285—**Newton's Jaundice Bitters**
No description available.

286—**Niagara Star Bitters**
Square amber. Roofed shoulder. Columned corners. Flat base with dome. Heavily indented panels. Two with arch-tops, two with square tops. Sloping four-sided roof with four arch-top panels, three with five-pointed ½ in. stars and one with "1864." Panel ribs extended on neck. Flanged and ringed mouth. Marked: "John W. Steele / Niagara (figure of star) / Bitters" in square-top face panel in two vertical lines. Reverse: "John W. Steele / Niagara Star Bitters" in two vertical lines. In arch-top panel an eagle facing left. 10 x 2⅞.
286-a—Variation: Square golden amber, marked same as above but with eagle facing to right and with thirteen stars in semi-circle above. 10 x 2¾.
286-b—Variations: In shades of amber.
Attributed to Lockport.

287—**Nightcap Bitters*****
Triangular clear. Beveled edges. Collared mouth. Marked: "Night Cap Bitters / Schmidlapp & Son. / Distillers / Cincinnati, O. / A Good Beverage." About ¾ quart.

288—**Obermuller's Bitters**
No description available.
OESTLING'S BITTERS—See Germania.

289—**O'Hara Bitters**
No description available.
OHIO BITTERS—See Sterki.

290—**Old Kentucky Bitters*****
Square amber. Domed base. Beveled corners. Flanged mouth. Wavy glass. Marked: "Old Kentucky Bitters" in two vertical lines in face panel. Reverse: "Brown & Wing," one vertical line. One side panel "Sole Proprietors" other plain. 9x3.
OLD CABIN BITTERS—See Kelly.

291—**O. K. Plantation Bitters*****
Dark amber trianguler. Two sides with seven vertical ¼ in. ribs. Other side with plain rectangular panel and smaller panel above with "O.K."—Plantation—1840," in three horizontal lines. On shoulder two panels with window lines; other panel with "Patented—1863." Heavy ring at base of convex neck. Tapered flanged mouth. Scarred base with dome and dimple. 11 x 3½.
O K BITTERS—See Drake.

292—Old Dr. Jacques' Stomach Bitters
No description available.

293—Old Continental Bitters
No description available.

294—Old Dominion Spice Bitters
No description available. The formula for this was common property and bitters under this name were manufactured and issued by many makers. Also known as Morning, Noon and Night Tonic.

295—Old Dr. Scroggins' Bitters
No description available.

296—Old Dr. Solomon's Indian Wine Bitters
No description available.

297—Old Sol Bitters
No description available.

298—Old Home Bitters***
Rectangular dense amber. About ¾ quart. Beveled edges. Collared mouth. Marked: "Old Home." Reverse plain. On sides: "Laughlin, Smith & Co." and "Wheeling, W. Va." All lettering in vertical lines in sunken panels.

299—Old Homestead Wild Cherry Bitters***
Square clear amber. In shape of log cabin. Four-sided roof with two sides with shingles indicated by lines. Marked: On plain roof side "Old / Homestead / Wild Cherry / Bitters" in four horizontal lines. Reverse: in plain panel between three rows of shingles "Patent." Round corners. One plain face panel. Reverse: Door with hinges and latch and five clapboards above. Two other sides with glassed window in each and three clapboards above. Flat base with dome. Straight short neck. Tapered flanged mouth. 9⅛ x 2⅞.
299-a—Variation: Olive amber. Shingles curved and more pronounced. All details sharper than 299. Sheared mouth. Hinges and latch on door show difference in design.
299-b—Variation: In ruby amber.
T. B. Slingerland & Co., Rome, N. Y. Circa. 1870.

300—Old Jamaica Bitters
Handled amber jug like Flora Temple flask. About ¾ quart. Identified by label. 9 in. high.

301—Old Sachem Bitters
Amber barrel shape. About ¾ quart. Flanged mouth. Short neck. Domed base. Marked: "Old Sachem (curved) Bitters / and / Wigwam Tonic" (curved) in horizontal lines on plain band about middle of body. Horizontal ribbing (hoops) above and below band. 9 x 3¼.
301-a—Variation: In red amber with smaller and more hoops.
301-b—Variation: In wine or puce color.
301-c—Variation: In golden amber.
OPERA BITTERS—See Griffith.

302—Opodeldoc Bitters
No description available. Attributed to Williamstown, N. J.

— GROUP B: MEDICINALS

303—Orange Bitters
No description available. Bettman—Johnson Co.

ORANGE GROVE BITTERS—See Baker.

304—Ordway's Sulphur Bitters
No description available. A. P. Ordway & Co., Boston, Mass. Circa. 1880.

OSWEGO BITTERS—See Austen.

305—Oxygenated Bitters
Bluish-aqua rectangular. Collared neck. Pontail scarred base. Marked: "Oxygenated Bitters—For Dyspepsia, Asthma and General Debility." 6¼ x 2¼ x 1¾.
305-a—Variation: Rectangular bluish-aqua. Marked: "Oxygenated" on one side; "Bitters" in one side. On face: For Dyspepsia, Asthma and General Debility. 7½ x 2⅝ x 1⅝. Dr. Wistar's. Sold by Seth W. Fowle & Co., Boston. Circa. 1885.

OXYGENATED BITTERS—See Green.

306—Ozark Stomach Bitters
No description available.

307—Pabke's Iron Bitters
No description available.

308—Pale Orange Bitters
No description available. Bettman-Johnson Co., Cincinnati Ohio. Circa. 1910.

309—Panama Bitters
No description available.

PANACEA BITTERS—See Franck.

310—Panknin's Hepatic Bitters
No description available. Charleston, N. C.

311—Parmelee's Mandrake and Dandelion Bitters
Twelve-sided aqua. Scarred base. Rounded shoulder. Straight neck. Flanged mouth. Identified by label. 6 x 2. Dansville N. Y. Circa. 1868.

312—Parmelee's Hop, Iron and Buchu Bitters
Square dark amber. Beveled edges. Domed shoulder. Flat base with dome. Tapered neck. Tapered flanged mouth. Marked: "E. M. Parmelee" and "Dansville, N. Y." in two vertical lines in two arch-top panels. Reverse plain. 8¼x2½.

313—Pepsin Bitters
No descriptin available. R. W. Davis Drug Co.

314—Pepsin Calisaya Bitters***
Rectangular emerald green. Beveled and fluted corners. Rounded shoulder. Flat base with rectangular indent. Tapered neck. Tapered flanged mouth. Marked: "Pepsin-Calisaya Bitters" in two vertical lines in panel. Reverse: "Dr. Russel Med. Co." in one vertical line in panel. Two arch-top plain face panels. 7¾ x 4¼ x 2½. See Augauer Bitters.

315—Pepsin Magen Bitters*
Round clear. Ringed base. Two graduated and heavy rings at base of neck. Bulged neck. Flanged and ringed mouth. About quart. Identified by label which reads: "Pepsin Magen Bitters / Stomach Bitters / Ludwig Steinwig." Picture of ship in oval medallion supported by lions and medals.
315-a—Variation: Another in pint size. Bettman-Johnson Co., Cincinnati, Ohio. Circa. 1910.

316—Pepsin Stomach Bitters
No description available.

317—Peptonic Stomach Bitters
No description available.

318—Peruvian King Bitters***
Triangular amber. Long SCM depression in base. On two shoulders: "O. H. P. Rose—Patd. June 21, '76". On one side: "O. H. P. Rose—EG—RI." Paper labels on three sides, reading, "O. H. P. Rose's Great Peruvian King Bitters, East Greenwich, R. I."

318 (2)—Peruvian Bitters
No description available.

319—Perry's Vegetable Bitters
No description available.

320—Peter Paul Stomach Bitters
No description available.

321—Dr. Petzold's Genuine German Bitters***
Oval dense amber. Collared mouth. Corrugated sides divided by broad central rib. About ¾ quart. Marked: "Dr. Petzold's Genuine German Bitters / Inco. 1862" in panels. Heighth 10½ in.

322—Phoenix Bitters****
Rectangular aqua. Beveled corners. Scarred base. Collared mouth. About half pint. Flat base with dome. Corners ¼ in. bevel. Rounded shoulder. Short straight neck. Square flanged mouth. Marked: "Phoenix / Bitters" in two vertical lines on face. Reverse: "John (curved) Moffatt" in two vertical lines and ½ in. letters. On sides "New York" and "Prince $1.00." 5⅝ x 2½ x 1¾.
322-a—In amber.
322-b—"John Moffatt" in one line and different style letters. Reverse: "Price One Dollar." Folded lip. Pontil scarred base.
322-c—Olive green. Scarred base. Tooled mouth. Marked: "Phoenix / Bitters" in two vertical lines on face. Reverse: "John Moffatt" in one vertical line. On one side "Price 1 Dollar." Diagonal mould.
322-d—Variations: In clear, light aqua, green-aqua and shades of amber.

PINEAPPLE BITTERS—See Bar Bottles for Bitters.

323—Pioneer Ginger Bitters
No description available.

PLANTATION BITTERS—See Drake and O. K.

— GROUP B: MEDICINALS

324—Pocahontas Bitters***
Aqua barrel shape. Marked: Original Pocahontas Bitters V. Ferguson." with lettering in circular depressed panel.

325—Pocahontas Indian Bitters***
Square amber shape of square-face gin bottle. Straight neck. Flanged mouth. Beveled corners. About quart Identified by label which reads: "Pocahontas Celebrated Indian Herb Stomach Bitters" with medallion with head of Indian girl.
325-a—Variation: Same in pint size.

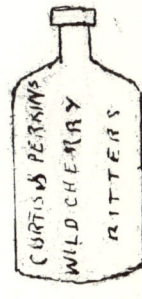

326—Poland Wine Bitters
No description available. Struzynski Bros. Chicago.
Note: One of the brands of Bitters issued to circumvent Prohibition laws.

327—Pollard's Bourbon Whiskey Bitters***
Dark amber barrel shape. Flat scarred base. Short straight neck. Square flanged mouth. Ten rings or hoops above and below central band on body. Marked: Bourbon Whiskey" (curved) / Bitters." About ¾ quart. Identified further by label showing girl in red skirt and blouse and marked "Pollard & Co., Boston, Mass."
322-a—Variations: In golden amber and other shades.
Note: Often confused with bottle for Greeley's Bourbon Whiskey Bitters.

328—Pierce's Bitters
No description available.

329—Polo Club Stomach Bitters
No description available.

330—Poor Man's Bitters
No description available.

331—Poor Richard's Bitters
No description available.

332—Porter's Bitters
No description available.

333—Prairie Flower Bitters
No description available.
PRAIRIE BITTERS—See Harvey.
PRAIRIE BITTERS—A name given by early plainsmen to a concoction of buffalo gall and water.

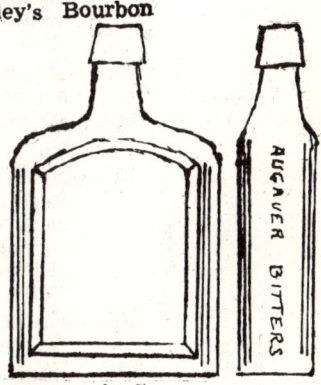

334—Price's Celebrated Aromatic Stomach and Tonic Bitters (IXI)***
No descrpition available. James W. Price & Co., New Orleans, La. Circa. 1870.

335—Prickley Ash Bitters
No description available. Prickly Ash Bitters Co., St. Louis and Kansas City, Mo.

336—Quaker Bitters
No description available.

337—Old Dr. Warren's Quaker Bitters****
Rectangular aqua. Marked: "Old Dr. Warren's / Quaker Bitters / Flint & Co. / Providence, R. I." 9¾ x 3⅜ x 2¼.

338—Dr. Flint's Quaker Bitters*
Rectangular aqua. Marked: "Dr. Flint's / Quaker Bitters."
Heighth 9 in.
338-a—Variation: Another style bottle.
QUININE BITTERS—See Evans.

339—Dr. Rattiger's Bitters
No description available.

340—Red Jacket Bitters*
Round amber. Marked: "Bennett, Pieters & Co. / Red Jacket Bitters." 9¾ x 2¾.

341—Reed's Bitters*
Round dense amber. About quart. Very long bulged neck. Collared mouth. Marked: "Reed's Bitters" in one vertical line in large letters.
341-a—Variation: Round golden amber. Long bulged neck. Square flanged and ringed mouth. Domed base. Marked: "Reed's / Bitters" in two vertical lines of 1 in. letters, and on shoulder, "Reed's (curved) Bitters." 12¼ x 3¼.

342—Rex Kidney and Liver Bitters**
Square amber. Rounded corners. About ¾ quart. Collared mouth. Marked: "Rex Kidney and Liver Bitters." Reverse: "Rex Bitters—Nothing Else."

343—Dr. Reusser's Allether Krauter Bitters
No description available.

344—Rheinstrom Stomach Bitters
No description available.

345—S. C. Richardson's Bitters
Rectangular aqua. Pint. With wide beveled corners. Scarred base. Flanged mouth. Marked: "S. C. Richardson's" in one vertical line. Reverse: "South Reading." On two sides, "Bitters" and "Mass." Heighth 7 in.
Tufts, Grosvenor & Co., New York. Circa. 1870.

346—Richardson's Jaundice Bitters
No description available.

347—Richardson's Sherry Wine Bitters
No description available.

348—Rising Sun Bitters*
Square amber. Marked: "Rising Sun Bitters." Reverse: "John C. Hurst, Philadelphia."

349—Rivaud's Cocktail Bitters
No description available.

350—Dr. Rivenburg's Indian Vegetable Bitters**
Rectangular aqua. About ¾ quart. Scarred base. Marked: "Dr. Rivenburg's / Indian Vegetable / Bitters / N.Y." in sunken panels.
ROMAINE'S BITTERS—See Crimean.

351—John Root's Bitters
No description available.

352—John Roach Bitters*
No description available. Bottle attributed to Lancaster.

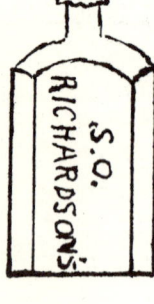

— GROUP B: MEDICINALS

Bottles number 338 (Quaker Bitters) and number 369 (Seaworth Bitters).

353—Roback Stomach Bitters***
Amber barrel shape. About ¾ quart. Collared mouth. Flat base. Straight neck. Marked: "Dr. C. W. Roback's Stomach Bitters / Cincinnati, Ohio" in lines around shoulder.
353-a—Variation: Light amber barrel shape. Straight neck. Applied tapered flanged mouth. Ten hoops above and below plain body band. Marked in body band: "Dr. C. W. Roback's (curved) / Stomach Bitters / Cincinnati, O." (curved). Reverse has hoops cut to six above and below band. 9½ x 3.
353-b—Variation: Another 9¼ x 3. Dark amber.
353-c—Variations: In shades of amber.
Circa. 1856.

354—Rohrer's Bitters
No description available.
ROOT BITTERS—See Frazier, Langley, etc.

355—Royal Pepsin Stomach Bitters***
Rectangular dark golden amber. Deep block design at top and bottom. Petal design on shoulder up to neck. Two rings on neck. Ringed mouth. Open cork with amber glass stopper. Marked: "Royal Pepsin / Stomach Bitters / L. A. Scharff, Sole Agents / St. Louis, U. S. A. and Canada" in five horizontal lines. Crown with lion at either side of lettering on face. 9¼ x 4¼.

356—Rush's Bitters**
Square amber. About ¾ quart. Double collared mouth. Straight neck. Marked: "Rush's Bitters / A. H. Flanders, M. D. / New York" in three depressed panels. Other side plain and flat. Height 9 in.
356-a—Variation: Rectangular amber. Marked as above in three sunken panels. 9 x 2⅝ x 3.

357—Russ's San Domingo Bitters****
Square olive green. Pint. Beveled corners. Collared mouth. Marked: "Russ's / San Domingo Bitters" in two vertical lines. Reverse: "New York" in one vertical line.
St. Domingo Manufacturing Co., Patent Medicines, 34 Dey Street, N. Y. Circa. 1865-1870.
357-a—Variation: With "St." instead of "San."

358—Dr. Ryder's Clover Bitters
Rectangular amber. Heavily rounded corners. Flat base with rectangular indent. Rounded shoulder. Straight neck. Flanged mouth. Marked: "Dr. Ryder's / Clover Bitters" in two vertical lines on face. Reverse plain. 7¼ x 3 x 1¾.

359—Saint Jacob's Bitters*
Square amber. About quart. Beveled corners. Rounded shoulder. Straight neck. Flanged mouth. Identified by label which reads: "Celebrated Saint Jacob's Bitters" with picture of ancient beside modern looking fireplace. Saint Jacob's Bitters Co. Cincinnati, Ohio.
359-a—Variation: In pint size.

360—Sarasina (Saracenia) Bitters
No description available.
San Domingo Bitters—See Russ.

GROUP B: MEDICINALS

361—Saracenia Life Bitters**
Square amber. About pint. Beveled corners. Marked: "Saracenia Life Bitters" with circle enclosing device of three kicking legs and feet. Reverse: "Tucker, Mobile."

362—Dr. Sawen's Life Invigorating Bitters***
Square golden amber. Beveled corners. Flat base with dome. Flanged mouth. Rounded shoulder. Four arch-top panels. "Dr. Sawen's / Life / Invigorating Bitters" in three vertical lines in face panel. Reverse plain. 10 x 2¾.
362-a—Variation: Square amber. Marked on reverse: "Utica, N.Y."
Circa. 1870.

363—Sazar Aromatic Bitters****
Round milk glass. Long bulged neck. About half pint. Collared mouth. Marked: "Sazar Aromatic Bitters" on base; P.H.D. & Co." in ring on shoulder. 12 x 3½ with 6 in. neck.
363-a—Variation: Marked in sunken circle and in ring on shoulder.

364—Sazerac Aromatic Bitters****
Round milk glass. Scarred base. Long 6 in. neck with bulge. Marked: "Sazerac Aromatic Bitters" in sunken circle on face, and "P.H.D. & Co." in ring on shoulder. Thick and uneven glass. 12 x 3½.
364-a—Variation: Round milk glass with longer neck than above. Marked: "Sazerac Aromatic Bitters" on base, and monogram of "P.H.D. & Co." on base.
NOTE: Sazerac Bitters were originally a flavoring bitters originating in New Orleans.

365—Scheetz's Celebrated Bitters Cordial***
Rectangular amber. Pint. Heavy tapered flanged mouth. Short straight neck. Domed shoulder. Marked: "Scheetz's / Celebrated Bitter Cordial" in two lines in panel. Reverse plain. Sides panelled.

366—Schier's Famous Bitters
No description available.

367—Schmidt's Celebrated Strengthening Bitters
No description available.

368—Schroeder's German Bitters**
Round amber. Long 6 in. neck. About pint. Marked: "Schroeder's Bitters / Louisville, Ky."

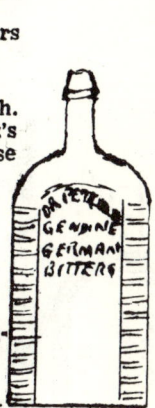

369—Seaworth Bitters****
Light amber shape of lighthouse. Plain base. About pint. Marked: "Seaworth Bitters Co. / Cape May, N. J., U. S. A."

370—W. F. Severa's Stomach Bitters***
Square amber. Beveled corners. Domed base. Rounded shoulder. Tapered neck. Square flanged mouth. Marked: "W. F. Severa" in one vertical line. Reverse: "Stomach Bitters" in one vertical line. 9¾ x 2¾. W. F. Severa Co., Cedar Rapids, Iowa.

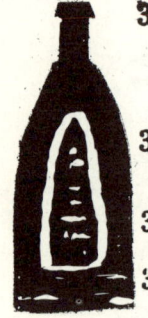

371—Sharp's Mountain Bitters***
Square dark amber. Beveled corners. About ¾ quart. Collared mouth. Depressed panels on three sides. Marked: Sharp's / Mountain / Bitters" in three vertical lines in face panel.

372—Shepard's Compound Wahoo Bitters
No description available. C. A. Shepard, Grand Rapids, Mich. Circa. 1870.

373—Sherman's Prickly Ash Bitters
No description available.

374—Dr. Siegel's Angostora Bitters
No description available.

375—Simon Aromatic Stomach Bitters
No description available.

376—Simon's Centennial Bitters****
In shape of bust of Washington. Aqua. Smooth slightly domed base, extended to form ring. Neck extends from top to head. Collared mouth. Marked: "Simon's Centennial Bitters" on band of circular base. In rear of base and on band: "Trade Mark." 10¼ x 5¼ across shoulders. Diameter of base 4⅛.
376-a—Variations: In amber, light green and blue-aqua. Attributed to Lyndeboro. Circa. 1875.
Note: Most duplicated or faked of all bitters bottles. Reproductions are easily detected because of faint lettering, colors and size, and the fact they have pontil scar in base.

377—Dr. Skinner's Celebrated 25-Cent Bitters****
Rectangular aqua. Pint. Beveled corners. Scarred base. Collared mouth. Marked: "Dr. Skinner's / Celebrated / 25-Cent Bitters / So. Reading, Mass." in four vertical lines on four sides.
SLINGERLAND'S BITTERS—See Old Homestead.

377 (2) Dr. Skinner's Sherry Wine Bitters
Aqua rectangular. Pint. Scarred base. Collared mouth. Wide-beveled corners. Marked: On one front panel: "Dr. Skinner's Sherry Wine Bitters"; on another bevel: "So. Reading Mass."
Note: This bottle identical with one for Black's Aromatic Bitters.

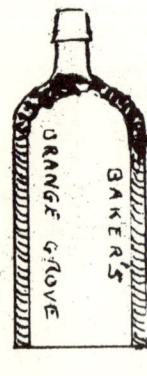

378—Smith's Bitters
No description available.

379—Smith's Vitalizing Bitters
No description available.
SMITH'S DRUID BITTERS—See Druid.

380—Snyder Bitters
No description available. J.H. Snyder Medicine Co., Jonesboro, Ark.

381—Sol Franck's Panacea Bitters****
Round amber. Shape of lighthouse. About pint. Marked: "Sol. Franck's Panacea Bitters" around neck. On body: "Franck, Mayman & Rhine, Sole Proprietors, N.Y."

— GROUP B: MEDICINALS

Many trade cards used to advertise bitters made a strong appeal for their use as medicines for juveniles, despite their high alcoholic content.

382—Solomon's Strengthening Invigorating Bitters***
Square blue. Beveled corners. About quart. Roofed shoulder. Heavy flanged mouth. Marked: "Solomon's Strengthening and Invigorating Bitters / Savannah / Georgia."

383—Spangerl's Bitters
No description available. C. O. Spangerl, Millerstown, Pa.

384—Snyder's Celebrated Bitter Cordial***
Square amber. Marked: "Snyder's Celebrated Bitter Cordial / H. G. Leisenring & Co., Philada." 9¾ x 2¾.

385—Old Dr. James M. Solomon's Indian Wine Bitters
No description available.

386—Sonoma Wine Bitters
No description available. C. A. Richards & Co., Boston, Mass. Circa. 1868.

387—Speer's Standard Wine Bitters
No description available. A. Speer, New York. Circa. 1865.

388—St. Nicholas Stomach Bitters
No description available.

389—Steinkonig's Stomach Bitters
No description available.

390—Dr. Sterki's Ohio Bitters
No description available. Dr. V. Sterki & Co., New Philadelphia, Ohio. Circa. 1900.
STOMACH BITTERS—See American, Augustiner, Belevedere, Bonekamp, Bokers, Bryne, Chasteney, DeWitt, Didier, Eureka, German, Hamburg, Hart, Herb, Hoffmann, Holtzermann, Home, Hopkins, Hortenback, Indian, Jenkins, Jerome, Jones, Karle, Karlsbader, Koehler, Kreuzberger, Lee, Lekko, Litthauer, Lutz, Lyon, Marks, Mexican, Izark Price, Rheinstrom, Roback, Royal, Pepsin, Simon, St. Nicholas, Steinkonig, Toneco, Union, Wallace, Warner, Westphalia, Wilder, Wingold.

391—Stomachic Bitters
No description available. A trade name used by Dyott.

392—Stifferine Bitters
No description available. "Doc. E. Ford's / Trade / Stifferine / Mark / Bitters. Richford Chemical Co., Richford, Vt."

393—Dr. Stoughten's National Bitters
Square amber. One side convex. Marked: "Dr. Stoughton's National Bitters / Patd. / Hamburg, Pa." 9¾ x 2¾ x 2½.

394—Stoughton Bitters
No description available. T. B. Slingerland & Co., Rome, N. Y. Circa. 1870.

395—Stoughton Bitters
Round amber. Tapered from domed shoulder to base. Long 5 in. bulged neck. Square flanged mouth. Flat base. Identified by label which reads: "Stoughton Bitters" over picture of female with amphora and male on tripod holding drinking bowl.
NOTE: The formula for Stoughton Bitters was common property and it is likely that many bitters of this name were issued

— GROUP B: MEDICINALS 229

by various concerns. However, the type of bottle seems to have been standardized and is listed in catalogues of druggists' supplies.

396—Suffolk Bitters****
Amber shape of pig. Marked: "Philbrook & Tucker / Boston / Suffolk Bitters." 10 in. long.

397—Sulphur Bitters
No description available. A. P. Ordway & Co., New York.

398—Dr. Kauffmann's Sulphur Bitters
Oval clear. Rounded shoulder. Straight neck. Ringed mouth. Marked: "A. P. Ordway && Co." in base. 8 x 3½ x 1½.

399—Sulphur Dandelion Bitters
No description available. Tilton.
SWEDISH BITTERS—See Diamond.

400—Dr. J. Sweet's Strengthening Bitters***
Square aqua. Pint. Beveled edges. Single ringed mouth. Marked: "Dr. J. Sweet's / Strengthening Bitters."

401—S & B Bitters*****
No description available. Such a marked bottle is known to have been made at Willington, Conn.
TEMPERANCE BITTERS—See Franklin, Whitwell.

402—Dr. Thompson's Wild Cherry Bitters**
Square clear. Round shoulder. Straight neck. Square flanged mouth. Broken ring on shoulder. Identified by label which reads: "Dr. Thompson's Wild Cherry (Head of deer) Bitters. Powerful Nervine and Tonic. Dr. Thompson Medicine Co., Cincinnati, Ohio."

403—Thorn's Hop Compound—The Best of All Bitters
No description available.

404—Dr. Thorne's Bitters
No description available. Brattleboro, Vt.

405—Tilton's Dandelion Bitters***
Red amber wicker covered. With glass medallion showing girl in white cap, red scarf and blue dress and lettering. Stopper attached by chain. About pint.

406—Tippecanoe Bitters**
Round golden amber. About ¾ quart. Very heavy flanged mouth. Marked: "Tippecanoe" in 1 in. letters in vertical line. Large canoe vertical. "H. B. Warner & Co." Long plain panel for label. In base: "Pat. Nov. 20, '83 / Rochester, N. Y." Bottle covered with bark design.
406-a—Variation: With smaller letters.
406-b—Variations: In aqua, dark amber and clear.
Attributed to Lancaster.

407—Toneco Stomach Bitters**
Square light aqua. Rounded corners. Flanged mouth. Marked: "Toneco / Stomach Bitters" in two vertical lines. Reverse: "Appetizer & Tonic" in one vertical line. 9¼ x 2⅝.
TONIC BITTERS—See Atwood, Blake, Boyce, Brown, Caldwell, Chapman, Clarke, Columbo, Crescent, Germania, Gray, Highland, Howes, Jacobs, Lamb, Price, Wheeler, Wild Cherry, **Wallace.**

408—Old Dr. Townsend's Celebrated Stomach Bitters**
Light amber jug. Applied and folded handle. Square flanged mouth. Scarred base. Marked: "Old / Dr. / Townsend's / Celebrated / Stomach / Bitters" in six horizontal lines. Reverse plain. 8¾ x 6.

409—Townsend's Bitters
No description available.

410—Traveler's Bitters***
Oval light amber. About ¾ quart. Collared mouth. Scarred base. On face heavily raised figure of man with hat, short beard and cane, almost like figures on Pike's Peak flasks. Marked: "Travelers Biters" on sides. On shoulder "1834."

411—Turner Brothers Bitters**
Barrel shaped smoky amber. About ¾ quart. Collared mouth. Marked: "Turner Brothers / New York." Turner Brothers, Cordial Distillers, 350 Washington St., New York. Circa. 1858.

412—Dr. Wm. H. Tutt's Golden Eagle Bitters
Square amber. Further description not available.

413—Tyler's Standard American Bitters**
Square amber. About ¾ quart. Collared mouth. Scarred base. Marked: "Tyler's / Standard American / Bitters."

414—Underberg Boonekamp Maag Bitters
No description available.

415—Union Bitters
Note: The formula for Union Bitters was common property (non-proprietory) and it is likely that bitters under this name were issued by many concerns. While Union Bitters bottles were listed as standard in catalogues of druggists' supplies, no marked bottle is now known.

416—U. N. O. Bitters
Square amber. Shape of schnapps bottle. Rounded shoulder. Straight neck. Flanged mouth with ring. Identified by label which reads: "U. N. O. Stomach Bitters (Picture of man in Colonial dress with upraised finger). "Trade Mark—For a Funny Feeling—Makes You Feel Good."
UNION STOMACH BITTERS——See Hopkins.

417—Valleix Bitters
No description available. George C. Starke, Petersburg, Va. Circa. 1880.

418—Vermont Bitters
No description available. C. C. Doty & Co., Bradford, Vt. Circa. 1865.

419—Vigo Bitters
No description available.
VINEGAR BITTERS—See Walker.

420—Van Der Heyde's German Bitters
No description available.

421—Dr. Van Hopf's Curacoa Bitters**
Square amber. Marked: "Dr. Von Hopf's / Curacoa Bitters / Chamberlain & Co. / Des Moines, Iowa." 9½ x 2¾.

GROUP B: MEDICINALS

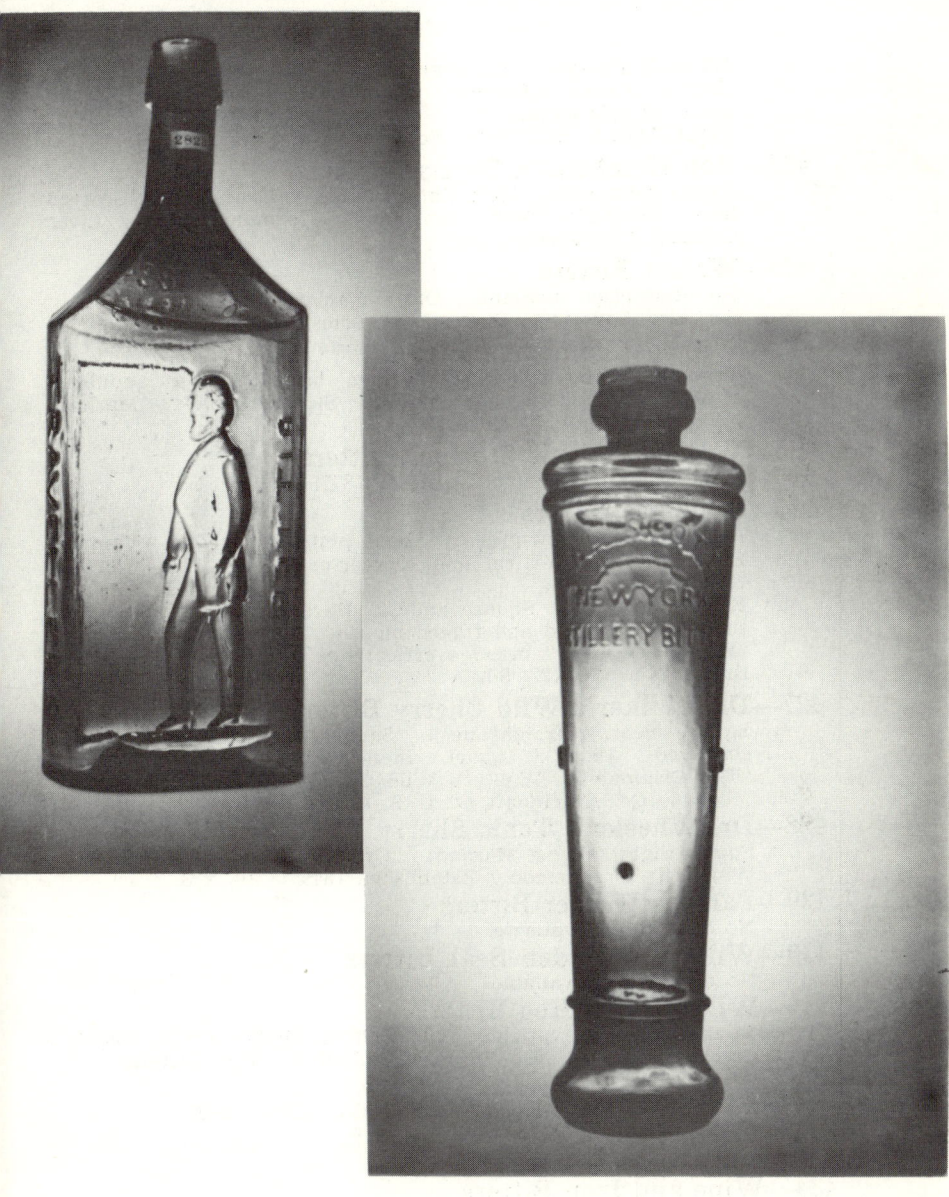

Two Rare Bitters Bottles: number 410 (Traveller's) and number 500 (Gen. Ssott's Cannon).

421-a—Variation: Rectangular amber. Marked: "Dr. Von Hopf's / Curacoa Bitters / Chamberlain & Co. / Des Moines, Iowa" in side panels.
VEGETABLE BITTERS—See Andrews, Perry, Rivenberg.

422—**Von Humboldt's German Bitters******
Rectangular aqua. Half pint. Double collared mouth. Scarred base. Marked: "Von Humboldt's / German Bitters / Liver Complaint, Dyspepsia, &c." 7 x 2 x 1¾.

423—**Wahoo Bitters**
No description available. Old Indian Medicine Co. See also Loveridge, Shepard, Wilson, Bishop.

424—**Wahoo Chamomile Bitters******
Triangular amber. Plain scarred base. Roofed shoulder. Heavily tapered flanged mouth. Straight neck. Marked: "Wahoo Chamomile Bitters."

425—**Wallace's Tonic Stomach Bitters**
No description available. Circa. 1875.

426—**Wampoo Bitters******
Rectangular yellow-green. About pint. Marked: "Wampoo Bitters" in one vertical line. Reverse: "Blum Siegel & Co., New York."
426-a—Variation: Square amber. Beveled corners. Rounded shoulder. Flanged and ringed mouth. Deep panels. Marked: "Wampoo Bitters" in one vertical line. Reverse: "Siegel & Bro. / New York." 9¾ x 2½.

427—**Dr. Walker's Wild Cherry Bitters**
Square clear. Straight neck. Square flanged mouth. Sides concaved. About ¾ quart. Identify by label which reads: "The Original Dr. Walker's Wild Cherry Bitters. Dr. Walker Medicine Co., Cincinnati, O., U. S. A."

428—**Dr. Wheeler's Tonic Sherry Wine Bitters*****
Square light green. Marked: "Dr. Wheeler's / Tonic Sherry Wine Bitters / Boston / Established 1849." 9½ x 3.

429—**Famous Weiner Bitters**
No description available.

430—**Willard's Golden Seal Bitters**
No description available.

431—**Wilson's Wa-Hoo Bitters**
No description available. Old Indian Medicine Co., Battle Creek, Mich. "O. K. Wilson's Original Wa-Hoo Bitters."

432—**Wine Bitters**
No description available. Bush & Co. Circa. 1849.

433—**Wine Bitters Tonic**
No description available.

434—**Wine and Iron Bitters**
No description available.

435—**Warner Stomach Bitters**
No description available. H. B. Warner & Co., Rochester, N. Y. In pint and quart sizes.

— GROUP B: MEDICINALS

436—Warner Safe Bitters
No description available. H. B. Warner & Co., Rochester, N.Y. Dr. Warren's Quaker Bitters—See Quaker.

437—W. C. Bitters***
Round amber. About ¾ quart. Long 4 in. neck. Collared mouth. Barrel shape with three hoops at top and bottom of body. Marked: "W. C. Bitters" on shoulder. In two vertical lines: "Brobst & Renstchler / Reading, Pa." Heighth 10½ in.

438—Westphalia Stomach Bitters
No description available.

439—Wheat Bitters***
Rectangular amber. Beveled corners. Arched shoulder. Flat base with ring. Short straight neck. Tapered flanged mouth. Marked: "Wheat / Bitters" in two vertical lines in two arch-top panels in ½ in. letters. 9½ x 3½ x 2⅛. Wheat Bitters Co., New York.
438-a—Variation: In milk glass.

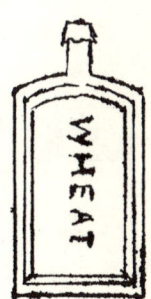

440—White Cross Bitters
No description available.

441—Whitwell's Temperance Bitters*****
Rectangular aqua. Pint. Beveled corners. Scarred base. Collared mouth. Marked: "Whitwell's / Temperance Bitters / Boston." J. B. Whitwell & Son, Battery March St., Boston. Circa. 1847.

442—Edward Wilder's Stomach Bitters****
In shape of a building. Clear. Square with roped edges. About ¾ quart. One side represents front of five-story building, with three doors on ground floor and three windows on each of four floors above. Marked: "Edw. Wilder's / Stomach Bitters / Edw. Wilder & Co. / Wholesale Druggists / Louisville, Ky." Lettering on two sides.

WHITE MOUNTAIN BITTERS—See Copp.

WILD CHERRY BITTERS—See Curtis, H. P. Herb, Harter, Mackenzie, Old Homestead, Thompson, Woods.

WINE BITTERS—See Chapman, Clarke, Imperial, Masten, Solomon, Poland, Richardson, Sonoma, Wheeler.

443—Wingold Brand Stomach Bitters
No description. Arrow Distilleries Co., Peoria, Ill. Circa. 1910.

444—Wild Cherry Tonic Bitters***
Square milk glass. Marked: "Dr. R. T. Hylton's / Patd. 1867 / Wild Cherry Bitters / Philada." 9 x 2⅝.

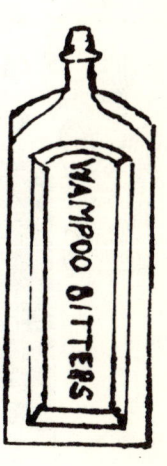

445—Wild Cherry Bitters****
Pea green log cabin shape. About ¾ quart. Collared mouth. Marked: "Wild Cherry (figure of tree) Reverse plain. On two sides of roof: "Bitters."

446—Wild Cherry and Sarsaparilla Bitters
No description available.

447—Dr. Wood's Sarsaparilla Wild Cherry Bitters***
Rectangular aqua. Pint. Wide beveled corners. Scarred base. Collared mouth. Marked: "Dr. Wood's" in one line on bevel; "Sarsaparilla and Wild Cherry in three lines on face; "Bitters" in one line on bevel. Reverse plain.

448—Woodbury's Brand Bitters
No description available.

449—Wahoo and Calisaya Bitters***
Square smoke amber. Columned corners. Sloping roof. Short neck. About ¾ quart. Collared mouth. Marked: "Wahoo & Calisaya Bitters" at top of face; on face of shoulders, "IM OK Y! Y!" On other faces in vertical lines "Jacob Pinkerton."
449-a Variation: In aqua.
Jacob Pinkerton 36 Dey Street, New York. Circa. 1856.

450—Wallace's Tonic Bitters
Square amber. Marked: "Wallace's / Tonic Stomach / Bitters." 9¼ x 2¾.

451—Dr. Walker's Vinegar Bitters***
Round aqua heavy glass. Domed shoulder. Heavy flanged mouth. Marked: "J. Walker's - V. B." in circle in base. 8½x3.

452—Worme's Gesundheit Bitters
No description available.

453—Yamara Cordial Bitters
No description available.

454—Zien's Stomach Bitters
No description available.

455—Zion Bitters
No description available.

456—Zingari Bitters
No description available.

— GROUP B: MEDICINALS 235

Added descriptions for Bitters Bottles listed as numbers 1 to 456: Consult original listing for numbers given below and add these new marked-in-glass facts:

27— Ben Hur Bitters (only square amber; 31 (2 sizes)
35— Bismark Bitters (only) ½ pt. Amber rectangular
41-43— Bonehamp Magen (not stomach) Bitters, Tall Round Amber label only on some
44— Rectangular Amber; "Herzberg Bros., New York
50— Pt. Hannibal, Mo. oval aqua
58— Burdocks Blood Bitters, Toronto aqua; (a Canadian variant)
64— ¾ Q. Cylindrical Cal. Extract of Figs, Los Ang.
71— Carters Liver Bitters (amber)
85— Clark's Serry Wine Bitters (variant) Rockland. M.
90— Amber square L. E. Jung, New Orleans, La.
104— Damena Bitters, Baja, Cal. Round aqua
105— Also, Beggs****
122— Rect. Aqua ½ pt. Dromgool, Louisville, Ky
151— NOT marked: Paper labels
176— Greeleys Boubon Bitters: rare marking
190— Label only "Hartshorn Family Medicines" on reverse in glass marking
216— Iron Bitters: Brown Chemical Co. square aqua
217— D. Hanley's Wild Grape Root Bitters. Round Aqua 12 in. high. 239—Square Aqua
261— Description is wrong (fits a Lithuanian Bitters with paper label) correct should read square milk glass and clear patd. 1864, Jos. Lowenthal, Berlin
293— Old Continental Bitters on sunken panelled ends. Rectangular golden amber in quart size: Folded collar and flattened corners attribuated to Chicago, Ill.. **1860**
296— **Also Great Indian B**itters Rectangular ½ pt. aqua
318— Mack & Co. for amber square Perivian Tonic Bitters, W. T. Phillips & Co.
328— Dr. Pierces Indian Restorative Bit., Lowell, Mass.**
329— ¾ Q. Amber Square
330— Poor Man's Family Bitters ½ pt. rectangular****
354— Wild Cherry Tonic***   373—(see No. 335)
378— Dr. A. H. Smith's Celebrated Old Style Bitters ¾ Q. aqua
451— (also green & chartreuse)
456— Cylindrical, long, neck with bulge, amber

THE 175 NEW FORMS THAT HAVE BEEN UN-COVERED SINCE THE FOREGOING (1947) LIST.

457—Dr. Abell's Improved Spice Bitters***
458—African Stomach Bitters**
459—Allen's Iron Tonic Bitters***
460—Alpine Herb Bitters***
461—Aromatic Life Bitters*****
462—Aromatic Orange Stomcah Bitters
463—David Andrews Veg. Jaundice Bitters
464—Argyle's Bitters
465—Dr. Atherton's Dew Drop Bitters 1866
466—Barto's Great Gun Bitters Reading, Pa.***
467—Barber's Indian Vegetable Jaundice Bitters**
468—Beck's Herb Bitters, York, Pa.
469—Bejamin's Sulphur Bitters
470—Begg's Dandelion Bitters**
471—Berliner Bitters, Pat'd. applied for
472—J. C. Brady's Stomach Bitters***
473—Dr. Josiah Brigg's Bitter Bark Bitters***
474—Berliner Bitters
475— C-Eye-O Bitters (Siesax)****
476—California Wine Bitters
477—Cabin Tonic Bitters (see old list, other names)
478—Old Cabin Bitters**** R. Holtzermann
479—Canteen Bitters***
480—Canton Star Bitters*****
481—Carcacas Bitters
482—Capuziner Stomach Bitters
483—Carmeliter Bitters
484—Caroni Bitters, (Round Amber, Pt.)
485—Celebrated Chill-Chili Bitters
486—Cider Wine Bitters*****
487—Collins Valley Bitters***
488—Colleton Bitters***
489—Dr. Corbett's Renovating Shaker Bitters*****
490—Cotton Patch Bitters
491—Daniziger Magen Bitters***
493—Demuth's Stomach Bitters
494—Dunker's Bitters
495—(Dromgooles) English Female Bitters***

— GROUP B: MEDICINALS 237

Bottles Number 461 (Aromatic Life Bitters) and Number 480 (Canton Star Bitters).

Bottles number 477 (Cabin Tonic Bitters) and number 473 (C-Eye-O Bitters).

— **GROUP B: MEDICINALS**

Bottles number 478 (Old Cabin Bitters) and number 495 (C-Y-O Varcant).

496—Eastman's Yellow Dock
497—Economy Boneset
498—Dr. Gregory's Scotch Bitters
499—German Balsam Bitters
500—Genl. Scott's (N.Y.) Artillery Bitters, Amber Cannon and very rare******
501—Gilbert's Rock and Rye***
502—Gilbert's Sasaparilla Bitters
503—Geo. C. Goodwin Indian Veg. & Sarsaparilla Bitters
504—Wm. F. Goodwin Bitters
505—Dr. S. Griggs (Detroit) Aromatic Bitters
506—Dr. Hartshorne's J. & D. Bitters
507—Hart's Star Bitters, Phila.***
508—Havis Iron Bitters
509—Headache Bitters******
510—Horseshoe Bitters*****
511—Hercules Bitters***
512—Hall's Spice Bitters. A label on a Hall Brandy Bottle, really a powder to put in brandy.
512B—H. V. S. Asparagus Bitters
513—Heirapicra Bitters
514—Hunkidori Bitters***
515—W. C. Hibbard's Bitters
516—Thomas Hurley's Stomach Bitters, Louisville***
517—Hutchins Anti-Dyspepsia Bitters
518—Jackson Stonewall Bitters*****
519—J. T. Higby's Tonic Bitters, square golden amber
520—Jamaica Stomach Bitters; also 520B Jamaica Ginger Root Bitters***
521—Juniper Bitters
522—Kaskareta Bitters Froser Thornton Co.
523—Keen's Sulphur Bitters
524—Klein's Aromatic Bitters
525—L. Kuffer's Sulphur Bitters
526—Dr. Leathe's Aromatic Life Bitters (Adv. 1861)
527—Lorimer's Juniper Tar Bitters, Elmira, N.Y.***
528—Lowell's Invigorator
529—Layman's Dandelion Bitters
530—McGuire's Curdurango Bitters***
531—Malarion Bitters: Snyder Gue & Condell St. Louis, Mo.

— GROUP B: MEDICINALS

Bottles number 243 (asparagus Bitters) and number 511 (Hercules Bitters).

532—Dr. Mampes Herb Stomach Bitters****
/ John Thielen / Sole Agents / Oskosh WK aqua /
533—Mansfield's Bitters
534—Marshall's Bitters—The Best Laxative and Blood Purifier
535—**Miller's Tansy Bitters**
536—H. L. Mishler's Keystone Bitters
537—Mohican Bitters, Roth and Co.*****
538—Moulton's Oloroso Bitters (Trade Mark Pineapple)*****
539—Mountain Root Bitters, S. J. Smith & Co, Chicago, Ill.***
540—A. B. L. Myersam Rock Rose Bitters, New Haven****
541—National Tonic Bitters
542—Dr. Newton's Anti-Bilious Bitters, Norwich, Vt.
543—Night Cap***
544—Old House / Orange Bitters (label only)
545—Old Time Bitters
546—Orroro Bitters, (round aqua; 5th)
547—Orinth Bitters, J. Mariston, Jr., Square Amber***
548—Parker's / Celebrated J.P.C. monogram Stomach Bitters
549—Perry's Excelsior Aromatic Bitters
550—Peruvian / Bitters II f II H and K (monogram in shield); Peruvian Bitters P. B. Co. (also see 318)
551—Barto's Great Gun Bitters, Reading, Pa.*****
552—Dr. Leow's Celebrated Stomach Bitters & Nerve Tonic & Dr. Leow & Sons, Cleveland, O., Rectangular ¾ quart Aqua.
553—Peychaud's American Aromatic Bitters Cordial***
L. E. Jung Sole Proprietor, New Orleans II c.
554—L. Peychaud's American Aromatic Cocktail Bitters***
555—Dr. Geo. Pierce's Indian Restorative Bitters, Lowell, Mass. 2 sizes .see 328)
556—Pendleton's Pineapple Bitters, Nashville *****
557—Dr. Planett's Bitters
558—Old Father Bitters(Amber Tapering)
559—Polo Club Trade F & M (monogram) Mark Stomach Bitters*** (see 329)

— GROUP B: MEDICINALS 243

Bottles number 509 (Headache Bitters) and 510 (Horseshoe Bitters).

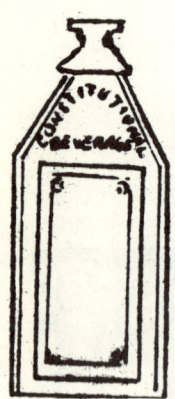

560—Pond's Bitters II f II, An Unexcelled Laxative Bottom Diamond with '76 in center; rectangular like Lash bottles.
561—Pond's Kidney and Liver Bitters Laxative II f.
562—Mr. Zadoc Porter's Medicated Stomach Bitters See 332)
563—Port Wine and Rock Rose Bitters (See also 540)
564—Ramsey's Trinidad Bitters
565—Ranch Bitters, Omaha, Nebraska
566—Dr. Renz Herb Bitters, Square Amber***
567—L. Reed's Bitters (see 341)
568—Dr. Renz Herb Bitters (Sq. Green & Brown)
569—Rex Kidney & Liver Bitters (See 342)
570—Richard's Life Preserver***
571—W. L. Richardson (sam as S. O. Richardson except initials***
572—Richardson's Dry Bitters
573—Dr. Richardson's Justly Celebrated Vegetable Purifying Bitters
574—Rock Mountain Bitters
575—Victor Roeberg's Prussian Bitters
576—Roger's Sherry Wine Bitters
577—Root's Bitters, Rectangular Amber (Adv. only)
578—H. P. Rose's Peruvian King Bitters (Triangular)
579—Rosenbaum's Bitters, N. B. Jacobs & Co., San. Fr.
580—Royce's Sherry Wine Bitters, Rectangular pt. Aq.
581—Saxlehner's Hunyadi Janos Bittersquelle
582—Eugene Schoening's Sweedish Bitters of Peruvian Bark, Philada.
583—Schroeder's Bitters, Louisville, Ky.*****
584—Swiss Stomach Bitters, Amber***
585—Sagur's Golden Seal***
586—L. Shaw Peruvian Bitters Prepared by P. Shaw M.D., Portland, Pa.
587—Dr. J. G. B. Siegert and Sons, Dr. J. G. B. Siegert and Sons on Base Angurtura Bitter (See 374 also)
588—Dr. J. G. B. Siegert II and Hijos / b / Dr. J. G. B. Siegert and Hijos (See 374 also)
589—Dr. Siegert Baliver
590—Skandinavian Bitters (Label only)

GROUP B: MEDICINALS

Bottles number 518 (Stonewall Jackson Bitters) and number 520 (Gentian Root Bitters).

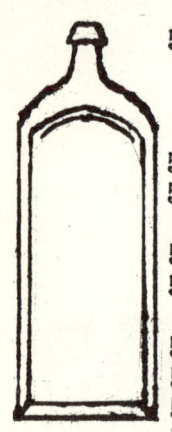

591—A. H. Smith's Celebrated Old Bitters. The Standard Tonic and Blood Purifyer. Square Amber
Standard Tonic and Blood Purifyer O. S. 2781, Square Amber (see 378)
592—Dr. A. H. Smith's / Old Style Bitters O S / 2781
593—Snyder's Celebrated Bitter Cordial, H. G. Leisenring and Co., Phila., Pa.
594—Old Dr. Solomon's Great Indian Bitters***
595—Old Dr. Solomon's Indian Wine Bitters (see 385)***
596—King Solomon's*****
597—Speer's Old Rye Bitters
598—Speer's Peruvian Bitters
599—Spencer's Bitters
600—Spring and Summer Bitters
601—Sumpter Bitters, Charleston, S. C., Dowie, Morse, Davis Wholesale Druggists, Sq. Amber*****
602—Star Kidney and Liver Bitters
603—John W. Steele's Niagara (star) Bitters, John W. Steele's Niagara Star Bitters (eagle); another with different eagle; another with 13 stars over eagle & 1864 (see 286)
604—Steinfield's French Cognae Bitters***
605—Staketee's Blood Purifying Bitters, ½ pt. Square)***
606—Dr. H. C. Stewart's Tonic Bitters
607—Stoever's Tonic Herb Bitters 1837
608—Sukey's Indian Vegetable Bitters***
609—Sunny Castle Stomach Bitters*****
610—Dr. Chas. Sweet Restorative Wine Bitters Oval A
611—Swain's Bourbon Bitters (Amber)
612—Taft's Brain and Nerve Bitters
613—Trowbridge Dandelion Bitters
614—Dr. Turk's Wine Bitters
615—Tuft's Tonic Bitters, Plymouth, N. H. (Label only)
616—Tyree's Chamomile Bitters***
617—Uncle Tom's Bitters (Tom Foulds & Co.)*****
618—U. S. Gold Bitters***
619—U. T. K. Hop & Iron Bitters
620—Webber's Strengthening Bitters
621—Dr. W. L. Wilbur's Aromatic Bitters
622—Dr. Wheeler's Bitters

— GROUP B: MEDICINALS

623—Wheeler's Berlin Bitters, Baltimore******
624—West India Stomach Bitters***
625—Watson's Balsam Bitters
626—Yerba Buena Bitters, San Francisco, Calif. Amber***
627—Yochum Bros. Celebrated Stomach Bitters
628—Zingari Bitters** Aqua Variant
629—Zu Zu Bitters***
630—Dr. Wilson's Herbine Bitters, oval aqua. pt.
631—Sal Villes Delaware Bitters; aqua round w/ paper label for dyspepsia, aque, etc. A. Saville 512 Market St., Wilmington, Delaware.

Bitters Bottle Numbers 623 and 624 from Gardner Collection: See Listings above.

A NOTE ABOUT FORM, SHAPE & DESIGN

That Bitters bottles so closely follow commemorative and historical flasks in the regard of collectors is due chiefly to the fact that Bitters bottles, while adopting some of the features that had been peculiar to flasks, were maker originators of a new American bottle form.

Designers of Bitters bottles ventured into new fields of bottles form when they added contour design to mere ornamentation of glass. Flasks had been held to a few simple and basic contour forms. None of these forms were comfortably adapted to packing in large lots. The flask makers had only to consider the uses and conveniences of owners of but a single bottle. The purveyors of Bitters needed to look after convenience and economy in packing bottles in lots of a dozen or more. They discovered that, even within the restrictions of a practical economy they could still make bottles that would have decorative appeal as well as a convenient and space-saving bulk. Thus the Bitters bottles may reasonably be credited with originating a new art-form.

Square	Round
Mischler's	Red Jacket
Home	Schroeders
Wampoo	Ben Franklin
Wayhoo & Calisaya	Halls
Cannon	Favorite
Rectangular	Greeleys
Burcock	Keystone
Congress	St. Jacobs
VonHopfs	Pocohontas
Solomons	**Jugs**
Travelers	Old Dr. Townsend
Fancy	Alpine
Gen. Scotts	**Flasks**
Oloroso	Yerba Buena

The Bitters bottles were designed with a consciousness that the flasks had been proven to have a strong popular appeal because they added decorative design to otherwise plain glass; but there was, probably, also an understanding that while Bitters may have been a downright hypocritical evasion and were in the closest analysis nothing more than alcoholic beverages disguised as medicines, there must be no overt association in the popular mind of medicine and alcohol. Therefore another reason is argued why the designers of Bitters bottles avoided repetition of the familiar flask form that was recognized as a badge of John Barlycorn. **ONLY TWO BRANDS OF BITTERS DARED TO OFFER THEMSELVES IN THE FORM OF FLASKS.**

Comparison of the Bitters bottles in fancy contour forms or cylindrical and oval shapes with the large numbers of bottles in square and rectangular shapes makes it evident that the square and rectangular forms may be taken as the standard or "norm" for all Bitters bottles. This design was undoubtedly influenced by a need for bottles that could be handled in numbers with a maximum economy. In various sizes the square and rectangular bottles (direct descendants of case bottles) were excellently adapted to safe and convenient transportation. Their design was so efficient that it at once set a pattern for other medicine bottles.

But the designers found that, even within the limitations of geometric design, they could devise decorative variations, and they turned with ingenuity and alacrity to many embellishments that have made Bitters bottles so attractive to collectors. To mention a few of these designs that give distinction to Bitters bottles: Beveled or champfered or roped or columned corners, fancy panels, roof designs, fluting or ribbing and inscriptions and pictorial designs.

The appearance of cabin-shaped bottles, the most frequent elaboration of the square design and a form that was seized upon by many makers, in considerable numbers is due to the influence of the "Hard Cider" campaign, and, also to a belief that an appeal to homely American instincts for the rough-and-ready pioneer sturdiness would be commercially profitable. The barrel-shaped bottles, which also appear in the Bitters category,

FANCY CONTOUR FORMS
Berkshire—Pig
Dinger's Napoleon Cocktail
 —Drum
Eagle Angostura Bark—Globe
Dr. Fish's—Fish
The Fish Bitters—Fish
Brown's Indian—Indian Queen
Parazyn Indian—Indian Queen
McKeever's Army—Drum
National—Ear of Corn
Seaworth—Lighthouse

SQUARE FORM
Baker's Orange Grove
Big Bill Best
Brown's Iron
Prof. Geo. J. Bryne's
Burdock Blood
Century
Congress
Crimean
DeWitt's
Doyle's Hop
Electric Brand
Fletcher's Cocktail
Fox & Co. Hygeia
Creer's Eclipse
Harvey's Prairie
Dr. Hoffman's
Home
Dr. Hopkins'
Hops and Malt
Hostetter's
Humulus
Johnson Calisaya
S. Kaufmann's
Landsburg's
Lash's
Leipziger
Litthauer
Dr. Lovegood's
Dr. Loveridge's Wahoo
Mishler's
Mountain
National Tonic
Niagara Star
Old Kentucky
Parmelee's Hop

ROUND FORM
Foerster's Teutonic
Old Jamaica
Tilton's Dandelion
Sazerac

CABIN FORM
American Life
Cannon
Drake's Plantation
H. P. Herb Wild Cherry
Holtzermann's
Jacob's Cabin
Kelly's Old Cabin
Old Homestead
Wild Cherry
Pure Apple Brandy
Dr. Chandler's Jamaica
Schroeder's German
Solomon's
Snyder's
Dr. Stoughton's
Dr. J. Sweet's
Dr. Thomson's
Toneco
Tyler's
U. N. O.
Dr. Von Hopf's
Wampoo
Dr. Wheeler's

RECTANGULAR FORM
David Andrews'
Augauer
Dr. M. C. Ayer's
Dr. Ball's
Dr. Bell's
Bender's
Dr. Bishop's Wahoo
Dr. Blake's
Boerhave's Holland
Burdock Blood
Calabash
California Grape
Carey's Grecian Bend
Chapman's
Clarke's
Congress
Constitution
Constitutional
Deutscher Aromatique
Dewey's Manila
Druid
Excelsior
Fenner's Capitol
Germania
Dr. Manly Hardy's
Hubbell's Golden
Indian Veg. Sarsaparilla

in impressive numbers, are obviously hints that they might contain more stimulating draughts than suggested by their labeled contents.

After the square and rectangular forms of Bitters bottles the most predominent form is round, the persistant sovenir of days when bottles were blown without moulds. There may have been some timidity in accepting this round or cylindrical design more largely because it had already become a standard form of container for alcoholic beverages·

In the ensuing lists Bitters bottles are classified according to form and shape, and reference to these lists will confirm the points made herein, and also serve as a guide to collection of specialized shapes.

A NOTE ABOUT COLOR: Amber in all its variegated shades may be taken as the class color of Bitters bottles, for it is most frequent in occurrence. However aquamarine, clear, green, blue and puce bottles follow amber in their order as typical Bitters bottles colors. Amber was adopted as the most frequently used color because of some real or fancied effect of light upon the chemical composition of the contents of the bottles.

As in the case of contour and other design, the designers of Bitters bottles had, also, an interest in the popular and aesthetic appeal of color, and devised formulas that produced lovely and artistic color variations. Not yet have collectors of Bitters bottles become so color-conscious as have the flask specialists, but for those who desire to collect and distinguish color variants there is among Bitters bottles every tint and shade that is emphasized as desirable in the category of flasks.

As has been pointed out before, the large circulation of Bitters bottles led to coincidental manufacture of bottles for some popular brands in several factories. This provides many variations in mould design, color and factory markings. Variants may be accumulated in great numbers, and those that are distinguished by the known marks of famous glass factories are decidedly worthy of identification and preservation.

This preparation, once selling for $1.00, when found with original box and contents is now in great collector demand. On a dare, the writer once got $100.00 for selling his own Museum's specimen and gave it to the cause.

— GROUP B: MEDICINALS

CHAPTER X   OTHER MEDICINALS

One may start out with just Bitters Bottles, but before he knows it, the collector tends to get caught up in related proprietary medicines that are not marked Bitters, that usually contained alcohol as part of their taker-appeal and that are just as old and interesting to the student of "nostrum residua." Many books have been written on the Patent Medicine Craze that preceded passage of the pure food and drug act in 1906. While this required (among other things) paying excise on alcoholic contents in excess of limiting requirements, the patent medicine advertising had already turned from the euphoria pitch to one of relief of constipation, general debility and all sorts of pain-hypochondria flesh can be made heir to. This is not the place to go into the psycho-social history of the medicine show, or pandering to "female weaknesses" and "loss of male virility." Instead the writer confines himself to the bottles the imbibers left behind and proposes a secondary classification list of Sarsaparillas, Tonics, etc. which could well substitute for the alcoholic bitters also a third classification of all proprietary medicine bottles up to 1875 which fall in our overall Group B ("medical?") category. One, may ask of all or any, "are these collectable, just as old and interesting as some Bitters?" The answer is yes! Just look at these random advertising notes on the contents of and drawings made from samples the writer picked up on a recent southern tour. That should be enough to challenge the true collector of what has sometimes been called "The Golden Age of Quackery: More advertising samples will follow in whatever pages remain for this grouping; Now to the 2nd and 3rd classification of the medical nostrum bottles that follow the true marked bitters.

Whereas the early flask designs were tapered from shoulder to base to make the bottle "easy on the draw," the medicinals of later age were "spoon fed." Designers of medical nostrums were free from the compulsion of such pocket needs. Such bottles were not intended to be portable by their purchasers. Thus was permitted a new freedom to allow ease of shipment to have a part in design, and Bitters bottles began to assume forms that were adapted to a mass market. Already the forms of case gin bottles and the schnapps or "square-face" bottles had proven convenient for packaging and transportation. The earlier rounded forms, largely the result of blowing bottles from tubes and without benefit of moulds, such as the Ludlow and Hogarth types, were extravagant of space, and calabash and other early scroll forms were also impractical. It was not difficult for the medicine bottle makers to find a rectangular pattern well suited to their demands. However, the traditional round shaped bottle persisted in many instances, not only with the true Bitters Bottles of the previous chapter but also occasionally in the related medicinals listed in pages which follow.

Once having distinguished and set down in an exclusive list those bottles specifically marked with the title of Bitters, the compiler is confronted with the problem of properly and satisfactorily classifying the large number of bottles that had been commonly known as Bitters bottles, although not so specifically marked, before the arbitrary and exclusive classification was made. This problem is not easily solved because the bottles excluded from the primary list partake in almost every particular of the characteristics of Bitters bottles, having the same physical specifications and designed to contain liquids of the same chemical and pharmaceutical nature as bitters. Included in the category of these bottles are large numbers whose contents were known as Sarsaparillas, Tonics, Elixirs, Cordials, etc. It is evident that these medicines differed from bitters only in name.

Many a worthy example of American bottle-making will be excluded from the category of Bitters by this jealous distinction, and there is no intent of detracting from the antique or other value of bottles because of this exclusion. A mere glance at the index of bottles that do not bear the specific title of bitters makes it apparent that their great numbers pose to the collector and compiler alike a perplexing if not discouraging problem. It, too, must appear that if one of these bottles be admitted to the select Bitters category then, in justice, all must be admitted. And that, again, is to invite a further confusion.

In preparation of the secondary list no attempt has been made to rate bottles by any rule of antiquity. However, it has been deemed best for reasons of economy to exclude from such a listing any bottles issued after 1875. Otherwise this list includes bottles varying widely in age.

Ayer's Sarsaparilla
Allen's Cherry Pectoral
Allen's Sarsaparilla
Angeline (Dr. Kaufman's)
American Compound
Angier's Petroleum Emulsion
Athlophorus
Ayer's Compound Sarsaparilla
Anti Apoplectine
Arabian Blood Purifier
Dr. N. Angell's Rheumatic Gun
Bristol's Sarsaparilla
Browder's Syrup of Ind. Syrup
Brandt's Ind. Pulmonary Balsam
John Bull's Sarsaparilla

Burnside's Purifico
Buchan's Hung. Balsam of Life
A. H. Bull Sarsaparilla
Brandriff's Vegetable Antidote
Burnett's cocaine
Boschee's German Syrup
Brow's Salicyline
Barker's Pain Panacea
Bristol's Sarsaparilla
Bavarian Malt Extract
Bull's Herbs and Iron Comp.
Buckout Dutch Liniment
Batchelor's Liquid Hair Dye
Bateman's Drops
Beef, Iron and Wine (Parker)

GROUP B: MEDICINALS

By the turn of the past century there were at least 110,000 proprietary liquid medicines on the American market, and a great majority of these were held in containers that have become collectible. In the past and before the arbitrary and select classification of Bitters bottles was proposed, all medicine bottles were admitted to the same category. It is obviously now impractical to continue such an all-inclusive catalogue if there is to be maintained a decent and orderly system for interchange of information concerning collectible bottles.

There was necessity for decision, and it seems that in the case of bottles relegated to a secondary classification it must remain with the individual collector to decide how he shall catalogue and classify these specimens —at least until a further and definitive catalogue or check list is made of them. However, because there is a need for a common system of classification and reference, an arbitrary ruling must be accepted. This may be founded upon such a classification as is proposed herein: To set up a secondary classification of Bitters bottles which will admit bottles of known rarity and worth that partake of the general character of Bitters bottles but are not so specifically marked. Such bottles are generally known to collectors and are not so many in number that they may not be properly catalogued and described. In this secondary classification, then, will appear titles of bottles that for reasons of age, origin, physical characteristics and historical or folkways significance are worthy of some special consideration.

If this arbitrary solution of the problem be accepted and bottles whose descriptions fulfill requirements of worthiness be admitted to this secondary classification of Bitters, there still remains to be decided what shall be done with the remaining thousands of collectible bottles that have heretofore so carelessly been permitted admission to the Bitters category. This may be solved by setting up a third classification which, until a further separation is decided upon, will admit all the great numbers of medicine bottles.

There will always enter into consideration the individual interests of collectors: whether their major concern shall be with mere numbers or whether they shall be concerned with the lore of glassmaking or whether they shall be interested in the intangible collaterals.

THE COVERS of a pamphlet promoting The Mormon Elders Damiana Wafers, one of countless nostrums promoted with a sex pitch. Courtesy of the Bella C. Landauer Collection in The New-York Historical S

GROUP B: MEDICINALS

Blackman's Gen. Heal. Balsam
Wm. Jay Barker's Hirsutus
Bromo Seltzer
Bromo Caffeine
Carter's Spanish Mixture
Comstock's Sarsaparilla
Constitutional Beverage
Cook's Balm of Life
Cordial Balm of Gilead
Crook's Wine of Tar
Curtis Cherry Syrup
Clinic Blood Purifier
McClintock's Dyspeptic Elixir
Churchill's Specific Remedy
Calcura Solvent
Coe's Dyspepsia Cure
Cummings' Vegetine
Campbell's Curo-Compound
Constitutional Water
Cooper's New Discovery
Curtis' Cherry Syrup
Clapp's Malt & Cod Liv Oil Cd.
Christie's Magnetic Fluid
Curative Jasnogorski Wine
Clover & Burdock Wine—Blood
Chamberlain's Cough Remedy
Castoria
Chamberlain's Pain Balm

Callan's Brazilian Gum
Celery Malt
Celery Compound
Chamberlain's Liniment
Osgood's India Cholagogue
Caldwell's Syrup Pepsin
Clickemer's Purgative Pills
Curtis' Inhaling Hygeia Vapor
Cantaur Liniment
Cherokee Liniment
Denison's Sarsaparilla
Duffy Malt Whiskey
Pierce's Golden Med. Discovery
Dana's Sarsaparilla
Drake's Palmetto Wine Comp.
Darby's Prphylactic Liquid
Daniels' Triple Ex. Hamamelis
Drees-Bentheim Liq. Fer. Alb.
Dillingham's Plant Juice
Dyke's Elixir
Dalley's Magic Pain Extractr
Dalby's Caminative
Drake's Croup Remedy
Eilert's Ext. of Wild Cherry
Espey's Fragrant Cream
Ely's Cream Balm
Elderkin's Egyptian Balsam
Evans' Camomile Pills

Fahrney's Rel. Old Time Prep-
F. E. C. Kidney Remedy
Fenner's Blood & Liver Rem.
Forestine
Fowler's Ex. of Wild Strayb'ry
Fahnestock's Vermifuge
Fenner's Kid. & Backache Cure
Foley's Sarsaparilla
Fellows' Syrup of Hypophos.
Food's Pectoal Syrup
Faucine
Forni's Alpenkrauter Blut.
Fenner's Peoples Remedy
Father John's Medicine
Flanders Grecian Drops & Oil
Foster's Anodyne Cordial
Foley's Honey and Tar
Floraplexion
Fenner's Golden Relief
Frink's Eczema Ointment
Freeman's Velcutine
Folger's Olconian
Green's Nervure
Guysott's Yel. Dock & Sarsap.
Gorfrey's oCrdial
Gardner's Ind. Bal. of Liverwort
Gardner & Smith Hair Dyne
Gordak's Jelly of Pom. Prep.

Gosnell's Cherry Tooth Paste
Halsey's Forest Wine
Healy & Bigelow Ind. Sagwa
Hood's Sarsaparilla
Houck's Patent Panacea
Howe's Sarsaparilla
Household Panacea
Hygeia Wild Cherry Phosphate
Hartison's Pulmonic Mixture
Hoofland's German Tonic
Hobo Medicine
Hayden's Viburnam Comp.
Himalya
Halsey's Wine
House's Indain Tonic
Howe's Arabian Milk Cure
Heine's Golden Specific
Hailton's Balsam
Haskins' Turkish Hair Tonic
Hartshorn's Family Medicine
Hunt's Liniment
Houston's Pepsin
Hohnstock's Vermifuge
Hanford Balsam of Myrrh
Hirsutus
Hemlock Oil
Haarlem Oil
Hind's Honey and Almond Crm.

— GROUP B: MEDICINALS

Iodine Liniment
Improved Trommer Ex. of Malt
Jayne's Expectorant
Jayne's Alterative
Jayne's Extract Ginger
Jayne's Cayminative Balsam
Jordan's Cholera Remedy
St. Jacob's Oil
Kine's Aro. Digestive Cordial
King of the Blood
Kilmer's Cough Cure Con. Oil
Kennedy's Favorite Remedy
Kilmer's Swamp Root
Ka-Ton-Ka
King's New Discovery
King's Nervine
Kilmer's Female Remedy
Kennedy's Rheumatic Dis.
Kilmer's Oc. Weed Heart Rem.
Kennedy's Tonic Port
Kalamazoo Cel. and Sarsap.
Kermott's Extract Blackberry
Kennedy's Salt Rheum Oint.
Kelly's Ovals
Kier's Medicine
Kendall Spavin Cure
Kemp's Balsam
Kennedy's Rheumatic Liniment

Lake's Indian Specific
Lindsey's Blood Searcher
Log Cabin Sarsaparilla
Log Cabin Extract
Log Cabin Tonic
Liebig Malt Extract
Lindenfeld's Veg. Worm Syrup
Lyko
Lane's Am. Worm Specific
Larned & Baker
Liebig Extract of Beef
Miles Restorative Nervine

Magee's Emulsion
Mother's Friend
Maguire's Ex. of Benne Plant
Moore's Magnetic Pain Killer
Morgridge's Fam. Veg. Med.
Mathewson's Infallible Rem.
Modoc Indian Oil
Munyon's Inhaler
Mellin's Food
Munyon's Paw-Paw
McClintock's Dyspeptic Elixir
McArthur Syr. of Hypophosph.
McGrew's Liq. Herbs of Youth
Masury's Sarsaparilla Cathartic
McMinn's Elixir of Opium

McLane's Am. Worm Specific
Moxie Nerve Food
Morse's Celebrated Syrup
Newton's Panacea
Nevin's Catarrh Remedy
Nuxated Iron
Nivalis
Neave's Food
Opodeldoc
Old Padre's Wine
Otto's Cure
Pierce's Favorite Prescription
Paine's Celery Compound
Pavle's Spark. & Per. Sherbet
Perrine's Apple Ginger
Peters' Blood Vitalizer
Pine Tree Tar Cordial
Pettit Blood Purifier
Peruna
Pond's Extract
Psychine
Pinkham's Medicine
Pinkham's Vegetable Compound
Pisco's Cure
Paskola
Phillips' Emulsion
Poland's White Pine Comp.
P. B. Wait's Celery Malt
Pierce's Golden Med. Discovery

Pitcher's Castoria
Paul's Russian Oil
Pain Killer
Porter's Pain King
Peckham's Veg. Heal. Cgh. Bal
Pedine
Perrin's Fumigator
Peery's Vermifuge
Pabst Extract
Pinaud's Elixir Dentrifice
R. S. Rheumatic Syrup
Rohrer's Ex. Wild Cher. Tonic
Red Clov. & Burdock for Blood
Royal Digesto
Riker's Expectorant
Rogers' Liverwort, Tor & Can.
Raqam's Micrabe Killer
Ransom's Hive Syrup and Tola
Root Juice Compound
Radway's Sarsaparillian
Rowland's Macassar Oil
Sand's Sarsaparilla
Schenck's Seaweed Tonic
Schenck's Pulmonic Syrup
Scoville Blood & Liver Syrup
Shaker Syrup
Smith's Green Mountain Reno-
Sparks' Perfect Health
Swaim's Panacea

— GROUP B: MEDICINALS

Shoop's Sarsaparilla & Iron
Samaritan Nervine
Saxlehner—Bitterquelle
The Great Shoshonees Remedy
Sanford's Liver Invigorator
Southworth's B. and K. Remedy
Sheehan's Can. Malt Whiskey
Scott's Emulsion
South Carolina Dispensary
Shoop's Family Medicine
Swain's Vermifuge
Shilch's Cough Remedy
Syke's Sure Cure for Catarrh
Townsend Sarsaparilla
Turner's Sarsaparilla
Trommer Extract of Malt
Tanlac
Tyndall's Eucalyptus
Thom' Copaiba Sarsaparilla
Turlington's Balsam
Tobias' Venetian Liniment
Tricopaphic
Thomas Eclectric Oil
Thompson's Eye Water
Trask's Magnetic Ointment
Tarrant's Aperient

Vaughan's Veg. Lithon. Mixture
Vinol
VanWert's Balsam
Vernal Palmetone
Vandeveer's Medicated Gin
Vincent's Dendan
Vitaline

Wayne's Diuretic Elixir
Weaver's Canker & Salt R. Sy.
Wister's Balsam of Wild Cherry
Wood's Aromatic Spirits
Wynkoop's Kath. Hon. Sarsap.
Wait Celery Malt
Wilber's Cod Liver Oil
Warren's Tonic Cordial
Wetumka Dispensary
Wood's Elixir
Weller's Stone Root and Gin
Wine of Chenstokow
Warner's Safe Kid. & Liv. Cure
Warner's Safe Rheumatic Cure
Warner's Safe Cure
Warner's Safe Tonic
Warner's Safe Diabets Cure
Winslow's Soothing Syrup
Westlake Vegetable Ointment
Warner's Lithia Water
Wilcox Specific
Witch Hazel Jelly
Wright's Indian Veg. Syrup

We may curtly dismiss a large number of bottles from consideration for inclusion in the third classification as merely old medicine bottles; but, even then, we must, if all things are considered, be careful in separating the worthy from the unworthy. It is rapidly becoming apparent to collectors of bottles that only a small beginning has been made in the study of their importances; as the processes of time enlarge the definition of antiquity relative importances will be altered. Any present attempt to classify and catalogue must be mindful of a future importance and usefulness, and so in the third category of bottles will appear many which have no present value in the opinion of present-day collectors...

While it is not to be inferred that any great numbers of bottles in the following index are of considerable present interest, this third list is appended as a guide to collectors who desire to specialize in this category.

In compiling this third list it has been possible to refer to druggists' inventories and to catalogues of dealers in drugs and medicines, so that the index may be taken as a reasonably complete catalogue of proprietory medicines in general circulation before 1875. Presumably many medicines that had but a local popularity are omitted from the list. For reasons of convenience the bottles in this list have been placed in divisions according to the nature of their contents.

Lest the following formidable list be considered a dismaying deterrent to collecting in this specialized field of bottles, it may be said that only a comparatively small number of these medicine bottles were so distinguished by design, origin or background that they are desirable collector's items. Many titles, it will be discovered, are repeated from much earlier lists, and in these instances it may be assumed that later bottles are reproductions.

If the following list be considered an amazing exhibition of the American capacity to consume medicinal nostrums, it may be pointed out that 1875, before which year all these bottles were issued, was even before the so-called "patent medicine era" had reached its peak, and that in the years from 1875 to the end of the century and to the time of the restrictive Pure Food and Drug laws thousands more of such medicines were poured onto the market, until the total of glass-contained preparations reached to more than 110,000.

— GROUP B: MEDICINALS

AN INDEX TO PROPRIETARY MEDICINE BOTTLES SOMETIMES RELATED TO BITTERS CIRCA. 1875

****

Alkethrenta
Jayne's Alterative
Jayne's Spanish Alterative
Pierce's Alterative
Kendall's Amboline
Reeve's Ambrosia
Ring's Ambrosia
Sterlin's Ambrosia
Anakesia
Disbrow's Anisette
Hedge's Annihilator
Wolcott's Annihilator
Grove's Anodyne
Shaker's Anodyne
Horton's Antidote
Jeffries' Antidote
Watts' Antidote
Anticholerine
Allan's Anti-Fat
Bailey's Aperient
Tarrant's Aperient
Close's Aperient
Fish's Aperient
Frothingham's Aperient
Aspargo
Aporo
Brown's Assimilant
Green's August Flower
Robare's Aureoline

BALMS
Brown's Woodland Balm
Cook's Life Balm
Brandt's Balm
Graefenberg's Balm
Hagen's Balm
Harter's Lung Balm
Lawrence's Balm
Marsden's Balm
Metcalfe's Balm
Miller's Balm
Quirk's Balm
Persian Balm
Rush's Lung Balm
Townsend's Balm
Zane's Hindo Balm
Thousand Flowers Balm

BALSAMS
Adamson's Balsam
Allen's Lung Balsam
Arnold's Balsam
Becker's Eye Balsam
Bishop's Cough Balsam
Blackman's Balsam
Brandt's Balsam
Buchan's Hungarian Balsam
Cheeseman's Arabian Balsam
Christie's Balsam
Coe's Balsam
Dame's alsam
Denton's Balsam
Fitch's Pulmonary Balsam
Folger's Balsam
Hall's Lung Balsam
Horton's Horehound Balsam
Foyle's Balsam
Foley's Balsam
Hayne's Arab Balsam
Hill's Honey Balsam
Hyatt's Life Balsam
Jackson's Magic Balsam
Keating's Balsam
Knapp's Cough Balsam
Mast's Pulmonary Balsam
Miller's Balsam
Kemp's Balam
Lawrence's Balsam
W. C. Parks' Balsam
Peckham's Balsam
Pettit's Canker Balsam
Porter's Balsam
Powell's Balsam
Prior's Balsam
Palmer's Balsam
R. & C. Pulmonary Balsam
Roman Eye Balsam
Seabury's Balsam
Silliman's Balsam
Turlington's Balsam
U. S. Blackberry Balsam
VanDeusen's Balsam
Wells' Throat Balsam
West's Balsam, also Wood's

Wilcox Pulmonary Balsam
W. C. Wister's Balsam
Upham's Banisher
Brown's Blood Purifier
Howe's Blood Purifier
Roback's Blood Purifier
Wilson Blood Renewer
Linsay's Blood Searcher
Laird's Bloom of Youth
Baker's Broma
Tilden's Bromo Chloraium
Bronchine
Dalby's Carminative
Dixon's Blackberry Carminative
Fitley's Carminative
Hart's Carminative
Jayne's Carminative
Louden's Carminative
Marsden's Carminative
Nelson's Carminative
Carboline
Allen's Casinai
Marchisi's Cathlicon
Marshall's Catholicon
Grown's Chlorodyne
Platt's Chlorides
Osgood's Cholague
Cloverino
Kay's Coaguline
Phalen's Cocin
Burnett's Cocaine

COMPOUNDS

Clark's Antibilious Compound
Gardiner's Rheumatic Comp.
Berman Worm Compound
Hayden's Viburnam Compound
Johnson's Rheumatic Comp.
Juhlin's Hydrastic Compound
Larookah's Sarsaparillia Comp
Poland White Pine Compound
Rush's Fever and Ague Comp.
Simmons' Hepatic Compound
Wilson's Sarsaparilla Compound
Green's Ague Congueror

CORDIALS

Arnold's Soothing Cordial
Bower's Infant Cordial
Brown's Nursery Cordial
Fitler's Kidney Cordial
Fosgate's Cordial
Foord's Tonic Cordial
Godfrey's Imiation Cordial
Holden's Cordial
Jacobs' Cordial
Jay's Apple Ginger Cordial

Mrs. Kidder's Cordial
Kennedy's Diarrhoea Cordial
McLean's Cordial
Monelt's Teething Cordial
Morse's Invigorating Cordial
Stabler's Diarrhoea Cordial
Swayne's Bowel Cordial
Swett's Female Streng. Cordial
Wishart's Pine Tree Tar Cordial
Wishart's Crdial
Warren's Tonic Cordial
Fitch's Heart Corrector
Fitch's Biliary Corrector
Wade's Liver Correcto

"CURES"

Aver's Augue Cure
American Cough Cure
Adams' Forest Cure
Alden's Catarrh Cure
Beddau's Liver Cure
Benett's Quick Cure
Benson's Skin Cure
Caldwell's Cough Cure
Caldwell's Dyspepsia Cure
Crosby's Cure
Coe's Dyspepsia Cure
Chile's Spas. Cure
Clarke Clinic Cure
Cutler's F & A Cure
DeCosta Radical Cure
Dodd's Fever Cure
Fenner's Kidney Cure
Fenton's Asthma Cure
GALLEY TWO
Farnham's Asthma Cure
Farrar's Ague Cure
Fowles' Piles and Humor Cure
Gregary's Instance Cure
Guild's Green M. Asthma Cure
Harter's F & A Cure
Hartshorn' "No. 18" Cure
Hermance's Asthma Cure
Himrod's Asthma Cure
Howe's Ague Cure
Howe's Arabian Milk Cure
Jayne's Ague Cure
Knapp's Throat Cure
Kennedy's Catarrh Cure
Kentz' Chill Cure
Langley's Pimple Cure
Laubuch's Worm Cure
Marsden's Cholera Cure
Magic Cure
Mrs. Belcher's Female Cure
Norton's Catarrh Cure
People's Cure
Poor Man's Cot. Cure

— GROUP B: MEDICINALS

Pisco's Cure
Remington's Foot-Rot Cure
Rhodes' F & A Cure
Rogers' Fever Cure
Sandford's Catarrh Cure
Seward's Cough Cure
Simrod's Pain Cure
Shildoh's Consumption Cure
Talcott's Magic Cure
Uncle Sam's Cough Cure
Upham's Asthma Cure
Weaver's Canker Cure
Wellington's H. A. Cure
Wilton's Catarrh Cure
Whittlesey's Dyspepsia Cure
Warner's Safe Diabeses Cure
White Lily Catarrh Cure
Vincent's Dendan
Curtis' Dentiline
Anderson's Dermador
Kennedy's Discovery
Pierce's Golden Discovery
Nattan's Crystal Discovery
King's Discovery

DROPS
American Life Drops
Austin's Drops
Augsberger's Drops
Bateman's American Drops
Bardott's Worm Drops
Francis' Water of Hap. Drops
Hamburg Drops
Harter's Soothing Drops
Hurlburt's Soothing Drops
Hurlburt's Trachael Drops
Kirby's Cholera Drops
Kornoran's Pie Tar Drops
Lindenfeld's Cholera Drops
Lyons' Female Periodical Drops
Marshall's Pine Tree Tar Drops
Miner's Botanic Drops
Rice's Worm Drops
Rushton's Baby Drops
Skinner's American Life Drops
Wilson's Neuropathic Drops
Wishart's Worm Drops
Eau de Fees, Felix
Eau de Melisse des Carmes, Bys

ELIXIRS
Acker's Elixir
Barr's Pectoral Elixir
Caswell, Hazard & Co.'s Elixir
Delluc's Calisaya Elixir
Down's Elixir
Ducros' Elixir
Governor's Blood Root Elixir
Habuteau's Iron Elixir
Hegeman's Calisaya Elixir
Hegeman's Ferrateo Elixir
Hubbell's Elixir
McMunn's Elixir of Opium
Nichols' Val Ame Elixir
Burdock Elixir
Shaker Malt Elixir
Tilden's Elixir
Wayne's Diuretic Elixir
Wright's Lung Elixir
Wright's Rejuvenating Elixir
Roberts' Embrocation
Roche's Embrocation

EMULSIONS
Griffith's Emulsion
Robinson's Emulsion
Hawley's Pancreatic Emulsion
Savory & Moore's Pan. Emul-
Scotts Cod Liver Oil Emulsion
Smith's Emulsoin
Angiers' Emulsion
Becker's Emulsion
Frey's Emulsion
Frey's Emulsion
McGee's Emulsion
Bovieau's Ergotin
Cutler's Eucalyptus
Sanders' Eucalyptus
Reynolds' Eyewater
Thompson's Eyewater

EXPECTORANTS
Fitch's Expectorant
Hegman's Expectorant
Jayne's Expectorant
Jacque's Spanish Expectorant
Louden's Expectorant
Rose Expectorant
Stabler's Expectorant
Tutt's Expectorant
Bell's Expedient
Brown's Floral Bloom
Bogle's Hyperion Fluid
Darby's Prophylactic Fluid
Upham's FurlingC Fluid
Children's Friend
Lawrence's Woman's Friend
Poor Man's Friend
Stewart Woman's Friend
Valentine's Nurses' Friend
Gastoria
London Cordial Gin

TONICS

Filkins Co. Tonic
Harrison's Chaly. Tonic
Harter's Iron Tonic
Hoofland's Tonic
Tippecanoe Tonic
Howe's Arabian Tonic
Hurley's Ague Tonic
Jones' Red Clover Tonic
Kress' Fever Tonic
Laubach G. S. Tonc
Liebig Cola Tonic
Liebig Cica Tonic
Marsden's Tonic
Austin's Tonic
Rohrer's W. C. Tonic
Schenck's Sea Weed Tonic
Smith's F & A Tonic
Parker's Tonic
Reed's Tonic
Van Deusen's Tonic
Buren Ladies' Tonic
Wilder's Chill Tonic
Wilhoft's Ague Tonic

VERMIFUGES

Brown's O.P. Vermifuge
Fahnestock's B.A. Vermifuge
Fahnestock's B.L. Vermifuge
Frey's Vermifuge
Jayne's Vermifuge

WATERS

Barnes' Magnola Water
Constitution Water
Kennedy's Eye Water
Poor Richards' Water
Reynolds' Eye water
Lanman & Kemp's Florida Water
Hegeman's Florida Water
California Water
What Is It? Water

Fellows' Hypophosphites
Honey Dew
Cutler's Inhalant
VanBuskirk's Liver Invigorator
Sanford's Liver Invigorator
Battle & Co's Iodia
Burnett's Kalistan
Rowland's Kalydor
Lyon's Kathairen
Arnold's Cough Killer
Allen's Indian King
Kalident
Katonka
Watson's Neuralgia King

Ransom's King of the Blood
Bull's King of Pain
Knight's King of Pain
Lactopeptine
Parker's Lethean

LINIMENTS

Allen's Nerve and Bone Lin.
Ander's Iodine Liniment
Baker's Hoof Liniment
Barrell's Ind. Liniment
Burdsell's Liniment
Bennett's Golden Liniment
Bishop Soule's Liniment
Bragg's Arctic Liniment
Centaur Liniment
Coffeen's Chinese Liniment
Cherokee Liniment
"Doctor" Liniment
Child's Liniment
Donnelly's Electric Liniment
Dustin's Horse Liniment
Farrell's Arabian Liniment
Farrell's Arab Liniment
Fennimore's Matchless Lin.
Fitch's Pulmonary Liniment
Frontfield's Liniment
Four Fold Liniment
Gates Horse Liniment
Giles Iodine Liniment
Grant's German Liniment
H. H. H. Liniment
Hamilton's Horse Liniment
Harter's Liniment
Hart's N & B Liniment
Henry's Vermont Liniment
Herrick's Horse Liniment
Hunt's Liniment
Jadwin's Liniment
Jayne's Liniment
Johnson's Anodyne Liniment
Kellinger's Liniment
Johnson Liniment
Kennedy's Rheumatic Liniment
Kennedy's Scattering Liniment
Laubach's Liniment
Low's Magnetic Liniment
Low's Liniment
Lepper's Liniment
Martin's N & B Liniment
H & H Arnica Liniment
McLean's Vol. Oil Liniment
Mustang Liniment
Parker's N & B Liniment
Risley's Liniment
Robinson's Liniment
"Rub It In" Liniment

— GROUP B: MEDICINALS 267

Saawen's Oil Liniment
Sawen's Arnica Liniment
Seabury's Oleaginous Liniment
Sleeper's Arnica Liniment
Sterling's Liniment
Sweet's Liniment
Thorne's Liniment
Tobias' Venetian Liniment
Wells' N & B Liniment
Young American Liniment
Copeland's BB Liquid
Moyle's Catarrh Liquid
Batley's Cinchonae Liquor
Batley's Opil. Liquor
Lavill's Gout Liquor
Lee's Lithontriptic
Bartin's Family and Horse Lot
Bally's Lotion
Church's Lotion
Gowland's Lotion
Craefenberg's Lotion
McClintock's Lotion
Malvina Lotion
Perry's Moth and Freckle Lot.
Robinson's Horse Lotion
Shaw's Mouth and Freckle Lot.
Whitcomb Lotion

MIXTURES
Butters' Mixture
Braddock Cough Mixture
Brazilian Mixture
Chapman's Worm Mixture
Carter's Spanish Mixture
Fennimore's Cough Mixture
Foutz's Mixture
Hegeman's Tonic Mixture
Humboldt's Swamp Mixture
Jayne's F & A Mixture
McClintock's C & C Mixture
Paschall's F & A Mixture
Risley's Colic Mixture
Bowland's Tonic Mixture
Strickland's Cholera Mixture
Worthington's Cholera Mixture
Wright's Worm Mixture
Taylor's Pectoral Mucilage
Bullock's Nephreticum
Bunter's Nervine
Dodd's Nervine
Neuralagine
Richmond's Nervine

COD LIVER OILS
Baker's Cod Liver Oil
Burnett's Cod Liver Oil
DeJongh's Cod Liver Oil
Fongera's Cod Liver Oil
H C. & Co. Cod Liver Oil
Frey's Cod Liver Oil
Hegeman & Co. Cod Liver Oil
Marsden's Cod Liver Oil
Marvin's Cod Liver Oil
Moller's Cod Liver Oil
Nichols' Cod Liver Oil
Cliffe's Cod Liver Oil
Peck's Cod Liver Oil
Rogers' Cod Liver Oil
Rushton's Cod Liver Oil
Savery & Moore's Cod Liver Oil
Scott's Cod Liver Oil
Wilbor's Cod Liver Oil
Walker Cod Liver Oil

OILS
Carter's Oil
Caban Oil
DeCrath's Electric Oil
Dove's Turf Oil
Green Mountain Oil
Hamlin's Wizard Oil
Haarlem Oil
Sylvester's Haarlem Oil
Hoofland's Greek Oil
Kayton's Oil of Life
Kellogg's Oil of Life
Langworthy's Oil
Lightning Oil
Little White's Oil
Merchants Gargling Oil
Page's Arnica Oil
Parker's Nipple Oil
Renne's Magic Oil
Thomas Electric Oil
Walker's White Oil
Walker's Black Oil
Indian Oil
St. Jacob's Oil
St. John's Oil
Society Oil
Stafford's Olive Tar
Newton's Liquid Opodeldoc
Steer's American Opodeldoc
Seabury's Opodeldoc
Dalley's Pain Extractor
Perry Davis Pain Killer
Wolcott's Pain Paint
Marsh's Pain Reliever
Baker's Pain Panacea
Curtis & Brown Panacea
Fahrney's Blood Cleaner Pan.
Graefenberg's Panacea

Houck's Panacea
Household Panacea
Rush's Pain King
Shaker Pain King
Hawley's Pancreatine
Fairchild's Pancreatine
Papoma
Paullinia, Grimault
Ayer's Cherry Pectoral
Pierce's Purgative Pectoral
Wynkoop's Iceland Pectoral
Phenol Sodiqiue
Philtoken
Kennedy's Prairie Wood
Pierce's Favorite Prescription
King's Prescription
Protagon
Brown's Blood Purifier
Stearn's Sweet Quinine
Baker's Quinelixir
Delangrenier's Racahout
DuBarry's Rayalenta
Bradfield's Female Regulator
Emerson's Bowel RRegulator
Grave's Heart Regulator
Pearson's Rejuvenator
Bartholic's Mother's Relief
Chamberlain's Relief
Davis Home Relief
Flagg's Relief
Farnham's Electric Relief
Hart's Great Relief
Morgan's Relief
Radway's Ready Relief
Read's Asthma Relief
Shaw's Sure Relief
Sloan's Instant Relief
Caldwell's Dyspepsia Relief
Constitutional Rheum Relief
Durang's Rheum Relief
Fenner's Catarrh Relief
Frieligh's Remedy
Graefenberg's F & A Remedy
Harper's Cough Remedy
Hunnewell's Cough Remedy
Hunt's Remedy
Acker's Remedy
Kern's Rheumatism Remedy
Langwell's Asthme Remedy
Leonard's S A Remedy
Lockwood's Catarrh Remedy
Metcalfe's Rheumatic Remedy
Popham's Asthma Remedy
Norton's Catarrh Remedy
Packard's Sorofuls Remedy
Pardee's Remedy

Pisco's Catarrh Remedy
Rush's Female Remedy
Sage's Catarrh Remedy
Seelye's Catarrh Remedy
Strickland's Ague Remedy
vanDeusen's Remedy
Valpau's Remedy
Whitcomb's Asthma Remedy
White's Diamond Cat. Remedy
Williams' Asthma Remedy
Wilson's Consumption Remedy
Poor Man's Remdy
Rush's Remedy
Shiloh's Remedy
Brown's Scalp Renovator
Kerr's Scalp Renovator
Rugg's Digestive Renovator
Smith's Green Mt. Renovator
Radway's Resolvent
Cireassian Hair Restorative
Revivum
Philogene
Meyer's Rock Rose
Lawrence's Rosadalis
Sagwa
Salicyline
Lamplough's Pyretic Saline

SARSAPARILLAS
Ayer's Sarsaparilla
Jno. Bull's Sarsaparilla
A. H. Bull's Sarsaparilla
Bristol's Sarsaparilla
Corbett's Sarsaparilla
Graefenberg's Sarsaparilla
Guyscott's Sarsaparilla
Helmbold's Sarsaparilla
Hurley's Sarsaparilla
Hood's Sarsaparilla
Larcokah's Sarsaparilla
Nichols' Sarsaparilla
Rush's Sarsaparilla
Sands' Sarsaparilla
Cilden & Co's Sarsaparilla
Jonnson's Sarsaparilla
Old Dr. Townsend's Sarsaparilla
S. P. Townsend's Sarsaparilla
Wilder's Sarsaparilla

SPECIFICS
Appleby's Specific
Bullock's Catarrh Specific
Cameron's Gout Specific
Campo's Specific
Carey's G. E. S. S. Specific

GROUP B: MEDICINALS

Crossman's Specific
Gray's Specific
Donne's Specific
Fenner's St. Vitus Dance Spec.
FilRins' Catarrh Specific
Harter's F & A Specific
Humphrey's Specific
Japne's Tape Worm Specific
Lalleman's Specific
Ludlum's Specific
Popham's Asthma Specific
Powers' Specific
Reynolds' Gout Specific
Stoddard's Gout Specific
Tnompson's Caarh Specific
Upham's Tape Worm Specific

SYRUPS

Atherton's Cough Syrup
Aubergier's Lactucraium Syr.
Bailey's Soothing Syrup
Barrets Syrup
Berthe's Codeia Syrup
Blackwell's Syrup
Blanchard's Syrup
Boschees German Syrup
Boykins' Syrup
Brown's Syrup
Bull's Syrup
Bumstead's Syrup
Carrington Croup Syrup
Burrington Croup Syrup
Campbell's Tar & W.C. Syrup
Chapman's Croup Syrup
Clark's Worm Syrup
Johnson's Syrup
Clark's Peruvian Syrup
Constitution Life Syrup
Corbin's Worm Syrup
Crook's Poke oot Syrup
Davis' W.C. & Tar Syrup
Edwards' Tar and W.C. Syrup
Fahnestock's Syrup
Foord's Pectoral Syrup
Globe Flower Syrup
Gould's Pin Worm Syrup
Fenner's Syrup
Graefenberg's Sysent. Syrup
Gregg's Constitution Life Syrup
Grimault's Syrup
Frey's Syrup
Hassan's Tar Syrup
Hastings Syrup of Naptha
Hatch's Cough Syrup
Gregory & Dover Syrup
Hobensak's Worm Syrup

Hooker's Cough Syrup
Hufeland's Tar Syrup
Jardella5s Blackberry Syrup
Laubach's Worm Syrup
Kenkel's Worm Syrup
Lera's Syrup
Livingston's Tar Syrup
Low's Worm Syrup
Marsdens Carminative Syrup
Mason's Tar Syrup
Marshall's Syrup
McClintock's Pectoral Syrup
McArthur Syrup
Miller's Horehound Syrup
Miller's Baby Syrup
Mother Noble's Healing Syrup
Morris Tar Syrup
Munson's Cough Syrup
Mitchell's Special Syrup
Page's Syrup
Philips' Syrup
Parrish's Syrup
Peruvian Syrup
Parker Worm Syrup
Peterson Syrup
Ransom's Hive Syrup
Retter's Tar Syrup
Rogers' Tar & Canchalagua Sy.
Rogers' Worm Syrup
Rowland's Blackberry Syrup
Rush's Buchu and Iron Syrup
Rheumaic Syrup
Schenck's Pulmonic Syrup
Scovill's B. & L. Syrup
Seabrook's Soothing Syrup
Seller's Cough Syrup
Smith's Tonic Syrup
Swann's Syrup
St. John Cough Syrup
Swayne's Syrup
Talft's White Pine Syrup
Weaver's Salt Rheum Syrup
Webster's Cough Syrup
Whitcomb's Soothing Syrup
Wilder's Worm Syrup
Winchester's Syrup
Winslow's Soothing Syrup

Woods' Syrup
Tincture D'Or
Cooper's Anti Pain Tincture
Sweet's Mother Tincture
Tongaline
Barry's Tricopherous
Veradia
Vegetine

PE-RU-NA
FOR CATARRH AND ALL CATARRHAL DISEASES.

— GROUP B: MEDICINALS

SELLING EUPHORIA

The collecting of 19th century proprietary medicine bottles, specifically those marked "Bitters," has now reached the stage where many are bringing the same price as historical flasks; yet the majority date only from the last half of the century, were made in vast quantities as compared to the historicals and usually are far less artistic examples of bottle-making art. One reason for today's collecting craze may be its humorous backward glance at the customers who originally bought these bottles for their contents. After unbridled early American effort the Temperance Movement finally gained a firm footing. By 1876 it was in full cry. At this same time Americans were being persuaded by patent medicine firms that they were in poor health and needed to take "medicine." 'Bitters' (well laced with alcohol) was the perfect answer to the country's ever present need for bottled Euphoria. Even the ladies of Frances Willard's WCTU could go to the drug store and pick up Lydia Pinkham's nostrum for satisfying their "female complaints." Today's bottle collector often gets snide tongue-in-cheek amusement from studying why so many different medical nostrums were made and why so many were once actually sold: he needs but a basic Bitters bottle terminology before going out to acquire such empties as have escaped destruction. Here once lay Euphoria!

Various peoples at various times have evidenced in mass manias a common variation from the norm of human behavior. From tarantism to boogie-woogie, from obeah and voodism to mental healing, such departures from normality have taken hold on popular ways and, for shorter or longer periods, have influenced mass behavior. Such manifestations are the effects of causes bedded deep in the subconscious and hidden well-springs of human desires. While there is no present intent to inquire at length into the long-growing causes of the Patent Medicine fever that for a century held a pertinacious grip on America, acquisition of the bottles that are the tangible relics of such a mania requires that something should be known of the intangible backgrounds that give them interest and value.

No more prolific field exists for the growth of popular manias than the human desire for physical health and comfort. It is in this field that medicinal nostrums have flourished and that many a cult that promised bodily ease to its followers has grown and prospered. There is a word in the language of medicine that at once defines and expresses this altogether human desire to feel well-"euphoria." As such euphoria may be induced either by mental suggestion or by administration of drugs or stimulants, the one who provides systematic stimuli to delusion or narcotism has at hand a means to induce a mass mania. It appears that makers of Bitters were well and shrewdly aware that one of the most potent agents for euphoria is alcohol. They were also aware of a pre-

— GROUP B: MEDICINALS

vailing conscience that obeyed a code that regarded indulgence in alcoholic stimulants as a sin. A still more prevalent human characteristic was a willingness to esteem euphoria desirable if produced by medicine. With these understandings in their possession the Bitters makers were able to make a commercial assault on the stronghold of popular conscience and to impel a popular mania.

The most important thing to know about Bitters is that they were highly alcoholic in content. Whatever herbs or drugs or flavorings that were held in suspension in the alcoholic base were gratuitous and had little or no medicinal value. Despite the loud protestations of some Bitters vendors that their concoctions were "temperance," it remained a chemical impossibility for such fluids to retain any potency without alcohol. Here, then, is the salient point in any definition or understanding: that the very chemical or pharmaceutical composition of Bitters implied an evasion, a hypocrisy and a poular form of self-delusion that persuaded the very large numbers of Bitters drinkers to a seemingly innocent violation of an otherwise strictly obeyed code.

How greatly this mass delusion and evasion was responsible for changes in customs and character may be guessed by the fact that the Bitters industry rose to the highest brackets in American commerce, and that it had a great influence in propelling the glass industry upward with it to commercial success.

Commemorative or historical flasks were issued in small numbers compared to the output of Bitters bottles. If a ratio be established between the original number of flasks and the original number of Bitters bottles and the present known numbers of each, amazement will increase that so few of the Bitters bottles are now available.

This rarity may, too, be traced to the almost indefinable psychologic quality that surrounds Bitters taking. The same conscience that was deluded to a belief that bitter tasting stimulants could be imbibed innocently in the guise of medicine turned more honest in a fear of discovery of its pecadilloes, and was impelled to destruction of the evidences of its secret tippling. Great numbers of Bitters bottles were broken up due to this impulse.

For bottle collectors who are stimulated to a search for advertising materials and pictures of the old-time medicine shows, such collaterals will provide a wealth of entertainment, information and a large assortment of memorabilia. This includes the almanacs, pictures, brochures, pamphlets and temperance exhortations as shown on pages which follow. But with all this fun about Selling Euphoria, one should not forget the most important records of all, namely those showing the long and finally successful struggle of the Government to assess upon the proprietary medicine dispensers a Pure Drug Code and a proper Revenue Tax.

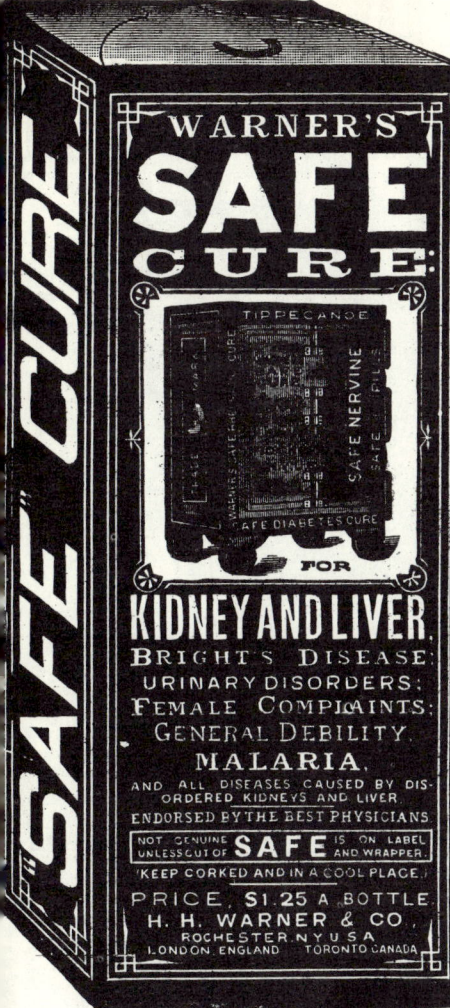

Fig. 1.

Apparent ONE-FOURTH Size Fac-Simile Views of "Warner's SAFE Cure" Caddy or Wrapper, and "Warner's SAFE Cure" Bottle.

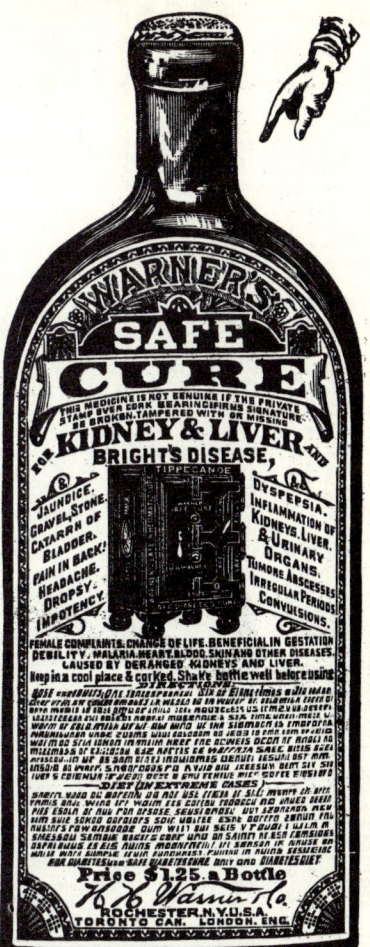

IMPOTENCY or general Loss of Power before Old Age, is generally caused by mental and Physical overwork, and is especially hastened by Bladder diseases, Catarrh, Congestion, Abscesses, Venereal diseases, etc. Kidney diseases produce unhealthy water, which irritates the bladder, destroying in a large measure virile power. Many of those who have passed the prime of life, report what they regard as wonderful results from the use of Warner's SAFE Cure and Warner's SAFE *Pills* for this condition. Try it to-day.

ANALYSIS OF URINE.

THIS is always of value, and many times absolutely essential to a diagnosis. To enable us to make a diagnosis and give you the information you seek, you must carefully observe the following instructions for sending urine: Fill a clean, strong half-pint bottle at least half, but not over two-thirds full (urine first passed in the morning preferred); attach paper giving name, full post office address, and quantity of urine passed in twenty-four hours (by measurement);

Under no circumstances is any Dealer authorized to remove the Stamp over the Cork of "Warner's SAFE Cure," nor is he authorized to repurchase our bottles, wrappers or boxes! If he offers to do this, we will be obliged if our patrons will report the case to us. The proceeding is Criminal, and we shall prosecute Rigorously! Take no bottle of "Warner's SAFE Cure" (or other liquid SAFE Remedies) unless it has a Chocolate-tinted Private Stamp affixed over the Cork, as shown in Fig. 4, page 2.

GUIDE TO HEALTH.

1890   **189**

CIRCULATED FOR THE BENEFIT OF SUFFERING HUMANIT

BEWARE OF FRAUD AND IMPOSTERS

I have spent years of untiring effort in building up a professional character and reputation. There are persons who are using my name and imitating my circulars and pamphlets in order to deceive and in-

veigle innocent sick people to buy their nostrums and injurious compounds. I receive letters quite frequently asking if I prepare such and such a remedy, giving some name. For the benefit of the unsuspecting public, I will say that the name of the medicines that I make, and sold by druggists and agents will be found in this "Guide to Health." All other are

frauds. Thirty days from Jan. 30th, 1890 all persons circulating fraudulent printed matter with my name thereon and selling or trying to sell

See that my likeness and address, Binghamton, N.Y., is on all outside and inside wrappers of my remedies and on all of my circulars.

The Physician At Work. } **S. ANDRAL KILMER, M. D., BINGHAMTON, N. Y.** { The Inval Benefacto

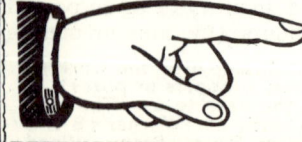

Any Person Picking up this Book with the intention of passin hour or two in reading funny stories, receipts or jokes, will be di pointed. But if you are interested in the welfare of your health that of your friends, then it will repay you to read and preserve future reference this "GUIDE TO HEALTH."

"Dr. Kilmer's Standard Herbal Remedies."

1890

Consulting Rooms, Dispensary and Laboratory, of Dr. Kilmer & Co.,
BINGHAMTON, N. Y.

S. Andral Kilmer, M. D., — The Great Specialist.

Office Hours — 8 A. M. TO 11 A. M., AND FROM 2 P. M. TO 5 P. M.

INVALIDS from a distance should call on either **Tuesday, Wednesday or Thursday.** On these days persons out of town will have preference, and will not be detained any longer than is necessary. No charge for consultation.

SWAMP-ROOT

The wonderful Specific for Rheumatism, Gravel, Diabetes, Bright's Disease, Catarrh of the Bladder, and all urinary difficulties.

The Great KIDNEY Remedy,

Swamp-Root has the largest sale of any Special Kidney Remedy in the World.

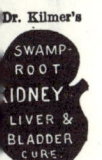

Dr. Kilmer's SWAMP-ROOT KIDNEY LIVER & BLADDER CURE.

Price 50c. LARGE SIZE **$1.00**

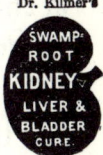

Dr. Kilmer's SWAMP-ROOT KIDNEY LIVER & BLADDER CURE.

READ THIS GUARANTEE — Swamp-Root is the only Kidney Remedy that is POSITIVELY GUARANTEED — All we ask of you is to use the contents of **one** bottle faithfully, then if you are not benefited, return the bottle to your druggist, and he will refund the price paid, only requiring you to write your name and address as **evidence of good faith,** and as a record which we desire to preserve.

SOLD, RECOMMENDED AND GUARANTEED BY

BURDOCK BLOOD BITTERS ALMANAC.

BAD BLOOD

1890

the "Golden Age" to Me

A large majority of diseases owe their existence to poverty, impurity, or poisoning of the blood. Scarlet fever, smallpox, diphtheria, consumption, rheumatism and cancer are all due to the presence in the blood of poisonous matters peculiar to each of these diseases; the unpleasant effects of dyspepsia, biliousness and constipation arise from the blood being impregnated with food-poisons, the result of imperfect assimilation and elimination, and many skin diseases take their origin in the same cause. Scrofula is due to impoverished blood, and rickets to a deficiency of lime salts therein. But to enumerate all the affections which depend upon an unnatural condition of the blood would take more space than can be given to the subject here. The moral is that purity of the blood is a condition essential to health, for "the blood is the life." Into it is received, in a soluble state, the nutritious portions of the blood which go to make bone and muscle and fat, and laden with this it is carried to all parts of the body, bathing every tissue and organ and supplying it with the nourishment necessary to the proper performance of its functions. But the duties of the blood do not end here. Not only does it supply the tissues with food, but it also removes from them the waste products which are continually being formed, and which unless carried off would speedily cause disease and death.

I have received much benefit from Burdock Blood Bitters. I was seriously troubled with a breaking out on my face, and it has cured me. Have recommended B. B. B. to many friends, some of whom are using it with good results.

THE COMPLIMENTS OF THE SEASON.

We have pleasure in presenting you with a new and attractive Almanac containing many useful suggestions. With grateful acknowledgements to our patrons for past favors, we would add that our present stock is carefully assorted and complete to satisfy the requirements of all in choice goods and at low prices.

We also keep in stock in addition to other popular medicines
BURDOCK BLOOD BITTERS
Dr Thomas' Eclectric Oil · Burdock Pills · Hanson's Corn Salve
AND
Dr Fowler's Extract of Wild Strawberry

WISHING YOU A PROSPEROUS NEW YEAR.

Use Thomas' Eclectric Oil for Strains, Sprains, and Bruises of the Skin.

HOSTETTER'S STOMACH BITTERS
Gives that Physical Vigor which is the Main Safeguard of Health and Strength

This represents the Bottling Department of The Hostetter Company.

HOSTETTER'S ILLUSTRATED ALMANAC FOR 1892,
With accurate tables, and full of information, now being gratuitously distributed, offers a means of relief to all who are suffering from Dyspepsia, Malaria, Fever and Ague, and all diseases arising from inaction or disorders of the Stomach, Bowels, Liver and Kidneys, and submits testimony to its efficacy from physicians who have prescribed it, and patients who have experienced its reviving and curative powers. Prepare to enjoy the coming year by renewing your physical man with a course of the Bitters. Ask your Druggist for an Almanac, and ponder the message it brings.
For Sale by all Druggists and Dealers in Proprietary Medicines.

D. HERBERT HOSTETTER, President.	**M. L. MYERS**,	**THE HOSTETTER CO.**, Proprietors,
THEO. R. HOSTETTER, Vice-President.	Sec'y and Treasurer.	PITTSBURGH, PA.

Bitters advertising missed no bets, and appealed to all

Medicine Showman

once upon a time credulous buyers responded to this.

The writer's father once had a big troupe modelled after one nation-wide touring company—the Kickapoo Indian Show that peddled Sagwaw and other dark bilge products of this famed Connecticut company (yes, there actually *was* a Kickapoo "joy juice"). People believed in his medicines.

— GROUP B: MEDICINALS

The Medicine Show Dr. Larry Freeman

The earliest memory of my father has him pulling off with his spanking horse team and its wagon covered with signs of old Dr. Wood's medicines, "good for man or beast." The year was 1905 and Dad, who had been a New York City specialty salesman, was somewhat dubious about the future of taking over a "down-at-the-heels medicine show" inherited by his mother's third husband, the now-deceased "Dr." Wood. I guess the probable "take" must have looked lucrative to Dad; anyway he later once said, "It was all probably a mistake, for the medicine show was then in its last days." But while it lasted everyone (including the customers in the "sticks") had fun.

Here we are concerned only with those people who made a commercial business out of "patent medicine" and especially those who sold the brews via a travelling medicine show. Everyone has heard of Lydia Pinkham's Compound for Female Troubles and the business she started on the kitchen stove,— also how her boys gave this a major shove by becoming "showmen with wagons." But long before its mid-century heyday, concoctions bottled by so-called "Doctors" and "Indians," medicine men were roaming the countryside with their own nostrums. Just when they took to carriages with a troupe for free entertainment in tow can not be precisely dated. Probably as soon as primitive roads became wagon passable, some enterprising soul saw here a new way to "drive" his way to wealth by selling health.

People in backwoods territory and village hamlets were starved for entertainment. There were no theatres or home talent plays; pioneer churches looked askance at having fun. But if a strolling minstrel and his troupe were to stop at the crossroads, open the wagon's back-flap and give a free entertainment, people would flock to see from miles around. What is more, with a good "spiel," they would buy. In this way was the medicine man and later his elaborate tent show born.

A typical early "show" began with a straightforward statement that one's health was his most precious possession and that Dr. Quack was here to help. Next he introduced his partner or (if he only travelled alone) re-introduced himself as a world famous performer of magic, music or song; thus the show got under way. This was followed by bringing out the medicine bottles and extolling their virtue. Then more music or clog dancing and with everything going real lively, a final exhortation to buy. "Step right up ladies and gentlemen and put your quarter on the line. Money back if no cure within twenty-four hours . . . I can help everyone of you."—And with the cash jingling in his pocket away the Medicine Man drove for the next port of call.

As the "take" grew progressively bigger with each year and expanding settlements, the proprietor added more entertainers until it became expedient to carry a tent and "set up" in one spot for several days. Some proprietors gave up the circuit ride in favor of just making and bottling the medicine, then letting independent showmen go out and sell it as they pleased. The greatest entertainment feature seems to have been the Indian (or Indians), dressed in alleged tribal costume and dancing wildly about or uttering gutteral nonsense as he smoked the peace-pipe; a Negro with his banjo made good music, and of course, the proprietor could play anything or any part as the situation demanded.

The alleged virtues of Indian remedies were so generally accepted that many wagon and tent shows billed themselves as "Indian Medicine Men," Here are Dad's reminiscenses.

"Well, the man who went out and got extra boys needed to play in the show was the boss—the promoter—the manager and incidentally the barker who did all the announcing. We had a band of Indians but only one of them was real. The talent consisted of several old-time professional actors and a rather poor band of only three pieces, consisting of a small street organ, a cornet and a banjo. The manager picked out a good vacant lot, their pack wagon arrived filled to capacity with equipment, scenery and properties. Immediately a rough enclosed stage and cover was erected, seats were placed in front, planks laid on soap boxes; clothes-line was strung around the enclosure and a small stand for the barker was placed near the entrance. On a high pole a calcium light was erected (for night use) and people were beckoned in—"It's all free." The Kickapoo Show was now ready. Indians marched down the aisle doing a war dance while the band played a lively tune or the Star Spangled Banner. The manager then went on the stage and welcomed the audience and hoped they would enjoy this healthful show. Then the feature of the eve-

GROUP B: MEDICINALS

"Patent Medicine" Advertising of the BITTERS Era, missed no bets. Counterfeits and Imitations.

TERLING articles, in universal request, are always counterfeited and imitated, and the corsairs of trade, who pick up a living by depredating upon the rights of eminent firms, and cheating the public, have not overlooked PLANTATION BITTERS in their nefarious career. Both in the home and foreign markets they have contrived to introduce their villainous compounds, in some instances boldly affixing the name of the great cosmopolitan tonic to their philtres, and adopting slightly different names, in which, however, the word "Plantation" is conspicuous. Some of the parties to these atrocious deceptions have been prosecuted, and made to suffer the penalties which the law prescribes for counterfeiting trade marks; but in spite of the efforts of the proprietors to protect themselves and the community against fraud, considerable quantities of the noxious trash referred to, are sold. The public are therefore cautioned not to buy any article purporting to be PLANTATION BITTERS, which is not verified by the name, in full, on the bottle and Label, and the same put up in bottles, a fac-simile of the above. By exercising proper care in these particulars, the genuine preparation may always be obtained, and the tricks and dodges of the counterfeiters and imitators of the article will be effectually baffled.

Plantation Bitters as a Spring Specific.

WHEN the sun of Spring breaks up the snow and ice embargo, a vast cloud of moisture ascends from the surface of the earth and water. For weeks this evaporation continues, and the atmosphere becomes saturated with elements of intermittent fever, bilious fever, phthisic, and diseases that affect the stomach and the bowels. With the first advent of Spring, therefore, recourse should be had to the STANDARD PROTECTIVE MEDICINE of the age. Brace up the nervous system.

Plantation Bitters as a Summer Restorative.

HOT weather takes a large amount of vital force out of every one. It relaxes the muscles, reduces the flesh, unstrings the nerves, evaporates through the pores elements that are needed in the blood, diminishes the vigor of the brain, and debilitates the body generally. To enable the system to bear up against the constant drain to which it is subjected by a high temperature, a tonic is needed. The digestion should be stimulated, and the blood, which is always impoverished by profuse perspiration, should be reinforced with all the nutritive material that a perfect assimilation of the food taken into the stomach can supply. By these means emaciation and debility may be prevented and the body kept in as healthy a condition when the thermometer is among the nineties, as if the sun were in a milder mood. The agent, the only certain agent, by which this desirable condition of the physique can be brought about and maintained in the summer months, is PLANTATION BITTERS. Unmedicated stimulants are pernicious. They excite, but do not strengthen; and impair, instead of promoting digestion. Persons who are subject to bilious colic, diarrhœa, dysentery, indigestion, languor, nervous prostration, or ailments that are more prevalent in summer than at other seasons, should frequently resort to the BITTERS as a preventive, and it may be added, that for all sudden attacks vertigo, exhaustion from heat, disturbances in the bowels, oppression after eating, biliousness, and nervous headaches, this pure Vegetable Tonic and corrective is unequaled as a remedy.

Plantation Bitters as a Fall Medicine.

FOR the same reason that has popularized PLANTATION BITTERS as a spring specific, it should be taken in the Fall as a defensive medicine and as a restorative. At both seasons the air contains an unusual amount of deleterious moisture and the same diseases prevail in Autumn as during the vernal months. In Autumn, however, the organization having been enervated by long continued heat, is perhaps still more unfit to resist the morbid atmospheric elements, than in the Spring. By all means, therefore, put the system through a renovating course of the BITTERS in September and October. Indeed there are good and sufficient reasons why it should be resorted to occasionally, at all seasons; and thousands who take a single dose daily throughout the year, are of opinion that they owe health and vigor (under Providence), in a great degree to its regular and systematic use. They may be right; and persons with feeble constitutions unquestionably are right in adopting this plan. In an article on malarious fever, in another portion of this book, the extraordinary value of the BITTERS, as a preventive and curative of chills and fever, bilious remittents, etc., is fully shown. Chronic indigestion is generally aggravated by the sudden and marked variations of temperature which occur in the Fall months, and for indigestion in all its stages, the BITTERS may be safely pronounced infallible.

Plantation Bitters as a Winter Stimulant and Tonic.

WE need more food in Winter than at any other season, for food is the fuel of the system, and a large amount of caloric is required for vital purposes in inclement weather, because of the greater quantity of vital heat abstracted from the body by the severe cold. In order to enable the primary generator of animal heat, the stomach, to digest the additional amount of nourishment which the appetite demands and the physique requires in winter, a wholesome stimulant and tonic is often necessary. Spirits and strong wines, are therefore considered necessary to a greater extent during that season than at any other period of the year, on the supposition that they assist digestion. This, however, is a mistake. The liquors and wines of commerce are *stimulants;* but in their simple state, they are *not tonics* in the true sense of the word. It is only when a spirituous liquor exceptionally pure, is medicated with the finest vegetable invigorants and alteratives, as in the case of PLANTATION BITTERS, that a tonic of the highest excellence is produced. The BITTERS deservedly stand at the head of all the anti-dyspeptic medicines which pharmacy and chemistry have as yet given to mankind. Consequently the standard restorative is an article of pure necessity to persons whose systems need more food than their stomachs are able to digest thoroughly. As a stimulant and invigorant for individuals with weak stomachs it is perfectly invaluable as a winter medicine.

MORNING, NOON, AND NIGHT.

Plantation Bitters as a Summer Restorative.

HOT weather takes a large amount of vital force out of every one. It relaxes the muscles, reduces the flesh, unstrings the nerves, evaporates through the pores elements that are needed in the blood, diminishes the vigor of the brain, and debilitates the body generally. To enable the system to bear up against the constant drain to which it is subjected by a high temperature, a tonic is needed. The digestion should be stimulated, and the blood, which is always impoverished by profuse perspiration, should be reinforced with all the nutritive material that a perfect assimilation of the food taken into the stomach can supply. By these means emaciation and debility may be prevented and the body kept in as healthy a condition when the thermometer is among the nineties, as if the sun were in a milder mood. The agent, the only certain agent, by which this desirable condition of the physique can be brought about and maintained in the summer months, is PLANTATION BITTERS. Unmedicated stimulants are pernicious. They excite, but do not strengthen; and impair, instead of promoting digestion. Persons who are subject to bilious colic, diarrhœa, dysentery, indigestion, languor, nervous prostration, or ailments that are more prevalent in summer than at other seasons, should frequently resort to the BITTERS as a preventive, and it may be added, that for all sudden attacks of vertigo, exhaustion from heat, disturbances in the bowels, oppression after eating, biliousness, and nervous headaches, this pure Vegetable Tonic and corrective is unequalled as a remedy.

Plantation Bitters as a Fall Medicine.

FOR the same reason that has popularized PLANTATION BITTERS as a spring specific, it should be taken in the Fall as a defensive medicine and as a restorative. At both seasons the air contains an unusual amount of deleterious moisture and the same diseases prevail in Autumn as during the vernal months. In Autumn, however, the organization having been enervated by long continued heat, is perhaps still more unfit to resist the morbid atmospheric elements, than in the Spring. By all means, therefore, put the system through a renovating course of the BITTERS in September and October. Indeed there are good and sufficient reasons why it should be resorted to occasionally, at all seasons; and thousands who take a single dose daily throughout the year, are of opinion that they owe health and vigor (under Providence), in a great degree to its regular and systematic use. They may be right; and persons with feeble constitutions unquestionably are right in adopting this plan. In an article on malarious fever, in another portion of this book, the extraordinary value of the BITTERS, as a preventive and curative of chills and fever, bilious remittents, etc., is fully shown. Chronic indigestion is generally aggravated by the sudden and marked variations of temperature which occur in the Fall months, and for indigestion in all its stages, the BITTERS may be safely pronounced infallible.

Plantation Bitters as a Winter Stimulant and Tonic.

WE need more food in Winter than at any other season, for food is the fuel of the system, and a large amount of caloric is required for vital purposes in inclement weather, because of the greater quantity of vital heat abstracted from the body by the severe cold. In order to enable the primary generator of animal heat, the stomach, to digest the additional amount of nourishment which the appetite demands and the physique requires in winter, a wholesome stimulant and tonic is often necessary. Spirits and strong wines, are therefore considered necessary to a greater extent during that season than at any other period of the year, on the supposition that they assist digestion. This, however, is a mistake. The liquors and wines of commerce are *stimulants;* but in their simple state, they are *not tonics* in the true sense of the word. It is only when a spirituous liquor exceptionally pure, is medicated with the finest vegetable invigorants and alteratives, as in the case of PLANTATION BITTERS, that a tonic of the highest excellence is produced. The BITTERS deservedly stand at the head of all the anti-dyspeptic medicines which pharmacy and chemistry have as yet given to mankind. Consequently the standard restorative is an article of pure necessity to persons whose systems need more food than their stomachs are able to digest thoroughly. As a stimulant and invigorant for individuals with weak stomachs, it is perfectly invaluable as a winter medicine.

VENTILATING CHAMBERS.—If a lamp or candle, or a very little fire, is kept burning in a fire-place at night, a draught is created up the chimney, by which the foulest air in the room is carried out with great rapidity.
In all cases where there is a fire-place in a chamber, it should by all means be kept open.

—.GROUP B: MEDICINALS

ning took place, usually a comedy lasting not more than half an hour. Next the barker announced. "Folks, we have a few bottles of wonderful liniment to cure all pains and aches at 25c a bottle, but our special is Indian Sagwaw at $1.00 a bottle guaranteed to cure coughs, colds or pains in the stomach." The Indians would then go down the aisles and sell the medicines like hot cakes. A few people (always connected with the show) would stand up and give their testimonials as to the miraculous cures derived from the medicines they had bought at the show. Then, the barker would announce a ten minute intermission calling attention to the refreshment counter on the side (no free handouts there). The second part of the show started with the band and then a nervous tenor sang a piece like "Asleep in the Deep"; and a brief final sketch "Your Turn Next", lcosed the show. The barker, however, rose on his feet to announce that his famous hair tonic (made of rattlesnake oil) "will make hair grow on a bald head and can be obtained before you leave the grounds." And so it went, several times daily.

Medicine show men, even in its last days, put on a very crude performance, nothing much as far as the scenery and talent of modern theaters are concerned. In their day, however, Medicine Show men pleased people immensely. In fact, they were the forerunners of all of today's better types of entertainers. That they sold remedies of dubious worth is somehow quite beside the point. They did bring people together and gave them a boost to otherwise dull living. Whether the contents were primarily alcoholic or rain water, they set a pattern for health hopes through easy-to-take 'medical' dosage that persists in related form even now. And if you think that the exaggerated claims and fear-selling of today's advertising is modern, just look at the Bitters Bottles and Proprietary Medicines peddled by the *free* tentshowmen of yesterady. Department stores like Macy's and Gimbels, find most succesful "pitch" is selling health and beauty by a free show in the "Bargain (?) Basement! ! ! ! !" People gather around top pitchmen and women to be carried away by a fascinating dramatic performance. They still go for impulse buying, part easily with their money and carry their purchase away feeling highly elated. Once home, however, they tend to hide it in the cupboard so they will have a chance to test its alleged virtues in private and with none to criticise a rash purchase.

ADVERTISEMENT
OF AN
HONEST RUMSELLER
AS IT SHOULD BE!

FRIENDS AND NEIGHBORS:—Having just opened a commodious shop for the sale of "Liquid Fire," I embrace this early opportunity of informing you that, on Saturday next, I shall commence the business of making drunkards, paupers, and beggars, for the sober, industrious, and respectable portion of the community to support.

I shall deal in "familiar spirits" which will excite men to deeds of riot, robbery, and blood; and, by so doing, diminish the comforts, augment the expenses, and ENDANGER THE WELFARE of the community.

I will undertake, at a short notice, for a small sum, and with great expedition, to PREPARE VICTIMS for the Asylums, the Poor-Houses, the Prisons, and the Gallows.

I will furnish an article which will increase the amount of fatal accidents, multiply the number of distressing diseases, and render those which are harmless incurable.

I shall deal in drugs, which will deprive some of life, many of reason, most of property, and all of peace, which will cause the fathers to become fiends, wives widows, children orphans, and all mendicants.

I will cause many of the rising generation to grow up in ignorance, and prove a burden and nuisance to the nation.

I will cause mothers to forget their offspring, and cruelty to take the place of love.

I will sometimes even corrupt the ministers of religion, obstruct the progress of the Gospel, defile the purity of the church, and cause temporal, spiritual, and eternal death; and, if any should be so impertinent as to ask why I have the audacity to bring such accumulated misery upon a comparatively happy people, my honest reply is, MONEY.

The Spirit Trade is lucrative, and some professing Christians give it their cheerful countenance.

I have a License; and, if I do not bring these evils upon you, somebody else will.

I live in a Land of Liberty.

I have purchased the RIGHT to DEMOLISH the character, destroy the health, shorten the lives, and ruin the souls of those who choose to honor me with their custom.

I pledge myself to do all I have herein promised. Those who wish any of the evils above specified, brought upon themselves or their dearest friends, are requested to meet me at my BAR, where I will, for a few cents, furnish them with the certain means of doing so.

— GROUP C: HOUSEHOLDS

Bottle Collaterals; Advertising of bygone brands.

1 Preserve jar, olive amber; free-blown; 18th-early 19th century.

2 "Porter" or "beer" bottle, "black glass"; free-blown; late 18th-early 19th century.

3 Utility bottle, olive green free-blown; type used for various liquids from medicine to blacking; 18th-early 19th century.

4 Medicine bottle, pale aquamarine; free-blown; late 18th or early 19th century.

5 Medicine bottle, pale aquamarine; free-blo late 18th or early 19th century.

8 18th century-type pocket bottle; free-blown; ri green.

9 "Ludlow" bottle, light olive amber; about 11 capacity; free-blown; utility type used for liquo cider, vinegar, and, when covered with straw leather, as canteens and ranging in size fro miniature to more than a gallon.

10 Wine bottle, "black glass"; free-blown, 18 century, circa 1760; type undoubtedly made Wistarberg, N. J., the German-town Glass Wor

14 Panelled bottle for cologne, perfume and toilet waters, opaque "Sandwich" light blue; blown-molded in 12-sided form; very rare in color; mid-19th century.

15 Panelled bottle similar to No. 14, sapphire blue; blown-molded in 12-sided form; mid-19th century.

16 "Gothic" perfume and cologne bottle, colorless; blown-molded; rare in colorless glass; believed to be one of the "Gothic" patterns advertised by New Jersey bottlemakers in the 1840's and 1850's.

17 Perfume or cologne bottle; aquamarine; blown-

18 "Lion" perfume and cologne bottle, aquamar blown-molded; believed to be the "lion" advertised by New Jersey bottlemakers in 1840's and 1850's.

19 Panelled bottle similar to No. 14, amethyst, in color; blown-molded in 12-sided form; r 19th century.

20 Panelled bottle similar to No. 14, light b green, rare in color; blown-molded in 12-si form; mid-19th century.

21 Nursing or pocket bottle, brilliant green; pa molded in 12 vertical ribs and then blow finished; 18th-early 19th century.

ineral water bottle, deep c le, arc of sun rays above ICKLES.

Preserve jar, aquamarine; THE LADIES FAVORITE,

30 Turlington's aquamarine; obverse: BY/ KING'S/ROYALL/PATENT/GRANT/ED TO; rev ROBT/TURLI/NGTON/FOR HIS/INVENTED/BAL OF LIFE. Robert Turlington was one of the if not the first, to have lettered bottles fo patent medicine. He adopted this form in

31 Pickle bottle, golden amber; on one sid medallion depicting a monument, trees, ch and house, and three kegs, inscribed in frame: SKILTON, FOOTE AND CO'S BUNKER

— GROUP C: HOUSEHOLDS

CHAPTER IX HOUSEHOLD BOTTLES

OTHER THAN WHISKEY

Since bottles were the principal commercial product of 19th century American Glasshouses, it stands to reason that many were made for other uses than to hold whiskey and strong drink. In fact, a collector of specialties could find an almost infinite rarity of free-blown and pattern-molded bottles made originally for use by apothecary, doctor or general merchant. Here is a still relatively inexpensive field of collecting that will turn up a variety of small bottles, some with name marked in the glass, others with colors from pale green to deep amber and even blue, all with a great variation in size, shape and neck finish. Furthermore, if one extends the field beyond the blown and into the mechanically produced glass, a turn of century attempting this area has even more extended collector possibilities.

Such a miscellany of uses prevailed for bottles designed for something other than liquor, that the organizer of collectables in our third grouping has to make a number of arbitrary decisions. We have lumped them all together as containers for household products including also the bottles and jars made for druggists, doctors, barbers and other professional users. Under this general C Grouping we select 10 sub-categories each one of which has its own enthusiastic collecting fraternity. These include (1) Perfume, Scent and Snuff Bottles, (2) Beverage, Mineral and Soda Water bottles, (3) Pickles, Sauces and Syrups, (4) Milk Bottles, Nursers and Feeders, (5) Oil Bottles and Fruit Jars, (6) Ink and Blacking and Hair Dye Bottles, (7) Grenade, Target and Testing Bottles, (8) Barber Stand Bottles, (9) Apothecary Jars, Drug and Store Bottles, and (10) a final roundup for complexion and hair creams, liniment, ammonia, and other household aid containers. Each of these categories tended to develop its own style of bottle and many harbor examples which are as early as any found in the whiskey flask groupings. However, little attempt is here made to separate either age or rarity factors. In fact, the numbered listings given and pictured for each category are but a small sample of the individual varieties in shapes, color and markings that the diligent collector in different sections of the country will unearth by himself. Let us say simply that the great majority of bottles in this grouping are from the 19th century and that a liberal sprinkling of glasshouse catalog pages from that era should be most helpful in spotting aberrant types. We start then with one of the oldest and earliest collecting fads (the perfume bottles) and go down the line to more prosaic household and human aid containers. In that progression we shall hope to start many new enthusiasts and so open new vistas of bottle collecting.

BOTTLES — STUDY IN CONTRASTS.

Photographs from collections will serve as aid to memorial promised Mrs. Van Rensselaer before her passing. Also, a complete listing of all varieties of the same type is out of place in a general reference book. In fact, the Van Rensselaer classification has itself been somewhat condensed.

THE BOTTLES SHOWN   HOLD UP TO FOUR OUNCES.

— GROUP C: HOUSEHOLDS

THE HOUSEHOLD BOTTLES

INTRODUCTION

Our third grouping covers an odd assortment of containers used for all household and personal needs not associated with strong drink or medicine. Van Rensselaer, McKearin and Gardner were pioneer collectors of some of these food, perfume, ink and related early blown bottles in these categories. But today the list of collectables has grown almost out of hand due to interest in similar mass-produced items of the early 20th century. A good place to start is with typical Van Rensselaer listings, followed by added examples turned up by Mr. Gardner and other bottle collectors who are still with us. Little attempt will be made to date the later examples or their place of manufacture. It is far more important at this time to show the variety of types and sub-classifications of household containers so that one who wishes to specialize on a certain phase of this broad field can say, "Those were usually used to carry "hair dye and blacking, those are target and testing bottles," etc., etc. While it is possible that the same bottle was sometimes used for diverse purposes, many (especially those marked in the glass) are forever identified with a product such as Walker Hair Dye, Moxie Nerve Food or Pluto Water for the Bowels.

Since the *perfume or cologne* bottles were the first items in this field to hold collector interest, it is only fitting that our study begin here. Everyone has probably heard that a Stiegel perfume in Amythest with the diamond daisy pattern mold is the hearts desire of advanced collectors. Actually these half pint early chestnuts can seldom be attributed to Stiegel, also they were often called ladies' flasks and used almost as often for whiskey nips as for cologne. The cologne need is as explainable as the whiskey nip. In the days when any kind of bath was a luxury, people doused themselves with cologne to hide any body odor. Traveling by coach to visit a distant friend or relative, a lady often supplied herself with two small flasks, one with drinks to help stay the fatiguing journey, the other to help overcome the stench of close communion with other passengers. These early Stiegel types here are the true rarities. But also now in great demand (if not just fakes and repros) are the cologne bottles of the 1850's in the violin and scroll type pattern. Then if one wants to move into a later category there is a wealth of perfume atomizers of the late 19th century (many in colored glass) or even the patented designs of cologne and perfume bottles used by present day promotors of the belief that the perfume is what charms the man. Some of each era are shown in the hope that this field will be of even greater collector interest in the future.

8
Stiegel perfume in Amythest

These 'Stiegels' are the field's Rarities. Blown from amethyst non-lead glass and pattern-molded, these might be contrasted with some Stiegel type 'pocket flasks' (See Chapter IV)—Hunter referred to these 'Toilet Bottles,' Van Renssalaer called them 'perfumes in the Diamond and Daisy-in-Square' patterns. Note: The Gemels or Twin Bottles (see page 305) may have held perfume, though we usually think of the large varieties as for Oil and Vinegar.

— GROUP C: HOUSEHOLDS

Violin flasks were made at Wheeling, West Virginia; Zanesville, Ohio; Pittsburgh, Pennsylvania and probably at Wellsburg, Steubenville and Martins Ferry, Onio, and some of the smaller factories in Indiana, and of course at Louisville, Kentucky and Lancaster, N. Y.

Many minor and not noteworthy variations occur, denoting a wide range of production.

GRAND OLD AMERICAN BOTTLES

THE MODERN

GIFT PERFUME

Modern Perfume Bottles—a few are hand cut rarities.

— GROUP C: HOUSEHOLDS

CHAPTER XI   PERFUMES AND SCENTS

SCENT, PERFUME AND SNUFF BOTTLES

Perfume and scent bottles form a natural category of human household needs. Collecting the earliest 18th century forms is both costly and elusive, that of the 19th and 20th more numerous and often even far more interesting shape and story. Desire to make one appear beautiful and attractive knows no era limits. In the days before baths and cleanliness were easy and expected, people in close congress tried to eliminate body odor by a liberal sprinkling of cologne and perfume. Stiegel type expanded-mold perfumes form our first instance of 18th century and aside from differences seen by experts, have very much the same form. Contrast these pocket flasks or the small colognes with the great variety of 19th century perfumes listed and shown in a following section. Then turn to the more miniature scent and smelling salts bottles where you see some very fine instances of the glass blowers art. Note also that some bottles are for a sweet smell, others for a strong ammonia scent designed to revive a woman who was fainting from tight laces or just to act the 'elegant vapors' that status decreed was a Victorian gentlewomans special loot. In between somewhere, we give a small section over to the double scent bottle of late 19th century, many the work of costly jewelers art. Then, with greater personal cleanliness in common practice, the more subtle appeal in the 20th century, gave rise to expensive channel 5 and other French gift perfumes to add "allure." Finally look back at a few 17th and 18th century snuff bottles where the practice of snuffing snuff so as to clear the nose (a mild tobacco habit) is no longer considered the mark of a fine lady. This certainly puts a kind of finus to the whole perfumery and scent business—another type of bottle euphoria.

SNUFF BOTTLES

Imperishable Perfumes

Standard Odors ......

Unapproachable Excellence.

VIOLETS OF SICILY (Trade Mark)   The Finest Violet Odor Ever Produced.

BLUE LILIES (Trade Mark).   Of Exquisite Character.

ROSE OF SHARON.   A Wonderful Rose Odor.

Exquisite Odors.   Beautiful Packages.

OUR SPECIALTIES:
Cairo Violets,   Satanita,   Dorothy,   Daphnea,

Cherokee Rose,   Lady May,   Duchess Rose, Almond Blossom.

19th Century **Perfumes**
Bottles and association collaterals at writer's Yorker Yankee Village, Watkins Glen, N. Y.

— GROUP C: HOUSEHOLDS

Perfume Bottles

Top row, soldier, height 9½ inches. Lower row master bottle in centre. height 7¾ inches, others 4½ inches to 8¼ inches in height. (U). P 2.

Height 2 inches to 5½ inches. (U). P. 3.

Top Row. Plate 4.
    1. Height 3½ inches to 5½ inches. 6 has original label. (U).

Lower Row.
    1. Clear glass, ribbed to right and upward, height 3½ inches (U).

    2. "Sea horse" shape with volieted ends and applied glass filament scrollings. Clear glass, length 1¾ inches (U).

    3. Sunburst design, amethyst, length 2¾ inches (U).

    4. 3 Fleur-de-lis surmounted by crown. Reverse: 3 hearts and floral motifs, floral edging, amber, height 3½ inches (U).

    5. Bellows, length 6¾ inches, aquamarine. (U).

    6. Like 4 but deep blue, pewter top missing. (U).

    7. Sunburst design, beaded sides, green, height 2⅞ inches. (Kn).

    8. Ribbed to right and upward, deep green, height 3 inches. (U).

    9. Intricate design of fine latticing with twisted open work ribbons, red and opaque, vertical line through centre of bottle each side and edge. Clear glass, height 4⅛ inches (U).

Master bottle (centre top row), height 9 inches, others from 5 inches (U). P. 5.

Top master bottle (center) height 10½ inches, lower master bottle (center) 8¼ inches, others 4¾ inches to 6½ inches in height. (U). P 6.

Plate 7 (U)

Later type, height 1 inch to 4¾ inches (U). P. 8

GROUPED EXAMPLES

GROUPED EXAMPLES

GROUPED EXAMPLES

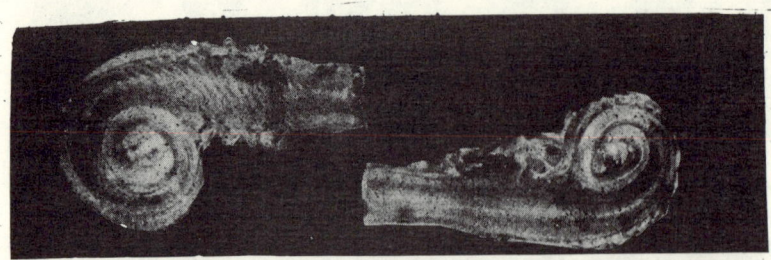

MINIATURE SCENT BOTTLES

— GROUP C: HOUSEHOLDS

SCENT

Another fascinating field of bottle collecting are the little scent and smelling bottles made for the days by both Stiegel and Sandwich and continued in others even after these factories had closed. A Stiegel account book of 1769, still extant and in possession of the Historical Society of Penna. lists among the inventory at the Manheim glass store, 584 Smelling Bottles. These Stiegel type smelling bottles (often in Cobalt even from 2½ to 3 inches long and calculated to slip into a glove or reticule. They were free-blown-pattern mold in small dip-piece molds and with decorations ranging from the family seahorse type to those of highly individual shape depending on whim of the blower. But scent bottles do not end with the tiny ones of blown-molded origin. A little later in the 19th century, the Victorian era of tight corsets and swooning ladies was upon us; and by the middle of that century a slightly larger smelling salts bottle in pressed glass was being made for the reticule and parlor table. Still later in this century (1870's) we even began to see the double scent bottle which combined the invigorating ammonia for the fainting on one side and the sweet smell of attar of roses on the other. Since this 1870-1880 craze seems to have come over from England, we give you a description of the type of collectable (both then and here) and that winds off scent or smelling bottle for all time. Some had jewels in them and most were in silver and gold. Exactly what is the modern accompaniment for the pocket lipstick, this man would not know. But with a look at the double scent bottle of Victorian times, certainly a new era in bottle collecting is well on its way.

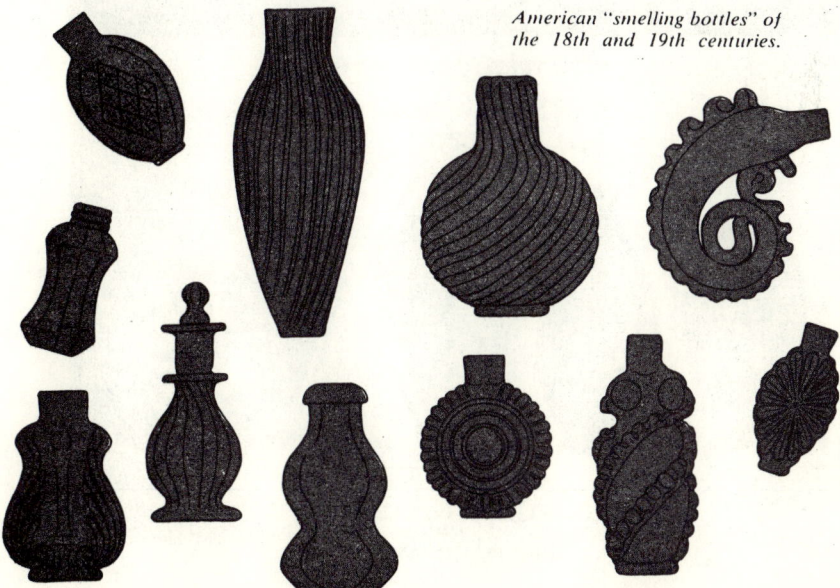

American "smelling bottles" of the 18th and 19th centuries.

MINIATURE SCENT BOTTLES

MINIATURE SCENT BOTTLES

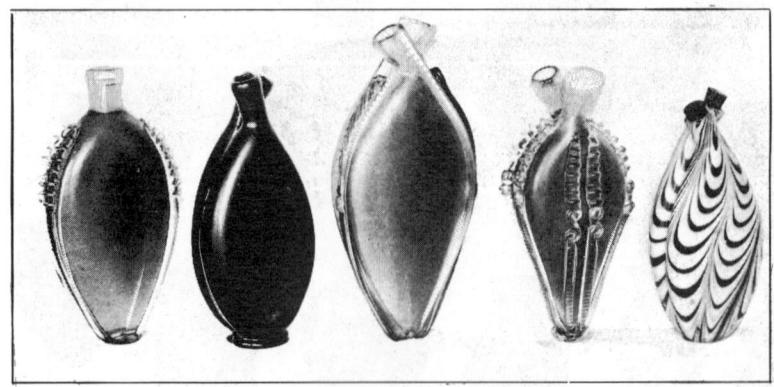

Gemel BOTTLES

GROUPED EXAMPLES

MINIATURE SCENT BOTTLES

COLOGNE BOTTLES.

Pressed, Blown and Engraved, etc.

Fig. 585.

The following cuts represent but a few of the many styles of Colognes, Pungents, &c., constituting our extensive assortment and to which we are frequently making additions. To an inspection of this assortment we would especially call the attention of those who contemplate visiting our establishment.

These goods are worthy the attention of those seeking novelties for the coming holiday season.

COLOGNE BOTTLES.

MOULDED AND PRESSED.

Fig. 538. Per doz.	Fig. 539. Per doz.	Fig. 540. Per doz.
1 oz. $0.75	½ oz. $0.70	8 oz. $2.00
	1 " 0.75	12 " 2.25

PUNGENT OR SMELLING SALT BOTTLES.—Continued.

 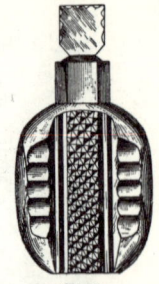

Fig. 588. Per dozen $3.00

Fig. 589. Per dozen $3.50

Fig. 590. Per dozen $3.00

Fig. 591. Per dozen $3.75

COLOGNE BOTTLES.—Continued.

Fig. 559.

	Pressed Stoppers. Per doz.	Cut Stoppers. Per doz.
1 oz.	$1.20	$2.00
2 "	1.50	2.30
4 "	2.10	3.25
8 "	2.63	3.60
12 "	3.00	4.00

Fig. 560.

	Cut Stoppers. Per doz.
1 oz.	$1.88
2 "	2.25
4 "	3.20
6 "	4.10
8 "	5.00
12 "	6.25
16 "	8.00

CUT.

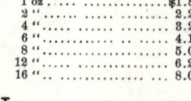

Fig. 561. Per pair.	Fig. 562. Per pair.	Fig. 563. Per pair.
16 oz. $2.50	16 oz. $4.00	12 oz. $2.50

COLOGNE BOTTLES.—Continued.

Fig. 541. Per doz.	Fig. 542. Cut Stoppers. Per doz.	Fig. 543. Cut Stoppers. Per doz.
1 oz. .... $ .75	½ oz. $1.60	1 oz. $1.75
2 " .... .88		
4 " 1.15		
8 " 1.88		
16 " 2.80		

Fig. 544. Per doz.	Fig. 545. Per doz.	Fig. 546. Per doz.
1 oz. $1.25	1 oz. $1.25	1 oz. $1.20
2 " 1.75	2 " 1.75	2 " 1.50
4 " 2.50	4 " 2.50	4 " 2.00
6 " 4.20	8 " 4.20	8 " 3.00

PUNGENT OR SMELLING SALT BOTTLES.—Continued.

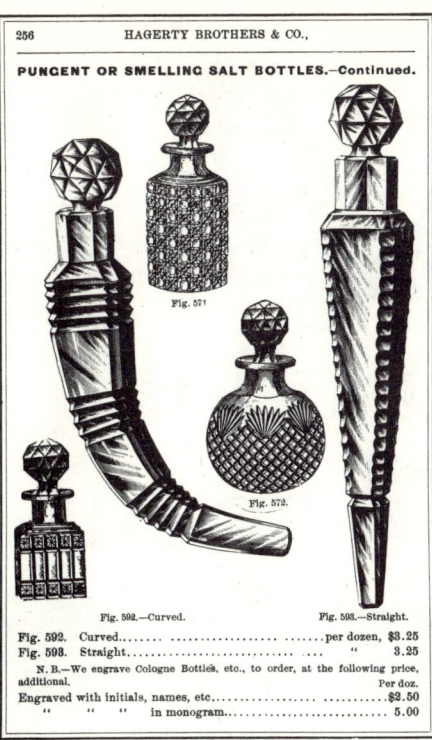

Fig. 592.—Curved.   Fig. 593.—Straight.

Fig. 592. Curved................................ per dozen, $3.25
Fig. 593. Straight................................ "   3.25

N. B.—We engrave Cologne Bottles, etc., to order, at the following price, additional.

	Per doz.
Engraved with initials, names, etc.	$2.50
" " " in monogram	5.00

PUNGENT OR SMELLING SALT BOTTLES.—Continued.

Fig. 581. Assorted Styles, per doz.... $1.50   Fig. 582. Per dozen............ $2.00

Fig. 583. Per dozen.......... $1.50   Fig. 584. Assorted, per dozen........ $3.40

COLOGNE BOTTLES.—Continued.

Fig. 547. Per doz.	Fig. 548. Per doz.	Fig. 549. Per doz.
1 oz............$1.25	1 oz............$1.25	1 oz............$1.25
2 "............ 1.75	2 "............ 1.75	2 "............ 1.75
4 "............ 2.50	4 "............ 2.50	4 "............ 2.50
6 "............ 3.50	6 "............ 3.50	6 "............ 3.50
8 "............ 4.20	8 "............ 4.20	8 "............ 4.20

Fig. 550. Per doz.	Fig. 551. Per doz.	Fig. 552. Per doz.
1 oz............$1.20	1 oz............$1.25	1 oz............$1.20
2 "............ 1.50	2 "............ 1.75	2 "............ 1.50
4 "............ 2.00	4 "............ 2.50	4 "............ 2.00
6 "............ 2.63	8 "............ 4.20	6 "............ 2.63
8 "............ 3.00	12 "............ 5.00	8 "............ 3.00

COLOGNE BOTTLES.—Continued.

Fig. 553. Pressed Stoppers. Per doz.	Cut Stoppers. Per doz.	Fig. 554. Per doz.	Fig. 555. Per doz.	Cut Stoppers. Per doz.
1 oz.. $1.20	$2.00	1 oz............$1.60	1 oz........	$2.00
2 "... 1.50	2.25	2 "............ 2.10	2 "........	2.30
4 "... 2.00	2.75	4 "............ 2.50	4 "........	3.10
6 "... 2.63	3.50	6 "............ 3.00	8 "........	3.60
8 "... 3.00	4.00	8 "............ 3.50	12 "........	4.00
16 "... 4.50	5.75			

Fig. 556. Pressed Stoppers. Per doz.	Cut Stoppers. Per doz.	Fig. 557. Pressed Stoppers. Per doz.	Cut Stoppers. Per doz.	Fig. 558. Pressed Stoppers. Per doz.	Cut Stoppers. Per doz.
1 oz.. $1.30	$2.00	1 oz.. $1.20	$2.00	1 oz.. $1.20	$2.00
2 "... 1.65	2.50	2 "... 1.50	2.30	2 "... 1.50	2.30
4 "... 2.30	3.50	4 "... 2.10	3.25	4 "... 2.10	3.25
8 "... 2.75	4.00	8 "... 2.63	3.60	8 "... 2.63	3.60
12 "... 3.50	4.50	12 "... 3.00	4.00	12 "... 3.00	4.00

Double scent

A SILVER mount *three examples of hinged scent bottles. Left, Bristol blue glass with heavy brass mounts and a vinaigrette grille by S. Mordan and Co.; centre, dark green glass; right, ruby glass with gilded mounts and a photograph in the centre.*

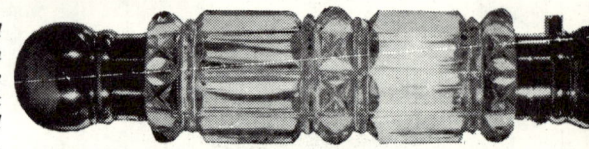

Below: top, blue twist glass bottle with hinged cover and tiny stopper; centre, finely hand-cut glass still containing small scraps of sponge; below, opaque opal glass which glows in rich sunset colours when held up against the light.

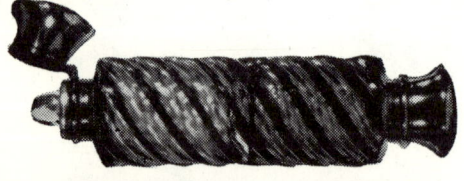

Above: top, a heavy specimen weighing 6 ounces and measuring 6 inches, richly hand-cut with roman pillars and cross-cut diamonds; centre and below, two specimens in metal, the top one is hallmarked for 1881 and the centre portion of the other is of plaited silvery nickel alloy.

bottles

GROUP C: HOUSEHOLDS

NAPOLEON BONAPARTE bathed his head and shoulders every morning in eau-de-Cologne, refreshed by the mind-stimulating rosemary attar and citrous distillations of this grape-spirit diffusion. The Empress Josephine drenched her apartments with the lingering scent of musk. The whole 19th century was enchanted by perfumes.

The new craze of the 1870s and 1880s was the invigorating ammonia of the smelling bottle, the new shape the double scent bottle. Collectors are only beginning to look for these articles, completely Victorian but as varied and charming as glassmaker, silversmith and gilt metal manufacturer could devise.

Smelling salts, inexhaustible salts, sal volatile, under various names the revivifying scents needed by the over-dressed Victorian in her over-furnished rooms were based upon pungent ammonia. A drachm each of English lavender and rosemary attars, half a drachm each of bergamot and cloves, would together enrich a pint of liquid ammonia.

The immense popularity of the bottles under review may be attributed to the fact that the design incorporates two bottles, joined base to base, so that one half could be filled with the fashionable salts, while the other contained a more endearing perfume—one of the sweet flowery "handkerchief scents" then equally appreciated, tuberose, violet or powerful patchouli.

In most of these bottles the centre part is of glass. Two bottles were blown separately and welded together. Some bottles are of china, some of glass-lined silver or imitative nickel alloy. At each end is a metal lid, silver perhaps, or more often merely of gilded brass alloy. This may be delicately tooled or stamp-embossed in an all-over foliate pattern or engraved with severe engine turning.

OCCASIONALLY the ends are mounted with tiny turquoises or other inexpensive gems, and a fashion of the 1870s put a coloured glass "gem" in the centre of each mount, matching the glass bottle, ruby, sapphire or emerald.

It was important to the user to differentiate at a touch between the ends of her bottle. Usually one end springs open on a hinge by pressure on a small stud: this is the end for the smelling salts. Inside the lid is a glass-covered metal disc.

There are several variants. One of the most attractive harks back to the vinaigrette and the hinged cover springs open to reveal a fretted grille over a sponge once saturated with aromatic vinegar. Some of the smaller bottles made in the 1850s and '60s, $2\frac{1}{2}$ to $3\frac{1}{2}$ inches long, disclose such intricate fittings. A more elaborate style is hinged in the middle where the two bottles meet, one bottle being plain-based, the other based with a delicate perforated vinaigrette.

Mainly, however, the collector finds variety in the rich colours and fine cutting of the glass. Translucent deep blues, sea greens and ruby reds tone splendidly with the gilded mounts, but other tints range from a manganese amethyst to a uranium opaline green. Some specimens are in flashed glass, the clear flint glass thinly covered with colour so that patterns cut through to the clear glass are emphasised by the coloured background.

The knowing collector distinguishes these from the specimens shaped not by cutting but by blowing into a patterned mould and coloured by brush-staining. This was somewhat cheaper although the colour still needed a kiln firing to fix it, and finishing touches on the cutting wheel.

Many of the most impressive specimens, 6 or 7 inches long, 6 ounces in weight, are in clear flint glass deeply cut on the wheel, and these too are cleverly imitated, and only slightly less sharp-edged, by blowing the molten glass into patterned moulds. All the familiar designs of the glasscutter are to be found
—long smooth diamonds, sharp starry points of light where diamond shapes have been cut across and across, bold Roman pillars, and whirling ribbons of square-edged panel cutting. A rarity is a bottle with flowers engraved on the flat glass panels.

-Bottling natural mineral water.

— GROUP C: HOUSEHOLDS

CHAPTER XII   MINERAL WATERS

From mid-19th century on, Americans have consumed millions upon millions of gallons of soda pop and other sparkling waters. Each specially bottled brand has usually had its own distinctive glass container, if not at least its own name marked in the glass. Everyone is familiar with the distinctive trademarked Coca-Cola and Pepsi bottles (of which 1″ miniatures are alone a bit hard to find) and the early Bromo Seltzer containers and Pluto Mineral Water for the bowels. But classification wise, what is one to do with the quinine tonic ginger beers and ales or other effervescent products which certainly suggest fixers and mixers with alcoholic contents? Certainly there is no point of separating containers for natural mineral waters taken for health and the artificially manufactured thirst quenchers. One could have a whole category on beer bottles alone, for they were passed over very lightly in connection with our first or A Group of liquor flasks. But it is more historically correct to start this chatter with a listing of bottles first designed to hold natural mineral waters. The so-called Saratoga Spring Bottles date from mid-century when the public was first taught to take the foul-smelling waters foaming up from the bowels of the earth to aid an alleged faulty elimination or fix other human internal ills. The vogue of "taking the waters" at Saratoga and other spas can hardly be touched on in this book. However, we should mention that commercial exploitation of the vogue soon took the form of bottling and selling the waters in distant spots so that one could have the alleged benefits even without attending in person. Elsewhere we picture how the natural physics, etc., were first captured in glass bottles and then how they were made artificially by adding sulphur dioxide to a non-effervescent compound and so bringing on another product which eventuated in the sweet soda pop take overs of Coca-Cola, Mr. Pepper and other Pop Drinks, "Moxie Nerve Tonic," "Liquid Force." Our first listing is based on Mr. Van Rensselaer's list and shows a few typical bottles, usually bottle green and heavy sided so as not to "explode under carbon dioxide pressure." Then we give a listing and picture typical examples of the soda and other tasty soda pop bottles that are also beginning collector items. As far as bottle type goes some of early manufactured bubbly thirst quenchers are indistinguishable from the natural Sal-Hepaticas, Pluto Waters and Mineral Spring Health Aids. The writer has a different memory of each type of product, but he remembers the containers as very much alike. One memory is of a very old 1920 Sorority Housemother for whom he dishwashed his way through college: she always called for her "Pluto Water"

Double and Single Soda Waters 1799, derived their name ' from the peculiar mode of Preparation employed by A. & R. Thwaites & Co., which renders them highly useful to the powers of Digestion, improving the APPETITE and stimulating the HEPATIC FUNCTIONS'.

The method of production was simple. A strong solution of soda was poured into bottles. To each bottle was added a measured amount of acid sufficient to neutralise 50% of the soda content and at the same time generate carbon dioxide gas. Each bottle was then immediately corked and wired to resist gas pressure. Cork shrinks when dry, but the bottles used had round bottoms and would not stand upright. This ensured that the corks were kept moist and that a gas-tight seal was maintained.

The manufacture of soda water by the original method continued until Mr. W. F. Hamilton invented a mechanical method, whereby carbonic acid gas was generated in a gas chamber and pumped under pressure with water into saturating cylinders, from which the highly-charged water was bottled. A. & R. Thwaites & Co. purchased the time rights in Mr. Hamilton's patent in 1810 and continued the manufacture of soda water by this new method, calling it Patent Soda Water.

The old fashioned soda-water or 'pop' bottle was first modeled after the ancient amphora for wine. Its pointed base with deep blue or sea-green coloring is often described as a "bottle without a bottom." This is the rarity of the field.

— GROUP C: HOUSEHOLDS

at breakfast and could not be convinced it was not bottled at Saratoga which she had visited as a girl. The other memory is of the writer's father introducing "Liquid Force" to thirsty New Yorkers in 1905. Taking over at 5th Ave. drugstore window and with a big Greek fresh off steerage lifting bar bells after each drink of Liquid Force. The supersalesman took watchers off the street, gave them a free drink inside and sold them a case of bottles of dark Pluto-like brew that was guaranteed to give them all "plenty of Moxie." Liquid Force is long off the markets, and even Pluto Water may be gone too. But some of the bottles left from both types of alleged human betterment aids are now in the writer's collection at Yorker Yankee Old Village Museum—a source of much amusement to collectors who have previously thought only in terms of empty whiskey containers. Verily, verily, one man said, the gullible will drink anything that promises some kind of Euphoria. Question—does the soda pop of today even really quench thirst?

Drug Store Of 1900

Bottles and association collaterals at writer's Yorker Yankee Village, Watkins Glen, N. Y.

Soda Water NOVELTIES

Oscillating Glass Syrup Jars
THE FONTAINE

Smiles and Frowns?

Depends on whether you draw from your fountain

Hires Rootbeer

or a worthless substitute. This year we shall prosecute the dispensers of bogus stuff sold as HIRES.

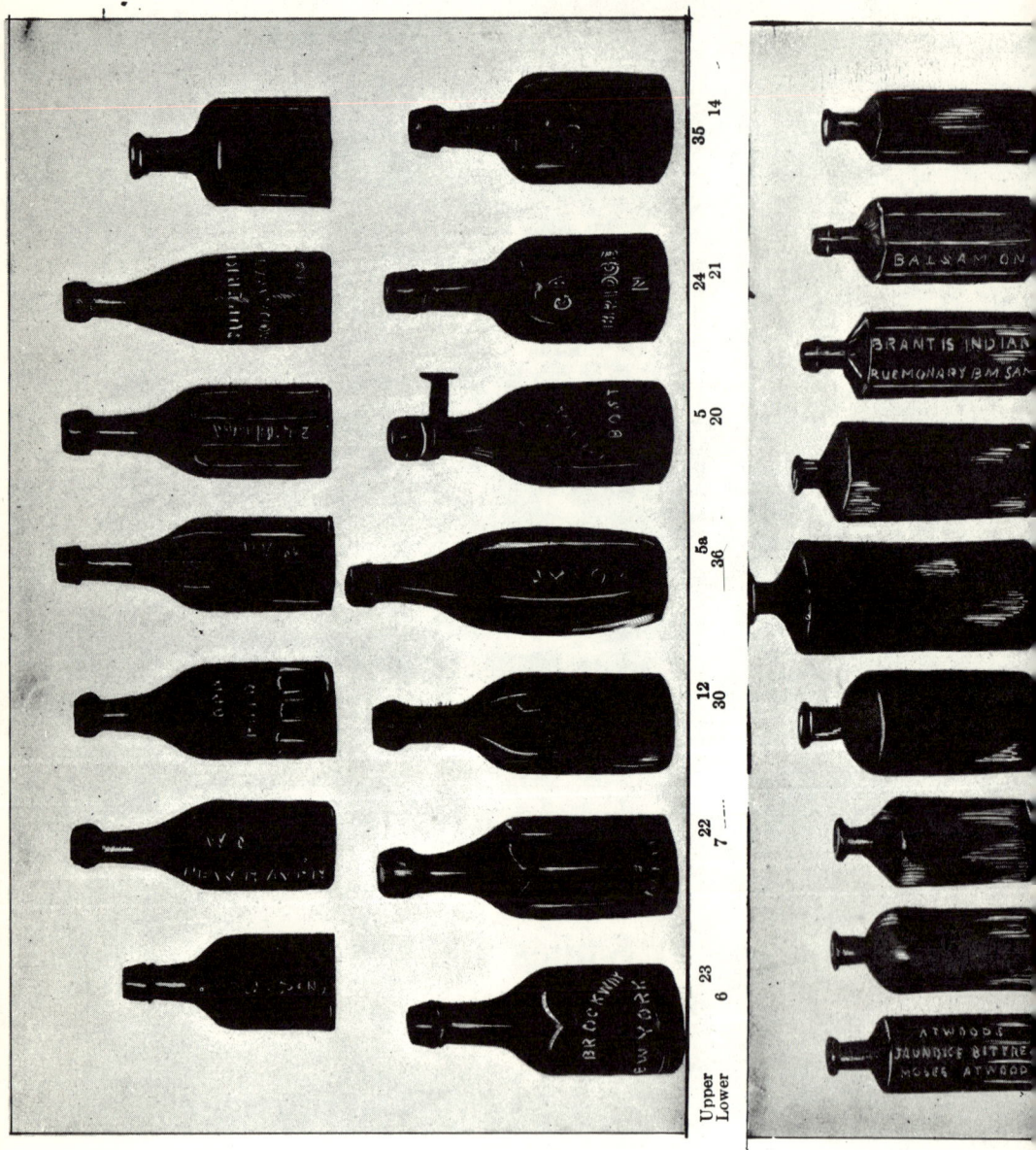

GROUP C: HOUSEHOLDS 317

I.—Mineral Spring Bottles

1. "Anthony". large block letters running around bottle. Green. c. m. (NL). 2. "Bartlet & Chase" About ½ pint—aquamarine.

3. "Luke Beard, Howard St., Boston" (3 horizontal lines.) Reverse: Five pointed star and "This bottle is never sold" (2 lines). Half pint—olive green. 1 s c m with ring. (U)

4. "BEARD'S" (large letters in semi-circle) below "Mineral Water" (straight line). Reverse: "F. & B" (large letters), below "Boston" (smaller letters). Deep green. (U)

5. Ten panels, on three of which is "Wm. Betz, Salem, O., Mineral Water." Light green, heavy c m. Height 7½ inches (U)

5a. Lettered "Betz & Co. Pitts." (U)

6. "W. E. Brockway & Co." (semi-circle), "New York". Pint—green, d c m. Height 6¾ inches. (86-88 E. 11th St., Soda Water makers in 1857-8)

7. "Buffum & Co.", "Pittsburgh", large letters encircling the bottle. Half-pint—bluish aquamarine. Heavy c m. (U).

8. "C. Cleminshaw, Troy, N. Y." Blue. (A).

9. Same. Reverse: C in circle, vertical ribbing.

10. "P. Conway, Philad." Reverse: "No. 8 Hunter St. 108 Filbert St. Mineral Waters" Blue—long neck. Height 7½ inches (Un)

11. "A. R. Cox, Norristown, Pa." Reverse: "Union Glass Works, Phila" in (semi-circle). "Superior" (in middle) "Mineral Waters". Pint—blue. c m Height 7¼ inches.

12. "M. T. Crawford". Reverse: "Superior Mineral Waters" (2 lines, semi-circles.) "Union Glass Works, Phila" above. Blue—10 flat panels extending around base and 1½ inches high. P. 123.

13. "Crystal Palace Premium Soda Water. W. Eagle, New York". Reverse: Crystal Palace and "Union Glass Works, Phila." About ¾ pint—sea green. h c m (Wm. Eagle 1851-52 premium soda and mineral water, Phila. and London porter XX and Scotch Ales, champagne, etc. 192-94 Fulton St. In 1857-58 Bottler at 71 Varick St.)

14. "J. Deane 164 Broadway" (3 lines). Pint—green. c m. Height 6⅝ inches (U)

15. "J. & A. Dearborn, N. Y." Reverse: "Albany Glass Works, New York". Pint—blue. Height 7 inches.

16. "Demott's Celebrated Soda or Mineral Waters" (4 lines). Reverse: "Hudson County" (semi-circle) "N. J." below. Blue—c m. Height 7½ inches (U) (1854-60).

17. "Dowdale" (U)

18. "Francis Dusch, This Bottle is Never Sold" (2 lines). Height 7½ inches, 1½ inches in diameter at base. (U)

19. Large eagle in flight, with ribbon overhead and in beak, perched on shield through which goes a ribbon lettered "E. W. & Co.", below cartouche lettered "Works". Aquamarine. Height 7½ inches. (E. W. & Co.)

20. "M. F. & Co" (large letters.) Reverse: "M. F. Fairbanks & Co." (semi-circle), below "Boston". Aquamarine. (Moses Fairbanks & Co. manufacturers of Belfast Ginger Ale, mineral waters, lemonade, etc., in bottles, barrels, half barrels and kegs, is found in the Boston directory from 1855 to 1860, etc.) (U)

21. "J. Gahre (quarter circle) Bridgetown, N. J." (three lines). Pint —yellow-green. c m. Height 6⅞ inches (Br)

22. "T. W. Gillet, New Haven". On one panel opposite the name is a six-pointed star. About ¾ pint—blue. Heavy c m s b. Height 7¾ inches. Octagonal. (Note: Thos. W. Gillet Soda Water Mfr. 1849-50, 9 Lyon St., 1851-56, 44 Court St.; 1857, 1 Veto St.) (NL)

23. "J. & S. W. Harbey, Norwich, Ct. Porter, Ale & Cider". Sea green. c m s b. Height 6 inches. (U)

24. "E. S. & H. Hart" (in semi-circle). Reverse: "Superior Soda Water, Union Glass Works". Pint—blue. c m Height 7½ inches.

25. "Vincent Hathaway & Co. Boston" (lettering lengthwise on one side in 4 lines). Half pint—deep green. rolled c m. Round base.

26. "W. Heiss Jr's Superior Mineral Waters, No 213 2d St Phila". Reverse: Large spread eagle, head to left, rays over head, perched on large shield and on each side flags and olive branches. Pint—deep blue. (Un)

27. "M. McCormack, This Bottle Never Sold" (2 lines). Green—height 7½ inches. (U)

28. "Knickerbocker Soda Water S. S." Blue—quintagonal. (U)

29. "Miller & Bro.". Reverse:' 'Hamburg, Pa." Pint—emerald green. c m. Height 7 inches. (U)

30. "Mineral Waters" (semi-circle). Pint—olive green, c m Height 7⅝ inches (U)

31. "R. C. & T. New York" (large letters). Pint—emerald green. c m. Height 7¼ inches (U)

32. "W. Roberts, Kensington". Pint—emerald green. c m s b. Height 7 inches. (K)

33. "Sloper & Frost". Blue (U).

34. "S. Smith, Auburn, N. Y." (2 lines). Pint—blue. c m. (U). P. 123.

35. "Superior Soda Water" (two vertical lines.) Reverse: Spread eagle. Deep blue lines. c m. (U).

36. "Taylor's Best", lengthwise on separate panels. Sexagonal, tapering at base and below neck. Pint—navy blue, round c m s b. (U).

— GROUP C: HOUSEHOLDS

37. "Taylor Never Surrenders". Reverse: "Union Glass Works, Phila." About pint—(shaped like Union soda water bottles)—blue. H c m.

38. "John Tweedle Jr's. Celebrated Soda and Mineral Waters, Barclay St., 41 New York". Dark green. (Soda Water and Malster, 41 Barclay St. and 2 Broome St., N. Y. City in 1851–2). (U).

39. "Loren J. Wicks, Bridgeton, N. J. Pat. Feb. 1st, 1870" surrounding a diamond. Pint—aquamarine full of bubbles. c m. Height 8½ inches (Br).

40. Green c m. Height 7 inches. (U).

41. Pint—green, octagonal. c. m. (N L).

42. Pint—rich dark golden amber. c m. Height 6¾ inches. Found on former site of Glass Works (St.)

43. Deep golden amber. (St.).

This list is appended merely as a guide for Collectors as to range and diversity of the bottles, but it is a partial catalogue only.

II.—SARATOGA DISTRICT AND OTHERS

1. ARTESIAN (Sa)
"Ballston Spa (semi-circle)
  "Lithia
   Mineral
   Water"
Reverse: "Artesian Spring Co." (semi-circle). Entwined A and S in open block letters. "Ballston, N. Y." Pint—green. s d c n.

2. CHAMPION SPRING (Sa)
"Champion Spouting Spring" (semi-circle) "Saratoga Mineral" (semi-circle).
  "Spring   Also large C (open block type) over the lettering.
   SS
Limited"   Reverse: "Champion
"Saratoga, N. Y."   Water". Pint—bluish green. s d c m.

3. CLARKE & WHITE (Sa., St.)
"Clarke & White" (semi-circle). Large "C". "New York" below. Reverse: Plain. Quart—round—olive green. s d c m. Also pint.

4. Another 1½ inch mouth, rolled lip.

5. "John Clarke, New York" on shoulder (running around). Quart—dark golden amber. s d   c n.
(Clarke & White, 98 Cedar Street, Soda Water (1865–66).

6. CONGRESS SPRING (Sa)
"Congress & Empire Spring Co." (¾ circle). "Hotchkiss Sons" (semi-circle). Large "E" (open block type). "New York". "Saratoga, N. Y." Reverse: "Empire (quarter circle) "Water". Quart—yellow green bubbly. s d   c m.

7. "Congress & Empire Spring Co." (¾ circle). Large "E" (open block type). "Saratoga N. Y." Reverse: "Empire" (semi-circle). Quart —sea green. s d   c m.

8. "Congress & Empire Spring Co." (semi-circle). Large "G" (open block type). "Saratoga N. Y." Reverse: "Congress" (quarter circle) "Water." Quart—sea green. s d   c m.

9. "Congress & Empire Spring Co." (¾ circle) Large "C" (open block type). "Saratoga N. Y." Reverse: "Congress" (semi-circle). "Water." Quart—sea green. s f   c m.

(Hotchkiss & Sons (1866-67) 92 Beekman St. and 58 Cliff St., N. Y. C. In Wilson's Directory of 1867-68 Hotchkiss & Sons had a page advertisement calling attention to their Columbian, Congress and Empire Mineral Waters. The company had a branch office in Saratoga Springs, N. Y.

10. "Congress & Empire Spring   These lines in semi-circle
          Hotchkiss Sons Co."
"C"   "New York
         Saratoga".   Reverse: "Congress Springs". Pint—green. s d c m.

11. Another different arrangement of lettering. Reverse: "Congress" (semi-circle) "Water". Pint—sea green. s d c m.

12. "Congress and Empire Spring Co." (¾ circle). Large "G" (open block type). "Saratoga, N. Y." Pint—sea green. s d   c m.

13. "Congress Spring Co." (semi-circle). Large "C" (open block type). "Saratoga, N. Y." Reverse: "Congress" (semi-circle) "Water". Pint—sea green. s d c m.

14. Another same, no lettering. Amber.

15. Another—pint—green. (Sa).

16. Quite similar to beer bottle shape, on base "Congress Spring Co. S S—N Y— 3—". Pint—sea green, heavy rolled c m.

(Note: Some of the Congress Spring bottles were made at the Box Factory at Stoddard, N. H., others were made at Saratoga, N. Y. It is, therefore, difficult to correctly designate the place of manufacture without having the bottle at hand.)

17. EMPIRE SPRING (Sa)
"Empire Spring Co." (semi-circle) Large "E" (open block type) "Saratoga, N. Y." Reverse: "Empire" (quarter circle) "Water". Quart—**sea green**. s d c m.

18. Reverse: Lettering in quarter circle. Pint—sea green.

19. EXCELSIOR (Sa)
"Excelsior" (semi-circle) "Spring"
                     "Saratoga N. Y." (semi-circle, up curved). Quart—sea green. s d c m.

Lower   43   39   26   39   33

20. GEYSER SPRING (Sa)
"Saratoga"
(In this rectangle
is a large "G" with
flower in center and
underneath on a panel
"Trade Mark".)
"Geyser Spring"   "The Spouting Spring"
This is a rectangular panel.
Reverse: "Geyser Spring" (semi-circle). "Saratoga Springs" (semi-circle). "New York". Pint—aquamarine. s d c m. Also quart—bluish aquamarine.

21. HATHORN SPRING (Sa) MT. FACTORY.
"Hathorn Spring". Reverse: "Saratoga, N. Y." Quart—dense amber. s d c m.

22. Larger lettering—sea green.

23. "Hathorn Springs" (semi-circle) "Saratoga, N. Y." Pint—dense amber s d c m. Another—sea green.

24. Larger lettering.

25. HIGH ROCK SPRING (St.)
"High Rock Congress Spring" (semi-circle).
    "1767"
    Rock
"C & W"
"Saratoga, N. Y." Pint—golden amber. s d c m. Also dark amber. (Sa.)

26. Date omitted. Olive green (St.) Box Factory.

27. "High Rock" (date omitted). Quart—yellow olive. (U).

28. "High Rock Spring" (semi circle) "Saratoga, N. Y." Pint—deep green. (St.) Box factory.

29. KNOWLTON
"D. A. Knowlton" (semi-circle) "Saratoga, N. Y." Quart—olive green. s d c m. (Sa also St).

30. 1½ inch mouth, rolled lip.

31. MISSISQUOI SPRINGS
"Missisquoi" in semi- circle, large "A"—below—"Springs". Reverse: Full length figure of squaw. Quart—greenish olive. s d c m. (St).

32. Reverse: Plain.

33. PAVILION
"Pavilion & United States Spring Co." (¾ circle). Large "P" (open block type). "Saratoga, N. Y." Reverse: "Pavilion" (semi-circle) "Water." Pint—sea green. s d c m. (Sa).

34. SARATOGA RED SPRING
   "Saratoga" (semi-circle)
   "Red
   Spring. Quart—sea green. s d c m. (Sa).

35. SARATOGA SELTZER
   "Saratoga Seltzer Water" (around shoulder). Rolled c m. Pint—bluish green. (Sa).

36. No lettering, height 5⅝ inches. (Sa).

37. SARATOGA SPRING
   "Saratoga"
Large 5-pointed skeleton star
   "Spring". Reverse: Plain. Quart—olive green. s d c m . (Sa)

38. SARATOGA VICHY
   "Saratoga"
   "Vichy" (very large)
   "Water"
   "Saratoga, N. Y." Reverse: Large "V" (open block type). Quart—light amber. d c m. (Sa).

39. STAR
   "Star Spring Co." (semi-circle) "S" reversed.
   5-pointed skeleton star.
   "Saratoga, N. Y." Pint—golden amber. s d c m. Also r c m.
   (Size of Mineral Water Bottle).
   Distorted by the heat. Recovered from ruins after the fire. (Box Factory). (St).

40. TRITON SPRING
   "Triton Spouting Spring" (¾ circle). Large "T" (open block type). "Saratoga, N. Y." Reverse: "Triton Water", (lengthwise). Pint—light green, sd c m. (Sa).

41. UNION SPRING
   "Union" (quarter circle)
   "Spring"
   "Saratoga, N. Y." (semi circle up curved). Pint—sea green. s d c m. (Sa).

42. WASHINGTON SPRING
   "Washington Spring Co." (three quarter circle) surrounding Bust of Washington. "Ballston Spa, N. Y." Reverse: Large "C" (open block type). Pint—sea green. s d c m. (Sa).

43. WESTON
   "G. W. Weston & Co."
   "Saratoga, N. Y."   Lettering on shoulders. Quart—olive green. s d c m. (Sa).

43a. "Albergh" (semi-circle) below "A" (large open block type), below "Springs, Vt." Reverse: Plain. Quart—round—golden amber. 1 s c m. (St).

— GROUP C: HOUSEHOLDS

44. BUFFALO
"Buffalo" below woman. "Mineral Springs" to right and "Water" to left. "Trade mark" below. One-half gallon. Clear glass. c m. (U).

44a. "Lithia Nature's Materia Medica" to left and "Water" to right. "Trade Mark" below. (U).

45. GETTYSBURG
"Gettysburg Katalysine Water" (circle). Quart—olive green. dc m. (U).

46. MAGNETIC SPRING
"Magnetic Spring" in semi circle, below "Henniker, N. H." Quart—round—golden amber. Long d c m. Height 9 inches. (St).

47. MERCHANT
"Address C. W. Merchant & Co.
Lockport, N. Y.
Oak Orchard Acid
Springs." Quart—deep green. s d c m. (Lk).

48. MIDDLETOWN
"Middletown" (semi-circle)
"Healing"
"Springs"
"Grays & Clark"
"Middletown, Vt." Quart—rich golden amber. s d c m. (St).

49. POLAND
In shape of man with beard. "Poland Water" and "H. Ricker & Sons, Proprietors" Quart—aquamarine. c m. (U).

50. RICHFIELD
"Richfield Sulphur Water" (¾ Circle).   "B & R"
                                          "Richfield
                                          Springs, N. Y."
Pint—sea green. s d c m. (Sa).

51. VERMONT SPRING
"Vermont Spring (semi circle)
  "Saxe & Co."
  "Sheldon, Vt."   —sea green.   c m. (U).

Poland Water

18 D2

17 D2

324 GRAND OLD AMERICAN BOTTLES

Early Mineral Water Bottles often show mold marks. In background is a squat N. Y. Lockport bottle which bottled water from Acid Springs (Alabama swamp) which sold in Southern states for 25c each 100 years ago.

— GROUP C: HOUSEHOLDS

19th Century Soda—Pop Bottles

MINERAL AND SODA WATER BOTTLES

GRAND OLD AMERICAN BOTTLES

SODA WATER BOTTLES

it is quite likely that soda pop bottles in the American scene may date from the 1840s. We suspect the first ones were of stoneware. The glass bottle seems to have entered the scene in the 1850s. But bottle making for soda pop (or the making of bottles that made a popping sound when decorked or unsealed by a forcible punch) on a widespread scale had to wait for the widespread making of soda pop.

When there were soft drink production possibilities all over the U.S.A. it was the Illinois Glass Company at Alton that had the great opportunity to make pop bottles by the million . . . and did so. Why all this concern over pop bottles? Mark this well: Pop bottles are going to be collected! When the vogue starts we may well expect things like this to happen: a collector offers a green pop, marked Black & Rogers, Oklahoma Territory, for a clear glass Victorian Texas Bottling Works "pop". The scope of usage of pop bottles, upon examination, offers a variety of impressions, marks, brands, and tints that is comparable to the varieties of collectible book matches, or buttons.

Thanks to E. F. Loer of New Orleans we have secured catalog pages of actual pop bottles as made by Illinois. Here, then, is at least a large part of the pictorial Illinois Glass Company Pop Bottle story. Ponder it . . whether you are a beginning collector, a wary eyed dealer, or mere observer of the collecting scene. Someday, somehow, there will be an explosive start made in gathering in these bottles, now relics indeed of America's past. Who knows? Perhaps the carbonated beverage people themselves will start collecting these relics of their early days.

Concerning the illustrations no matter how much they appear to be alike, all the bottles are different,

ROBERT BREEDING

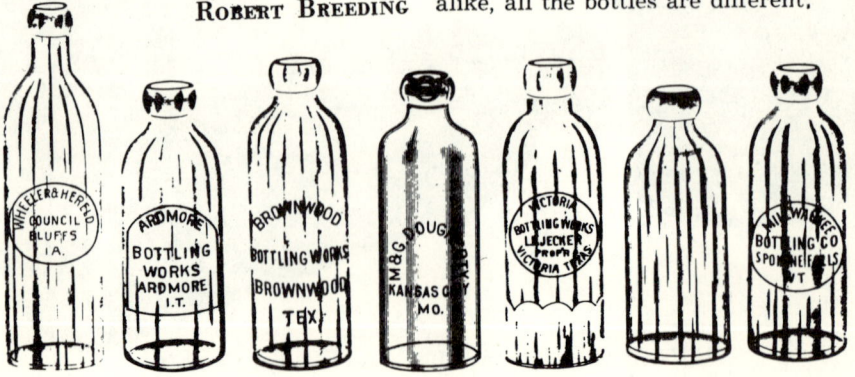

Taking the Saratoga Waters: These came in three strengths (1) Digestive Aids, (2) Mild Laxative, (3) Action in 15 Minutes.

Fruit Bottles from author's collection.

(1) Yeoman's Fruit Bottle (3 sizes—3 colors)
(2) Potter & Bodines Airtight Fruit Jar, Philad.
(3) Rare Fruit Bottle; with Lafayette impressed in glass
(4) Millville Atmospheric Fruit Jar
(5) Bromson's Barrel Fruit Jar (Amber)

— GROUP C: HOUSEHOLDS

CHAPTER XIII FOOD CONTAINERS

FOOD CONTAINER BOTTLES

This sub C-Grouping is three-fold and includes Pickles, Syrups and Sauces, Milk Bottles, Nursers and Feeders, and Oil Bottles and Fruit Jars. A full chapter could well be given to each; but because collector interest here is still rather dormant we shall cover the highlights of each type in a few paragraphs, then let representation pictures and descriptive literature indicate where further research and samples will lie. Certainly the field of Mason and related types of Fruit Jars hold a major upcoming interest, while early pepper sauce bottles are rather hard to find. In between lies the great and almost virgin field of collecting milk bottles and early infant feeders, especially those marked in glass and of mid nineteenth century origin. In this as in the other two categories there is much interest and value to be dug up by vigorous study and research.

FRUIT JARS

A relatively new field of collector interest is the 19th century containers especially designed for preserving fruit. About everyone knows the Mason Fruit Jar with its screwed on glass top cover, also the Ball Brand locked hinge-type which followed. But who can remember— much less has saved—the glass preserving jars which preceded these rather modern types. Who can recognize a Yoemar's Fruit Bottle which antidates 1850 and is in beautiful early bubble-marked glass (light green, blue or amber). Equally hard to find are the other marked-in-glass fruit bottles that are listed below. Let us consider why and how they functioned before going on the Mason Jar story which superseded all others. . . . Until around 1810 little bottling attempt was made to preserve food unless, of course, by imperishable alcohol! But with coming of Pasteur and his forerunners in Paris, the idea developed that food could be preserved by heating and sterilization. This meant that the cooked fruit, meat or vegetables would have to have an air-tight seal. These first seals, of course, were no more than cork plugs, (possibly held down with wax or other type of cement), and the amount of spoilage by air breaking the seal must have been tremendous. At least, as you can see by typical forms listed below all sorts of depressed glass rims and lay-ons were tried, as well as a variety of shapes. The thing that really worked did not come out until 1858 when the Mason screw on top was invented. The 5 types next shown are today prime collector items, and there may be may others unlisted. The story of the Mason Fruit Jar follows.

MASON JAR CENTENNIAL

GLASS CONTAINERS INSTITUTE
1858 – 1958

— GROUP C: HOUSEHOLDS

NOVEMBER 30, 1958, marks the one-hundredth birthday of the Mason jar, and this long famous and familiar glass container enters its second century as modern as it is historic.

While there have been modifications and improvements, Mr. Mason's basic invention has faithfully served American families for a full century. The ancestor of all glass containers with tops that screw on, the Mason jar is today a household article in literally millions of U. S. homes.

Many Mason jars are used, re-used and handed down from one generation to another, giving families fresh foods in winter for as long as three quarters of a century.

A letter in the April 5, 1958, issue of the Michigan Farmer illustrates how glass protects its contents from the effects of time. "We have a dozen one-quart Mason jars which my husband's grandmother gave us filled with fruit on our wedding day. I am still using them. We have been married 58 years."

It was in 1810—forty-eight years before John Landis Mason patented his jar on November 30, 1858—that Nicolas Appert, a French confectioner, published his principles of food preservation through sterilization.

Appert's theory was that heat would preserve fruits, meats, fish, and vegetables by arresting the natural tendency of foods to spoil. After fifteen years of experimentation, Appert was awarded a 12,000 franc prize by the Emperor Napoleon himself. The pioneer in food preservation had chosen glass containers because, he said, it was the packaging material most impervious to air.

It remained for John Mason to perfect a glass container that could seal in the harvest-time freshness of fruits and vegetables. Two years after Mason patented his jar, Louis Pasteur explained the reasons for Appert's theories: micro-organisms, responsible for food fermentation, could be destroyed with heat, and food could be kept fresh in air-tight glass.

Attempts to preserve foods were sporadic and very limited after Appert and before Mason. William Underwood packed pickles and condiments in bottles in Boston around 1819. And, about the same time, Thomas Kensett and Ezra Daggert experimented in packing salmon and lobster.

Winter diets were dreary indeed in the first half of the nineteenth century. Dried fruits and vegetables were the only things available, and fall spelled the beginning of monotonous menus.

The Mason jar proved a blessing to housewives on farms and in cities alike. The chemically inert qualities of glass preserved fresh flavors. Clear, transparent jars permitted housewives to see contents at a glance. Easy to clean and re-use, Mason jars could be effortlessly stored by the hundred. And it is not hard to imagine the joy and delight of having, for the first time throughout the winter, juicy peaches, pears, plums, berries, tomatoes, stringbeans, corn, and many other fruits and vegetables packed at the peak of their perfection.

The son of a Scottish farmer, John Mason was born in Vineland, New Jersey in 1832. As a young man, he moved to New York where he first conceived of the idea of a jar

GROUP C: HOUSEHOLDS

Here are letterheads from typical glasshouses that made our 19th century Bottles (Shoe-fly, Picnics, Bitters, Foods, Liquors and Medicinals.) Best source for a Household Bottles Check-list and the papers and catalogs of 19th Century Glasshouses and druggist supply houses.

№ 22,186.   Patented Nov. 30, 1858.

J. L. Mason,

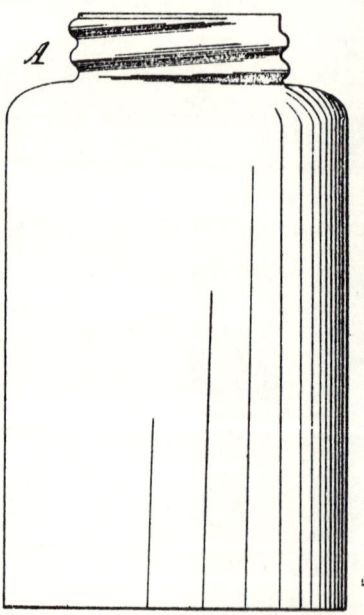

Witnesses:
W. P. N. Fitzgerald
J. McMurray

Inventor:
John L. Mason

| Look for the ENAMEL Lining!  To expert canners the cream-white enamel lining on Ball DOME Lids means *extra* protection. This smooth, clean-looking inner surface prevents corrosion. Folks, too, prefer the seal they can SEE ... Ball DOME down, jar sealed. To be sure, say *Ball* DOME Lid! | Sort Those Jars   1920  Look over your old jars and eliminate those with nicks! Count how many new Ball Mason Jars you'll need to replace them—plus those you'll want for that *extra* bit of canning. *Now*'s the time to buy your Ball Mason Jars, the ONLY jars that come with Ball DOME Lids. Dept. E 94, BALL BROTHERS Co., |

— GROUP C: HOUSEHOLDS

In the middle of November, 1858, Mason took out his first patent for a mold which could turn out a glass jar with a threaded top. On November 30, 1858—a date which was to become a landmark—Mason took out his patent for the "Improved Jar." This famous legend, "Mason's Patent, November 30, 1858," was to be inscribed on glass jars for the next three-quarters of a century.

That winter, Mason moved his business to 257 Pearl Street where he formed a partnership with T. W. Frazier, Henry Mitchell and B. W. Payne. This modest enterprise was the start of a mighty industry. Mason and his partners made the tops on Pearl Street. The jars were ordered from glass blowers who had made molds, generally costing less than $10, according to the specifications of Mason's patent.

The first such producer was a man named Samuel Crowley who operated a small glass shop in southern New Jersey. Crowley's glass blower, Clayton Parker, it is recorded, blew the first Mason jar. How many followed is beyond estimation, but certainly over 100 billion.

With the exception of jams and jellies that had sufficient sugar content to remain unspoiled without hermetic seal, very few foods were packed commercially at the turn of the century. Home canning was the greatest provider of preserved vegetables and fruits. People everywhere found that the Mason jar served their purpose perfectly.

By 1900 the jars were packed in cartons of a dozen, and the caps and rubber rings were put in the straw-lined packages with the jars. Families bought them by the dozen.

GRAND OLD AMERICAN BOTTLES

FOOD CONTAINER BOTTLES
INTRODUCTION

Cathedral

Moxie
Nerve
Food

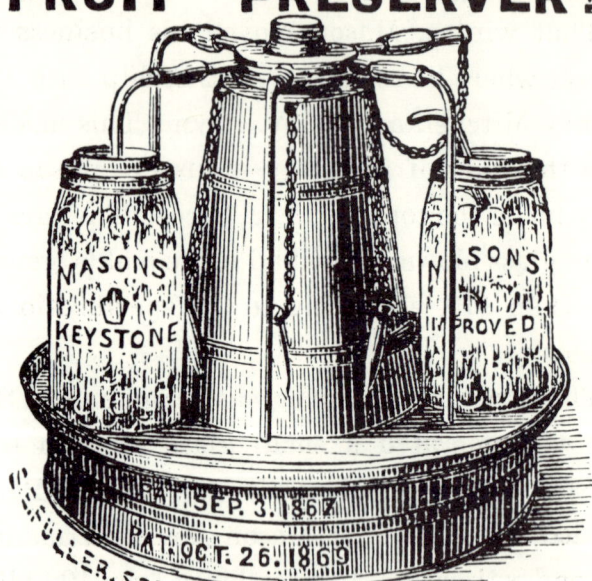

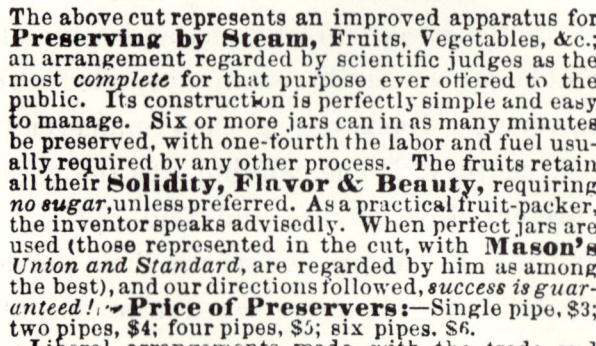

PAYNE'S IMPROVED, or THE COMMON-SENSE
FRUIT PRESERVER!

PAT. SEP. 3, 1867
PAT. OCT. 26, 1869

The above cut represents an improved apparatus for **Preserving by Steam,** Fruits, Vegetables, &c.; an arrangement regarded by scientific judges as the most *complete* for that purpose ever offered to the public. Its construction is perfectly simple and easy to manage. Six or more jars can in as many minutes be preserved, with one-fourth the labor and fuel usually required by any other process. The fruits retain all their **Solidity, Flavor & Beauty,** requiring *no sugar,* unless preferred. As a practical fruit-packer, the inventor speaks advisedly. When perfect jars are used (those represented in the cut, with **Mason's** *Union and Standard,* are regarded by him as among the best), and our directions followed, *success is guaranteed!* **Price of Preservers:**—Single pipe, $3; two pipes, $4; four pipes, $5; six pipes, $6.

Liberal arrangements made with the trade and good canvassers. For particulars, address
WILLIAMS & CHASE, 35 Park Place, N. Y. City.

—GROUP C: HOUSEHOLDS

American Bottles Old and New

Preserving Jars, Old Style

Medicine Bottles, Old Style

The First Thatcher Milk Bottle is said to be the one showing Dr. Thatcher milking a cow.

In earlier days one went for milk to have his needed allotment dipped from a large milk can making the rounds of various town houses.

— GROUP C: HOUSEHOLDS

MILK, BABY AND FEEDING BOTTLES

Closely associated with the Mason Fruit Jar development (and the Atlas and Ball Brothers preserving bottles which followed) was the problem of proper preservation and distribution of fresh milk. The presence of proper hygienic glass milk bottle on the doorstep every morning is only a little over 50 years old. In earlier days one went for his milk direct to the farmer (who might squirt from the cows teat directly into the consumers tin pail) or else have his needed allotment dipped from a large milk can making the rounds of various town houses. A Dr. Thatcher of Pottsdam, N. Y., is credited with developing the first open-mouthed glass milk bottle with a special cap to be bottled under hygenic conditions and delivered to the door. Here is his story. Due to added costs, the glass milk bottle did not catch on rapidly. In fact, not until infections and the need for Pasteurization became a point of hygienic life, did a large glass company named after Thatcher swing behind the new trend and develop cheap returnable milk bottles with special seal-tight caps. From round to square shapes, from high to squat forms, from easy seal glass lids to plug cap and wire handle, one can form a rather unique show of milk bottles.

But the prize collection is and always will be the nursing bottles and feeding equipment developed in the 19th and early 20th century for infant or invalid care. Of course, the use of nursing bottles was long frowned on in favor of breast feeding. Infants who could not be so fed by their own mothers were turned over to "wet-nurses" (women who could keep up their flow for long periods, doing a wholesale business by managing 3 or 4 infants a day). The use of cows or goats milk was regarded as fraught with danger and "likely to bring on the watery gripes." Another authority feared the infant "might imbibe with the milk the evil passions and frisky habits of the animal supplying the milk.

It was not until the end of the 18th century that crude feeding bottles began to make their appearance in England and America. Thereafter every year saw new and improved devices. The collector will not be especially interested in pottery or pewter bottles, but of the glass types shown in accompanying pages he will find a full range. The first had a small opening for the baby to suck on and a hole at the side to pour in the milk. Later there was perfected a variety of nipple or tubes, or when these did not work a sucking sugar tit rag could be used. This brings us to a related type of feeding bottle or pap boat—also when a long spout is provided it is called an invalid feeder for pouring liquids down the throat. All these and more besides are collector challenges.

GRADUATED NURSING FLASKS.

Fig. 228.

These Flasks are graduated in fluid ounces and half-ounces, or tablespoonful.

The Flasks are stamped on left hand side "Tablespoonful," and on the right hand side "Ounces."

The interior surface of Flask presents no angles for the collection of milk; it is easily cleaned, and the graduated scale is convenient for nursing purposes.

Originally introduced in July, 1887.

				Per gross.
6 ounce		Fig.	228,	$4.50
8 "		"	228,	5.25
12 "		"	228,	7.50
Old Style Nursing Bottle.	Flint glass, hole in side	"	227,	54.00
Hagerty's,	green glass	"	215,	3.75
Manhattan,	" "	"	222,	5.00
"	flint "	"	222,	6.25
Hagerty's Alexandra,	" "	"	217,	7.50
Nichols',	" "	"	216,	7.00
Nichols', Improved,	" "	"	218,	7.00
Gem,	" "	"	220,	6.00
Hagerty's Improved,	" "	"	220,	6.00
No. 1. Peerless,	" "	"	222,	8.50
" 2. "	" "	"	222,	8.50
" 3. "	" "	"	222,	8.50
" 4. "	green "	"	222,	6.00
Triumph,	flint "	"	221,	7.50

BREAST PUMPS.

Fig. 231.

Fig. 232.

INHALING BOTTLES.

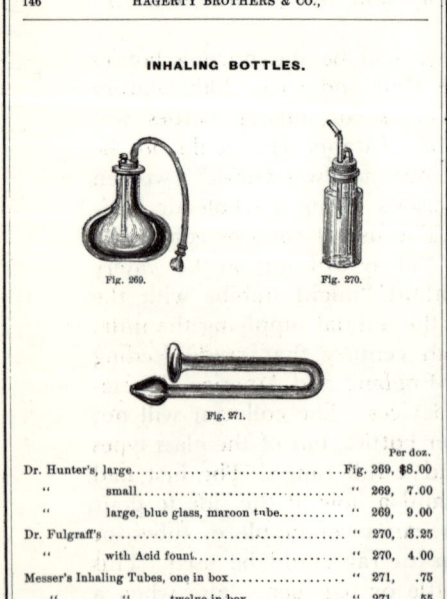

Fig. 269.   Fig. 270.

Fig. 271.

			Per doz.
Dr. Hunter's, large	Fig.	269,	$8.00
" small	"	269,	7.00
" large, blue glass, maroon tube	"	269,	9.00
Dr. Fulgraff's	"	270,	3.25
" with Acid fount	"	270,	4.00
Messer's Inhaling Tubes, one in box	"	271,	.75
" " twelve in box	"	271,	.55
Nichols', "			.63
Dr. Strong's, "			3.00
Nasal, with two nose pieces			9.50

NURSING BOTTLES.

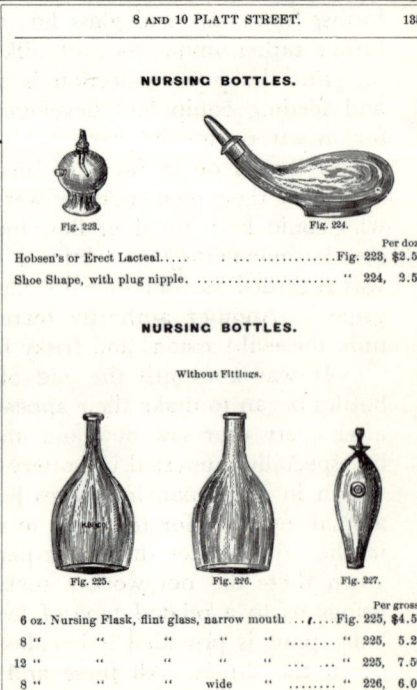

Fig. 223.   Fig. 224.

			Per doz.
Hobsen's or Erect Lacteal	Fig.	223,	$2.50
Shoe Shape, with plug nipple	"	224,	2.50

NURSING BOTTLES.

Without Fittings.

Fig. 225.   Fig. 226.   Fig. 227.

						Per gross.
6 oz. Nursing Flask, flint glass, narrow mouth					Fig. 225,	$4.50
8 " " " " "	"	"	"	"	" 225,	5.25
12 " " " " "	"	"	"	"	" 225,	7.50
8 " " " " "	"	wide	"		" 226,	6.00

HAGERTY BROTHERS & CO.,

NURSING BOTTLES.—Flint and Green.

With Fittings.

Fig. 215. Fig. 216.

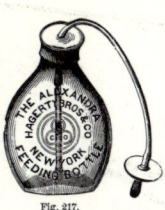
Fig. 217.

No.			Per doz.
1.	Fig. 215.	Hagerty's, green glass, wood tops, 1 doz. in a box	$1.00
2.	" 216.	Nichols', flint glass, porcelain tops, with brushes, each in paper box	2.25
3.	" 217.	Hagerty's Alexandra, flint glass, porcelain tops, with tube and bottle brushes, each in paper box,	3.50
4.	"	Manhattan, green glass, bent neck, with jet top and shield, ½ doz. in box	1.10
5.	"	Manhattan, flint glass, bent neck, with jet top and shield, ½ doz. in box	1.35
6.	"	Manhattan, flint glass, bent neck, jet top and shield, with brushes, each in paper box	1.50

Fig. 218.

Fig. 219.

Fig. 220.

---

8 AND 10 PLATT STREET.

BREAST PIPES.

Fig. 236.

Fig. 237.   Fig. 238.

		Per gross.
Hagerty's, No. 1	Fig. 237,	$18.00
" " 2	" 236,	24.00
Nechols', " 2	" 238,	18.00

NIPPLE SHELLS.

Fig. 239.   Fig. 240.

		Per gross.
Nipple Shells	Fig. 239,	$7.50
" with ring	" 240,	12.00

HAGERTY BROTHERS & CO.,

NIPPLE SHIELDS.

Fig. 241. Fig. 242. Fig. 243.

Fig. 244. Fig. 245. Fig. 246.

		Per doz.
Wood, untrimmed	Fig. 241.	$ .30
Rubber, white	" 242,	.50
" black	" 242,	.60
" maroon	" 243,	.60
Glass	" 243,	1.25
Nichols', with Bone Guard, each in a wooden box	" 244,	1.25
New York, with Bone Guard, each in a paper box	" 244,	.75
Hagerty's, with Rubber Tube, and Cleaning Tube, each in paper box	" 245,	1.25
Needham's Patent, each in paper box	" 246,	2.50

EYE BATHS.

Fig. 247.

		Per doz.
Eye Baths, plain glass	Fig. 247,	$ .40
" porcelain	" 247,	1.00
Vapor Eye Bottles, with Glass Stoppers		5.60
" " Blue,		8.00

HAGERTY BROTHERS & CO.,

THE PEERLESS NURSER.

With Double Valve.

Fig. 222.

Trade Mark Registered March 21. 1878.

We take pleasure in presenting to the Trade a New Nursing Bottle, **The Peerless Nurser,** which is constructed on the Double Valve principle—a decided improvement upon the ordinary Nursing Bottle, and one which secures ease and comfort to the child while nursing. It has these advantages:

In the materials of which it is composed: Crystal Glass and Pure Rubber; dispensing with lead, wood and cork entirely.

In its shape: being without seams or corners, the contents cannot secrete and become sour.

In the facility with which it can be cleansed after having been used.

The impossibility of its getting out of order.

Its use cannot, in the slightest degree, prove injurious to the youngest or most delicate infant.

The Double Valve: by the use of this contrivance, the slightest compression of the lips, or the least effort at suction, or both actions combined, upon the rubber nipple will cause the fluid to flow with facility, and to do so continuously and regularly, as the fluid when once drawn up in the tube cannot again descend; hence the least effort of the child, even when fretful or crying, is made available, and not lost as in the case of the ordinary Nursing Bottle.

This Nurser is put up in a neat and attractive style, and at the following low prices:

No.			Per doz.
1.	Fig. 222.	Each Nurser, of Crystal Glass, with Glass Top and Maroon Rubber Tube and Nipple, in an elegantly finished wooden box	$3.75
2.	" 222.	Each Nurser, of Crystal Glass, with Glass Top and Black Rubber Tube and Nipple, in a neat and handsome paper box	3.00
3.	" 222.	Six Nursers, of Crystal Glass, with Enameled Tops and Black Rubber Tubes and Nipples, in a neat paper box	2.25

We also manufacture the Nurser of Green Glass, same shape and style as the Crystal, with an Enameled Top and White Rubber Tube and Nipple, to which we attach the Double Valve improvement, and call it our

No. 4.	Twelve Nursers, in a wooden box	$1.40

To clean the above bottles, use tepid water and the brush enclosed in the box with the Nurser; to clean the Tube, remove it from the bottle, and insert the valved end into the tepid water, compressing the Nipple until the Tube is thoroughly cleaned.

Early Nursing and Milk Bottles: The "Cornucopia blown" could have housed an old man's snuff or an infant's pap; take your choice.

— GROUP C: HOUSEHOLDS

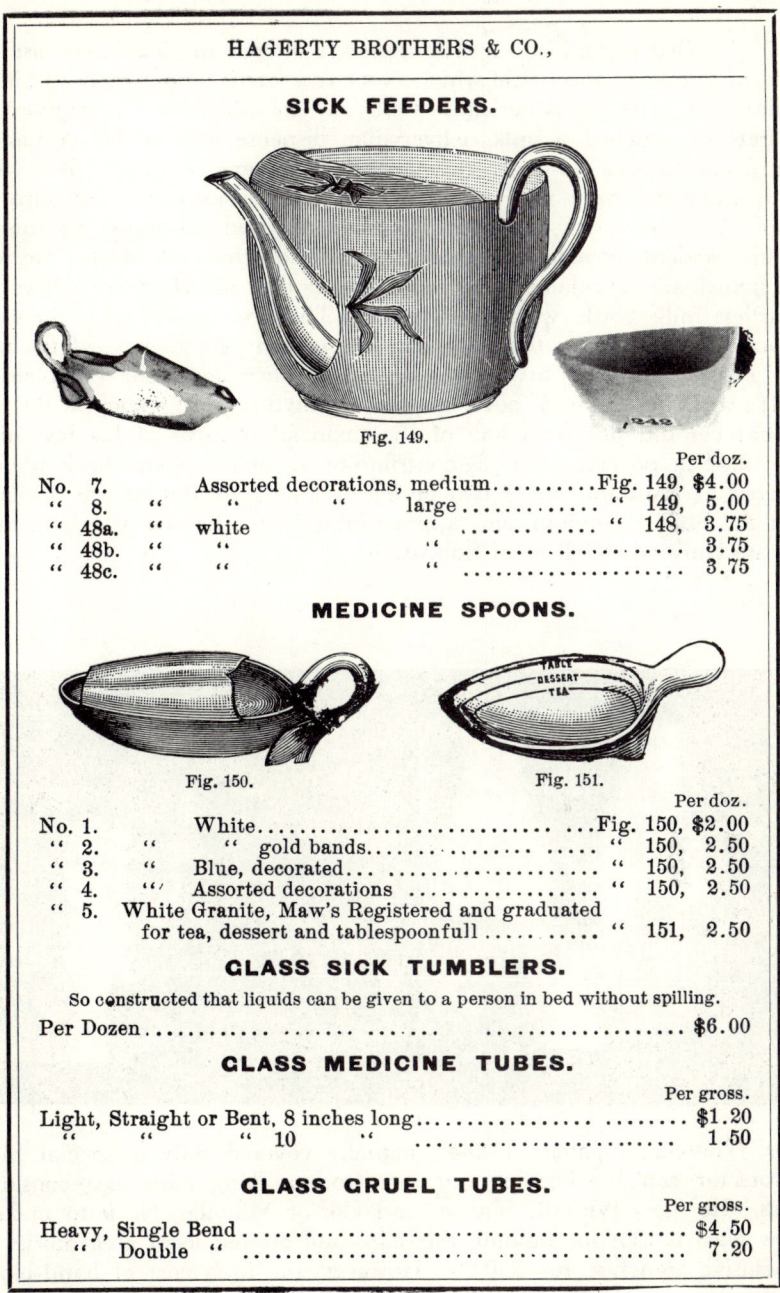

HAGERTY BROTHERS & CO.,

SICK FEEDERS.

Fig. 149.

					Per doz.
No. 7.	Assorted decorations, medium	....	Fig. 149,	$4.00
" 8.	"	" large	....	" 149,	5.00
" 48a.	" white	"	....	" 148,	3.75
" 48b.	" "	"	....		3.75
" 48c.	" "	"	....		3.75

MEDICINE SPOONS.

Fig. 150.   Fig. 151.

				Per doz.
No. 1.	White	....	Fig. 150,	$2.00
" 2.	" " gold bands	....	" 150,	2.50
" 3.	" Blue, decorated	....	" 150,	2.50
" 4.	" ' Assorted decorations	....	" 150,	2.50
" 5.	White Granite, Maw's Registered and graduated for tea, dessert and tablespoonfull	....	" 151,	2.50

GLASS SICK TUMBLERS.

So constructed that liquids can be given to a person in bed without spilling.

Per Dozen..$6.00

GLASS MEDICINE TUBES.

Per gross.
Light, Straight or Bent, 8 inches long.................$1.20
"   "   "   " 10   " 1.50

GLASS GRUEL TUBES.

Per gross.
Heavy, Single Bend..$4.50
"   Double   " 7.20

In fact youth and old age are so much alike in dietary needs that many collectors of the feeders will probably direct all energy to baby bottles too.

A soiled ragged doll and a druggist's interest in cleanliness inspired the invention of the bottle which every year carries more than 10 billion quarts of milk to Americans. One day in 1884, as Dr. Hervey D. Thatcher watched a milk deliveryman dispense milk to his customers, as usual from a 40-quart tin can at three cents a quart. But while the milkman's back was turned, a small girl dropped her doll into the can. On noticing it, he calmly fished it out and continued his rounds. This incident moved Dr. Thatcher to develop the milk bottle. He took a homemade wooden model to an ink bottle manufacturer where the earliest milk bottle were hand-blown. The first dealer using them became annoyed when the jostling of his wagon caused most of the milk to spill. Returning to the older method once again, he complained: "It's a failure and will never amount to anything." We know it did, but Thatcher did not reap any of the financial rewards of his invention; he died in poverty. For his contribution to public health he is remembered at Potsdam where two of his original milk bottles are displayed at the Public Museum, and a new dining hall is named after him at its State University College of Education.

Dr. Thatcher's patent (1884) actually covered only a special milk-protector cap for keeping out dirt from milking pails and consumer tins. He got Whitall, Tatum and Co. of Millville, N. J. to make a few glass bottles for holding the 'cap' and offered local area dairies an exclusive franchise for $50.00. However, the high cost of hand-blown bottles attracted few takers. Not until the early 1900's (with invention of mechanical Bottle Blowing and expiration of the patented protector cap) did the glass milk bottle finally 'catch-on.'

— GROUP C: HOUSEHOLDS

HOUSEHOLD BOTTLES:- PEPPER SAUCE, PICKLES, SYRUPS

Some very unusual 19th century bottles were made to hold Pepper Sauce, Pickles, Syrups, Ammonia, blacking and other household staples. We give you a sample pickle-form listing, followed with a brief general look into the entire field. Note that there is little attempt here to differentiate rarity or to carefully define usage. Bottles may have been made for one sort of contents, the mold sold or the design pirated for an entirely different product. Along with many of these food bottles and jars go others that served for alleged "beauty aids." We shall list only ten of those marked in glass and indicate by line drawings the typical shapes involved. No attempt is yet made at order and completeness, but rather to open a new field of bottle collecting.

(1) Mondox Hexagonal Pepper Sauce (for family use)
(2) Indian Chocologue (Syrup)
(3) B & D Jelly
(4) R. Eakirts Patent Japan Sponge Varnish
(5) Military Blacking — A. A. Cooley, Hartford, Conn.
(6) Pompeian Complexion Cream
(7) 7 Sutherland Sisters Hair Restorer
(8) Mandy's Home Need
(9) Mandy's Pancake Syrup
(10) Ma's Household Cleaner (Ammonia)

Bottles and jugs for syrup as well as special containers for molasses and honey were fairly common household necessities until around 1900, when a change in public taste caused marked reduction in per-capita consumption of these edible sweets. All such are collector items today especially those with corrosive metal tops. Nine molasses cans sold by Heisey in the late 1890's are shown and were used interchangeable for syrup, molasses and even honey. Honey jars, however, in the shape of old-type beehives or with the design of honey bees in the glass are especially sought by some who also may collect special jars (jelly jars and patented sweet-meat containers usually made after the turn of the present century).

As for mustard, pickle, oil, vinegar, and catsup containers one has only to look at some of the 1890 glasshouse catalogue pages here reproduced to note the shapes, sizes, and wholesale prices of the leading types or varieties. Beside the *castor bottles* which were sold in sets to go into a revolving silver lazy-susan stand, there are the straight and castorized mustards conspicuous by its shortness and a small side-opening at the mouth for insertion of a small ladle. A mustard bottle with a novel top and spoon was patented in 1873 by H. J. White of Boston. Other mustard containers in form of novelties were made by Tiffen Glass Co. and Atterbury, of which we show a few samples. Some of their animal dishes are shown in the character bottle or D Grouping that follows. Less common are the catsup, horseradish containers shown on accompanying plates.

1. Pepper sauce, aquamarine—height 8½ inches.

2. Four indented panels, spray of wheat top and bottom. Original tin foil label marked "Home Made Pickles Prepared by Wells & Provost, Pure Malt Vinegar, Principal Warehouse 215 & 217 Front St., New York". Aquamarine—c m. Height 8¼ inches. (U). P. 86.
("Pickles, preserves, patent preserved meats, 217 Front St. 442 Water St. and 193 Cherry St. 1849".)

3. "William Underwood & Co., Boston". About quart and a half—light green. c m. Height 11½ inches, 4¼ inches round. (U).

4. Original glass stopper, marked "A. Kline, Pat'd Oct. 27, 1863". 2 quarts—aquamarine. c m. Height 17 inches. (U).

5. Deep green. Height 11¾ inches. (U).

6. Pepper sauce—green. Height 10¼ inches. (U).

7. Pepper sauce—green. Height 6⅛ inches. (U).

Four Gothic panels. Large raised ring around neck. About 2 quarts—beautiful golden amber. Height 13½ inches. 3½ inches square. (Wn).

In form of Bunker Hill Monument. Lettered "Skilton, Foot & Co., Bunker Hill Pickles, Trade Mark". Picture of monument, barrels, etc. Light—clear amber. 1½ inches. c m. Height 8 inches. NOT ILLUSTRATED.

Round—about pint, jar shaped, light—clear amber. b c m. (U).

Sexagonal panel each side, Gothic top. In the top of each arch are two floral motifs of different designs. Original label lettered. "Gerkins from W. K. Lewis & Bros. 93 Broad St., Boston, Mass. Manufacturers of pickles, preserves, condensed milk, hermetically sealed articles, &c." Two quarts—aquamarine. (U).

— GROUP C: HOUSEHOLDS

Castors were common until World War I; but even before that time bottle used to hold food products were rapidly discarded when the contents were gone or else they were put into a table castor. In contrast with a quick discard, we now refer you to the double-duty containers of the 1890's. For then, as now, commercial products were often placed in appealing glass containers with an eye to reuse. Consider the sample catalogue page of the Githans, Rexsamer Co. of Philadelphia. It shows the packing of foods and beverages in containers useful as vases, goblets, tumblers, and refrigerator jars. This "new idea" was the general thing even 75 years ago. Grecian and Etruscan form glass vases in clear or aquamarine tinting are now being sold in antique shops without some purchasers realizing they were originally "olive bottles." This company also made delightful early prune jars, sausage and meat pots, pickle jars and mustard containers which are now being avidly collected even by some of the *elite* of the antiques fraternity. When the neophyte now finds such items, the catalogue pages here shown will let him know what these were for and what they are.

Mustard Jar, of Githens, Rexsamer & Co   Philadelphia, the 1890

SMALL Grecian Vase,   LARGE Grecian Vase,   32 oz. Etruscan Vase,   20 oz. Etruscan Vase,

Relatively few bottle collectors have yet branched out into this field of specialization. As a result the early remainders have mostly been thrown away or destroyed in the pursuit of their natural use.

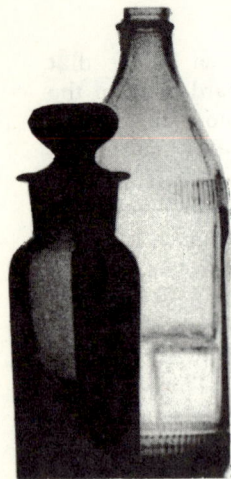

Some modern glass containers may become rare if enough are destroyed: opposite a check list of 1890 varieties.

HAGERTY BROTHERS & CO.,

PICKLE JARS.

Square Pickle Jars. Wide-Mouth. Brandy Fruit.

Square and Fancy.
			Per gross.
Pint,	8 ounce weight		$12.00
"	10 " "		14.00
Quart,	13 " "		18.00
"	14 " "		19.00
"	15 " "		20.00
½ Gal.,	20 " "		28.00
"	22 " "		30.00
1 Gal.,	35 " "		45.00
"	44 " "		56.00
1 Gallon Hexagon			61.00

Round English Pickle Jars or Chow-Chows.
			Per gross.
Pint,	13 ounce weight		$18.00
Quart,	20 " "		28.00
½ Gal.,	35 " "		45.00

JELLIES OR PRESERVE JARS.
	Per gross.
6 ounce	$ 9.00
8 " Half Pints	10.50
R 10 ounce	13.00
12 ounce	15.00
16 "	17.00
20 "	20.00

BRANDY FRUITS, Etc.
	Per gross.
½ Pint	$11.50
1½ "	19.50
Brandy Cherries	23.50
Pie Fruits and Oyster Bottles, 18 to 20 oz. weight	27.00

LUBIN EXTRACT BOTTLES.

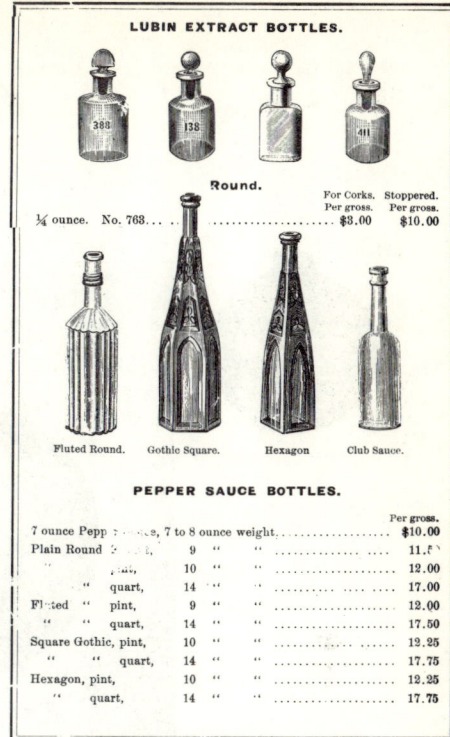

Round.
			For Corks. Per gross.	Stoppered. Per gross.
¼ ounce.	No. 763		$3.00	$10.00

Fluted Round. Gothic Square. Hexagon. Club Sauce.

PEPPER SAUCE BOTTLES.
			Per gross.
7 ounce Pepper Sauce, 7 to 8 ounce weight			$10.00
Plain Round "	9 " "		11.50
" "	10 " "		12.00
" " quart,	14 " "		17.00
Fluted " pint,	9 " "		12.00
" " quart,	14 " "		17.50
Square Gothic, pint,	10 " "		13.25
" " quart,	14 " "		17.75
Hexagon, pint,	10 " "		12.25
" quart,	14 " "		17.75

HAGERTY BROTHERS & CO.,

CLUB SAUCE BOTTLES.
	Per gross.			Per gross.
½ Pint Club Sauce, 6 oz	$9.50	Quart Club Sauce, 20 oz		$25.00
" " 8 "	11.50	" " 22 "		28.00
Pint " 0 to 11 oz	13.75	" " 24 "		30.00
" " 12 oz	16.00	Club-Stoppers, large		3.75
" " 14 "	18.75	" " small		3.75

CATSUP BOTTLES.

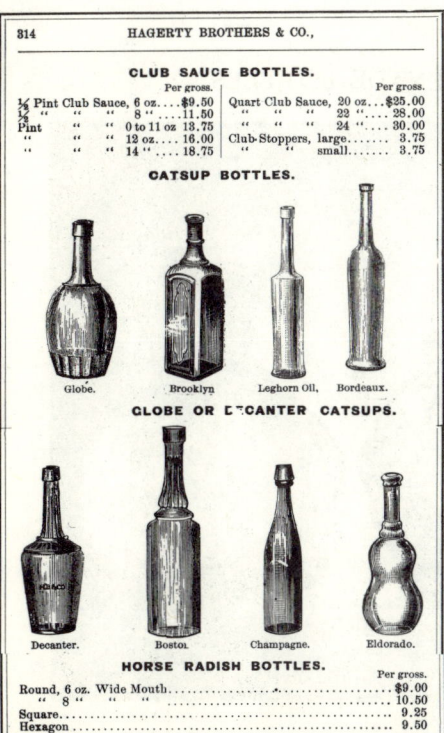

Globe. Brooklyn. Leghorn Oil. Bordeaux.

GLOBE OR DECANTER CATSUPS.

Decanter. Boston. Champagne. Eldorado.

HORSE RADISH BOTTLES.
	Per gross.
Round, 6 oz. Wide Mouth	$9.00
" 8 " " "	10.50
Square	9.25
Hexagon	9.50

---

8 AND 10 PLATT STREET.

MUSTARD BOTTLES.

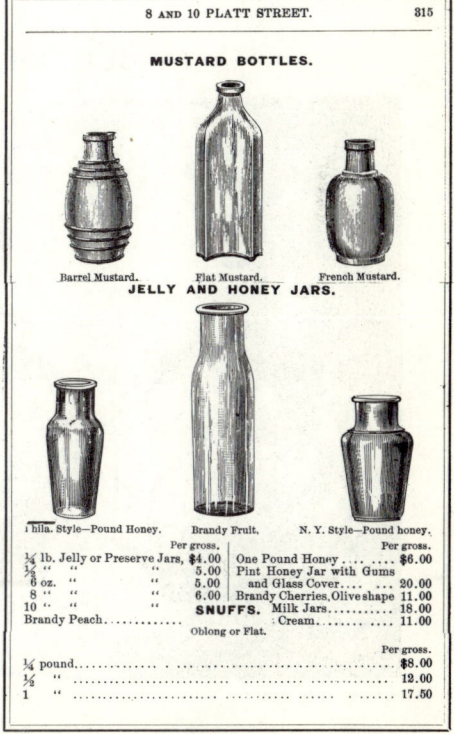

Barrel Mustard. Flat Mustard. French Mustard.

JELLY AND HONEY JARS.

Phila. Style—Pound Honey. Brandy Fruit. N. Y. Style—Pound honey.

		Per gross.		Per gross.
½ lb. Jelly or Preserve Jars,		$4.00	One Pound Honey	$6.00
¼ " " "		5.00	Pint Honey Jar with Gums	
6 oz. " "		5.00	and Glass Cover	20.00
8 " " "		6.00	Brandy Cherries, Olive shape	11.00
10 " " "			SNUFFS. Milk Jars	18.00
Brandy Peach			" Cream	11.00

Oblong or Flat.
	Per gross.
¼ pound	$8.00
½ "	12.00
1 "	17.50

GRAND OLD AMERICAN BOTTLES

TARGET AND GRENADE-BOTTLES

— GROUP C: HOUSEHOLDS

CHAPTER XIV HOUSEHOLD NEEDS

HOME MAKING NECESSITIES

This chapter's Subgrouping C is also threefold, and includes those bottles and containers which originally purveyed products which while not food or drink, were considered necessities for keeping a family up to snuff in personal appearance, polite correspondence and approved togetherness. As in the previous chapter, one can find collectors of the different specialties involved. But here we have lumped various types rather willy-nilly into three categories described as follows: Hair Dye, Blacking and Ink Bottles, Grenade, Target and Testing Bottles, and Toiletries and Barber Stand Bottles. We cover the highlights of each field only, listing representative samples and descriptive literature leading on to further research. For the person interested in sub-specialties there are a few articles noted in the bibliography. But a book on any one of them would have questionable value at the present state of collector interest and knowledge. That many such bottles are as old as any of the more desirable Bitters is seen by our description of 28 bottles of the blacking and other types (first listed back in the early 1920's) and here added as 'fillip.'

GRENADE, TARGET AND TESTING BOTTLES

Relatively few bottle collectors have yet branched out into this field of specialization. As a result the early remainders have mostly been thrown away or destroyed in the pursuit of their natural use. For Grenade, Target and Testing Bottles were largely broken up and thrown away.

Take the grenade bottle: it was a first extinguisher, a bulbous ball of green or light blue glass whose liquid contents were destroyed by using the full grenade as a bomb thrown into a blazing fire: No one knows how many overheated stoves, oil lamp fires, etc., were prevented from spreading by use of these fire extinguisher grenades. We do know that examples are quite rare and highly collectable.

Or take the Target Bottle: these were the clay pigeons of the 19th century, small blown bottles that you could throw in the air and try to hit with a rifle shot. They were stuffed with feathers and the proof of good markmanship was how many feathers you bring down in a given period of time. Famed collector Charles Gardner tells me that he recalls Annie Oaklie once in the Buffalo Bill Show giving a demonstration with these target bottles; someone (i.e. Mr. Gardner) got two that sure-shot Oaklie let fly by.

Testing bottles, these were once thought to be for testing whiskey.

THE BOGARDUS SHOOTING BOTTLE

Glass balls were first used for trapshooting in England and transferred to America around the 1850's.

During the 1830 to 1865 period, shooting clubs in America first used box traps and live pigeons. This system was most uncertain, since the pigeons would not always fly in the direction wanted. It became necessary to find a better way.

Charles Portlock, of Boston, Massachusetts, first introduced the glass ball for use in target shooting in the United States.

Captain Adam H. Bogardus, the champion of the sport of trap shooting saw the shortcomings in the way of throwing the first glass balls into the air; and set about to contrive a new method to assure better targets for the competing sportsmen, and built a mechanical device for throwing the glass balls into the air

This tossing machine, helped to increase the interest in the sport, and glass ball shooting became widespread in the sporting clubs throughout the country in the late 19th century

In America all shooting balls were blown in molds. Designs were more for purpose than appearance. At first these spheres were plain; then came ornamental patterns; and lastly, a band was added on which was impressed the name of the maker or the source.

In the beginning, clear glass was used, then colored glass, blue or amber, was substituted as it increased the visibility of the ball against the background.

The smooth surfaced ball was later given a corrugated surface to decrease the chance of the shot glancing off the surface without breaking the ball.

The glass balls were generally made of thin glass, ranging from 2½" to 3" in diameter. All the balls have an opening about ½" in diameter.

These small glass globes, or bottles, were filled with confetti, feathers, silk ribbons, smoke, or remained empty. They were tossed into the air by hand or by the mechanical slingshots that were made to be used with them. The marksman tried to shatter the targets with rifle or pistol fire as they were shot into the air.

During the early years of the target ball there were at least a dozen competitive firms supplying the glass globes and ball traps used to toss them into the air.

But about 1880, a Cincinnati inventor, conceived the idea of a pressed clay pigeon, and this clay flying disk soon retired the glass shooting ball to disuse and oblivion.

— GROUP C: HOUSEHOLDS

TESTING BOTTLES

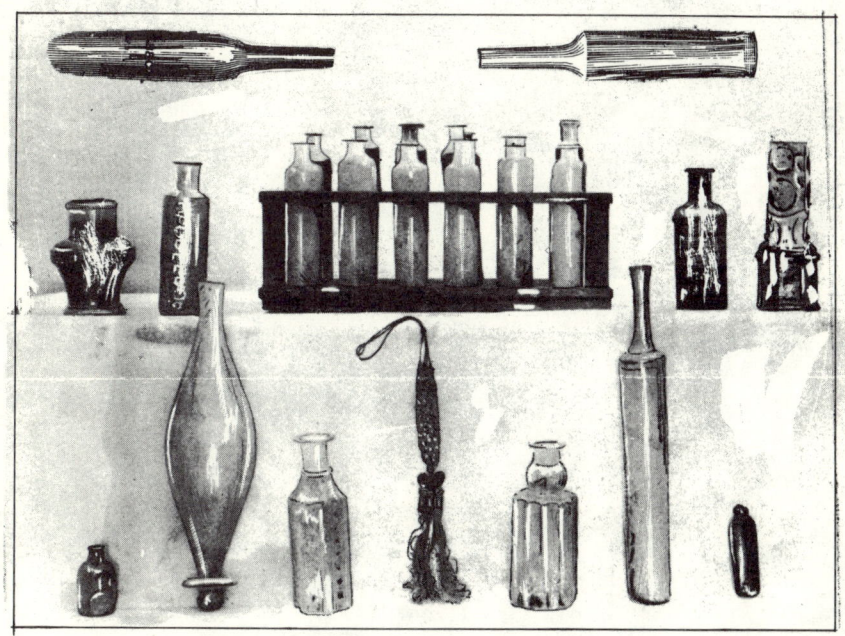

Testing bottles, these were once thought to be for testing whiskey. More likely they tested sperm oil because most have been found around old whaling centers like New London and New Bedford. Anyway, their purpose was for testing liquid in drums and containers not open to full view. Samples of this type appear in accompanying photographs.

A word might be added on the Testing Bottles (see picture) once thought to have been used to test whiskey (being dropped by wire down in a barrel), it is even thought they were sometimes used to test liquids intended for infant or invalid consumption, or even more likely, for testing quality of sperm oil brought in by the whalers for lamp lighting. Whatever their purpose, feeding, testing and nursing bottles these are really early 19th or late 18th century and figure among the rarities in any bottle collection.

The RISING SUN STOVE POLISH

— GROUP C: HOUSEHOLDS

SNUFF, HAIR DYE, BLACKING AND INK

These "household necessities" also had their character types of bottles in 19th century America. The snuff bottle is usually thought to be one of the earliest needs so packaged. Some cut from quartz or China jade were highly prized exportables, others free-blown or blown-molded with a wide top are also hard to come by today. The late snuff bottles are quite plain, early ones sometimes highly elaborate since it was considered good breeding for a lady to take the bottle from her reticule and, apply a pinch of snuff to the nasal passages and thus bring on a delighted sneeze. Later, when snuff taking was regaled to the backcountry one sees pottery snuff jars, others had square shapes with rare impressions on glass. The hair dye bottles of the late 19th century are of very different character, often with marked-in-glass directions for using preparations No. 1 or No. 2; one small glass bottle actually called this dye a "mustache conditioner" and another was an early eye-shadow bottle (forerunner of Maybeline); blacking (whether for shoes or stove or hair) was packaged in blacking bottles some quite early and some very late (with a dauber).

The ink bottles on the other hand are of such interest that sometimes whole sections have been given to them in special books. A representative sample is again all this study can presently offer. Attribution in terms of glasshouse and shape is indeed often possible. They were made in great quantities and one collector, having found a very heavy pyramid type that resembled the first telephone insulators in green glass, suggests the latter should also be collected and preserved. Of the ink bottles, look for the early blue Carter's (sometimes large sized) and always keep in mind that many late 19th century low and high ink shapes are going to become collectors items. But keep the label if you wish to know the original use of some of these 19th century household bottles.

Mottled orange and yellow glass

SNUFF-BOTTLES

GRAND OLD AMERICAN BOTTLES

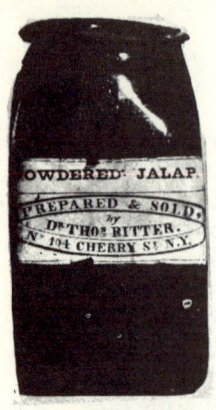

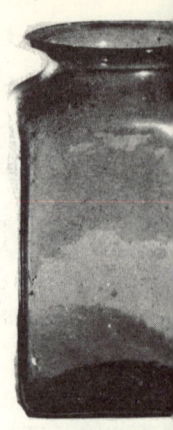

1. Light olive 2. Olive green; 3. Clear green; 4. Pale ye

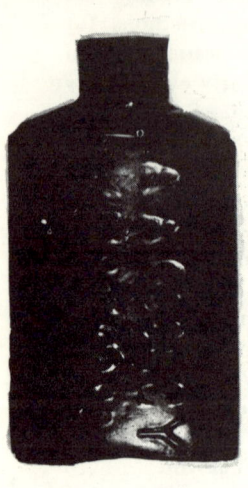

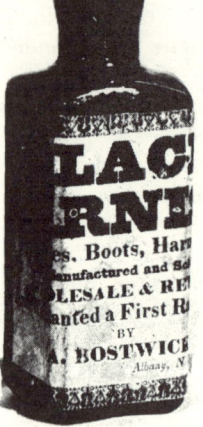

6. Olive amber 7. Olive green 8. Olive green 9. Olive

Blacking Bottles courtesy McKearin Collection.

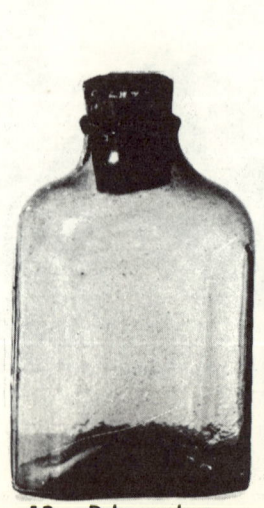
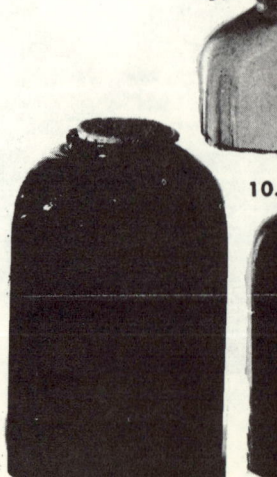

11. Clear brilliant amber 12. Pale amber, 13. Dark Olive green

— GROUP C: HOUSEHOLDS 357

MISCELLANEOUS
(Those not previously listed)

1. Raised circle with anchor in the middle. Reverse: Half pint—deep olive amber. Sheared and collared mouth. s b.

2. Apothecary's Bottle Green. r m s b. 8 inches arm. (Supposed to be Wistarberg). (U).

3. Apothecary's Bottle. Green—11½ inches high.

4. Basket Weave Flask. Half pint—clear glass.

5. "A. BISSELL'S
GENUINE WATER-PROOF LEATHER PRESERVER,
AND POLISH BLACKING.
SUPERIOR TO ANY ARTICLE OF THE KIND
EVER PREPARED.
It has been tested by the most scientific men of Boston and elsewhere, who pronounce it the best they ever tried. A fair trial will satisfy the most incredulous.

Wardsboro', Vt., March 1, 1855.
AUSTIN BISSELL."
(Above on printed label). Light aquamarine, 1¾ inches square—4½ inches high. Folded lip. s b. (U).

6. "Hutchins"
and Mason"   "s" reversed, one side
"Waterproof
Blacking", other side. Golden amber. s m. s b. 1¾ inches square. (St.)

7. "THAYER'S
Real Japan
Sponge Blacking.
For Boots, Shoes, Military Caps, Harnesses and Morocco.
───────
This article, for beauty of Color and Polish, is equal to anything of its nature ever invented. On the application of it to the Leather, it instantly dries on the surface with a smooth and brilliant appearance.
19 Haverhill Street,
BOSTON."
"THAYER'S
Sponge Blacking
───────
DIRECTIONS
The Leather should be dry and clean, and well oiled or greased:—the sponge must be pressed against the mouth of the Jug until it is pretty dry; then apply it gently to the Leather.
Each bill signed by the fac simile S. Thayer.
Lettering on printed label. Light golden amber. 1⅝ inches high. s m s b (U).

8. "Water Proof Blackin" (no g) "Prepared by A. Ensign" "West Hartland, Conn." Olive green. 4½ inches square, height 1⅝ inches, s m   s b. (W)

9. Flat shape, like the clock flask but covered all over with small bull's eyes. Pint—clear glass c. m. Height 6¾ inches. (U)

10. Cruet bottle, clear glass. s b (U).

11. Diamond pattern. Half pint clear glass. (U).

12. Fitted with whiskey glass.

13. Pint, like No. 11.

14. Quarter pint with label space.

15. Diamond Pattern. Pint—blue. s m   s b. (Type XII). Two mold. (U).

16. Eight Gothic panels, aquamarine. 3¼ inches high, 1¾ inches in diameter. (U).

17. Olive amber gin bottle.

18. Green amber gin bottle.

19. Green amber, marked "A. van HOBOKEN & CO. ROTTERDAM." Reverse: Same, other two sides plain. Seal on shoulder marked "AVH,"

20. Yellow amber. Seal on shoulder marked "L M & C."

21. Beautiful green amber.

22. Olive green, s b. Height 11½ inches. (U).

23. Olive green, s b. Height 11½ inches (U).

24. LONDON MUSTARD (FW). (No description but have data to authenticate.)

25. Miniature Bottle, dark golden amber. Very deep pontil, holds one drink. 3⅞ inches. (U).

26. NURSING BOTTLE (U).
Bulbous, 2¼ inches foot like wine glass, tapering to 1½ inches, shoulder, surmounted by nipple, hole in base for pouring in milk. About half pint—clear glass. Height 5 inches.

27. Nursing bottle, clear glass. Height 9¼ inches.

28. Pewter capped bottle. Half pint, clear glass. (U).

— GROUP C: HOUSEHOLDS

17   18   19   20   21

29. Quart—golden amber. d c m. (St.)

30. Same but pint.

31. Pint—olive green. s m   s b. (U), from Ohio.

32. Half pint—olive c m. (U)

33. Porter bottle, light golden amber. s c m. (St.)

34. TESTING BOTTLE
Length 6 inches, crimped mouth, 1⅝ inches at center, ⅝ inches at base, which is solid for 2 inches. Clear glass. (U).
(These interesting and very rare little vial like bottles were used for testing wine or liquor. The weighted base not only prevented it from "upsetting" but carried it into the liquid. The crimped mouth held the cord used in dropping it through the bung.)

35. Round, tapering to neck, twisted to left. About pint—pale shaded smoky blue. Height 6¼ inches, 2¼ inch base. f m   s b. (U).

36. Scrolls on each side. Half pint—clear glass. f m   s b. (U)

37. Sunbursts and bulls eyes below vertical ribbing. Reverse: Same. Half pint—clear glass, ring on neck. d c m. (U).

39. Half pint, light green, s m. Wicker covered. Height 5¼ inches.

40. About quart and a half, olive green. s m with ring, s b. Wicker covered. Height 13 inches. (Kn). P. 29.

11   12   14   13   5   4   28

JAYNE'S AMERICAN HAIR DYE,

Which, if strictly applied according to the directions, will change the hair from any other colour to a beautiful **Auburn**, or a perfectly jet **Black**, without staining the skin.

DIRECTIONS.

This Dye is in the form of a powder, put up in wide-mouth four-ounce bottles, and when used, should be put into a tea-cup, or some such vessel, and sufficient cold water added to mix it into a stiff batter; — then, after having well washed the hair to free it from dirt and grease, spread the Dye, with the blade of a knife, evenly and liberally all over the hair, so thick that the hair is completely hidden by it. Then take a towel, or muslin or linen cloth, three or four double, and after wetting it through by dipping it in water, bind it on closely over the hair, so that it may keep the Dye moist; for it ceases to colour as soon as it becomes dry.

To change white hair to red or auburn, requires the dye to be kept on the hair for about three hours, and then to make it a perfect black requires two or three hours more; that is, to change **White** hair to **BLACK**, the Dye should remain on the hair for from four to six hours. By this time the Dye has usually become dry, and should be worked out of the hair as much as possible with the fingers. After which the hair should be well washed, so as to remove any remaining portions of the powder which may still adhere to the hair or skin. Then slightly brush the hair the way you wish it to remain, and the work is done. In cleaning the Dye out of the hair, be careful not to chafe and irritate the skin by rubbing the dry, hard particles against it.

Prepared only by Dr. D. JAYNE, No. 84 Chestnut, below Third Street, Philadelphia.

JAYNE'S HAIR TONIC,
FOR THE PRESERVATION, BEAUTY, GROWTH,
AND RESTORATION OF THE HAIR.

This valuable preparation excites the scalp to a new and healthy action, cleanses it from Scurf and Dandruff, prevents the hair from falling off, or becoming prematurely GRAY, cures those eruptive diseases which often appear upon the head, and in a majority of cases produces a fine growth of new hairs. It also gives the hair a rich and beautiful appearance, unequalled by any thing of the kind.

Ladies and Gentlemen—Do you wish elegant, luxuriant, and beautiful hair? I know you will answer yes. Hear, for one moment, the cause of its loss, why it turns gray, rusty, and coarse, harsh and unpleasant in its appearance, and finally falls off. Each hair has a root in the skin, and is itself a hollow tube, through which there is a constant circulation of fine blood. By this circulation the hair is nourished and held fast, its glossy colour is given and preserved, and it is covered with the finest oil. Now any thing which injures the skin of the head, or diverts or takes away the blood from it, will prevent or impede the circulation through the tubes of the hair, stop its growth, and cause it to fall off or turn gray, or both. Hence it is that any cause that obstructs or weakens the circulation of the blood through the skin, or that diverts the blood to other parts of the system, will take away the lively, fresh, and youthful appearance of the hair, arrest its growth, turn it gray sooner or later, and in thousands of instances causes premature baldness. For this reason—

All kinds of Fevers—Dyspepsia—Child-bearing and confinement—Low Spirits—Dissipation and excessive thought—allowing the hair to grow too long without cutting—long and continued Headaches—Liver Complaints—Grief, Fear, great alarm, excesses of all kinds—Debaucheries—unclean and neglected condition of the scalp and hair—great mental uneasiness—old age, &c. &c.,—will always, unless proper remedies are used, more or less, sooner or later, produce generally or partially, gray hairs and premature baldness. The cure is perfectly effected by preserving a healthy and brisk circulation of the blood through the skin of the scalp and head. Could this always be done, the hair never would fall off or turn gray.

That the Hair Tonic will produce this happy effect in a perfect and permanent manner, is beyond all doubt, and places it at the head of all other remedies for the cure of baldness and the preservation of the hair in the fullest luxuriance and beauty.

Gentlemen, who wish to improve their whiskers, will find this a most valuable assistant, giving them a thick, glossy, fine, and curling appearance. For this purpose it is all that can be desired.

For the toilet, the ladies will find this an admirable article, as it gives a luxuriant brilliancy to the hair and curls.

It removes all unnatural harshness and dryness of the hair, which often precede its loss, and should never be permitted to continue without using remedies.

Persons taking journeys or sea voyages will find this a most valuable assistant for preserving the health of the hair, which at those times is so apt to fall off.

Mothers who wish to encourage the growth of luxuriant hair on their children, their daughters especially, when the hair is light and thin, will find that the use of the HAIR TONIC will confer on them beautiful and luxuriant heads of hair.

All persons during sickness, indisposition, and fevers, and when recovering from them—at which times, in thousands of instances, the hair becomes very tender, and the slightest touch will cause it to

SPRINKLE-TOP COLOGNES

With Metal Screw Tops, of Extra Quality, Superior Finish, and well-corked; thus preventing the Tops from tarnishing or leaking.

Fig. 589.

Fig. 590.

Lubin Shape.
Fig. 589.   Per
1 oz., round shoulder. ..

Taper Shape.
Fig. 590.   Per gross.
No. 548..........$14.00

Fig 588.

CRYSTAL BOTTLES, CUT STOPPERS, AND ENGRAVED LABELS.

No. 830.   Fig. 588.

	Per doz.
½ pint.............	$7.50
1 "	10.50

TABLET BOTTLES.—Flint Glass.

With Nickel Plated Metal Caps, screwing on the neck of the bottle. Suitable for Tablets or Soda Mint, and of convenient shape for carrying in the pocket. (Cuts the exact size of bottles they represent.)

No. 1. Fig. 310.   No. 2. Fig. 311.

No. 3. Fig. 312.   No. 4. Fig. 313.

TABLET BOTTLES.

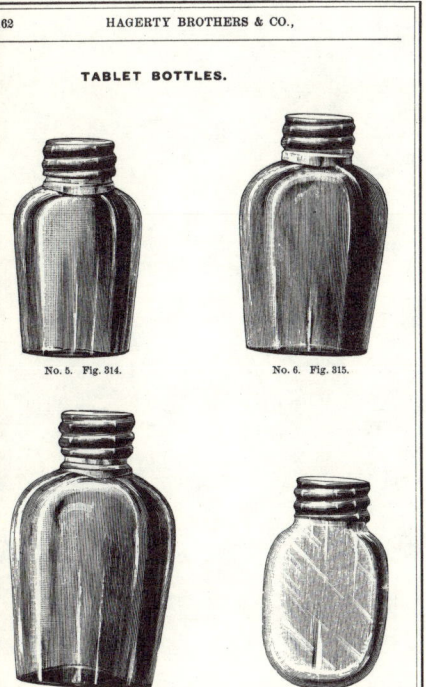

No. 5. Fig. 314.   No. 6. Fig. 315.

No. 7. Fig. 316.   No. 8. Fig. 317.

FLINT B.

COMMONLY CALLED GERMAN FLINT WARE.

This is a quality of Ware, medium, between Flint and Green, but far superior to the latter, and nearly equal to the former, and much less expensive; preferred by those who make price the leading consideration.

This Ware is sold in "Package Quantities" only; Plain, not Lettered.

NO CHARGE FOR ORIGINAL PACKAGES.

PLAIN, ROUND SHOULDER PRESCRIPTION VIALS.

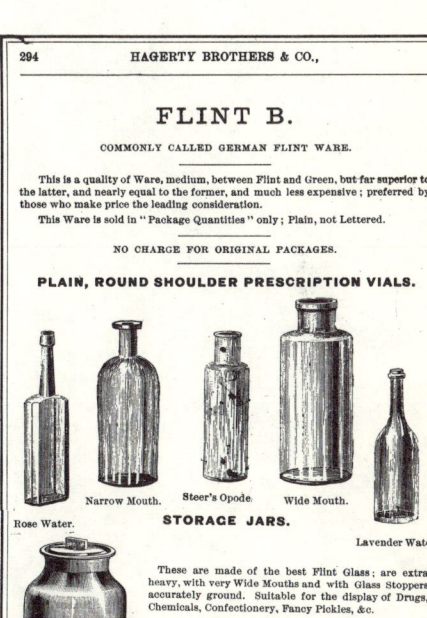

Rose Water.   Narrow Mouth.   Steer's Opode.   Wide Mouth.

STORAGE JARS.

Lavender Water.

These are made of the best Flint Glass; are extra heavy, with very Wide Mouths and with Glass Stoppers accurately ground. Suitable for the display of Drugs, Chemicals, Confectionery, Fancy Pickles, &c.

Capacity.	Height.	Width.	Width of Mouth.	Per doz.
2 gallons	16 inch.	7½ inch.	4 inch.	$28.00
3 "	18½ "	8 "	5 "	45.00
4 "	21 "	9½ "	6 "	67.50
6 "	22 "	10 "	7 "	90.00

Bottle Collaterals; Advertising of bygone brands.

— GROUP C: HOUSEHOLDS

"The Bottle" and Its Refills

Plate I. — The Bottle Is Brought Out for the First Time: The Husband Induces His Wife "Just to Take a Drop" illustrations from Michelin's lithographic edition of Cruikshank's eight etchings of "The Bottle"

Early Ink Bottles (wooden molds whittle-carved).

CONDENSED PRICE-LIST
OF THE
LEADING BRANDS OF INK,
AMERICAN MANUFACTURE.

CARTER'S
American Writing Inks.

TRADE DISCOUNT:

40 & 10 per cent.

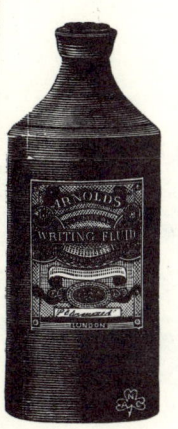

Arnold's Ink

in the same shape packages as are used by our domestic manufacturers.

This enables us to fill small orders with greater dispatch, and the price **includes cost of packing and cartage.**

Jobbers will find it a most desirable way of handling the Ink in this form, as it saves labor of unpacking and repacking, and largely economizes in space for storing it.

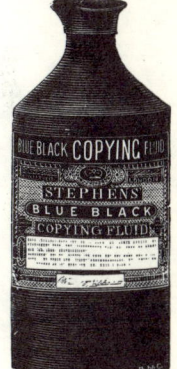

CAW'S
Popular Inks

Trade Discount:

50 per cent.

	Quarts.	Pints.	½ Pints.	4 Ounce.	3 Ounce Stands.	1½ Ounce Stands.
Black	$9 00	$4 80	$3 00	$1 80	$1 20	$0 60
Black Fountain Fluid with Patent Filler	....	....	....	....	3 60	2 40
Black Fountain Fluid with Patent Filler. Each Bottle in Wood Case	....	....	....	....	6 00	3 60
Black Fountain Fluid with Patent Filler. Each Bottle in Wood Case	12 00	7 80	4 80	3 00	....	....
Green	12 00	7 80	4 80	3 00	....	1 20
Blue	12 00	7 80	4 80	3 00	....	1 20
Carmine	24 00	15 00	9 00	4 80	....	1 20

Prices subject to change without notice.

GROUPED EXAMPLES

INK BOTTLES

Top Row.
1. 3¾ inches x 2½ inches x 3½ inches high, clear.   (U)

2. 3¼ inches base, 2⅛ inches s b. (weighted) clear.   (U)

3. 4¼ inches base, 1⅝ inches s b., golden amber.   Original label. "Palmer's Superior Dark Blue Writing Ink".   (St.)

4. 4½ inches x 2¼ inches, s b., blue. "Harrison's Columbian Ink" (horizontally 3 lines).   (U)

5. 7¼ inches x 4⅛ inches, s b. 12-sided "Harrison's Columbian Ink" (vertically 3 lines) aquamarine.   Also gallon size.   (Wn).

6. 5 inches x 1⅞ inches, s b. golden amber (St.) original label.   (U)

7. 4 inches x 2 inches, s b., octagonal "Harrison's Columbian Ink" (vertically 3 lines), aquamarine.   (U)

8. 3¾ inches x 1 15-16 inches, octagonal, s b., golden amber.   "Farley's Ink" (Vertically 2 lines).   (St.)

9. 1¾ inches x 2⅞ inches, height 3 inches, s b., clear. "Harrisons". Reverse: "Tippecanoe".   (Wn).

Lower Row.
1. 1⅞ inches base, height 2 inches, blue, cupped spout.   (U)

2. 1¾ inches, height 1½ inches, octagonal, s b., original label "Ne Plus Ultra Ink" "Will not rust or corrode a pen.—Put up by Newman & Co., Gilsum, N. H." Olive green (Kn).   (U)

3. 3 inches high, 1⅝ inches, 12 sided, golden amber (St.), s b., flanged mouth, (broken off) (no lettering).   (U)

4. Length 5¼ inches, height 1⅝ inches, aquamarine (U).

5. 6½ inches, height 4⅞ inches, aquamarine.   Spout m. s b.   (U). "Segur's Record Ink" (3 horizontal lines), square, bevelled corners.

6. Height 2 inches, length 4 inches, blown, dark golden amber, two mouths.   (U).

7. Height 3⅛ inches, 2½ inch base, s b., 16 sided, aquamarine. (U)

8. 2½ inches x base 2¼ inches, deep green, s b.   (U) octagonal.

9. 2 inches x base 2⅛ inches, deep green.   (U) octagonal.   Also gallon size.

Others
1. Rectangular—aquamarine (FW).

2. Ink bottle, olive green full of bubbles, height 4¼ inches, 1½ inches diameter.   Original label "Black writing Fluid, suitable for records with quill or steel pens, prepared by Moses Brickett, New Ipswich, N. H."   (Kn.).

(Note: Moses Brickett of New Ipswich, N. H. made and sold 100 barrels of ink, 30 barrels of Japan blacking and great quantities of Paste Blacking, essences, Oils, etc.—From "History of New Ipswich".)

3. Ink bottle—golden amber (St.).

4. "Williams" on one side, opening for insertion of pen, 4 inches square, 5½ inches high, c m. light green.   (U).

5. About pint, olive amber, bubbly, spout mouth.   (Kn.)

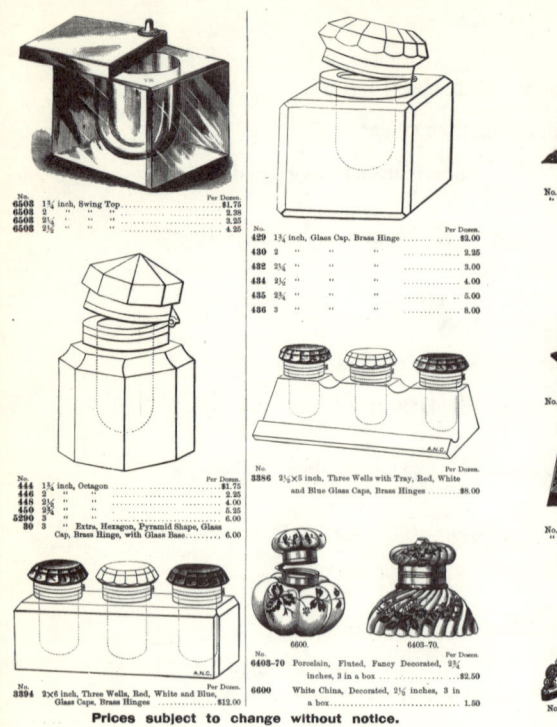
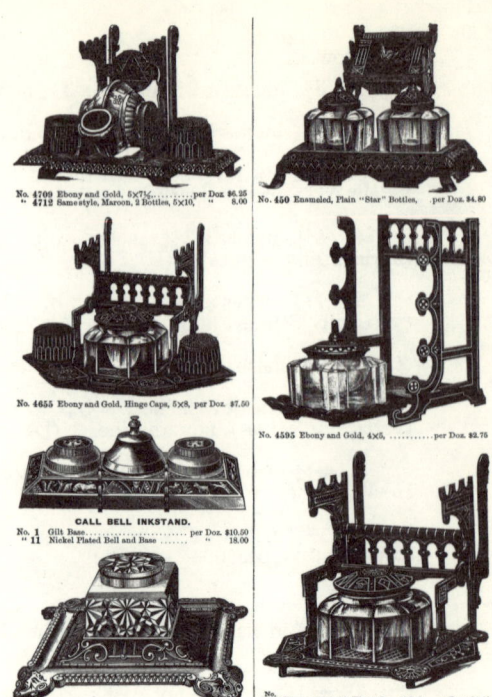

GLASS INKSTANDS.

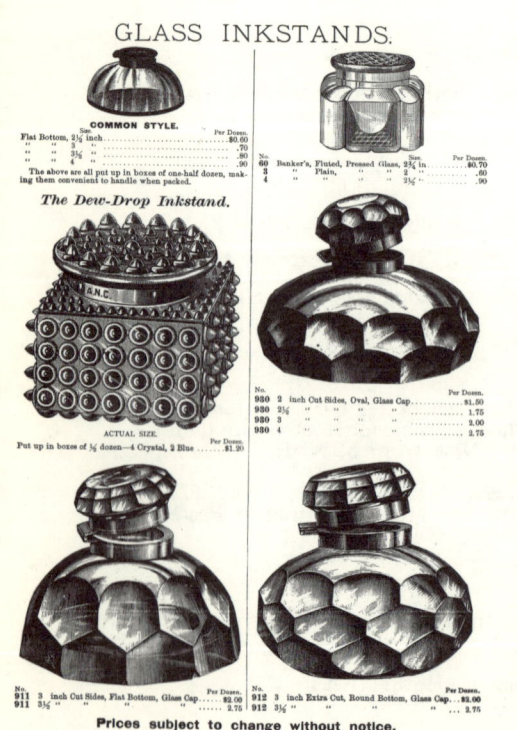
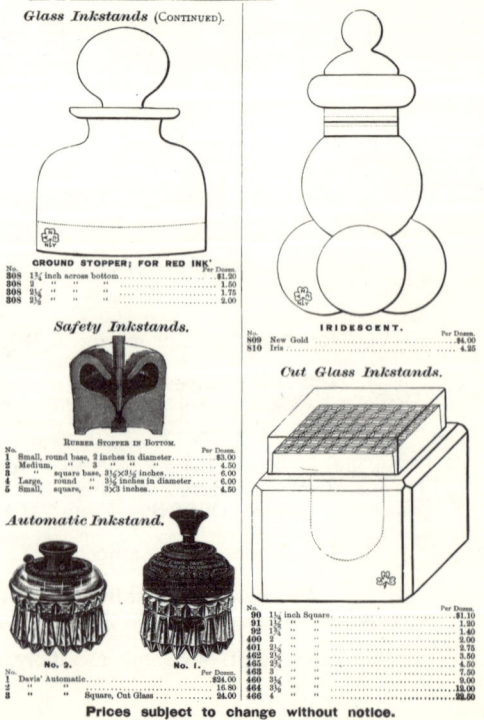

Prices subject to change without notice.

CATALOGUE OF STATIONERY. 155

	Per Doz.
ed Brass, 5¼×8⅜	$8.00
r Relief, 5¼×8⅜	9.60

No. 4130B Cast Brass, 5×6½ inch ... Per Dozen $14.00

ed Brass Base, 5×8¼ ... $8.00

ed Brass Base, 5×8¼ ... $8.00
r Relief, 5¼×8⅜ ... 10.25

No. 4134B Cast Brass, 5×6 inch ... Per Dozen $17.50

No. 4132B Cast Brass, 5×6½ inch ... Per Dozen $20.00

ed Brass Base, 6×11 ... Per Dozen $10.00

No. 0207 Nickel & Silver Bronze, 6×8 ... Per Dozen $14.50

Prices subject to change without notice.

---

150 THE AMERICAN NEWS COMPANY'S

ASSORTED INKSTANDS.

Nos. 6634½ 3454.

No.		Per Dozen
3454-1¼	Pressed Glass, Assorted Colors, Fancy Decorated, 1¼ inch square, 6 in a box	$1.00
3454-1⅜	Pressed Glass, Assorted Colors, Fancy Decorated, 1⅜ inch square, 6 in a box	1.20
6634½	Cut Glass, Assorted Designs, Fancy Decorated, 1½ inch square, 6 in a box	1.25

Nos. 3792. 3792.

No.		Per Dozen
3792	Cut Glass, Assorted Octagon and Diamond, Decorated, 1⅜ inch square, 6 in a box	$2.00
3556-57	Cut Glass, Assorted, Square and Octagon, Fancy Decorated Top and Bottom, 2 in. square, 6 in a box	2.75

Nos. 6612. 6626-1½ 6626-2.

No.		Per Dozen
6612	China, Gilt and Flowers, Decorated, 1½ in. on 3¼ in. tray, 3 in a box	$2.00
6626-1½	Porcelain China, Fancy Decoration, Gilt and Colors, 1½ inch, 3 in a box	2.25
6626-2	Porcelain China, Fancy Decoration, Gilt and Colors, 2 inches, 3 in a box	3.50
6622-2	Porcelain, Gilt, Assorted Colors, Round, 2 inches, 3 in a box	3.50
6404-2	Fancy Color, Shaded, Porcelain, Fluted, Square, 2 inches, 3 in a box	2.75
6404-2½	Fancy Color, Shaded, Porcelain, Fluted, Square, 2½ inches, 3 in a box	5.00

Nos. 6456-57 6581-1½ 3964
6306 6520 6309
6521

No.		Per Doz.
6581-1½	China, Fancy Decorated, Gilt and Flowers, 1½ inch square, 3 in a box	$0.90
6520-1¾	China, Fancy Decorated, Gilt and Flowers, 1¾ inch square, 6 in a box	.90
6521-2	China, Fancy Decorated, Gilt and Flowers, 2 inch square, 3 in a box	1.25
3964-1½	China, Fancy Decorated, Gilt and Flowers, 1½ inch square, 6 in a box	1.20
6446-1½	China, Fluted, Fancy Decorated, 1½ inch square, 3 in a box	1.20
6447-1½	China, Fluted, Fancy Decorated, 1¾ inch square, 3 in a box	1.20
6456-57	Porcelain, Assorted, round and square, Fancy Decorated, 1¾ inch, 3 in a box	2.00
6308-2¼	Porcelain, Square, Fancy Decorated, 2¼ inch, 3 in a box	4.00
6309-2	China, Octagon and Square, Gilt Decorated, 2 inch, 3 in a box	2.95
6291-3¼	Porcelain, Square, Gilt Decorated, 3¼ inch, 1 in a box	5.40

Nos. 6404. 3931-32. 6580.
6622. 6485.

No.		Per Doz.
3931-32	Glass, Gilt, Fluted, Assorted, Round and Square, 1¾ inch, 6 in a box	$2.12
6580-98	Glass, Gilt Ball, Fluted, Assorted, Round and Square, 1½ inch, 3 in a box	2.40
6485-2¼	Glass, Gilt, Fluted, Dewdrop, Round, 2¼ inches, 3 in a box	3.75
3932-2¼	Glass, Gilt, Fluted, Hinge Top, 2¼ inches Square	4.80
3983-2	Fancy Pressed and Cut Glass, 2 inches Square	2.00
3983-2½	" " " " 2½ "	3.00

Prices subject to change without notice.

THE AMERICAN NEWS COMPANY'S

ass Inkstands (CONTINUED).

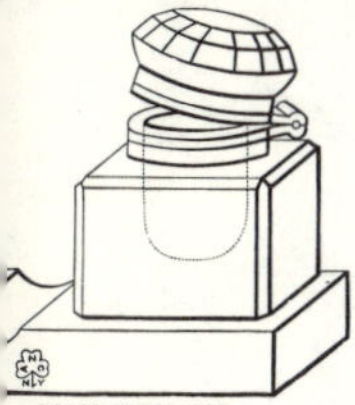

BRASS HINGE TOP.

	Size	Per Dozen
Tray, 1 Bottle	1½ inch	$2.75
" 1 "	2 "	3.32
" 1 " cut bottom	2½ "	6.50
" 1 "	2½ "	9.00

BRASS HINGE TOP.

ed Glass, Double Inkstand on Tray, Ink and 1½ inch, Tray 2¾×4 inch ... $3.50
Tray, 2 Blue Bottles, 1½ inch, red tops, 7.75

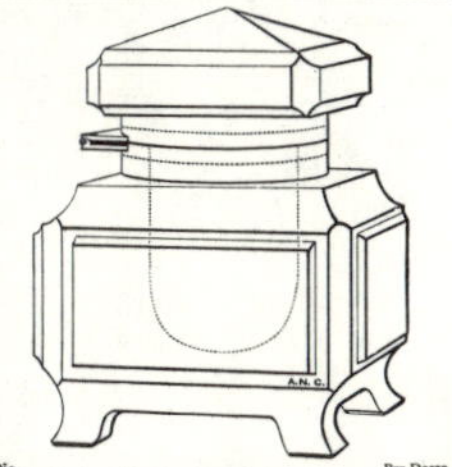

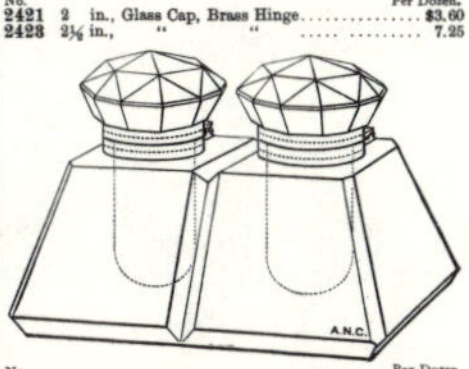

No.		Per Dozen
2421	2 in., Glass Cap, Brass Hinge	$3.60
2423	2½ in. " "	7.25

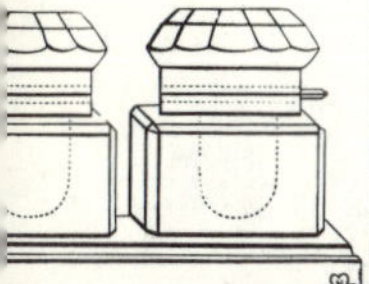

No. 3632 2×4 inch, Corrugated Bottom, Colored ... Per Dozen $6.00

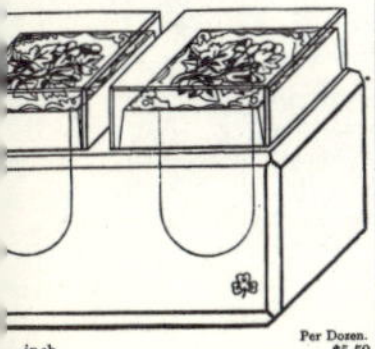

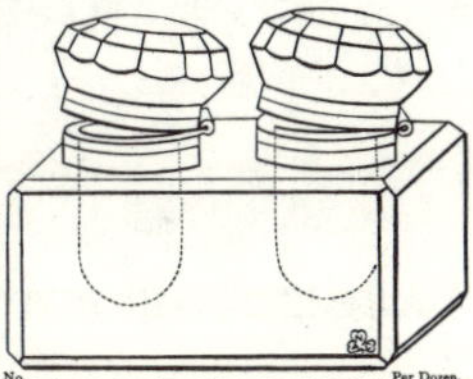

No. 184 Double Cut Glass Inkstand, 1½×3×3½ inch, Decorated in front, Flowers and Pearl Shell ... Per Doz. $6.00

	Per Dozen
inch	$5.50
½ "	8.00
2 "	11.25
2½ "	18.00
3 "	21.00

No.	Double Cut Glass	Per Doz.
498	2×4	$7.25
499	2¼×4¼	9.00
500	2½×5	13.50
506	2¾×5½	18.00
507	3×6	24.00

Prices subject to change without notice.

The Victor.

Automatic, Non-evaporating, Cheap, Cleanly, Perfect.
Put up one in a Box, ½ dozen in Carton.
Net Trade-price ... $4.00 per doz.

The Popular Automatic Inkstands.

THE DAISY. THE COMMERCIAL.

	Per Dozen
"Daisy," (holds 2 ounces)	$1.25
"Commercial," (holds 4 ounces), Nickel top	7.00
" " " " Black Hinge top	8.00

Screw Cap Inkstands.

No.			Per Dozen
1	Low, 1¾ inch, square		$0.60
2	" 1½ " "		
3	" 2 " "		
1	High, 1¾ " "		
2	" 1½ " "		
3	" 2 " "		

Traveling Ink-stands.

Glass Ink Wells.

		Per Doz.
For School Desks		$1.50
7443	Leather or Plush covered, 1¾ in. Diam.	1.50
7444	Leather or Plush covered, 1¾ in. Diam.	2.00

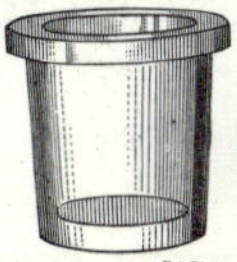

Wood Pocket Inkstands.

Screw.

No.	FULL SIZE.	Per Dozen
1	Lignum Vitæ, Screw	$1.25
2	" "	1.12
3	" "	1.00
	Barrel Screw	2.00
2	" "	1.75
3	" "	1.50

Rubber Pocket Inkstands.

Our illustrations represent actual size.

No.		Per Dozen	No.		Per Dozen
10—2	Round	$1.50	7	Flat	$2.00
20—5	Oval	1.63	30—6	Round	$2.75
25—4	Round	2.00			

Prices subject to change without notice.

GRAND OLD AMERICAN BOTTLES

"Stand Bottles"

BARBERSHOP BOTTLES

Bohemian Glass "Stand Bottles"; Shaving Paper Vase at bottom; two pomade cups.

-- GROUP C: HOUSEHOLDS

BARBER STAND BOTTLES AND TOILETRIES

Glass collectors have always loved the barber bottles which once held urgents for plastering their hair down and toning up the skin of a man after his shave. Some of the most desirable were of the opalescent hobnail variety, made at Sandwich and in bewitching blues and yellow colored glass. Some may have been on the male's home dressing table, but mostly they adorned the dresser of the barber shop. A common invigorator was bay rum, another was witch hazel. Still others were the alcoholic rubs said to help restore hair on a bald scalp, the skin bracers and "Tiger Rub." Besides these aids to sartorial perfection, there was a whole variety of containers of hair cream (Bear Grease) and other toiletries that are today collectable. Of course the major interest still goes to the Barber Bottles, some made in Sandwich, some with Mary Gregory decoration, some with pointed hobnail base. But a coming field is the Barber Stand Bottle, in clear glass with the owner's name on it in gold.

The use of these barbershop bottles became extremely popular in the early 1870's, and continued through the early 1900's.

Bay rum, the favored tonic made from distilled liquid and leaves of the bayberry bush was a leading barbershop unguent, so was bear grease.

Most barbershops had the standard set of shelf bottles, and for their preferred or regular customers there was a personalized bottle or set. This was placed in a wall shelf for the customer's own use. His name usually appeared in gold across the top of the bottle and the name of the tonic across the bottom. Just as he kept his shaving mug and name on it and went every day.

Most of these personalized bottles had a picture of a then-reigning stage favorite in full color in the center, while some had romantic scenes. These pictures were lithographed on a thin paper, pasted on the bottle in a frame, and over this was placed a glass panel label. The lettering was underpainted. The glass was bent to the contour of the bottle and cemented down over the picture. The bottles were press-blown with pewter screw tops.

In a high class barbershop personal accessories would include owner's own shaving bowl, a 3/12 ounce stand bottle, his pomade jar or a small stand bottle with a shaving-paper vase. When men began to shave at home, most of these personal sets were left behind at the shop and so destroyed.

Many of the early bottles were highly decorated and came from Bohemia, Bristol and other English glass plants. Some, of course, were made of American glassware, especially the pomade jars in milk glass. Better class shops did not use enameled decorated bottles, but had cut glass or silver deposit bottles on their shelves. All of these and the pomade jars in cut glass too, are very collectable.

Window Show Bottles.

No. 2. Grecian Vase.
Pineapple. Four Pieces.
No. 5. Grecian Vase.
Wayne. Four Pieces.
No. 4. Grecian Vase.
No. 6. Grecian Vase.
No. 7. Grecian Vase.

EACH.

	THREE PIECES.		FOUR PIECES.	
PINEAPPLE.	Plain.	Engraved.	Plain.	Engraved.
½ gallon	$2 00	$3 10	$2 40	$3 70
1 gallon	2 40	3 80	3 00	4 50
1½ gallon	3 20	5 00	3 70	5 70
2 gallon	3 60	5 80	4 20	6 50
3 gallon	4 70	7 60	5 50	8 60
WAYNE.				
1 gallon	3 00	4 80	3 50	5 60
2 gallon	4 60	7 20	4 80	7 60
3 gallon	5 90	9 40	6 90	10 50

GRECIAN VASE.
2 Gallon. Height, 32 inches.

	Each.
Plain	$7 00
Engraved	9 50
No. 2, Richly cut	26 00
No. 4, Richly cut	19 00
No. 5, Richly cut	23 00
No. 6, Richly cut	24 00
No. 7, Richly cut	37 00

— GROUP C: HOUSEHOLDS

CHAPTER XV   DRUG STORE BOTTLES

DRUG AND STORE BOTTLES

Both the early druggist and general country storekeeper often carried much the same bottle products; both were a market for glasshouses that produced whiskey, medicine, fruit, candy and other containers. In this chapter we shall be looking primarily at Drug Store Glassware as shown in two typical catalogs. One (1890) before the advent of the machine-made bottle and one of 1901, two years after that momentous invention which further cheapened the cost and enhanced the use of bottles. You will see in the pages which follow a unique array of bottles, flasks, jar shapes and uses, together with their correctly designated names, any or all of which are well worth collecting. Not many, of course, have use marked-in-the-glass, but sometimes the druggist or storekeeper's name is so marked, and locally that makes such bottles rather unique.

Note that by 1900, shapes were determining type of contents, hence a collector can now assemble his groups accurately. Perhaps he will want to keep to marked-in-glass medicinals (non-alcohols like liniments); if so it is in our lists; or he may go in for variety in types of use. Besides the common light green bottle-glass, one can find almost any color in some shapes—dark green and blues being the most desired and variations in amber used often for special contents. Note also that patent stoppers, tumbler stoppers and locked-flask tops were now beginning to come into the fore. A collection of extract bottles even would be fascinating since both color, taste and scent liquids were often bottled at the retail store from a larger container and using individually designed small colored bottles. We have used a great variety of actual catalog pages in this section to enhance new collector interest. Those who want a listing of some typical bottles in each class (but marked in glass) can see the description in end of this chapter; all before 1900 and a start on any non-alcoholic (Group C) bottle collecting. Note especially the Drug Show bottles—worth today $50 to $100 depending, also the ink and hair dye bottles we have listed earlier; small and cheap to collect, these are very nice to look at in a sunlit window.

Best loved household collector's bottle was "some say" the Apostles or Monk's Bottle. A plump red-amber bottle decorated with the figures of six monks standing in gothic archways, it was one of the great "mistakes" of modern bottle making, it failed to please the Catholic clergy and was a financial failure to its sponsors who soon discontinued. The writer does not know, but maybe some repros have been made.

Here are letterheads from typical glasshouses that made our 19th century Bottles (Shoe-fly, Picnics, Bitters, Foods, Liquors and Medicinals.) Best source for a Household Bottles Check-list are the papers and catalogs of 19th Century Glasshouses and druggist supply houses.

INDEXING HAGERTY & DEAN-FOSTER CATALOGS OF DRUGGISTS' BOTTLES

The next 50 pages (378-428) have been given over to reproducing catalog drawings (and prices) from the leading late 19th Century drug bottle suppliers. There is no surer way to date bottle types already described in earlier chapters than by use of the Fig. nos. appearing on such pages. So that you can refer to individual shapes (in corresponding with other collectors or in locating actual examples from your own collection) we suggest use of the special catalog index prepared at the end. Note these catalog pages are numbered as x 48 etc., for Dean-Foster bottle types and z 318 etc., for Hagerty bottle types. Thus a Liquor shape which appeared on these z pages would be referred to as z 318, fig. 211, etc.; while one that appeared on an x page would be referred to as x 32, Cut 144.

— GROUP C: HOUSEHOLD: MEDICINALS

Factory and Warehouse, Eastern Avenue, Boston, Mass.

WE HAVE, WITHOUT QUESTION, the largest and best facilities for meeting the requirements of the drug trade of any house in our line in this country. Our immense warehouse in Boston enables us to carry a very large and well-assorted stock of GLASSWARE AND DRUGGISTS' SUNDRIES for prompt delivery.

Situated as it is on the water-front, together with a spur track of the Union Transfer Company running to the doors, thus connecting us with all of the railroads centering in Boston, it enables us to ship goods to all parts of the country by either water or rail with ease and despatch. All orders, except for goods to be made, are shipped within twenty-four hours after they are received.

As no Bottle Glassware is manufactured in the New England States, it is necessary, in order to avoid vexacious delays, to carry a much larger supply of ware in Boston than is the case in other sections of the country.

OUR SALESROOM AND OFFICE on Blackstone Street, Boston, is accessible, and has long been identified with the druggist glassware business. Here we are always glad to meet our friends, and to show them the latest novelties.

CHARLES L. DEAN — ELMER G. FOSTER

Price List
DEAN, FOSTER & COMPANY

MANUFACTURERS OF

GREEN, AMBER BOTTLE GLASSWARE, FLINT, VIALS, DRUGGISTS' SUNDRIES AND CORKS

14 BLACKSTONE STREET, BOSTON

ESTABLISHED 1849.

HAGERTY BROS. & CO.,

NOS. 5, 8 & 10 (OFFICE & SALESROOM, NO. 10) PLATT ST., NEW YORK.

Factories: PENNSYLVANIA, NEW JERSEY and BROOKLYN, N. Y.

MANUFACTURERS, IMPORTERS AND EXPORTERS

In Stock, and Manufactured or Imported to Order.

APOTHECARIES' STORES

Labeled throughout in the best and most artistic manner, and furnished with everything pertaining to the business.

PRIVATE MOULDS MADE TO ORDER AND PARTICULARLY ATTENDED TO.

NEW YORK:
E. P. COBY & CO., PRINTERS, 21 PLATT STREET.

HAGERTY CATALOG PAGES INDEX

bottle types and z 318 etc., for Hagerty bottle types. Thus shape which appeared on these z pages would be referred to as z 318.

A.

	Page.
Acid Bottles, Coin Test	81
" " Green	308
" " Measures, Graduated, Porcelain	98
" Syphons, Glass	83
Adapters, for connecting Retorts and Receivers	78
Alcohol Lamps	81
Anatomical Specimen Jars	84
Aspirator Bottles, (Tubulated Tinctures)	19
Atomizers, Perfume, Steam, Throat, etc.	234–236

B.

Balsam or Oil Bottles, American	15
Balsam or Oil Bottles, with Cut, etc. Bottoms	16
Balsam or Oil Bottles, English	16
Balsam or Oil Bottles, American, No. 360 Ware	13
Balsam or Oil Bottles, English, No. 360 Ware	13
Balsam or Oil Bottles, Recess	18
Bandages, Suspensory	225, 226
Baths, Eye	142
Batteries, Electro-Magnetic	168
Battery Jars, Flint	85
Beaker Glasses	79
Bed Pans, White and Yellow	98
Bell Glasses	82
Blow Pipes, Brass	125
Blue Essential Oil Bottles	198
" Steeple-Top Jars	88

	Page.
Blue Syrup Bottles, Dispensing	15
" Tincture and Salt Mouths	11
" " " No. 360 Ware	13
Bottles, Acid, Green	308
" Bulk Extracts	285
" Castor Oil, Green	307
" Cod Liver Oil, Green	307
" Emulsion, Green	307
" Dispensing Syrup	15
" Essential Oils, Hand Made, Flint and Blue	198
" Ether	16
" Hair Oil	289, 290, 299
" Hot Water, Rubber	222
" Inhaling	146
" Ink, Green	311, 312
" " Flint	290
" Lager Beer	323
" Lubin Extract	287–289
" " Dentine	259–260
" Magnesia	291, 308
" Medicine Chest	183, 184
" Morphine	291
" Mucilage	290
" Nursing	132–136
" Patent Medicine	309
" Prescription, Flint	270–280
" " B 294–298
" " Green	302–304
" Quinine	291
" Sachet Powder	257
" Saddle Bag	184
" Sample	194–199
" Sewing Machine Oil	299

	Page.
Bottles, Show	48–56
" Soda Syrup	237
" Sprinkler Tops	258
" Tablet, with Screw Tops	161–163
" Tooth Powder	259, 260
" Wash	260
" Wheat Sample	199
" Wine, Amber	318
" Flint B	325
Bougies and Catheters	151
Boxes, Cold Cream	90
" Gill's Seamless Tin	166–168
" Tooth Powder, Opal Glass	157
" Turned Wood	160
" Twine, Glass, Iron, Brass, etc.	75, 76
Brackets, Window	122, 128
Breast Pipes	141
" Pumps	140
Brushes, Bottle	138
" Throat	150
" Tube	138
Bulb Nasal Douches	232

C.

Cans, Herb	262
Carmine Ink Bottles, Flint	290
" " B	299
" " Green	312
Case Vials	193
Cases, Physicians' Vial	179–182
" Sample	182
Casseroles, Porcelain, Covered and Uncovered	93, 94
Catheters and Bougies	90
Catsup Bottles, Flint B	301
" " Green	314
Chemical and Philosophical Glass Ware	77–86
Chemical Flasks	79
China Medicine Spoons	102

	Page.
China Sick Feeders	101, 102
Chloroform or Ether Bottles	16
Clinical or Fever Thermometers	154
Club Sauce Bottles	314
Coal Oil Stoves	129
Coin Test Bottles	81
Cold Cream Pots	90
Collapsible Tubes	157
Cologne Bottles, Burnett's	284
" " Caswell, Round	285
" " Caswell, Square	285
" " Cut, Pressed, etc.	243–250
" " H	284
" " For Covering with Silk, etc.	250
" " Nichols'	286
" " Violet	286
Combs, Hard Rubber	209–217
Combination Pocket Syringes	191
Cork Borers	125
" Pressers	120
" Screws, Hard Rubber	208
Corn and Bunion Plasters	151
Counter Jars, Flint Ring	21
" " French Ring	21
" " English	22
" " Richly Cut	24
Counter Jars, Venetian	23
Counter Urns	22
Contents of Original Packages	332
Creamometers	177
Cupping Glasses	143
Cushions, Invalid	221
Cut Shelf Ware	12–14

D.

Decorated Jars, Pedestals, Vases, etc.	57–61

INDEX

	Page
Designs for Lettered Plates	268, 269
Demijohns, Covered	324
Dishes, Evaporating, Agate Iron	124
Dishes, Evaporating, Iron, Porcelain Lined	123
Dishes, Evaporating, Porcelain	93
Dishes, Evaporating, Porcelain Nested	93
Dispensing Syrup Bottles	15
" " Blue	15
" " Cut	13
" " No. 360 Ware	12, 13
Douche Bottles	148
Douches, Nasal	147
Drawer Knobs, Porcelain	31
" Pulls, Hagerty's	32–36
" " Porcelain	30
Drug Mills	126, 127
Druggists' Prescription Vials, Flint	270–280
Druggists' Prescription Vials, Flint B	294–298
Druggists' Prescription Vials, Green	302–304
Druggists' Scales, Weights, etc.	103–113
Druggists' Shelf and Counter Ware	9–18
Druggists' Sieves	172, 173
" Sundries	149–171
" Twine	76

E.

Eagles, Gilded	62
Ear Cleaners	152
" Trumpets, Hard Rubber	208
Elastic Bands, Rubber	221, 222
" Bulb Syringes	227–230
Electro-Magnetic Machines	188
Essential Oil Bottles	198

	Page.
Evaporating Dishes, Agate Iron	124
Evaporating Dishes, Iron, Porcelain Lined	123
Evaporating Dishes, Porcelain, Berlin	93
Evaporating Dishes, Porcelain, German	93
Evaporating Dishes, Porcelain, Nested	93
Eye Baths	142
Explanation of Bottle Lips	267
Extract, etc. Bottles	287–289
Extra Fittings for Fountain Syringes	231

F.

Feeding Bottles	132–136
" Bottle Fittings	137
" " Fixtures	138
Feeders, Sick	101, 102
Fever or Clinical Thermometers	154
Filtering Bags	153
" Paper	152
" Racks	153
Finger Cots, Rubber	220
Fish Globes	242
Flasks, Chemical	79
" Flint, with Plated Metal Screw Caps	329
Flasks, Pocket	321, 322, 328
" " Olry's	331
Flat Top Jars, American	89
" " German	89
Flint Ring Jars	21
Florida Water Bottles, Green	310
Folders, Powder	125
Fountain Syringes	230, 231
French and English Porcelain Ware	87–98
French Pipettes	151
" Ring Jars	21

	Page.
French Squares, Flint	276, 277, 279
" " B	297
" " Green	304
Funnels, Glass	66
" Patent Ribbed	67
" Hard Rubber	207
" Porcelain	97
" Wedgwood	98

G.

Gallipots, White, Nested	90
" China, Wood Tops	90
Gallipots, White China, Uncovered	90
Gallipots, Yellow	91
Gas and Oil Stoves	128, 129
Gauge Glasses, Scotch	114
Gilded Eagles	62
" Mortars	62
" With Eagles	62
Gill's Seamless Tin Boxes	166–168
Glass Eye Baths	142
" Labels	27–29
" List of	37–46
" Letters and Numbers	31
" Medicine Tubes	102
" Mortars	74
" Ointment Pots	158, 159
" Patch Boxes, Opal	165
" Stirring Rods	86
" Syringes	187–191
" Tooth Powder Bottles	259, 260
" Wash Bottles	260
" Tubing	86, 114
" Twine Boxes	75
Glasses, Beaker	79
" Bell	82
" Cupping	143
Graduates, Glass	70–73
" Porcelain	98

H.

	Page.
Hagerty's Drawer Pulls	32–36
" Perfume Stands	63
Hair Oil Bottles	289, 299
Hard Rubber Combs	209–217
" Ear Trumpets	208
" Funnels	207
" Goods	200–217
" Speculums	207
" Syringes	200–207
Herb Cans	262
Holders, Soda and Mineral Tumbler	240, 241
Holders, Twine	75
Homœopathic Vials	192–199
Honey Jars	315
Horn Scoops	170
" Spoons	171
" Spatulas	171
Hydrometers	84
Hydrometer Jars	85
Hypodermic Syringes	155
" Needles	155

I.

Ice Bags	220
Infusion Jars	92
Inhaling Bottles	146
" Tubes, Messer's	146
Ink Bottles	290, 299, 311, 312
Insect Powder Bottles	310
Invalid Cushions	221
Iron Cork Pressers	120
" Evaporating Dishes	123
" Mortars	118
Irons, Plaster	124
Iron Retort Stands	119

J.

Jars, Anatomical Specimen	84
" Battery	85
" Decorated	57

INDEX.

	Page.
Jars, Flat Top, American	89
" " German Porcelain	89
" Flint Ring	21
" French Ring	21
" Fruit	330
" Glycerine Jelly	165
" Hydrometer	85
" Leech	91, 92
" Mason, Fruit	330
" Patent Pyramid	25, 26
" " Section	25
" Percolating	69
" Pomade	292
" Precipitating	83
" Specie	19, 20
" " New Style	20
" Sponge	24
" " Cut	24
" Steeple Top Blue	88
" " White	88
" " White China Gold Band	88
" Steeple Top, White Granite, Gold Band	89
" Storage	21
" Tie Over or Jelly Cans	91
" Venetian	23
" White Infusion	92

K.
Knives, Putty	117
Knobs, Porcelain Drawer	31

L.
Labels, Glass	28, 29
" Fac-Simile Sheets of	28
Lager Beer Bottles	323
Lamps, Alcohol	81
Lavender Salts Bottles, Emerald Green	291
Leech Jars	91, 92
" Tubes	144

	Page.
Lettered Ware, List of Plates for	265
Lip Salve Boxes	168
List of Names for Glass Labels	37–46
Lubin Extract Bottles	287
" Dentine "	259, 260
Liquor Dealers' Glass Ware, Amber	318–321
Liquor Dealers' Glass Ware, Flint, B	325–328
Liquor Thieves	199

M.
Magnesia Bottles	291, 308
Measures, Graduated, Glass	70–73
" " Porcelain	98
" Seidlitz	152
" Standard, Tin	261
Medicine Chests	178
" Chest Bottles	183, 184
" Droppers	151
" Glasses	74
" Spoons, China	102
" Tubes, Glass	102
Medical Saddle Bags	179
Metal Syringes	186
Mills, Drug	126, 127
Mineral Water Bottles, with Patent Stoppers	322
Miscellaneous Ware, Flint	291
" " B	300, 301
Mixed Ware, Green	313–316
Mortars, Gilded	62
" Glass	74
" Iron	118
" Porcelain	96
" Wedgewood	94, 95
Moulds, New	264
" Suppository	156
Mucilage Bottles	290, 312
" Caps and Brushes	290

	Page.
Mugs, Spit	100, 101
Mustard Bottles, Flint, B	300
" " Green	315

N.
Nasal Douches	147, 148
" " Bulb	282
" Douche Bottles	148
" Inhalers	146
New Moulds	264
Nipples, Rubber	218, 219
Nipple Shells	141
" Shields	142
Nursing Bottles	132–136
" Untrimmed	135, 136
" Bottle Brushes	138
" Fittings	137
" Fixtures	138
Nursers, Peerless	184

O.
Oblongs, Flint	279
" B	297, 298
" Green	304
Oil or Balsam Bottles	13, 14, 15, 18
Oil Bottles, Castor, Green	307
" Cod Liver	307
" Emulsion	307
" Essential	198
" Hair	289, 290, 299
Oil Bottles, Sewing Machine, Flint B	299
Oil and Gas Stoves	128, 129
Ointment Pots, Glass	158, 159
Opal Patch Boxes	165
" Tooth Powder Boxes	157
Ovals, Flint	274–276
" B	295, 296
" Green	303

P.
Panel Bottles, Flint	280
" Green	305

	Page.
Panel Bottles, Ball Neck, Flint	281
" " Flint B	298
" " Green	304
Patch Boxes, earthen	89
" Opal Glass	165
Patent Medicine Bottles, Green	309
Patent Section Jars	25
" " Pyramid	25, 26
Pearl Agate Iron Water Baths	124
Pedestals, Marbleized	60
Percolators, Glass	67, 68
" Tin	69
Percolating Jars, Graduated	69
Perfumers' Glassware, Flint	284–292
" " Green	310
Perfume Stands	68
Pepper Sauce Bottles	313
Pessaries, Glass	145
" Hard Rubber	145
" Soft Rubber	144
Physicians' Vial Cases	179–182
Pickle Jars	316
Pill Machines	121
" Rollers	152
" Silverers	152
" Tiles, Earthen, Graduated	96
" " Glass "	96
Pipes, Breast	141
" Blow, Brass	140
Pipettes, French	151
Plasters, Corn and Bunion	151
Plaster Irons	124
" Spreading Machines	124
Pocket Cook Stoves	129, 130
" Flasks, Amber	321
" " Flint	328
" " Plated Caps	329
" " Olry's	331
Pomades, with Caps	292
" without Caps	292
Porcelain Evaporating Dishes	93
" Casseroles	93, 94

INDEX.

	Page.
Porcelain Funnels	97
" Mortars	96
Pots, Cold Cream	90
" Glass, Ointment	158, 159
Powder Bottles	283
" Folders	125
Precipitating Jars	83
Prescription Vials, Flint	270–280
" " B	294–298
" " Green	302–304

V.
Vases, Decorated	58, 59
Vaseline Bottles	292
Vial Cases	179–182
Vials, Homœopathic	192–194
" Medicine Chest	183, 184
" Patent Medicine	309
" Prescription, Flint	270–280
" " B	293–298
" " Green	302–304

Q.
Quinine Bottles	291

R.
Recess Glass Labeled Shelf Ware	17, 18
Recess Glass Labeled Shelf Ware, with Cut Stoppers	18
Receivers, Plain & Stoppered	78
Retorts	78
Retort Stands	119
Ring Jars	21
Rods, Stirring Glass	86
Rubber Bandages	222
" Bands, Elastic	221
" Bottles, Hot Water	222
" Combs	209–217
" Cushions, Invalid	221

U.
Urinals, Earthen, White	98
" Glass	99
" Graduated	91

	Page.
Urinometers	84
Urns, Counter, Plain	22
" " Fluted	22
" " English	22
" " Richly Cut	24
" " Venetian	23

S.
Sachet Bottles	287
Saddle Bags	179
" Bag Style	184
Salt Mouth Bottles	10, 11, 12, 14
Sample Bottles, Cone Shaped, Heavy	196
Sample Bottles, Flat, on Foot, Stoppered	195
Sample Bottles, Flat, no Foot	196
Sample Bottles, Round, on Foot, Stoppered	195
Sample Bottles, Square	198
" " Flat on Foot	196
" " Liquor	199
" " Round, Oil, Straight	197
" " Venetian	196
Scales, Counter	104
" Counter, Robervahl, French	105
Scale Pans	109
Scales, Pocket	109
" Prescription	105–108
Scoops, Horn	170
Screw Neck Tube Vials	164
Scotch Gauge Glasses	114
Seamless Tin Boxes	166–168
Section Jars	25
" " Pyramid	26
Seidlitz Boxes, Tin	168
" Measures	152
Select Powder Bottles	283
Shop Furniture Bottles	9–18
Show Bottles, Gilded Mortars, etc	48–62
Show Jars, Decorated	57

INDEX.

	Page.
Sick Feeders	101, 102
" Tubes	102
" Tumblers	102
Sieves, Tin, Brass, etc	172, 173
Sinking Proof Glasses	199
Smelling Salts, or Pungents	251–256
Soda Syrup Bottles	237
Soda and Mineral Water Tumblers	237–239
Soda and Mineral Water Tumbler Holders	240–241
Soft Rubber Goods	218–224
Spatulas, Horn	171
" Steel	116, 117
" Pocket	117
Specie Jars	19, 20
" " New Style	20
Specimen Jars, Anatomical	84
Speculums, Silvered, etc	143
Spirit Lamps, Glass	81
Spit Mugs	100, 101
Sponge Jars	24
Spoons, Horn	171
" Medicine, China, etc	102
Sprinkler Tops	261
" Top, Colognes	258
Standard Measures, Tin	261
Stands, Retort	119
Stethoscopes	148
Stirring Rods, Glass	86
Stoppers, Rubber	224
Stoppers, Style of	266
Stoves, Oil	129
Style of Stoppers	266
Stoves, Gas and Oil	128
" Pocket	129, 130
Sundries, Druggists'	150–168
Suppository Moulds	156
Suspensory Bandages	225, 226
Sweet or Olive Oil Bottles	300, 314
Syphons, Glass, Acid	83

	Page.
Syringes, Elastic Bulb	227, 230
" Infant Rectal	227
" Fountain	230, 231
" Glass	127–131
Syrup Bottles, Dispensing	13, 15, 18
" Soda	237

T.
Tablet Bottles, Screw Top	162, 163
" Glass, for Fittings	138
" Glass Gauge	114
" Inhaling, Messer's	146
" Leech	144
" Medicine, Glass	102
" Test	80
Tub'ng, Glass	86, 114
" Rubber	223
Tabulated Tinctures (Aspirator Bottles)	19
Tumbler Holders	240, 241
Tumblers, Mineral	239
" Sick	102
" Soda	237, 238
" Chemical or Laboratory	176

W.
Wine Bottles, Amber	318
" Flint, B	325–327
Thieves, Liquor	199
Wheat Sample Bottles	199
White Opaque Glass Ware	291
Tiles, Pill, English	96
" Glass	96
Tin Boxes, Seamless	166–168
Tincture Bottles	9, 10, 11, 12, 13, 14, 17
" Pressers	126
Tooth Powder Bottles	259, 260
" " Boxes, Glass	157
" " Wash Bottles	260

HAGERTY BROTHERS & CO.,

FLAT POCKET FLASKS.
With Glass Tumbler Stopper.

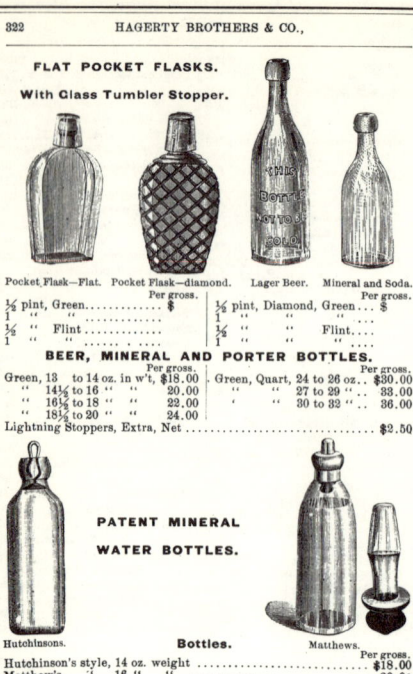

Pocket Flask—Flat.	Pocket Flask—diamond.	Lager Beer.	Mineral and Soda.

	Per gross.		Per gross.
½ pint, Green,	$	½ pint, Diamond, Green...	$
1 " "		1 " " "	
½ " Flint.		½ " Flint....	
1 " "		1 " " "	

BEER, MINERAL AND PORTER BOTTLES.

	Per gross.		Per gross.
Green, 13 to 14 oz. in w't,	$18.00	Green, Quart, 24 to 26 oz..	$30.00
" 14½ to 16 " "	20.00	" " 27 to 29 " .	33.00
" 16½ to 18 " "	22.00	" " 30 to 32 " .	36.00
" 18½ to 20 " "	24.00		

Lightning Stoppers, Extra, Net $2.50

PATENT MINERAL WATER BOTTLES.

Hutchinsons.	Bottles.	Matthews.

	Per gross.
Hutchinson's style, 14 oz. weight	$18.00
Matthew's " 16 "	20.00

Stoppers.
	Per gross.
Hutch[inson's] [Sp]ring, Extra, Net......................	$2.50
Matt[hew's] " "	3.00

LIQUOR DEALERS' GLASS WARE,
FLINT B.
BRANDIES, WINES AND FLASKS.

Brandy or Wine.	Squat Brandy.	Seal, No. 322.

Brandy or Wine Bottles.
	Per gross.
8 to the gallon, 1 gross in a box.......	$26.00
6 " " 1 " "	30.00
5 " " 1 " "	32.00
4 " " 1 " "	35.00

Squat Brandies.
	Per gross.
8 to the gallon, 1 gross in a box.......	$26.00
4 " " 1 " "	35.00

Seal, No. 322. Plate Mould.
	Per gross.
8 to the gallon, 1 gross in a box.......	$26.00
6 " " 1 " "	30.00
5 " " 1 " "	32.00

HAGERTY BROTHERS & CO.,

BRANDIES, WINES AND FLASKS.—Continued.

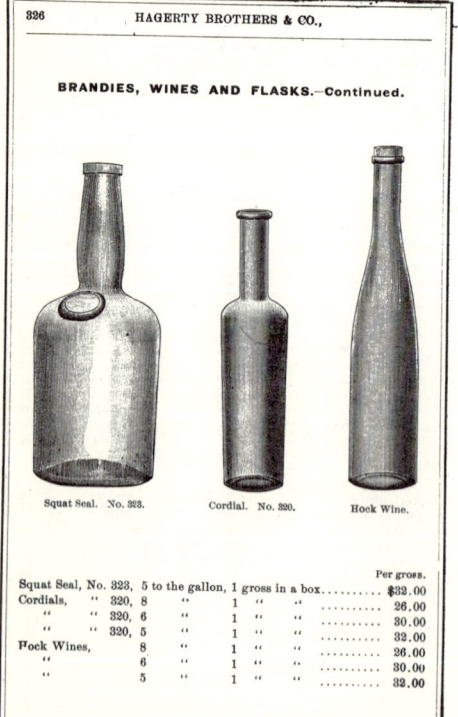

Squat Seal. No. 323.	Cordial. No. 320.	Hock Wine.

		Per gross.
Squat Seal, No. 323, 5 to the gallon, 1 gross in a box.........		$32.00
Cordials, " 320, 8 " " 1 " "		26.00
" " 320, 6 " " 1 " "		30.00
" " 320, 5 " " 1 " "		32.00
Hock Wines, 8 " " 1 " "		26.00
" 6 " " 1 " "		30.00
" 5 " " 1 " "		32.00

POCKET FLASKS.
OLRY'S PATENT.

The Screws are Fastened with METAL instead of Cement.
LEAKAGE IMPOSSIBLE.

These flasks (American made) are alone in the market with metal-fastened screws on neck; all other makes are fastened with plaster or various compositions which cannot prevent leakage. The OLRY FLASK is free from such risk.

Nos. 8, 9, 10, 11, 12 and 13.	Nos. 514, 515, 516, 517 and 518.

LEATHER COVERED; GLASS.
With Britannia Metal Cups.

Nos.	DESCRIPTION.	MEASURES. Per dozen.				
		1/16 Pint.	⅛ Pint.	¼ Pint.	½ Pint.	Pint.	Quart.
8,	Plain Sheepskin..... $	....	9.00	11.00	12.50	15.00	18.00	30.00
9,	Colored Leather, asst..		9.00	12.00	14.00	17.00	21.00	33.00
10,	Russia Leath. open sides	11.00	12.00	16.50	21.00	24.00	30.00	42.00
11,	Hogskin...............			13.50	15.00	18.00	24.00	36.00
12,	Turkey Morocco......	11.00	11.00	13.50	15.00	18.00	24.00	36.00

With Inverted Cups.

Nos.	With Plain Metal Cups.	MEASURES.—Per dozen.		
		¼ Pint.	½ Pint.	¾ Pint.
514,	Assorted Sheep.................	$13.50	$16.50	$19.50
515,	Russia	15.00	19.50	24.00
516,	Hogskin	15.00	19.50	24.00
517,	Morocco........................	15.00	19.50	24.00
518,	Fancy Leathers.................	15.00	19.50	24.00

GLASS; COVERED ALL OVER WITH LEATHER.
Without Cups.

Nos.	DESCRIPTION.	MEASURES.—Per dozen.				
		⅛ Pint.	¼ Pint.	½ Pint.	¾ Pint.	Pint.
1,	Colored Leather, Assorted......	$8.25	9.50	11.00	13.50	16.50

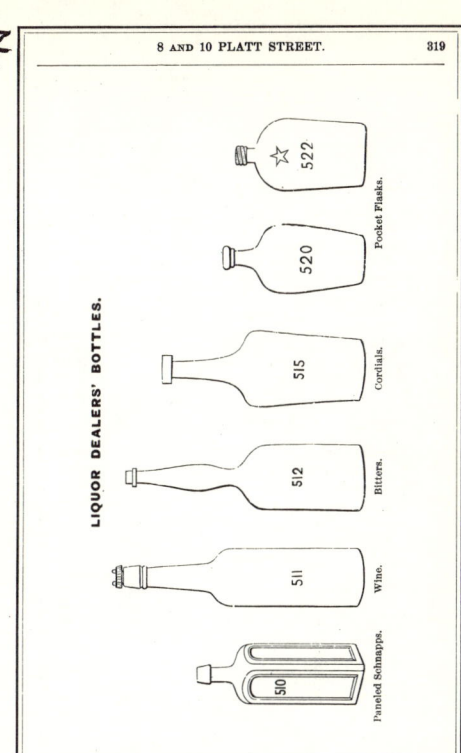

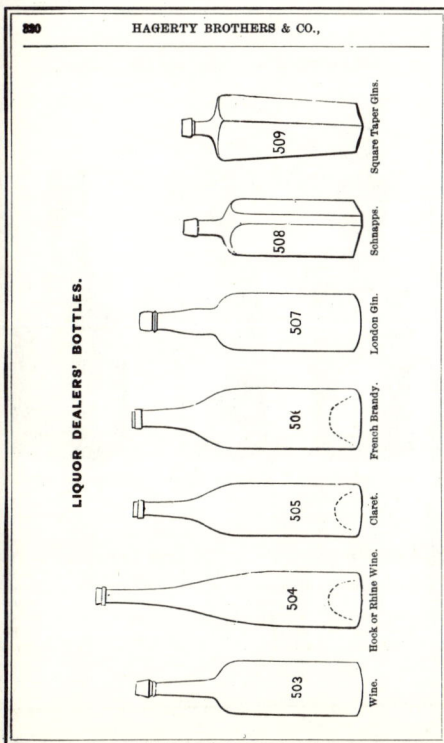

LIQUOR DEALERS' GLASS WARE.

No Charge for Original Packages.

WINE BOTTLES.
Amber or Green. Fig. 503.

			Per gross.
4 to the gallon, 24 to 26 ounce weight, ½ gross in a box			$30.00
5 " 18 to 20 " 1 " "			23.00
5½ " 17 to 19 " 1 " "			22.00
6 " 16 to 18 " 1 " "			21.00
7 " 15 to 16 " 1 " "			20.00
8 " 12 to 14 " 1 " "			17.00
10 " 10 to 12 " 1 " "			15.00
12 " " 1 " "			14.00
16 " " 1 " "			12.00

WINE BOTTLES.
Amber Color, of Superior Quality and finish. Fig. 503.

	Per gross.
5 to the gallon, 22 to 24 ounce weight, 1 gross in a box	$27.00
5½ " 20 to 22 " 1 " "	25.00
6 " 18 to 20 " 1 " "	23.00

HOCK OR RHINE WINE BOTTLES.
American, Iron Mould, Fig. 504

	Per gross.			Per gross.
5 to the gallon, 20 to 22 oz.	$27.00	5 to the gallon		$
6 " 18 to 20 "	27.00	6 "		
1 pint Colognes Hock Shape, Iron Mould, American, 15 to 16 oz.				22.00
½ " " " " 7 to 8 "				13.00
Clay Mould Hocks. $2.00 per gross extra, net.				

CLARET BOTTLES.

American.	Fig. 505.	Per gross.	German.	Per gross.
Pint, 15 to 16 oz. weight,		$22.00	Pint	$
Quart, 18 to 20 "		27.00	Quart	
Clay Mould Clarets, $2.00 per gross extra, net.				

FRENCH BRANDY BOTTLES.
Fig. 506.

	Per gross.
American	$
German	

LONDON GIN BOTTLES.
Light Green Glass. Fig. 407.

	Per gross.		Per gross.
5 to the gallon	$24.00	6 to the gallon	$22.00

Glass Stoppers and Corks, extra.

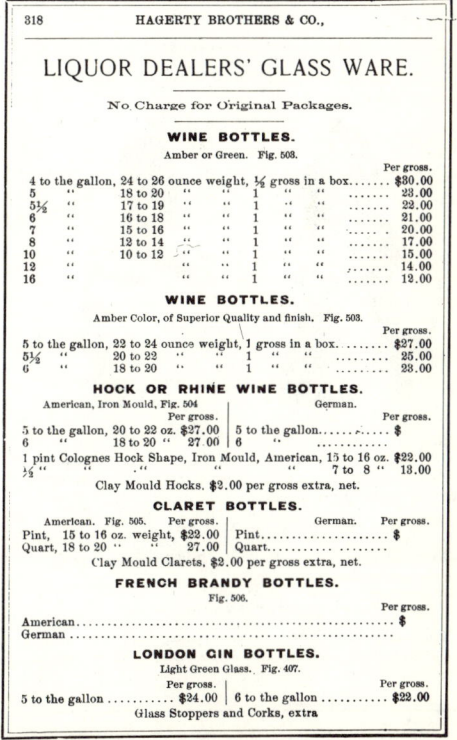

HAGERTY BROTHERS & CO.,

POCKET FLASKS

Pic-nic Flask.

Shoo-Fly Flask.

Pic-nic.

		Per gross.
½ pint, 1 gross in a box		$10 00
½ " ½ " "		12.00
1 " ½ " "		19.00
1 quart, ½ " "		30.00

Shoo-Fly.

		Per gross.
½ pint, 1 gross in a box		$10 00
½ " ½ " "		12.00
1 " ½ " "		19.00
1 quart, ½ " "		30.00

Shoo-Fly.
Full Measure.

		Per gross.
½ pint, 1 gross in a box		$15.00
1 " ½ " "		22.00
1 quart, ½ " "		35.00

Union.

		Per gross.
½ pint, ½ gross in a box		$12.00
1 " ½ " "		19.00
1 quart, ½ " "		30.00

FLINT FLASKS.
With Cork Lined and Plated Metal Screw Caps.

Union.

Saratoga.

Union.

		Per gross.
½ pint, ½ gross in a box		$6.25
1 " ½ " "		7.50

Saratoga.

		Per gross.
½ pint, 1 gross in a box		$6.25
1 " 1 " "		7.50

FLINT FLASKS.
With Plated Metal Screw Caps. Handsomely Finished.

			Per gross.
No. 755. Capacity, 2½ ounces			$6.00
" 1960. " 8 "			10.00
" 2063. " 12 "			15.00

LAGER BEER BOTTLES.
With Patent Lightning Stoppers.

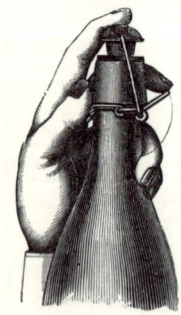
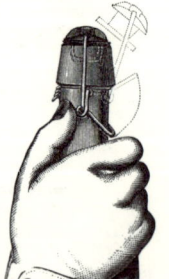

	Per gross.
½ pint, 13 to 14 ounce weight	$18.00
1 " 14½ to 16 " "	20.00
1 quart, 27 to 29 " "	33.00
Lightning Stoppers, Extra, Net	2.50

Putting on Stoppers, 25c. per gross, Extra, Net.

Every description of Bottles furnished at the shortest notice, and at the lowest manufacturer's prices.

Private moulds made to order and particularly attended to.

Possessing superior facilities for manufacturing Glass Ware, we would solicit orders, particularly for ware requiring great care and superior workmanship.

BRANDIES, WINES AND FLASKS.—Continued.

Export Beer. No. 325.

Champagne. No. 329.

Squat Seal. No. 327.

						Per gross.
Export Beer, No. 325,	pint,	1 gross in a box				$28.00
" " 325,	quart,	1 "	"	"		38.00
Champagnes, " 329,	pint,	1 "	"	"		28.00
" " 329,	quart,	1 "	"	"		38.00
Squat Seal, " 327,	6 to the gallon,	1 "	"	"		35.00
Taper Gins, " 330,	6 "	1 "	"	"		32.00
Schnapps, " 331,	6 "	1 "	"	"		30.00

Castor, Round and Oval, and Cod Liver Oil Bottles.

MUCILAGE BOTTLES.

CITRATE OF MAGNESIA.
Plain or Lettered.

Mucilage. Plain. Fluted. Flat.

Citrate of Magnesia. Flat Bottom Citrate. Round Bottom Citrate.

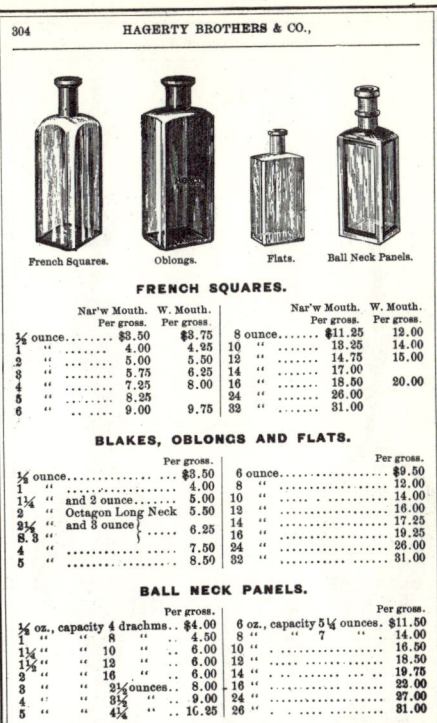

French Squares. Oblongs. Flats. Ball Neck Panels.

FRENCH SQUARES.

	Nar'w Mouth. Per gross.	W. Mouth. Per gross.		Nar'w Mouth. Per gross.	W. Mouth. Per gross.
½ ounce	$3.50	$3.75	8 ounce	$11.25	12.00
1 "	4.00	4.25	10 "	13.25	14.00
2 "	5.00	5.50	12 "	14.75	15.00
3 "	5.75	6.25	14 "	17.00	
4 "	7.25	8.00	16 "	18.50	20.00
5 "	8.25		24 "	26.00	
6 "	9.00	9.75	32 "	31.00	

BLAKES, OBLONGS AND FLATS.

	Per gross.		Per gross.
½ ounce	$3.50	6 ounce	$9.50
1 "	4.00	8 "	12.00
1¼ " and 2 ounce	5.00	10 "	14.00
2 " Octagon Long Neck	5.50	12 "	16.00
2½ " and 3 ounce }	6.25	14 "	17.25
3, 3 "		16 "	19.25
4 "	7.50	24 "	26.00
5 "	8.50	32 "	31.00

BALL NECK PANELS.

	Per gross.		Per gross.
½ oz., capacity 4 drachms	$4.00	6 oz., capacity 5¼ ounces	$11.50
1 " " 8 "	4.50	8 " " 7 "	14.00
1¼ " " 10 "	6.00	10 "	16.50
1½ " " 12 "	6.00	12 "	18.50
2 " " 16 "	6.00	14 "	19.75
3 " " 2½ ounces	8.00	16 "	23.00
4 " " 3½ "	9.00	24 "	27.00
5 " " 4¼ "	16.25	26 "	31.00

SQUARE SAMPLE BOTTLES.
For Exhibiting Sugars, Fine Chemicals, Etc.

The Cuts are one-half the size of bottles they represent.

Fig. 386. Fig. 387. Fig. 388.

WHEAT SAMPLE BOTTLES.
For Exhibiting Fine Drugs, Chemicals, Pills, &c.

	Per doz.
1 ounce	$2.00
2 "	2.00
4 "	2.50
8 "	3.00
1 pint	3.50
1 quart	4.00
½ gallon	9.00
1 "	12.00
2 "	24.00
3 "	40.00
4 "	48.00
5 "	60.00

Fig. 389.

LUBIN DENTINE BOTTLES.
With Metal Screw Top. For Tooth Powder.

Fig. 600. Fig. 601. Fig. 602. Fig. 603.

Fig. 604. Fig. 605. Fig. 606. Per gross.

2 ounce, Inclined Shoulder				Fig. 600.	$7.50
3 " " "				" 600.	8.00
4 " " "				" 600.	8.50
2 " Round "				" 601.	7.50
3 " " "				" 601.	8.00
4 " " "				" 601.	8.50
1½ " No. 597, Square, with slip or acorn top				" 602.	9.00
3 " " 598, " "				" 602.	10.00
1½ " " 645, Round, "				" 603.	9.00
3 " " 646, " "				" 603.	10.00
2 " " " Oblong, "				" 604.	9.00
2 " " " Square, "				" 605.	9.00
2 " " " Round, "				" 606.	9.00
2 " " " Oval, "					9.00

Figure 605 represents a "slip," and Fig. 606 an "Acorn" top. When ordering please state which of the two styles of tops you prefer.

HAGERTY BROTHERS & CO.,

CUT MEDALLION SHOW BOTTLES.

Richly Cut.

Fig. 61.

Height.		Each.
1 gallon,	36 inches	$4.75
2 "	54 "	6.25
4 "	60 "	9.50

ROMAN VASE SHOW BOTTLES.

Richly Cut. A new and unique designs.

Fig. 60.

Height.		Each.
½ gallon,	33 inches	$3.50
1 "	36 "	4.50
2 "	42 "	6.00

Fig. 60.   Fig. 61.

HAGERTY BROTHERS & CO.,

Fig. 27.   Fig. 28.   Fig. 29.

RICHLY CUT ENGLISH URNS.

Cut Shield and Flat Diamonds.

Fig. 22.   Fig. 23.   Fig. 24.

Plain Counter Urns.   **Fluted Counter Urns.**

HAGERTY BROTHERS & CO.,

PEERLESS SHOW BOTTLES.—Moulded.

New, Cheap, Brilliant, Attractive.

These bottles are new and unique in design; are brilliant, sparkling and attractive, and will reflect a most brilliant light. In appearance they resemble richly cut bottles.

Fig. 47.   Fig. 48.

PINE APPLE SHAPE.

Fig. 47.—With Two Stoppers.

	Height.		Per doz.
½ gallon,	26 inches		$20.00
1 "	30 "		24.00
2 "	35 "		36.00

Fig. 48.—With Three Stoppers.

	Height.		Per doz.
½ gallon,	32 inches		$24.00
1 "	36 "		30.00
2 "	40 "		42.00

---

8 AND 10 PLATT STREET.

THE SPIRAL SHOW BOTTLE.—Moulded.

Fig. 57.

The Bottle is new and unique in design, is brilliant, sparkling and attractive, and will reflect a most brilliant light. It is made of the purest crystal glass, and is heavy and fire polished. We make two sizes, gallons and half-gallons. The gallon size has three stoppers, two of which are spiral, the other (the upper one) a cut lapidary; the half-gallon has two stoppers, the lower a spiral; the upper a cut lapidary. None but an expert can tell them from a genuine cut bottle.

			Each.
½ gallon, 27 inches high			$4.00
1 " 39 "			6.00

ROMAN VASE.—Punty Cut.

A new and handsome style; will reflect a most brilliant light.

Fig. 58.

			Each.
½ gallon, two stoppers, 28 inches high, Fig. 52			$6.00
1 " three " 42 " " 52			8.00

PATENT SECTION JARS.

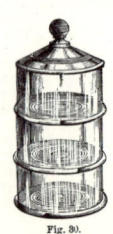  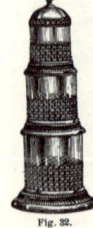

Fig. 30.   Fig. 31.   Fig. 32.

HAGERTY BROTHERS & CO.,

RICHLY CUT SHOW BOTTLES.

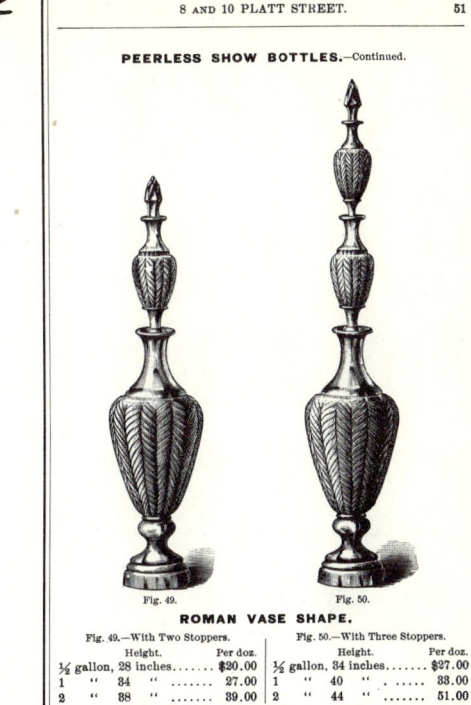

Fig. 57.   Fig. 58.   Fig. 59.

PEERLESS SHOW BOTTLES.—Continued.

Fig. 49.   Fig. 50.

ROMAN VASE SHAPE.

Fig. 49.—With Two Stoppers.

	Height.	Per doz.
½ gallon,	28 inches	$20.00
1 "	34 "	27.00
2 "	38 "	39.00

Fig. 50.—With Three Stoppers.

	Height.	Per doz.
½ gallon,	34 inches	$27.00
1 "	40 "	33.00
2 "	44 "	51.00

HAGERTY BROTHERS & CO.,

EGYPTIAN SHOW BOTTLES.
With Two Stoppers.

Fig. 51.   Fig. 52.   Fig. 53.
Cut Vine.

	Height.		Each.
1 gallon,	25 inches.	Fig. 51	$5.00
1½ "	28 "		6.00

Cut.—Single row of Raised Leaves.

	Height.		Each.
1½ gallon.	25 inches.	Fig. 52	$10.00

Cut.—Double row of Raised Leaves.
Form same as Fig. 52.

	Height.		Each.
1½ gallon.	25 inches		$12.00

WAYNE SHOW BOTTLES.
Handsomely Cut.
Fig. 53.

		Per doz.
1 pint, Single Stopper		$18.75
1 quart, "		22.50
½ gallon, "		30.00
1 " Three Stoppers		56.40
2 " "		76.80
3 " "		105.00

---

8 AND 10 PLATT STREET.

RICHLY CUT SHOW BOTTLES.
With Two Stoppers. Will reflect a brilliant light.

Fig. 54.   Fig. 55.   Fig. 56.

PUNTY CUT.
Fig. 54.

	Height.		Each.
½ gallon	21 inches		$6.00
1½ "	25 "		7.20
2 "	28 "		9.00

RICHLY CUT SHOW BOTTLES.
With Double Stoppers.
Fig. 55.

The whole surface cut and polished. The Globe and Stoppers cut in flat diamonds. A most brilliant reflector.

	Height.		Each.
½ gallon	21 inches		$9.00
1½ "	25 "		12.00
2 "	28 "		13.50

The Globe and Stopper cut in hollow diamonds. Will reflect a brilliant light.
Fig. 56.

	Height.		Each.
½ gallon	21 inches		$9.00
1½ "	25 "		12.00
2 "	28 "		13.50

HAGERTY BROTHERS & CO.,

STOPPERS.

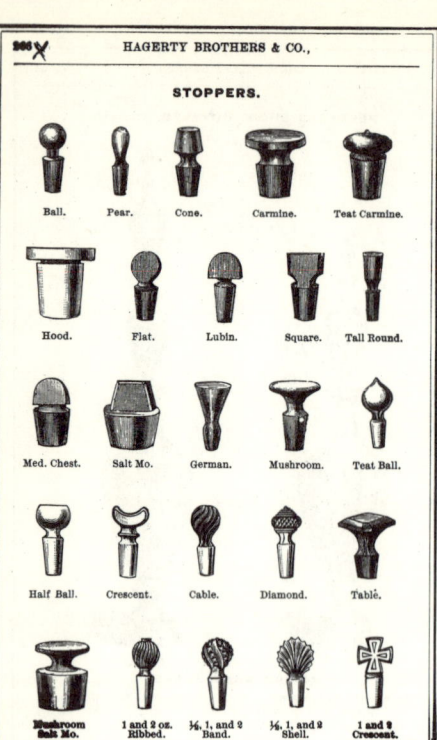

EXPLANATIONS.

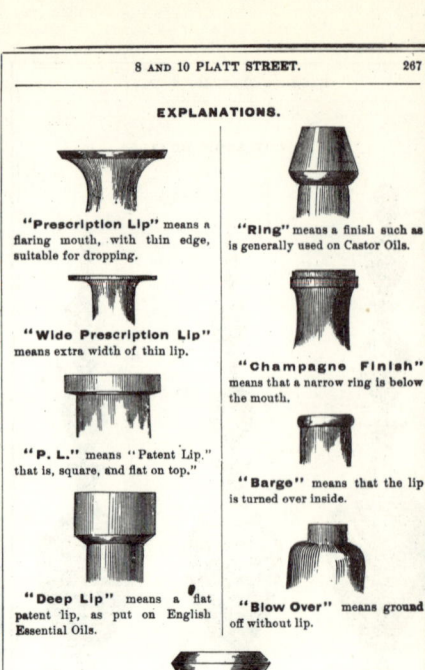

"**Prescription Lip**" means a flaring mouth, with thin edge, suitable for dropping.

"**Ring**" means a finish such as is generally used on Castor Oils.

"**Wide Prescription Lip**" means extra width of thin lip.

"**Champagne Finish**" means that a narrow ring is below the mouth.

"**P. L.**" means "Patent Lip," that is, square, and flat on top."

"**Barge**" means that the lip is turned over inside.

"**Deep Lip**" means a flat patent lip, as put on English Essential Oils.

"**Blow Over**" means ground off without lip.

"**Double Ring**" means a ring such as in Ayer's Ware.

DESIGNS FOR LETTERED PLATES.

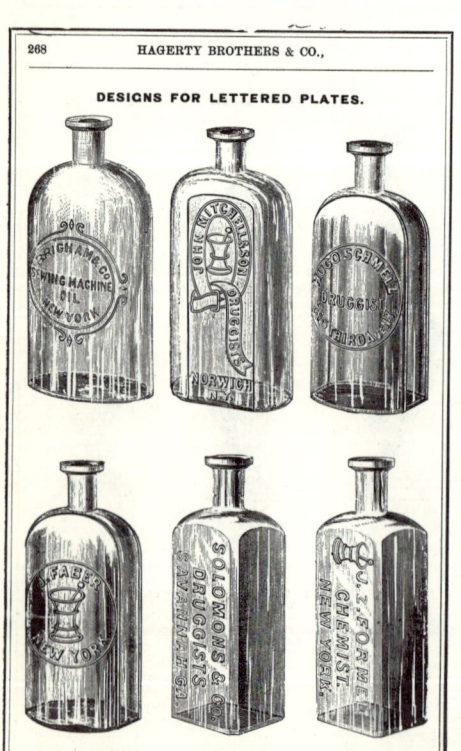

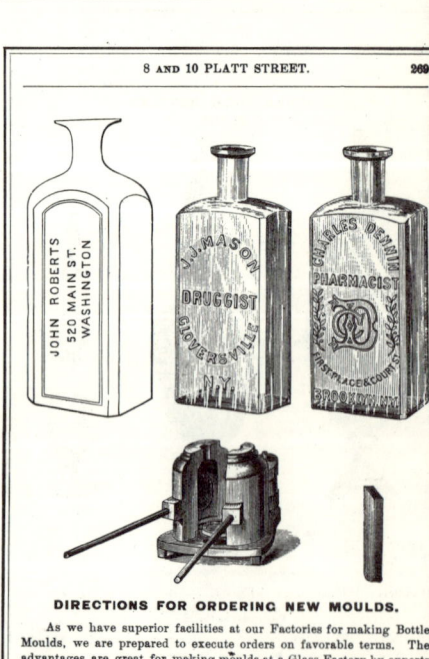

DIRECTIONS FOR ORDERING NEW MOULDS.

As we have superior facilities at our Factories for making Bottle Moulds, we are prepared to execute orders on favorable terms. The advantages are great for making moulds at a Glass Factory by experts knowing the special requirements for making a mould that will deliver smooth and regular Bottles. When desired, samples can be blown and forwarded before lettering or finishing up the mould, so as to allow of modification of style.

In ordering moulds, it is well to select a bottle as near as possible to the kind desired, and send it with directions for any variations to be made in the new mould.

OFFICIAL NATIONAL FLINT BOTTLE LIST

Quinines.
(Fluid Measure.)

	Per gross
½ oz	$ 6.00
1 "	6.50
2 "	7.75
3 "	8.75
4 "	9.75
5 "	10.50
6 "	12.00
7 "	13.50
8 "	14.00
9 "	15.50
12 "	19.00
16 "	24.00

Essential Oils.

	N. M.	W. M.
5 oz	$10.00	$10.50
10 "	15.00	16.00
20 "	25.00	26.00
40 "	40.50	41.50
80 "	67.00	69.00

Glycerines and Chloroforms.

12 oz	$21.50

Sterilizers.

6 oz	$14.00
7 "	14.75
8 "	15.50
12 "	20.50
16 "	25.00

Mustards.
(Round, French, Pot or Barrel.)

	Per gross
3 oz	$ 8.25
4 "	9.25
6 "	11.50
8 "	13.50
12 "	17.50
16 "	22.50

Olive Oils.

4 oz	$10.00
6 "	12.50
8 "	14.50
12 "	18.50
16 "	23.50
20 "	25.50

Oil Sample Bottles.

2 oz	$14.75
3 "	18.00
4 "	23.00
6 "	27.00
8 "	29.50

Carmine Inks for Corks.

½ oz	$5.50
1 "	6.00
1½ "	6.50
2 "	7.25
3 "	8.25
4 "	9.25

Nursing Bottles.
(Plain or Graduated.)

	Per gross
6 oz. Balto. or Decanter	$12.50
8 " "	13.50
12 " "	19.00
8 " Bent Neck	15.50
8 " Alexandria	15.50
8 " Millville	13.75
6 " American, W. M.	13.75

Brandies.

4's	$33.50
4½'s	33.50
5's	30.00
5½'s	30.00
6's	28.00
8's	24.00
10's	18.00
12's	17.00
16's	14.00
20's	12.00
32's	10.00
3 oz	9.00
2 "	8.00

Hock Wines.

4's	$33.50
5's	30.00
6's	28.00
8's	24.00

Gins.

	Per gross
3's	$40.00
4's	35.00
5's	31.00
6's	29.00

Schnapps.

4's	$33.50
5's	30.00
6's Paneled	29.00
6's	28.00

Flasks.

3 oz., 1 gross cases	$10.00
4 " 1 "	10.00
5 " 1½ "	12.00
5½ " 1½ "	12.00
6 " 1½ "	12.00
7 " 1½ "	13.50
8 " 1½ "	15.00
10 " 1½ "	19.00
12 " 1½ "	19.00
14 " 1½ "	20.50
16 " 1½ "	22.00
20 " 1½ "	26.00
24 " 1½ "	30.00
26 " 1½ "	31.50
28 " 1½ "	32.50
32 " 1½ "	35.00

For all bottles above standard weight, add $1.50 to list prices for each additional ounce.

For Discount see last page.

FLINT GLASS PRESCRIPTION BOTTLES.

Hollis Ovals.

Cut No. 18

Size	Cases contain	List per gr.
½ oz.	6 gr.	$3.00
1 "	6 "	3.75
2 "	5 "	4.75
3 "	4 "	5.50
4 "	3 "	7.00
6 "	2½ "	8.50
8 "	2 "	10.50
12 "	1½ "	13.75
16 "	1 "	16.50
32 "	⅔ "	30.00

Eastlake Ovals.

Cut No. 20

½ oz.	6 gr.	$3.00
1 "	6 "	3.75
2 "	5 "	4.75
3 "	4 "	5.50
4 "	3 "	7.00
5 "	3 "	8.00
6 "	2½ "	8.50
8 "	2 "	10.50
10 "	2 "	12.25
12 "	1½ "	13.75
16 "	1 "	16.50
32 "	⅔ "	30.00

Westlake Ovals.

Cut No. 21

½ oz.	6 gr.	$3.00
1 "	6 "	3.75
2 "	5 "	4.75
3 "	4 "	5.50
4 "	3 "	7.00
6 "	2½ "	8.50
8 "	2 "	10.50
12 "	1½ "	13.75
16 "	1 "	16.50
32 "	⅔ "	30.00

Philadelphia Ovals.

Cut No. 19

Size	Cases contain	List per gr.
¼ oz.	6 gr.	$3.00
½ "	6 "	3.00
1 "	6 "	3.75
2 "	5 "	4.75
3 "	4 "	5.50
4 "	3 "	7.00
5 "	3 "	8.00
6 "	2½ "	8.50
7 "	2½ "	9.50
8 "	2 "	10.50
10 "	2 "	12.25
12 "	1½ "	13.75
14 "	1 "	15.25
16 "	1 "	16.50
24 "	1 "	24.00
28 "	1 "	28.00
32 "	⅔ "	30.00

Chicago Ovals.

Cut No. 22

½ oz.	6 gr.	$3.25
1 "	6 "	4.00
2 "	5 "	5.00
3 "	4 "	5.75
4 "	3 "	7.25
6 "	2½ "	9.00
8 "	2 "	11.25
12 "	1½ "	14.25
14 "	1 "	17.00
16 "	1 "	18.50
32 "	⅔ "	31.00
*3 "	4 "	6.25
*4 "	3 "	8.00

* Wide Mouth.

Drug Ovals.

Cut No. 24

Size	Cases contain	List per gr.
½ oz.	6 gr.	$3.00
1 "	6 "	3.75
2 "	5 "	4.75
3 "	4 "	5.50
4 "	3 "	7.00
6 "	2½ "	8.50
8 "	2 "	10.50
12 "	1½ "	13.75
16 "	1 "	16.50
32 "	⅔ "	30.00

Gas City Ovals.

Cut No. 25

½ oz.	6 gr.	$3.00
1 "	6 "	3.75
2 "	5 "	4.75
3 "	4 "	5.50
4 "	3 "	7.00
6 "	2½ "	8.50
8 "	2 "	10.50
12 "	1½ "	13.75
16 "	1 "	16.50
32 "	⅔ "	30.00

Marion Ovals.

Cut No. 31

½ oz.	6 gr.	$3.00
1 "	6 "	3.75
2 "	5 "	4.75
3 "	4 "	5.50
4 "	3 "	7.00
6 "	2½ "	8.50
8 "	2 "	10.50
12 "	1½ "	13.75
16 "	1 "	16.50
32 "	⅔ "	30.00

Klondike Ovals.

Cut No. 26

Size	Cases contain	List per gr.
½ oz.	6 gr.	$3.25
1 "	6 "	4.00
2 "	5 "	5.00
3 "	4 "	5.75
4 "	3 "	7.25
6 "	2½ "	9.00
8 "	2 "	11.25
12 "	1½ "	14.25
16 "	1 "	18.50
32 "	⅔ "	31.00

Hub Ovals.

Cut No. 27

½ oz.	6 gr.	$3.00
1 "	6 "	3.75
2 "	5 "	4.75
3 "	4 "	5.50
4 "	3 "	7.00
6 "	2½ "	8.50
8 "	2 "	10.50
12 "	1½ "	13.75
16 "	1 "	16.50
32 "	⅔ "	30.00

Kellogg Ovals.

Cut No. 28

½ oz.	6 gr.	$3.00
1 "	6 "	3.75
2 "	5 "	4.75
3 "	4 "	5.50
4 "	3 "	7.00
6 "	2½ "	8.50
8 "	2 "	10.50
12 "	1½ "	13.75
16 "	1 "	16.50
32 "	⅔ "	30.00

Windsor Ovals.

Cut No. 29

Size	Cases contain	List per gr.
½ oz.	6 gr.	$3.00
1 "	6 "	3.75
2 "	5 "	4.75
3 "	4 "	5.50
4 "	3 "	7.00
6 "	2½ "	8.50
8 "	2 "	10.50
12 "	1½ "	13.75
16 "	1 "	16.50
32 "	⅔ "	30.00

Baltimore Ovals.

Cut No. 30

½ oz.	6 gr.	$3.00
1 "	6 "	3.75
2 "	5 "	4.75
3 "	4 "	5.50
4 "	3 "	7.00
6 "	2½ "	8.50
7 "	2 "	9.50
8 "	2 "	10.50
12 "	1½ "	13.75
14 "	1 "	15.25
16 "	1 "	16.50
32 "	½ "	30.00

FLINT GLASS PRESCRIPTION BOTTLES.

Packed Eastern Size Cases.

Short Blakes.

Wide Mouth.

Cut No. 35

Size	Cases contain	List per gr.
½ oz.	6 gr.	$3.50
1 "	6 "	4.50
1½ "	5 "	5.75
2 "	5 "	5.75
3 "	4 "	6.50
4 "	3 "	8.50
6 "	2½ "	10.25
8 "	2 "	12.50

These moulds can be lettered.

Flint Packers.

Cut No. 32

½ pt.	1 gr.	$10.50
Pint	1 "	16.50
Quart	½ "	28.50
½ gal.	¼ "	47.00
Gallon	1 doz.	55.00

These moulds cannot be lettered.

Paris Square Prescription

Cut No. 676

½ oz.	6 gr.	$3.25
1 "	6 "	4.25
2 "	5 "	5.25
3 "	4 "	6.00
4 "	3 "	7.75
6 "	2½ "	9.50
8 "	2 "	11.75
12 "	1½ "	15.50
16 "	1 "	19.50
32 "	½ "	33.00

Our very latest shape in Prescription Bottle, being entirely different from anything now in the market. Anyone wanting a striking appearing package would do well to investigate this line. These moulds can be lettered.

French Squares.

Homeopathic Wide Mouth.

Cut No. 33

Size	Cases contain	List per gr.
½ oz.	6 gr.	$3.25
1 "	6 "	4.00
2 "	5 "	5.00
3 "	4 "	5.75
4 "	3 "	7.25
6 "	2½ "	9.00
8 "	2 "	11.25

These moulds can be lettered.

French Square.

Wide Mouth.

Cut No. 36

½ oz.	6 gr.	$3.50
1 "	6 "	4.25
2 "	5 "	5.50
3 "	4 "	6.25
4 "	3 "	8.00
6 "	2½ "	9.75
8 "	2 "	12 00
12 "	1½ "	15.50
16 "	1 "	20.00
32 "	⅔ "	34.00

These moulds can be lettered.

French Square.

Round Corners.

Cut No. 38

½ oz.	6 gr.	$3.25
1 "	6 "	4.00
2 "	5 "	5.00
3 "	4 "	5.75
4 "	3 "	7.25
6 "	2½ "	9.00
8 "	2 "	11.25
12 "	1½ "	14 75
16 "	1 "	18.50

These moulds can be lettered.

French Squares.

Round Cornered.

Medium Wide Mouth.

Cut No. 37

Size	Cases contain	List per gr.
½ oz.	6 gr	$3.50
1 "	6 "	4.25
2 "	5 "	5.50
3 "	4 "	6.25
4 "	3 "	8.00
6 "	2½ "	9.75
8 "	2 "	12.00
12 "	1½ "	15.50
16 "	1 "	20.00

We carry this style in stock in amber glass, also for pills or powders.

These moulds can be lettered.

Indiana Prescription.

Cut No. 39

½ oz.	6 gr.	$3.00
1 "	6 "	3.75
1½ "	5 "	4.25
2 "	5 "	4.75
3 "	4 "	5.50
4 "	3 "	7.00
6 "	2½ "	8.50
8 "	2 "	10.50
12 "	1½ "	13.75
16 "	1 "	16.50
32 "	½ "	30.00

The Indiana is our latest pattern bottle and combines several of the most striking features we have originated.

These moulds are fitted for lettered plates.

Tall Blake.

Cut No. 40

Size	Cases contain	List per gr.
½ oz.	6 gr.	$3.25
1 "	6 "	4.25
2 "	5 "	5.25
3 "	4 "	6.00
4 "	3 "	7.75
6 "	2½ "	9.50
8 "	2 "	11.75
12 "	1½ "	15.50
16 "	1 "	19.50
32 "	⅔ "	33.00

These moulds can be lettered.

Short Blakes.

Cut No. 41

½ oz.	6 gr.	$3.25
1 "	6 "	4.25
2 "	5 "	5.25
3 "	4 "	6.00
4 "	3 "	7.75
6 "	2½ "	9.50
8 "	2 "	11.75
12 "	1½ "	15.50
16 "	1 "	19.50

These moulds can be lettered.

French Square.

Cut No. 42

½ oz.	6 gr.	$3.25
1 "	6 "	4.00
2 "	5 "	5.00
3 "	4 "	5.75
4 "	3 "	7.25
6 "	2½ "	9.00
8 "	2 "	11.25
12 "	1½ "	14.75
16 "	1 "	18.50
32 "	⅔ "	31.00

These moulds can be lettered.

Union Ovals.

Cut No. 43

Size	Cases contain	List per gr.
½ oz.	6 gr.	$3.00
1 "	6 "	3.75
2 "	5 "	4.75
3 "	4 "	5.50
4 "	3 "	7.00
6 "	2½ "	8.50
8 "	2 "	10.50
12 "	1½ "	13.75
16 "	1 "	16.50

These moulds can be lettered.

Boston Round Prescription.

Cut No. 44

½ oz.	6 gr.	$3.00
1 "	6 "	3 75
2 "	5 "	4 75
3 "	4 "	5.50
4 "	3 "	7.00
6 "	2½ "	8.50
8 "	2 "	10.50
12 "	1½ "	13.75
16 "	1 "	16.50
32 "	⅔ "	30.00

These moulds can be lettered on the bottom only.

Tall Blakes.

Wide Mouth.

Cut No. 34

½ oz.	6 gr.	$3.50
1 "	6 "	4.50
2 "	5 "	5.75
3 "	4 "	6.50
4 "	3 "	8.50
6 "	2½ "	10.25
8 "	2 "	12.50

These moulds can be lettered.

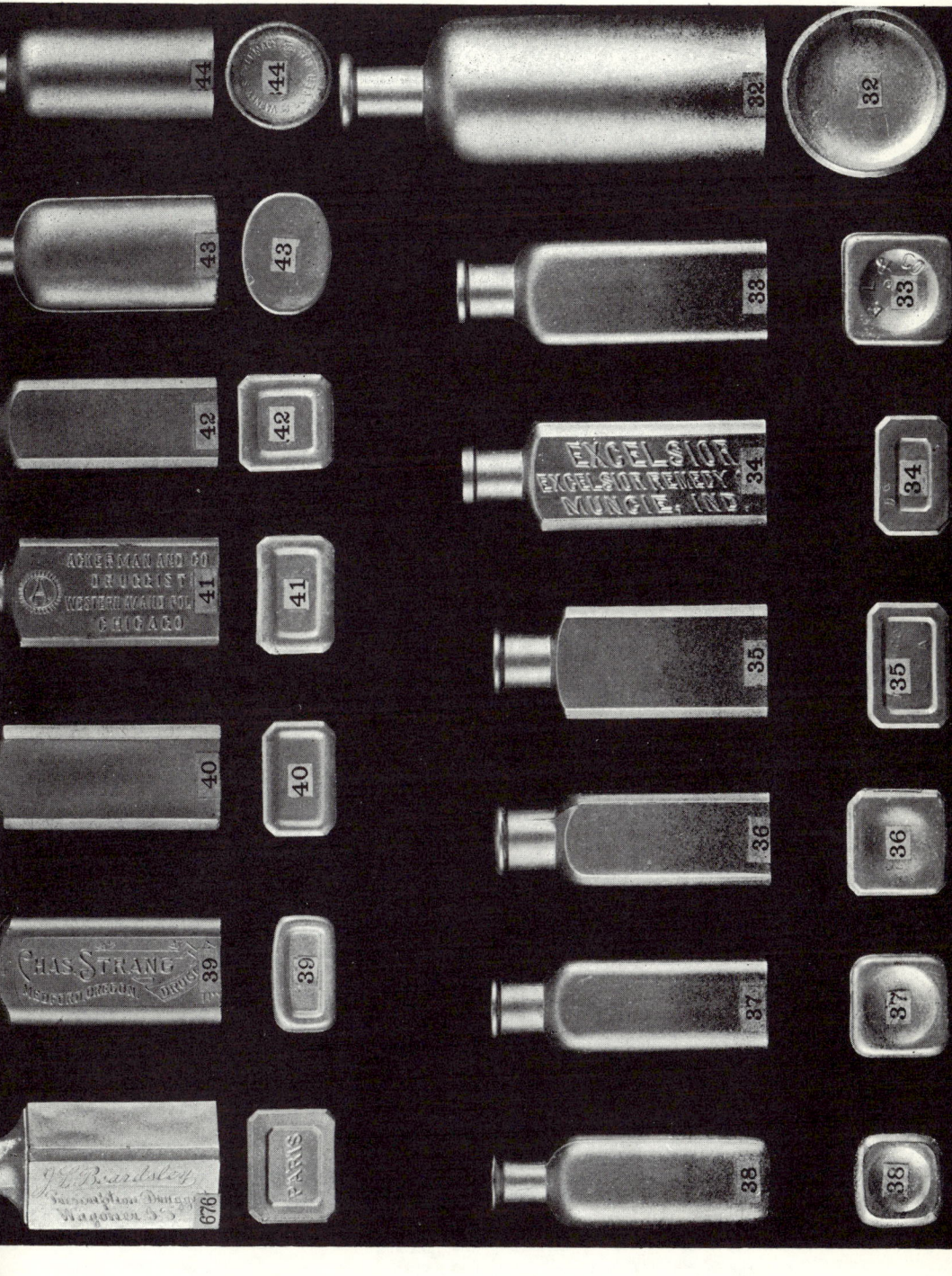

FLINT GLASS PRESCRIPTION BOTTLES.

No. 13 Tall Ball Neck Panel.

Cut No. 44

Size	Actual capacity	Cases contain	Height (in.)	Width (in.)	Thickness (in.)	List per gr.
1/2 oz.	3 1/2 drams	5 gr.	4 9/16	1 9/16	3/4	$4.75
1 "	7 "	4 "	5	1 5/8	13/16	5.50
1 1/4 "	9 "	4 "	5 1/2	1 13/16	7/8	5.75
1 1/2 "	11 "	4 "	5 3/4	1 13/16	7/8	5.75
1 3/4 "	1 3/4 "	3 "	6	1 13/16	7/8	6.75
2 "	1 7/8 "	3 "	6 5/8	1 7/8	15/16	6.75
2 1/2 "	2 1/4 "	3 "	6 7/8	2	15/16	7.75
3 "	2 3/4 "	2 "	7 1/4	2 1/16	1 1/16	8.75
4 "	3 3/4 "	2 "	7 3/4	2 1/4	1 1/8	12.50
5 "	4 1/2 "	2 "	7 7/8	2 5/16	1 3/16	14.00
6 "	5 1/2 "	1 "	8 1/8	2 7/16	1 5/16	16.00
8 "	7 1/4 "	1 "	8 3/4	2 5/8	1 7/16	19.00

This is the largest appearing panel now on the market, especially adapted for cartoning. These moulds are arranged to take lettered plates.

Plain "O" Panels.

Cut No. 47

Mould No.	Size	Cases contain	Weight	Height (in.)	Width (in.)	Thickness (in.)	List per gr.
28	1 oz.	5 gr.	2 1/2 oz.	4 3/8	1 9/16	11/16	$4.00
28	2 "	5 "	4 "	5 1/2	1 15/16	7/8	5.50
28	4 "	3 "	6 1/2 "	6 3/8	2 1/4	1 1/4	8.00
310	2 "	5 "	4 "	5	1 13/16	1	5.50
316	3 "	3 "	5 "	6 1/4	2	1 1/16	7.25
311	4 "	3 "	6 "	6	2 3/16	1 3/16	8.00

These moulds can be lettered.

This line of plain panels are very flat, and appear to hold much more than they actually do. They are paneled on three sides and plain on one side.

Regular Ball Neck Panels.

Cut No. 45

Actual capacity	Cases contain	Wt.	Ht. (in.)	Width (in.)	Thick. (in.)	List per gr.
3/4 oz.	5 gr.	1 1/2 oz.	4 3/8	1 9/16	3/4	$4.75
1 "	5 "	2 1/2 "	4 5/8	1 3/4	13/16	4.75
1 1/4 "	5 "	3 1/4 "	5	1 3/4	7/8	5.50
1 1/2 "	5 "	3 1/2 "	5 1/8	1 13/16	15/16	5.50
1 3/4 "	5 "	1 3/4 "	5 5/16	1 13/16	15/16	5.75
2 "	5 "	4 "	5 5/8	1 7/8	1	5.75
2 1/2 "	3 "	4 1/2 "	5 7/8	1 15/16	1 1/16	6.75
3 "	3 "	5 "	6 1/8	2	1 1/8	7.75
4 "	2 "	6 1/2 "	6 1/4	2 1/4	1 5/16	8.75
6 "	2 "	8 1/2 "	7	2 1/2	1 3/8	13.00
8 "	1 "	11 "	7 7/8	3 13/16	1 9/16	17.00
12 "	1 "	14 "	9 1/2	3 1/8	1 13/16	21.00

In all of our Ball Neck Panels the length of neck and size of cork-age will be found to run unusually uniform, which renders

Poison Bottles.

Blue Glass, covered with Diamond Points.

Cut No. 65

Size	Per gr.
1/2 oz.	$3.25
1 "	4.25
2 "	5.25
3 "	6.00
4 "	7.25
6 "	9.50
8 "	11.25
Asstd.	7.00

Cannot be

Obert Panels.

Cut No. 12

Size	Cases contain	List per gross
1 ounce	3 gross	$4.75
1 1/4 "	3 "	5.50
1 1/2 "	3 "	5.50
3 "	2 "	7.75

These moulds can be lettered.

Morphine Bottles.

Cut No. 104

Size	Cases contain	List
1/2 ounce	5 gross	$4.00
1 "	5 "	4.50
1 1/2 "	4 "	5.25
2 "	3 "	5.25
3 "	3 "	6.00
4 "	2 "	7.75

Cannot be lettered.

Castor Oil Panels.

Three Sides Paneled.

Cut No. 191

Size	Cases contain	List
3/4 ounce	5 gross	$4.75
1 1/2 "	3 "	5.50
2 1/2 "	2 "	6.75
3 1/2 "	2 "	8.75
6 "	1 "	13.00
8 "	1 "	17.00
12 "	1 "	21.00
16 "	1 "	27.00

Cannot be lettered.

Square Carmine Inks.

Cut No. 103

Size	Cases contain	List
1/2 ounce	5 gross	$3.75
1 "	5 "	4.50
2 "	3 "	5.50

Cannot be lettered.

Sewing Machine Bottles.

Cut No. 55

Size	Cases contain	List
1 ounce	5 gross	$4.75
1 3/4 "	5 "	5.75
2 1/2 "	3 "	6.75
4 "	2 "	8.75

Lettered "Sperm Sewing Machine Oil."

These moulds ar also arranged for lettered plates.

Long Neck Panels.

Panele on Fou Sides.

Cut No.

Size	Cases contain	List
1 1/4 ounce	5 gross	$6.50

Round Prescriptions.

Wide Mouth.

Cut No. 101

Size	Cases contain	List per gross
1/2 ounce	5 gross	$3.25
1 "	5 "	4.00
2 "	5 "	5.25
3 "	4 "	6.00
4 "	3 "	7.75
6 "	2 1/2 "	9.25
8 "	2 "	11.50
12 "	1 1/2 "*	14.50
14 "	1 "	16.75
16 "	1 "	19.00
32 "	1/2 "	30.00

These cannot be lettered.

Quinine Bottles.

Cut No. 102

5 ounce Liquid Meas. or 1 oz. Quinine. 2 gross $8.75

Cannot be lettered.

Oval Ball Neck Panels.

Full Capacity.

Cut No. 51

Size	Cases contain	Weight	List per gross
1 1/2 oz.	5 gr.	3 1/2 oz.	$5.50
2 "	4 "	4 "	5.75
2 1/2 "	3 "	4 1/2 "	7.75

These cannot be lettered.

Taper Panels.

Paneled on Four Sides.

Cut No. 50

Size	Cases	Weight	List
1 oz.	5 gr.	3 oz.	$4.75
1 1/2 "	3 "	4 1/2 "	5.50
3 "	2 "	6 "	7.75

These moulds can be lettered.

Ball Neck Panel.

Round Shouldered. Four Sides Paneled. Exact Capacity.

Cut No. 46

Size	Cases	Weight	List
1 oz.	5 gr.	2 1/2 oz.	$4.75
1 1/4 "	5 "	3 1/4 "	5.50
1 1/2 "	5 "	3 1/2 "	5.50
*1 3/4 "	4 "	3 3/4 "	5.75
3 "	2 "	5 "	7.75
†2 "	4 "	4 "	5.75

These moulds can be lettered.

* Mould No 608.

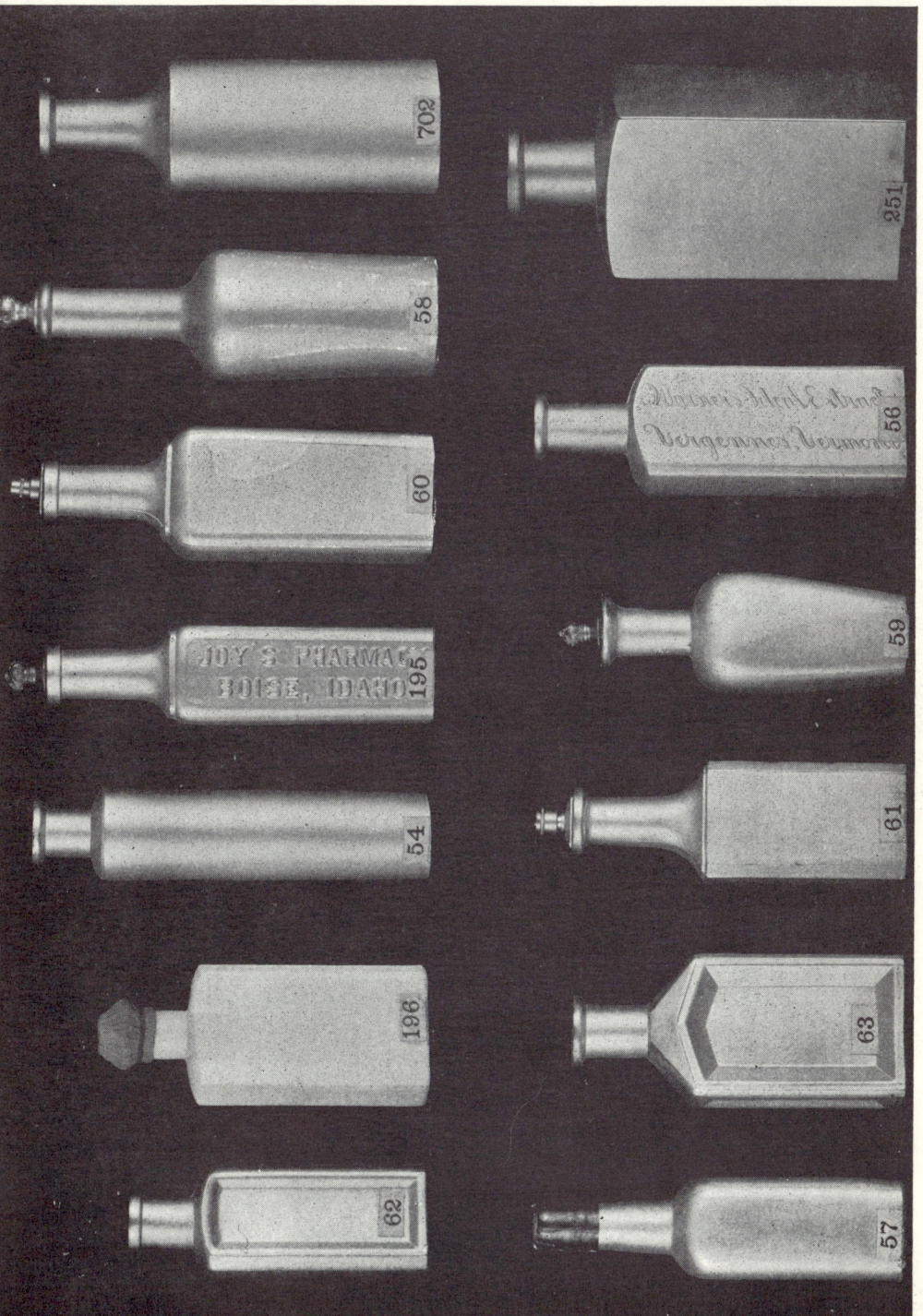

FLINT BOTTLES.

Cod Liver Oil Panels.
Round Shoulder.

Cut No.	Mould	Size	Capacity	Weight	List per gross
53	303	16 ounce	14 ounce	19 ounce	$22.00

Cod Liver Oil Panels.
Three Sides Paneled. Long Neck.

Cut No.					
52	301	16 ounce	12 ounce	15 ounce	$20.00
	305	16 "	16 "	17 "	22.00

Perfume Ware.

Cut No.	No.		Size	Actual Capacity	List, per gross Cork Stoppers	List, per gross Glass Stoppers
130	100	Square Lubin	½ oz.	3 drachms	....	$11.00
	100	" "	1 "	6 "	....	12.00
	100	" "	2 "	14 "	....	14.00
	747	" "	½ "	½ ounce	$4.00	11.00
	749	" "	1 "	1 "	5.00	12.00
	750	" "	2 "	2 "	6.00	14.00
	748	" "	¾ "	¾ "	4.75	11.75
131	560	Cologne	½ "	3 drachms	....	12.00
	560	" "	1 "	6 "	....	13.00
	560	" "	2 "	12 "	....	16.00
132	370	Oval	½ "	3 "	5.00	11.00
	370	" "	1 "	6 "	6.00	12.00
133	420	Round Lubin	½ "	3 "	4.00	11.00
	420	" "	1 "	6 "	5.00	12.00
	420	" "	2 "	14 "	6.00	14.00
202	1310	Fancy	½ "	½ ounce	....	13.00
	1311	" "	1 "	1 "	....	15.00
	1312	" "	2 "	2 "	....	18.00

Perfume Ware. Caswells.

Cut No.	Mould No.	Size	List, per gross Cork Stoppered	List, per gross Glass Stoppered
125	544	4 ounce square	$9.00	$18.00
	545	8 " "	12.00	26.00
	639	12 " "	15.00	32.00
	546	16 " "	18.00	36.00

Perfume Ware.

Cut No.	No.	Size		List per gross
643	350	1 ounce	Oval Shape	$36.00
	350	2 "	" "	42.00
	350	4 "	" "	60.00
644	315	1 "	Round Shape	36.00
	315	2 "	" "	42.00
	515	4 "	" "	60.00

Cut Glass Stoppers accurately ground in.

Nichols' Perfume.

A large looking bottle, blown heavy to hold exact capacity.

Cut No.	Size	Cases contain	List per gross
134	½ ounce	5 gross	$4.00
	1 "	5 "	5.00
	2 "	4 "	6.00

Dropping Bottles.
Glass Stoppered.

A groove on one side of the neck of the bottle and a vent on the other connect with two grooves in the peg of the stopper, and allow the contents to flow out drop by drop. A quarter turn of the stopper closes the bottle tightly.

Cut No.	Size	List, per doz. Round	List, per doz. Square
135	½ ounce	$2.15	$2.15
	1 "	2.25	2.25
	2 "	2.35	2.35

FLINT BOTTLES.

Citrate of Magnesia Bottles.

Cut No.		Capacity	Cases contain	List per gross
122	Old Style	12 ounce	1 gross	$16.00
123	Tall, for Cork	12 "	1 "	16.00
124	With Metal Stopper	12 "	1 "	20.00
124	With Porcelain "	12 "	1 "	23.00

These moulds are arranged to take lettered plates.

Small Perfume and Cologne Ware.

Cut No.		Capacity	Paper boxes contain	List per gross
90	Raymond	2 drachms	6 gross	$5.00
91	Taper	1½ "	6 "	5.00
93	Fluted	½ "	6 "	5.00
	Diamond	1½ "	6 "	5.00
94	"	½ ounce	6 "	5.00
	"	1 "	6 "	6.00
	"	3 "	3 "	10.00

All of these patterns are made especially for so-called Card Perfumes or for dispensing extracts in very small quantities.

Tablet Bottles.

Nickel Plated, Screw Cap

Cut No.	No.	Capacity	Mould No.	Paper boxes contain	List per gross
36	2	4 drachms	840	3 dozen	$5.25
36	3	5 "	841	3 "	5.50
	5	8 "	842	3 "	5.75
96	4	4 "	899	2 "	5.50

These moulds are arranged to take lettered plates.

Saddle Bag or Traveling Bottles.

Ground Glass Stoppers with Heavy Nickel Caps.

Cut No.		Per dozen		Per dozen
64	1 ounce	$2.00	6 ounce	$3.50
	2 "	2.50	8 "	4.00
	4 "	3.00		

A very handsome bottle for putting up Tooth Wash or other liquid preparations suitable for travelers.

Glass Stoppered Bottles.

French Square.

Cut No.		Narrow Mouth Per gross	Wide Mouth Per gross
126 / 127	¼ ounce	$10.00	$11.00
	½ "	10.00	11.00
	1 "	11.00	12.00
	2 "	12.50	13.75
	3 "	15.00	15.50
	4 "	17.00	18.00
	6 "	20.00	21.00
	8 "	24.00	24.50
	12 "	29.00	31.00
	16 "	34.00	36.00
	32 "	48.00	

Round Boston Prescriptions.

Cut No.		Narrow Mouth	Wide Mouth
128 / 129	½ ounce	$10.00	$11.00
	1 "	10.75	12.00
	2 "	12.25	13.00
	3 "	14.00	15.00
	4 "	16.25	17.25
	6 "	18.25	19.00
	8 "	20.75	22.25
	12 "	26.50	28.00
	16 "	31.50	33.00
	32 "	44.00	47.50

For Discount see last page.

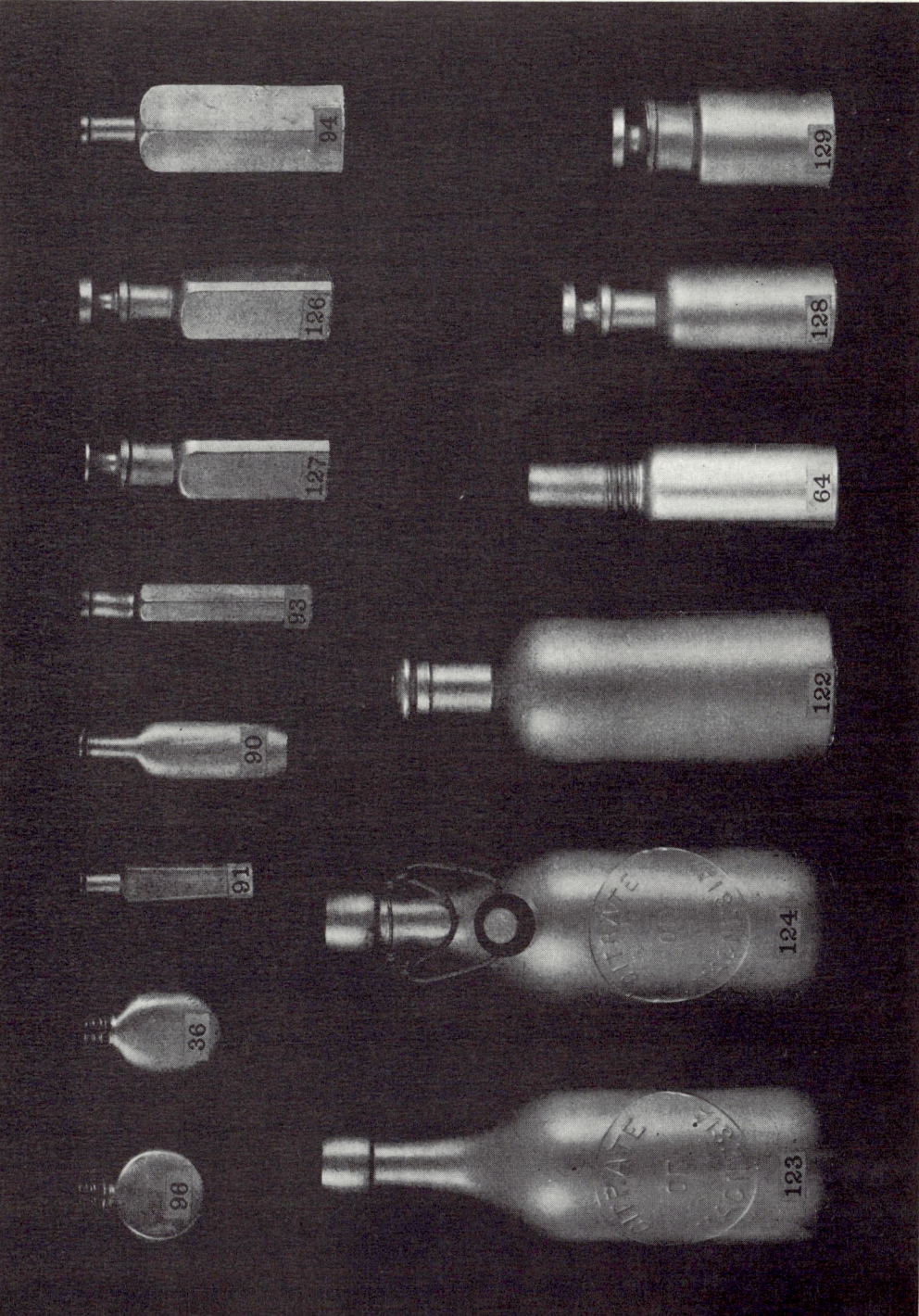

PLAIN FLINT BOTTLES.

Tooth Powder Bottles.

Cut No.	No.	Capacity	Cases contain	List per gross
77	{613	2 ounce	5 gross	$6.00
	613	5 "	2 "	12.00
79	{902	2 "	3 "	8.00
	904	4 "	2 "	12.00
80	903 Paneled	3 "	2 "	11.00
81	{735	1½ "	3 "	7.00
	736	3 "	3 "	10.00
82	{184	2 "	3 "	8.00
	185	3 "	3 "	10.00
84	43	2 "	3 "	8.00
85	806	3 "	3 "	9.00

Above moulds can all be lettered, except Nos. 902, 904.

Prices quoted are for Bottles alone, without Metal Tops. For prices of Tops see page 52.

Tooth Powder Bottles,

Complete with Metal Caps.

Cut No.	No.	Capacity	Case contains	Metal Caps	List per gross
72	88	2 oz.	5 gross	Nickel Plated	$15.00
73	785	2 "	5 "	"	15.00
74	98	2 "	5 "	"	18.00
75	{784	3 "	2 "	"	16.00
	784	4 "	2 "	"	18.00
76	988	3 "	2 "	"	16.00

The above moulds are arranged to take lettered plates.

Gold Plated Caps can be furnished with above at an additional cost of $1.25 per gross, net.

TOOTH WASH BOTTLES.

Cut No.	No.	Capacity		Cases contain	List per gross
67	815	2 oz.	Flat	3 gross	$8.00
68	Gas City	2 "	Oval Back	3 "	8.00
69	103 Plain	2 "	"	3 "	8.00
83	103 Paneled	1¾ "	"	3 "	9.00
70	835	4 "	Flat Oval	2 "	9.00
71	784	3 "	"	2 "	9.00
35	1900	4 "	Oblong	2 "	12.00
43	Richmond	2 "	Flat Oval	5 "	9.00

These moulds can be lettered.

Prices quoted are for Bottles alone, without Metal Tops. For price of Tops, see page 52.

OPAL GLASS PATCH BOXES.

Round.

Cut No.	Size	Cases contain	List per gross
112 (Panel Cover)	¼ ounce	12 gross	$6.50
	½ "	8 "	7.50
110 (Plain Cover)	1 "	6 "	9.00
	2 "	4 "	13 00

Plain or Paneled Lids same price.

Square.

Cut No.	Size	Cases contain	List per gross
111	½ ounce	5 gross	$9.00
	1 "	3 "	13.00

Oblong.

Size	Cases contain	List per gross
1 oz., round cor.,	5 gross	$17.00
1 " square "	5 "	17.00

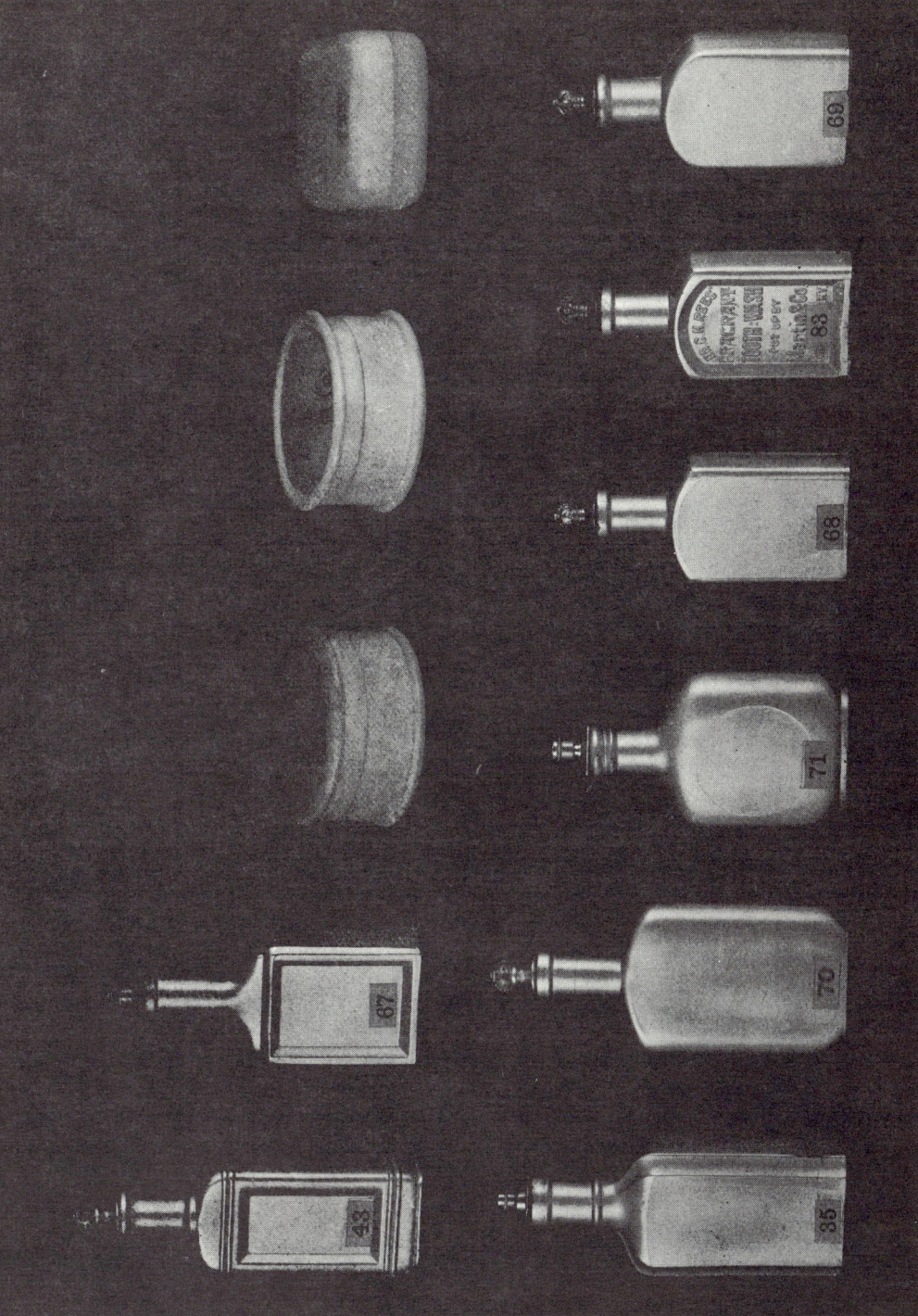

OINTMENT JARS.

No. 1890 Cup Bottom Jars.
Nickel Plated Screw Caps.

Capacity	Cases contain	List per gross
¼ ounce	5 gross	$5.00
½ "	5 "	5.50
1 "	3 "	7.00
2 "	2 "	9.00
4 "	1 "	12.50
8 "	½ "	20.00
16 "	¼ "	30.00

Amber, opal and flint glass carried in stock. Special price on quantities.

Cut No. 104

No. 1894 Ointment Jar.
Nickel Screw Cap.

Mould No.	Capacity	Cases contain	List per gross
1894	¼ ounce	5 gross	$5.50
1894	½ "	5 "	6.00
1894	1 "	5 "	7.50
1894	2 "	5 "	9.50
1894	4 "	3 "	13.00

Can be made in either flint, opal, amber or blue glass. Lettered with special names in full case lots without extra charge. We carry in stock only the opal glass.

Cut No. 106

No. 83 Cold Cream Jar.
Opal Glass.

83	2 ounce	2 gross	$13.00
83	1 "	3 "	12.00

No. 83 Jar can be made in either flint, amber or blue glass on special orders.

Cut No. 107

No. 1897 Plain Tall Opal Jars.
Nickel Plated Screw Cap.

Capacity	Cases contain	List per gross Amber & Crystal	Opal
¼ ounce	5 gross	$4.25	$4.75
½ "	5 "	4.75	5.50
1 "	3 "	6.00	7.50
2 "	2 "	7.75	10.50
3 "	2 "	9.00	12.00
4 "	1 "	11.25	14.25

The above jar can be made in amber blue or flint glass on special orders. The jars can be lettered same as our No. 1894 Jar on special orders. We carry in stock only the opal glass.

Cut No. 105

Queen Mary Ointment Jar.
Flint Glass only

Size	Capacity	Cases contain	List per gross
	2 ounce	3 gross	$8.00
	4 "	2 "	9.00

Cut No. 108

Glycerine Jelly Jars.
Nickel Plated Screw Caps.
Pressed Glass. Heavy Bottoms.

½ ounce	5 gross	$6.00
1 "	3 "	7.00
2 "	2 "	9.00

This jar can be made in amber, opal or blue glass on special orders.

Cut No. 109

Blown Jelly Jars. Flint.
Nickel Screw Caps.

4 ounce	2 gross	$11.00
8 "	1 "	15.00
12 "	1 "	18.00
16 "	½ "	20.00
32 "	½ "	24.00

Selected quality; blown flint glass.

Cut No. 101

No. 14 Sample Jars.
Nickel Plated Screw Cap.

Size	Capacity	Cases contain	List per gross
	2 ounce	3 gross	$9.00
	4 "	1 "	11.00
	8 "	1 "	15.00
	12 "	1 "	18.00
	16 "	½ "	21.00
	32 "	¼ "	30.00

Special price on quantities. Flint glass only.

Cut No. 101

No. 675 Ointment Jars.
Nickeled Caps.

½ ounce	3 gross	$6.00
1 "	3 "	7.00
2 "	2 "	10.06

Cut No. 705

Square Tablet Jars.
Screw Capped.

1 ounce	4 gross	$8.00
2 "	3 "	8.00
4 "	2 "	12.00
8 "	1 "	18.00

These moulds are so arranged that they will take 1 oz., 2 oz. and 4 oz. Rx Plates for 2 oz., 4 oz. and 8 oz. sizes respectively. Special price on quantities.

Cut No. 102

Vaseline Bottles.
Screw Capped.

Mould No.	Capacity Liquid oz.	Cases contain	List per gross
1605	2 ounce	5 gross	$4.50
70	3 "	3 "	6.00
80	5 "	2 "	8.00

Price is for plain Tin Caps. Lacquered Caps can be furnished at an advance of 15c., and heavily Nickeled Caps at an advance of 50c. per gross *net*. These moulds cannot be lettered.

Cut No. 99

For Discount see last page.

DEAN-FOSTER CATALOG PAGES INDEX

NURSING BOTTLES.

Plain Flint.

Cut No.	Name	Capacity			Cases contain	List per gross
113	Columbia	8 oz.	Graduated		1 gross	$12.00
19	Universal	8 "	"		1 "	12.00
115	Boston	8 "	Plain		1 "	12.00
20	Chicago	8 "	Graduated		1 "	12.00
17	No. 5 Flask	8 "	for Nipple		1 "	12.00
118	No. 7 Flask	8 "	"		1 "	10.00
	No. 8 Flask	12 "	"		1 "	14.00

The above moulds are arranged to take lettered plates.

STERILIZER BOTTLES.

Cut No.	Mould No.	Capacity	Cases contain	List per gross
119	11	7 oz., for Sterilizers	1 gross	$10.00
	12	6 " " "	1 "	9.00
	13	8 " " "	1 "	12.00
120	Rubber Cork and Glass Plug for Sterilizer			18.00

VASELINE BOTTLES.

Cut No.	No.	Capacity		Cases contain	List per gross
97	77	2 liquid ounces		5 gross	$5.50
98	605	2 " "		5 "	5.50
	7	3 " "		3 "	7.00
	761	3 " "		3 "	8.00
200	29	8 " "		1 "	12.00
100	7 wood top 3	" "		3 "	14.00

These moulds cannot be lettered.

AMBER GLASS.

Amber glass, if wanted in any style bottle, can be made to order. We show several different patterns which are largely used in amber glass, and make very striking packages for different preparations where a distinctive style bottle is wished.

Cut No. 247 { Is our Round Corner French Square Bottle, largely used for Pills or Powders. (For List price see pages 5, 10, 16.)

Cut No. 248 { Shows our No. 13 Ball Neck Panel, used largely for Cough Syrups or other preparations where it is desirable to conceal a slight amount of sediment. (For List price see pages 6, 12, 18.)

Cut No. 249 Hollis Oval. (For List price see pages 5, 8, 14.)

Cut No. 250 Our Boston Prescription. (For List price see pages 5, 10, 16.)

These are two popular prescriptions, and when made in amber glass, make a very striking appearance, and are highly recommended for anyone who wishes a very distinctive prescription bottle.

Amber Glass Ware

Schnapp Bottles.

			Dimensions in Inches			Plain	Paneled
Cut No.	Size	Cases contain	Height	Width	Thick.	List per gross	List per gross
243 Plain	10 to gallon	1 gr.	8¾	2 5/16	2 5/16	$18.00	$19.00
	8 "	1 "	9	2 5/8	2 5/8	19.00	20.00
	6 "	1 "	9 7/8	2 3/4	2 3/4	24.00	23.00
245 Paneled	8 " (Mould 100)	1 "	9 3/4	2 5/8	2 5/8		19.00
	4½ ounce No. 1024	2 "	7½	1 7/8	1 7/8		13.00

All paneled moulds have one plain side with the exception of Mould No. 100, which has all four sides paneled.

These moulds are fitted for lettered plates.

Amber Blakes.

Round Bottom, Wide Mouth.

		Cases		List
	Size	Mould No.	contain	per gross
	¼ ounce	35	6 gross	$3.50
	½ "	36	6 "	3.50
	1 "	37	5 "	4.50
	1½ "	38	5 "	5.75
	2 "	39	4 "	5.75
Cut No. 246	3 "	40	4 "	6.50
	4 "	41	3 "	8.50
	6 "	42	2 "	10.25
	8 "	43	2 "	12.50
	10 "	44	1½ "	15.00
	12 "	45	1 "	16.50
	14 "	46	1 "	19.50
	16 "	47	1 "	20.50
	18 "	48	1 "	23.50
	20 "	49	½ "	27.00
	22 "	50	½ "	28.00

These moulds can be lettered only on the bottom.

These moulds are medium tall shapes, and make a very handsome bottle for emulsions and other proprietary preparations where a distinctly colored bottle is wished.

Olive Oil Bottles.

Flint Glass.

			Cases	List
	Size	Capacity	contain	per gross
Cut No. 121	½ Pint	5 ounce	2 gross	$15.00
	Pint	12 "	1 "	18.00

DEAN, FOSTER & CO., BOSTON.

PLAIN FLINT BOTTLES.

Brandy, Wine and Whiskey Bottles.

Cut No.	Name	Capacity	Cases contain	List per gross
388	Seal French	Quart	1 gross	$27.00
	"	Pint	1 "	19.00
389	Belle of Bourbon	4 to gal.	1 "	27.00
	"	5 "	1 "	25.00
	"	Pint	1 "	19.00
390	Square Wine	4 ounce	2 "	8.00
	"	8 "	2 "	12.00
	"	16 "	1 "	19.00
	"	6 to gal.	1 "	21.00
	"	5 "	1 "	25.00
	"	4 "	1 "	27.00
391	Round Wine	4 ounce	2 "	8.00
	"	8 "	2 "	12.00
	"	16 "	1 "	19.00
	"	6 to gal.	1 "	21.00
	"	5 "	1 "	25.00
	"	4 "	1 "	27.00
392	Boker Bitter	5 "	1 "	25.00
393	Champagne	4 "	1 "	27.00
	"	8 "	1 "	19.00

Brandy, Wine and Whiskey Bottles—Continued.

Cut No.	Name	Capacity	Cases contain	List per gross
394	Baltimore Brandy	4 to gal.	1 gross	$27.00
	"	5 "	1 "	25.00
	"	6 "	1 "	21.00
	"	8 "	1 "	19.00
395	Taper Gin	3 "	1 "	30.00
	"	4 "	1 "	28.00
	"	5 "	1 "	26.00
	"	6 "	1 "	20.00
396	No. 411	4 "	1 "	27.00
397	" 920	4 "	1 "	27.00
398	" 912	4 "	1 "	27.00
	" 512	5 "	1 "	25.00
	" 812	8 "	1 "	19.00
399	" 76	5 "	1 "	25.00
400	" 26	5½ "	1 "	25.00

Cocoa Wine Bottles.

Cut No.	Mould No.	Capacity	Cases contain	List per gross
387	25	25 ounce	1 gross	$25.00
	625	20 "	1 "	21.00
	825	16 "	1 "	19.00

These moulds cannot be lettered. See page 52 for prices of metal caps to fit these bottles.

FLINT LIQUOR OVALS FOR DRUG TRADE.

No. 500 Ovals.

Cut No.	Capacity	Finish	Cases contain	List per gross
144	7 ounce	R X	2 gross	$11.50
	14 "	"	1 "	20.00
	7 "	Wine	2 "	11.50
	14 "	"	1 "	20.00

Excelsior Ovals.

Cut No.	Capacity	Finish	Cases contain	List per gross
145 Wine finish	7 ounce	Wine or R X	2 gross	11.50
	8 "		2 "	12.50
	14 "		1 "	20.00
	16 "		1 "	21.50
208 R X finish	29 "		2/3 "	30.00
	30 "		2/3 "	30.00
	32 "		2/3 "	32.00

Philadelphia Ovals.

Cut No.	Capacity	Finish	Cases contain	List per gross
146	7 ounce	Wine or R X	2 gross	11.50
	8 "		2 "	12.50
	14 "		1 "	20.00
	16 "		1 "	21.50
	28 "		2/3 "	28.50
	30 "		2/3 "	30.00
	32 "		2/3 "	32.00

Klondike Ovals.

Cut No.	Capacity	Finish	Cases contain	List per gross
147	8 ounce	Wine	2 gross	12.50
	16 "		1 "	21.50
	32 "		2/3 "	32.00

English Ovals.

Cut No.	Capacity	Finish	Cases contain	List per gross
209	7 ounce	R X	2 gross	12.00
	8 "		2 "	13.00
	14 "		1 "	20.50
	16 "		1 "	22.00
	30 "		2/3 "	30.50
	32 "		2/3 "	32.50

Liquor Flasks.

Cut No.	Name	Capacity	Cases contain	List per gross
148	1/4 Pint Shoo-Fly	3 ounce	1 gross	$10.00
	1/2 " "	6 "	1/2 "	12.00
	Pint "	12 "	1/2 "	19.00
	Quart "	24 "	1/2 "	30.00
	1/2 Pint full	8 "	1/2 "	15.00
	Pint "	16 "	1/2 "	22.00
149	1/2 Pint Chicago	6 "	1/2 "	12.00
	Pint "	12 "	1/2 "	19.00
	Quart "	24 "	1/2 "	30.00
151	1/2 Pint Union, full	8 "	1/2 " { Moulds lettered "Registered Full."	15.00
	Pint " "	16 "	1/2 "	22.00
	Quart " "	32 "	1/2 "	35.00
154	1/4 Pint Picnic	2 "	1 "	10.00
	1/4 " Ring Neck	3 "	1 "	10.00
	1/2 " Picnic	6 "	1/2 "	12.00
	Pint "	12 "	1/2 "	19.00
	Quart "	24 "	1/2 "	30.00
152	1/2 Pint Jo-Jo	6 "	1/2 "	12.00
	Pint "	12 "	1/2 "	19.00
	Quart "	24 "	1/2 "	30.00
150	1/2 Pint Union	7 "	3/2 " { Moulds lettered "Warranted"	13.50
	Pint "	14 "	1/2 "	20.50
	Quart "	28 "	1/2 "	32.50

Cut No.	Name	Capacity	Cases contain	Net per gross
153	No. 785 Columbian	2 ounce	5 "	5.00
	" 786 "	3 "	1 "	5.50
	" 787 "	6 "	1 "	6.50
	" 788 "	12 "	1 "	7.50
	" 1786 "	4 "	1 " { Nickel Capped.	6.00
	" 1787 "	8 "	1 "	7.00
	" 1788 "	16 "	1 "	8.00

Moulds for Shoo-Fly, Chicago and Union Flasks are fitted to take lettered plates. Columbian and Jo-Jo moulds cannot be lettered.

Baltimore or Philadelphia Ovals. Screw Capped.

Cut No.	Size	Cases contain	Net per gross	Size	Cases contain	Net per gross
663	7 ounce	2 gross	$5.50	14 ounce	1 gross	$7.00
	8 "	2 "	5.50	16 "	1 "	7.00

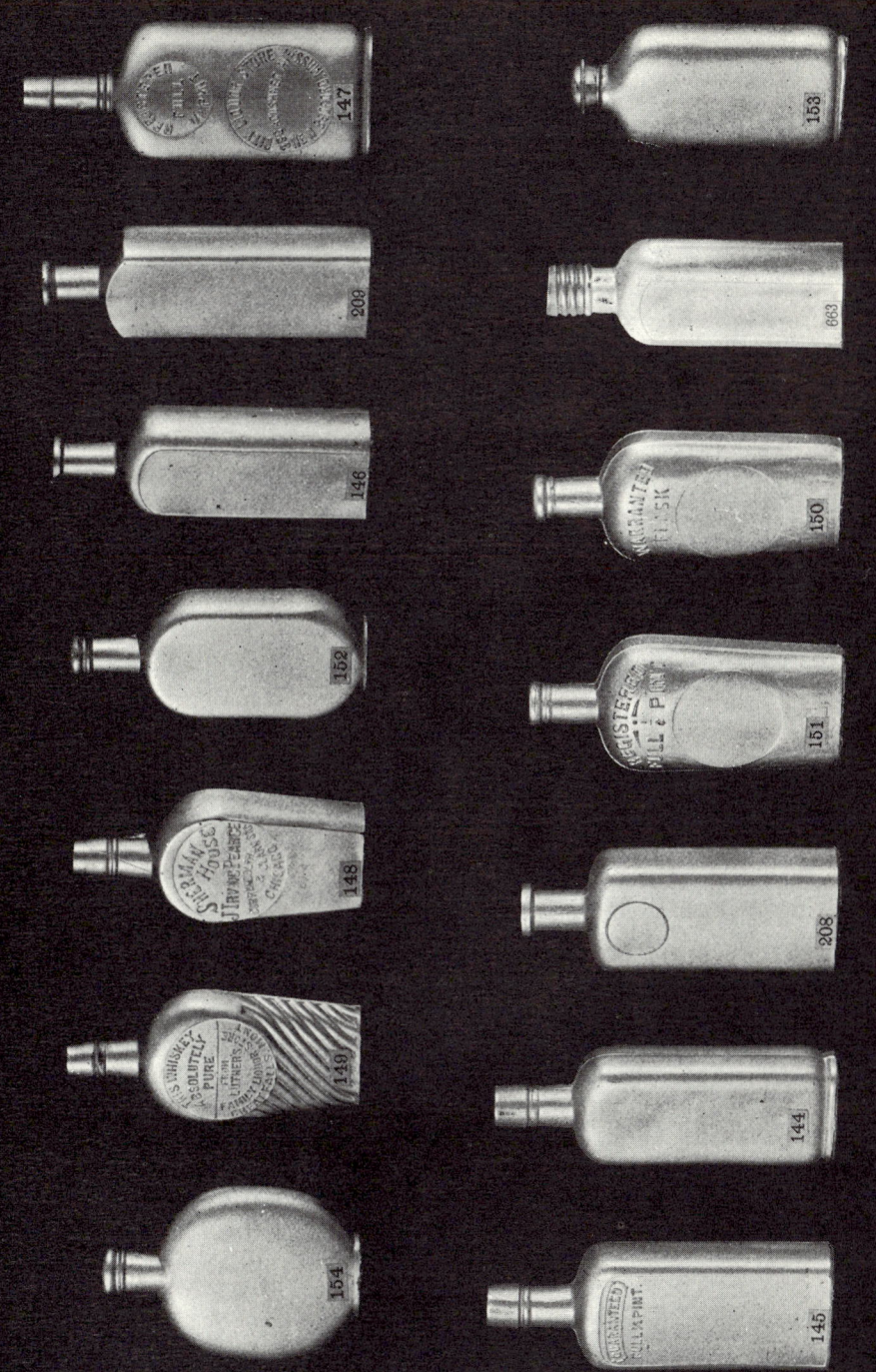

TOILET WATER BOTTLES.

Dark Green.

Cut No.	Mould No.	Capacity	Cases contain	Shape	List per gross
86	{ 516	4 oz.	2 gross	Round	$12.00
	753	8 "	1 "	"	18.00
87	844	4 "	2 "	Square	12.00
78	852	6 "	1 "	"	15.00
87	846	8 "	1 "	"	18.00
88	132	8 "	1 "	Oblong	20.00
89	4711	3 "	1 "	Round	20.00

These moulds are not fitted to take lettered plates.

LAVENDER SALT BOTTLES.

Dark Green, Glass Stoppered.

Cut No.	Size	Capacity	List per gross
42	2 ounce	2 ounce	$20.00

These moulds cannot be lettered.

HOCK BAY RUM BOTTLES.

Amber glass.

Cut No.	Size	Capacity	Weight	Cases Contain	List per gross
99	½ pint	5 oz.	8 oz.	2 gross	$13.00
	½ "	7 "	10 "	1 "	18.00
	Pint	12 "	16 "	1 "	22.00
	6 to gal.	20 "	20 "	1 "	27.00
	5 "	22 "	22 "	1 "	27.00

These moulds cannot be lettered.

No. 50 TOILET WATER BOTTLES.

Flint Glass.

Cut No.	Size	Cases Contain	List per gross
95	2 ounce	5 gross	$8.00

These moulds cannot be lettered.

The prices quoted are for bottles without Sprinkler Tops. See page 52 for prices of Sprinkler Tops, Metal Caps, etc.

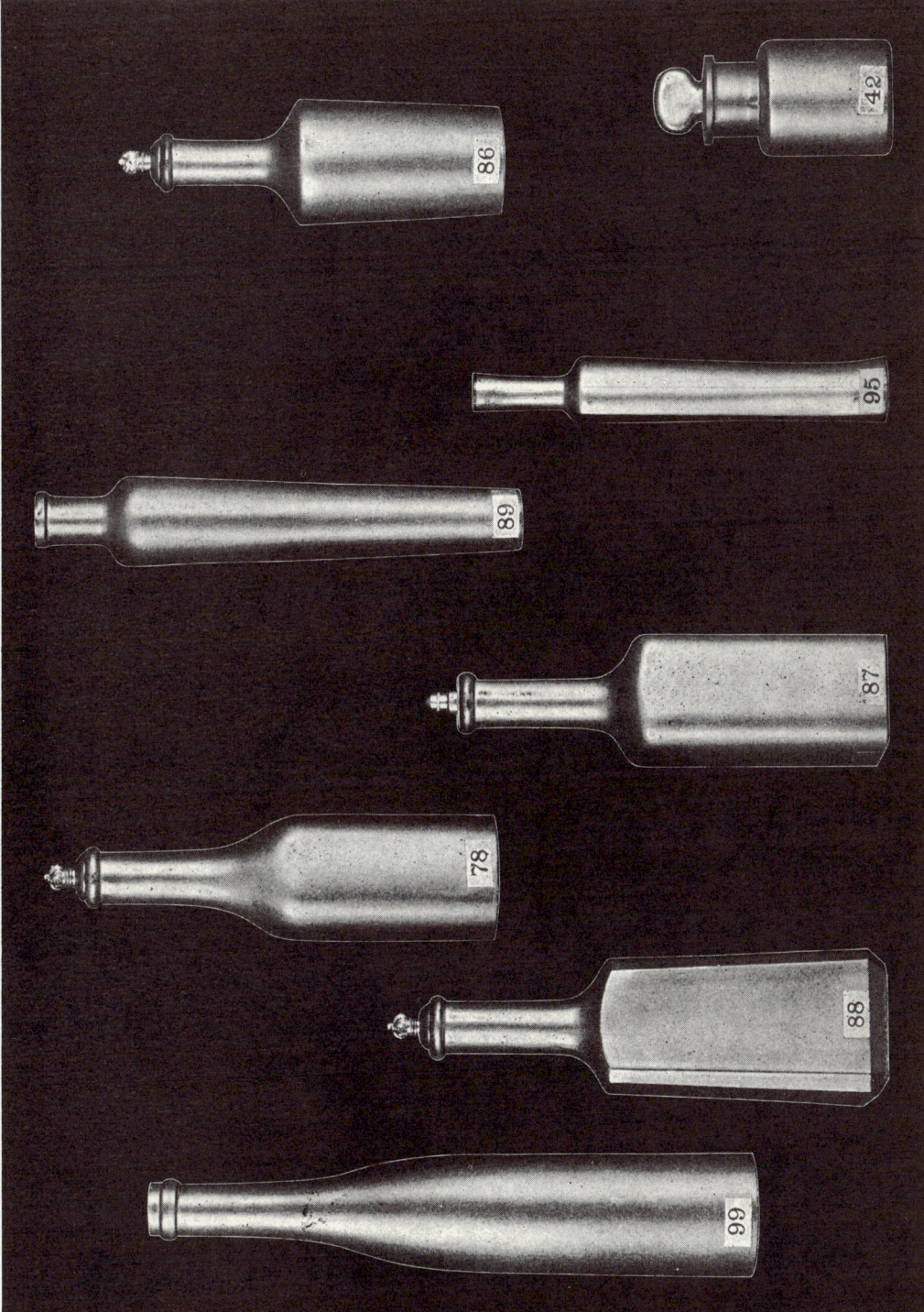

GREEN GLASS WARE.

Our Green Glass is made with every reference to handsome shapes, nice color, and heavy weights, and is the best line of Green Glass made by any manufacturer.

We have recently taken our leading green glass factory and changed it entirely to our brilliant "crystal flint," which, in a great many particulars is as good as the regular flint glass which is being quoted at so-called low prices by many manufacturers.

By comparing the price of our crystal flint with the prices others charge for what they call regular flint, quite a saving would be noticeable.

We are running some of our other furnaces, however, on the old-fashioned green glass, so that those who prefer it can get the same.

Ginger Panels.

(One Side Plain.)

Cut No.	Size	capacity	Height (Dimensions in inches)	Width	Thick.	Cases contain	List per gross
216	1 ounce	¾ ounce	4⅛	$\frac{15}{16}$	⅝	5 gross	$4.00
217	2 "	1¾ "	$5\frac{5}{16}$	$1\frac{11}{16}$	1	5 "	5.50
218	V 3 "	2¼ "	5⅝	1⅞	1	4 "	7.00
219	Plain Ginger	3½ "	6¾	2¼	1⅛	3 "	9.25
219	T 4 ounce	3¼ "	6¼	$2\frac{1}{16}$	$1\frac{3}{16}$	3 "	8.00
220	T 6 "	5¼ "	7	2¼	$1\frac{5}{16}$	2 "	10.50
220	G 6 "	4½ "	6¾	$2\frac{5}{16}$	$1\frac{5}{16}$	2 "	10.50
220	M6 "	5½ "	7⅝	$2\frac{9}{16}$	$1\frac{7}{16}$	2 "	10.50
221	T 8 "	7¼ "	7¾	2⅝	1½	1½ "	13.00
221	T 12 "	10½ "	8¾	$2\frac{15}{16}$	$1\frac{13}{16}$	1 "	17.50
167	No. 19, 12 oz.	10½ "	8⅞	$3\frac{3}{16}$	$1\frac{15}{16}$	1 "	17.50
167	14 ounce	13½ "	8⅞	3⅛	1¾	1 "	18.75
167	16 "	15½ "	9	3⅛	2	1 "	21.00
167	24 "	20 "	10	3¾	2¼	1 "	26.00

These moulds are arranged to take lettered plates.

This line of moulds has been very carefully made, and make the most distinguished line of Ginger Panels made by any manufacturer; are very large in appearance, and made very heavy so that they make a very distinguished bottle and the price is no higher than others charge for a much inferior line.

Oval Panels.

(One Side Plain for Label.)

Cut No.	Size	capacity	Height	Width	Thick.	Cases contain	List per gross
162	1 ounce	1 ounce	4½	1½	¾	6 gross	$4.00
222	1¼ "	1¼ "	5	1¾	¾	5 "	5.50
222	1½ "	1½ "	5	1¾	⅞	5 "	5.50
222	2 "	2 "	5	$1\frac{13}{16}$	$\frac{15}{16}$	5 "	5.50
223	3 "	3 "	6¼	2	1	3 "	7.00
224	4 "	4 "	6¼	2	1¼	3 "	8.00

These moulds are arranged to take lettered plates.

For Discount see last page.

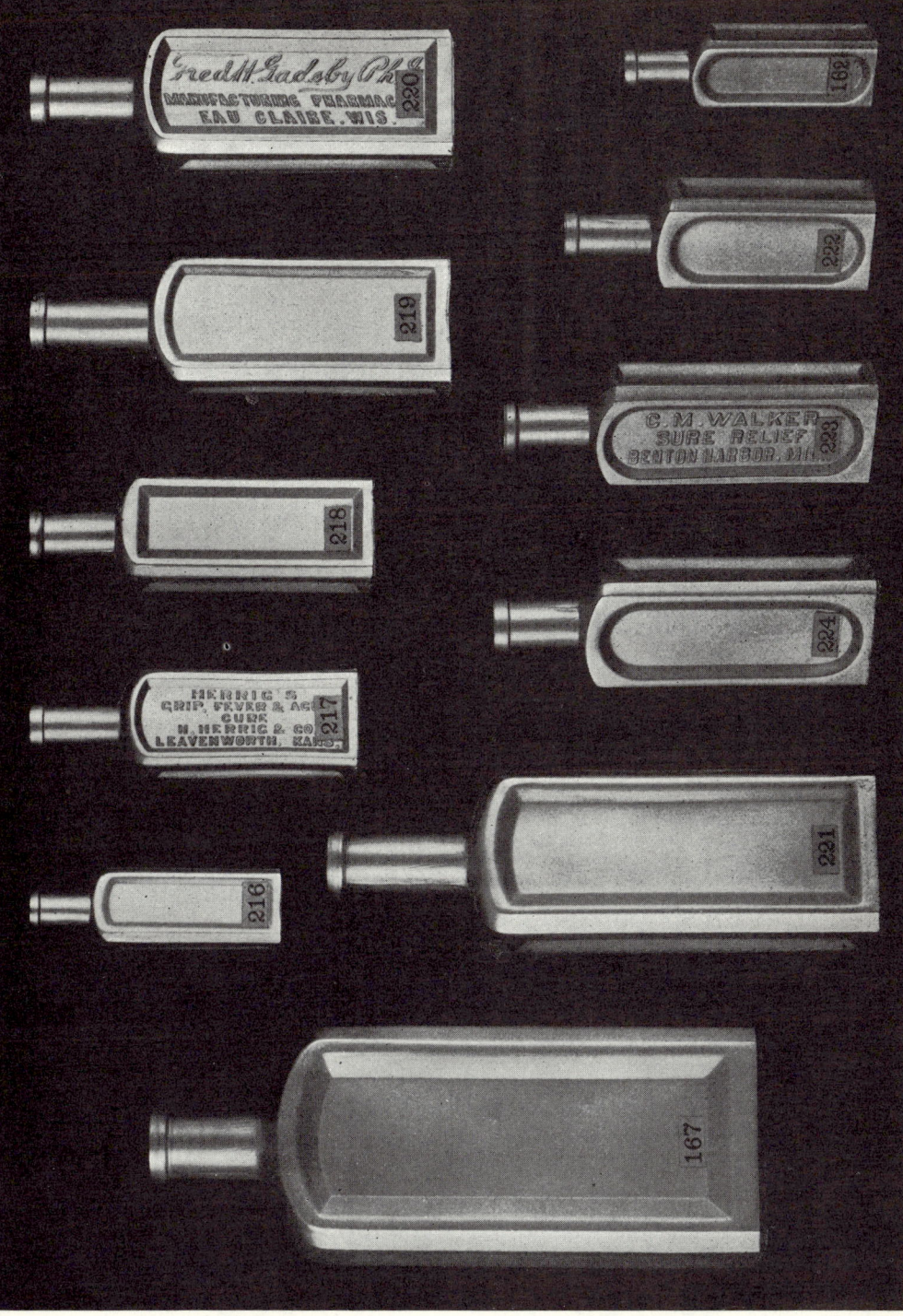

GREEN GLASS WARE.

Sarsaparilla Panels.
Hood Style.
(One side plain for label.)

Cut No.	Size	Actual Capacity	Dimensions in Inches — Height	Width	Thickness	Cases contain	List per gross
161	12 oz.	11 oz.	$9\frac{1}{4}$	3	$1\frac{3}{16}$	1 gr.	$17.50
226	10 "	$9\frac{1}{2}$ "	$8\frac{1}{2}$	$2\frac{5}{8}$	$1\frac{3}{4}$	$1\frac{1}{2}$ "	15.50

These moulds are arranged to take lettered plates.

Ball Neck Panels.

Cut No.	Size	Capacity	Cases contain	List per gross
	1 ounce	1 ounce	6 gross	$4.50
	$1\frac{1}{4}$ "	$1\frac{1}{4}$ "	5 "	6.00
	$1\frac{1}{2}$ "	$1\frac{1}{2}$ "	5 "	6.00
	2 "	$1\frac{3}{4}$ "	5 "	6.00
165	Z 3 "	2 "	4 "	8.00
	S 3 "	$2\frac{1}{2}$ "	4 "	8.00
	S 4 "	3 "	3 "	9.00
	L 4 "	4 "	3 "	10.50
	6 "	5 "	2 "	11.50
	8 "	7 "	2 "	14.00

These moulds are arranged to take lettered plates.

Emulsion Panels.

Cut No.	Size	Actual Capacity	Dimensions in Inches — Height	Width	Thickness	Cases contain	List per gross
166	12 oz.	$11\frac{1}{2}$ oz.	$9\frac{5}{8}$	$2\frac{5}{16}$	2	1 gr.	$21.00
225	8 "	7 "	$7\frac{1}{2}$	$2\frac{3}{8}$	$1\frac{1}{2}$	2 "	15.00

Dixie or X Panels.

Cut No.	Size	Actual Capacity	Height to base of neck Inches	Width Inches	List per gross
	$1\frac{1}{4}$ oz.	1 oz. scant	$3\frac{5}{8}$	$1\frac{5}{8}$	$5.50
	2 "	$1\frac{1}{2}$ "	4	$1\frac{3}{4}$	6.00
	3 "	$2\frac{2}{5}$ "	$4\frac{3}{8}$	$2\frac{1}{4}$	7.25
164	4 "	3 "	$4\frac{7}{8}$	$2\frac{1}{4}$	8.75
	6 "	4 "	$5\frac{1}{4}$	$2\frac{5}{16}$	10.50
	6 " Ginger	$4\frac{1}{2}$ "	$5\frac{1}{4}$	$2\frac{5}{16}$	10.50
	8 "	6 "	$5\frac{7}{8}$	$2\frac{9}{16}$	13.00
	10 "	8 "	$6\frac{3}{4}$	$2\frac{7}{8}$	15.50
227	16 "	12 "	$7\frac{1}{4}$	$3\frac{1}{4}$	21.00
	24 "	16 "	$8\frac{1}{4}$	$3\frac{1}{2}$	26.00

These moulds are arranged to take lettered plates. These moulds have extra deep panels, making them very large appearing, with a very scant capacity.

For Discount see last page.

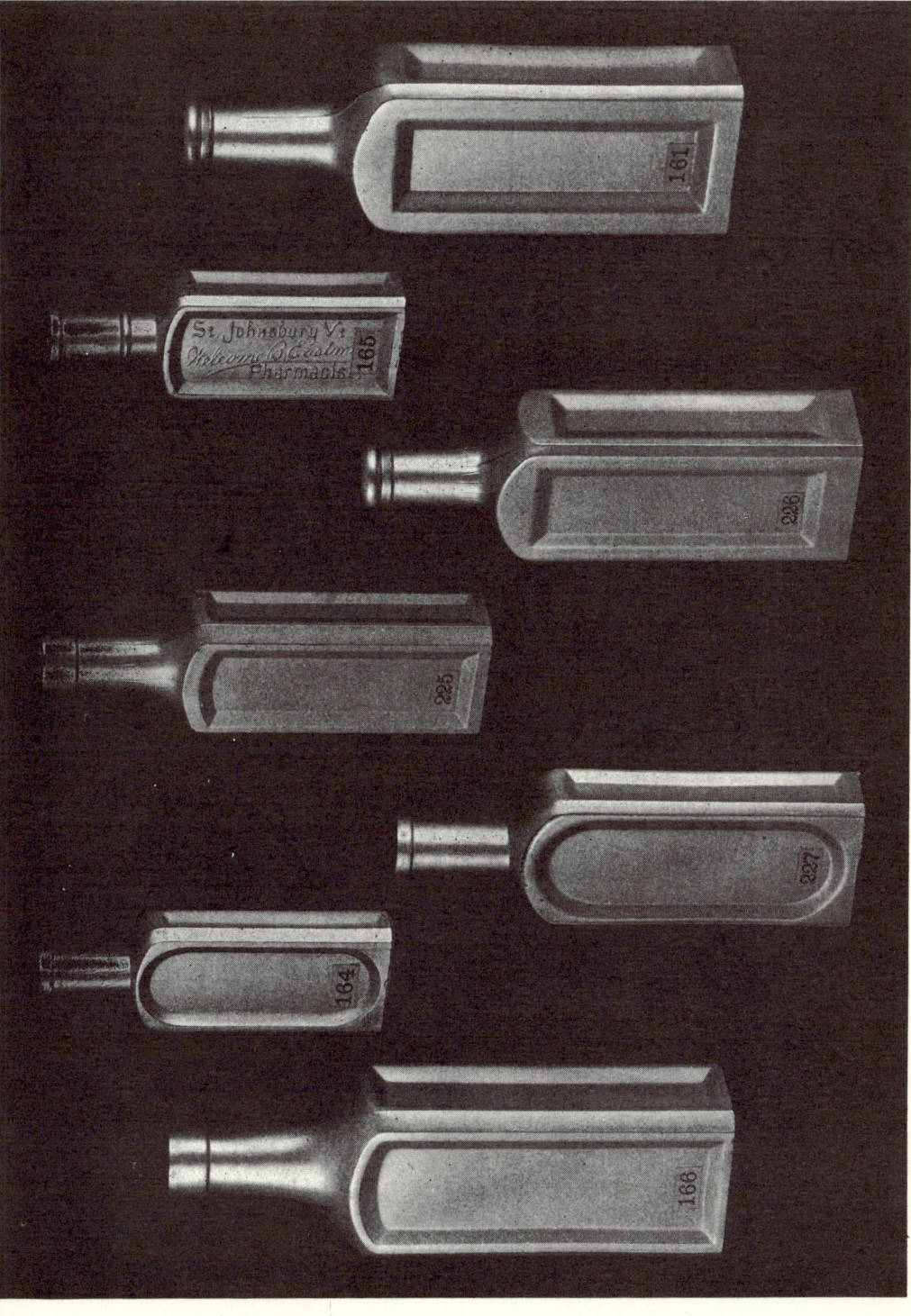

GREEN GLASS WARE.

Ginger Panels.
Four Sides Paneled.

Cut No.		Size	Actual Capacity	Height	Dimensions in inches Width	Thick	Cases contain	List per gross
239		$\frac{1}{2}$ ounce	4 drachms	$3\frac{3}{4}$	$1\frac{3}{16}$	$1\frac{1}{16}$	6 gross	$3.50
238		6 drachm	6 "	4	$1\frac{5}{16}$	$1\frac{1}{16}$	6 "	4.00
228		1 ounce	7 "	$4\frac{1}{4}$	$1\frac{7}{16}$	$\frac{3}{4}$	6 "	4.00
229	{	$1\frac{1}{2}$ "	$1\frac{1}{2}$ ounce	$5\frac{1}{4}$	$1\frac{9}{16}$	$\frac{7}{8}$	5 "	5.50
		2 "	$1\frac{1}{4}$ "	$5\frac{1}{4}$	2	$1\frac{5}{16}$	5 "	5.50
230	{	T 2 "	2 "	$5\frac{3}{4}$	$1\frac{7}{8}$	1	5 "	7.00
		C $1\frac{3}{4}$ "	$1\frac{3}{4}$ "	$5\frac{7}{8}$	2	1	3 "	8.00
231		3 "	$2\frac{1}{2}$ "	$5\frac{3}{4}$	2	$1\frac{1}{8}$	4 "	7.00
232		4 "	$3\frac{1}{2}$ "	6	$2\frac{1}{8}$	$1\frac{1}{4}$	3 "	8.00
233		G $2\frac{1}{2}$ "	$2\frac{1}{2}$ "	$6\frac{1}{4}$	$2\frac{1}{8}$	$1\frac{1}{16}$	3 "	8.00
234	{	No. 9-5 "	4 "	$6\frac{1}{4}$	$2\frac{5}{16}$	$1\frac{5}{16}$	3 "	10.50
		No.16-5 "	$3\frac{1}{2}$ "	$6\frac{7}{8}$	$2\frac{1}{4}$	$1\frac{3}{16}$	3 "	10.50
235	{	L 6 "	6 "	7	$2\frac{1}{2}$	$1\frac{1}{2}$	2 "	10.50
		L 8 "	8 "	$7\frac{1}{4}$	$2\frac{5}{8}$	$1\frac{3}{4}$	$1\frac{1}{2}$ "	13.00
236		12 "	12 "	$8\frac{1}{2}$	$2\frac{3}{4}$	$1\frac{7}{8}$	1 "	17.50
237	{	14 "	13 "	$8\frac{1}{2}$	3	2	1 "	18.75
		16 "	16 "	$9\frac{1}{4}$	$3\frac{1}{4}$	2	1 "	21.00

These moulds are arranged to take lettered plates.

These bottles are made extra heavy and are a very large appearing line.

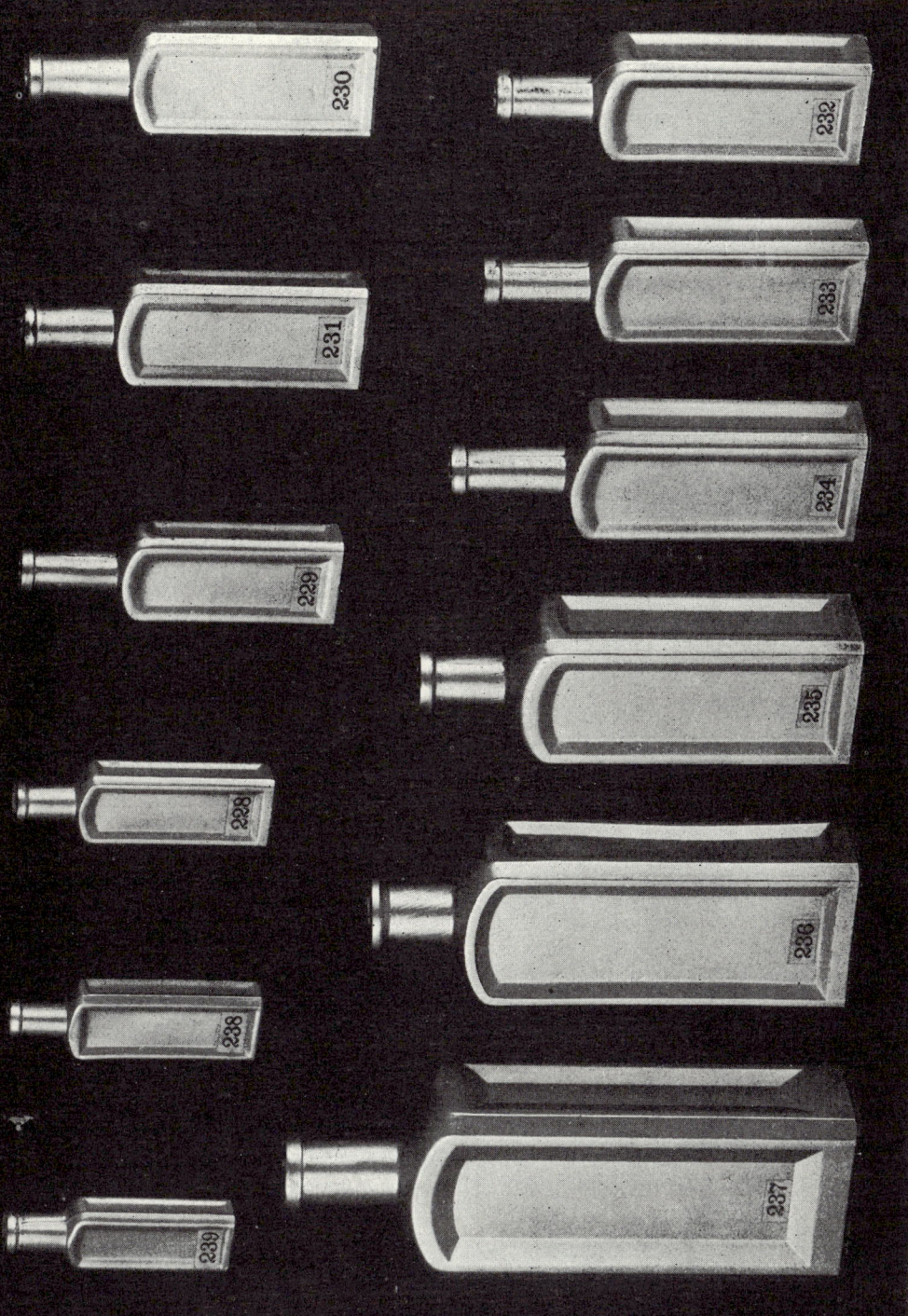

GREEN GLASS WARE.

French Squares.

Cut No. 168 Narrow Mouth. 178 Wide Mouth.

Size	Capacity	Cases contain	Narrow Mouth List per gross	Wide Mouth List per gross
½ oz.	½ oz.	6 gr.	$3.50	$3.75
1 "	1 "	6 "	4.00	4.25
2 "	2 "	5 "	5.00	5.50
3 "	3 "	4 "	5.75	6.25
4 "	4 "	4 "	7.25	8.00
6 "	6 "	3 "	9.00	9.75
8 "	8 "	2 "	11.25	12.00
10 "	10 "	2 "	13.25	
12 "	12 "	1½ "	14.75	15.50
16 "	16 "	1 "	18 50	20.00
32 "	32 "	¾ "	31.00	34.00

Round Prescriptions.

Cut No. 201 Narrow Mouth. 240 Wide Mouth.

Size	Capacity	Cases contain	Narrow Mouth List per gross	Wide Mouth List per gross
½ oz.	½ oz.	6 gr.	$3.25	$3.50
1 "	1 "	6 "	3.75	4.00
2 "	2 "	5 "	4.50	4.75
3 "	3 "	4 "	5.50	6.00
4 "	4 "	3 "	6.75	7.50
6 "	6 "	3 "	8.25	9.00
8 "	8 "	2 "	9.75	10.50
12 "	12 "	1½ "	13.75	15.00
16 "	16 "	1 "	15.25	16.25
32 "	32 "	¾ "	24.50	25.50

Castor Oils and Lemon Syrups.

Cut No. 169

Size	Capacity	Cases contain	List per gross
1½ ounce	1½ ounce	5 gross	$5.00
1⅞ "	1⅞ "	5 "	5.00
2 "	2 "	5 "	5.00
3 "	3 "	4 "	6.00
4 "	4 "	3 "	7.00
6 "	6 "	2 "	8.50
7 "	7 "	2 "	9.25
8 "	8 "	2 "	10.50
14* "	14 "	1 "	15.00
16 "	16 "	1 "	16.00

* Lemon Syrups.

Philadelphia Oval. Cut No. 171 — Baltimore Oval. Cut No. 172

Union Oval. Cut No. 173 — Plain Oval. Cut No. 174

Size	Capacity	Cases contain	List per gross
½ ounce	½ ounce	6 gross	$3.25
1 "	1 "	6 "	3.75
2 "	2 "	5 "	4.75
3 "	3 "	4 "	5.75
4 "	4 "	4 "	7.00
5 "	5 "	3 "	8.00
6 "	6 "	2½ "	8.50
7 "	7 "	2 "	10.25
8 "	8 "	2 "	10.25
10 "	10 "	2 "	12.25
12 "	12 "	1½ "	14.25
14 "	14 "	1 "	15.75
16 "	16 "	1 "	17.50
24 "	24 "	½ "	24.00
28 "	28 "	½ "	25.00
32 "	32 "	½ "	25.00

Square Sponge Varnish. Cut No. 178

Oblong Sponge Varnish, Paneled. Cut No. 179

Size	Capacity	Cases contain	List per gross
2 ounce	1½ ounce	5 gross	$4.50
2 "	2 "	5 "	5.00
3 "	3 "	4 "	5.50
3½ "	3½ "	4 "	6.50
4 "	4 "	3 "	7.00
4 "	4 "	3 "	7.50
6 "	6 "	2 "	7.50
8 "	8 "	2 "	8.50
10 "	10 "	1 "	11.00
12 "	12 "	1 "	12.00

Fluted Prescription. "F. P. L."

Cut No. 170

Size	Capacity	Cases contain	List per gross
1 ounce	1 ounce	6 gross	$3.75
1¼ "	1¼ "	5 "	4 50
1½ "	1½ "	5 "	4.50
1¾ "	1¾ "	5 "	4.50
2 "	2 "	5 "	4.50
3 "	3 "	4 "	5.50
4 "	4 "	4 "	6.75
6 "	6 "	3 "	8.25
8 "	8 "	2 "	9.75
16 "	16 "	1 "	16.50

Long Neck Ovals.

Cut No. 175

Size	Capacity	Cases contain	List per gross
2 ounce	2 ounce	3 gross	$4.75
3 "	3 "	2 "	5.75
4 "	4 "	2 "	7.00
6 "	6 "	1 "	8.50
8 "	8 "	1 "	10.25
12 "	12 "	1 "	14.25
14 "	14 "	1 "	17.00
16 "	16 "	1 "	17.50

Long Round Prescriptions.

Cut No. 177

Size	Capacity	Cases contain	List per gross
½ ounce	½ ounce	10 gross	$3.50
1 "	1 "	6 "	4.00
2 "	2 "	5 "	4.50

Godfrey Cordial.

Cut No.	Size	Capacity	Cases contain	List per gross
180	2 ounce	2 ounce	5 gross	$4.50

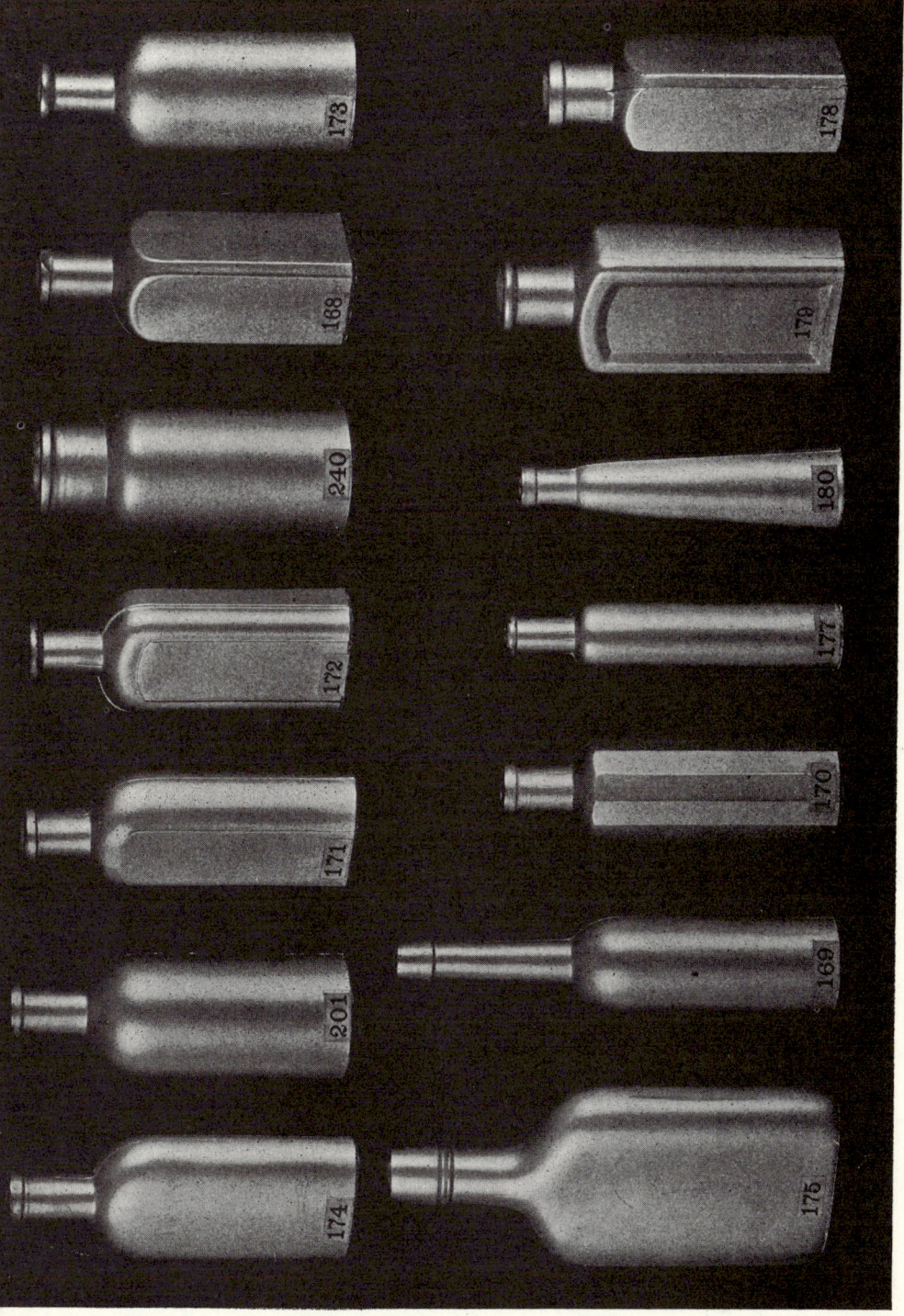

GREEN GLASS WARE.

Druggists' Packing Bottles.

Cut No.	Size	Capacity	Cases contain	Cut No. 279 Narrow Mouth	Cut No. 277 Wide Mouth
279 Narrow Mouth	½ pt.	½ pt.	2 gr.	$9.75	$10.50
	12 oz.	12 oz.	1½ "	14 75	15.50
	1 pt.	1 pt.	1 "	15.25	16.25
	1½ "	1½ "	1 "	19.50	21.00
	1 qt.	1 qt.	1 "	24.50	25.50
277 Wide Mouth	3 pt.	3 pt.	½ "	37.75	40.00
	½ gal.	½ gal.	½ "	39.00	40.00
	5 pt.	5 pt.	⅓ "	55.00	56.00
	1 gal.	1 gal.	¼ "	56.00	57.00
				Net	*Net*
	2 "	2 "	1 doz.	5.25	5.50

Baltimore Pickle Bottles.

Square.

Cut No.	Size	Capacity	Weight	Cases contain	List per gross
542	Pint	6 oz.	6 oz.	2 gr.	$9.00
	"	7 "	7 "	2 "	11.00
	"	8 "	8 "	2 "	12.00
	Quart	16 "	12 "	1 "	14.00
	"	17 "	13 "	1 "	15.00
	½ gal.	32 "	24 "	1 "	25.00
	1 "	50 "	34 "	½ "	40.00

Acids and Tinctures.

Dark Green or Amber.

Cut No.	Size		Per gross
278	½ pt.	(Ground Stoppers)	$36.00
	12 oz.	" "	40.00
	Pint	" "	42.00
	Quart	" "	55.00
	½ gal.	" "	85.00
	Gallon	" "	115.00
	Chloride of Soda or Stoppered Wines		48.00

Melrose Salad Cream.

Nickeled Screw Caps. Net

Cut No. Size Capacity per gross

Milk Jar Baskets.

Made of extra heavy wire.

Cut No.	Hold	Per dozen
242	6 pts.	$18.00
	6 qts.	21.00
	4½ gal.	24.00
	4 qts. } 2 pts. }	18.00

Demijohns.

Rattan Covered.

Cut No.		Each
276	¼ gal.	$0.30
	½ "	.40
	1 "	.55
	2 "	.80
	3 "	1.00
	5 "	1.25

Carmine Ink Bottles.

Cut No.	Size	Cases contain	List per gross
176	½ ounce	6 gross	$4.00
	1 "	6 "	5.00
	2 "	5 "	5.50

Florida Water Bottles.

Cut No.	Size	Cases contain	List per gross
544	8 ounce	1½ gross	$12.00
	4 "	3 "	7.00
	3 "	4 "	6.00

Only the 8 oz. mould is lettered

Olive Oil Bottles.

Crystal Flint.

Cut No.	Size	Capacity	Cases contain	List per gr.
543	½ pt.	5 oz.	2 gr.	$12.00
	Pint	12 "	1 "	15.00

Round Horse Radish.

Cut No.	Size	Capacity	Cases contain	List per gr.
277	5 oz.	5 oz.	3 gr.	$8.00
	6 "	6 "	3 "	9.00
	7 "	7 "	2½ "	9.50
	8 "	8 "	2 "	10.50
	10 "	10 "	1½ "	12.00
	12 "	12 "	1½ "	14.00

Ammonia Oval.

Cut No.	Size	Capacity	Cases contain	List per gr.
266	¼ pt.	4 oz.	4 gr.	$7.00
	½ "	7 "	2 "	10.25
	Pint	12 "	1 "	15.75
	"	14 "	1 "	17.50
	"	16 "	1 "	17.50
	Quart	28 "	⅔ "	25.00
	"	30 "	⅔ "	25.00
	"	32 "	⅔ "	25.00

Screw Cap Catsup.

Crystal Flint.

Cut No.	Size	Capacity	Cases contain	List per gr.
546	½ pt.	8 oz.	2 gr.	$20.00
	1 "	16 "	1 "	22.00

Round Chow Chow or English Pickle.

Cut No.	Size	Capacity	Cases contain	List per gr.
547	8 oz.	7 oz.	2 gr.	$10.50
	10 "	9 "	2 "	11.00
	14 "	10 "	1 "	12.00
	16 "	12 "	1 "	14.00
	20 "	13 "	1 "	15.00
	32 "	17 "	1 "	20.00

Extra Seltzers.

(Extra Size and Weight.)

Cut No.	Size	Narrow Mouth	Wide Mouth
279	½ pt. and 9 oz.	$12.25	$13.25
	12 oz.	15.00	16.00
	Pt., 18 to 20 oz.	19.50	20.50
	22 oz. to 24 oz.	24.00	25.00
	Qt., 35 to 40 oz.	30.00	31.00
	3 pt.	40.00	41.00
	½ gal., 80 oz., (5 pt.)	55.00	56.00
	3 qt.	63.00	64.00
	1 gal.	70.00	71.00

O.K. Pickle or Oyster Jar.

Cut No.	Size	Capacity	Cases contain	List per gr.
548	½ pt.	8 oz.	2 gr.	$10.00

Cream Jars.

Tin Screw Cap.

Cut No.	Size	Capacity	Height	Net per gr.
545	½ pt.	8 oz.	4¼ in.	$4.00
	½ "	8 "	4¾ "	4.00
	1 "	16 "	6 "	6.00

Patent Stopper Milk Jars.

Flint Glass.

Cut No.	Size	Cases contain	Net Prices Gross	Net Prices Dozen
268	½ pt.	1 gr.	$8.00	$0.75
	1 "	½ "	10.00	1.00
	1 qt.	½ "	12.00	1.25
	2 "	½ "	18.00	1.75

Seal Milk Jar.

Cut No.	Size	Gross	Dozen
267	½ pt.	$6.00	$0.75
	1 "	8.00	.90
	1 qt.	10.00	1.00
	2 "	15.00	1.50

The Thatcher Paper Disk to seal

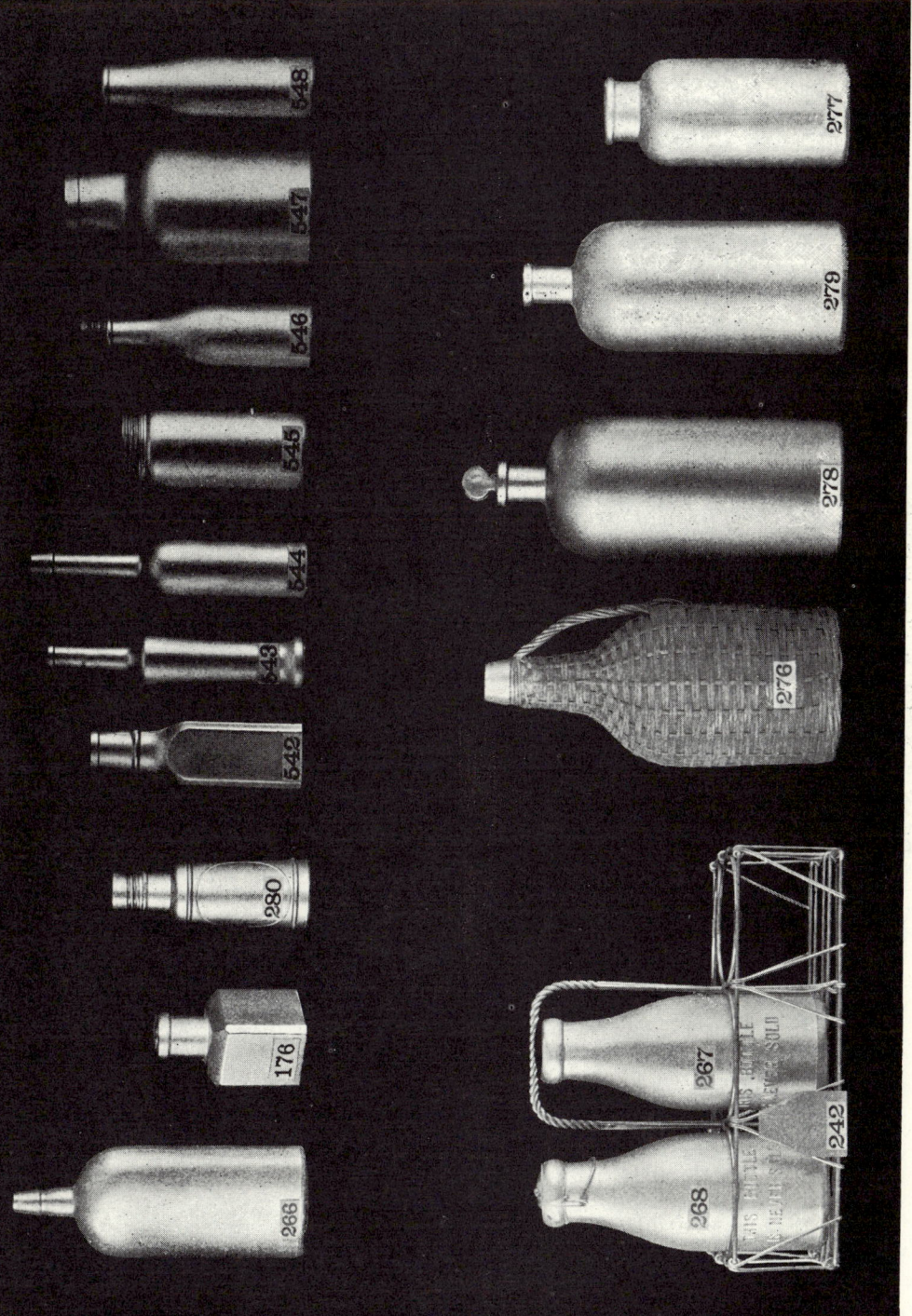

GLOBE CANDY JARS.

Ground Glass Stoppers.

Diameter	Height	Capacity	List per doz.
2 in.	4 in.	2 oz.	$3.75
3 "	6 "	8 "	4.50
4 "	8 "	16 "	6.75
5 "	10 "	1 qt.	10.25
6 "	12 "	3 pt.	14.50
7 "	14 "	3 qt.	20.50
8 "	16 "	4 "	26.25
9 "	18 "	7 "	35.00
10 "	20 "	9 "	47.00

Order by diameters.

Cut No. 233

No. 1900 JAR.

Ground Stopper. An unusually fine Show Jar for Druggists' use.

No.	Height	Capacity	List per doz.
1	16 in.	2 pints	$14.00
2	21 "	5 "	30.00
3	26 "	9½ "	48.00

Cut No. 238

GLASS TABLET JARS.

With Ground Stoppers.

Cut No. 518.
(Square Shape with Round Corners.)

Cut No. 519.
(Round Style.)

Size	Per doz.		Per doz.
2 lb.	Square, $4.75	Round,	$4.50
4 "	" 6.00	"	5.40
5 "	" 7.00	"	7.00

TALL SAMPLE JARS.

Ground Glass Stoppers.

Height	Per dozen
6 inches	$5.00
9 "	6.50
12 "	9.50
15 "	14.00
18 "	20.00
21 "	31.00
24 "	40.00
27 "	52.00
30 "	70.00

These jars are used for sampling soaps, puffs, or other small and fragile articles, and make an inexpensive but handsome show jar for one using colored liquids in show windows. They are carefully selected and free from blemishes.

Cut No. 522

EGYPTIAN SHOW JARS.

Ground Glass Stoppers.

Height	Capacity	List per doz.
5 inches	6 ounce	$3.00
6½ "	12 "	4.50
8 "	24 "	6.00
9¾ "	2½ pint	9.00
11 "	2 quart	13.00
13 "	7 pint	19.00
15 "	6 quart	25.00
17 "	2 gallon	31.00

Order by capacities

Cut No. 521

CANDY SCOOPS.

Glass, per doz.		$2.00
608 Nickel plated, each		1.50

Cut No. 608

CANDY TRAYS.

	No.	
No. 200 Glass Candy Trays.	422	
No. 300 Glass Candy Trays.	423	

	List per doz.
7 inch, actual size, 7⅛ x 4⅝ in.,	$2.50
8 " " 8 x 5½ "	3.00
9 " " 8¾ x 6¼ "	3.50

WINDOW SHOW BOTTLES.

Pineapple shape.

	Three Pieces		Pieces
	Plain Each	Engraved Each	Engraved Each
½	$2.00	$3.10	$3.70
1	2.40	3.80	4.50
1½	3.20	5.00	5.70
2	3.60	5.80	6.50
3	4.80	7.60	8.60

Cut No. 234

Roman Vase Shape.

	Each	Engraved Each
½		$6.00
1		8.00
2		10.00

Cut No. 235

WINDOW SHOW GLOBES.

No. 846

Plain glass globe
Engraved glass globe
Length of jar, fittings and chain
Length of bracket, 15 inches.
Capacity, 3½ gallons.

Style	Each
20 A	$15.00
20 C	20.00

No. 847

Plain glass globe, without base
     " with base
With engraved globe, without base
     " with base
Height, without base, 25 inches.
Height, with base, 28 inches.

	Each
2 A	10.00
	14.00
2 C	15.00
	19.00

GLASS SHOP FURNITURE.

Price of Bottles does not include Labels.

GLASS LABELS.

We present herewith our Shop Ware and Glass Labels. The cuts simply show the style. The quality will surpass that of any other manufacturer. We use the very best lead glass labels with finished edges, and unless otherwise specified, make the orders with Latin names.

Prices of glass labels.

Style	Each
No. 0, 1, 21, 51, 113	$0.20
" 2, 7, 11	.22
" 4, 41, 42, 64, 114	.24
" 13, 52, 63, 92	28
" 5	.26

The price of labels includes attaching to bottle when ordered complete.

Prescription Case Bottles

The label is blown in the glass, being ground so as to render it distinct. Amber bottles furnished for articles affected by light, and Blue bottles for poisons.

Cut No. 844

	Per doz.
¼ pt. Tinctures	$3.50

Cut No. 843

¼ pt. Salt Mouths	$3.86

Chicago Shelf Ware.

Cut No. 212

Round Recess, Crown Stoppers, Fire Polished.

Boston Recess.

Mushroom Stoppers, Fire Polished.

Cut No. 217 Square, 218 Round.

Tinctures.

Size	Height	Per doz.
4 oz.	6¼ in.	$1.40
8 "	7 "	1.80
16 "	9 "	2.65
32 "	10¼ "	3.70
½ gal.	12¼ "	6.20

Salt Mouths.

Size	Height	Per doz.
4 oz.	6 in.	$1.75
8 "	6⅞ "	2.25
16 "	8⅝ "	2.70
32 "	10⅛ "	3.80
½ gal.	12⅜ "	6.50

Syrups.

With Loose Stoppers.

Pints . . .	$2.65
Quarts . . .	3.70
½ gal. . . .	6.20

Oils.

Ground Stoppers with Loose Caps.

Pint . . .	$5.50
Quart . . .	6.50
½ gal. . . .	9.00

Standard No. 1.

Free from mould marks, hand made and fire polished. Surface Label.

Cut No. 207

Tinctures.

Size	Height	Per doz.
4 oz.	6 in.	$1.75
8 "	7¼ "	1.80
16 "	8⅛ "	2.65
32 "	10⅜ "	3.70
½ gal.	12⅜ "	6.20
1 "	14½ "	8.00
2 "	19½ "	18.00

Salt Mouth.

Size	Height	Per doz.
4 oz.	5⅝ in.	$1.75
8 "	7 "	2.25
Pint	8¾ "	2.70
32 oz.	10¼ "	3.80
½ gal.	12½ "	6.50
1 "	14½ "	10.00
2 "	18¼ "	21.00

Syrups.

Loose Stopper.

Cut No. 216

Size	Height	Per doz.
Pint	9 in.	$3.50
Qt.	10⅝ "	4.50
½ gal.	12½ "	7.50

Oils.

Ground Stoppers with Loose Caps.

Cut No. 215

Size	Height	Per doz.
Pint	10 in.	$5.50
Qt.	10⅞ "	6.50
½ gal.	12⅝ "	9.00

Congress Square.

Recess Label, Square Bottle, Rounded Corners.

Tinctures.

Cut No. 208

Size	Height	Per doz.
4 oz.	6 in.	$1.50
8 "	6¾ "	2.00
16 "	8⅜ "	2.90
Qt.	10¼ "	4.00
½ gal.	12 "	6.75

Salt Mouths.

Cut No. 209

Size	Height	Per doz.
4 oz.	5⅝ in.	$1.75
8 "	6¾ "	2.25
Pint	8¼ "	3.00
Qt.	10 "	4.20
½ gal.	12 "	7.00

Syrups.

Loose Stoppers.

Pint . . .	$4.00
Quart . . .	4.70
½ gal. . . .	6.00

Oils.

Ground Stoppers with Loose Caps.

Pint . . .	$6.00
Quart . . .	7.00
½ gal. . . .	8.00

Columbian Shelf Ware.

Extra Weight. Fitted with Crown Stoppers. Surface Labels.

Tinctures.

Cut No. 210

Size	Height	Per doz.
4 oz.	6¼ in.	$2.25
8 "	7¼ "	2.75
16 "	9⅛ "	3.50
32 "	10⅜ "	4.50
½ gal.	12⅜ "	7 00
1 "	14½ "	11.00
2 "	19½ "	20.00

Salt Mouths.

Cut No. 211

Size	Height	Per doz.
4 oz.	6 in.	$2.40
8 "	7 "	3.00
Pint	8¾ "	3.80
Qt.	10¾ "	5.00
½ gal.	12½ "	7.50
1 "	14½ "	12 00
2 "	18¼ "	22.00

Syrups.

With Loose Stoppers.

Pint . . .	$3.75
Quart . . .	5.00
½ gal. . . .	8.00

Oils.

Ground Stopper with Loose Caps.

Pint . . .	$6.50
Quart . . .	7.75
½ gal. . . .	12.00

DRAWER PULLS.

Cut No.	No.	Size, in.	Per doz.
838	386 Bronzed	4⅞ x 2⅜	$1.20
840	586 "	3⅝ x 1¾	1.00
8[illegible]	2228 "	4½ x 2	1.20

Glass Ointment Jars.

With Raised Glass Letters.

Cut No.	Size	Flat Top Height, in.	Amber Per doz.	Opal Per doz.	Size	Steeple Top Height, in.	Amber Per doz.	Opal Per doz.
	¼ lb.	3⅛	$2.25	$2.50	¼ lb.	4⅜	$2.50	$2.75
	½ "	4½	[illegible]	4.00	½ "	5¾	3.50	4.00

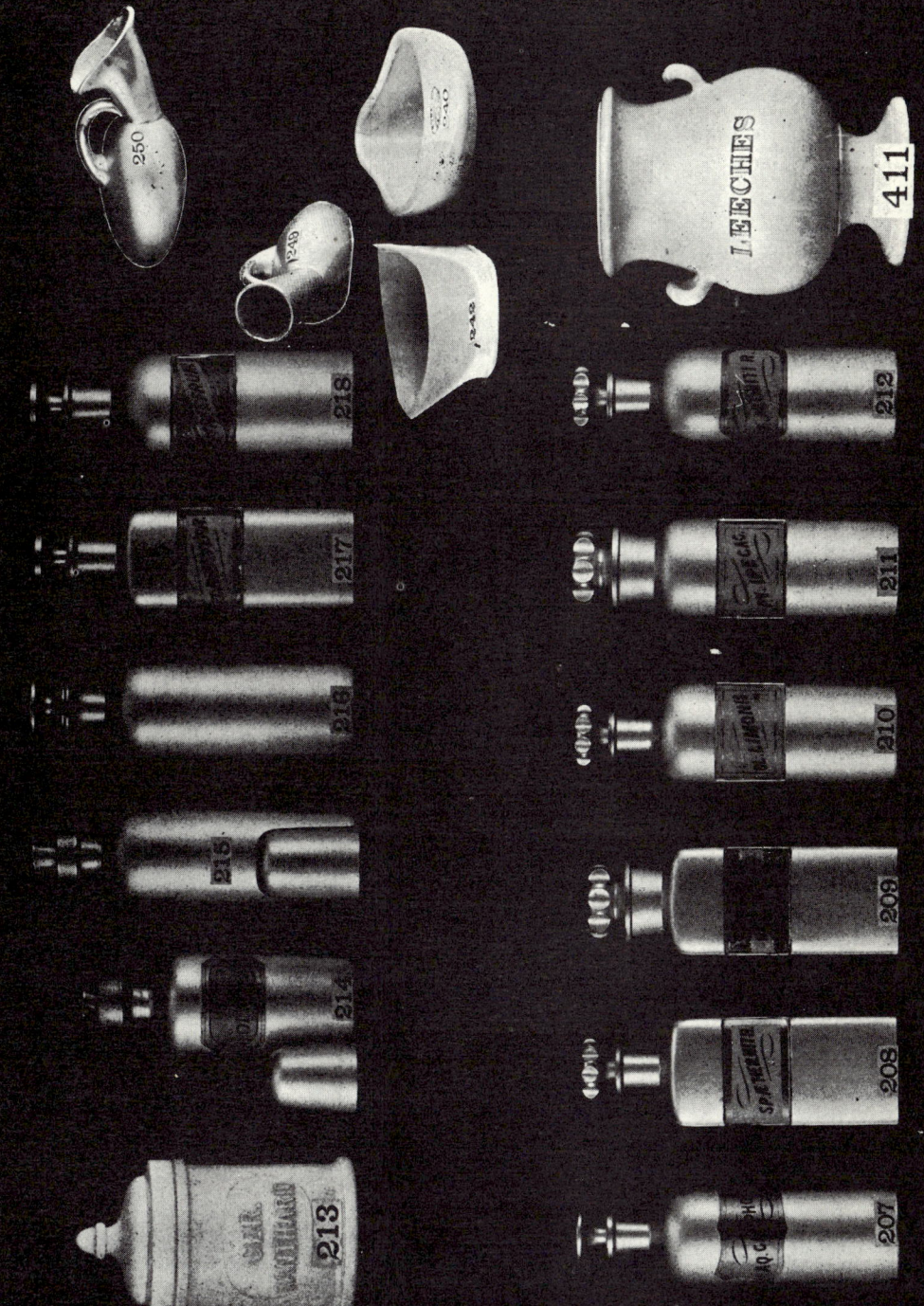

HOMEOPATHIC VIALS.

Scale of Millimeters.

Short Style.

Special size Vials made to order

Screw Cap.

Short Shape only.

The necks of these Vials are finished with threads and the caps screwed directly on the glass.

Size	List per gross
1 drachm	$3.00
2 "	3.75
3 "	4.00
4 "	5.00
6 "	8.00
8 "	10.50

Special lengths of this style can be made when desired

Homeopathic Vials.

Long and Short Styles.

	List per gross
⅛ drachm	$1.12½
¼ "	1.12½
½ "	1.12½
1 "	1.25
1½ "	1.50
2 "	1.70
3 "	2.00
4 "	3.00
6 "	4.00
8 "	5.00

Mouths being formed by patent tools are always regular and round.

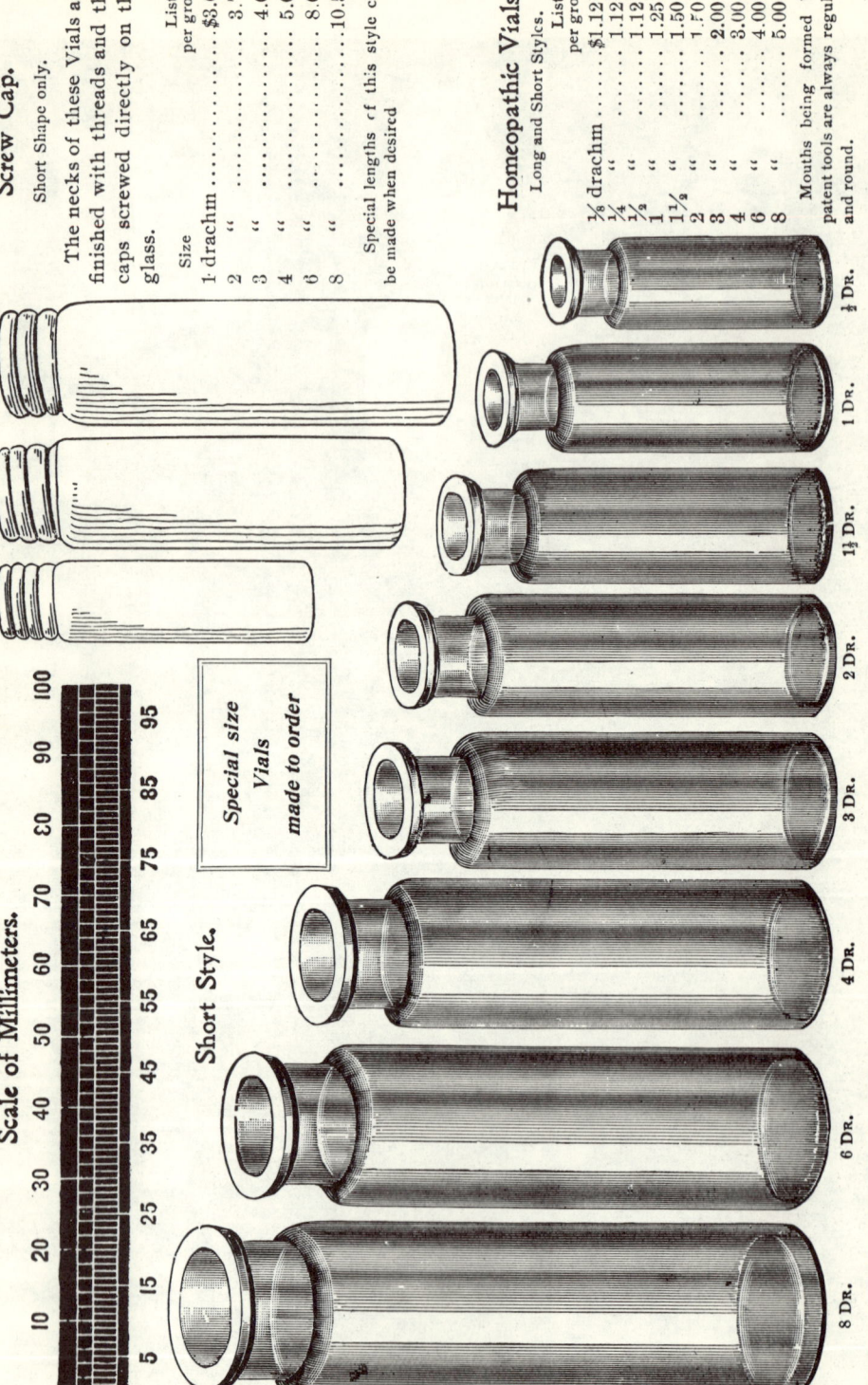

For Discount see last page.

GLASS LABELS

PV. IPECAC.
2

FL. EXT. CIMICIFUGÆ
41

TR. ACONITI R.
1

G. ACACIÆ
4

7

52

S. ÆTHER. NITR.
113

11

SYR. RHEI AR.
51

HAMLIN'S WIZARD OIL

THE GREAT MEDICAL WONDER.

There is no Sore it will Not Heal, No Pain it will not Subdue.

HAMLIN'S COUGH BALSAM

PLEASANT TO TAKE

MAGICAL IN ITS EFFECTS.

HAMLIN'S BLOOD AND LIVER PILLS

For Liver Complaint, Constipation,

AND ALL

Disorders of the Stomach and Digestive Organs.

PREPARED AT THE LABORATORY OI

HAMLINS WIZARD OIL COMPANY, CHICAGO, ILL.

A MUSICAL medicine show, one of many such aggregations sent forth by John A. Hamlin to sing the praises of Wizard Oil

— GROUP C: HOUSEHOLDS

CHAPTER XVI   HEALTH-HELP NEEDS

LINIMENTS, AMMONIA, ETC. FOR HOUSEHOLD

In this final roundup of Household and Kitchen bottles we must return to what some would call "medicinals"—the liniments, balsams, gargling oils and other ungents supplied to aid good health, and not drinkable. Primarily non-alcohol, they form a category which has been relatively neglected in bottle lore. We begin by giving you a representative listing of such bottles, all made before 1900 and now collectors items. Also we show the types of related advertising material and associated bottle lore a special collector can find in this relatively untouched field. It is hoped that these listings will spark others to continue and enlarge the whole field of the non-drinkable household and family aid bottles of the bygone past.

INDEXING HOME-BOTTLE NECESSITIES

1890 catalogs of the makers of drug and household glassware are the surest way toward a basic classification of shapes. In correspondence refer to picture as well as x or z page number.

The problem of creating check-lists for all C Group bottles that fall into our household-aids category has proved almost insurmountable. Not only is there a great variety of different shapes; the same shapes are found with an infinite variety of marked-in-glass name plates. As you have seen from the numbered drug catalog pictures of the last chapter, these wholesalers and glassmakers often changed the same basic mold so the name of a local store or some regional concoction could be impressed along the side of a standard bottle. Thus, if you are going to check-list and number even these most representative shapes which once held tablets, pomades, toothpowders, linaments and other health aids, the best present method is to use the figure numbers found on the old catalog pages that follow. In order to find a particular bottle that is pictured therein give it the call number shown under the figure and then add the x or z page number where it appears. In that way collectors in different parts of the country will be able to exchange bottles and information basic to further advancing the field. Remember, Household Bottle Collecting is not an established specialty. The basic 19th Century forms pictured herein as well as related ads that show the original paper labels are the surest way towards establishment of a definite Households Check-List. Aid is also supplied by consulting the Index which tells all the pages where bottles of a given Type are pictured or described.

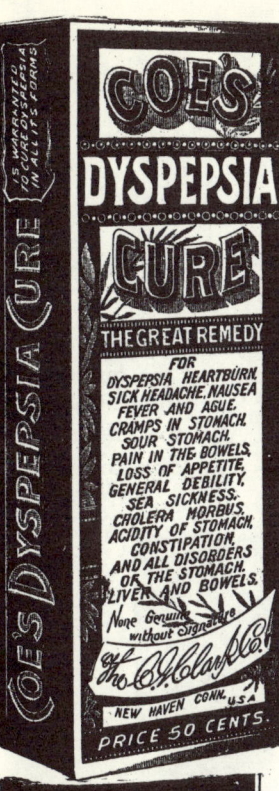

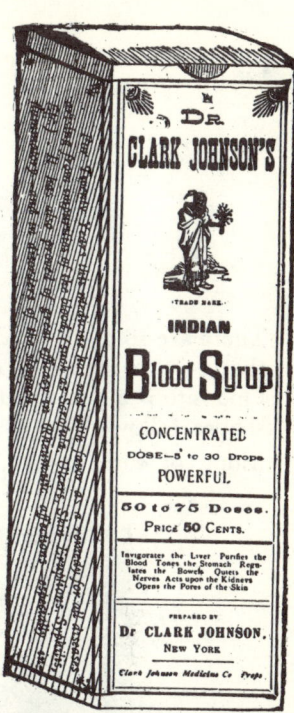

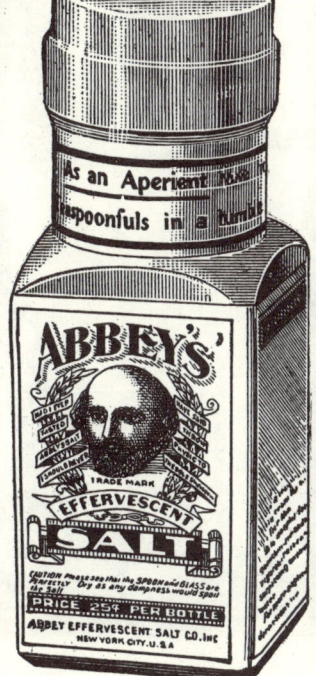
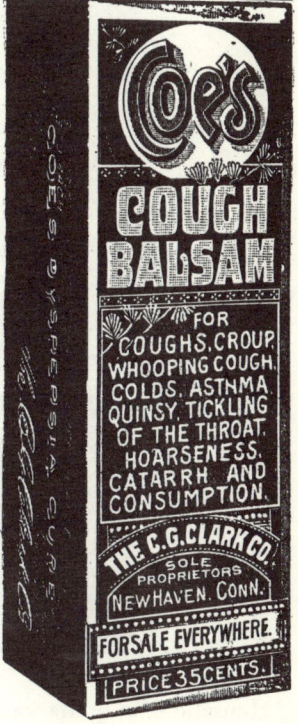

There are so many of these liniments, Syrups of Tansy, Eye Waters, etc., that even a listing of ads for such "sick helps" is out of the question. Opposite is a pamphlet of 1850, next comes a check list of typical bottle shapes followed by associated collateral materials. Also the check list listing of such bottles, all made before 1900 and now collector items.

Household gargling oils and other ungents supplied to aid good health

— GROUP D: FIGURALS, Etc.

Some very unusual 19th century bottles were made to hold staples. We give you representative sample listing, followed with a brief general look into the entire field. Note that there is little attempt here to differentiate rarity or to carefully define usage. Bottles may have been made for one sort of contents, the mold sold or the design pirated for an entirely different product. Along with many of these food bottles and jars go others that served for alleged "beauty aids." We shall list only ten of those marked in glass and indicate by line drawings the typical shapes involved. No attempt is yet made at order and completeness, but rather to open a new field of bottle collecting.

— GROUP C: HOUSEHOLDS

OTHER   BOTTLES

1. "Opodeldoc Liquid", height 4½ inches, aquamarine. 1¾ inches in diameter. s b. (1836) (FW) P. 83.

2. Wooden stand holding 12 vials used by a New Hampshire physician. s b. (U). P. 83.

3. Vial, height 9⅝ inches—aquamarine. s b. (U). P. 83.

4. Early Patent Medicine bottle. aquamarine 2½ inches in diameter, height 9½ inches. s b. (U). P. 84.

5. Medicine Bottle, diameter 3½ inches, height 8½ inches, clear glass. s b. (U). P. 84.

5a, 5b, 5c, 5d, 5e. Others similar but smaller. P. 84.

6. Turkish Hair Tonic, T. M. Haskins. Height 8⅜ inches (U). P. 67 and 85.

7. BUCKOUT
"Dutch Liniment" horse between lettering on sides of frame, "Prepared by E. A. Buckout, Mechanicsville Saratoga Co. N. Y." Reverse: Prancing horse, on sides of frame "The Only Genuine Liniment for a horse." "Price 50c". (U). P. 16.

8. "Dr. Moore & Co's. Magnetic Pain Killer", etc. (original label). Rectangular. bevelled corners, aquamarine. s c m s b. Height 6 inches (U). P. 66.

9. "Dr. Elderkin's Egyptian Balsam", etc. (original label). Round—aquamarine. f m s b. Height 6⅛ inches (U). P. 66.

10. Brouns Drops. Pentagonal—aquamarine. s m s b. (U). P. 66.

"Anti-Apoplectine, The Only Apoplexy Preventative and Paralysis Cure. Dr. F. S. Hutchinson & Co." Lettering on three sunken panels, other side flat. Square, about one-sixth pint—aquamarine. d c m. "Enosburgh Falls, Vt." on base. (U).

"Dr. J. Blackman's Genuine Healing Balsam."

"E. A. Buckout Dutch Liniment" and full figure of Dutchman. Reverse: "Prepared at Mechanicsville, Saratoga Co., N. Y." Aquamarine. c m. s b. Height 4½ inches (U).

Clickemer's Sugar Coated Vegetable Purgative Pills.

"Dalby's Carminative."

"D. Evans, Camomile Pills"

"Mrs. M. N. Gardner's Indian Balsam of Liverwort."

Note: Liberty tree—an old Elm in Boston so called—1765. By others it is assumed to be the famous Charter Oak.

Top Row. Height 4 inches to 7¼ inches.
1. Rectangular, sunken panels, plain.
2. Round, plain.
3. Round, plain.
4. Round, tapering, plain.
5. Round, plain.
6. Apothecary measuring bottle with scale on neck.
7. "Dr. Curtis Cherry Syrup, New York", rectangular with sunken panels.
8. Round, plain.
9. Round, plain.
10. Round, plain.
11. Square, plain.
12. Round, plain.
13. Elliptical, lettered "Swain's Vermifuge Disentary, Cholera-morbus, Despepsia". (Exact spelling).

Lower Row. Height 2 inches to 5¼ inches.
1. Round, plain.
2. Round, plain.
3. "Batchelor's Liquid Hair Dye, No. 2".
4. Round, plain.
5. Round, plain.
6. Round, plain, Nos. 7, 8, 9, 10 and 11 are round, plain.
12. Rectangular, beveled corners, lettered "M".
13. Rectangular, sunken panels, beveled edges, "Davis Vegetable Pain Killer."
14. Twelve sided, plain.
15. Round, plain.
16. Twelve sided, plain.
17. Five flat sides with round space for label.   (All U)

— GROUP C: HOUSEHOLDS

Top Row.
1. "Iodine Liniment, prepared by S. Ingersoll", sides lettered "Dr. John Roakes, N. Y." Rectangular.
2. "Doct. Curtis Inhaling Hygeia Vapor, N. Y." Rectangular.
3. Plain, elliptical.
4. "Glycerine Pure Distilled", diamond shaped panel with entwined "D H".
5. "Rushton, Clark & Co. Chemists, N. Y." Rectangular.
6. Plain, rectangular.
7. Elliptical, plain.
8. "Phallon & Son, Perfumers, N. Y." Rectangular.
9. "Mathewson's Infallible Remedy, price 50 Cents." Rectangular with sunken panels.
Height of above from 7¼ inches to 10 inches. (All U)

Second Row.
1. "Rowland's Macassar Oil for the Hair, Kirby St., London". Rectangular.
2. "R. E. Sellers, Druggists, Pittsburgh". Round.
3. "Moyer & Hazard, Philada". Rectangular, sunken panels.
4. Square, plain, clear glass.
5. Rectangular with bevelled edges, plain.
6. "Dr. J. S. Houston's Pepsin". Round.
7. Rectangular with bevelled edges, plain.
8. "Mrs. S. A. Allen's World's Hair Balsam, 355 Broome St., N. Y." Rectangular with sunken panels.
9. "Dr. Carrs Nonpariel Nerve and Bone Liniment". Rectangular with bevelled corners.

"Gardner & Smith, Hair Dye No. 2."

"By Dr. Gordak Only" Reverse: "Jelly of Pomeganate Preparate"
Rectangular, rounded sides with cut in corners. Pint—light green. 1 inch flanged mouth. (U).

"Dr Hartshorn's Family Medicines" on sunken panel. Reverse: Plain. Elliptical. Pint—aquamarine. c m height 9¼ inches. (U).

"Hunt's Liniment, Prepared by C. E. Stanton, Sing Sing, N. Y."

"Dr. D. Jane's Carminative Balsam, Philada."

"Kendall's Spavin Cure for Human Flesh", lettering on sides. Ten sides, about one-sixth pint—aquamarine. f m. On base "Enosburg Falls, Vt." (the place of manufacture of the cure), 1876.

"Kennedy's Salt Rheum Ointment."

"Doctor McLanes American Worm Specific."

"Dr. McMinn's Elixir of Opium".

MORBRIDGE BOTTLE (U)
Full figure of Indian holding bottle in right hand and "Dr. Morbridge's Family Vegetable Medicines". Reverse: Plain. About ¾ pint—aquamarine. c m s b.

"Dr. Tobias, New York, Venetian Liniment."

"R. & G. A. Wright, Phila; Alexander's Tricsbaphi."

"Turlington's Balsam" (four lines). Reverse: King's Patent" (two lines). Small, flat bottle, flanged mouth s b.
(Note: This bottle was found in Vermont, but it is known that such specimens were made at the Freewill Glass Works in New Jersey.)

(All U unless otherwise noted).

The foregoing list represents but a few of the vast numbers made.

    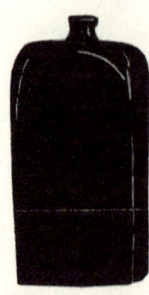

— GROUP C: HOUSEHOLDS

he Wonder of the World.

Leaurelle Oil Balm

The Elegant Toilet Requisite

R COMPLEXION, SKIN AND

Prevents Wrinkles or Ageing of the Skin.

Withering or Drying up of the Flesh and Skin.

NO-TO-BAC
MAKES WEAK-NERVED MEN STRONG

Don't Spit

NO-TO-BAC STOPS THIS.

Great Event.

We are now firing our new flint glass bottle furnace, recently completed, the largest in the East. Let your orders come, we can take care of you. Large contracts solicited Remember our New Red Star Oval Prescription, it's a beauty, plain or lettered. The Red Star Tooth Wash Bottle still leads— every live druggist wants it. A beautiful package like a beautiful woman, attracts. Write us.

Red Star Tooth Wash Bottle.

T. C. WHEATON & CO.,
MILLVILLE, N. J.

DR. KENNEDY'S SALT RHEUM OINTMENT,

rrison's Hair Hastener.

A GUARANTEE WITH EVERY BOTTLE.

IT CURES BALDNESS

when not of too long standing, removes dandruff, stops hair from turning gray, and imparts new life and vigor to the glands of the scalp.

WILL SEND FREE

an ample supply of advertising circulars, glass and water-proof signs, etc. For full particulars as to introductory terms, address

The Excelsior Medicine Co., Kalamazoo, Mich.

PHALON'S CHEMICAL HAIR INVIGORATOR

Dr. Kennedy's SALT RHEUM OINTMENT

Cleveland

— GROUP D: FIGURALS, Etc. 441

CHAPTER XVII   FIGURAL BOTTLES

Our final Grand Old American Bottle Grouping deals with the Figurals. These fully depict some individual or object and are distinctly different from Bas-relief faces seen on some early flasks. Of course, a few full figure-moldeds have appeared in perfume and liquor categories; but the rarest of the type are 'whimseys,'—not especially made for commercial use. Avid figure bottle collectors are always writing, "I hear there is a list of 600 known shapes", or "The French are said to have produced over 700 different types": yet the writer has never been able to locate a single published listing! One California collector reports over 300 she has seen or studied (but not always owned) at first hand. Mr. Hubbard reports even more.

These were an outgrowth of the glass industry's insatiable urge to capture a new market for its product. After the mechanized mold blowing was perfected, at the end of the 19th century, bottle designers began trying to see how intricate a mold could be used. So called 'figure' bottles were then designed and patented in large numbers. Some of these glass replicas of Presidents and famous personages were used as whiskey containers; but a far greater number were sold to manufacturers of less stimulating liquids—medicine, soft drinks, household ammonia and sugar syrup. A complete listing of all the Figure bottle mold patents found among U. S. Patent papers is not here warranted. Many such were never made. And of those that did get into production, some found no popular market for their products and so are quite rare. In this section we shall show you some of the fairly common as well as rare figure bottles, mostly made after turn of the century are now classed as collectors items. These bottles usually came in clear, though sometimes in colored glass and were often retained by their original owners after the contents were used up. Mr. Charles Hubbard has made an outstanding study of such bottles and a report on his collection follows this chapter. Here we show typical figure bottles that commemorate some human person of event and the names by which they are identified in the antique trade. The Uncle Sam Bottle is a real find, Moses (Poland Water), African, Victor Hugo, Bob Fitzsimmons, Mexican Madonna, Spanish Americans, Girl in Basket, Coachman, Englishman's Port Bottle, Seaman Port Bottle, Boy on Rooster, George Washington Bud Bottle, Grover Cleveland, Boy-Girl Climbing Tree, Rastus Serving Bottle, Bathing Girl, Monks Cathedral Bottle, Baby Head, Up-ended Nude, Man In the Moon Bottle, and of course, the Indian Queen Bitters Bottle. There are several varieties for some of these bottles for a good thing was often copied.

Figural Bottles, Courtesy Mr. Hubbard

These bottles were often retained by their original owners after the contents were used up. Mr. Charles Hubbard has made an outstanding study of such bottles and a report on his collection follows.

Character Bottles shown on preceding pages reading left to right are usually referred to under the following names, Page 442; Top — Elephant, Trick Dog, Gambetta; Bottom, Garfield, Victor Hugo, Henry Ward Beecher. Page 443: Top—Girl Climbing Tree, Bathing Beauty, 3 Cherubs, Hand Revolver1 ; Hand Whiskey Bottle, Negro Wanted, Old Soldier; Bottom — Sad Hound, Man on Barrel, Miner (Sailor), Washington's Bitters, Budda, Cary Notions and Old Santa Claus. A few more typical examples appear on the next four pages (444-447) (photos courtesy the Holmbergs, Glass Bottle collectors in California). Left to right these list as follows: Grover Cleveland, Webster; Top— 5 Santa Claus Bottles; Bottom — Three Cherubs Holding the Globe, Boy-Girl Climbers, Cherub Holding Clock; Top—Klondyke 4 Nugget Flask, Octopus, Tiny Baby Head, 2 Eye-Openers (all in Milk Glass); Bottom—Revolvers in Hand; Top—2 Clock Bottles. Bottom—Standing Pig, Poodle, Bull Dog and Goat.

The listing above is far from complete and no attempt is made to indicate date of original molding. Especially interesting is the fact that our first bottle (Moses) was an originally designed figure mentioned to carry Poland Water (from a Saratoga Health Spring) became so popular that by the time prohibition arrived, the bottle was often used to carry illegal rum. With the repeal of prohibition, one enterprising distiller hit upon the idea of using the same bottle to house legal gin. All this bottle maker had to do was to get the distillers name stamped in the glass along with that essential notation, "'Federal Law Forbids Sale or Reuse of this Bottle." A perfect facsimile of the original Poland Water Bottle has that notation plus the name of the distiller Hiram Ricker and Sons stamped in the glass. It comes in pint and quart sizes and contained the first legitimate gin on the market after the repeal of prohibition. We wonder how many figure bottle collectors have such an item?

Some Figure Bottle Collectors also include along with those that show actual molded figures those which have a raised figure on side of a more conventional shape, this impressed in the glass. Among such types of commemorative figural we might list the Columbus perfume bottle, John Paul Jones Flask (1901-1905), Statue of Liberty Preserving Jar, Octopus, Silver Dollar Bottle (against silver as coin of realm 1901), the G.A.R., Dewey, and McKinley-Roosevelt Canteens, The Columbian Exposition (1892), and World's Fair (1939) bottles; TVA (Norris Dam Bottle), Jenny Lind, and Washington Calabash type bottle, The Lafayette Preserving Bottle, Peace Bottle of Philadelphia, 1900, and Pan American Bottles 1901,—(Uncle Sam), the General McArthur flask and many others. Those numbered here are shown on accompanying pages and include perfume or salt type such as Columbus, Franklin, General Shafter, etc. Also perfume bottles as the pair which depicts Garfield and the Vice President who ran with him in that campaign.

— GROUP D: FIGURALS, Etc.

Figural Bottles, Courtesy R. Holmberg

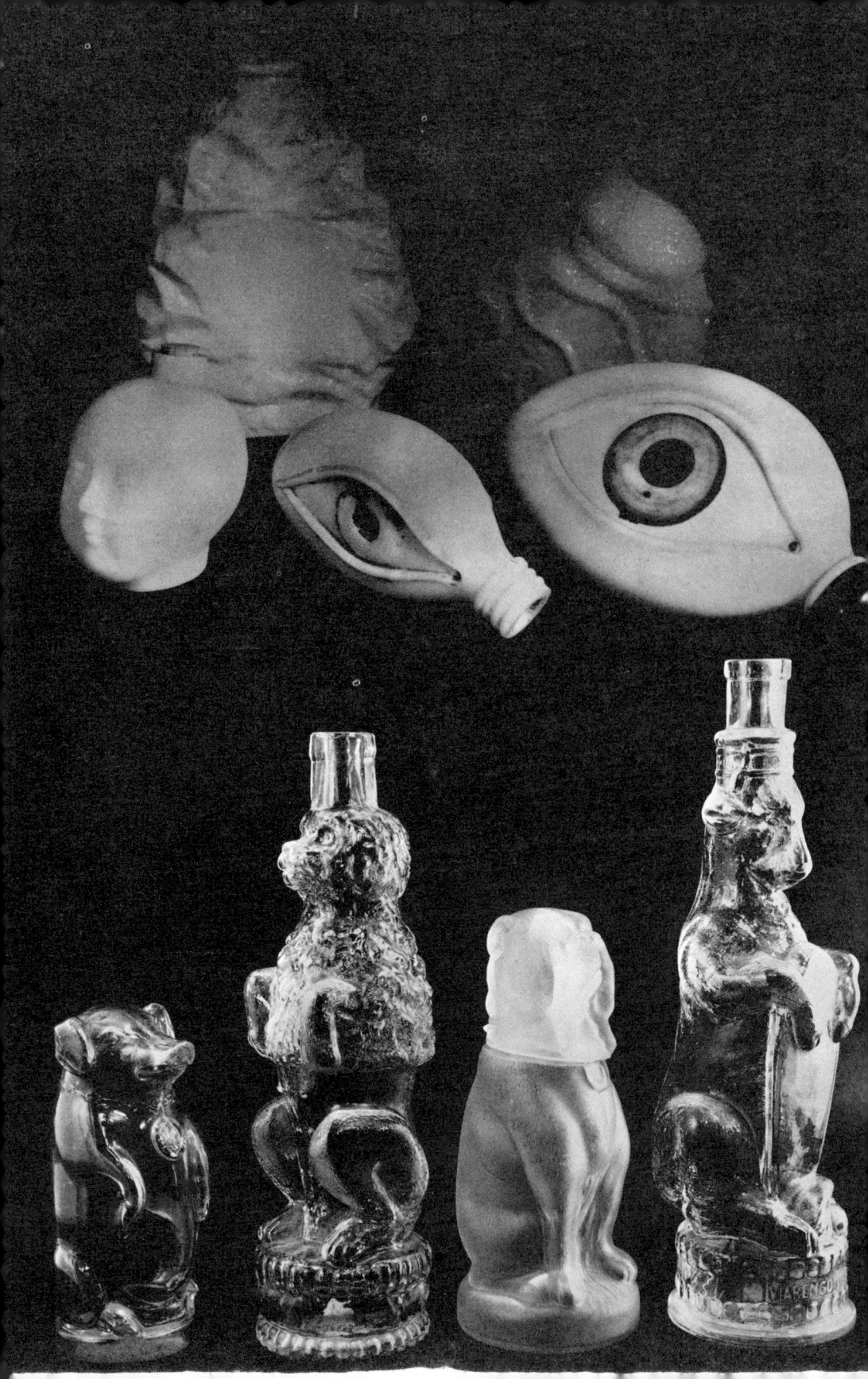

Uncle Sam Bottle

A *clear glass bottle*, nine and one-half inches tall, is molded in the shape of Uncle Sam, the neck of the bottle shaped to represent the tall hat. His left hand grips a musket which stands beside him.

Design, No. 29,331, was patented by George A. Flaccus, of Wheeling, West Virginia, Sept. 13, 1898. The patentee described his design as representing "Uncle Sam — standing in an upright position on a pedestal and wearing a hat."

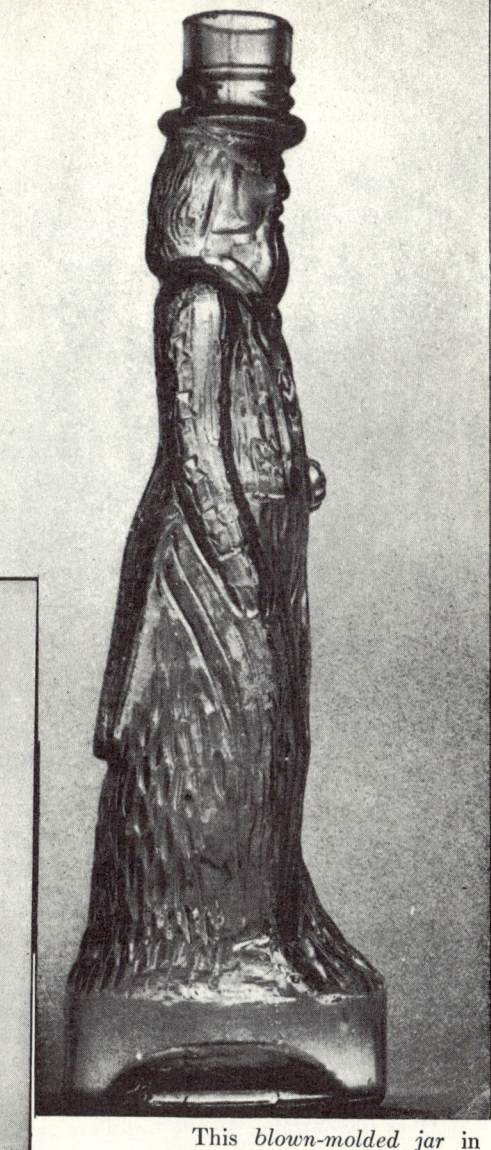

This *blown-molded jar* in clear glass, twelve and one-half inches high, has a design of the Statue of Liberty molded on its side. The lower portion of the jar is molded to simulate the foundation on which the "Lady of Liberty" stands. Beneath the figure is a large American spread eagle.

A *glass bottle* fashioned in the shape of a mail box bears the inscription "Patented Ent. Dec. 15, 1891." On the two sides we find a plain rectangular panel; on the two ends, the inscription "U.S. Mail," and an eagle in flight. It is of quart size and is made of clear glass. The date on the bottle gives information as to about the time it was produced. One can safely conjecture that the occasion for its appearance was to commemorate.

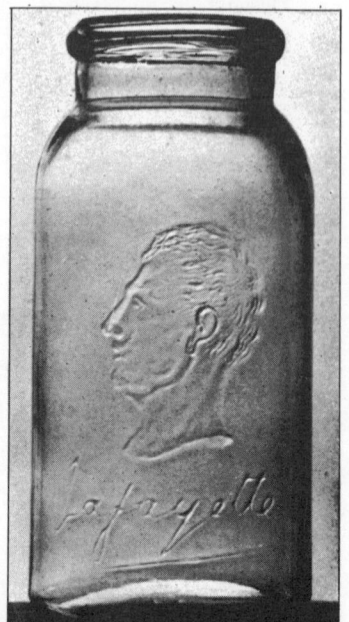

A glass *preserving jar*, in aqua color, has a left-facing profile portrait under which is the name "Lafayette," in script. In this item we find that our early citizens preserved not only food but also memories of one who befriended our nation.

Grant's Tomb Bottle, *Circa 1897*

An opaque white glass *bottle* molded in the shape of Grant's tomb in Riverside Park, New York City, is eight inches tall. It is a rare item. Grant's tomb was built by volunteer contributions of the people, who held the General in high esteem. It was dedicated on his birthday, April 27, 1897. Over the entrance to the tomb are the words, "Let Us Have Peace."

At the dedication ceremonies the oration was delivered by General Horace Porter who had been Aide-de-camp to General Grant (1864–1865).

The formal Roman-style mausoleum, in which General and Mrs. Grant are buried, is on Riverside Drive. It is one hundred sixty-five feet high

A small four ounce *bottle* in milk-white glass is molded to represent an octopus with its eight arms sprawling over both sides of the bottle, molded to simulate an American silver dollar, as though it had a strangle hold on the coin. On the obverse is the head of Liberty and on the reverse the American Eagle under which is the date "1901" molded in the glass.

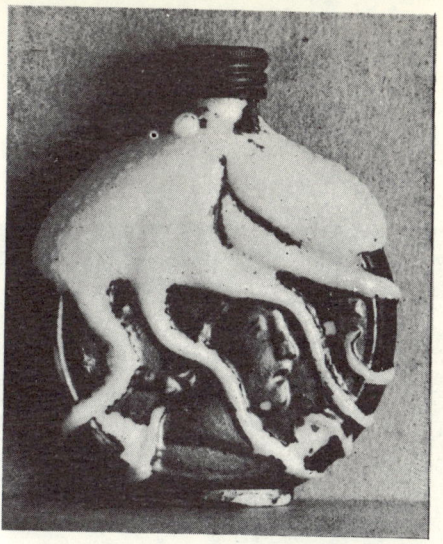

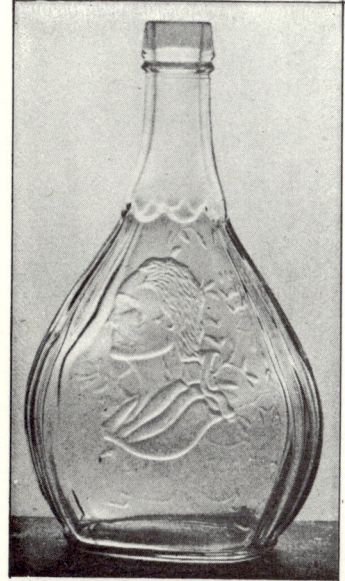

A *calabash bottle*, in clear glass, has a left-facing portrait of Washington on the obverse and a tree on the reverse. Under the tree are the dates "1732–1932," which indicates that it was a bi-centennial commemorative of his birth. This portrait of Washington was made from a medal designed by Charles Cushing Wright.

The tree design on the reverse may refer to the traditional cherry tree, chopped down by the boy Washington, or it may have been intended to represent the Charter Oak of Colonial fame.

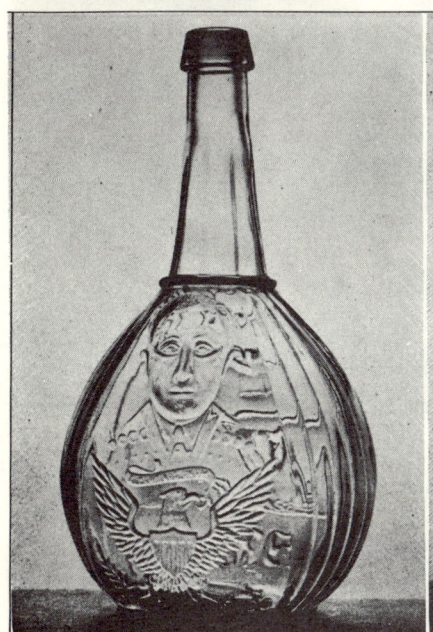

Even electric power is commemorated in glass! Senator George W. Norris.

Frosted Bull Dog, Courtesy F. Holmberg

Some Figure Bottle Collectors also include along with those that show actual molded figures those which have a raised figure on side of a more conventional shape, this impressed in the glass.

— GROUP D: FIGURALS, Etc.

ANIMAL BOTTLES

One can only guess how many different ones can be turned up by the persistent searcher. We picture some of the more common and make no allegations as to date. Of course, the Sandwich Bear (milk glass and actually on old time pomade bottle or jar) would take a collectors first. Many search for the early butterfly bottle, while dogs, squirrels, fish, pigs and cats are also having their day with bottle collectors. Original contents could have been everything from perfumes and unguents to shoe blacking and beetle nut droplets. Pigs have always been a special pet of the animal bottle designers with roosters, fish, squirrels and dogs not far behind. Our numbered picture sampling does not include some of the ultra new Teddy, Piggy and Smokey the Bear bottles which are being sold filled with a concentrated soft drink liquid and whose slitted caps can later be used to make the bottle serve as a Piggy Bank. In fact, we may be on the verge of a whole series of modern animal bottles to help sell food products. If so, you can be sure that bottle collectors will buy a number of unwanted or unneeded products just to have the containers.

Probably the great appeal here, as with all figural bottles, is that there is human interest here for everybody. That is, one does not have to be an old glass specialist or a searcher for historical flask rarities to appreciate the side humor often anthromorphisized in the glass animal for a reverse of this), then when the liquid is gone, turn about and tokens. For instance, why not take a drink from a pigs snout (see page 140 for a reverse of this), then when the liquid is gone, turn about and use it as a bank to hold pennies. By saving the bottle a new collector is often born.

Sandwich Glass Bear Pomade Jars.

U
Liberty

Franklin

Columbus, Head

Dog

• REVOLVER BOTTLE

Rooster

Bear

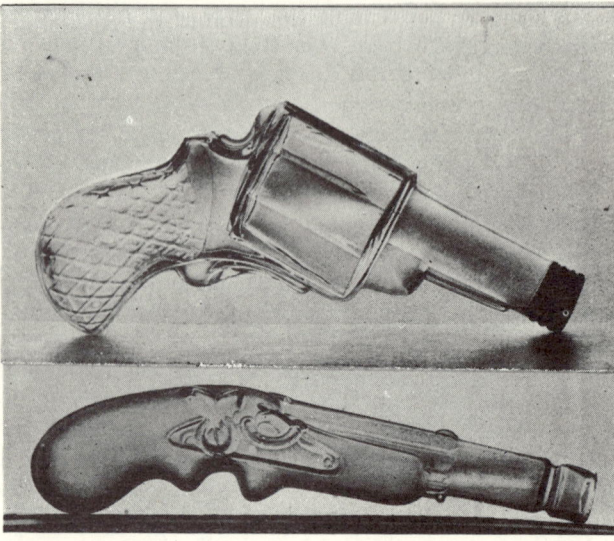

Excelsior • LINDBERGH CANDY CONTAINER

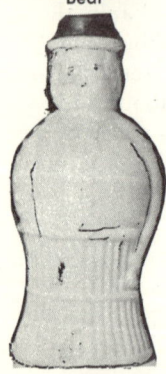
John Bull

Rabbit

Owl,

Space does not permit more than this sample of glass candy containers. Some were also used as Salt Cellars; Cf. Dr. Peterson...

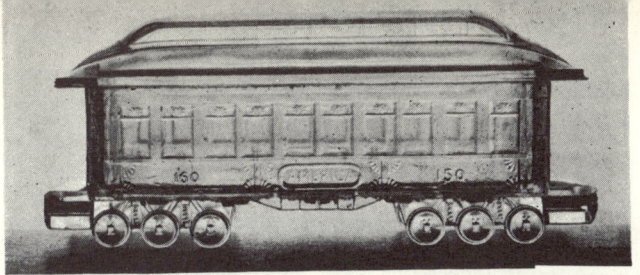

LOCOMOTIVE

A *covered dish* in the shape of an *outmoded locomotive* engine was among the souvenirs purchased at the Chicago World's Fair in 1893. A dish in this design was patented on December 20, 1892, by one D. E. Mapother, of Louisville, Kentucky, and registered in the United States Patent Office as design.

Made by Bellaire Goblet Co., Bellaire, Ohio, Circa 1886

The design was patented by Melvin L. Blackburn, of Bellaire, Ohio, and assigned to the Bellaire Goblet Company, of that city. It is recorded in the United States Patent Office as design No. 16,941, patented October 19, 1886.

Glass Candy Containers, etc., Courtesy T. Marsh

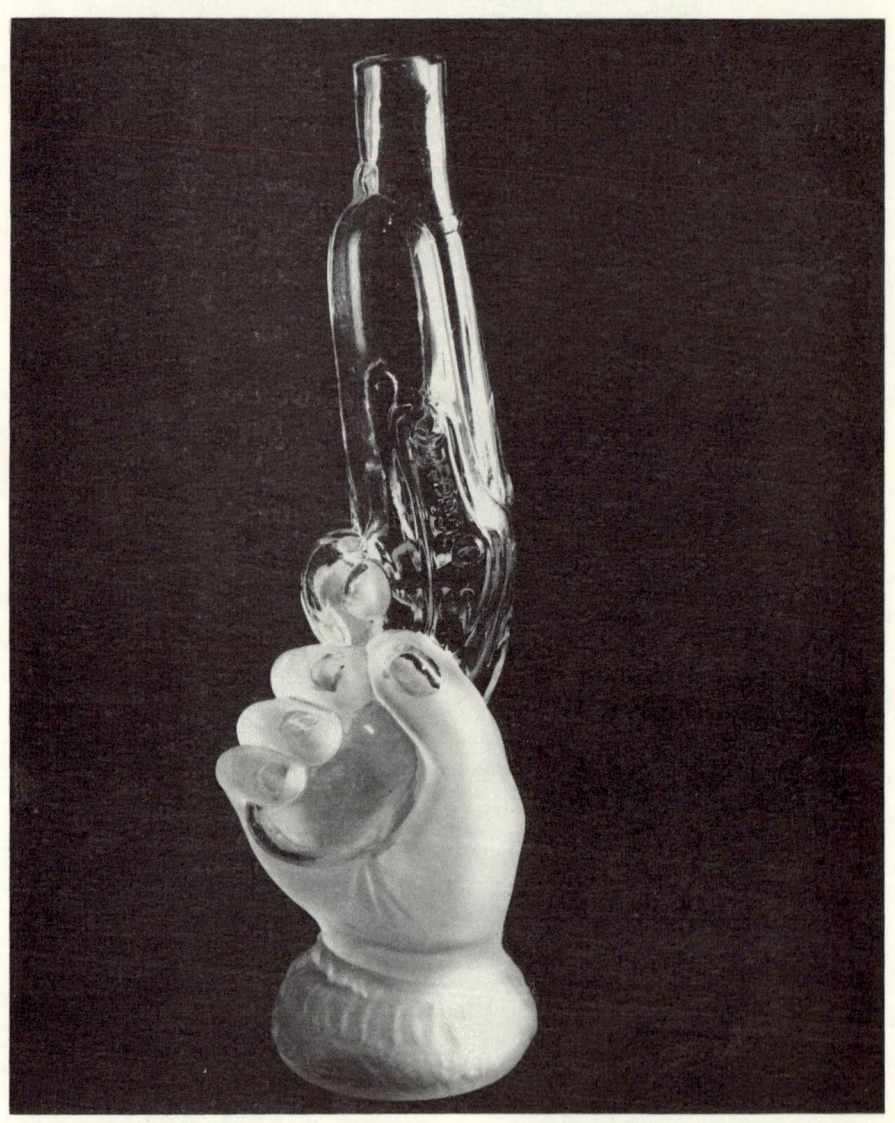

The Pistol Hand Bottle, Courtesy R. Holmberg

There are several varieties for some of these bottles for a good thing was often copied.

— GROUP D: FIGURALS, Etc.

OBJECT BOTTLES, OTHER THAN HUMANS AND ANIMALS

These form about the largest class of mass produced molded forms at turn of the century. Many are easily recognized by name and associated pictures. The more obscure ones probably won't get mentioned in this section. Here we see such old standbys as the Wicker cask, the barrel cask, pretzel and eye opener. Whisk broom, corn, claw, cigar, clam and violin bottles appear in various styles, usually by different makers. The same is true of the Dice, Bellows, Pillar, Cathedral, Bucket, Bullseye and Teardrop bottles. Especial attention should be called to the Mail Box and especially the Clock bottle. The latter is said to have originated with the Bininger Bottle family in 1848. This same bottle and its canteen type replicas was made through the late 19th and early 20th century, is still an old standby for one brand of Prune Juice. A whole chapter could be written on the Bininger products, but that we already covered in discussions of gin and related whiskey bottles. Other object bottle include powder flasks, horn, hand and a number of pistol bottles. Some of the late ones were used as candy containers; the large ones with hand holding pistol could have been for whiskey. So varied is size and make of object bottles that it is hard to identify their original use as containers. Some may have been perfume and medicine, others for varieties of drink. Candy bottles (as shown) form another fascinating sub-area. A fine collection can be made in glass alone; or if one wishes to branch over into pottery bottles *i.e.*, the Bennington Book and Pedlar, that is another beckoning field.

Best loved household collector's bottle was "some say" the Apostles or Monk's Bottle. A plump red-amber bottle decorated with the figures of six monks standing in gothic archways, it was one of the great "mistakes" of modern bottle making, it failed to please the Catholic clergy and was a financial failure to its sponsors who soon discontinued. The writer does not know, but maybe some repros have been made.
There is also a milk glass bottle in shape of the base of the Statue of Liberty, but on none have we seen a cap (might be Statue of Liberty itself is gone); it appears to have been made around turn of the century.

We could tell you many other tales of personality and personage bottles, such as the fact there are several recent ones that are found in food stores. One is the Lincoln (or man with stovepipe hat) that usually holds a juice drink to which one adds water. Another is the Aunt Jemima pancake lady in clear glass; or especially fine in amber glass, Mrs. Butterworth Pancake Syrup. These and many other later character bottles will find their place on collectors shelves. One, like the Monks Cathedral bottle, was designed to please the Priest and did not. What about the Carrie Nation Hatchet bottle, and the one of the sweet old long skirted grandmother clutching an umbrella? Happy hunting in this field, or if that tires you turn to other types of object bottles besides humans.

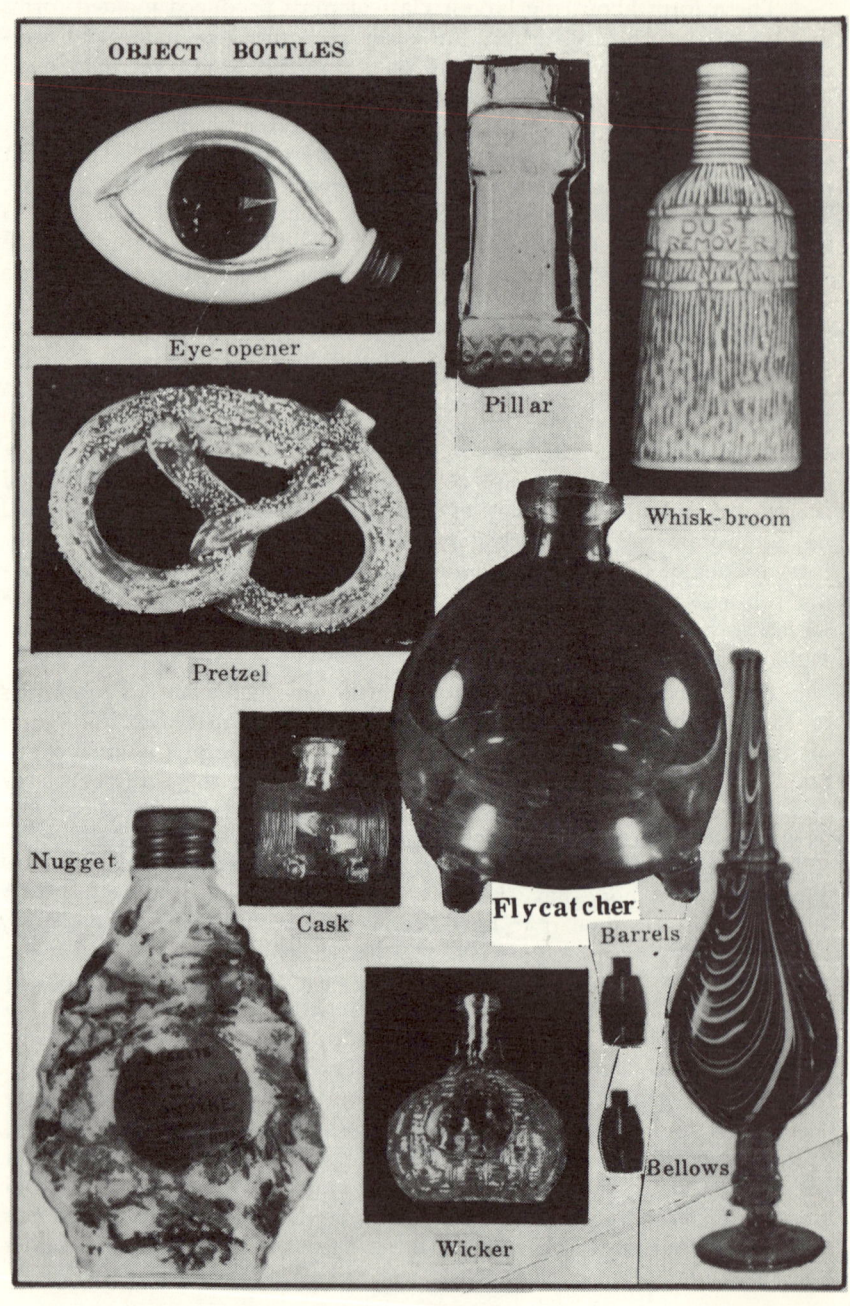

— GROUP D: FIGURALS, Etc.

OBJECT BOTTLES

Christmas Tree and Tall Santa are 12" Figurals

Many other Bottles shown (often perfumes) are much smaller.

— GROUP D: FIGURALS, Etc.

What are the real rarities in Non-Character figural bottle collecting? As the long time expert in this field, Mr. Hubbard, recently said, "The one important thing to be emphasized is that no two people can ever have the same collection. There are so many one of a kind bottles that each collector will obtain something the other fellow never finds."

Just why is that? Well, you might begin by recalling that at the start all figural bottles were glass blowers whimseys—*i.e.*, an offhand shaping of some hot glass gather left at the end of the days toil. Many of these offhand whimseys were a work of art and were carefully preserved by the workman's family or his friends down through generations until dug out by a diligent collector or sold over the auction block. That is why a listing of object bottles such as we picture and number on other pages is only representative. Most of those shown, of course, were produced in some quantity to sell perfume and other products.

THE CLASSIFICATION PROBLEM

By this time the Old Line Collector will have seen enough photographs of figured bottles to realize what an almost hopeless task this field presents to a devotee of check lists. Many years ago Mr. Hubbard of Connecticut proposed to do one but gave up the job as "well-nigh impossible." Mr. Wearin of Iowa has promised for years, but to date it has not appeared. So now the writer comes to grips with the matter and at least tries a rough preliminary "sort." At the end of this chapter is a check-list of several hundred figural bottles which we have been urged to publish 'as is' in the hope later collectors will extend and develop it further. Such a list has been broken down into these 3 categories: (1) Human Characters, (2) Animals and (3) Object Bottles other than Human and Animal Figures. No attempt is made to show the bottles as listed (though many can be easily identified with reference to the photographic pages); also no attempt is made to date or locate glasshouse where made. Within limits, naturally, we will try to indicate which bottles are American and which presumably foreign and show by asterisk which in opinion of collectors like Mr. Hubbard and Mrs. Holmberg are considered "important." Some important glass figure bottles are very rare while others are still fairly common. We are especially indebted to Mrs. Holmberg of The Glass Bottle, Lomita, Cal., for sending us a sample listing of typical Ceramic bottles; and because the figural collector frequently mixes the two mediums, we will add that to the end of the Glass Figure listings. Note: in examining such a checklist one will often find omitted figure bottles that have already appeared in one of our other major groupings, i.e., as Liquors, Medicinals, or Households and usually regarded as belonging there. A true figural should present the full-blown object, not just a raised portrait on some common bottle shape. The next four pages by Collector Hubbard makes the point very clear, while two on Collector Schmidt of California, gives numbered 13 modern examples courtesy Spinning Wheel) in contrast with old ones.

For those with limited funds for collecting, figural bottles offer a wide variety of selection. Even good examples need not be costly, though as any collector advances, the more the rare and unusual pieces tempt purse.

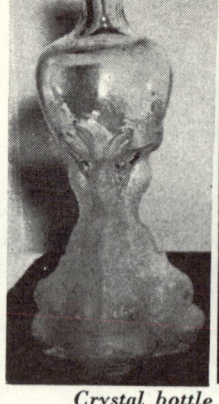
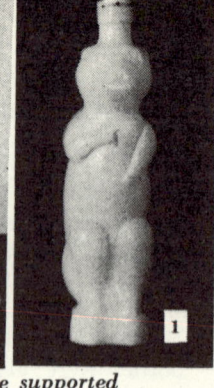

Crystal bottle supported   in camphor glass

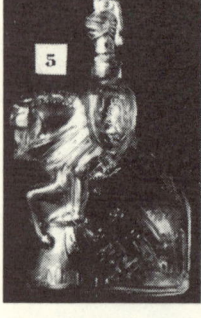

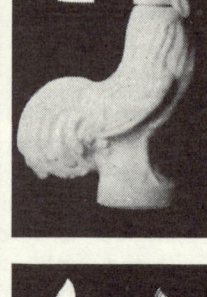

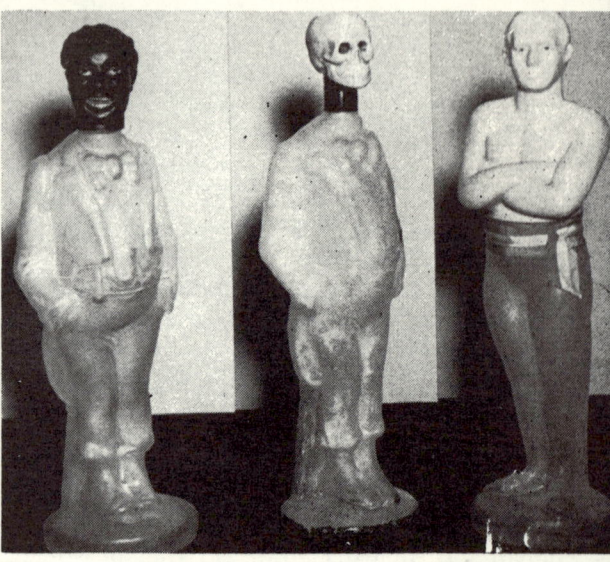

Negro porter, camphor glass body, black amethyst glass head; Skeleton with skull head of bone, camphor glass body; Bob Fitzsimmons, once world heavyweight boxing champion, camphor glass bottom, milk glass top, held liquor.

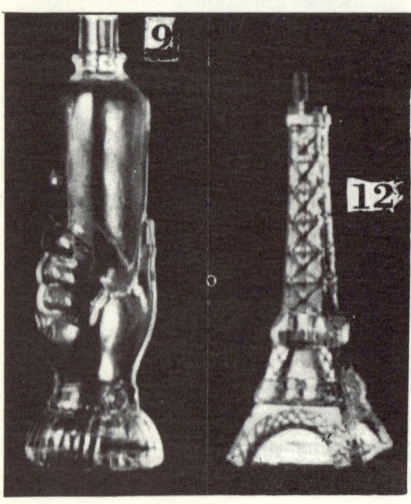

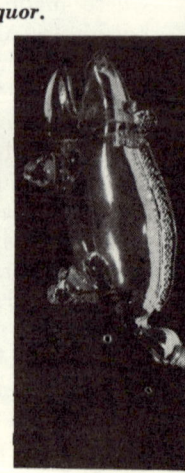

Figural Bottles
collection of Mrs. A. L. Schmidt

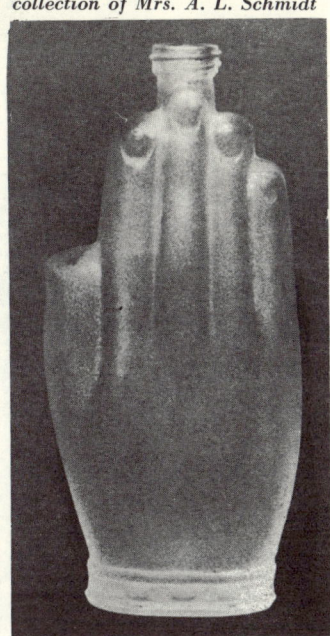

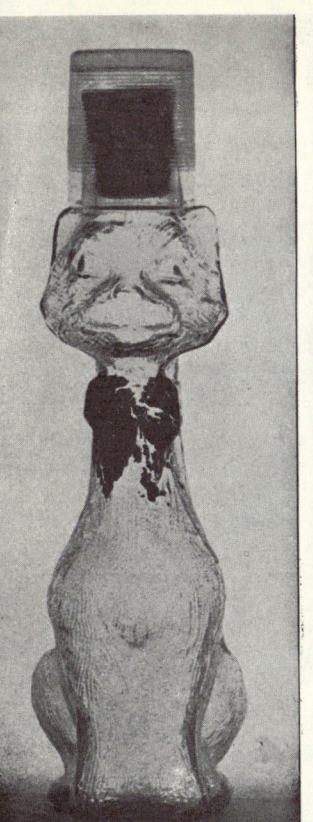

Left, smiling cat, pink glass, painted bow tie, 9" tall with cover, threaded "shot" glass cover fits over cork, unmarked, but known to be a commercial whiskey container. . Frosted hand, 4½" tall, 2" wide, lotion bottle, finger opening, marked on bottom "Pat. 85490. Nov. 10-31".

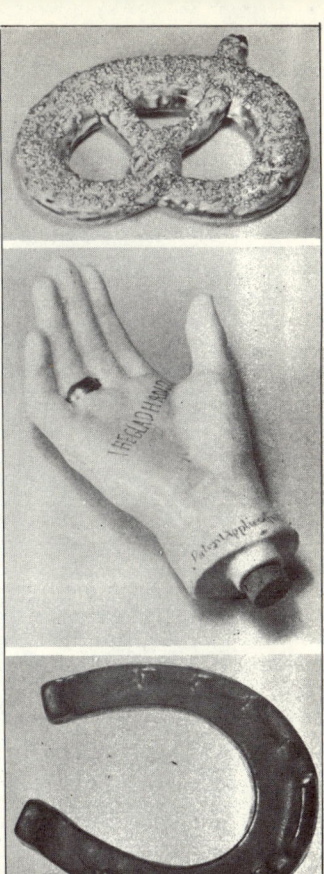

Watchman bottle, dark brown man holds lantern in one hand.

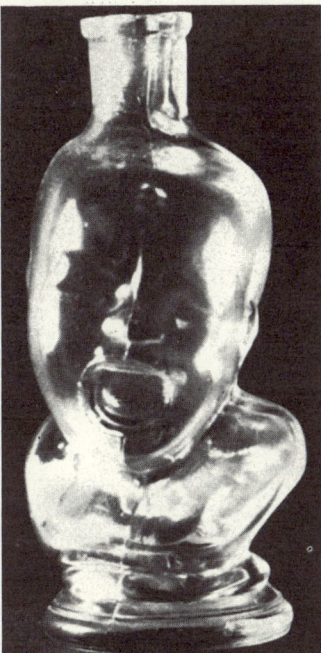

Above: Christmas and New Year greetings were given to holiday customers in many fancy shapes, such as this realistic ceramic pretzel; ceramic Glad Hand, simulated gold ring, neck opening at bottom of wrist, possibly both left and right hands were made; ceramic horse shoe, black finish, neck at back. All are unmarked and of 1890-1900 period. *Left:* Crying baby cologne bottle 6⅛" tall, clear glass, marked on back "Patented June 2nd, 1874" and on extended base "T.P.S. & Co" (T.P. Spencer & Co. of New York). *Below:* Teapot bottle 5" tall; honey-amber glass, applied deep blue-green handle, unmarked, blown-molded in 2-part mold, lid attached, spout forms bottle neck.

There is also a milk glass bottle in shape of the base of the Statue of Liberty, but on none have we seen a cap (might be Statue of Liberty itself is gone); it appears to have been made around turn of the century and is worth further study.

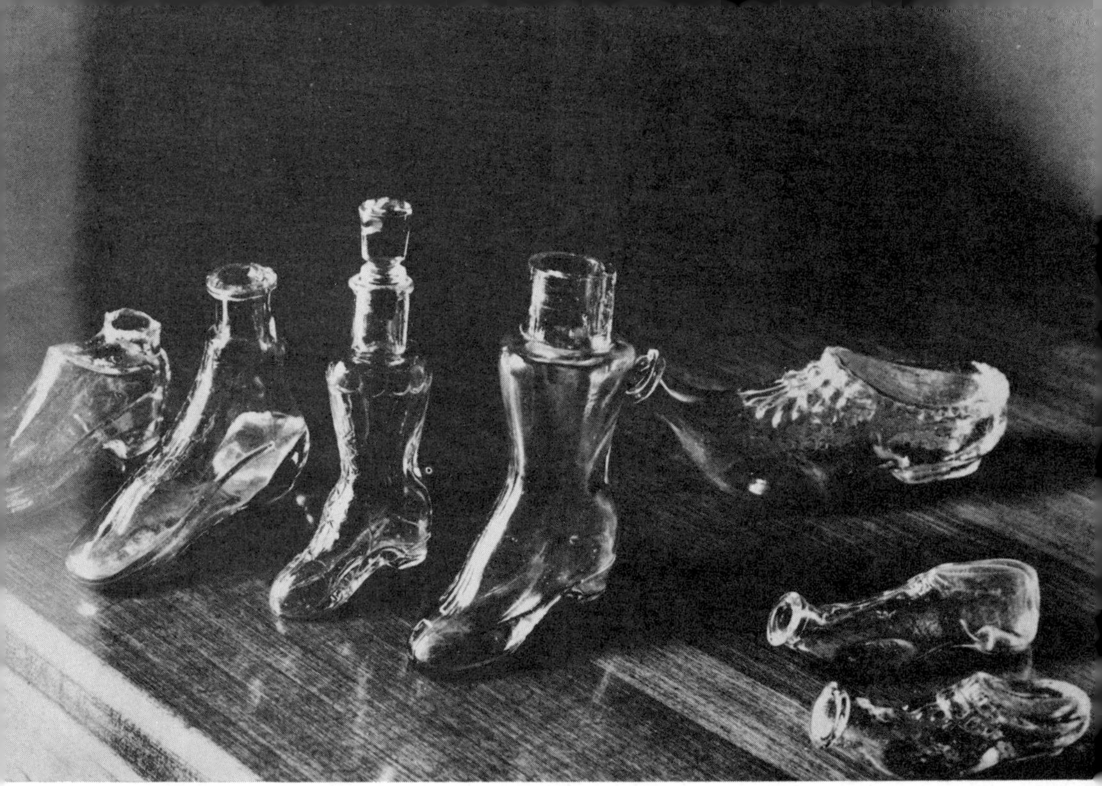

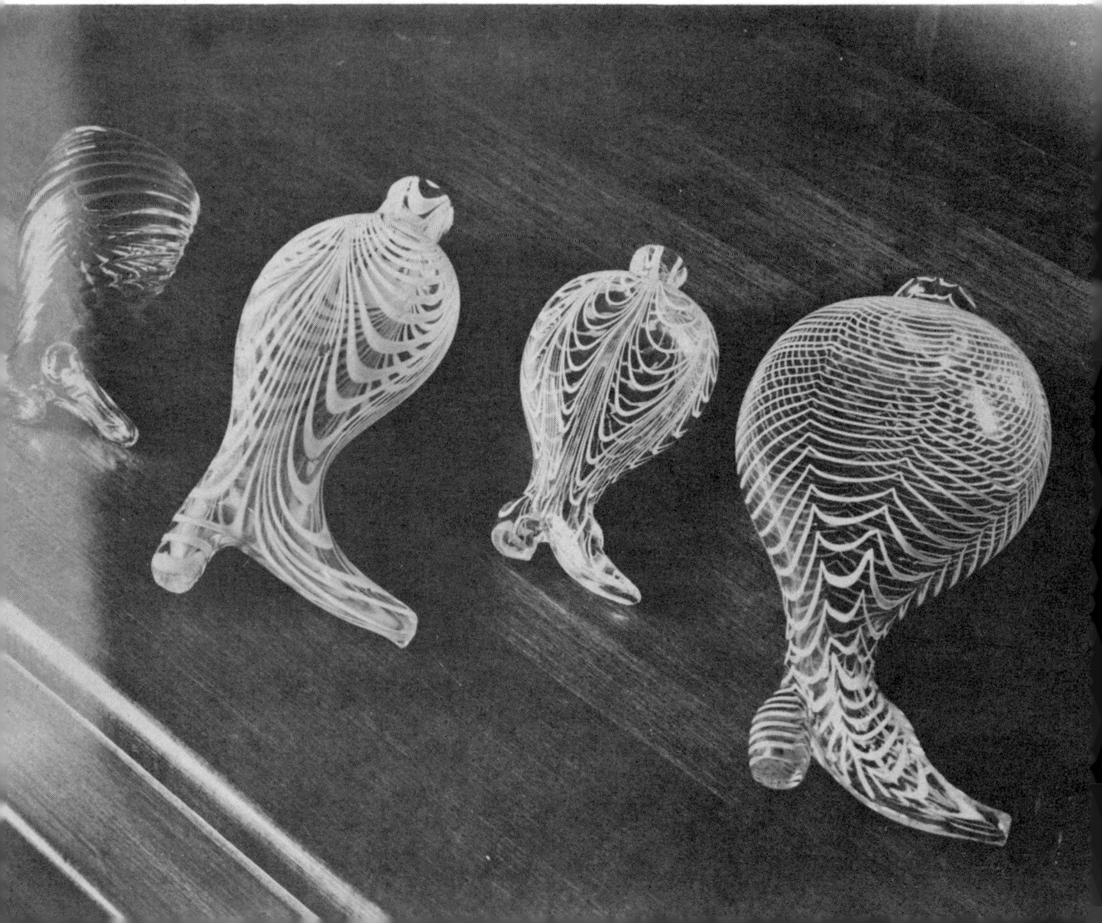

GRAND OLD AMERICAN BOTTLES

— GROUP D: FIGURALS, Etc.

SOME CONCLUDING REMARKS

As we reach the end of our four-type bottle groupings, the writer is acutely aware that much still remains to be done, especially in the figural field. With rarities being the off-hand whimseys never intended for commercial use, the great majority found have had real sales possibilities in mass markets. The field began that way,—is still true today.

Figurals are outgrowth of the glass industries' insatiable urge to capture a new market for its product. While it took a little while for any bottles to be made on these shores, already by 1776 some glass men were oogling the "acorn shaped" bottle brought over by the red-coat soldiers from England and containing Thurlington's Balsam Drink. This was a King's must in every British knapsack and probably the first "all purpose" remedy which hit Colonial America. Good for anything from gunshot wounds to "stomack disorders and general rejuvinator," it carried a patent grant from George the Third. Its container was somewhat later actually reproduced on these shores and some call this the "first figural bottle." Actually, one cannot exactly say who made the first character or figure bottles here—there are just too many of them. Also, an acorn bottle, or "chestnut" if blown, is hardly the figure bottles that one collects today. Instead the vogue now is to find bottles which depict a human character or allegorical figure like Uncle Sam.

Look, for instance, for the full length castings of George Washington, Carrie Nation and Mr. Pickwick, all originally used as vinegar containers selling for ten cents each or the slightly earlier Hessian soldier bottle. Very hard to find is the bust-bottle of Henry Ward Beecher, the great preacher and temperance man, brought out by the liquor interests but soon largely broken up when the Beecher family got hold of mold. But what of the Mersham Pipe and other seeming uniques. Is there a whole series of drug store bottles molded after a stump? Probably! Are there Christmas bottles other than the Santa Claus and Christmas Tree bottles shown? Undoubtedly. Let us close this section of our final bottle group then, with some excerpts from the man who has studied this field most thoroughly, Mr. Hubbard; thereafter move on to the even more fascinating sub field—the collecting of collateral materials, pictures, signs and pamphlets which relate to this and all other forms of bottle.

The thing that suggests itself as we close our account of Grand Old American Bottles is the feeling that it's best days are over—at least for quality commercial productions. The move of packaging experts is towards plastics, and while glass production of simple milk bottles will undoubtedly continue, the commercial figural bottle has had it best run. Only a few of these contoured bottles are being made today—mustard put out in a lighthouse, honey in a bear-shaped bottle, perfume in a chess figure, and *none* of President Kennedy. But just as a full glass whiskey bottle often ruined a man and a glass character bottle often *made* him politically, the collectors of empty bottles are exempt on both scores. So happy hunting with one of the best hobby hunches a man (or woman) could undertake.

PRIMARY CHECKLIST OF FIGURAL BOTTLES

OBJECTS (Ob.) CLASS.—
- Ob. 1. Airplane (Am.)
- Ob. 2. Alarm Clock (Am.)
- Ob. 3. Apple, blown (Am.)
- Ob. 4. Arc de Triumph (For.)
- Ob. 5. Autos, all var. (Am.)
- Ob. 6. Autos, Early Tonneau
- Ob. 7. Balloons, various (Am.)
- Ob. 8. Ball and Cue, Billiard
- Ob. 9. Banjo, various (Am.)
- Ob. 10. Barrels, many (Am.)
- Ob. 11. Basket, Pack (Am.)
- Ob. 12. Basket, Sewing (For.)
- Ob. 13. Bell, School (Am.)
- Ob. 14. Bell, Liberty (Am.)
- Ob. 15. Billy, Policeman (Am.)
- Ob. 16. Binoculars, many (Am.)
- Ob. 17. Bone-shaped, 'poison'
- Ob. 18. Boot, Logger's, clear
- Ob. 19. Milk, Basket of Bottles
- Ob. 20. Bucket (Am.)
- Ob. 21. Building, Empire State
- Ob. 22. Broom, Whisk, various
- Ob. 23. Bunch-Grapes (For.)
- Ob. 24. Bunch, Asparg'us (Am.)
- Ob. 25. Cabins, Log, various
- Ob. 26. Camera (Am.)
- Ob. 27. Canon, various (Am.)
- Ob. 28. Cap, Night (Am.)
- Ob. 29. Car, large 20" (Am.)
- Ob. 30. Carboy, Wicker (Am.)
- Ob. 31. Cello (Am.)
- Ob. 32. Chess Man Set (Am.)
- Ob. 33. Church, Steeple (For.)
- Ob. 34. Clock, Grandfather
- Ob. 35. Cigar, various sizes in clear and amber (Am.)
- Ob. 36. Coal Lump in black
- Ob. 37.*Cologne, nailsea glass Shoe, many varieties
- Ob. 38. Cologne, Shoe (For.)
- Ob. 39. Columbus Column
- Ob. 40. Comb, Honey (Am.)
- Ob. 41. Corn, Ear of, many
- Ob. 42. Crowns, many types
- Ob. 43. Crucible (Am.)
- Ob. 44. Cucumber, blown (For.)
- Ob. 45. Dagger, blown (Am.)
- Ob. 46. Dice (Am.)
- Ob. 47. Dice and Cards (For.)
- Ob. 48. Domino (For.)
- Ob. 49. Drum (Am.)
- Ob. 50. Engine, Fire, light blue (Am.)
- Ob. 51. Engine, Railroad, many
- Ob. 52. Glasses, Opera (For.)
- Ob. 53. Globe of World (Am.)
- Ob. 54. Grapefruit, blown (Am.)
- Ob. 54b Horn, Powder, many sizes (Am.-For.)
- Ob. 55. House, Tin Roof, several sizes, clear (Am.)
- Ob. 56. House with the Mansard Roof (Am.)
- Ob. 57. House, Thatched Roof (Am)
- Ob. 58. Klondyke, Gold Nugget milk glass (Am.)
- Ob. 59. Lamps, Kerosene, various sizes (Am.)
- Ob. 60. Lamp, GWTW (Am.)
- Ob. 61. Lamp Post (For.)
- Ob. 62. Lantern (Am.)
- Ob. 63. Lantern, Railroad, many
- Ob. 64. Lighthouse, several sizes clear and amber (Am.)
- Ob. 65. Lighthouse (For.)
- Ob. 66.*Locomotive, Steam, 12" (For.)
- Ob. 67. Locomotive, Steam, many different, (Am.)
- Ob. 68.*Mailbox, U. S. (Am.)
- Ob. 69.*Man in Moon (For.)
- Ob. 70. Monument, many varieties (Am.-For.)
- Ob. 71*Monument, Baltimore
- Ob. 72. Monument, Bunker Hill milk glass - clear (Am.)

— GROUP D: FIGURALS, Etc. 469

Ob. 73.*Monument, Columbus in Barcelona, Columbus St.
Ob. 74. Orange, blown (Am.)
Ob. 75. Oranges, Pair of (Am.)
Ob. 76. Pail, Full Dinner (Am.)
Ob. 77. Pear, blown (Am.)
Ob. 78. Pear, leaves and handle
Ob. 79. Pillar (Am.)
Ob. 80.*Pineapple Bar Bitters
Ob. 81. Pin, Rolling, various
Ob. 82. Pipe, amber mouth
Ob. 83. Pipe, clear (Am.)
Ob. 84. Pipe, Dutchman (Am.)
Ob. 85. Pipe, Turkish (Am.)
Ob. 86. Pistol, Duelling, blown
Ob. 87. Pistols and Revolvers, too many to list (Am.)
Ob. 88. Potato (Am.)
Ob. 89. Pretzel (Am.)
Ob. 90. Scissors (Am.)
Ob. 91. Shoes, Dutch (Am.)
Ob. 92. Shoe, depression-toe cut
Ob. 93. Shoes, High, many styles
Ob. 94. Shoe, Inkwell (Am.)
Ob. 95. Slippers, many sizes
Ob. 96. Sphinx (Am.)
Ob. 97.*Statue of Liberty, base milk glass (Am.)
Ob. 98.*Statue of Liberty Bottle (Am.-For.)
Ob. 99.*Steeple at Utrickt
Ob. 100. Stove, Parlor (Am.)
Ob. 101. Teapot (Am.)
Ob. 102. Three Sun Flowers Teardrop (Am.)
Ob. 103.*Tomb, Grant's in milk glass and clear (Am.)
Ob. 104. Teardrop (Am.)
Ob. 105. Tower, 3 sided
Ob. 105b. Tower, Eiffel, many
Ob. 106.*Tree, Christmas with Star Stopper, modern
Ob. 107. Tree, Frosted, modern
Ob. 108. Tree, Shell or Pine, modern (Am.)
Ob. 109. Umbrella, blown (Am.)
Ob. 110. Violins, 42 different
Ob. 111. Windmill (For.)

ANIMAL (An.) CLASS.—
An. 1.*Bear's Hair Oil (Am.)
An. 2.*Bear Sitting, Sandwich, Black or White Glass
An. 2.*Bear on Pole Black Glass
An. 3. Bear Sitting, modern painted black or white (Am.)
An. 4. Bear Bank Bottle, 3 sizes (Am.)
An. 5. Bird (Am.)
An. 6. Bird on Rock (Am.)
An. 7. Bull Dog, clear, candy c. (Am.)
An. 8.*Bull Dog, frosted head is stopper (Am.)
An. 9.*Butterfly (Am.)
An. 10. Cat, Smiling, many sizes and colors (Am.)
An. 11. Cat, vaseline (Am.)
An. 12. Canary Bird (?)
An. 13. Common Bug (Am.)
An. 14. Cat, small frosted head on stopper (For.)
An. 15. Cats and Rats (For.)
An. 16. Clam Shell, several sizes (Am.)
An. 17. Claw Holding Egg (For.)
An. 18. Dog with Ribbon (For.)
An. 19. Dog, applied feet and tail (?)
An. 20. Dog, Sitting (Am.)
An. 21. Dolphin (For.)
An. 22. Three Dolphins (For.)
An. 23. Duck, green with applied feet (For.)
An. 24. Duck (For.)
An. 25.*Duck Bottle, Atterbury (Am. Ptd.)
An. 26. Eagle (Am.)

An. 27. Elephant Bank Bottle
An. 28. Elephant, "Old Sol," Amber (Am.)
An. 29.*Elephant with raised Trunk (Am.)
An. 30. Elephant's Head (For.)
An. 31.*Elephant with Palaquin on Back (Am.)
An. 32. Elephant, S t a n d i n g, clear and amber (Am.)
An. 33.*Elk's Tooth, milk glass
An. 34. Fox (Am.)
An. 35. Fox Bank Bottle (Am.)
An. 36. Fox Reading B o o k
An. 37. Fish, Lying Down (Am.)
An. 38.*Fish, blown, non-standing for candy; scales painted (Am.)
An. 39. Fish, Standing on Tail, many Bitters versions
An. 40. Frog (For.)
An. 41. Goat on Haunches
An. 42. Ham Bone, amber (Am.)
An. 43. Horse's Head (For.)
An. 44. Humpty-Dumpty Bank Bottle (Am.)
An. 45. Kitten in Shoe (Am.)
An. 46. Kitten Bank Bottle
An. 47. Krazy Kat (For.)
An. 48. Lizards Climbing Tree
An. 49. Lobster (For.)
An. 50. Monkey (Am.)
An. 51. Monkey Climbing Bottle (Am.)
An. 52.*Octopus Grasping Gold Dollar, milk glass (Am.)
An. 53. Oyster Shell (Am.-For.)
An. 53a. Owl, many sizes (Am.-For.)
An. 54. Parrots (For.)
An. 55. Pelican, milk glass and clear (For.)
An. 56.*Peacock, 2 sizes (For.)
An. 57. Penguin Bank Bottle
An. 58. Pig, Bitters (Am.)

An. 59. Pig (Am.)
An. 60.*Pig. "Good Old Bourbon in a Hog's Hole" (Am.)
An. 61. Pig Sitting Up, opening in base (Am.)
An. 62. Piggy Bank (Am.)
An. 63. Poodle Sitting Up, large, clear (For.)
An. 64. Poodle, Standing (For.)
An. 65. Puss-in-Boots (For.)
An. 66. Rooster, head is stopper
An. 67. Rooster and Egg on Nest
An. 68. Rabbit, frosted - pink, cork in tail (For.)
An. 69. Rabbit (Am.)
An. 70. Roast Turkey (Am.)
An. 71. Reindeer (Am.)
An. 72. Snail (For.)
An. 73. Sad Hound, many sizes and colors (Am.)
An. 74. Scallop Shell (For.)
An. 75.*Shampoodle H o l d i n g Drum (Am. Ptd.)
An. 76. Sunfish (For.)
An. 77. Turkey Claw on Ball
An. 78. Turkey (Am.)
An. 79. Turtle, clear and amber
An. 80. Walrus (Am.)

HUMAN (Hu) CLASS.—
Hu. 1. Acrobat Standing on Head, several varieties
Hu. *2. Apostle Bottle, in panels (Am.)
Hu. 3. Aunt Jemima (Am.)
Hu. 4.*Bather on Rocks (For.)
Hu. 5.*Baby Crying (Am.)
Hu. 6. Baby Stuart (For.)
Hu. 7. Beau Pup (Am.)
Hu. 8.*Billikin, clear and milk glass (Am.)
Hu. 9. Bootmaker (For.)
Hu. 10. Boy with Cornucopia
Hu. 11. Boy on Velocipede
Hu. 12. Boer Soldier (For.)

— GROUP D: FIGURALS, Etc.

Hu. 13. Budda, amber headdress (Am.)
Hu. 14. Small Budda, frosted
Hu. 15. Busts of the following:
   Abraham Lincoln
   *Theodore Roosevelt
Hu. 16.*Alphonse XII of Spain (For.)
Hu. 17.*Henry Ward Beecher
Hu. 18. Hattie Carnegie (Am.)
Hu. 19.*Calvin Coolidge (Am.)
Hu. 20. DeWitt Clinton (Am.)
Hu. 21. Admiral Dewey (Am.)
Hu. 21b.*Grover Cleveland, 9½"
Hu. 22. Dr. Granger, connoisseur of etchings, 6½"
Hu. 23a.*Webster (Am.)
Hu. 23. James Garfield (Am.)
Hu. 24.*Gen. U. S. Grant (Am.)
Hu. 25.*G e o r g e Washington (Centennial Bitters) (Am.)
Hu. 26. G e o r g e Washington modern reproduction, also small Cobalt (Am.)
Hu. 27. Gen. Gambetta (For.)
Hu. 28. Gallileo (For.)
Hu. 29.*Jenny Lind, P. T. Barnum Bust Bottle (Am.)
Hu. 30.*Louis Kossuth (For.)
Hu. 31. Mazzantini, bust in high relief; also full body (For.)
Hu. 32.*Bob Fitzsimmons (Am.)
Hu. 33. Victor Emmanuel
Hu. 34. Victor Hugo (For.)
Hu. 35. Bust of Woman, wooden base (For.)
Hu. 36. Bust of Queen, wooden base (For.)
Hu. 37. Bust of Courtier, wooden base (For.)
Hu. 38.*Boy-Girl Climbing Tree various sizes (For.)
Hu. 39. Clown, various sizes (For.)

Hu. 40. Clown Bank Bottle (Am.)
Hu. 41. Chinaman (?)
Hu. 42. Seated Chinaman
Hu. 43.*Carrie Nation Standing viniger (Am.)
Hu. 44. Columbia (Am.)
Hu. 45.*Czar Nicholas II, 17" base opening (For.)
Hu. 46.*Cherubs (3) Holding Globe (For.)
Hu. 47. Charlie Chaplin (For.)
Hu. 48.*Cherub with Horn of Plenty (Am.)
Hu. 49. Cherub Holding Clock (For.)
Hu. 50. Draped Nude with Horn (For.)
Hu. 51. Dressmakers T o r s o Form (For.)
Hu. 52.*Van Dunck's Coachman (Am.)
Hu. 53. Elizabeth Arden, frosted portrait, 2 modern
Hu. 54. Egyptian on D r u m (For.)
Hu. 54a. Eye Opener, milk glass, (Am.)
Hu. 55. Foot on Hassock (For.)
Hu. 56. Feed the Baby (Am.)
Hu. 57. Francuelo (For.)
Hu. 58. Fisherman (For.)
Hu. 59. Frosted Sailor, small
Hu. 60. Golliwog, several sizes, frosted (Am.)
Hu. 61. Girl with Muff (Am.)
Hu. 62. Girl with Umbrella
Hu. 63. G e o r g e Washington, standing, regular (Am.)
Hu. 64. Head of Gypsy (For.)
Hu. 65. Hummel Figure Pair, modern, frosted (For.)
Hu. 66. Hessian Soldier (Am.)
Hu. 67. Hearts, too many varieties to try to list (Am.-

Hu. 68. Hand Holding Bottle (For.)
Hu. 69. Hand Holding Small Bottle For.)
Hu. 70. Hand Holding Gun. Many varieties (For.)
Hu. 71. Hand Holding Torch
Hu. 72. Hand Holding Mirror
Hu. 73. Hand Only, C. & F.
Hu. 74. Hand Palm Down (For.)
Hu. 75. Hand Holding Vase (For.)
Hu. 76.*Napoleon's Tomb(Figure stopper) (For.)
Hu. 77. Napoleon (For.)
Hu. 78. Indian Papoose (Am.)
Hu. 79.*Italian Royal Family, 3 on pedestal (For.)
Hu. 80. Indian Maid, frost. (?)
Hu. 81.*Joseph Smith on Barrel (Am.)
Hu. 82. *Joan of Arc, 13½" (For.)
Hu. 83. Joan of Arc on Horseback (For.)
Hu. 84. Joan of Arc at Stake (For.)
Hu. 85. Knight on Horseback, several colors and sizes (For.)
Hu. 86. Lady of Alsace (For.)
Hu. 87. Lady of Fatima (Am.)
Hu. 88. Lady of Lourdes (Am.)
Hu. 89. Lady of Guadalupe (Am.)
Hu. 90. Lady of Lorraine (For.)
Hu. 91. Lincoln Bank Bottle (Am.)
Hu. 92. Lafayette (For.)
Hu. 93. Matador (For.)
Hu. 94. Man Astride Barrel (For.)
Hu. 94b. Man Sidewise on Barrel (For.)

Hu. 95. Moses in Bullrushes, or Baby on Cabbage Leaf (Am.)
Hu. 96-99. Norris, Washington, Lafayette, Liberty (see page 450.)
Hu. 100. Mikado, shoe blacking, amber (Am.)
Hu. 101.*Moses, Poland Water Bottle (Am.)
Hu. 102. *Mr. Pickwick Standing vinegar (Am.)
Hu. 103 Mermaid (For.)
Hu. 104. Madonna and Child, 6" base opening (For.)
Hu. 105 *Noble Catcher, early ball player (Am.)
Hu. 106. Naughty Boy of Brussels
Hu. 107.*Principee Aelena (For.)
Hu. 108 *Small Baby Head, milk glass (Am.)
Hu. 109. *Uncle Sam (Am.)
Hu. 110. *Rebecca at Well, several sizes, clear and frosted (Am.-For.)
Hu. 111. Sailor (For.)
Hu. 112. Soldier (For.)
Hu. 113.Toby (For.)
Hu. 114.*Santa Claus; at least 5 different varieties (Am.-For.)
Hu. 115. Saints and Sinners
Hu. 116. Shriner (Am.)
Hu. 117. Tree Trunk with 3 children about (For.)
Hu. 118.*Tree Trunk with Dog and Goat at Base, Children Climbing (Am.)
Hu. 119. Waiter, frosted, black face (Am.)
Hu. 120. Waitress, frosted, black face (Am.)
Hu. 121. Woman's Torso in Corset, several sizes (For.)
Hu. 122. Woman's Torso (For.)

— GROUP D: FIGURALS, Etc.

CERAMIC (Ce.) FIGURALS
Ce. *1. Pretzel
Ce. 2. Hot Tamale
Ce. 3. Roast Chicken
Ce. 4. Majolica Cucumber
Ce. 5. Majolica Ear of Corn
Ce. 6. Loaf of Bread
Ce. 7. Hot Dog
Ce. 8. Apple
Ce. 9. Orange
Ce. 10. Pomegranate
Ce. 11. Dagger with stag handle
Ce. 12. Monkey on Potty
Ce. 13.*Bennington Coachman
Ce. 14.*Bennington Man on Barrel, several variations
Ce. 15.*Bennington Book, several
Ce. 16. Other Books, many
Ce. 17. Bennington Boots
Ce. 18. Depression Shoe, several
Ce. 19.*Duke of York, English Portrait
Ce. 20.*Queen Victoria, English
Ce. 21.*Queen Elizabeth, English
Ce. 22.*William IV, English
Ce. 23.*Lord Chesterfield, Eng.
Ce. 24.*Lord Russell, English
Ce. 25.*Sir William Pitt, Eng.
Ce. 26. Traveling Pistol
Ce. 27. Banana
Ce. 28. Old Crow
Ce. 29. Raven, held Tequila
Ce. 30. Skeleton in Sheet, sev.
Ce. 31. Dutch Boy
Ce. 32. Dutch Girl
Ce. 33. Hillbilly, Hatfield
Ce. 34. Hillbilly, McCoy
Ce. 35.*Large Key
Ce. 36.*Horseshoe
Ce. 37. Pipe
Ce. 38. Violin
Ce. 39. Elephant
Ce. 40. Donkey
Ce. 41.*Glad Hand, many var.
Ce. 42. Delft shoe
Ce. 43. Delft Houses, many var.
Ce. 44. Granfather's Clock
Ce. 45. Venus de Milo, 2 sizes
Ce. 46. Spanish Don, Royal Doulton, 2 sizes
Ce. 47. Monk, many variations
Ce. 48. German Tourist
Ce. 49. Majolica Cat with fish
Ce. 50. Majolica Girl standing
Ce. 51. Bartender, some **old ones**
Ce. 52. Madonna, various
Ce. 53. Elk's Tooth
Ce. 54. Barrels, many types
Ce. 55. Wolf
Ce. 56. Rooster
Ce. 57. Cabin, many
Ce. 58. Canteen
Ce. 59. Barmaid, bisque, etc.
Ce. 60. Bisque Bust of Woman
Ce. 61 Totem Pole
Ce. 62. Drunkard
Ce. 63. Old Hickory
Ce. 64. Japanese Lady
Ce. 65. Poodle
Ce. 66. Owl (one with music)
Ce. 67. Staffordshire Cat
Ce. 68. Staffordshire Fish
Ce. 69. Mr. Carter Ink
Ce. 70. Mrs. Carter Ink
Ce. 71 Money Sack
Ce. 72. Tobacco Pouch
Ce. 73. Whiskbroom, Dust Pan
Ce. 74. Majolica Rabbit
Ce. 75. Man with Pear
Ce. 76. Scotchman
Ce. 77. Duck
Ce. 78. Pheasant
Ce. 79. Dog, Garnier
Ce. 80. Clenched Fist
Ce. 81. Man's Hand, bisque
Ce. 82. Lemon
Ce. 83. Frog
Ce. 84. Pig, innumerable
Ce. 85. Giraffe
Ce. 86. Football
Ce. 87. Barrel Cactus
Ce. 88.*Kilted Scotsman

Spring Physick.
Dr. Dyott's Anti-Bilious Pills,
Which prevent and cure Bilious Complaints Malignant Fevers, &c. &c.

THE numerous known cures performed by these Pills has induced the inventor, at the solicitation of the many respectable citizens who have all experienced their beneficial and salutary effects, to make them publick for the good of mankind in general.

If timely administered they will surely counteract the causes which commonly produce the Yellow or the Bilious Fever, the Ague and Fever, Bilious Cholick, Pleurify, Dysentery, Worms, Bilious vomiting, Sick and Foul Stomach, Loss of Appetite, Flatulency Epileptick Fits, Hypochondria and Hysterical Complaints, Indigestion, Habitual Costiveness, Colds and Coughs, Asthma, Stranguary, Gravel, Rheumatism and Gout.

Also, an effectual cure for the scurvy, surfeit, scorbutick blotches, and for carbuncles—and all impurities in the blood yield to their happy effects, whether proceeding from constitutional ailment, or arising from indiscreet intemperance.

They are an infallible medicine for Female Complaints generally, and especially for removing those obstructions which are the source of their ailments at certain periods—they possess the eminent advantage over most other purgatives, that while they operate gently, they produce neither costiveness, debility, or too great excitement.

And whenever there is predisposition to receive disease from marsh effluvia or from a too copious use of ardent spirits, or from a vitiated state of the bile, these Pills will surely counteract it.

They are highly recommended to travellers by sea or land, and may be made use of with safety without change of diet, and in situations where no exercise can be used. They will be found particularly valuable for preventing diseases incidental to hot climates; they deterge and cleanse viscid humours, open obstructions, and promote the secretion of good bile, operate as an easy cathartick, as a powerful diuretick, and as a diaphoretick.

DR. DYOTT here, under the strong conviction of the power of his Pills to relieve the afflicted, when other medicines have failed, recommends the use of them (at least once a fortnight) during the spring and summer months, in which he feels assured that those who attend to his advice will find the benefit they seek.

Directions for using the Pills.

For a purge, from three to six pills are to be taken at bed time or early in the morning which may be done as often as the state of the body or circumstances may require; warm gruel, barley water, or any diluted liquids may be drank to aid their operation.

Children under one year old may take from half to a whole pill; those of two years, from one to one and half, and in proportion as they advance in years.

In weak and debilitated constitutions, female complaints, and in chronick disorders, they are to be used as an alternative medicine, and then taken by one pill at night, if the constitution can bear it, till six or seven pills have been taken; and then three or four pills must be taken as a purge—thus continuing the alterative and the purge, till the obstructions are removed and the desired relief obtained.

For the scurvy, surfeit, scorbutick blotches, and for carbuncles, &c. and impurities of the blood, or vitiated humours a full dose of these pills must be taken every three or four days; at the same time Dr. Robertson's much esteemed *Vegetable Nervous Cordial*, or *Nature's Grand Restorative*, may be taken according to the directions with good effect, as it will not only aid the cure, but prevent a return of any scorbutick complaint.

The female of the most delicate frame, or the infant, may take these pills with the greatest safety, their composition being perfectly innocent.

The price of the above pills is *fifty cents* per box—small boxes *twenty five cents*, with a very liberal discount to those who purchase to sell again, or for family use, purchasing not less than one dozen boxes.

Take Notice—Each genuine box of the above Pills is signed by the only Proprietor. His signature is on a piece of paper, pasted on the outside wrapper. None other can be depended on.

T. W. DYOTT, M. D.

Sold in Philadelphia, only by the Proprietor, at his Wholesale Drug and Medicine Warehouse, N. E. corner of Second and Race streets.

March 24   tf

Approved Plaster Cloth,
T. W. DYOTT, M. D.
Successour to Bouchony Lordenet, the late approved Preparer of this valuable Plaster.

Sold Wholesale and Retail in Philadelphia, only at the Proprietor's Drug and Family Medicine Warehouse, northeast corner of Second and Race streets; and retailed by his appointed agents throughout the United States.

Qualities of Mahy's Plaster.

THIS Plaster Cloth, so well known throughout the United States—and more generally in the City of Philadelphia, where its beneficial effects and surprising cures have procured for it the approbation and recommendation of the most eminent of the faculty.

It is a sure and safe remedy for Ulcers and sores, either fresh or of long durance—it stays, and prevents Gangrenes, and by a timely application will *preserve* many a *valuable life and limb*.

In cases of inveteracy of Ulcers, or a proneness of the affected parts to mortify (or Gangrene) it will be advisable for the unfortunate sufferer to resort to the use of some gentle purgative for a few days previous to using the Plaster, and continue the same till a cure is completed, which may be confidently expected in a reasonable time. No purgative more proper than Dr. Dyott's well known Anti-Bilious Pills.

The Matengers of the negroes, is ranked under the denomination of Ulcers; this valuable Plaster is also a certain cure for it, if the same treatment as above made be observed.

Cancers, erysipelas, wens, scrophula, fistula, white swelling, sore breasts, felons, whitlows, and bites are removed, and cure happily produced, by the use of this valuable Plaster.

It removes Abscesses and dissipates collected humours, it also cures Sprains, Bruises, Anthrax, Scalds Burns and all Sores and Wounds, tending to suppurate; it draws cauterized sores or Issues very successfully and without pain. It dissipates distressing pain from Gout or Rheumatism in a very short time, and is a safe and certain cure for Rheumatism and flying Rheumatick Pains, if the Plaster is constantly applied to the affected part for six or eight months by the application the parts affected become invigorated and a cure seldom fails to be completed—it is also successfully used for the cure of Corns.

Those useful men, Mariners, should never be without Mahy's valuable Plaster Cloth; it keeps any length of time equally good, and is particularly calculated to dry sores arising from green wounds, after they are suppurated, which it much aids. It is necessary it should be kept dry.

Manner of using Mahy's Plaster Cloth.

The Sore or Wound must be first well cleansed by washing it with luke warm water or milk, a piece of Plaster large enough to cover it completely, must be applied, and covered with a dry rag or Patent Lint (lint is best) the sore should be dressed twice a day, and washed clean with luke warm water. The plaster must be wiped clean of pus; either side of the Plaster may be used.

For the Gout or Rheumatism, Pains in the Limbs and White Swellings, a piece of plaster sufficiently large to cover the parts affected must be used, and changed once in six or eight days.

For Corns on the Toes—The Corn must be cut down close with a penknife, covered with plaster, renewed every three days, and the Corn every time cut or rooted out.

For a Fistula—The plaster must be rolled up in the form of a pipe, and introduced into the anus or fundament—a piece of thread fastened to it, in order to withdraw it when necessary.

For Abscess or Bile—Keep some plaster on till suppuration—wash the sore as before directed, wipe the plaster clean and reapply it.

For a large Green Wound—Stop the bleeding in the usual way; fill the cavity of the wound with lint, first free it from foreign matter, do this for a day or two, after which the plaster only must be used as before described; should the cavity of the wound be very deep, do not use lint, but roll the plaster into a form to fill the wound, and cover it with a flat piece of plaster.

TAKE NOTICE, each Genuine Plaster is signed by the only Proprietor; his signature is on a piece of paper, pasted on the folding wrapper. None other can be depended on.

T. W. Dyott, M. D.

Feb. 1—f

CHAPTER XVIII   COLLATERALS

BOTTLE COLLATERALS COLLECTING

When one is first caught by the fascination of empty bottles or their decorative use in home windows, he is not likely to think of anything else except the need to find more and different colors or shapes to the container he wants to collect. But after a spell of hunting for rarities and showing his collection off for admiring friends, it begins to dawn on him that unless he knows something of a bottle's use and history he is losing half the fun of it all. So he begins to acquire signs, pictures, pamphlets and beyond advertising placques which detect how his bottles were originally made, sold or distributed. And thus there has grown up a whole new field of association material—the contemporary collaterals of the Historical Flasks period. Medicinal advertising of the Bitters and Puritanical Tipplers era. Signs once hung in saloons, drug stores and other places where euphoric alcoholic concoctions, perfumery, candy and household needs were dispensed via attractive glass bottles. Here is the fun and fact galore. Soon the enthusiastic collateral collector has his own bar or hobby room with walls adorned with material such as shown in this final section, soon, too, his friends want samples of the testimonial where the Rev. Dr. McGregor extolls "Duffy Pure Malt Whiskey" as his personal life preserver. Even if not an ardent bottle collector, any American with the time and taste for nostalgia will get a bang out of thumbing this section. The writer's Yorker Yankee Old Village Museum has this material in quantity and often sells some of it to visitors along with an occasional duplicate empty bottle. The thing to do is get started now, before all such ephemera is either destroyed or tucked away in "father's private den."

PICTORIAL ASSOCIATION MATERIAL

For bottle collectors who are stimulated to a search for advertising materials and pictures of the old-time medicine shows, such collaterals will provide a wealth of entertainment, information and a large assortment of memorabilia. This includes the almanacs, pictures, brochures, pamphlets and temperance exhortations as shown on pages which follow. But with all this fun about Selling Euphoria, one should not forget the most important records of all, namely those showing the long and finally successful struggle of the Government to assess upon the proprietary medicine dispensers a Pure Drug Code and a proper Revenue Tax.

MY PIOUS FRIENDS AND DRUNKEN COMPANIONS Frank Shay

Ballads of Conviviality

The Female Smuggler
Fill the Flowing Bowl
The Foggy, Foggy Dew
Get Away, Old Man, Get
I Wish I Was Single Again
I'll Give My Love a Cherry
I've Been Workin' on the Railroad
Je Donnerais Versailles
Jesse James
Jim Fisk, Jr.
Little Brown Jug
Mademoiselle from Armentiers

"There was a period, not so long gone, a time contemptuously called Victorian, but which is now receiving the favorable attention of our most advanced historians, when we rose to the heights of tipple and song. It was our nearest approach to urbanity, a time when we sang and drank and danced, though we did all three quite badly. Like all drinkers, we were good fellows when we had it . . ."

Frank Shay wrote these words some 30 years ago, in the midst of Prohibition, but they still hold true: the Victorian era was America's greatest time for singing. Out of this time came most of the real live favorites of American song, the true folk drinking songs that we all learn when we're young, sing while we're in college, and hear around us all our lives.

Strangely, however, even though we all know the tunes to these songs, few of us know the words—perhaps because the songs are so popular no one thinks of printing a collection of them. And yet the lyrics provide more than half the fun, because all these songs tell a story, whether nostalgic, roughly humorous, or romantic, that makes for enjoyable reading.

Now you can learn the words to more than 100 of America's favorite songs, all By the way, don't expect to find among them "Drink to Me Only With Thine Eyes," or other "nice" literary, pallid songs; these are the real stuff—rough, vigorous, sometimes bawdy, filled with frontier humor and the colorful language of railroad men, miners, sailors, and other groups.

A special feature of this collection is the illustrations by John Held, Jr., the man who made the flapper world-famous and whose "magnificent" (to quote the artist himself) drawings are the perfect accompaniments to these songs of conviviality.

THE GILDED PALACE.—A DEN OF INIQUITY OF THE 19th CENTURY.

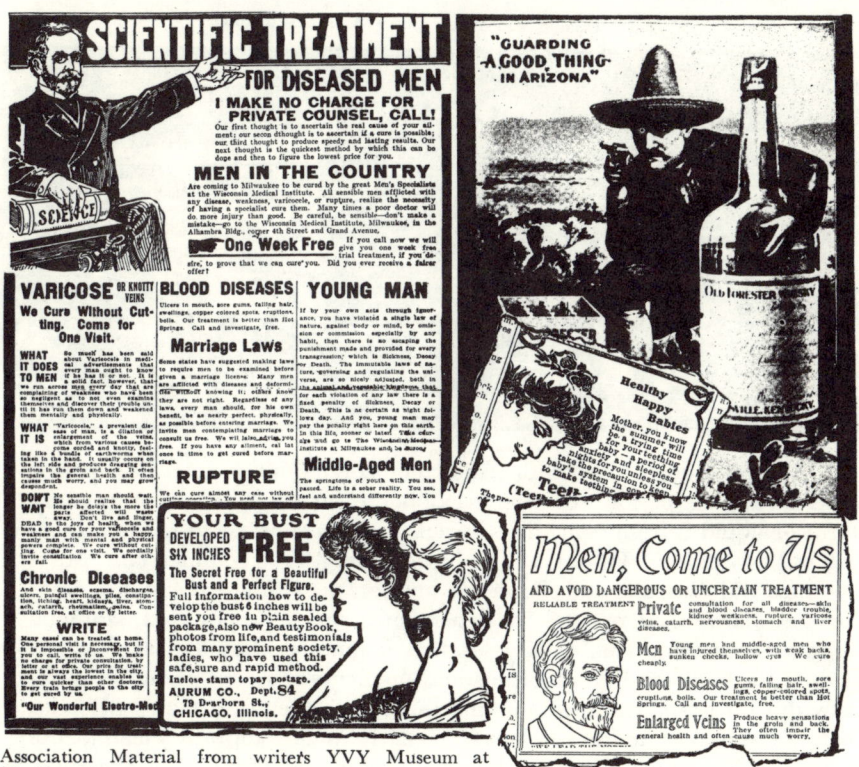

Association Material from writer's YVY Museum at Watkins Glen, N. Y.

> **Know all men by these presents:**
>
> We, William F. Berry, Abraham Lincoln and John Bowling Green, are held and firmly bound unto the County Commissioners of Sangamon County in the full sum of three hundred dollars, to which payment well and truly to be made we bind ourselves, our heirs, executors and administrators firmly by these presents, sealed with our seal and dated this 6th day of March, A. D. 1833. Now the condition of this obligation is such that, whereas the said Berry and Lincoln has obtained a license from the County Commissioner. Court to keep a tavern in the Town of New Salem to continue one year. Now if the said Berry and Lincoln shall be of good behavior and observe all the laws of this State relative to tavern-keepers, then this obligation to be void or otherwise remain in full force.
>
>   **ABRAHAM LINCOLN.** [Seal]
>   **WILLIAM F. BERRY,** [Seal]
>   **BOWLING GREEN.** [Seal]
>
> *A. Lincoln*

Taft's Holdup Saloon, Red Lodge, Montana, in 1900.

As one studies the bottle collecting colaterals of preceding pages, especially those period ads which extoll the virtues of some proprietary form of liquid refreshment, he is struck with its contrast to today's catering to "a Nation of Pill-takers" by hard-driving T.V. commercials. Maybe these old Cureralls and Euphoric boosters to Human Happiness were far less harmful than present dependence on high powered synthetic drugs. Since the virtue of any product is mainly what the taker *thinks* it does for him, the bygone bitters and medicine show proprietaries probably did far less harm in sciambling the body's chemistry than LSD pills, Benny's and Barbituates. This was recently made painfully clear to the writer by Robert Goldman's article on "Instant Happiness" as excerpted.

— GROUP D: FIGURALS, Etc.

More and more Americans are turning to drugs in a danger-filled attempt to escape from their troubles.

One out of six Americans today uses the pill bottle to change his mental attitudes and perceptions. This almost slavish dependence on medication by thirty million Americans has become one of the most serious and pressing problems of our time.

Drug overuse is destroying the physical and emotional wellbeing of uncounted men, women and children of all ages and social backgrounds. Indeed, it threatens almost every aspect of American life, school, job, marriage.

Doctors and health authorities are appalled by the constantly broadening scope of the "new drug kick." Teenagers and college students are indulging in wild orgiastic binges with the most powerful compounds ever known to mankind. Even eight-year-olds are using stimulants to blur their mental states, not realizing that these same stimulants may cause permanent damage to the brain. Today's pill-users know they can easily obtain products to make them high, or to grind down their feelings. They have even discovered that there is a bizarre reaction to such widely disparate substances as powdered nutmeg and morning-glory seeds. One fact emerges from cases documented at medical centers throughout the nation: your generation is willfully exposing itself to unknown dangers from drugs. Inevitably, death occurs in some of these tragic cases. This is not to say that many of the present-day tranquilizers, energizers and other related compounds do not have a vital place in therapy when properly prescribed for appropriate patients. They have helped a good many people over the most difficult emotional hurdles. However, drug abuse has become "the fashion of our times."

By Robert P. Goldman

So on this sadly solemn note we end our survey of Grand Old American Bottles—their contents "taken with discretion" and the empties studied "just for fun", — seems one of the safer ways to "help lift care" in this Aspirin Age.

NOTE ON THE EVOLUTION OF THE WINE BOTTLE.

BY

—— PRICE, Esq., F.S.A., Scot.

THE glass bottle for holding liquors has been known from the earliest times. Down to the beginning of the eighteenth century the hand-made globular bottle for the reception of wine and ale retained practically the same form in this country, and it was only in that century (which covers the most glorious period in the production of the artistic wine-glass) that its present cylindrical form was gradually evolved. The manufacture of glass bottles in England in the seventeenth century is shown by this fact, that when Henry Holden and John Colonet, in 1662, applied for a patent for a new invention for making glass bottles, their application was successfully resisted on the ground that Sir Kenelm Digby had made such bottles in 1632. Moreover, in the time of Queen Elizabeth, as Mr. Albert Hartshorne points out in an interesting note in *Old English Glasses*, ale was generally sold at the ordinaries in glass bottles, and in the seventeenth century the practice became more and more general of drawing liquors for use at the ordinaries or at table in glass bottles instead of in the "latten" or pewter vessels customary in medieval times.

Then, as now, wines were chiefly brought to this country in bulk, that is in wooden casks. The palate had not been educated to appreciate vintages and the maturing of wines or liquors in bottles. There must therefore have been many glass-houses in Great Britain for the making of bottles passed to the annealing house. Mr. Hartshorne, in *Old English Glasses*, quotes a passage from Markham's *English Housewife* (1675), which mentions "round bottles" with narrow necks for "Bottle Ale having the corks fast tied with strong pack thread."

The placing of names or initials or marks on glass ware has a very ancient origin. The custom fell into disuse, but was revived in England in the eighteenth century, and thus one finds names, initials, dates, coats-of-arms, crests, not only on glass ware, but on most other objects of art made during that period.

The "use" of impressing dates has enabled me to obtain a series of dated wine bottles extending in time over a period of 150 years, and showing in an interesting and concrete way, the variation of the shape of the bottle.

GROUP D: FIGURALS, Etc.

CHAPTER XIX: BOTTLE MAKING

This reference book (with pictures, checklists and association material built around four major groupings) was developed primarily for present and future collectors of all types of empty bottles. But no account of such grand old American Glass should end without a brief history of what was our FIRST GREAT AMERICAN INDUSTRY. . . . Glass Blowing was a guarded English secret, especially since they invented the lead (hard flint) mix which sparked Heavy Black-glass Seal Bottles (Chapter II) that followed the leather and clay containers of earlier time. We show Jamestown excavation fragments from such Seal Bottles that may well have been made there in the short period before this first American Glass-house was burned—with Indian Massacre besides. In England recently at the Vintner's Society headquarters, the writer was given information shown on an accompanying page that indicates few Seal Bottles were ever made here. Certainly, English Glass Blowers were bound to home-base by law; so to German immigrants like Baron Stiegel and Caspar Wistar, also Pitkin, goes the usual credit for blowing the first all American Flasks (see Chapter III). Even after the Revolution, England prohibited emigration of all Glassblowers and not until 1826 did the great Glass Artist, Thomas Leighton, escape illegally via France and formed (with six sons) a group of Master Gaffers at the Libbey Company (founded 1818 and still going strong).

In America the practice of jealously guarding the secrets of glassblowing was continued throughout the 18th and 19th centuries. Owners misled the public by passing out incorrect information. Visitors were not allowed in the factories and any newly developed technique was acquired only by raiding workers from one's competitors. That is why existing records of American Bottle production and methods are full of many inconsistencies and contradictions. In general, however, basic old procedures and new developments came about something like this:

Since glass is a 'metal' formed by heating (at 2700° F. or higher) a mix of silicic acids (like sand) and alkalies (like potash, soda ash, calcium, etc.), a 'gather' must be removed from this molten mass and blown into shape while still white-hot. Until just before First Century A.D., a glass bottle was formed by slapping the molten paste over a sand or plaster core that was later dug out leaving a hollow container. This brings us to the first of historic period of Glass Bottle Making.

Jamestown, Va

The Glass Bottle's First Golden Age coincides with the Roman Empire. Somewhere (probably in Syria) a nameless glass worker put a hollow iron rod into the hot molten mass and then blew the first glass bubble. At first free-blown only, soon mold-blown was also being tried. Just as today, these people cherished the wines and food containers for their aesthetic as well as their practical quality. Small glass perfumes like these shown here were the first pictorials. But with the fall of the Roman Empire, a long period of Western Darkness developed for the bottle until the Venetians of the 13th Century worked a delicate artistry in fairy-like vessels and sparked the Second Golden Age of the Glass Bottle (of which little now exists except in Museums).

This brings us to the Third Great Age of bottle making, practicing the free-blown method in 17th and 18th Century Europe and England —also somewhat here as well. The basic steps of bottle blowing are shown by accompanying drawings to proceed as follows: (0) the furnace is stoked with wood to heat as a "batch"; (1) then the long hollow-blow-pipe is dipped through the fire arch to pick up and pull out a 'gob'; (2) next the red-hot gather is rolled on a flat metal 'marver' to give it preliminary shape while the glass blower puffs a time or two into the blow pipe so the glass becomes a bubble. This is the embryo bottle; for a long-neck bottle the blower swings the pipe down and lets the thick taffy-like glass sag at the end, while for a flattened shape he swings the blowpipe around; (3) this bubble (now known as a 'parison') is now put into a hollowed wooden block for further shaping; then it is passed to a team-mate (called a 'Gaffer') who sits in a special 17th Century invented chair and (4) with left hand constantly rolling the blowpipe takes a pincers-like instrument known as a 'jack' and narrows the parison's neck to desired shape with further blows on the pipe. Now for free-blown, the base of the bottle must be flattened so it will stand up; and here another member of glasshouse team picks up an iron 'pontil rod' whose molten glass tip fuses the pontil rod to the bottle base (5) while the gaffer 'whets off' or frees the blowpipe with a sharp tap. (6) Further shaping of the bottle's lip (with the pontil rod still rolling on the frame) is made, and the gaffer knocks off the pontil rod with a brisk blow so the finished bottle can be put into a 'lehr' or tunnel-like oven to be annealed through gradual cooling.

While the use of molds to form glass bottles dates back to Roman and Syrian times, it was not until the beginning of the 19th Century that one finds much widespread use or new developments therein. This brings us to the 4th Golden Age of bottle making, the period of historical flasks, name-marked-in-glass-whiskies and other health or household containers. Blown-molded types were discussed in Chapter V, full mold-blown in Chapter VI and following. Here we should note that these molds were first whittled from wood, with the glassblower taking a few puffs on the rod and then lowering the red-hot bladder-shaped glass into a rough-hewn mold-block and blowing again until the glass pressed

GROUP D: FIGURALS, Etc. 483

firmly against the sides. It could be either left there to acquire its final shape or be quickly withdrawn to do a bit of expanded-mold-blowing to the pressed shape.

The earliest mold types were called 'post-holes' or 'open-tops' where only the bottom of the bottle was formed and quickly pulled out so the 'gaffer' could whirl the bottle neck into shape before it got off the blowpipe on its way to the annealing ovens. Molds first came in two parts; then, with ever more elaborate designs were cut into three-mold sections. Later in the 19th Century, the closed mold was developed in which the base and lip were both parts of the original mold.

Early American flasks blown in wooden molds often showed ridges left by the mold carver's knife and also the place where the molds came together. The molds were held wet to prevent ignition; but sometimes the sides charred and this made a cleaner glass contour, but as seen today are not nearly so rare as bottles that show the 'whittle marks.' These marks increase a bottle's value and cover the period 1820-1860, when the use of iron molds made for a general uniformity. First in demanding a smoother bottle surface (in imitation of expensive freeblowns) were the sellers of fine wines; to please them it was found that by turning a charred wooden mold while the completed bottle was still inside, one could smooth out undesired mold marks and ridges. This finding led to the use of paste in iron molds which would take up the mold-cracks as the mold was turned about the bottle's sides. Called 'turn-molds' or 'paste-molds', special turn-mold machines (1890-1900) became popular for giving bottles the lustrous low-mold-mark-register of semi-automation.

The 5th and final Golden Age of the great American Glass bottleblowing machine. Prior to its invention by H. Owen (see pictured story) every bottle produced had to be hand-blown by a man holding a blowpipe. The Owens machine was, of course, preceded by minor inventions which made the process semi-automatic, speeding up production by increasing helper efficiency and decreasing the use of sheer lung power. In 1881 came the use of mechanical air-pressure (providing one was adept in putting just the right amount down a blowpipe) and in 1898 a suction and blowing machine eliminating some hand action and semi-automatic creation of a bottle line. But the glass blower was still everywhere present and bottles were still being individually made rather than ganged on an endless chain. There was still the problem of the lip, and getting 'the gather' on and off the blow pipe.

A study of Bottle Lips forms a good preliminary to understanding the 1903 automatic bottle-making machine. In the hand-blown process, the mouth or lip is formed last, after being in the mold and freed from the blow pipe. The oldest 19th Century bottles (before 1840) show a sheared lip, formed by simply cutting the glass free from the blowpipe. From 1840 to 1890 glassmakers formed a laid-on ring, always applied by hand, using pincers or wooden paddle at the gaffer's seat. After that closed molds were designed so the lip could be formed at the same time as the rest of the bottle; however, it still had to be sheared from the blowpipe in the same manner as the original sheared top: and 'age' here, (as in the earlier ring-neck bottles) can be easily told by looking at the mold marks. All you have to do in order to see if you have an applied-lip bottle is check the mold seams. These will run the mold marks up to somewhere near the neck where they will end and is sure proof that the bottle was made before 1900. Even in the closed-mold (with fixed rather than applied lips) there will be a place ¼ or ½ inch from the bottle crest where the glass has protruded from the mold to the blowpipe and has once been cut off that short way. The thing to remember here is that with the wholly machine-made bottle the lip comes first and the mold lip is always used in its formation. Look at any modern bottle and YOU WILL FIND THE MOLD MARKS RUNNING FROM THE BASE OF THE BOTTLE THRU THE ENTIRE LIP AT NECK TO THE VERY TOP.

Note now the screw-top (another waymark towards invention of the automatic bottle making machine; which sends red hot bottles to the annealing ovens at incredible automated speed and without touch of human hands). Bottle men have always wanted a screw top for having a safer hold on a bottle's contents than a cork top; but the first progress there came with development on outside screw threads in food-preserving bottles. We should recall that the Mason Jar (1858) had a screw top. These threads were formed by the original mold which had to be broken away from the blow-pipe and sent to the annealing ovens in jagged condition. Only after the jars were fully cooled was the jagged rim-edge ground off by hand and fitted to the patent screw tops. It is said that this process was suggested by the small Sandwich Bear Pomade jars (black and white milk glass) whose heads could be locked on in such manner. Anyway, by 1891 the screw-thread problem was semi-automated so that by combining the sandwich plunger-pressing machine with automatic air pressure, on wide mouth jars the hot glass could be forced to the top of the mold with the lip formed first. By this method, the glass was blown into the mold tip first, then a metal plunger was forced through that bottle mouth and air pressure applied to body of the vessel to fill its sides, whereon the metal plunger was withdrawn leaving the screw top lid all finished. This speed-up process can be seen on later age Mason and Ball fruit jars which will not show the hand-top grinding of earlier years. But since the metal plunger device could not go through narrow neck vessels, it is obvious that the outside screw-top bottle had to await the fully automatic blowing machine. Of course, around 1898 some worker had discovered that you could twist a screw thread on the inside of a bottle neck after the hot glass had been separated from the blowpipe. But the rarity of this type of closed-mold bottle suggest it ran into complications or was made in very limited

GROUP D: FIGURALS, Etc.

quantity for buyers who planned its reuse. No, if you wanted to close or cap a bottle, even in 1900, you had usually either to wire the stopper down or use the new Crown-cap with its lip-indentation that allowed a capping machine to use the tin cap-seal (still used for pop bottles). The true outside screw-bottle-cap-thread is the product of the Owen automated machines of 1903 which marks the end of the bottle's Golden Age, and the most basic improvement in the mechanization of our First Great American Industry—Glass (since the invention of the blowpipe 2,000 years before). We show you pictures of this great bottle machine and a drawing of a modern automated plant which moves bottles from molten glass mix into annealing oven without touching human hands and with incredible speed.

One may ask in closing. Is this automation the end of Bottle Collecting for the Antiquarian Specialist. The answer is no—only another beginning! The earlier bottle froms are increasingly hard to find outside museum and private hoards. But new bottle forms, shapes, uses and colors are always appearing. Some of these so commonly discarded today are tomorrow's rarities. The forward-looking collector will try to anticipate which of today's 'common and lowly' will rise to tomorrow's status of 'highconnoisseuresteem.' Already the writer sees the lines forming for some, namely the minerals and soda-pop specialties and certain of the early 20th Century food containers, to say nothing of today's fine whiskey decanters.

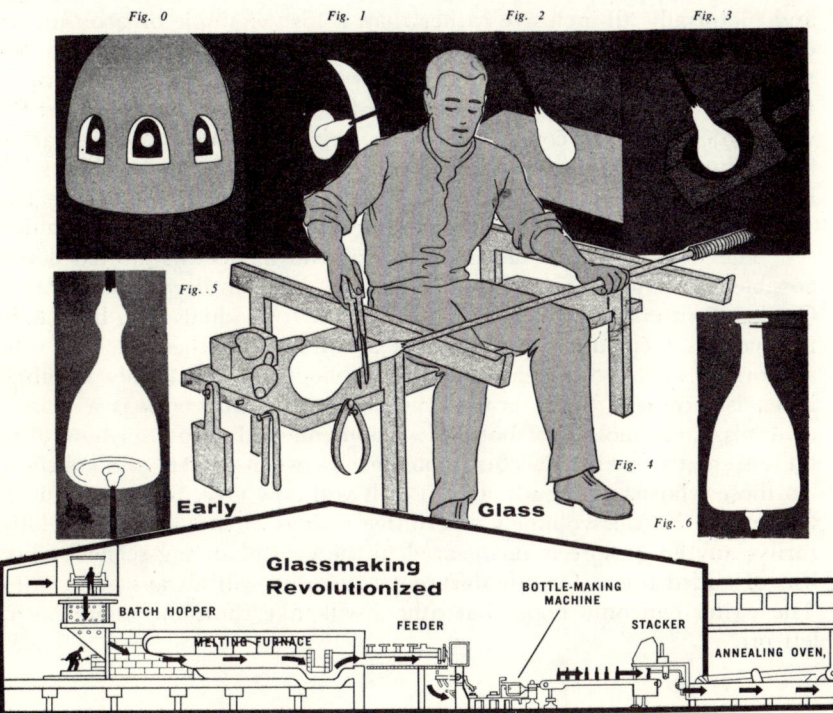

APPENDIX

The writer reaches this book's closing section with a sense of great fatigue and considerable frustration. After three solid years of study on the four different categories of bottle collecting: 1. Liquor, 2. Medicinals, 3. Household and 4. Figurals, many such fields have hardly been scratched. An "authority" on any one of these might possibly point out omissions or faulty attribution. Historical flask experts may feel our adaption of Van Rensselaer original classification system inadequate or out of date; collectors of more recent medicinals and figural bottles can point to many examples not in our check lists. Mr. Wearin reports a total of 1000 figurals in his yet-unpublished list to ours of only 400; those just entering the vast field of drug and household bottles, may wish less space had been given to pages showing collateral poster and catalog materials. The answer to all this lies in the major purpose behind our own endeavor, namely to **force some specific order on a very chaotic area.** Having himself created the books which brought the first order to such fields as toys, lamps, pricing antiques, iridescent glass, etc., the writer was induced by his publisher to attempt the same for "The Bottle Explosion — hottest item of current collector interest." This task however, proved Herculean and only the promise of long standing and great sacrifice to more pressing other interests brought this book to completion;—This is undoubtedly "the Doctor's last book he can do for his hobby field."

One may say this is a typical Century House book—fact-packed and pictorially all-inclusive rather than a lush example of book making old time collectors were taught to expect. In point of fact, it is a **New type of book,** created by this publishing house and a pace-setter for the future. Its lavish use of different type-faces and formats helps break a vast subject into its component parts, brings collateral paper material into proper juxtaposition with the bottles they sparked. Always, the focus is on "give the collector an **integrated picture** of what he has" and "always **expand ones vista for seeking new types of collectables.**"

The writer thanks the many toilers who made this limited edition possible: American Life Foundation and its Century House, Elmira Quality Printers and the Riverside Bindery. Individuals who have aided the writer's fact-hunt are already acknowledged in the text, and other authorities are so fully cited in the Bibliography that only a subject index is required. What is most needed in this appendix is a glossary of terms, a chronology of bottle developments and a note on how to use the different checklists in correspondence between dealers and collectors. To those who have already asked "will you now give us a price guide," the answer is "this volume's descriptive listings already indicate relative rarity; anything more is not geared to the ever-changing scene." Check lists of added forms for our different categories will always be in order. The writer can only hope that others will take these up where he has left off.

A CHRONOLOGY OF BOTTLE MAKING

1500 B.C. First glass containers—Egypt

1st cent., B.C. Invention of blowpipe

1st—4th cent., A.D. First Golden Age of Glass—Rome

1250—1650 Second Golden Age of Glass—Venice

1608 Jamestown, Virginia—America's first glass-house and first "industry"

1676 First "crystal" glass—England

1739 Caspar Wistar established America's first successful glass-house—New Jersey

1763 First Stiegel plant—Pennsylvania

1783 Pitkin glass-house opened—Connecticut

1819 William Underwood packed food in glass—Boston

1841 Nursing bottle patented

1850's Pressing methods adapted to bottle forms

1858 Mason jar patented

1903 Michael Owens perfected first fully automatic bottle-making machine

1938 Non-returnable bottle for beer introduced

Before advent of Bottle-making machine, children were paid from 5 to 25 cents for returning empties for reuse by the druggist.

How to Use the Check-Lists

If your collection features only one type of bottle, first consult subject index and open its pages. Next study all numbered listings until you find picture or description corresponding to bottle desired. Then, in correspondence **code** it by indicating the general group reference (A-D) and specific sub-grouping plus the page number where the same can be found. For example, marked 19th Century Jugs and Cruets are in general Group A (Whiskeys) whose listings begin on Page 140 in Chapter VII. If you were looking for bottle #7 on this page (Star Whiskey, N. Y.), you would describe it as follows: #7 on Page 140 in GAB (Great American Bottle) Group A, Liquors, Sub. 6; whereas, if you wanted to refer to an earlier 'sealed' bottle, you could ask for #3 on Page 135 in GAB, Group A, Sub. 6.

To aid one in running down a given bottle, we now show the extent and location of the different category check-lists.

GROUP A — LIQUORS:—
1. 40 Decanters 26- 29
   (3-Section mold, arched, geometric, baroque)
2. 78 Early Chestnut expanded mold pocket flasks . . 32- 38
   (54 Pitkin type—4 divisions I—24 Steigel types)
3. 80 Early full-mold blown flasks 42- 53
   (29 Masonic—21 Violin—Scrolls—20 Sunbursts)
4. 52 Miscellaneous flasks from 1921 Van Rensselaer plates 62- 72
5. 400 Historical flasks and related pictorials . . . 76-112
   (In Group I — 139 Varied subject; In Group II — 56 American Eagles—7 divisions; In Group III—51 Washington—4 divisions; In Group IV—29 Pikes Peak; In Group V—125 Non-Historicals)
6. 166—19th Century marked-in-glass whiskeys . . 120-147
   (30 Biningers; 58 other dated and lettered whiskey; 33 Jugs, cruets and decanters; 45 other descriptive)
7. 20th Century marked whiskeys 154-169
   (65 representative samples, pictorial and descriptive)

GROUP B — MEDICINALS—
1. 456 Marked Biters — the Thompson list with corrections 177-250
2. 166 Marked Bitters found in addition to original check-list 240-246
3. 300 Marked Sarsaparillas, Malt Whiskey and other early
      medicinals closely associated with bitters drinking 256-262
4. 620 Marked proprietory medicinal bottles prior to 1875 263-269

GROUP C — HOUSEHOLDS—
1. 52 Blacking and misc. household bottles . . . 356-359
2. (62 early blown ink bottles; and late 19th Century ink
      bottles and stands 364-309
3. 188 Perfumes and Scents 300-309
   85 19th Century mold-blown perfumes; 50 cologne bottles; 40 hand-cut scent bottlels; 13 Stiegel seahorse pocket perfumes & toilet bottles)
4. 130 Mineral and beverage bottles 317-326
5. 52 pepper sauce, mustard, pickle and other food containers 345-349
6. Drug Supply-House Glassware 372-427
   (Over 700 19th C. shapes related to all household categories pictured and wholesale prices in Hagerty and Dean-Foster catalogs. Index for the Hagerty list is on P. 376 & 377 and all Hagerty catalog pages can be marked by the distinguishing Z code. Index for Dean-Foster starts on 385, while bottle listings that follow are coded as 7X to 55X catalog pages). This section carries the most important identification lists for new collectors.
7. 120 Liniments and other home help aids . . . 429-440

GROUP D — FIGURALS—
1. 400+ Human, Animal and other Object Bottles . 440-473

GLOSSARY OF TERMS

ANNEALED BOTTLES
—Bottles which have gone through annealing oven for gradual cooling
APOTHECARY JAR
—A round widemouth hand blown bottle with ground glass stopper.
BARBER BOTTLES
—Hand blown, elongated neck bottles with sprinkle stopper for Barber Stand for holding bay rum, dandruff cure; some in pointed hob-nail, Mary Gregory, Bohemian glass, milk glass, even late 19th Century State-lady pictures forming decals.
BININGER BOTTLES
—Early 19th Century marked in glass, whiskey shapes and widely distributed by Bininger Companies.
BITTERS —
—19th Century blown in mold medicinal with this word and related "others" marked in the glass.
BLACK GLASS
—Due to impurities in the glass mix, early blown bottles which appear very black or dark green.
BLOW PIPE
—Long iron is dipped into hot glass mix and blown through.
BLOWN 3-MOLD BOTTLES
—A full blown flask, decanter etc., whose mold gives rise to 3 seams
"BOOZ" —
—The most famous marked in glass log-cabin shape; made for a Mr. Booze, a Philadelphia liquor dealer of the 1860's; many reproductions.
CALABASH
—1850 type of blown whiskey flasks, long neck and bulbous sides—sometimes called the Jenny Lind bottle.
CANDY CONTAINERS
—Small figural bottles with a metal cap opening for pouring pellets
CANDY JARS
—A wide-mouth squared bottle, panel sides, with ground glass stopper which keeps contents fresh; various sizes.
CARBOY
—A large blown container with small neck for whiskey, commercials, etc., with capacity over 5 gals.; frequently wickered or wooden-boxed.
CHESTNUT
—Small free-blown flasks which get their name from its nut shape.
CHESTNUT JUGS
—Mid 19th Century type with bulbous shape and applied handle
COLOR IN —
—Colored bottles are made by adding metallic oxides. Cobalt provides blue, chromes make greens, ambers and yellow are from iron.
COMMEMORATIVE —
—Usually refering to only pictorial flasks; but occasionally types differ such as Ball & Perisphere of 1939 World's Fair or 1942 Gen. McArthur

CULLET
—Broken glass bottles used to form part of the new mix in glass furnaces.
DECANTERS
—Fancy, long neck bottles for holiday spirits, identified by ground-in-glass stoppers in many designs; form of neck ring, also the amount of cut, engraved or pressed-mold formations varies with age and manufacture.
DEMIJOHN
—A smaller version of the Car-boy—usually holding under 5 gals.
DRUG TRADE BOTTLE FORMS
—Terminology developed by glass houses catering to the drug trade and called by such terms as **tablet** bottles, **atomizer** bottles, **mustard** bottles, **nursers, quinines, ginger panels,** and **sick feeders,** etc. See Chapter XV and its drug catalogs for full listings.
DUNMORE —
—Squat, flattened, 18th or early 19th Century type—similar to Hogarth, high kick-up long neck.
DRUG WINDOW —
—Show globes originally filled with red (artery) and blue (veinous) blood waters for shop display; and exhibiting a pyramid of shapes—small bottles are stoppered in larger ones; cut-glass and expensive.
ENAMELED GLASS
—Colorful hand-painted floral designs inscribed on some early Stiegel type bottles and set in the annealing oven.
FIGURAL —
—One which has been molded into shape of a human figure, animal or other object, properly distinct from commemoratives where figure is only raised on the side of a conventional bottle shape.
FLORA TEMPLE
—19th Century whiskey jug with applied handle and famous race horse impressed in paneled side.
FLYCATCHER —
—A large squat bottle to hold sugar-water and entice flies through top.
FRUIT —
—Special jar type with large indented open lip for inserting whole fruits; sealed with a wax plug; precedes advent of Mason jar.
GATHER
—Term referring to a blob of hot glass pulled out of the glass furnace by the blow pipe and used to form a bottle.
GAFFER
—A foreman of the gang—head glass blower.
GEMEL—
—A hand-blown two-mouthed (double) bottle for holding oil, etc.
GIN —
—Usually refers to early Holland type four-sided sloping, and short neck.
GLASS LABELS FOR —
—A thin curved sheet of glass with Latin Medical name enameled on back for affixing over label panel impressed on apothecary jars.

GRENADE—
—A squat, ball-shaped form for holding fire extinguishing liquids.
HOGARTH —
—The early globular wine bottle shown in Hogarth engravings (**i.e.** Rake's Progress) and phototype for most 18th Century forms. In America sometimes called a **Ludlow** and believed to have originated in Ludlow, Mass., around 1815.
HISTORICAL FLASKS
—Full-blown examples where historical figures are cut in the mold forms so design or/and name appears raised on the bottle's side.
HORSE—
—Very long-necked 19th Century bottle for ramming medicine down.
HIP FLASK
—A pocket container of the late 19th and 20th Century whose flattened form is curved to fit a man's back hip pocket.
HOUSEHOLD —
—So many different varieties only those of major importance are defined here. See Group C descriptions Chapters XI-XVII.
KIMMEL—
—A special type in form of Russian Bear originally holding cordial.
KICK UP
—Bottoms of blown bottles vary with age and type of treatment! Some early bottles got a high kick-up when pointed rod pushed the semi-fluid glass center upwards in the base. Late 19th Century bottle bottoms have low kick-ups (or none at all) except for Champagnes or other spirits that require strong resistance against internal pressure to prevent breakage.
LEATHER BOTTELLS
—The first containers for whiskey and other drink were made entirely from leather; sometimes known as a leather jack.
LILY PAD JUGS
—Popular design blown external decorative pattern used by N. Y. State glass houses in the 1850's.
LIQUOR —
—So many different varieties only those of major interest (**i.e.** Historical flasks) have been defined. See Group A.descriptions Chapters II-VIII.
MEDICINAL—
—So many variations only types of major current interest are defined: See Group B Description Chapters IX & X.
MINIATURE LIQUORS
—Specially designed forms for different brands given away or sold for 20th Century "nip" collectors. Brand's paper label important.
MOLDS
—Hollow forms whittled out of wood and stone or metal forms into which the glass gather is dropped and pushed against its sides by the blow pipe to form the bottle. Several types—2 mold—3 mold, paste mold, etc.

NECK-RING
—The practice of putting an applied glass ring or rings around neck of blown bottles or decanters (various types).

OWENS —
—A 20th Century bottle made by the Owen's Mechanical Bottle Machine. Can be identified becouse mold marks extend through the rough vertical opening due to the fact that here neck is always formed first, whereas lips of old-type bottle come after, blowing and show no mold marks.

PARISON
—A glass-blown bubble of preliminary shape which bottle blower holds into the hollowed out wooden block for further shaping.

PATENT STOPPERS FOR —
—Various inventions timed to seal a bottle from damage or theft of contents. Cf. Dr. Thatcher's milk top patent, Haynes whiskey bottle lock, and others.

PATTERN MOLDED
—Blown into a rough mold first, often redipped and further patterned; cf. also expanded mold.

PIG —
—Half pints, blown in form of pig with "hog's hole" serving as the bottle's mouth. Various marked-in-bottle whiskey slogans;—daily sustainer for Irishmen who built the Western railroads.

PERFUME —
—Free blown, pattern molded and full blown miniatures with special shape for holding scents; cf. also blown stiegel-type 'sea-horse form.'

PICNIC —
—A small ovoid shape with short neck and cork stopper—carried in pocket as a Traveler's Companion; often called a Picnic Nip.

PICTORIAL —
—Side of flask or bottle showing some form or scene usually not considered historical i.e., man with dog.

PILGRIM —
—A canteen type first used by Pilgrims on way to Canterbury and other religious shrines; much later versions have been developed for use with fruits, juices and other drinks.

PITKINS
—Pattern molded chestnut flask with gather dipped and blown in 2-part mold to make ribby or swirl effect.

PONTIL
—Iron rod used to take the blown bottle off the blow pipe and holds the semi-molten form while the tip is being shaped.

PONTIL MARK
—The rough scar remaining on the bottom of the bottle where the pontil rod is broken loose and the bottle is sent to the annealing oven.

PUNTS
—Hot wafer-like blobs of glass applied to outside of a blown bottle.

QUILTING
—Wavy lines swirled or cross-notched on outside of still-hot blown flask.
RIGAREE
—Glass ribbons are applied early in parallel lines to early blown flasks; cf. also **threads** and **looping**.
SADDLE —
—A free-blown slender-necked flask for carrying in early saddle bags.
SEAL —
—A blown Hogarth type bottle which has early 18th Century dated seal. Late 19th Century whiskey forms sometimes used fake seals.
SHEARED FORM
—Mouths of different bottles formed according as it was finished after taken from blowpipe and variously described as "sheared," "finished after form taking," "collared," "sloping," "rolled," "screw or thread," "flattened," "banded," "folded up," etc.
SICK GLASS
—A bottle with long time chemical deposit or scale which prevents it from washing clean.
SNUFF —
—Small, square rough blown jar with large mouth opening; also beautifully wrought flat pocket miniatures with silver mounts or cap opening.
SODA LIME GLASS
—A type of green bottle glass mix distinct from **flint** glass type.
STRIGILES AND OIL—
—Skin scrapers looking like small curved animal nails which hung from a ring and with the oil bottle. Used by the Romans in their baths.
STOPPERS OF —
—Many elaborately blown shapes and types for decanters, etc. Mass produced special types also including screw caps, sprinklers, tubular, dentrifice and soda pop plugs.
SUNBURST —
—Earliest full blown 2-mold flask of the ovoid shape with ridged sides sun burst intaglio center patterns.
SUN-TINTED —
—When left in the desert sun many not-so-old bottles take on an amythestine hue that Western collectors find highly desirable.
SWIRLED JUG FLASK
—Early 19th Century type produced by Mid-Western glasshouses.
TARGET —
—Small glass balls used in skeet shooting. Released by a spring, the marksman could prove he hit the ball if it was broken and released the feathers held therein. Antedates the clay pigeon.
VIOLIN AND SCROLL —
—Early flasks shaped like violin or heart scroll; many reproductions.
WHIMSEYS
—One of a kind free-blown; some are figurals,—some have a special hand blown name inscribed.

BIBLIOGRAPHY

BIBLIOGRAPHY ON BOTTLES

The only general reference list already out in this field is the first thing that serious students of the glass bottle should consult. Compiled by G. S. Duncan, this international numbered and indexed bibliography (from earliest records to 1940) was published in 1960 by Oceana Publications Co. The listings below include (1) American Books and Pamphlets, (2) Sales and Company Catalogs, (3) Magazine articles on bottles to date, with the following periodicals searched for references: **Antiques, Antique Journal, American Collector, Antiquarian, Apollo, American Life Collector, Connoisseur, Hobbies, Magazine of Old Glass** and **Spinning Wheel**. Various glass and Whiskey manufacturer's trade publications were not widely canvassed: cf. especially, Directory of Glass Factories (U. S. & Canada 1915) grouped by date, product and capacity.

1. Books and Pamphlets:

A.M.A. **Articles on Nostrums and Quackery,** Medical Assn. Press (1912)

Bacon, E. M. **How Glass Bottles Are Made** (Whitall-Tatum), N. J. (1935)

Bacon, O., **Black Jacks and Leather Bottells,** being some account of leather drinking vessels in England—London: Burrow & Co. (1921)

Barber, E. A., **American Glassware Manual for Collectors of Historical Bottles,** McKay (1900)

Beseker, W. J., **Glass Labels for Bottles,** Stationers Patent Office, London (1854)

Brannon, P. A., editor: **Catalog of Bottle Finds,** Montgomery (Ala.) Glass Collectors Mimeograph Series #1-10 (1937-38)

Carson, G., **One For a Man, Two for a Horse,** Garden City, Doubleday (1961); **History of Bourbon,** Dodd, Mead, N. Y. (1963)

Clifford, W., **Book on Bottles,** Dial Press, N. Y. (1930)

Cruikshank, G., **The Bottle, in Eight Plates,** London: D. Bogue (1847), Caricatures & Cartoons

Freeman, L., **Medicine Showman and His Bottles,** Century House, Watkins Glen, N. Y. (1957); **Grand Old American Bottles,** Century House, Watkins Glen, N. Y. (1964); **Nursery Americana** (1947).

Harrington, J. C., **Glass Making at Jamestown:** America's First Industry, The Dietz Press, Richmond, Va. (1952)

Heiges, G.L., **Henry William Stiegel,** Bibliography, Manheim, Pa. (1937)

Henrivaux, J., "**LeVerrect 6 Crystal . . . ,**" 2 Vols., Paris: Vicq. Dunod (1897).

Holbrook, S. H., **The Golden Age of Quackery,** Macmillan (1959)

Hunter, F. W., **Stiegel Glass,** Houghton Mifflin, Boston (1914) Bibliography
Innes, L., **Early Glass of the Pittsburgh District** (1797-1890), Carnegie (1949)
Kendrick, G., **The Antique Bottle Collector,** Western P & P Co., Nevada (1963)
Kilner, C. A., **50 Years Glass Bottle Trade,** Kilner Jubilee, London (1894)
Knittle, R. M., **Early American Glass,** Century, New York (1927)
McKearin, H., **Story of American Historical Flasks,** Corning Museum of Glass (1953)
McKearin, G. S. & H., **American Glass,** Crown, N. Y. (1941), Bibliography; **200 Years of Blown Glass** (1949)
McMurray, C., **Collector's Guide of Flasks and Bottles,** Dayton, Ohio (1927)
Maust, D., (ed.) **Bottle and Glass Handbook,** Uniontown, Pa. (1956); —**Bottle Price Guide,** Uniontown, Pa., Warman (1957)
Moody, B., **Packaging in Glass,** Hutchins, London (1963)
Minton, L. W., **History of Glass Bottle Blowers,** Merkle Press, Washington (1961)
Pittsburgh P. G. Co., **Glass History, Manufacturer & Application** (1823)
Reed, A., **Old Bottles & Ghost Towns,** Chalfant Press, California (1963)
Romaine, L., **Bibliography of Trade Catalogs,** Bowker, New York (1961)
Ruggles, S., **Sealed Bottles,** Country Life, Ltd. (1950)
Thompson, J. H., **Bitters Bottles,** Century House, Watkins Glen, N. Y. (1947)
Van Rensselaer, S., **Check List of Early American Bottles and Flasks,** Peterborough, N. H. (1926) (1st Ed., 1921)
Walbridge, W. S., **American Bottles, Old and New,** Owens Bottle Company, Toledo (1920)
Watkins, L. W., **American Glass and Glassmaking,** New York; Chanticleer (1950) Bibliography
Watkins, L. W., **Cambridge Glass,** (1818-1888), Boston, Little Brown (1930); **The Development of American Glassmaking,** Boston, Glass Club (1935)
Weigh, E., **Development of Automatic Glass Bottle Machines,** Glass Mfg. Assn:. London (1960)
Wilson, K. M., **Glass in New England,** Old Sturbridge Village, Mass. (1959)
Young, J. H., **Toadstool (patent medicines) Millionaires,** Princeton (1961)
The Glass Containers Mfg. Institute, **Billions of Bottles,** N. Y. (1959), 30
Thatcher Glass Co., **Story of a Milk Bottle** (1920), 11-24
Twaine Co., **Story Behind Mineral Water Bottles,** Dublin (1769-1959)

2. Periodical References:

Adams, A., Face of Independence: Grants' Hold Fast Whiskey, **Design For Industry** (January 1959), 35
Amber, W., A Home for Stray Bottles, **Century** (1896) 511; (1915), 27
Barber, E. A., Old American Glass, **Art in America** IV (1916), 162-72
Broadley, A. M., Evolution of the Bottle, **Country Home** (1910), 129
Brobeck, F., Old Toilet Water Bottles, **The Antiquarian** (1929), 54-56
Burbank, L. F., **The Keene Glass Works,** The Antiquarian, May 1926
Carleton, E., At Sign of the Carboy, **Century** (1902), 221
Carroll, D., Sellouts of a Century Ago, **Spinning Wheel** (1953-54)
Cohen, South Carolina Dispensary Bottles, **Antique Journal** (June 1947)
Cummings, J., The Dorflinger Glass Works, **N. Y. History** 1953 , 468-74
Davidson, M., The Similarity Between Ancient and Early American Glass, **The American Collector** (August 1942), 10-11, 14
Davis, T., Whiskey Bottle Shape Survey, **Design for Industry** (December 1959), 20-21
Decatur, S., Masonic Emblems on Glass, **American Collector** (April 1940), 8-9
Depla, Y., Bottles of Allure, **Design for Industry** (January 1959), 32-35
Dreppard, C. W., French Perfume Bottles and Jars, **Spinning Wheel** (1949), 18; also Cut Glass Perfume (1952), 16
Dudley, M. S., Irish Cut-Glass Decanter, **Antiques** (1928), 476
Freeman, L., Great American Bottle, **American Life Collector Annual** (1962), Vol. I, 49; Dorflinger Glass, (1940); **Heirlooms** (1941)
Gardner, C. B., New England's Many Bottles, **American Collector** (June 1934), 14; Bottles Made at New London, **American Collector** (May 1934), 14; Connecticut Glass, **Antiques** (1935), 101
Gillingham, H. E., Pottery, China, and Glass Making in Philadelphia, **Penn. Mag. History & Biography** (April 1930), 97-129
Griffinhagen & Young, Old English Patent Medicine in America, **Smithsonian Institute Bulletin** (1959), 159-183
Hartman, Double Duty Containers of 1890, **Spinning Wheel** (1954), 41
Holden, M., Notes on Old Bottles, **Antiquarian** (April 1926), 22-25
Hollander, D., Bottle Oddities, **Heirlooms** (1941), 22
Hubbard, C. T., Character Bottles, **Antiques** (1949), 444; Character Bottles Attract Collectors, **Antique Journal** (Jan. 1951), 18-19
Hudson, J. P., 17th Century Glass Wine Bottles and Seals Excavated at Jamestown, **Journal of Glass Studies** (1961), 27
Hughes, G. B., Old English Decanters, **Antique Dealer and Collectors Guide II** (1948), 40-42
Hume, I. N., Bottle in Colonial Virginia, **Journal of Glass Studies** (1961), 9-117
Kennedy, J.G., In Praise of Diversification, **Old Glass** (1938), 6
Keyes, F., The Springs, Glass Houses and Bottles of Saratoga Springs, N.Y., **N. Y. History** (1957), 212-23; Collectors Check List of Bottles

Keyes, H. E., Cruikshank's Bottle, **Antiques** (1931), 386; cf (Aug. 1925),
Knittle, Rhea M., New Notes on American Glass, **Antiques** (May 1928), 408-09; A Bit About Bottles, **The Antiquarian** (1926), 20; Violin Bottles, **Antiquarian,** (1930), 46; Ohio Spirit Flasks, **Antiquarian** (Oct. 1924), 201
Kumm, M., Sandwich Nursing Bottle, **Antiques** (1944), 311
LeFevre, E., Why I Collect Empty Bottles, **Sat. Ev. Post** (Oct. 19, 1929)
Laidaker, S., Bottles, **Old Glass** (1938), 23 (cf. also articles in his **American Antiques Collector**)
Law, M. L., Baron Stiegel and His Glass, **The Antiquarian** (June 1928), 41-43
Lee, R. W., Glass Cruets, **Spinning Wheel** (1955), 10
Little, W. H., The Evolution of the Bottle, **Trans. Cumberland Westmoreland Antig. Soc.** New Series (1904), 213-16
Loomis, L., Sandwich Glass Pomade Bears, **Old Glass** (Sept. 1938)
McKearin, G. S., Jenny Lind Bottles, **American Collector** (1937), 33; Wistarberg and South Jersey Glass, **Antiques** (Oct. 1926); Stiegel Blown Three Mold Decanters, **Antiques** (1930), 338; What Bottle Shall I Collect, **Old Glass** (1938-1939), 8-22
McLaughlin, W., History of Redford Glass Works, **New York History** (1945), 368-374
Mirkil, H., Booz and His Bottle, **Antiques** (Nov. 1926), 372
National Preservers' Assn., Standardization of Bottles, **Glass Container** (1928), 7 (12), 11
Newman, B., Pacific Glass Bottle Works, (1855), **Antiques** (Feb. 1943), 85
O'Connor, J., Keene Masonic Flasks, **Antiques** (1923), 37; The Lowell Railroad Bottle, **Antiques** (1923), 37
Pazaurek, G. E., Stiegel and Related Types, **Antiques** (1932), 27
Pears, T. C., First Flint Glass Factory in America, **Antiques** (Mar. 1927)
Pyre, F., Steigel Glass, **Antiquarian** (March 1924), 18-21
Ramsey, R., Violin & Scroll Flasks, **Hobbies** (1939), 61
Reifstahl, R. M., Early American Glass, **Int. Studio** (April 1926), 102
Romaine, L. B., Barbershop Glassware, **Spinning Wheel** (1952), 10
Sherd, I. M., Barber Bottles, **Old Glass** (**1939**), 6
Stow, C. M., Three Mold Flasks, **The Antiquarian** (1926), 31-100
Susswein, R., Early 19th Century New York Produced Fine Glass, **American Collector** (1934), 3, 10
Thompson, J. H., Give Bitters Bottles Their Due, **Antiques,** 6:230, 294 (Oct.-Nov., 1944), 230, 294
Thorpe, W. A., Evolution of the Decanter, **Connoisseur** (1929), 196-207, 271, 81
Van Nostrand, L. C., Three Mold Blown, **Old Glass** (1939); Glass Miscellany (1939), 6; Blown Decanters (1940), 5; Blown in Bottles, **Old Glass** (1938), 12

Van Tassel, V., Lady With Glass Cruets, **Antique Journal** (Apr. 1951), 18-19

Watkins, L. W., Distribution of Early American Glass, **Antiques** (1937), 10

Wenham, Pilgrim Bottles and Later Uses, **Antiques** (1929), 48

White, H. H., Kentucky Glass Works, **Antiques** (Feb. 1926); New View of Old Glass, **Antiques** (1933), 68, 118-110; Keene Bottles, **Antiques** (1927), 459; Mineral Water Bottles, **Angler** (1930), 40; N. Y. State Glass Houses, **Antiques** (1930), 220; Mt. Vernon Chestnuts, **Antiques** (1923), 98-100 & 135-138

White, J. M., Empty Bottles Full, **Antiques Journal** (Feb. 1946), 13-14; Demijohns in Decoration, **Antiques Journal** (June 1946), 6-8

Winkworth, W. W., Old Chinese Snuff Bottles, **Antioch College Record** (Jan.-Feb. 1949), 244

Winn, M. G., Dairy Bottles, **Spinning Wheel** (1948), 10-23

Wintermute, H. O., Carnegie Museum Exhibition of Early Pittsburgh Glass, **Antiques Journal** (Oct. 1949), 117

Writer's Survey of American Glass Made in 1832, **American Collector** (May 1935), 6-11; ....Baron Stiegel; Yeoman and Gentlemen, **Antique Journal** V 8 (Aug. 1950), 14; ....Evolution of the Wine Bottles, **the Cellerman**, London, (Aug. 1958); ....Glass Balls for Targets, **Antiques** (1943), 275; ....Perfume Bottles, International Studio (1923), 129; Know Your Glass, **Antiques Journal** (Dec. 1950), 26; ....Notes on Fancy Flasks (1840-60), **Hobbies Mag.** (Aug. 1949), 109; Perfume Bottles, **Antiques** (May & Aug. 1940-41); Pilgrim Bottles, **Antiques** (Jan. 1940), 18; **Spinning Wheel Bottle Notes:** Half Bottles, (Oct. 1955), 40; McKearin Flask Collection (Feb. 1955), 12; The Mason Jar (June 1955), 38; Soda Pop Bottles (Nov. 1955), 40; Scent Bottles (June 1955), 29; Barbershop Bottles (Oct. 1955), 40; Figural Bottles (June 1956), 24; Threaded Liquor Sets (1958), 1; (1959), 14; Bacarat Bottles (1952), 205; Westmoreland Mustards (May 1948); Glass Bottle Origins, **Wine Club of America Magazine,** ....Stiegel Glass Bottle Origins, **Wine Club of America Magazine** (June 1949), 13; ....Twined Water Bottles for S. California, **American Antiquity** (1955), 345-52

3. Sales and Manufacturers Catalogs

Brigham, H. H., (Collection) Early American Glass, New York: American Art Association (Oct. 15, 1937)

Buena Vista Glass Company, Price List . . . Flint Glass Bottles, Prescriptions, Brandies, Flasks, Beers, etc., Wheeling, West Virginia (1891)

Dean, Foster & Co., Glass Manufacturers Catalogs of (1890 & 1900)

Eisendrath, David B., Flasks of Fame, Greenwich, Conn. Fawcett Publication (1957)

Hagerty Bros. & Co., New York, Glassware Catalogs of (1876-1890)

Howe, W. T., (Collection) . . . notable examples of Ohio and Midwestern, South Jersey, New York, Sandwich Glass . . . group of historical flasks . . . New York: Parke-Bernet Galleries (Nov. 7 & 8, 1940)

Lawton, Herbert, (Collection) . . . Steigel, Wistarberg, Jersey, New York: American Art Association (Feb. 1-2, 1923)

McKearin, H., The Alfred B. Maclay Collection of . . . American Glass . . . New York: Parke-Bernet Galleries (March 23-24, 1939); Catalogue of the Exhibition of the John Hays Hamond Jr. Collection of Early American Glass, Philadelphia, Penn., Society of the Colonial Dames of America (1931); Exhibition of Mr. John Hays Hammond Jr.'s Collection of Early American Glass, N. Y., The Art Center (1930); Early American Glass, The Mrs. Frederick S. Fish Collection, N. Y., Parke-Bernet Galleries (Jan. 5 & 6, 1940); Early American Glass, The Frederick K. Gaston Collection, N. Y., Parke-Bernet Galleries (March 29 & 30, 1940)

McKearin, G. S., Collection, Sale of Early American Glass, N. Y., American Art Association (April 22 & 23, 1931 and Jan. 6 & 7, 1932); Sale of Reproduction of Flasks, Pennybacker, Reading (1963)

McKesson & Robbins, Prices current of drugs . . . etc., New York: McKesson & Robbins (18....)

Maris, (John M.) & Co., Catalog of Prices current of druggists' shop, furniture, glassware implements, appliances, sundries, etc. (1900)

Mason, H. D., (Collection) . . . Early American Glass . . . New York: American Art Association (Dec. 17, 1932)

Meacham, M. I., (Collection). The Early American Glass Collection of N. Y., Anderson Galleries (Oct. 26 & 27, 1926)

Osgood, C. D., Sale of Early American Glass Bottles and Flasks. (Also other U. S. Collections sold), Penny Packer Auction Center, Reading, Pa. (1956)

Owens-Illinois Glass Company, Glass Containers, Toledo, Ohio (1931), 507; The Romance of Glass, Toledo, Ohio (After 1900)

Hovenden & Sons, London. Ill. Catalog of Perfume Bottles (1875)

Temple, J. P. (Collection) Early American Glass, N. Y., Anderson Galleries (March 1-3, 1923), N. Y., American Art Association (Nov. 15-17, 1923)

Van Winkle, W. M., (Collection) American Glass, N. Y., American Art Association (April 27, 1934), N. Y., Parke Bernet Galleries (April 28 & 29, 1938)

Whittall Tatum Co., N. J., Glassware Catalogs of 1880 & 1900

White Cap Co., History of Glass Containers, Chicago (1956)

Many caltalogs from the writer's collection at Y.Y.V. Museum, including files of Polk & Calders, etc.; also National Druggist, American Druggist and other bottle trade papers.

INDEX

LIQUORS, BITTERS, MEDICINALS

American Eagle Flasks
  Listings 63, 68-71, 87-91
Apostle 103, 127
Aromatic Schnapps 161
Baron Stiegel 36
Bininger 113, 115, 124, 133
Booz Bottle 13, 104, 114
Bottle Hoax (Pig and
  Whistle 115, 148
Bottle Shapes, early 10, 16
Bottle Shapes, late 164, 165, 400
Calabashes 51, 62
Carboys 14, 19
Casks 19, 20
Chestnut expanded mold
  flasks 31, 36, 39
Corn Licker 20, 23, 59
Cornucopia Flasks 78, 79
Coventry Flasks (also
  Covetry) 31, 82
Collateral Material
  2, 8, 114, 116, 132, 144, 150,
  152, 153, 166, 170, 171, 172,
  174, 175

(Advertising Catalogs and
Signs, Photographs, Prints
and Paintings, Letters and
other Pictorial Paper Materials)

Dorflinger Bottles 24
Dated and Lettered Bottles
  and Flasks 135-139, 142
Decanters
  22, 23, 26-29, 163, 167, 168,
  169
  English blown 15, 25
  Irish 25

Deeming Jarves 36
Demijohns 12-15, 20, 23
Dyott, Thos. W., 55, 56, 57, 13
Empty Bottle Collecting 9
Enameled Drug Bottle 40, 41
English Bottle Making .. 14, 480
Free Mold Blown and Full
  Mold Blown
      19, 23, 39, 42, 43-53
Flask Values 11
Gemel (double flask) 40, 304
Gin, boxed nested bottles 21
Glass Works and Glass
  Manufacturers 73
Historical Flasks
  6, 53, 55, 58, 59, 74, 75, 76-112
Hogarth Bottle 6, 14, 39, 53
Holand Gin Bottle 14
Indian Grave, Bottle from .. 20
Indian Queen 67, 126
Jamaica Rum 20, 59
Jugs, Cruets, etc.
      140, 142, 145-147
Keene Works
      23, 26, 31, 45, 53, 59
Kimmel Bottle (Russian Bear)
      125, 127
Leather Bottel 60
Looping 36
Ludlows 39
Manchester Works 31
Manheim Works 36
Marked in Glass Whiskey
      151, 154-169
19th Century
Glass Whiskeys 113, 126, 128
131, 135, 143, 145, 146, 147
20th Century
Glass Whiskeys 101, 154-169

Masonic Flasks 39, 43-48, 81
Metal Molds 59
Miniature Liquors Bottles .. 161
Miner's Friend; Oldner's
Rye 147
Monk Bottle (Apostle), 103, 127
Mountain Dew 5, 132, 133
Non-Historical Bottles, 103-113
Owens Bottle Machine 484
Pioneer Bottle Collectors
9-12, 60
Paul Jones Flask 161
Philadelphia Glass Works 23
Picnic Nips 115, 133
Pig Bottles 147
Pike's Peak Flasks
68, 96-102, 149
Pittsburgh Glass Works 24
Pitkin Flasks
6, 31, 32, 33, 34, 35, 36, 37, 39,
53, 63, 64
Pocket Flasks 31
Prohibition (Volstead)
5, 113, 149
Punts 31
Quilting 36
Recipes for Old Drinks 114
Reproductions 54
Rigaree 36
Rye Whiskey 59, 113, 125, 147
Saddle Flask 115, 134

Sandwich Works 23, 36
Scroll Bottles 51, 53
Shoo-fly Bottle 115, 128
South Jersey Type Bottles
30, 31, 36
Spencer, Jared Bottle, 39, 43, 110
Stiegel 6, 23, 25, 38, 53
Stoppers 23-26
Seal Bottles
6, 13, 17, 18, 19, 20, 21
Soap-Stone Mold 59
South Carolina Dispensary
110, 130, 133
Square Bottles 115
Stenger 31
Sunbursts 6, 43, 52, 53, 63
Threading 36
Three Mold Blown, 25, 26, 27, 29
Traveler's Companion Bottle
111, 133
Types of Liquors 152
Van Rensselaer Listings 61
(Unclassified groupings
from his original 1921
plates VI-XVI) 62-71
(Backups for plates XIV,
XV, XVI) 72
Violin Flasks 49-52, 64
Washington Flask 72, 92-95
Wistarburg Glass Works
31, 36, 39

INDEXING HAGERTY & DEAN-FOSTER CATALOGS OF DRUGGISTS' BOTTLES

pages (378-428) (and prices) from the leading late 19th Century drug bottle suppliers. There is no surer way to date bottle types already described in earlier chapters than by use of the Fig. nos. appearing on such pages. So that you can refer to individual shapes (in corresponding with other collectors or in locating actual examples from your own collection) we suggest use of the special catalog index prepared at the end. Note these catalog pages are numbered as x 48 etc., for Dean-Foster bottle types and z 318 etc., for Hagerty bottle types. Thus a Liquor shape which appeared on these z pages would be referred to as z 318, fig. 211, etc.; while one that appeared on an x page would be referred to as x 32, Cut 144.

HOUSEHOLD BOTTLES, FIGURALS, ETC.

Advertising Blood Bitters .. 279
Food Preserving —
—Advertising 336
Hair Dyeing, Etc.—
—Advertising 360, 363
Holstetter and Wheat Bitters
—Advertising 280
Medicine Show Photo —
—Advertising 280
Plantation Bitters Booklet
—Advertising 283-284
Soda Dispensing —
—Advertising 313-314
Stove Blacking—Advertising 357
Swamp Root — Advertising
276-277
Temperance Poster —
—Advertising 286
Warners Safe Cures —
—Advertising 274, 278
Ball Fruit Jars 335
Barber Stand Bottles 370, 371
Bitters Bottles, (new forms) 236
Bitters Bottles, added description 235
Bitters Form, shape and
design 248
Bogardus Bottle 352
Bottle Chronology 487
Bottle Collaterals
443-439; 166-176; 428-432; 273
Bottle Molds 483
Bottle Making .... 481 ff
Bottle Making, Automated 485ff
Beauty Aids 434
Carters Ink 355
Color in bottles 151
Commemoratives .. 444, 449-451
Character Bottles, Animal 453ff
Character Bottles, Human .. 444
Crown Caps 485
Dean Foster Drug Trade
Bottles 385-427

Drinking vs. Pill-Taking 479
Drug Bottle Stoppers and
and Lips 384
Drug Store Glassware 373
Drug Show Bottles 372ff
Drug Window Show
Bottles 372, 383
Dunmore Bottle 16
Euphoria, selling 271
Fall of Shuman's Bottles 286
Figural Bottles 440ff
Figural Check List 468-473
Figurals, Modern 462ff
Food Bottles 328
Food Jars 329
Fruit Jars 330, 384
Fruit Bottle 328
Gargling Bottles 432
Glass Bottle Correspondence
—Photo 374
Glass Candy Containers 451
Glassology Revolution 485
Glassware, Drug Store 373
Bottle Supply 378-381
Grenade Bottles 350, 351
Hagerty Drug Trade
Bottles 352-385
Ink Bottles 364, 366, 368, 369
Jamestown, Va. Bottle
making 481
A Lincoln's Liquor License
and Last Chance saloon
photo (adv.) 492
Liniment 429ff
Mason Jars 330-335
Medicine show bottles 281
Medicinals 253ff
Milk Bottles 338, 339, 342, 344
Mineral Water Bottling —
Print 310
Miniature Scent Bottles 302-304

Mineral Water Bottles   317-324
Modern and Old Food Jars
   337, 348
Moxie Nerve Food 311, 312, 336
   Store—1900 Photo 313
Nursing Bottles 339-342
Object Bottles 458ff
Paper on Household Needs
   —Photo 289
Pepper Sauce and Pickle
   Bottles 345-349
Perfume Bottles 387-301
Perfume Bottles, Modern 296
Perfume Rarities
   (Stiegel Type) 294
Personal Aid Bottles, Check
   List 433-438
Pilgrim Bottle 328
Pious Friends and Drunken
   Companion (adv.) 490
Pluto Water 311, 312
Pop and Beverage Bottles
   325, 326
Pressing Machine 484
Proprietary medicines 263ff
Sandwich Bear glass 453
Saratoga Bottles 321
Sarsaparilla, advertisement .. 272
Scent Bottles—Double   308, 309
Screw tops 329
Seahorse Scents 302, 303
Seltzer Bottles 325
Sick Feeders 343
Smelling salts bottles 36, 37
Snuff Bottles 297, 355

Soda Water 325
Stove Blacking 354-355
Tablet and Prescription
   Vials 362
Taking Saratoga Waters —
   —Print 327
Target Bottles 352
Testing Bottles 351, 353
Thatcher bottle 339, 344
The Bottle: Cruck-shank
   lithographic scenes on the
   print 362
Thompson Bitters check
   lists 177ff
Violin colognes 295
Household Bottles
Brief Survey of Varied
   Types 350-450
Blacking, Hair Dye and
   other Misc. Households 356-359
Cologne Bottles 306, 307
Gemel Bottle 304, 294
Household, 4 oz. bottles col-
   lected by Van Rensselaer .. 361
Index Catalog of Hagerty
   Drug Glassware 376-377
Index Catalog of Dean-
   Foster Drug Glassware 389-430
Medicine Show 280-285
Nineteenth Century
   Perfumes 297-301
Origin of Bottled Soda
   Water 312
Pop Bottle—Amphoro Type 312
Pure Drug Act 350

Figurals

Representatives of all 4 Bottle Groupings (Liquors, Medicinals, Households, Figurals) from writer's collection at YYV; readers can try to match with check listings.